RITES OF PASSAGE
at $100,000 to $1 Million+

RITES OF PASSAGE
at $100,000 to $1 Million+

YOUR INSIDER'S LIFETIME GUIDE TO
EXECUTIVE JOB-CHANGING
AND FASTER CAREER PROGRESS
IN THE 21ST CENTURY

JOHN LUCHT

THE VICEROY PRESS

NEW YORK

Managing Editor: Monica Becerra
Senior Editor: Lenka Knowski
Editor: Jean Sanders

Library of Congress Cataloging-in-Publication Data
is available upon request

ISBN 0-942785-30-4

"This is what I tell my friends."
John Lucht

CONTENTS

Rites of Passage

at $100,000 to $1 Million+

Rites has been in scores of publications (several times in many), including: Business Week, Wall Street Journal, Forbes, USA Today, New York Times, Working Woman, Self, Boston Globe, Denver Post, Chicago Tribune, The Philadelphia Inquirer, Los Angeles Times, Chief Executive, Seattle Times, American Way, Financial World, Portland Telegram, Dallas Morning News, Omaha World-Herald, New York Daily News, Savvy, Salt Lake City Tribune, American Banker, Women's Wear Daily, Psychology Today, Minneapolis Star & Tribune, Industry Week, Newsday, Investor's Business Daily, St. Louis Post-Dispatch, Training, Publishers Weekly, San Antonio Express News, National Business Employment Weekly, Harper's Bazaar, Chicago Sun-Times, Board Room Reports, Newark Star-Ledger, Cleveland Plain Dealer, Baltimore Sun, El Paso Times, Wichita Eagle, Across the Board (The Conference Board), Men's Health, Personnel Executive, Training & Development Journal, Atlanta Journal/Constitution, Indianapolis Star & News, Executive Female, Manchester Union Leader, Personnel Administrator, Worcester Telegram, Akron Beacon Journal, Brandweek, Human Resource Executive, Madison State Journal & Capitol Times, Success, Albany Times Union, Career News (Harvard Business School Alumni Career Services), Corpus Christi Caller-Times, The Bricker Bulletin, Canadian Industrial Relations & Personnel Development, World Executive's Digest (serving Asia from Singapore), China Technology Market News (mainland China), and many more.

Chapter 1

Window on a Changing Scene...

RITES OF PASSAGE AT $100,000+ first appeared several years ago.

Business Week praised it. Others chimed in.* Immediately *RITES* became —and is today—America's #1 bestseller on executive job-hunting and career management.

Why? Because the *RITES* reader has an insider's view of how best to deal with executive recruiters...and with every other factor that—handled well —can accelerate executive-level career progress.

And now the Internet...

This newest *RITES* also exploits today's many opportunities to use the Internet and other modern technology to speed and ease an executive's upward mobility.

Technology puts exciting *new* tools in your hands!

*(See partial listing on prior page.)

The Person in Charge

Who's in charge of your career? Obviously, you are.

Does that fact change with the changing economy? With the changing fortunes of your employer? Your field?

With attitudes toward your: Experience? Education? Age? Gender? Race? Sexuality? Appearance? Physical challenges? Family life? Employment status? Achievements? Mistakes?

No, not at all. Countless factors may influence *how* you manage your career. But who *cares* enough about you to take on that responsibility never changes.

And most assuredly, who's responsible does not change when you're the subject of a commercial transaction...in the hands of an executive recruiter of any kind, or a career or outplacement counselor.

And just as surely not, when you're a Human Resource...in the hands of a company and its managers from the Chief Executive on down, whose

interest is mainly in the corporation's wants and needs, not yours.

You know the bottom line. If you don't pay attention and make sure you're getting what you really deserve and want from your career, you have no one else to blame.

Which brings us to the "Rites of Passage." Those so called "primitive societies" had a great idea when they took their young men and women off to the side for a few days or weeks and gave them knowledge that otherwise would have taken years to acquire.

As the saying goes, "We get too soon old and too late smart." With respect to career matters, let's fix that. And since we can't start yesterday, let's start now.

Rites of Passage

For the past 30 years, I've been an executive recruiter filling high-level positions for some of America's leading corporations. Day after day, year after year, I've observed...and brokered...those pivotal company-to-company transitions that launch a fast-rising career into higher orbit, and that restore momentum when an executive is underutilized or let go.

And whether the scenario is doing-better-elsewhere...moving-up-in-the-company...or seizing-victory-from-a-setback, what I've observed is that a very few exceptionally aware and self-secure executives...maybe the top 1/2 of 1%...seem to have a virtuoso's mastery of the job-changing process. Exceptionally able in doing their job, they're just as able when it comes to changing jobs.

They deliberately attract the attention of the top executive recruiters... something I want you to do, too. As a result, they're periodically told about attractive opportunities, most of which they turn down. That is, until there's something really worth moving for. Then they snap into action, and win out over tough competition. They don't move too often. But when they do, their careers surge ahead.

Even when they refuse to look at something a recruiter proposes, they build up future career momentum. The recruiter who called them realizes how secure and fast-rising they are with their current employer, so he or she resolves to offer something much better next time.

These people also take advantage of Internet technology to speed and improve their career management. They're wised up to the fact that head-hunters—from the sleaziest to the most prestigious—are now on the Web in ways that *look* similar, but must be treated differently.

Yet, successful as these executives are in handling recruiters, they also know when it serves their self-interest to ignore them entirely and go straight to the potential employer…something you too should do under the proper circumstances.

And when contacting a company directly, they shrewdly choose between two newly differentiated routes. One, classic and low-tech, approaches the decision-maker. The other, trendy and high-tech, enters through the HR department.

Indeed, it's knowing all of today's techniques and how differently they should be used under similar-appearing circumstances, that makes the most successful executives as impressive in managing their careers as they are in doing their work.

These able and observant men and women have mastered the art of executive job-changing, whether at $100,000+, $300,000+ or $1 million plus. At the executive level, the rules and methods change. There are more initiatives to take, more contacts and opportunities to explore. But also more pitfalls and misinformation.

So you and I are about to do something we saw years ago in Sociology class. Remember how those "primitive societies" took their "initiates" aside and gave them a cram course in what they ought to know for future well-being? They got life's practical knowledge once-and-for-all-in-a-hurry, instead of painfully by trial-and-error over the next 20 years. And of course, they also learned secrets they'd never have found out, unless an insider told them. "Rites of Passage" is what the professor called that process, and you and I are beginning a modern version of the same thing.

Here in *RITES*, I'll hand you all the advanced-level job-changing wisdom

I've picked up over the past 30 years from the executives who do it best. To that I'll add behind-the-scenes information on the executive search industry which even they haven't had access to. And, to complete the package, I'll demonstrate the latest Internet technology.

The result is a comprehensive cram course in accelerating your career. It's "Rites of Passage," updated and upscaled for you…an old idea in a new time and place.

But before we go any further,
let's look at one of the most important benefits of
knowing how to change jobs advantageously.

It's the self-confidence to push for faster
advancement right where you are.

Realizing that you can move efficiently if and when you decide to do so, you'll feel a lot freer to have periodic frank discussions with your current superiors, letting them know that you feel ready to step ahead, and drawing out their unvarnished reactions to your self-appraisal.

There's truth in the old saying, "The squeaking wheel gets the grease." The person who's doing an excellent job and has the self-confidence to ask about the company's tentative timetable for his own promotion is much more likely to get the next higher-echelon position that opens up than his equally-fine-but-silent co-worker. The reason:

> "We felt we had to do something for Jason pretty soon, or we
> might lose him."

And the person whose career is marked by a *series* of fully deserved but sooner-than-her-superiors-might-have-preferred promotions is the one who winds up "way ahead of her age level" in the corner office. By that time her equally able, hardworking, and loyal co-workers have stopped asking, "What's Kate got that I haven't?" It's obvious:

> "She's just got more on the ball. Why, she's moving up through
> the organization like a shot! She knows where she wants to go and
> she isn't wasting any time getting there. Mark my words, someday
> she'll be running this company!"

Momentum is its own reward.

Momentum is also a self-fulfilling prophecy. Kate's superiors don't want to be faulted by top management for not recognizing an exceptional talent when they see one...nor for petty jealousy. So they cheer her along, either as ready now to take their job so they can move up or, if that's not possible, as an ideal candidate for a higher-level position somewhere else in the company:

> "She's ready for more responsibility right now. Unfortunately, I just don't have it for her, unless you want to give her my job. She could handle it!"

Kate's current supervisor, Steve Steady, is being shrewd, not stupid, when he talks like that. The reply he gets proves it:

> "Certainly not, Steve. You're doing great right where you are. In fact, one of your many fine talents is your ability to recognize and help groom the future leaders of this company. You stand out like a beacon in contrast to some of the other old guys around here who'd feel threatened by a young superstar like Kate. That's why we like to put our up-and-comers through your department...to get your solid knowledge of the business, without holding them back and dampening their enthusiasm."

> "Incidentally, Kate speaks well of you too, Steve. She'll probably be giving you some promotions as the years go by!"

That's the way it works. Once career momentum takes hold, it builds. Ironically, having the solid self-confidence that comes from knowing there are plenty of attractive opportunities for you outside your current company *encourages you to press for maximum progress where you are.*

||| But please...no blackmail! |||

Don't misunderstand. I'm not talking about actually interviewing for an outside job, getting an offer, confronting your employer, and eliciting a counteroffer. That's a bad idea. Even if you get by with it once or twice... "three strikes and you're out." Nobody likes a blackmailer. And no one earmarks him for the future presidency of the company.

In fact, after a pivotal executive is "saved" by a counteroffer, he's usually not looked upon in quite the same favorable way. Instead of being slated for important future positions, he tends to be left out of organizational planning. Or he's categorized as an *alternate*:

> "Well, *if Ron's still with us*, we could *also* consider him for that job."

No, don't come in with an outside offer you hope your company will meet or beat. It serves you right if they just wave goodbye, and you're headed for a job and a company you don't really want.

Instead, take this approach. Tell your boss:

> YOU: "Got a call today from a recruiter looking for a Vice President of Marketing for a $550 million specialty foods company. I told him I wasn't interested, but I'd call back with some suggestions. He didn't name the company. Who do you think it might be?"

> HE: "Maybe NutriCroft. They're about that size and they just put in a new President. Maybe she's reorganizing. Who called you?"

> YOU: "A guy I know, Hunter Probe, at Randolph Ripley Associates. I like it here, and I haven't personally been interested in anything he's had so far. But I've pointed him toward other people, so he keeps calling. Remember my friend Carol Stevens? Hunter put her into Clarendon Foods as Marketing VP...a big jump for her."

> HE: "I didn't know you knew anyone at Randolph Ripley Associates. How'd you meet Hunter Probe?"

> YOU: "Oh, he just called one day last fall. He was looking for a head of Brand Management at Modern Consumer Foods, and some people mentioned my name. I told him I like this company, and he'd have to come up with a lot bigger job than that to attract me away. However, they were offering a bushel of money...about $40,000 more than I'm making now, even after that big raise you pushed through for me in January."

> HE: "You never told *me* any of this!"

> YOU: "I didn't see any need to, Bill. I knew you were doing everything you could to fix the salary situation. No point in trying to put pressure on you. What I'm really hoping, is for you to get Sally's job when she retires next summer, so maybe I can have your job."

> HE: "*You and three other people!* And they've all been here a lot longer than you have. But I must admit, Randi, you're doing *excellent* work. You've got our attention. We're planning a great future for you. In fact, when Alex approved your raise, he said..."

Now you've got the right idea. You can't whack a relationship into place with a sledge hammer. You're likely to shatter it. An occasional gentle tap on the shoulder will do far more good...and less harm...than one big dramatic hit.

It's almost never too late for the right move.

And it's possible to look outside, without risking the job you have.

Let's go back to Kate's boss, Steve Steady, the older fellow whose department the company likes to put its "young superstars" through…to get his "solid knowledge of the business, without holding them back and dampening their enthusiasm." Obviously the company likes him a lot better than it does "some of the other old guys around here who'd feel threatened by a young superstar like Kate."

But is Steve happy? Is he enjoying enough status, and making enough money, to justify relegating himself to "unsung hero"? He's got job security. But does he have job satisfaction?

Maybe not. Maybe somewhere under Steve's 25-years-with-the-company recognition pin beats the heart of a striver, who still craves challenge, status, and rewards. Actually, he's in quite a good position to pursue them. True, he's 56. But he's also more comfortably established and more mobile than a younger person. His pension is vested. His home is paid for. And his youngest child is almost out of college.

Steve can afford to take risks. Since he's no longer on the "fast track," his compensation isn't particularly high. Even if Steve has bad luck in the first outside job he takes, he can surely duplicate what he earns now in *some* subsequent position. And knowing Steve's ability and commitment, *he won't fail!*

Moreover, the outside world will be receptive. Steve has a consummate knowledge of his industry, gained in one of its most respected companies. Chances are, a hot young growth company can greatly profit from his experience…and possibly even from his mature image, which will lend credibility to sales and/or investor presentations led by an under-30 CEO. And a dynamic, youthful company—possibly even a "dot com"—may provide an exciting equity opportunity that Steve could never hope for where he is.

Steve's problem is to identify his best outside opportunities *without letting his employer know he's looking.* How to do so by using both traditional and Internet methods is something else you and I will cover before we part company at the end of this book.

For some executives, even a lateral move can be attractive...

and sometimes a counteroffer should be accepted.

Let's look in on Steve Steady's 54-year-old sister Sandra, who runs a large out-of-the-mainstream department in an altogether different company. Unlike Steve, Sandra is a specialist. Aided by a leading search firm, the Chief Operating Officer of a competitor is asking her to join Next-Co in the very same job she's always handled brilliantly at Current Corp.

The incentive to switch: Considerably higher compensation...about 15% more than industry-average pay for her job, whereas Sandra's now making 25% less than industry-average. That's actually a 53% improvement in cash, plus a company car, which she doesn't have now.

Should she accept? She'd be a fool not to. In fact, Sandra resigned yesterday.

But her boss, shocked and upset, asked her "not to say anything about this to anyone else for 24 hours, and until you and I have talked again." Obviously, there's a counteroffer in the wind.

Usually it's a big mistake to forego a leap-ahead opportunity and stay in response to a counteroffer.

But Sandra may be an exception.

As a specialist, she now heads her function in one of the largest corporations. She's gone about as far as she can reasonably expect to go. Unfortunately, for that reason and because her superiors have assumed that no outside company would identify and grab her, Current Corp. has been neglecting her compensation. Now that she's resigned to join Next-Co, Sandra's superiors are suddenly waking up:

> "Face it, Adam, we've been getting by with murder. We knew Sandra loved her job, and loved that department she's built. We figured she'd never try to leave, and we never imagined that anyone would swoop in here looking for her. So we haven't been paying what she's worth. She'll be getting $265,000, including first year's bonus *guaranteed*, plus a car, plus options. You know what we're paying her? Assuming she earns full bonus, $172,500!"
>
> "If we have to replace Sandra, we'll probably have to come up with about the same money they're offering which, with the car,

comes to more than $280,000. And it'll cost us an extra $90,000 or $100,000 just to hire a recruiter to look for somebody."

"Therefore, I say let's hit Sandra with $300,000, including bonus, and no car, since we have a policy against cars. But let's also throw in an EVP title, which will qualify her for Class A stock options. And let's include a new office for her when we remodel the East Wing. Let's give Sandra the recognition she deserves. We've got the best person in the industry! Let's at least try to keep her."

Well, Sandra, under your unusual circumstances, maybe they're coming up with a counteroffer you should seriously consider. It's too bad your bosses didn't "get religion" sooner. But now that they realize you're visible to the outside world, they're not going to be so casual about your "care-and-feeding" again. You love the department you've built. Maybe you should stay.

Obviously, Sandra, your superiors don't even suspect that *you drew yourself* to the attention of the executive recruiting community.

And we won't tell them. Congratulations. Mission accomplished!

Out of a job?

That's when you can take full advantage of all the "Rites of Passage" right away.

Nearly all of the most successful senior executives I know have been out of work at least once in their careers…and many, several times. The difference between these "winners," and others less successful, is in how creatively and aggressively they've handled their unemployment. Much of the help in this book comes from observing them. Read on, and you'll soak up their knowledge and experience.

On the other hand, by far the most misunderstood job-changing resource… at all points of an executive's career…and *especially when he or she is out of work*…is the executive search industry, including its widely misunderstood role in the online job sites. You can't get past the myth and misinformation, until you have an insider's perspective on upper-level recruiting. And that's what you'll have when you're halfway through this book.

Later, when the remainder of this book has prepared you for it, you can take a postgraduate course. It's in Appendix I. See a search through the recruiter's eyes. When you've finished *Rites*, you'll know as much about recruiting as if you've actually been a recruiter yourself.

| | | **Internet Savvy? Or Internet Shy?** | | |

Probably you're somewhere in between...not a dope, but not a savant either. As we cover all the main issues in managing an executive career—most of which are *not* high-tech—I'll fill you in on the modern ways to remove drudgery from the process. I'll also classify the many—currently estimated at over 80,000—job sites on the Internet, showing you their advantages and pitfalls. And I'll show you *RITE*Site, the minimally-commercial Executive Information Exchange I've set up to assist *RITES* readers and the recruiters who comprise the list of outstanding search firms you'll find in Appendix II.

To Investigate: Access an infinite fund of information on companies, industries, professions, salaries, geographic data...the resources are endless. Also turbocharge your networking by using the Internet to locate key contacts you've known but lost touch with, and also to figure out who you know that knows—and hence can introduce you to—someone you're eager to meet.

To Deliver: Use the Net as an alternative to the Postal Service in making yourself known. Participate wisely in the online employment sites. These days, they're infinitely numerous. Informed, you can achieve the right balance of dignity and confidentiality vs. all-out speed.

So now you know what we'll be doing together.

Let's just glance at a bit more of what's to come, and then we'll get down to business.

By the time you complete these "Rites of Passage," you'll clearly understand the motives and methods of every sector of the "people business." Everyone from the employment agency that got you your first couple jobs after college (which today calls itself a "management consulting," or "executive search" firm)...right through the most prestigious recruiters...to the Internet job sites which—at long last—merit your participation...to the "outplacement" and "executive marketing" segments of the industry.

As an upwardly-mobile executive, you're likely to be involved with all of the "professions" that move executives around. Therefore, it's worthwhile to take this once-and-for-all-in-a-hurry opportunity to see how you should deal with each to best serve *your self-interest*, which often does not match theirs. For example, one of many practical suggestions is as simple as this:

"Watch the money change hands!"

That's a good rule in general. And especially helpful, when you're the subject of a commercial transaction.

Of course, dealing with "professionals" in the "people business" isn't the only way to advance your career.

We'll polish every facet of your game…from handling your own personal contacts…to "networking" among helpful strangers…to telephone technique with recruiters to smoke out whether what they're calling about is in your best interest…to researching and contacting potential employers on the Internet… to creating a really persuasive resume…to interviewing with both employers and recruiters for your maximum advantage…to conducting a direct mail campaign or its paperless on-line alternative…to negotiating your employment agreement. And lots more.

Whatever could put you a thought or a step ahead in the advancement of your career we'll cover. And wherever a "professional" in the "people business" may be a step ahead of you, we'll even the odds. Beyond that, everything is up to you.

Five Main Ways to Go

I can't know your situation at this moment.

Your degree of job satisfaction may range anywhere from totally delighted to utterly disgusted. You may even be unemployed and in the midst of an all-out search for your next position.

You may be so pleased with your current employer and your progress that you don't want to hear about any opportunity unless it can advance your career at least three to five years. At the other extreme, you may be delighted to hear about anything even remotely close to your latest job.

Over the years, your circumstances will vary. And you'll probably come back to this book at different stages of your career. Therefore, we'll proceed on the broadest possible assumption...that you're interested in everything you can possibly know about changing jobs. This is a complex and fascinating subject, but it centers on just a few fundamentals.

The Five Methods
Four are classics. One is new.

Until nearly the end of the '90s there were only four basic routes to an executive-level job outside your current company. Anything else was a minor variation.

1.   Personal Contacts...getting in touch with people you already know.

2.   Networking...getting in touch with a series of people others refer you to.

3.   Executive Recruiters...dealing with the various species of "headhunters."

4.   Direct Mail...letting the Postal Service take your message more places than you can visit and phone.

These days there's also a fifth way.

5.   The Internet...taking advantage of modern technology in job-hunting and career management.

> ### With No. 5—the Internet—everything is new
> ### ...and yet nothing is *really* new.
> ### It's just the application of technology to Nos. 3 and 4.

Look at Monster.com and the others. They're really just incredibly low cost vendors of classified advertising. Newspapers have huge costs—reporters, editors, paper, printing, delivery, etc. Electronic Web sites have virtually none of those expenses. Therefore, they can offer unbelievably cheap advertising rates.

First, No. 3 - the Executive Recruiter Dimension: Who's advertising job openings on the employment Web sites? The same people who've always used newspaper ads...headhunters (No. 3) and corporations. Later, we'll discuss headhunters in detail...the various games they play, and how to protect and advance yourself, regardless of what they're up to. Just remember that the headhunters posting on the job sites are the same type of firms that advertise in the newspaper...except, perhaps, less well-financed and less responsible, because the cost of being present on the Web is far less.

And Secondly, No. 4 - the Direct Mail Dimension: What are you doing when you post your resume on a Monster.com-type web site? Basically, the same thing you're doing when you mail an unsolicited resume to a search firm or a company. You're *sending out* your information in the hope that they'll have or get an opening you fit. Now, however, you're using wires instead of paper and stamps. And, of course, zapping is a lot quicker, easier, and cheaper than mailing.

But who are your recipients?

Are they the same firms you'd address your envelopes to in a well-thought-out direct mail campaign? No! Most of the headhunters paying the small fees required to post their openings on an employment site and to view its resume database are *not* the ones you would intentionally mail to.

Why not? Well, just hang on. We'll cover that...and so much more.

Structuring Our Time Together

Before we're finished, we'll not only cover the essentials, we'll also sweep up a number of minor related possibilities...such as answering newspaper ads. Also an intriguing alternative that doesn't aim for a corporate payroll but may put you there anyway...becoming an independent consultant. Plus many other matters, such as resumes, interviews, "outplacement," the implications of e-mailing vs. "snail-mailing" your paperwork, and all the issues involved in negotiating your compensation. But let's format our discussion around the five most basic and powerful job-changing methods.

Each of those five will get enough attention to exploit all of its possibilities and avoid its pitfalls: one chapter each, for Personal Contacts and Networking; plus six for Executive Recruiters and three for Direct Mail. We'll point out Internet implications everywhere they're an option throughout those eleven chapters. Then we'll blitz the Net with its own mega-chapter. These matters will take up over half of our time together...12 of 20 chapters...so I've organized with them. But there's lots more to know, and we'll deal with it all.

The End Game

Remember those earliest video games, "Pac Man" and "Pac Woman"? They came quite close to illustrating the ultimate in career proficiency. Whether you're a recent college grad or a merged-and-purged CEO, we'll work together to polish your "Pac Person" skills. Then, as you go through the career maze, you'll avoid making wrong turns. And if anybody's in your way, you'll gobble 'em up.

Does that mean you should play tough and nasty?

Not at all! But bear this in mind: you will almost never be the sole candidate for any promotion or new job. So get ready to reach out for whatever you desire *and deserve*, recognizing that others will be desirous and deserving too. The outcome will depend to some extent on your skills as a player. Please play fair. Be a person you can fully respect at all times. But don't hesitate to become skillful...and play *to win*.

WHAT'S GOING ON HERE?

RITES is not quite what it appears to be.

It looks like a reference book...and it will be when you come back to it later.

But right now it's more of a novel.

So kick off your shoes, relax, and go straight through. That's the only way to get what's really in *RITES*.

If you read 100% by skipping around, you'll see about 50% of what's going on...and not even the better half, because the real story is sequential and beneath the surface.

Chapter

Personal Contacts:
Pursuing the People You Know

Approaching and surpassing $100,000, you've got something you didn't
have early in your career...*valuable personal contacts*.

Pick up the phone. Senior officers at most of your competitors will accept
your call or call you back.

So will lots of other high-level people who do business in your industry...
from direct customers, wholesalers, and distributors...to suppliers of raw
materials, components, sub-assemblies, and packaging...to providers of
services such as engineering, contract manufacturing, accounting, banking, advertising, management consulting, market research, and PR.

A few of these people have hire-and-fire power over jobs that could be excellent next steps in your career. And nearly all are in a position to hear about openings that might interest you, and possibly even to make an appropriate introduction.

Personal contacts are the resource you'll turn to first, when you think of changing jobs.

People you already know are your #1 asset.

If you can get your ideal job just by talking to them, why do anything more?

There's a big difference between talking to someone you've known awhile... possibly very well, and maybe for years...and talking to a stranger whose name you've just been given. In the next chapter, we'll discuss "networking" the strangers you meet at the suggestion of someone else. But let's start right now by getting in touch with people you already know.

True personal contact has advantages over Networking, Executive Recruiters, Direct Mail, and even your usual interface with the Internet.

Greater Impact. Talking with friends and associates is easier and more effective than with strangers.

Better Confidentiality. Long before you're ready to "go public," you can speak to the people you trust.

Less Need to Persuade and Sell. People who already know your professional skills and like you personally don't have to be convinced.

Maximum Efficiency. Why bother writing a resume? And why deal with lots of letters, phone calls, and appointments...if you don't have to?

No question about it. If you can get the career-advancing job you want through Personal Contact, it's the quickest, easiest, and most pleasant way to go.

Unfortunately, *LUCK* plays a starring role in what you accomplish through personal contacts. *Who* do you know? And does your inquiry come at the *opportune time* when someone you know happens to have, or know of, the right position? If so, great! If not, you'll have to proceed to other job-changing methods we'll discuss later on.

But now let's look at my all-time favorite "case history" of successful job-changing through a Personal Contact. We'll see one of America's most gifted marketing-oriented general managers get into the position of needing a job change...and then actually achieving one. And he does both in what I believe to be the prevailing world-record time. These events happened. Only the identities have been changed to protect the guilty:

> Several years ago Matt Marketczar, a suave, marketing-oriented general manager from New York City, became President of SpecialFlavor Foods Co. in a smallish city we'll call Elmdale. SFC markets nationwide under a famous brand name, just like any other big corporation. However, it's actually a cooperative owned by growers of the main ingredient of the company's products.
>
> Unfortunately, at the time Matt arrived, America's appetite for foods containing the key ingredient was declining, and supply was increasing...trends that threatened the financial health of the farmers who owned the company.
>
> Happily, within just a few years Matt accomplished a management miracle. He brought out hugely successful new products based on the special ingredient, and producer prices rose 300%, while costs declined slightly. The growers were delighted.
>
> Matt was assisted by his brilliant secretary, Lucy Local, wife of Larry Local, a lifetime Elmdale resident. Besides accompanying Matt to his frequent business meetings in the nearby town of Midday, which were usually held at the Midday Motel, Lucy also took care of his expense reports, which she documented by saving his American Express bills and vouchers from Midday Motel.
>
> On Monday of the eventful week that interests us, Matt determined that Lucy's services were no longer required...strictly a management decision, and one in which Lucy did not concur.
>
> So, resourceful to the very end, Lucy filled an envelope with expense account documentation, and mailed it to Matt's clever wife, Sylvia Fox Marketczar. Lucy didn't bother to include a note, figuring that Sylvia would know what to do.

Mrs. Marketczar indeed required no explanation, and added none her-self, as she merely transferred the data to a fresh envelope, which she then forwarded to Lucy's husband, Larry Local, at his business address.

That's why, early Saturday morning, when Larry might otherwise have gone squirrel hunting, he arrived on the front lawn of the Marketczar residence, with his trusty rifle, and opened fire on the front windows. Matt grabbed a pistol and returned the fire, while Sylvia hurriedly summoned the sheriff.

That afternoon, with Larry safely in custody, a hastily convened meet-ing of the Board of Directors of SpecialFlavor Foods accepted Matt's resignation.

Early that same Saturday evening, Matt made just one phone call which proves, more graphically than any other example I know of, the advan-tages of Personal Contact over all other job-changing methods.

Matt called Bernie Bigdeals, who'd been Matt's boss several years earlier. Bernie, now Chief Executive of a huge diversified corpora-tion, picked up the phone at his home, halfway across the U.S., and received an unvarnished account of the circumstances under which Matt was now offering his services.

Result? Monday morning...approximately 38 hours after a single Personal Contact phone call...Matt reported to work as President of the Foods Division of Bernie's corporation.

Before Larry was even out on bail, Matt was already at his desk in a stylish office more than a thousand miles from Saturday's unpleasant-ness, holding meetings and making decisions as the much-more-highly-paid President of a corporate subsidiary several times the size of SpecialFlavor Foods in Elmdale.

How's that for an eventful weekend? As they say, "Truth is stranger than fiction."

In 30 years of executive recruiting, plus over a decade as an executive myself, I've never come across a more perfect example of job-changing by Personal Contact. Absolutely every aspect was at its optimum, including the accident of *timing*. Not only did Bernie Bigdeals have hire-and-fire *control* of an attractive job, the job happened to be *open*. And not only did he *know* Matt, he'd *directly supervised* him, and had firsthand knowledge of his ability and personality. Moreover, there was *no possibility that Matt's performance had declined since they worked together*, because his success at SpecialFlavor Foods had been widely publicized in the trade press. And of course Matt's *reason-for-leaving* couldn't have been clearer.

The moral of this story, if there is any, certainly isn't that crime pays. In the long run, it doesn't...for marketing geniuses, or anyone else. But we can all have a lucky, or an unlucky, day. And apparently it's possible to have notable amounts of both kinds of luck on the same day.

The point is that luck is fully as important...and often more so...as skill in determining what you'll achieve through your personal contacts on any given day, or in any three- or six-month period that you happen to be interested in a career change.

Fortunately, however, there are techniques that will polish your proficiency and improve your odds. Let's look at them.

Take inventory of all your personal contacts.

Arrange them in priority order, and focus on the ones who can be most helpful.

Personal contacts can be time-consuming.

True, just one out-of-the-blue phone call to a former boss, that lengthened into a three-hour employment interview, solved Matt Marketczar's problems with possibly-world-record speed. But everything just happened to work perfectly. Matt enjoyed a moratorium on Murphy's Law on that one day in his life when he needed it most. Unfortunately, Murphy keeps pretty close watch on you and me. Personal Contact, for us, involves a long series of lunch and break-fast dates, other appointments, and countless phone calls which, added together, take up lots of time.

Therefore, it's extremely important to plan your personal contact campaign carefully. Before you reach for the phone, try to think of everyone you know who might be worth contacting. Only when you've identified all the people you might call, can you determine whom you should call, and in what order.

Matt Marketczar obviously chose to make his first call to his most likely con-tact. And if Bernie Bigdeals hadn't solved Matt's problem, you can bet Matt's *second* call would have gone to his second-most-likely contact, not to his thir-teenth. Moreover, if a more subtle across-the-lunch-table approach would have been more likely to succeed, Matt would surely have employed it.

Determining Priority:
Who to contact earlier...and spend more time with... is a trade-off between two issues:

1. **Relevance:** how likely to control, or at least know of, appropriate jobs, and

2. **Knowledgeable Enthusiasm:** how likely to react favorably to your availability.

Obviously, if you know her well, the Chief Executive of the company in your industry you'd most like to work for should be number-one priority. She controls at least one job you'd want...maybe several. But if you merely shook hands at a convention four years ago, and she's unlikely to remember, then you'd better get a new introduction. Or write her a letter, as you would any other important stranger.

On the other hand, a first-class former subordinate who's always considered you a genius, and who now runs a small but respected supply, distribution, or service company in your industry, might also be a high-priority contact. There's no spot for you in his organization. But he knows what's happening in your field; he's enthusiastic about you and eager to help; and he's intelligent and discreet...not an oaf who might smudge your image while trying to polish it. His eyes and ears could be very beneficial.

Above all, beware of the perverse natural tendency we all have, to get in touch with the people we know best and are most comfortable with, rather than the ones who can do us the most good. Remember:

> You can make a relevant contact more enthusiastic, but you can't make an enthusiastic one more relevant.

Allocate your time accordingly.

Here's a hierarchy for ranking the twin trade-offs:

Relevance

1. **Control of Jobs**. These top-priority people have hire/fire power, or at least influence, over a job you'd want. Think of CEOs, outside

Directors, and heads of functions such as Human Resources, Finance, Marketing, Manufacturing, R&D, etc.

2.   Vantage Point.   Lower-priority, but still valuable, these contacts are extra eyes and ears. Consider middle managers in companies that interest you, and other people in your field...suppliers, customers, and consultants.

3.   Neither Control nor Vantage Point.   Lowest in relevance are the people outside your field altogether. Some may be widely connected, and you may be interested in off-the-wall suggestions. So there's no harm in an occasional try for serendipity. But give it low priority.

And now the opposite trade-off. How well and how favorably does the contact know your achievements, and how well does she like you personally?

Knowledgeable Enthusiasm

1.   Co-Workers.   First-priority goes to your former supervisors, subordinates, and peers. No need to convince. Just update them on your latest exploits, and they're automatically enthusiastic. On the other hand, if you suspect their opinion from the past is negative, don't bother. Nothing you say now will overcome what they believe they saw with their own eyes.

2.   Closely Dealt-With Outsiders.   Suppliers, customers, consultants, and others you've dealt with also have enthusiasm...or lack of it...based on prior direct experience. Moreover, they've probably heard about you from your superiors and subordinates. They can't be quite as sure as if they'd seen you from inside your company, but they're capable of justified enthusiasm. If it exists, take advantage.

3.   By-Reputation-Only Contacts.   You've met these people and know them slightly. And, although they've never done business with you, they've surely heard others speak about you. Consider trade press editors, trade association executives, competitors you've met at industry functions, suppliers who've solicited you and customers you've solicited where no business ensued, etc. There's a little more going for you than with a stranger, but not much.

4.   Non-Business Connections.   These are the very same people listed as number-3 under "Relevance." You may know them very well indeed, but they're not part of your business milieu. Hence, they're "long shots" as job-advancement contacts.

Scoring Your Contacts

The purpose of these lists is merely to encourage you to think about all your possible contacts and emphasize the ones most likely to be helpful, rather than the ones you'd most enjoy getting in touch with.

However, you can use the lists for a combine-the-numbers game, if you temper it with judgment. The lowest total number, 2, is obviously best, as Matt Marketczar demonstrated. The highest, 7, is least likely to be helpful. And the numbers in between provide roughly comparative rankings.

Now the most valuable suggestion I know on how to handle personal contacts:

Ask for a reference instead of a job.

This technique was pointed out to me many years ago by the President of a New York advertising agency. And the logic behind it is so compelling that... to this day...it's still my most helpful tip on personal contacts.

Imagine the following conversation. You're not out of a job. However, you could be, and all the same logic would apply. But for our example, let's just say you're definitely fed up and want to make a change. Today you've asked a former boss to lunch. You admire each other and enjoy working together, and you've both made outstanding progress since leaving the company where he supervised you. So you pop the question:

> YOU: "FlamingTiger.com has been a great learning experience. The venture capitalists made sure that I got a ton of stock when they brought me in as CEO, in order to dress up the management prior to the IPO. They believed I could take our flaky concept, build a business behind it, and actually make a profit if anyone could. And they promised they'd raise as much cash as we needed for as long as we had to keep burning it. So I signed on. At the peak of the pop after the IPO, my shares were worth—on paper— nearly $70 million.

> "But that was then and now is now. We've actually got a good little business going. We'd even turn a small profit if we didn't have to keep on with more media advertising than we ever dreamed we'd need, in order to fend off all those copycat competitors that have come out of the woodwork. If the VCs would only keep their word on funding, I believe we could make a go of it. The VCs

admit that I've got the business going as well as anyone could reasonably expect. But now that we really *are* a business, they're beginning to talk as if the size of the opportunity is too small in comparison to a couple of other irons they have in the fire.

"Those bastards!

"If I leave, the stock will totally tank. But I don't give a damn. My stock is $10 under water, now that we're at $3.25 a share. My $70 million that I never really had is gone in a puff of smoke. I feel sorry for the staff. We've all worked so hard. But they're a bunch of great young people, and what they've learned is priceless. They'll do just fine. In fact, they're beginning to get raided out already.

"So frankly, Jim, my reason for wanting this lunch with you is to see if you might have anything for me over there at SolidGrowth Corp. I tremendously enjoyed working for you at Early Corp. What do you think? Is there something I can do for you?"

JIM: "Gosh, Bill, I'd love to have you on my team again. In fact, you're one of the best people I've ever had the pleasure of working with.

(Long pause)

"But, unfortunately, no. I just don't have anything for an outstanding financially-oriented general manager right now. In fact, I just went outside a couple months ago to fill a Divisional slot that would have been perfect. Got a good person. But I'd rather have you...especially with your e-commerce experience. I wish you'd called me then. I'll definitely give you a ring next time a job like that opens up."

That's it. You asked. He answered. Matter closed. You both order coffee, split the check, and get on with the remainder of a busy day.

But now let's go back and change your script. Let's have you ask for a reference instead of a job:

YOU: "So frankly, Jim, my reason for wanting this lunch with you is to ask a favor. I've decided to leave FlamingTiger.com within the next six to nine months...as soon as I can line up something worth moving for. I'm already putting out feelers. And at some point I'll need some confidential references. Would you be willing to talk to a few people about what I did for you at Early Corp.?"

JIM: "Yes. Absolutely! I'd be delighted. You're one of the very best people who ever worked for me. In fact, as you recall, I was the one who persuaded you to get out of finance and go into marketing, working for me. I told you you'd get into general management faster that way. And of course you did, because a year and a half later I gave you that sick little division in North Carolina, where you not only had your own finance and marketing, but also your own manufacturing as well. You turned out to be a 'natural' as a General Manager."

YOU: "What made you think I'd do well as a GM?"

JIM: "Well, you were such a practical finance person...not just a 'green-eye-shade' type. You had so much curiosity and creativity. In short, you were a problem-solver. I was particularly impressed when you went down to Savannah and worked out that inventory-control system that we later installed in all locations worldwide.

"Of course the rest is history. I moved you up to Division Manager in the shortest time of anyone who ever worked for me. The skeptics fought me tooth and nail. But I said, 'What can we lose? We've been trying for years to sell that operation, and nobody will touch it. We'll probably have to shut it down anyway, so why not give the kid a chance?'

"Frankly, I was as surprised as everyone else with the turnaround you accomplished. And your strong financial and systems background had a lot to do with it.

"Bill, I'd be delighted to be a reference. I just wish I had a spot for you at SolidGrowth. That opening a couple of months ago would have been perfect! Damn! I'd much rather be getting you myself, than just recommending you to someone else!"

See the difference?

In both instances you told Jim you've decided to leave FlamingTiger. And in both he told you he's sorry, but he doesn't have anything for you at Solid - Growth.

However, something very different happened when you asked for a reference than when you asked for a job.

Answer to a reference: "Yes. Absolutely!"

Answer to a job: "Unfortunately, no."

So you could say that the answers are as different as *Yes* and *No*. That's true. But, in fact, they're even more different. When you asked about a job, you got *one* answer: No. But when you asked about a reference, you got two answers: the job answer, No, plus a resounding Yes on serving as a reference. *The reference inquiry achieved everything the job inquiry did, and more, too.*

Moreover, the reference question served as a *springboard for further conversation about you.* Jim did what all newly recruited references do: discussed the background of the "referencee." If we'd listened longer, we'd have heard him probing for even more information...further recollections of what you did for him, and news of how you've "kept up the good work" since he lost track of you.

Above all, the biggest advantage of your asking for a reference, rather than a job, is the *positive and open-ended frame of mind* Jim takes away with him as he leaves this thoroughly enjoyable lunch with you.

Ordinarily, under similar circumstances, Jim is directly asked for a job. The accident of timing almost always guarantees that he won't have an opening. And it's always awkward to have to say so...especially to a colleague who, unlike you, may be out of work, and whom Jim might want to think about for several days (and possibly meet alternative candidates) before offering to rehire.

So when Jim is asked if he has an appropriate job, he normally hastens to say No...*and then piles on convincing reasons why not.* That way the asker won't suspect that Jim has any hesitancy about *him.* Your requesting a reference rather than a job was a refreshing change. It allowed Jim to reassure you by talking about your merits, rather than why he has no job. You let him say:

> "Bill, you're great! *And here's how great I think you are.*"

You didn't force him to say:

> "Bill, you're great! *And here's proof that I have no job for you.*"

Therefore, Jim's commitment to you is far more open-ended...both in outward promise, and psychologically as well. If you'd asked for a job, Jim would have coped with your query right on the spot by explaining that there wasn't one, and why not. The matter would have been finished.

But you asked for a reference. *Jim accepted an assignment.* Follow-up is forthcoming. Jim leaves the lunch table recalling what it was like working with you, and preparing to tell others.

Too bad, Jim muses, *that I don't have something for Bill. Everything I said was true. He really is one of the best people who ever worked for me. So versatile! And a real problem-solver. Wish I could be hiring him, instead of just recommending him.*

A month goes by. You've almost forgotten your lunch with Jim. And then out-of-the-blue, your assistant says he's on the line:

JIM: "Bill, I've just had an idea. You wouldn't consider going back to Finance, would you?"

YOU: "It's certainly nothing I've had in mind. I love general management for the same reasons you do. And besides, it was you who took me away from Finance back in 1996. Are you admitting you gave me a bum steer?"

JIM: "Well, hear me out. I've kept thinking about you off-and-on since our lunch, and frankly I couldn't quite figure out why. But then the light clicked on. It's because I'm bucking for President and Chief Operating Officer of the entire corporation over here in about four years, when Caroline retires, and Ken moves up to Chairman.

"So I've got to groom a successor. My General Managers are doing okay with their own relatively small units. But they're all up from Marketing or Operations. None is really strong in Finance. And I have a hard time believing that any of them will ever be able to monitor and supervise several businesses.

"Now, what brought all this thinking to a head is that Friday Ken, our President, asked me if I might consider giving up my Financial Officer, Sue Stacy, to our Energy Industries Group. They've got problems—and they haven't even started in B-to-B e-commerce. I'd like to cooperate. You don't score points for being selfish. But up to now, Sue's been my ace in the hole. I've been bringing her into monitoring the businesses, and in a couple years I planned to have one or two of them report to her...sort of gradually building her into my successor.

"But Bill, with your e-commerce experience, you've got even more to offer than she does in terms of my agenda. So here's what I propose: Come to my Group as CFO. Since you're already a proven General Manager, I'll announce that the two large businesses we have 'on probation' for possible divestiture will report directly to you...I'll remove them from our regular divisional structure. And I'll also announce that you're our key person in looking for acquisitions for the Group...something we'll get active on if we can dress up and sell off something we already have.

"Clearly you'll come in with Group Officer overtones. As CFO and basically my chief lieutenant, you'll be in on the Management Reviews of all the operating units. Plus you'll have two good-sized businesses of your own. They're sick ones, but that's not so bad, because if they stay sick it's not your fault, and if they get better, you're a hero. So you're line, as well as staff. You'll update your credentials at a higher level as a Financial Officer. You'll get experience in acquisitions and divestitures. And you'll have one foot in the door as Group Officer and my successor, if we both play our cards right and you help me look good.

"What do you say, Bill? Can we have lunch and talk about it?"

Wow! Sounds like a great opportunity. Aren't you glad you didn't get to Jim until after he filled that Division Manager job that "would have been perfect"?

And aren't you also glad you asked him for a reference, rather than a job? That was a good tactical move. You left Jim with a refreshed memory of your skills and achievements, and what it's like to work with you. When you and he shook hands outside that restaurant, he walked away with an open-ended assignment to think about you and to tell others about you. As it turned out, the person he convinced was himself.

What about purely social contacts?

Generally they're low-priority in advancing your career. But the rare exceptions can be wonderful!

So far, we've only concerned ourselves with your business contacts.

Indeed, our priority-list "numbers game" ranked purely social contacts at the bottom...3 on Relevance and 4 on Knowledgeable Enthusiasm. They don't control or influence jobs in your industry...or even know about them. And, not having worked with you in business, they probably haven't observed your professional abilities closely enough to be knowledgeably enthusiastic about them, even though their unbounded personal enthusiasm for you may have them convinced...rightly or wrongly...that you're outstanding in your work.

Moreover, your close friends may subscribe to the generally wise policy against hiring friends as business subordinates. Trying to nudge them in that direction may prove both embarrassing and frustrating. Certainly it puts your friendship at risk.

And when a purely social acquaintance recommends you to someone else, the potential employer may be wise enough to realize that the recommendation isn't backed by any firsthand knowledge of your professional competence. You'd be better off, if possible, coming in under more knowledgeable and less biased sponsorship.

And if you take a job-changing campaign with you into the recreational parameters of your tennis, golf, or athletic club, there's the very real danger of becoming thought of as "poor old Joe, down on his luck and bending everyone's ear"...a hapless aura that will lower your self-esteem, further depress your spirits, and probably rub off on your family members in the same social orbit.

Now, having duly pointed out the downside, I must also tell you that there are marvelous exceptions to the generally wise policy of not trying to use purely social contacts to advance your career.

Time and time again I've seen marginally appropriate...and even marginally competent...executives catapulted into prominent positions they would never even have been considered for on any objective basis. On rare occasions I've seen these appointments occur even when the employer had a slate of ideally qualified candidates, several of whom he or she would actually have preferred to hire. An opportune personal contact tipped the scale!

Nowhere is it written that you have to be the best obtainable candidate for a job in order to turn in an acceptable performance. Therefore, I can not report to you that less-than-optimum choices inevitably fail and are thrown out. It's just not so. Indeed, some have become my clients, and I've watched them succeed brilliantly...largely because they're very intelligent and have lots of common sense. But in part, too, because together we quickly recruited outstanding subordinates for them, who really *do* know the fundamentals of the businesses involved. And of course, within a year or two, the competent "surprise" choice will have filled in any significant gaps in background.

Moreover, serendipity knows no bounds. A widely connected social friend just might introduce you to an employer who needs precisely what you offer. Stranger things than that happen every day.

The Bottom Line: Diminishing Returns

After you've depleted your ideal business contacts, you may indeed want to try a few of your likeliest social contacts. Only your own good judgment can tell you what you should and shouldn't ask of someone you know.

However, here's a suggestion that applies to every job-changing activity, including every variation of Personal Contact: *Don't do too much of it!*

There are several techniques to advance your career, and we'll look at all of them. Since the amount of time you can devote to career development is necessarily limited, it's important not to spend so much time on any one activity that you neglect the others. Take advantage of the most obvious opportunities that all the techniques offer, and don't pursue any to the point that your time could more productively be spent on something else.

You see what to do. But, sadly, you've lost contact with some of the former colleagues you should be talking to.

Let the Internet come to your rescue!

What to do is clear. Ask for a reference, rather than a job. It's an amazingly helpful and versatile technique...absolutely the best way to approach the people you know from all your years in business who may be in a position to hire you into—or recommend you for—the ideal next step in your career.

Unfortunately you—like me and just about everyone I know—haven't kept in touch with all of your former bosses, subordinates, peers, customers, fellow board members of civic and charitable organizations, etc. whom you'd now like to phone.

Make that *doubly* unfortunate. Not only do these folks merit recontacting because of the warm mutual respect you vividly recall, some of them—since you last talked—have risen to far higher and more powerful positions. Today their opinion of you is just as favorable as ever. But now they're much more able to help...a pleasant surprise that awaits, if and when you can reconnect.

But your Roll-O-Dex has been comatose for the past 7 years, and your Palm Pilot hasn't yet been introduced to these people. How do you find them?

Personally, I'm amazed at how easy it is to locate lost friends using even the most basic tools available on the Internet.

Search Engines and Their "People Finder" Functions

Your Internet browser is almost certainly Netscape Navigator or Internet Explorer. Both have default search engines that immediately perform any function shown on the browser's home page.

For example, I use Netscape. To look for someone, I click "People Finder." On Internet Explorer, you'll click "White Pages." Now we have an engine ready to search the white page listings of every listed phone in the U.S. and Canada. Just fill in the blanks on the questionnaire.

You may need some creativity and experimentation to find your person. For example, confronted by a simple questionnaire, I input the name of my high school classmate Dick Vanner, plus WI, our state in those days. Nothing. Then I try *Richard* Vanner. Bingo!

But when I input Ralph Lauren and NY...nothing. Why? Unlisted residential phone. But then I try the business listings. Bingo! Of course. His name's included in the name of his firm. Might your lost person now be in business as an independent consultant?

Your "Wild Card"

The more specific your information input is the better. However, there's even a way—called "wild card"—to use *fragments* of information. Put in as many letters as you're sure of...and then an asterisk. Say you're looking for Richie Delgado. You don't know if he's Richard or Ricardo. Maybe he's even switched to Rick, which he once mentioned wanting to do. Try Ric* or Ri* Delgado. Or could it have been Delga *t* o? Try Ric* Delga*. With a name as distinctive as RD's you're likely to find him if you specify the right city or even the right state. Try several possibilities. Cinci* serves as well as the perfect spelling of the Ohio city, whereas a wrong spelling of Cincinnati will *defeat* your search.

What about unlisted phones?

So far, so easy. But the game will get far more challenging. Many of the contacts you and I will want to locate have *unlisted* phones. Creativity must come to the rescue. Think up questions to ask yourself.

Does the person have children who would now be 10 to 19 years old? Do you remember their names? They may have a phone and it probably *will* be listed. *"Is your dad there?"* Or an older child, as you recall, became a lawyer or an MD or a DDS and is likely to be living and practicing...where? Professionals will have listed office numbers.

Do you remember a close friend of your lost contact, whom he or she may have kept in touch with? The friend's phone may be listed.

Or try for an e-mail address.

Most of the sites that check phone listings also search for e-mail addresses. Some folks who'd never list their phone don't even try to hide their e-mail address. Often it's their last name, plus maybe a first initial or some other prefix to make it unique at the mail server that follows their @ symbol. The different search sites vary widely in finding even the most obvious clues in e-mail addresses. Try several. And at each, besides first naming as requested, try for the last name alone as your clue, using an * for first name, or an initial, or whatever your left brain *and* your right brain tell you to try.

Or become Sherlock Holmes

In seeking the person/friend/child, become Sherlock Holmes. Ask yourself wider-ranging questions. Are there any special interests, hobbies, college alumni or professional rosters, church or temple affiliations, etc. that could be accessed online or phoned at headquarters or locally for (1) published information or (2) a conversation with a "Good Samaritan," whom you might be able to chat into helping you by bending non-disclosure rules.

Maybe you'll wind up with a "Samaritan" who *knows* but won't *tell*. If so, try to strike a deal to send Ms. or Mr. S a letter to forward to your target person, asking him/her to contact you. If you do, I suggest you leave the stamped forwarding envelope unsealed, so that your brief note inside can be perused. "I've left the envelope open," you'll say, "so if you want to, you can enclose a note before you seal and send it." That way, your merciful helper can see that he or she isn't forwarding a blackmail demand or a dunning letter. Your note (on your stationery with address and phone numbers) will be very brief:

> "Bill —
> I've lost track of your address since we were together at Acme
> Corp. Ms. Samaritan is protecting your privacy, but has been kind
> enough to forward this to you. Please give me a call.
> > Regards, Aaron"

More Search Engines to Try

I'm confused—you will be too—by the myriad of sites that have "people finding" capability to search white and yellow page phone numbers and e-mail addresses. Moreover, resources that don't have this capability them-selves link you somewhere else that does. Also, an entity you're exploring for the first time will take you to its "people finding" destination, and you'll find your browser has already color-changed the name because you've already been there via a different route.

Moreover, "search engines" are inconsistent. One will instantly cough up target person #1. Fabulous! You've found the perfect tool. Then you try for person #2. Nothing. Damn! Then you go to the next resource. Person #2 in a breeze. The perfect tool! But being a good scientist, you try for person #1 on this new paragon. Nothing. And so on. And so on!

Frustrating, yes. But utterly wonderful that you've found your two people. Who cares that you had to go to two places to find them. The people who already know and enthusiastically respect the quality of your work are worth their weight in gold when you're job-changing.

These search engines/directories are among the famous general content ones: *Yahoo!*, *AltaVista*, *Excite*, *HotBot*, *Lycos*, *GoTo*, *Snap.com*, *WebCrawler*. Others are more specialized in finding people, and each site has interesting extra services: *BigYellow.com*, *WhoWhere.com*, *Bigfoot.com*, *PeopleFind.com*, *Canada411.com*, *WorldPages.com*, *411Locate.com*, *555-1212.com*.

When just sifting phone numbers—white and yellow page—these sites will yield reasonably similar answers. But they'll vary widely in answering your other queries. You'll find additional search engines among the many resources at the end of Chapter 14. But before you spend lots of time with the individual search engines, let's look at an even more exciting marvel of the Internet.

Metasearch Sites...
Masters of the Search Engine Universe

You may be as pleasantly surprised as I was to learn there are sites that will submit your query to several major search engines simultaneously, get answers from all of them and—in the same time it'd take to do one search on a single engine—get you the results of, for example, 12 searches done on 12 engines simultaneously.

These sites help you with your "Sherlock Holmes" searching. You've struck out with phone listing and e-mail address searches. Now you are coupling the person's name with a word that characterizes their occupation, industry, civic involvement, interest or hobby...a word the individual you seek might be connected with. You can also try just to use the first and last name alone... and you might hit if the name is distinctive. I've seen this happen, where a

person retired and now runs a bed and breakfast. I was sent right to the site...
and to Terry Target, "host."

These sites give you a choice of how they'll match your words: "any," "and,"
and usually also "as a phrase." Choose "***and***," because you only want sites
that include the first and last names of the person, plus the third word you've
chosen as a topical tag.

The Prominence/Time Trade-off

Since there is virtually an infinite amount of content on the Internet, even
people who are not famous ***do*** appear in something that's posted, if the computers look long enough for them in all of the sites and documents that have
the topic word. If a person is well-known and frequently written about and
so is their occupational category or other topic you've connected them with,
you'll almost instantaneously get several positive "hits" of first-and-last-
name-plus-topical-tag.

Take headhunters, for example. "Gerard" or "Gerry"—either works but different articles may be found—"Roche," plus "recruiter" or "headhunter"
almost instantly brings up the world's most famous person in this field.
Because of this book being widely written about, the same brief period will
find some—but fewer—mentions of me if my names are accompanied by
"recruiter" or "headhunter" or "author." Other recruiters who do superb
search work may be less written about. Therefore, it may take slightly longer
to find something on the Internet that mentions a specific one of them.

Metasearch engines present "hits" in declining order of relevance. First
come the ones that include all three (or however many) words...***if*** any sites
are found so quickly that do. Then will come ones with only the topical
word present. Or maybe that word, plus the first or last name but not both
(and therefore not our person). Why do the sites do this when specifically
asked for "all"? The reason is that some search engines queried on a
"metasearch" cannot make the distinction between "any." and "all."

So in searching for your person-plus-topic, take advantage of any opportunity the site gives you to *p r o l o n g* the search. Obviously, you're not
going to get much time on any important computer when you pay nothing
for service (aside from looking at advertising while you wait). But competition among these sites will gradually increase the amount of extra
time (and therefore thoroughness) beyond an instant flash report these
sites are willing—at your option—to provide.

All of these sites have different features and several have links to additional types of searches that you can pay for. Sometimes the same sort of search is done free on one site and charged for at another. Explore. Play! You'll be glad you discovered this resource for more purposes than just job-changing.

Here are some Metasearch Engines to try:

SavvySearch One of my favorites. Includes the opportunity to customize your own metasearch protocol choosing from 100 resources including not only search engines and "guides" (directories), but also online encyclopedias, business media, newspapers, magazines, TV, sports, travel, foreign, music, and other resources.

MetaCrawler This outstanding metasite gathers results from the top search engines and directories, cuts out duplication, scores results, and produces a comprehensive list of relevant sites.

Cyber 411 includes AltaVista, Excite, HotBot, Google, InfoSeek, Lycos, Magellan, GoTo, Snap.com, WebCrawler, Yahoo! and FindWhat search engines. Can be customized as to time spent on any one search, number of hits per search engine, and number of hits listed per browser page.

Highway 61 An entertaining site which sprinkles humor in among the search criteria and even provides inspiring quotes while you wait for results. Searches can be customized as to length of time spent searching and number of hits.

DogPile Incorporates search engines and directories, and lists results by source. Can also search stock quotes and usenet sites.

ProFusion Customize your search by type of phrasing, number of results shown, and which of 9 search engines to use. Will also check links if you choose that option.

See Chapter 14 for a further list of search engines, directories and metasearch sites.

Chapter 4

Networking:

Pursuing the People You Don't Know

Networking is a form of Personal Contact. But much *less personal* than getting in touch with people you already know.

Networking is contacting people your *contacts* know...and people *their contacts* know...and people their contacts' *contacts* know.

Because it's done face-to-face, Networking is "personal contact" in that sense. And since someone you've met introduces you to...or lets you use his or her name with...the next person you see, it's also "personal contact" in that sense.

Unfortunately, there's a big difference between asking people you already know for help and suggestions, and making the same requests of strangers you're sent to.

That's why we're looking at the two techniques separately, even though a lot of people prefer not to distinguish between them. And why we'll concentrate on getting only the good out of networking, and avoiding its pitfalls.

Networking is the single most powerful job-changing tool, so you should learn to use it effectively. Whether you give it heavy emphasis, or just let it happen spontaneously, some networking is inevitable every time you seek a new or better job.

First let's look at the advantages and disadvantages of Networking, including its most famous advantage:

"Networking increases your contacts geometrically."

For people who are actually out of work, Networking may well be the most popular method of finding another job. Certainly it's the most widely recommended way...particularly among the "outplacement" companies that employers hire to help fired employees find new jobs.

As those experts point out:

"Networking increases your contacts geometrically."

The concept is that everyone you approach, while probably not personally in control of a job that would interest you, can at least refer you to several additional people. And each of those can send you to several more. If each person only passed you along to one further person, your progress would be *linear*. But each Networking visit leads to multiple further visits, so your progress is *geometric*.

Everyone has at least a few contacts. Through Networking, those few can mushroom. Consider the following advantages:

More people meet and know about you. Your finite circle of acquaintances expands infinitely.

People who want to help can help. Only one hard-to-find person will provide your ideal job, but everyone can suggest additional people to see.

There's high impact in a face-to-face visit. Particularly in comparison to a printed resume arriving in the mail or posted on the Internet.

Here's a process you can initiate. Rather than passively waiting for a recruiter's call, you can be as active as your time and energy permit.

The job you find probably won't require relocation. Local visits lead you toward local jobs.

Appealing as its advantages are, Networking also has some disadvantages:

It's time-consuming. Making and keeping Networking appointments is slow, arduous work.

There's no confidentiality. You can't network without making your intentions public.

You reach relatively few people. You're doing well if you make and keep 2 or 3 Networking appointments per day...not enough to survey the overall employment marketplace very quickly.

Requesting favors from strangers isn't easy. Asking help from friends is hard enough; pursuing other people's friends is tougher still.

Focus is random and local. If you want to scour the nation for jobs in a particular field, a series of random local visits isn't the way to do it.

At its best, Networking is Personal Contacts. The big difference is that you're not limited to the few people you already know. At its worst, Networking is like dealing with Personal Contacts on a mass-production basis, with virtually all of the "personal" removed. Where on the spectrum you position your own version of this highly individualistic medium is entirely up to you.

Now let's look at Networking in practice.

Some of its implications are obvious, but others are not.

Let's go back to Jim, who wanted you to consider becoming his CFO and potential successor, and let's change the situation. Now let's say that he's *not* "bucking for President and Chief Operating Officer in about four years, when Caroline retires, and Ken moves up to Chairman." Let's say, instead, that Jim just got to SolidGrowth nine months ago. He's still consolidating his own position, and the Caroline/Ken scenario is at least 8 years away.

We'll also change the facts to make your problem immediate. Flaming-Tiger.com is one of five "dot com" startups...all financed and controlled by the same family-dominated venture capital operation. The five were show-cased together in a *Wall Street Journal* campaign for the VC firm, which dubbed them "*4 Hot Dots.*" "Tiger"—under your leadership—is the only one of the four that has built a reasonably strong and growing business. All four had dramatically successful IPOs in 1999. But today, at $3.25 a share, Tiger is the only one still reported as a Nasdaq stock in the daily papers. The others are virtually worthless. Now the family patriarch, who controls the VC operation *and* these startups, has decided to merge the other three into "Tiger" and put his stepson, who's headed the failed three from their inception, in charge of the merged company. You and virtually everyone in all of the companies but Tiger are suddenly out of work. Confidentiality is no longer a factor in your job-changing efforts.

However, Jim feels exactly as he told you. He's sorry he didn't know of your availability when he had that "perfect spot a couple months ago." Unfortunately, he doesn't foresee having another opening for a General Manager in his Group for at least the next couple years, and by then you'll already be somewhere else.

But Jim *does* want to help. Let's listen as he calls his friend and favorite customer, Norma Nice, Co-Founder and CEO of a young fast-growing multi-divisional marketing company that sells mainly business-to-business:

> JIM: "Norma, last week I had lunch with one of the best young General Managers who ever worked for me, Bill Versatile. In fact, I promoted him into his first general management job several years ago, when I was at Early Corp. Gave him a division that had been a loser for years...one we'd tried to sell and couldn't *give* away.

We were almost ready to shut it down. Well, he pulled off an amazing turnaround...improved efficiency, lowered costs, modified the product line, and brought in some new customers. He got the thing very respectably into the black and kept it there for two years. In fact, he put it on a good growth trend, so that we had no trouble unloading it at a favorable price.

"Bill's done a lot of equally fine work since then, most recently an amazing job at FlamingTiger.com., the only success in that stable of four startups you saw advertised in *The Wall Street Journal* as '4 Hot Dots.' Well, it's a sordid tale with some not-too-nice people in it, but they're merging the other three essentially defunct companies into Tiger and the Chairman of the VC outfit that controls the whole mess is putting his step-son, who fell flat on his face heading the three losers, in charge of the surviving company, which will really be nothing but Tiger. So Bill, who's done another extraordinary job, is out of work!

"As you know, I've filled my Division Manager opening. If I'd had any idea I could have got Bill, he'd be here right now. I'd even fire a couple people to fit him in, but I can't make another change so soon after getting here myself. That's why I thought of you, because you're looking for a President of that B-to-B e-commerce company you just bought. Of course I say that selfishly, because with someone like Bill in charge, that business would take off, and you'd be buying a lot more of our stuff to sell through it."

NORMA: "You really think he's that good?"

JIM: "Darn right. I only wish I could have him myself!"

NORMA: "Well, on a recommendation like that from you, Jim, I think I've got to at least meet him. But, unfortunately, I'm in about the same position you are. I finally found a candidate I like for that job, and he's agreed to take it. In fact, I sent him an offer letter last night by Federal Express. Unless they come up with a big counteroffer, my job is filled. But have Bill call me and come over. There's always the chance my deal may fall through."

JIM: "And even if it doesn't, maybe you can refer him to some other people. He's really great, and I'd appreciate any help you can give him."

NORMA: "I'll certainly try. Thanks for thinking of me, Jim."

There you have an ideal example of Networking. Everything is operating entirely in your best interests. You can only gain from Jim's effort to be helpful.

Jim: 1. knows you well,
        2. enthusiastically recommends you, and
        3. unequivocally asks help for you.

Norma: 1. knows Jim well,
        2. respects his judgment, believes his recommendation, feels a friendly obligation to him, and
        3. is very likely either to have a job for you, or to be able to refer you to someone else who can be helpful.

When you meet Norma, you've got almost as much going for you as when you met with Jim. At least Jim has tried to set it up that way. Indeed, given Jim's top-notch credibility with Norma, she may even be hoping that her deal with the other candidate falls through.

But alas, your cookie crumbles. The signed-and-returned employment contract from Norma's new Division President is on her desk by the time you arrive for an interview tomorrow morning. Norma likes you on a personal basis and wants to oblige Jim. So she treats you to an early lunch. And afterward, she makes several phone calls in your behalf. One is to Sam Supplier, from whom Norma buys a lot of what she sells:

> NORMA: "Sam, I don't know whether you need a Division Manager over there or not, but I just had a very impressive young man in my office that you ought to take a look at. He's one of the casualties at that dot com mess that was advertised as '4 Hot Dots.' Well they're cold now. But he's a *very* able guy, according to a friend of mine, who thought he'd be good for President of that e-commerce company I just bought. But it's too late. I just hired somebody else. Could you meet him and see if you can use someone like him? And if you can't, could you maybe introduce him to some other people who might need a really good 'e-executive?'"

> SAM: "Sure, Norma. I'd be happy to help. I really don't think I need anyone at quite that high level. But let me meet him and see what I can do to refer him to others who might."

> NORMA: "Thanks, Sam. I knew I could count on you."

No question about it. Sam Supplier will cheerfully see you to oblige Norma, who's one of Sam's biggest customers. He'll also set up further appointments for you. He almost has to. But this time there's no specific job in mind. And Norma can only relay Jim's endorsement. She doesn't speak from firsthand knowledge. So Sam doesn't hear quite the same glowing words Norma did.

And by the time Sam sees you and begins passing you along to people who owe him a favor, the transaction may be on quite a different footing. There may even be a disclaimer thrown in:

> SAM: "Say, Phil, would you do me a favor and see a guy who's looking for a job? He was sent to me by my biggest customer, Norma Nice at Buyathonics, and I've got to show I've tried to help. His name's Bill Versatile. I don't personally know how good he is, since I've never worked with him. But he seems like a reasonably intelligent guy. He's one of the crew they dumped out of that disaster that used to be called the '4 Hot Dots.' And Phil, if you possibly can, please try to pass him along. I did almost 15% of my total volume with Buyathonics last year."

> PHIL: "Okay, I'll help...even though you've hit me at a really busy time. But, *I* did pretty good business with *you* last year. And I appreciate it. You can count on me, Sam, anytime."

And so it may go. As you get further away from the people who know you and believe in you, there may be less interest in you as a potential employee and in helping you find employment. And as that phenomenon sets in, Networking, which is basically your most useful job-changing technique, becomes less worthwhile. You spend lots of time on appointments, and yet the value of that time may be considerably less than outward appearances suggest.

We've just looked at classic "please-help-him-as-a-favor-to-me" Networking.

Today there's a more modern and aggressive form: Networking-as-a-contact-sport.

You should know about it. But use good judgment in practicing it.

I call it *NFL Networking.*

Consider it Networking-as-the-ultimate-scrimmage. What used to be a rather prim and polite pastime, not too far removed from lawn bowling and croquet, has been transformed into one of the roughest contact sports in the business world today.

Unemployment is a nasty thing...especially for the executive well above $100,000. Cutting off his income is like trying to choke off his air supply. He'll fight for life just as fiercely as any other wounded and cornered animal. Motivation he's got. Give him a strategy and he'll execute.

So, long before it appeared as a major national sport, the stage was set for NFL Networking. There were plenty of players available...all of them adequately motivated, without resort to Pro Football's megabucks. The only things needed to get a good rough game going were aggressive coaching and a new set of rules.

Enter the "Outplacement Counselors." Pervasive growth of the outplacement industry, which is paid by employers to help fired executives find jobs, has provided the missing factors: an aggressive and creative coaching staff which, in turn, has provided appropriately revised rules. Networking is the number-one favorite job-changing technique among these professionals, and they have contributed greatly to the advancement of the game.

The basic problem with the classically polite lawn-bowling-and-croquet form of Networking...the please-help-him-as-a-favor-to-me version...is its passivity, its lack of vigorous combat. The job seeker is put into play by someone else, who wishes to be helpful and therefore opens doors and makes appointments that the executive might otherwise have difficulty achieving on his own. Merely capitalizing on these thoughtfully-provided opportunities, the unemployed executive keeps these dates, presents himself and his achievements as pleasantly and persuasively as he can, and graciously accepts whatever is offered at the conclusion of each appointment...employment, offers of further help, or merely good wishes. Regardless of the outcome, he expresses genuine appreciation for the time he's been given, and he may attempt to kick an extra point with a "thank you" note.

How bland and wimpish! In these days when there's more mayhem in a love song on MTV than there used to be on *The Untouchables*, the game of Networking was obviously long overdue for an update. That modernization has been brilliantly accomplished in NFL Networking.

The breakthrough change has been to free the job-seeking executive from prior restrictions on his actions in the game. Indeed, he's now encouraged to seize and retain, if possible, total initiative for every aspect of play. No longer does he passively wait to capitalize on play-making opportunities created for him by others. Under professionally-coached NFL rules, the job-seeker initiates every phase of play, and fiercely defends his prerogative not to surrender the initiative to any other player. Let's first scan the new rules, and then I'll interview Axel Bludgeon, reigning world champion NFL Networker.

Rules of NFL Networking

1.   Never fail to get into the office of anyone whose name is mentioned to you.

2.   Never depart with less than 3 new names.

3.   Never leave follow-up solely in the hands of the person you just saw.

Now let's talk to Axel Bludgeon, who's emerged victorious for the past three years as the most aggressive job-seeking executive in the U.S. under NFL Networking rules.

JOHN: "Congratulations, Axel. You've won again! When you first got into NFL Networking, did you ever imagine that you'd become champion and hold the title three years in a row?"

AXEL: "Thank you, John. But before I answer your question, I also want to thank all those executives who helped me win. A big annual victory like mine is just a series of daily skirmishes. And if those guys and gals hadn't let me beat them down to get an appointment and come in, then I couldn't have forced them to give up the three names so I would leave. So thanks, fellas...and ladies...I owe it all to you!

"Okay, now I'll answer your question. No, when I first started Networking in NFL competition, I had no idea I could stay unemployed for three years, despite meeting close to 1,000 executives *in their offices*. Surely, I thought, somebody would want to hire me, and then I'd be out of contention. But early on, I met some of my competition...like in corporate reception rooms, where we were both waiting to see different executives. And when I saw what wimps they were, I was pretty confident. Did you ever meet Pete Polite, or Carl Courteous, or Cathy Considerate? I think the longest any of them lasted was four or five months!"

JOHN: "Axel, NFL Networking as a contact sport is something some of our readers may not be familiar with. Would you please explain how it works?"

AXEL: "Sure, gladly. First, somebody has to give you a name to get started. And then you go right ahead as if it were standard old-fashioned pre-NFL Networking. You call up the person at their office and say:

> 'Hello, I was talking to so-and-so, and she told me to call you. I'm in the process of a career change, and I'd like to come in and see you for just 15 minutes to get the benefit of your thoughts and suggestions. Now, I'm *not* going to ask you for a job. It's just that so-and-so speaks so highly of you, and she feels your advice could really be helpful. When would you like me to come in?'"

JOHN: "What if this person is too busy to see you, or maybe doesn't believe you're going to be out of there in 15 minutes? What if he'd rather just tell you what you want to know on the telephone? Then he or she can hang up when your 15 minutes are over."

AXEL: "NOBODY is too busy to see me. That's NFL Rule #1, *Never fail to get into the office of anyone whose name is mentioned to you.* I can't let them cop out on 'busy,' or I'd never get to see anyone important. And I sure can't go ahead on the phone. That's clearly against the rules, precisely because they can hang up on me in 15 minutes. Of course, *nobody*, even Cathy Considerate, would be in-and-out of an *office* in 15 minutes. Who ever heard of a 15-minute meeting on any subject? It's impossible. Once I'm in there, I'm good for a half-hour at least. And pretty often 45 minutes. How do you think I got to be National Champion? Under-promising and over-staying is an important technique."

JOHN: "Another question on your basic spiel. If so-and-so really wants this person to see you, why doesn't he call the person himself?"

AXEL: "Good question. Look at NFL Rule #3, *Never leave follow-up solely in the hands of the person you just saw.* I never leave anybody without finding out who they have in mind for me to talk to. That's NFL Rule #2, *Never depart with less than 3 new names.* If they say they'll call a few people and try to set up some appointments, I demand to know *who* they intend to call. That way, I'm no longer at their mercy. If they don't bother to follow up, I can go right around them, call the people they mentioned, and say they wanted me to meet those people, which of course they did. That was one of the first things my coach taught me."

JOHN: "Speaking of your coach..."

AXEL: "Excuse me, John. But let me just go back to your other question about why not have the person call for my appointment instead of calling myself. That question shows that you just don't grasp the fundamental change in Networking from the old sissy way to the new NFL tactics. Under the old rules, I *could* leave it up to the person I just saw to call and arrange my meeting with the next person. Because, under the old way, the person I just saw would know and like me enough to really *want* the next person to see me. Or at least he'd have a good dollars-and-cents *business* reason to pass me along. Under those circumstances he really would follow up. And I could walk out of his office without forcing him to tell me the names of the people he was thinking of calling in my behalf. Under the old style, people would be seeing me because *he wanted them to*. The fundamental motivation of the game would be *him* saying:

> *'Help Axel as a favor to me.'*

"But today, under NFL rules, I've got to see lots more people and get lots more referrals. And many of those referrals have got to come from stone-cold strangers, who don't know me from a hole-in-the-wall, except that I'm in their office and I won't leave until they give me names. If I simply walk out, do you think they're going to call their friends and business contacts and tell them they've got to see me? Don't be naive! Under the new rules, it's up to *me* to keep the game going. Since the guy I just saw isn't likely to put much pressure on, *I* apply the pressure, and say he told me to do it. Instead of trying to get him to say, 'Help Axel as a favor to me,' I say...or at least I imply:

> *'Help me, or I'll see to it that you're in trouble with him.'*

"Now of course I can't *really* get the guy I'm calling in trouble with the one who told me about him. But *he* doesn't know that! Get my drift? The guy whose name I'm using doesn't care much one way or another whether I get my next appointments...certainly not enough to call for them himself. In fact, he'd be too embarrassed to call and be as pushy in getting me an appointment as I can be when I use his name to get my own appointment. So you see the new rules put *me* in charge of the game and don't depend nearly so much on how other people feel about me."

JOHN: "Very interesting, Axel. I see you've really given a lot of thought to your game."

AXEL: "I've had to. You see, the intimidation of NFL Networking is psychological, not physical. So the entire game is mental strategy. It's not easy to get a no-agenda meeting with a really busy person. And the ones who aren't really busy aren't important enough to want meetings with. And besides, I'm not the only job-changer who's calling them. Some senior executives get several calls a week just like mine. So I've got to be the one who gets in when the others are turned away. I've done a lot of thinking about the psychological handles I can use to manipulate these people...first to get an appointment, and then to get the names I came for, so I can leave. Do you want to hear what I've come up with?"

JOHN: "Why yes, if you feel you want to give away such strategic information."

AXEL: "No problem. Just because other people know what the levers are doesn't mean they'll be able to pull them as hard as I do. Here are the psychological weaknesses I can appeal to in getting what I want, and I try to go for as many as possible in each case:

Friendship. Personal friends want to help if they can.

Altruism. The desire to help another human being in need. There's a streak of 'Good Samaritan' in everybody.

Greed. The desire to do business with the person whose name I mention...in the present and the future.

Fear. Concern that if they don't do what I want, it will prejudice business and personal relationships with the person I name.

Guilt. The feeling that if they don't do what I ask, they'll be letting down the person I mention, who probably *would* do what I want for somebody they sent to him.

Charm. The idea here is that if I'm face-to-face with people for a half hour, I can get them to do anything I want...from hiring me to spilling all the names they know. I always go in counting on charm as my main leverage, and then I wind up using anything else that works better."

"Now, John, there are two other possibilities I've thought about but never used, because they're against the rules...even the rougher, more realistic rules of the NFL. They're *Sex* and *Bribery*. The closest I've come to those is that I've sometimes used a CEO's *really significant other* as the name that referred me. Since, technically, that's just using one name to get another, it's perfectly within the rules. And it *does* get attention!"

JOHN: "Well, Axel, you've certainly been generous in sharing your expertise with us. One final question...and I'm almost embarrassed to ask it so late in our interview...but what is the exact connection between the National Football League and the NFL Networking title you hold?"

AXEL: "Don't be embarrassed, John. We're now a well-established sport, but just about everyone still asks that question. There's no connection. My sport is purely an individual one-on-one activity...not a team sport, and nothing to do with the National Football League. It's the *Networking by Force League.*"

JOHN: "Thank you, Axel Bludgeon. And best wishes for another year of unemployment through obnoxious Networking by Force."

There you have it: up-to-date, truly aggressive Networking, as practiced by a master. Axel Bludgeon is managing to get into the offices of a great many executives...and to walk out with the names of plenty of additional executives, whose offices he'll also penetrate. He has a virtuoso's mastery of the techniques of modern high-pressure Networking. It's the objective he's lost sight of. *Axel is not getting hired.*

There's a "catch 22" in basing a job campaign on the aggressive new style of Networking.

Using force to generate appointments offends the people you're trying to impress.

Let's look at this problem...and ways to overcome it.

If you're in a high-profile position...in control of attractive jobs, or likely to know about them...chances are you're up against a lot of Axel Bludgeons. Either you're *seeing them and resenting them*, or you're *fighting them off and feeling guilty*. "After all," you think, "just a slight turn of the corporate-wheel-of-fortune could throw *me* into Networking. And then how would I want people to react to me?"

But your work week is more than filled with your job. And if anyone's going to get an extra half or three-quarters of an hour from you, it ought to be a family member or a friend...not some stranger who drops a name and insists on an *appointment* for a "15-minute" matter, instead of straightforwardly handling it by phone.

On the other hand, if you're currently out-of-a-job, you're in an even worse position. What are you supposed to do...ignore the most widely recommended job-seeking method? Walk away from advice your former employer may have paid $5,000 to $50,000 for? Possibly delay restoring proper income to your household? And all because you're too prissy or sissy to do what others are doing every day?

If you're the appointment-giver, you're weighing the "clout" of the name that's dropped. How much do you revere or fear it? What's it worth in business gained or lost? Would the "name" see someone you sent her? *Would* you send her anyone? Is your caller *really* close to the "name" he's using? How busy are you? Do you *like* the caller's manner? Do you *want* to help him? Does he sound willing to accept your best efforts right now on the phone, or must you flatly say "No"? Or are you willing...*or forced*...to say "Yes"? Only you can decide. And only on a call-by-call basis.

In this situation one thing is clear. If you're the appointment-seeker, you've got the more difficult decision to make. Pressure or no-pressure? And how much pressure? If you push too hard, you can alienate the person you're approaching...even if she feels obliged to see you and even if she gives you further names.

Moreover, you could easily lose the respect and sponsorship of the "name" you're using. Regardless of what you imply, you only have a slight and probationary acquaintance. If you wield the "name" like a war club, there's a good chance the person you're approaching will ask the "name" about you. He'll find out your relationship is tenuous at best, and he'll feel obligated to let the "name" know about your foolhardy use of his most precious asset. Then you'll be on two you-know-what lists.

Overaggressive Networking can backfire into "mop-up" calls disclaiming connection with you. I make such calls. And I always inform my friends and contacts when their name is inappropriately used with me. My loyalty is to them...not to the strangers they've mistakenly tried to help.

Obviously you don't want to portray yourself negatively, while seeking appointments to present yourself positively. Here are some ways to get around that dilemma:

Emphasize close, rather than distant, contacts. The nearer along the networking chain you are to the people who know, respect, and genuinely want to help you, or have a business reason for doing so, the less pressure you'll have to use in getting appointments. Consider shifting to widely connected purely social contacts before relentlessly pursuing reluctant strangers.

Consider leaving appointment-solicitation in the hands of the person you've just seen. If someone says she'd rather call her contacts than have you call them, back off...even though this violates NFL rule #3. If she does set up dates, you're way ahead. You walk in with no prior record of bullying. If she doesn't follow up, you can probably make one discreet reminder call and offer to save her bother by calling the contacts yourself. If she fails to proceed on either basis, you've probably lost the right to use her name with those people. But you never really had it anyway. Maybe someone else will introduce you. Or you can write letters and introduce yourself.

Listen carefully during your self-introductory phone call. Tune to the "vibes," as well as the words. Whether you're being obnoxiously pushy is subjectively up to this listener, at this moment, of this call. It's not up to you, nor to any "Counselor" who has instructed you. If you've only met your sponsoring "name" during a brief networking visit, no matter how cordial, she's not *your* friend. She's the friend of the person you're calling. The only interpretation of this phone call she'll ever receive and believe will come from her long-standing contact...the person you're talking to. Don't sacrifice a successful prior networking contact through insensitive handling of a later one.

Also, reactions to your networking calls will differ with each person you phone, and even with the day and moment your call happens to come in. Be alert and flexible.

Consider accepting immediate help on the phone, rather than holding out for a visit. There's inherent weakness in your logic when you insist that you must have a face-to-face appointment, and yet you'll "only take 15 minutes" and "not ask for a job." If it's true that you only want "the benefit of your thoughts and suggestions," and only 15 minutes of them, then why not accept them right now on the phone?

Of course, what you *really* want is to *display your personality and charm,* which you expect will expand the 15 minutes into a pre-employment interview, or at least a "we-forgot-all-about-the-clock" brainstorming session. After dozens, and even hundreds, of calls like yours, and plenty of appointments like you're asking for, the person you're calling knows exactly what you want. If he's refusing it, and offering a valuable substitute, be smart. Accept and benefit. Make the most of what you *can* get. Otherwise, you may exhaust the time your respondent is willing to give you and wind up with neither on-the-phone help, nor an appointment.

Realize this. Calls like yours are frequent. And everyone's delivering the same high-pressure get-an-appointment script. When the person you call tries to get you to deal with him in the efficient and logical way he prefers, you have two choices: (1) Do so, and stand out from the crowd; you may so impress him with your alertness, common sense, and flexibility that he may decide to see you after all. Or (2) stick to the script and increase the pressure; prove your ability to follow instructions, while disproving your flexibility and resourcefulness.

One further point: Armed with the kind of resume you should be using (which we'll thoroughly discuss later on), you'll feel more confident than you do right now, to speak by phone and follow up by sending your resume by mail or messenger.

Make lots of polite contacts, keep records, and use time as your ally. Rather than besiege and bully a few key contacts, deal lightly-and-politely with lots of them. And be sure to keep careful records. That way, you can graciously leave follow-up in the hands of others, if they prefer. You won't forget to inquire about loose ends. And with lots of contacting underway, you won't be tempted to push anyone too soon or too stridently.

Concentrate on your current industry, where talking to you will seem most relevant. Except for your own purely social contacts, the people likeliest to grant you appointments will be in your industry, not unrelated fields. They'll expect an interesting conversation, which may even include new competitive scuttlebutt gained in your job-searching travels. So besides helping you, they'll figure there may also be some benefit for them.

Try to have something other than just your employment interests to talk about. The most irksome aspect of a networking appointment is its one-sidedness. Unlike almost every other business meeting, this one has nothing in it for your host...that is, unless he might want to hire you. And 99% of the time, he knows in advance he won't. He spends time, possibly risks valuable contacts, and maybe takes on a follow-up assignment. Yet he personally has nothing to gain. No wonder he's unenthusiastic!

Try to think of a topic that may interest your host, and offer it as part of the agenda:

> "I'd really appreciate your thoughts and suggestions. And maybe, since you're planning to build your own plant in Brazil, you'd be interested in some of the things we found out."

Who knows? Besides melting your host's resistance, you may get scheduled for more than 15 minutes. Incidentally, Chapter 18 is devoted to consulting which, if it matches your career objectives, enables you to conduct a meeting of genuine interest to your host, while still doing the same self-selling you'd do in an ordinary Networking session.

Trust your own good instincts, good manners, and good taste, whenever they conflict with what "experts" are telling you to do. You're just as able to judge what behavior will and won't turn people off, as any "expert" urging a commando raid. And unlike Axel Bludgeon, you want to get hired. Most people don't hire foot-in-the-door vacuum cleaner salesmen...or subtle extortionists...into high-level executive positions. And they're not comfortable entrusting their valuable contacts to them either. Through Axel's type of manipulation, someone may have to see you. But he doesn't have to like you. And you'll be a lot better off if he can do both.

Above all, don't fall for the "informational interview" strategy naively advised by many outplacement counselors. The concept is to present yourself as a sponge eager to soak up knowledge. Convey this idea: "You're so smart and I'm so dumb (or at least weak and needy at this moment); let me come in and drink from the font of your wisdom. Here we need Joan Rivers to shout, *"Oh, come on!"* A fresh young college grad can plead ignorance and ask for charity. An experienced executive cannot. Before the merger, you were a brilliant competitor. Today, downsized, you're no less able. Otherwise, who'd want you? The only time this flattery-plus-obsequious-modesty approach could possibly work would be in trying to switch to an entirely new industry or function. But even then you have far better approaches, and this chapter has shown them to you.

Use all the various job-changing techniques for what each can do best. Many "outplacement" advisors urge Networking almost to the exclusion of everything else. By the time we've examined all the "Rites of Passage," you'll see Networking in clear perspective among all the various job-changing methods, and you'll have the skill to use each when it's most appropriate.

If you're ever out of work, Networking will be your #1 most powerful technique...and the one you turn to most frequently. It's always available as a productive, open-ended outlet for your time and energy. After you've done about all you can with your Personal Contacts and Executive Recruiters, and perhaps you've even conducted a Direct Mail Campaign and also used the Internet productively, Networking will still beckon to you:

"Make another contact, and get several more to make."

That's Networking. Used sensitively, it can be richly rewarding.

||| **Now let's Network in reverse.** |||

Instead of meeting everyone your contacts send you to, let's pick someone you especially want to meet and find a contact who can introduce you.

I call this technique "Targeted Networking." And you'll benefit from it, even if you never change jobs.

Is there a Chief Executive you want to meet?

Maybe he's a CEO whose head of a division, or a corporate function, is nearing retirement with no replacement in sight. Or possibly a CEO with a division or a function so mismanaged that he *should* be looking for a new executive, whether he is or not. Or maybe she's a CEO who's searching for candidates, but using a recruiting firm that can't propose you because your company also gives it some business. Or perhaps a CEO with a corporate asset that's well-managed, but falling far short of its potential, because nobody in her organization sees that potential as you do.

Who do you want a personal introduction to? A high-ranking business or financial executive? Or perhaps the head of a university, a scientific association, a philanthropic foundation, an art museum, a professional sports league, a labor union, a charity, or an opera/symphony/ballet company? The possibilities are endless. But the method of identifying someone you already know, who also knows the person you want to meet, is the same.

First, find out everything you can about Mr. or Ms. Target. If he/she is prominent enough to control a job you'd be interested in, he or she is surely listed in a few of the directories shown in Appendix III. Besides naming the publications, my Research Director includes their prices and their publishers' phone numbers (many are no-charge 800s). The prices, however, will probably send you to a library to get your milk without buying the cow. Knowing which books you need, phone ahead to various libraries to make sure they have the ones you want.

Or better yet, stay home, relax, and let the Internet deliver everything you want to know. Visit the Web site of the organization you want to join. Probably there's a roster of key executives and quite an extensive biography of the CEO, if that's your person. A corporation's Proxy statement (available online) will have biographical information on its Directors. A nonprofit's Web site will have similar information. And with such a prominent person, the Metasites we just discussed in Chapter 3 should provide lots of background information.

Let's say you now know you want to meet:

> ARNOLD P. ACCESSIBLE
> CHAIRMAN AND CHIEF EXECUTIVE OFFICER
> ADVANTAGEOUS CORPORATION

Probably your online investigation has yielded essentially the same information you'd find in some basic—and very expensive—books in the library. But if not, drop in and check *The Reference Book of Corporate Managements*, published by Dun's Marketing Services, a division of Dun & Bradstreet, or *Standard & Poor's Register of Corporations, Directors, and Executives*. You'll see something like this:

> **CH BD CEO—ACCESSIBLE, ARNOLD P.**, b 1950; m;
> 1972—Univ of Michigan, BBA; 1974—Dartmouth Coll Amos
> Tuck Sch, MBA; 1974-1976 Army; 1976-1978 Entry Corp, Reg
> Sls Mgr; 1978-1984 Advancing Corp, Sls & Mktg Mgr, VP;
> 1984-1992 Larger Corp, VP Mktg, Sr VP Mktg; 1992-present
> Advantageous Corp, 1992 Pr Consumer Products Gp, 1996
> EVP, 1999 Pr COO, 2003 Ch CEO, now Ch Bd CEO Ch EC;
> Dir.

You may also find Mr. Accessible in Marquis *Who's Who in America*:

> **ACCESSIBLE, ARNOLD P.** corp. exec.; b Petersburg, Va., July
> 7, 1950; s. Franklin and Julia (Keys); m. Sally Slade, 1975 (div.
> 1991); children: Nancy L. (Mrs. Thomas Morse), Paul D.,
> Stephen K.; m. Lacey Tracey Parker Aug. 12, 1991; Children:
> Ralph T., Adam N. B.B.A. U. Mich., 1972; M.B.A. Amos Tuck
> Sch., Dartmouth Coll.; LL.D. (Hon.) Pepperdine U., 1999; asst.
> sls. mgr., reg. sls. mgr., Entry Corp., 1976-78; sls. & mktg. mgr.,
> v.p. mktg., Advancing Corp., 1978-84; v.p. mktg., sr. v.p. mktg. &
> sls., Larger Corp., 1984-92; pres. consumer products group,
> 1992-1996, exec. v.p., 1996-99, pres. & chief operating officer,
> 1999-2003, chmn. bd. & chief exec, officer, Advantageous Corp.,
> 2003, also dir.; dir., Diversified and Amalgamated Corp., Global
> Triumph Corp., Consolidated and Conglomerated Corp.; bd. dirs.,
> Center for Enlight-ened Thinking; bd. dirs., Foundation for
> Fostering Progress; chmn. bd. dirs., Fashionable Ballet Theatre
> Foundation; chmn. exec. com., dir., Drug Rehabilitation Outreach

Services; mem. Sigma Alpha Epsilon, Phi Beta Kappa. Presbyterian. Clubs: Metropolitan, Century, Sleepy Hollow. Home: 641 Fifth Avenue, New York, N.Y. 10022. Office: 345 Park Avenue, New York, N.Y. 10022.

Those entries are typical. You'll usually find a business history, plus varying amounts of personal and outside-activity/interest information, depending on how expansively the "biographee" filled out each publication's questionnaire. Therefore, the directory entries vary and it's worth checking all of them. On the Internet, of course, the information will be scattered among lots of sites and publications. But however you choose to get it, you'll have plenty of information to proceed.

Let's see who Mr. Accessible is sure to know. Anyone you know too? The possibilities are obvious:

Former Companies. He worked at Entry Corp., Advancing Corp. and Larger Corp., before joining Advantageous Corp. Scan your memory for prominent people you know, who were at those places when he was, and might have stayed in touch. Chances are 3 or 4 possibilities come to mind.

Present Company. Look at the senior officers (8) and particularly the outside directors (11) listed for Advantageous Corp. Know any?

Services to Present Company. Directories will tell you who Advantageous Corp. uses for Accounting, Investment and Commercial Banking, Advertising, and Law. From perhaps 6 to 10 such firms, you probably know 3 or 4 people who might be working closely with Accessible.

Fellow Corporate Board Members. Now we really hit pay dirt! Accessible is on the boards of Diversified Amalgamated, Global Triumph, and Consolidated & Conglomerated. These average about 14 members each, and insiders can introduce you just as well as outsiders; so here are 42 people (14x3) to consider.

Fellow Nonprofit Board Members. Another treasure trove! And each of the nonprofits has an Internet site you can visit to see who's on their board. Mr. Accessible is on these boards: Center for Enlightened Thinking, Foundation for Fostering Progress, Prestige

Ballet Theatre Foundation, and Drug Rehabilitation Outreach Services. A couple are very large boards. Figure an average of 17 members (not counting Accessible), so four boards yield 68 people who could introduce you to Mr. A. Know any of them?

So far, then, here are your potential "introducers":

People at Former Companies	3
Senior Officers at Present Company	8
Outside Directors at Present Company	11
Suppliers to Present Company	3
Fellow Corporate Board Members	42
Fellow Nonprofit Board Members	68
Total potential contacts so far:	135

Plus Purely Social Contacts. All 135 people we've identified so far are working with Mr. Accessible in a business context...or at least serving with him on the board of a nonprofit organization. If none of the 135 contacts is a "natural," his memberships in the Metropolitan Club, the Century Club, and the Sleepy Hollow Country Club may provide a link. Ask your closest friends in those clubs if they happen to know Mr. A well enough to make a friendly introduction. It's a long shot, but worth a try.

A Few Parting Comments About Targeted Networking

Targeted Networking is a lot of work. You won't do it, unless there's a very compelling reason...probably to meet someone who controls an ideal job for you. And that job either is open...or looks from your vantage point as if it should be.

Then an all-out effort to reach your "target" may be justified. But when you get your introduction and make your pitch, be sure you're easy to say "Yes" to. Use the strategy we discussed in asking for a reference, rather than a job. Don't frontally attack. Instead, do lots of listening and subtle questioning. Maybe toss in one or two of your best ideas as possible approaches you might explore if, on closer inspection, things are as they appear.

The strongest response you can hope to get at the end of your meeting is:

> "This has all been very interesting. I'll be thinking about our discussion, and we probably ought to get together again."

If the best way the person you've reached can use you is to fire whoever has the job you're aiming for, he or she may ultimately decide to do so. On the other hand, he or she may come up with a different way of using your talents that appeals to you even more. But one thing is almost certain: If you go in with guns blazing, naming names and suggesting tough action, you'll get the fast, easy answer..."No"...rather than the one you want..."To be continued."

Networking is your #1 tool. But use it carefully.

Networking—"targeted" and otherwise—is your single most valuable job-hunting tool. But always bear in mind that the further Networking takes you away from people who actually know you and can vouch for you, the weaker your referrals will be. And if you push too hard to get appointments with reluctant strangers, your behavior may become stridently self-defeating. In asking for your appointment, try to imply that you're inclined—and able—to *give*, not just take:

> "There is *one* good thing about job-hunting. And that's getting up-to-date on the really important things going on in the industry. I couldn't do that when I was chained to my desk. For example, those new wholesaler incentives that Acme has put in, trying to get the industry to adopt their e-commerce format as a standard... At least four of the major companies I've talked to are saying they're not going to meet them..."

Unfortunately, only a few of the people you'll meet while Networking will *at that moment* control a suitable opportunity...or know of one. Which brings us to the topic we'll soon be pursuing, Executive Recruiters, who are often knee-deep in situations you'd love to find out about.

What about Online Networking?
Is there such a thing? And if so, is it sufficiently
worthwhile not to waste the time of anyone
far enough along in a business life
to be reading RITES OF PASSAGE?

The answer is: No. And Yes.

I wondered about those questions and asked a fair number of people who are quite Net savvy to recommend their best suggestions. Most simply said, "Don't bother." Others suggested various sites on which to *hunt* for potentially useful Web forums, Usenet newsgroups, Listserv mailing lists, etc. Which I did. But only long enough to kill one frustrating rainy Saturday afternoon. By then I'd wholeheartedly joined the "Don't bother" crowd.

Everything I saw was trivial, stale, sophomoric...or worse. Nothing related in any worthwhile way to anything we're discussing. Clearly, I could have spent more time beating the bushes, but I'll leave that up to you.

Credentialed-Member Online Forums

However, the above comments relate only to the groups and forums available to the general public.

A Chief Information Officer I respect tells me that there's an online forum for CIOs that she says is *very* useful, because its membership is by application only and is firmly restricted to CIOs. As a result, members feel free to be quite frank in their exchange of information, much of which, she says, concerns vendor references.

"Basically," she says, "it's a discussion board with several threads you can post to, and in that way it's similar to a Usenet. The threads last anywhere from a week to several months. There's an administrator, called the Discussion Facilitator, who screens postings to eliminate redundancy and irrelevance. And once a week she issues a summary by e-mail." There also happens to be a job posting board through which this woman made a move at the CIO level.

According to my informant, the very able administrator is "the core of the thing and the main reason it's successful. Without monitoring and strict membership requirements, people wouldn't take the time to read it. They also wouldn't feel free to open up and offer comments, if they knew vendors and junior people in their own organization would be reading it."

Sadly, as I write this, I know something that my friend does not know. The Discussion Facilitator who is centrally responsible for this forum's success is about to change jobs. Will the forum be as worthwhile when moderated by a successor to the present paragon? Time will tell.

Is there a worthwhile online forum for you?

Why not check around? Ask your peers if they are participating in an online forum they find really valuable. If so, perhaps you should join.

There is something similar for CEOs. Is it valuable? How formidable are the CEOs who participate?

If currently there's no online forum that's open only to legitimately credentialed people at your level in your field, then perhaps you should think about starting one.

Chapter 5

Executive Recruiters:
Two Types, Depending on How They're Paid

You couldn't be at, or even reaching for, $100,000+ and not already know
a lot about executive recruiters.

Probably you've been placed in one or more jobs yourself by a "headhunter." And chances are, you've also used professional help in identifying people to work for you.

So, what can you possibly find out that you don't already know?

Plenty! Because we're going to look at recruiters from an entirely new
angle...*your self-interest*. And that's *not* the way they've been presented
to you up to now.

There are, of course, two kinds: contingency and retainer. The difference is in how they're paid. The contingency firms get paid only if and when someone they submit is actually hired. And the retainer firms are paid for their professional skill and effort, *regardless of whether anyone they provide is hired*.

Even though the employer pays both types...and you never do...your self-interest is very different, depending on which type you're dealing with. And often that's not easy to determine. These days, both look the same and call themselves by the same names. Even more confusing, both types may switch their compensation method, when it suits their self-interest...not yours...to do so.

Moreover, it's not a matter of "good guys" and "bad guys." Your self-interest very seldom lines up with either type. So in this and later chapters, you and I will figure out:

1.   What's best for you with both types, and

2.   How to tell them apart...in person, on the phone, and on the Internet.

Even when a recruiter you've known for years shifts opportunistically from one mode to the other, you'll recognize that shift, and react accordingly.

But we won't stop at polishing your reactions. You're going to reach out to these people, and get them to do more for you.

When we're finished, you'll know as much about recruiters as if you'd spent a decade of your life working in their industry.

WARNING

You are approaching Dullsville...the only speed trap in this book. Before you exit this chapter you'll say: "Why is John slowing me down with the history and business methods of the recruiting indus-try? I just want to be a candidate; I don't want to run a firm!"

"Why," you'll say, "can't you just slide me onto the Internet and fulfill my career goals in 72 hours?"*

Bear with me. Obey the speed limit. Master every concept. In the following chapters, when we're whizzing along the beltline, you'll see why we took this tour of the downtown business district.

---

*Think that way, and you're obviously not interested in being where the action is in terms of career opportunity at the executive level. Two facts will illustrate: The parent company of Monster.com (TMP, Inc.), is using its cash and stock from Monster's success to buy up prestigious retainer-compensated search firms and already ranks #3 in that field (behind Korn/Ferry and Heidrick and Struggles). Meanwhile, the largest search firms (K/F, H&S, and others) have launched major Internet employment sites (FutureStep, LeadersOnLine, etc.) which they insist are entirely separate from their traditional search activities.

Understanding their hidden financial arrangements is the first step toward understanding all headhunters who come your way.

On the surface, contingency and retainer recruiters are far more alike than different. Both:

Fill executive positions. Recruiting is the same function, regardless of payment method.

Are paid by the employer. You won't pay either type.

Range in size from small, intimate firms to multi-city giants. You can't tell them apart by the number and size of their offices.

Have handsome quarters. Neither type has a monopoly on ambience.

Call themselves by the same names. "Executive Recruiters," "Management Consultants," "Executive Search Consultants." Both types use all the same words. And the public calls both kinds "headhunters."

Keep vast numbers of resumes. Both will accept your unsolicited resume, whether you mail it in, fax it, e-mail it, or submit it online, and both may keep it on file, along with the resumes of people they've interviewed.

Fill jobs from resumes in their databases and on-paper files. That's why they both maintain extensive records.

Telephone employed executives. When your phone rings, either type may be calling.

The fundamental distinction between the two kinds of firms is in how they're paid.

Contingency Payment

Contingency recruiters are paid by employers only if and when someone they submit is actually hired. They may just go through their information and send over a few resumes. Or they may do telephone investigation and persuasion to develop candidates, and then interview them, to screen a highly appropriate group for the "client" to see. Either way, these recruiters are operating strictly "on contingency"...on the *chance* that someone they submit will actually get hired. Otherwise, there's no fee. If the employer hires his or her in-law, a next-door neighbor, somebody who mailed in a resume, someone submitted by a different contingency recruiter, or nobody at all, the contingency recruiter gets nothing for his efforts.

Retainer Payment

Retainer recruiters, on the other hand, *are paid by the employer regardless of whether anyone they submit is actually hired*. They're compensated for their professional skill and effort. Like the doctor, who's paid whether the patient lives or dies, and most lawyers, who're paid whether their case is won or lost, the retainer recruiter is paid merely to *attempt* a solution. He or she is not required to achieve one. In-laws, neighbors, contingency-recruiter-submissions, mailed-in resumes, internal promotions, and positions left unfilled don't keep the retainer recruiter from being paid.

Does it sound like the retainer recruiter has the better deal?

Why doesn't every recruiter operate on retainer, rather than contingency?

Everyone always asks these logical questions.

Approximately half of the executive recruiting organizations in America today operate "on contingency," and the other half work "on retainer." With equal numbers on each side of the compensation issue, the answer certainly isn't that the contingency firms don't know what the retainer firms are doing. Indeed, many contingency firms also accept retainer assignments, and retainer firms sometimes glide opportunistically into the contingency mode.

Percentage fees are about equal for both types.

Clearly, which method of payment a firm chooses is not explained by the amounts involved, because fees for both are very similar. The leading retainer firms charge one-third...33.3%...of estimated first-year's compensation of the executive sought.

Most of them bill that amount in monthly thirds or fourths during the three- or four-month period the search is expected to require; searching beyond that point, if necessary, continues without further fee. If, when the search is over, the recruited executive earns more than the early estimate, a final bill brings the fee to 33.3%. A few price-competitive retainer firms charge 30% and fewer yet charge 25%, but 33.3% is typical among top-ranking firms. A very rare few charge a fixed negotiated fee for each project, which may come to even more than 33.3%. All retainer firms allow cancellation of the project, which stops the billing when work is stopped. If termination comes after the three- or four-months of billing, the recruiter keeps the full fee.

On the other hand, the typical fee for a contingency firm is "1% per thousand, up to a maximum of 35%." Under this formula, the contingency firm gets 35% of estimated first-year's compensation on positions over $35,000, whereas their charge on a $26,000 job is 26%. Retainer recruiters hardly ever work on positions under $75,000, whereas contingency recruiters often do.

Recruiters are also taking all or part of their fee in stock.

These days, recruiters are just as eager to gamble on a likely stock speculation as anyone else. They never used to be. For decades, search fees were strictly a cash transaction. But then came the Internet and its "dot com" mega-million-dollar deals in the late 90s.

Recruiters saw venture capitalists and investment bankers making gigantic on-paper fortunes by getting hold of founders' or very-early-stage stock in hot new start-up companies. So—in a chorus—they said, "Let us in on the action!"

Today, recruiters—retainer and contingency—tend to be willing and even eager to help a fledgling company conserve its meager cash by taking all or a part of their fee in stock, warrants, or options...negotiating a separate and different deal for each young company based on its circumstances and perceived potential.

Indeed the very largest retainer-compensated firms have acquired vast amounts of stock in lieu of cash. And now they've added venture capital activity in various forms as another part of their ongoing business activity. But that's another story for another time.

Suffice it to say that the "approximately one-third" concept is still a jumping-off point for negotiations as a search firm discusses accepting stock for all or part of its fee. The actual deal will be unique...not based on any formula.

Recruiters choose retainer or contingency status,
depending on whether or not they want to be obligated.

The reason a recruiting organization chooses one payment method over the other is the *degree of commitment it's willing to undertake*. The retainer recruiter promises to search diligently—even exhaustively—for qualified candidates. The contingency recruiter does not.

A retainer recruiter accepts full payment for doing a successful search as his three- or four-month billing cycle elapses. Having taken the money, he's under a heavy obligation. He's been paid for success. So he'd better come up with it. Otherwise his reputation and the future of his business will suffer. Even if the client is capricious in rejecting candidates, or makes unrealistically low offers, or in any other way fails to recognize good candidates or drives them away, the retainer recruiter must try to deliver the desired result to someone who's already paid for it.

The contingency recruiter, on the other hand, has no such problem. His or her "client" pays absolutely nothing for effort, nothing for candidates...unless and until someone the recruiter submits is actually hired. If what the employer wants proves difficult to find, or hard to deliver at the intended salary, the contingency recruiter shifts her attention to an easier target.

Here's the contingency recruiter's philosophy, as summarized to me by one of the finest people in that field:

> "I don't mind if I don't get paid for every speck of work I do. I can fill three easy ones, John, in the time it takes you to do one hard one on retainer. And at the end of the year, I'll bet I count up as much or more money than you do. And everybody I collect from is somebody who actually got an employee from me. I tried retainer, and I stopped. When you accept a retainer, the employer thinks he *owns* you. I value my freedom!"

Touché! The point is well taken. After 30 years as a retainer recruiter, I agree. "Three easy ones" can be done on contingency as quickly as one "hard one" on retainer. However, retainer assignments tend to be at higher salaries, so fees tend to be higher. What makes the "easy ones" less difficult is that they're usually at a lower level, where both the number of openings and the supply of good candidates are more numerous.

So who knows who's ahead on total fees at the end of the year...retainer or contingency recruiters? Both types have coexisted for 60 years, and the industry today is split about 50 / 50. Chances are, we'll have both types for many years to come.

> ## Now you know the two payment methods, and why a recruiter chooses one or the other.
>
> ## As we'll see later, your self-interest is different with each type. Therefore, it would be convenient if each would stick to his or her chosen method.
>
> ## Unfortunately, some recruiters of both types switch back and forth.

You can probably guess why some recruiters sometimes shift gears.

Contingency firms also accept retainers.

Many contingency firms "also accept retainers," or "also do search" (meaning the same thing). The idea is to get the employer to pay a fee for the firm's attention, and thus nail down more time and effort than his or her opening would otherwise merit under the "easiest-first" priorities of contingency operation.

There's also another interesting wrinkle when a contingency firm accepts an optional "retainer." Normally the contingency firm is one of many such firms "working on" the employer's "listing," and must race the others to fill it. The retainer arrangement gives the firm an "exclusive" on the job, and a respite from the race. Nonetheless, being accustomed to focusing on openings that are easily filled, the contingency firm may still balk at giving too much time to a resistant project "on retainer."

The solution: accept retainer payments during several months of exclusivity, and afterward, if the job proves hard to fill, merely refund all or most of the retainer...thus pleasing the "retainer" client with the firm's "honesty," while winding up no worse off than if the same work had been devoted to the opening on a non-exclusive contingency basis. Such a refund is *never* made by a true retainer recruiter.

Retainer recruiters sometimes "lob one in" on contingency.

Occasionally, a retainer recruiter may volunteer a candidate without being paid on retainer to look. But not often. *And only under cover of an excuse* (more about this later).

The reason for the retainer recruiter's furtiveness about his or her rare grab for a contingency fee is that, if it becomes known that he's willing to provide candidates without being paid to find them, then clients will ask for more "freebee" candidates, rather than pay the customary retainer.

Since retainer payment is more stringent and prestigious than contingency, the contingency recruiter can accept retainer assignments without jeopardizing his or her contingency status. On the other hand, the retainer recruiter can *not* toy with contingency activity without endangering his or her retainer status.

> ### So much for the two compensation systems...and the fact that their proponents may sometimes switch.
>
> ### Contingency and retainer recruiting are different businesses: brokerage, and consulting.
>
> ### They have different "roots"...and methods... which you should know about.

Despite their surface similarity when you deal with them as an executive intent on forwarding your own career, contingency and retainer recruiters are really operating two different kinds of businesses. And that's true, even though each may sometimes resort to the other's payment method.

The contingency recruiter is basically a broker, and the retainer recruiter is fundamentally a consultant. This clear distinction prevails, even though the contingency recruiter often gives the employer valuable advice, and the retainer recruiter has to deliver employees; advice won't suffice.

Contingency recruiters are in the brokerage business.

Contingency compensation...payment only if and when an introduction leads to a sale...is the central characteristic of all brokerage businesses.

The real estate agency is a perfect example. No matter how much work the broker puts in...no matter how many prospects are shown the property... there's no fee until there's a sale or lease. It's a volume business. The more properties "listed," the more chance of having what any buyer wants. It's a competitive business. Lots of other brokers are trying to make matches among the same prospective buyers and sellers. So speed is important. Move fast, or the seller will have sold...or the buyer will have bought...through another broker.

"Roots" of the Contingency Recruiting Business

The contingency executive recruiting firm is today's highly evolved version of the "employment agency" and the "personnel agency" of the '50s, '60s, and '70s. Up until the mid-'60s, the employee paid the low fee...6% to 12% of annual compensation. As the demand for good employees heated up in the booming '60s, employers began paying agency fees as a way of competing for the best people. And with employers paying, the agencies raised their fees to the 20%-to-25% range that had been successfully pioneered by the retainer recruiters.

Contingency firms then adopted the retainer firms' terminology...becoming "management consultants" doing "executive search," and submitting "candidates" rather than "applicants." "Personnel" and "agency" were dropped from company names. Along with upscale prices and terminology came elegant offices, and the solicitation of truly executive-level listings. Twenty years ago, contingency firms would never have been "working on" jobs at and beyond $100,000+. Today many of them are, even if most of their work is at lower levels.

Newspaper and Internet Advertising
and Telephone Solicitation

Contingency firms always have—and still do—run a lot of advertising in newspapers and trade publications. Today, of course, they're doing lots of advertising on Internet job sites. Advertising is the fastest way to bring in plenty of candidates to submit on the jobs listed with them...their "searches," under modern terminology. Most truly retainer firms never advertise any particular job they fill. This is true throughout the U.S., although not in Canada and the U.K. So if you see a firm advertising its jobs, it probably does most of its work on contingency. Conversely, *not* advertising strongly suggests...but doesn't prove...that a firm is primarily "retainer."

As percentage fees and salary levels both rose, the contingency firms could afford to put more effort into attempting to fill each of their higher-level openings. When newspaper ads didn't draw enough of the right candidates, they began telephoning employed executives, exactly the same way retainer firms do. Today both types of firms telephone extensively.

Industry Specialization

Historically, most but not all contingency firms have tended to specialize in a single industry, such as consumer products, publishing, retailing, health care, high-tech, banking and brokerage, e-commerce, etc.; and/or a particular category, such as marketing, sales, finance, IT, engineering, law, etc. Not being guaranteed payment for their efforts, they gear up for high-volume cost-efficiency, and that generally means moving around lots of similar people in the same industry.

Today many industry-specific contingency firms have evolved to the point of requesting retainers for almost every job opening presented to them. Yet they still do not accept "searches" that require looking beyond the people their ads are bringing in, plus a not-too-burdensome number of phone calls to contacts they already know. If a firm does any contingency work, chances are it tends to do all of its work in its accustomed contingency-oriented manner.

Interviewing and Screening

Because the contingency recruiter isn't assured payment, he or she usually can't invest large amounts of time in interviewing and screening candidates for any particular opening. The decisive employer who lists frequently, gives clear specifications, and actually hires what's asked for will, of course, get more attention than someone who provides less business and is vague and capricious. However, in a brokerage business like contingency recruiting, the more candidates any employer is shown, the more chance of achieving the placement. So the rule-of-thumb is:

> "When in doubt, send 'em out!"

In other words, do not screen restrictively.

Non-exclusivity and the Need for Speed

An employer who uses contingency recruiters likes to list the same job simultaneously with lots of them. After all, she pays nothing for their efforts. And since they're not obligated, she's unsure how much, if anything, any of them will do for her.

Not having an "exclusive" on the job, the contingency recruiter must act quickly...if he decides to act at all. He's in competition with other contingency recruiters, and also with all the executives who may be sending their resumes directly to the employer...not to mention the employer herself, who may promote from within or hire her next-door neighbor.

Financial bias precludes a consulting relationship.

Since the contingency recruiter is paid only if and when one of his candidates is hired, he's financially biased. Therefore, he hardly ever acts as a consultant to the employer. Unless he enjoys extraordinary personal rapport with the employer, he's never asked to evaluate any candidates he doesn't supply, and he never interviews internal candidates.

Where's the price-tag?

In contingency recruiting, the price-tag is *on the head of each candidate* submitted by the recruiter. The more candidates, the more chances this broker has to make a sale.

On the other hand, if there are several obviously appropriate candidates in the marketplace that the contingency recruiter *hasn't* contacted and tagged, then each one of them represents a definite risk that he'll lose the sale. Therefore, at levels high enough for candidates to be clearly apparent, and in industries the contingency recruiter is familiar with, he'll certainly get on the phone and attempt to affix his price-tag to the head of *everyone* who's at all likely to be hired into the job that's listed with him. Indeed, he may even try to get his tag on the heads of all the most obvious candidates, even if the opening has *not* yet been listed with him.

At or beyond $100,000+, you're now a high-profile target for the contingency recruiters serving your industry. Sometimes it will be very much in your self-interest to go along with what they propose. Other times it will *not* be. Subtle and fascinating issues and tactics are involved, and we'll examine them in the next chapter.

But now let's look at retainer recruiters.

||| Retainer recruiters are in the consulting business. |||

Unlike the contingency recruiter, who's presumed to be biased in favor of the candidates he'll make money on, and against all others, the retainer recruiter is in an economic position that allows him to be objective. Moreover, his professional prestige and expertise are usually substantial enough to be considered part of what his client is paying for.

Therefore he's a consultant. But he'd better come up with some very impressive people. Words alone won't justify his fee.

"Roots" of the Retainer Recruiting Business

With the exception of one narrowly specialized New York firm, retainer executive recruiting didn't exist until after World War II. But as America returned to a prosperous peacetime economy in the late '40s and the '50s, and boomed in the '60s, many corporations needed more and better managers than they were developing internally.

The solution: Hire an aggressive third party to scout the best managers at competitive companies and persuade them to consider a career-advancing move. No more settling for the ad-answerers and the unemployed as served up by the agencies. And no need to become involved in the tacky matter of directly soliciting a competitor's key employees.

A New Process...with No Advertising

Retainer recruiting was a radical idea in the late '40s and the '50s, when it first took hold. Employers were asked to pay an expert in the identification, evaluation, and persuasion of executives to address time and skill to the filling of a key opening, *without any guarantee, or even a promise, that he or she would succeed.* And the fee was a hefty *20% to 25% of annual salary.*

Tough terms. And during the early years, a tough sale.

But 25% of annual compensation is only three months' salary for the position (even today's 33.3% is only four months). *Not* unreasonable, if it provides a truly different and superior recruiting process.

Obviously, running ads and screening applicants could never have supplied the necessary point-of-difference. Employers were already doing their own advertising and screening. So were the agencies, who didn't charge unless there was a hire.

The retainer recruiter's answer to hesitant employers...from the beginning, and still today:

> "We don't just advertise and hope that somebody good will see the ad and feel like *approaching us.* We research the companies and

industries of interest to you, and find out who the *very best people* are. Then *we approach them.* The best people are usually well challenged and generously rewarded where they are. They're busy with their fast-rising careers, not answering employment ads. They're the ones you want...and we find and solicit them for you."

After fifty years, the original promise of retainer recruiting still represents its highest expression. Whenever an excellent retainer recruiter is sufficiently unimpeded by entangling client relationships, he or she can study an entire industry and select its finest people as candidates. Then the client can hire the very best person, and thereby shift the competitive balance of management power in the industry. As I tell my clients:

"Somebody's got to have the best person. Why not you?"

So the pioneers of retainer executive recruiting turned their backs on advertising. Instead, they reached for the *telephone.* Among retainer recruiters, it's been that way ever since. Even in Canada and the U.K., where many prominent retainer recruiters *do* advertise, telephoning is their primary technique.

Here Comes the Internet!

For 50 years the retainer firms have proudly differentiated themselves from the contingency firms by not getting their candidates through advertising. Newspaper advertising existed, but the retainer firms always made it a point never to use it.

Suddenly the Internet exploded into view, with "employment sites" growing like mushroom clouds. Rather than ignore this mighty new phenomenon, the largest retainer firms decided to launch their own Internet sites. Korn/Ferry brought out *FUTURESTEP*, a joint venture with *The Wall Street Journal.* Heidrick and Struggles soon followed with *LEADERSONLINE.*

"Yes we have a site. But it doesn't do what we do!"

Both Korn/Ferry and Heidrick and Struggles stress that these sites are *totally separate from the parent firm's traditional retainer search practice.* These Internet units, they explain, provide a different, lower-level, service...a slate of candidates delivered very fast, by sifting the database of people who've registered on the site. And, of course, since the Internet operation is not the parent company, there's no logical inconsistency in advertising the site and/or the jobs it's filling. This new service, they explain, is appropriate for filling middle management jobs, where candidates are numerous and inter-changeable. At upper management levels, they say, the firm's traditional no-advertising telephone-based search services are still required, because candidates are fewer and require the customary telephone identification and persuasion.

Later on we'll thoroughly cover how you should take advantage of all types of Internet job sites. However, the point for now is just that any ads you see for retainer-firm-sponsored sites such as FutureStep or LeadersOnLine or the jobs they're filling does not mean that their prestigious retainer-firm parents have changed their classic telephone-rather-than-advertising way of doing business...even though they may have subsidiary units that run ads.

Specialists in Senior Managers...Not in an Industry

The vast majority of truly retainer firms—the ones making absolutely no referrals "on contingency"—are "generalists." They do *not* specialize in any industry, although some of the largest firms have certain recruiters who work mainly in specific fields. Retainer recruiters do specialize, however, in the *higher levels of management.* Corporations willingly accept a pay-regardless-of-hiring fee-structure when looking for senior managers. And of course salaries...and hence fees...are higher at the higher echelons. So the retainer recruiters seek upper-level assignments, while shunning lesser ones.

Moreover, at the senior levels, target people in the target companies are highly visible...even to a non-specialist. Also, any significant degree of industry-spe-cialization tends to severely restrict the number of companies the retainer recruiter can tap, because of "don't-bite-the-hand-that-feeds" considerations. Most retainer recruiters would rather serve lots of industries with minimal restriction, than just one in a handicapped manner.

Full Participation in the Hiring Process

Paid regardless of who's hired, the retainer recruiter normally *is* used by his clients as a *consultant.*

Unlike the contingency recruiter, who's presumed biased in favor of the can-didates who'll earn him or her a fee, the retainer recruiter is often asked to interview and evaluate candidates whom the employer finds on his own, and internal candidates too.

Where's the price-tag?

The retainer recruiter's price-tag is on his *professional services*, not on your head.

Far from being a broker operating on contingency...and thus owed nothing unless a purchase is made, the retainer recruiter *has a professional relationship* with the employer. He's brought in as an outside expert...fully-paid, fully-involved, and fully-trusted.

Moreover, since he's being paid to look for exactly what's needed, the retainer recruiter's candidates are presumed to have been *found specifically for the client who's footing the bill.* Therefore, the retainer recruiter *must never offer the same candidate to more than one client at a time*, whereas the contingency recruiter always offers the same candidate to as many potential employers as possible, as fast as possible.

The professional relationship between the retainer recruiter and his clients...and his firm's clients...creates two severely restrictive "off-limits" barriers against you:

1. He may not be able to touch you, even when you're the best person in the world for his client's position.

2. If he can show you any jobs at all, he can't show you many.

The way a retainer recruiter is paid...for his or her skill and effort, rather than on contingency...creates a professional relationship between the search firm and the employer. And that relationship creates two barriers that prevent you from seeing all but a very few...and perhaps *all*...of the jobs you'd want, which are "searched" by any retainer firm, no matter how large.

Even if the retainer firm handles dozens...or hundreds...of jobs per year that you'd be appropriate for:

1. *You may not hear about ANY,* and

2. If you do hear about some, chances are it *won't be more than two or three within any 12-month period.*

Two different aspects of the retainer recruiter's "don't-bite-the-hand-that-feeds" relationship with clients create these severe limitations. And there's seldom any way around them, no matter how many of the search firm's offices you visit, nor how many of its recruiters you know personally.

Barrier #1: The You-Work-for-a-Client "Off-Limits" Rule

Let's begin with the barrier that can keep you from seeing any jobs at all.

Because the retainer recruiter is being paid to strengthen the client organization, he or she has a corresponding duty *not to tear it down*. When the client agrees to pay the recruiter to attempt to fill an empty office, she has a right to expect that the recruiter won't simultaneously...or shortly afterward...try to empty another office.

Indeed, no employer will ever willingly contribute to the financial health of any recruiting organization that currently is...or soon will be...working against the health of the employer's organization.

As a Result: The Industry's Traditional "Off-Limits-for-Two-Years" Rule

How long should a retainer recruiter have to consider a client's employees "off-limits," after being paid for a consulting assignment?

For a while, at least. But certainly not forever. Over the years, the retainer recruiting profession has almost universally upheld the industry's traditional "**Two Years Rule**." Its essence:

> *For two years after accepting a retainer fee to strengthen a client company's management team, the ethical firm will not weaken that team by recruiting away any of the client company's people.*

The rule means that any company that pays a retainer recruiting firm to assist it is "off-limits" to that recruiting firm for the next 24 months. If, during that time, another assignment is received, the "off-limits" boundary extends *24 months from the completion of the latest assignment.*

Large retainer firms with dozens of recruiters and multiple offices handle hundreds...and in the largest thousands...of jobs per year. Therefore, at every moment they may be handling dozens—perhaps even hundreds—of jobs that would be right for you. Unfortunately, they also have hundreds of client companies "off-limits," and there's a strong chance that yours may be among them. If so, you'll hear of *no* opportunities from that search firm.

Examples will illustrate the dimensions and evolution of this phenomenon. *Fortune* Magazine of 10/9/78, reported Heidrick & Struggles as having 2,000 client companies off-limits...a disclosure that stirred considerable comment among corporate users of recruitment. When *Forbes* 7/10/89 studied America's four largest retainer firms, it found these numbers of client companies off-limits: Korn/Ferry 2,150; Russell Reynolds 1,567; Heidrick & Struggles 1,289; and SpencerStuart 1,250. And when Heidrick & Struggles went public in 1999 its 4/26/99 S-1/A filing with the U.S. S.E.C. was reported in the May '99 issue of *Executive Recruiter News* as having stated that the firm "worked for more than 1,800 clients in 1995 and over 3,100 in 1998."

With numbers like those, it's likely that your employer may be "off-limits" to several of the sizable retainer firms...especially if you work for a major company, since big companies are the ones most likely to have used several of the major recruiting firms recently.

Regardless of how outstanding you are, you probably won't hear about any job *suitable for you* from any firm your employer has used in the past 24 months. You may, however, be called to suggest people for jobs that obviously *wouldn't* interest you.

Moreover, the barrier isn't removed if you contact the firm and ask to be considered.

It doesn't solve the "off-limits" problem if you approach the retainer recruiter yourself, instead of waiting for him or her to call you. If she were unethical, she'd approach her client's employees and, with their cooperation, merely claim that they approached her. Therefore, the recruiting firm protects itself from any seeming impropriety by not involving you at all in its projects. The ethical retainer recruiter won't empty offices in any company where she's been paid to help fill them...at least not for two years, according to long-standing industry practice.*

---

*Up until early '96, the "Two Years Rule" was written into the "Code of Ethics" of the AESC, a trade association of retainer recruiters. In '96 the "Code" was stripped of almost all prohibitions. Nonetheless, nearly all fine retainer firms still automatically provide this traditional client protection, and almost all knowledgeable client companies still demand it in writing from any who do not.

Barrier #2: The You're-Allocated-to-Another-Recruiter-Within-the-Firm "Off-Limits" Rule

Under this rule, which is virtually universal among retainer recruiting firms:

You'll never hear about more than one-job-at-a-time
...probably no more than two or three per year.

You may simultaneously be asked to suggest candidates for several jobs that would *not* interest you. But on jobs you'd personally be interested in, virtually all retainer firms will only let you know about one-at-a-time.

The way it works is that only one-recruiter-at-a-time is given permission within the firm to contact you. And he's only allowed to tell you about one-job-at-a-time. Not until you declare yourself uninterested in job #1 do you have any chance of being told about job #2. And unless the very same person you turn down has a second job he wants to ask you about, chances are that weeks or months of inside-the-firm red tape will have to unwind, before another of the firm's recruiters can tempt you with something else.

Searches usually take three to four months, plus a while afterward during which administrative assistants "close out" completed searches and return non-recruited executives to the "pool." Therefore, even if you're given maximum exposure, you probably won't see more than two or three...or conceivably four...of any retainer firm's appropriate-for-you opportunities per year.

Not allowing prospective candidates to know about more than one search at a time is based on two compelling business reasons:

1. *Clients of retainer firms pay handsomely for each candidate.* On a $250,000 position, the recruiter bills upwards of $80,000... more than $16,000 each, if there are five candidates. *Client A* would be furious if any of his $16,000 candidates were simultaneously provided to *Client B*, against whom he'd then have to compete in the hiring process.*

---

*With contingency recruiters this consideration doesn't apply, because clients pay nothing for candidates and are billed only when someone is actually hired. Therefore, contingency firms introduce all candidates to as many employers as possible, but sometimes with sad results for the candidates, as we shall see in the next chapter.

2. *Filling jobs is the objective; accommodating executives is not.* Therefore, any executive who is shown any job...unless she refuses to consider it...must not be distracted by alternatives. Suppose an executive lives in Greenwich, CT, has two kids in high school, a spouse with a lucrative local job, and a beautiful house with a 6% mortgage. Even so, she's willing to consider an attractive position in Nome, Alaska.

Needless to say, she'd better not find out about an equally or more attractive situation only twelve miles from her home.

Point (2) above also has an unfortunate corollary for the *unemployed* executive. He's presumed to be "hungrier" for a new position than someone who's happily employed. Therefore, he's more likely to be shown jobs involving unattractive features...relocation, lateral responsibility, modest compensation, unstable and small companies, etc. And he won't hear about anything more attractive until the first project chosen for him has been disposed of.

How These Barriers Operate Within the Recruiting Firm

It's simple. Every recruiter in a retainer firm is forbidden to phone any executive as a prospect for a job until he or she checks to determine that the executive:

1. *doesn't work for a client*

AND

2. *hasn't been allocated to a different recruiter* doing a different search.

Only if the retainer recruiter is lucky enough to hurdle both barriers, does he have permission within his firm to tell you about a career opportunity. Otherwise, it doesn't matter that you're his closest personal friend, or that he knows you're extremely unhappy with your current circumstances which, if allocation-to-another-recruiter is the problem, *may even include unemployment.*

The recruiter who wants to "use" you as a candidate simply cannot break the "off-limits" rules under which virtually all retainer firms operate. These rules are for the economic benefit of the firm and its individual recruiters. When one firm member helps himself by breaking the rules, he hurts his company and his colleagues. *Such behavior is not tolerated.*

Isn't there some way around the retainer firm's off-limits rules?

Not if the firm is ethical, and looks out for its own interests, rather than yours.

The you-work-for-a-client barrier will always prevent you from being called as a potential candidate. However, it usually won't prevent your being called as a *"source"* of suggestions of other potential candidates. But only if the job would clearly be inappropriate for you...too junior if it's within your function (a Chief of Financial Planning, if you're a CFO), or in a different function (Marketing, rather than Finance). But even then, the recruiter will ask you only for executives *not currently working for your off-limits company.* She'll want people who've been there and left, and people at competitive companies.

If the job might appeal to you personally, you will *not* be called, *even for suggestions*, because of the obvious danger that when you express personal interest and are told you're off-limits to the recruiter because of client conflict, you'll merely go straight to the employer. After all, you don't care about the recruiter's "don't-bite-the-hand-that-feeds" problem. It's not your problem...nor that of the recruiter's client, whom you'd like to work for, and who'd be delighted to have a chance to consider you.

If a job represents a fine career opportunity for you, and you'd be an ideal candidate, then both you and the potential employer are hurt...not helped...when the recruiter has to keep you apart. Therefore, the recruiter doesn't want you showing up on his client's doorstep and illustrating what fine candidates he's forced to withhold. And he certainly doesn't want your present employer to find out that he's emptying your office, after just being paid to fill the one down the hall. For both reasons he'll steer clear of you.

Moreover, it wouldn't be any excuse to say that you went ahead on your own after the recruiter specifically told you he couldn't make an introduction because of the You-work-for-a-client "Off-limits" Rule. After all, tempting you with the job, and then telling you that *he* couldn't introduce you is exactly the way he'd manipulate you into the hands of his latest client, if he were a sleazy operator with no ethical policy.

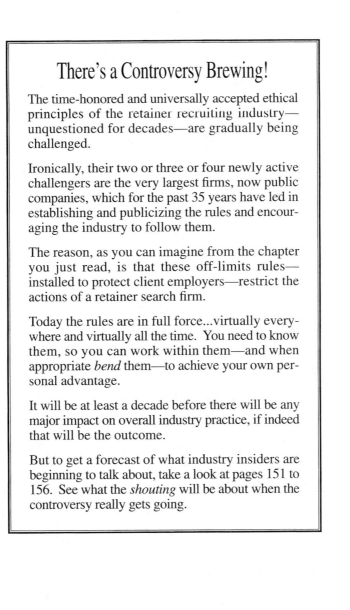

There's a Controversy Brewing!

The time-honored and universally accepted ethical principles of the retainer recruiting industry—unquestioned for decades—are gradually being challenged.

Ironically, their two or three or four newly active challengers are the very largest firms, now public companies, which for the past 35 years have led in establishing and publicizing the rules and encouraging the industry to follow them.

The reason, as you can imagine from the chapter you just read, is that these off-limits rules—installed to protect client employers—restrict the actions of a retainer search firm.

Today the rules are in full force...virtually everywhere and virtually all the time. You need to know them, so you can work within them—and when appropriate *bend* them—to achieve your own personal advantage.

It will be at least a decade before there will be any major impact on overall industry practice, if indeed that will be the outcome.

But to get a forecast of what industry insiders are beginning to talk about, take a look at pages 151 to 156. See what the *shouting* will be about when the controversy really gets going.

Looking Five Chapters Ahead

That's it. Now you know the ground rules.

All the basic facts that govern your dealings with recruiters...both contingency and retainer...were in the chapter you just finished reading. From here on, we'll look at the *implications* of those facts.

Think of dealing with recruiters as a game. You now know how the game works. But there's still a wide-open opportunity to improve your skills as a *player*.

The stakes are high. If you play expertly, and have a little luck, you may never have to do anything more to achieve career advancement outside your current company than just to handle recruiters effectively. Don't worry about what recruiters *won't* do for you. What they *will* do, if you treat them right, can still be the most favorable of all outside influences on your career.

That's why we'll pay special attention to the subject of executive recruiters. To polish this extremely important part of your career-advancement game, I'm not just going to hand you some written instructions, and walk away.

Far from it. You're going to get the nearest thing to *actual practice* that a book can provide. Rather than just tell you how to hold the bat and how to swing, I'm also going to throw you a systematic series of all the fastballs, curves, sinkers, and spitballs that you're likely to encounter in big league play at...above...and even *far* above $100,000+.

What's more, you're going to meet the same concept more than once, and in more than one context. So, as you read on, don't feel that you must take notes or mark pages whenever you hit an intriguing new insight. Just understand it...and zip right along. Chances are, I'll throw you the same pitch again, from a slightly different angle, until it's a permanent part of your business sophistication.

In the next few chapters you're going to develop a whole new set of *reflexes*. From now on, you'll automatically reach for your maximum advantage every time you encounter a recruiter. You'll be thoroughly accustomed to major league pitching. And you'll be batting 1000...or darn close to it.

Here's how we'll proceed. First we'll check out *your self-interest* when you deal with *contingency recruiters* (Chapter 6) and *retainer recruiters* (Chapter 7). And then, knowing what's best for you with both types, we'll make sure you get it when *you call them* (Chapter 8), when *they call you* (Chapter 9), and when you *do business* with them (Chapter 10).

And finally, after you've absorbed this entire book as background, you'll get a postgraduate course in Appendix I. There you'll witness the filling of a high-level executive position through the eyes of a fine retainer recruiter at a large and prestigious firm. After you've seen the process through his eyes, it will never look quite the same to you again.

Of course, I can't absolutely guarantee that this regimen will make you a life-long whiz at dealing with recruiters. But I'll be very surprised if it doesn't.

Chapter 6

Contingency Recruiters:
Look Out for Yourself

This chapter...and the entire book...aims relentlessly at one objective:
your self-interest.

What's best for *YOU*! **Not for contingency recruiters. Not for retainer
recruiters. And possibly not for your current employer, who'd rather
not lose you to a better opportunity.**

**Early in your career, your self-interest neatly matched the interests of
contingency recruiters. Chances are, one or more of them gave you
invaluable help in entering the business world, and possibly in climbing
the first few levels of the corporate pyramid.**

But beyond $100,000, your interests are no longer quite the same as those of *any* recruiter...contingency, or retainer.

Sorry about that!

You're on your own now. And in this chapter we'll focus on your self-interest whenever the recruiter you're dealing with is working "on contingency"...whenever he or she gets paid *only if you're hired*.

||| **Chances are, your career got some of its early momentum with the help of a contingency recruiter.** |||

Forget how special you are now.

Years ago you were a commodity in vast supply: a management trainee; a financial analyst; an assistant account executive or an AE at an advertising agency; a "member of technical staff" in an R&D lab; an engineering manager; a plant superintendent; a computer programmer or analyst; a lending officer in a bank; a field salesman or a zone manager; a copy editor; an assistant or full product manager...I could go on and on, but you get the idea.

Early in your career, you were just another face in the crowd of bright young people striving to get ahead. You needed all the exposure you could get. So you were properly grateful to find a friendly "counselor" at an agency (which today probably calls itself an executive recruiting or search firm), who saw the good qualities in you.

This "counselor" sent your resume...and extolled your "potential"...to HR departments and middle-managers all over town. Finally, you landed the job you wanted. You appreciated your "counselor's" help, and you may have kept in touch with her for years. Maybe you got a subsequent job through her. And perhaps you've used her as a source of junior- and middle-management people reporting to you, as you've moved further up.

Most of us who've climbed the corporate pyramid have warm memories of several fine contingency recruiters who touched our lives in a very positive way. Certainly I do, and I'll bet you do too.

Very helpful earlier, the contingency recruiter
no longer serves your self-interest the way he used to.

Now you're at, or within striking distance of, the senior-management level. You're already earning upward of $100,000...and probably *way* upward. You've outdistanced the crowd. You now have an impressively responsible position. You've made a track record. Your resume speaks for itself. Remember the contingency recruiter saying, "Keep it on one page"? That was because you hadn't done enough yet to justify more. And besides, she was your spokesperson in the Human Resources Department.

Today you don't need an advocate trying to break down HR Department doors for you. And when it comes to contacting the CEO or any other senior executive who'll take the initiative in bringing you into a company, you *don't want an advocate*. You can write your own covering letter and submit your own resume. And doing so will be considered more straightforward and dignified than if you're served up on a platter by a headhunter with a financial stake in promoting an introduction.

Avoid having a price-tag on your head.

Whenever a contingency recruiter introduces you to a company, you arrive with a price-tag on your head...usually more than $80,000 if, for example, you're making about $250,000 (see page 66-67 for fee explanation).

It doesn't matter whether or not the recruiter has been specifically requested to offer candidates for an open position. The price-tag is firmly affixed. Maybe he's just taking a flyer and sending your resume with no prior request for it, and possibly no prior contact at all with the employer he sends it to.

Nevertheless, if it's the recruiter who draws the company's attention to you, you can't be hired without his being owed a fee. Standard industry practice is that such referrals are "solid" for at least six months. All incoming resumes are date-marked—physically or in a database—in the HR Department. And if two contingency recruiters submit the same person, the recruiter whose submission arrives first is the one who gets paid.

Racing You to Your Employment

Anyone paid on contingency has this objective: *to receive a fee when someone is hired.*

Ideally, the recruiter pursues her goal by securing a listing from an employer with a specific job that she and other recruiters are invited to try to fill. She then *races the other contingency recruiters to fill the job.*

But suppose a contingency recruiter...or a retainer recruiter who shifts opportunistically into the contingency mode...encounters an exceptionally desirable *employee*. Then, despite having *no listed job* that this employee fits, the recruiter may nevertheless decide to attach his or her price-tag, and *race to all the companies this employee is likeliest to wind up working for.* After all, new job openings occur every day. There may be one the recruiter doesn't know about.

Let's assume that you're not just good, but outstanding. You're one of those exceptional executives that companies will surely hire if they have an opening. "Seen is as good as sold."

Moreover, the list of companies in your industry that might want you is just as obvious as your excellent record and personal attributes. Those companies, of course, are the ones you'll logically contact first when you're interested in changing jobs. They're also the ones where you may already have your own personal contacts. And they're where, even if you're not already personally acquainted, a letter and resume from you may spark immediate interest.

Therefore, the contingency recruiter has no time to lose. Since you're talking to him, you're probably talking to *other headhunters too.* And soon you'll be in touch with the most obvious *employers* as well.

So he may immediately submit your resume to all the companies most likely to hire you. If he's ethical, he gets your verbal okay first; if not, he doesn't bother. Either way, he moves quickly, to get your resume submitted before any other recruiter does...*and before you do.* After all, if your resume gets there before his submission arrives, he'll be out-of-luck. Therefore, he "covers" you at all the companies you're most likely to join. A copy of your resume, an envelope, and a stamp—or merely an e-mail—just might produce a $80,000+ fee...or at least insure against losing one.

Would a recruiter be so brassy as to write and phone a CEO or another key officer he didn't already know personally?

Absolutely. CEOs and other senior executives I work with on a retainer basis have shown me this kind of mail many, many times. Moreover, their secretaries say it's often followed by persistent phone calls...especially if an opening has been reported in the trade press. Of course the more usual and circumspect submission will be to the HR Department in any company the headhunter normally does business with. There, he can't afford to overreach the people who give out the contingency listings of lower- and middle-management jobs.

The Harm That's Done to You

What's wrong with the above scenario from your point of view? After all, you're not paying. You don't care who does or doesn't collect a fee. You just want to find the right job to advance your career. Isn't it a good idea to be introduced by a professional who'll do everything possible to promote the idea that you ought to be interviewed?

No. The entrée you achieve by personal contact, networking, or an impressive letter and resume you send is likely to be more, rather than less, persuasive than a headhunter's. The recruiter may have saved you some effort, but it's not likely that she's enhanced your image.

Assuming you get interviewed and hired and the headhunter gets paid, it's true that you haven't been economically hurt, since these days the employer always pays employment fees.

But the sad fact of the matter is that you're far less likely to get seen...much less hired...than if you'd arrived under your own steam, with no $80,000+ price-tag attached.

||| Behind-the-Scenes After an Unsolicited |||
Referral by a Recruiter

Notice I did *not* say "by a *contingency* recruiter." Any referral that is not specifically requested by the employer is "on contingency," even if made by a prestigious retainer firm in a convenient lapse from publicly professed behavior.

Step One:

> Letter and resume arrive; perhaps followed by phone calls from the recruiter.

Step Two:

> Material is duly filed in the central HR Department.

Step Three:

> You make contact. Through personal contact, networking, or your own mailing. Or even a fortunate accident.

> Maybe you meet Mr. Decisionmaker on an airplane, or on the golf

course, or at a trade show, or at your daughter's swimming meet... whatever kismet the fates send or you can contrive. Impressed, he begins to think about meeting you in his office, with an eye toward potential employment. He doesn't have anything specific right now, and your background may be a little offbeat. But he's intrigued with you and thinks, "Let's have her in here. We can shoot a few ideas around, and I can at least pick her brains. Maybe nothing will come of it; even so, no harm done."

Step Four:

Mr. Decisionmaker follows proper company procedure. He calls the HR department first, as everyone is supposed to before scheduling a meeting that could lead to employment. Let's listen:

DECISIONMAKER: "Have we got anything on a Judy...or more likely it's Judith...(fill in your last name)? She's over at Stodgy Corporation. I met her last evening and she impressed me. I don't exactly have an open slot and maybe I won't be too interested after I know her better. But then again, I've been thinking of several ways I might do some reorganizing."

PERSONNEL ASSISTANT: "Oh, yes, Mr. D. I've found her in our file. Judith A. (you!)...the Stodgy Corporation. Yes, we have her full resume here."

DECISIONMAKER: "How could we? I just met her last night."

PA: "The resume was sent in by a Mr. Ralph Quick of Quick Associates, a headhunter firm...letter dated the 14th and we got it on the 19th. Mr. Quick also phoned us, and I see he also sent a letter to Mr. Big, which Alfred sent down here for us to file."

DECISIONMAKER: "Well, what does all that mean to me? I met her at my daughter's swimming meet. Diane beat her daughter by just one second. They were both awfully nice...congratulated us as we were leaving...and she and I got to talking. No connection at all with Quick Associates, whoever they are."

PA: "They're a pretty decent headhunter firm, and we've listed with them from time to time. I think they hit with a manager for our New England Region a year or so ago. I suppose that if anything *did* develop between you and Ms. (you!), we could call them and tell them about the swim meet and all and maybe they'd..."

DECISIONMAKER: "No, never mind. It's not worth the trouble. I really don't have my thinking squared away yet. 'Bye now. Thanks!"

Sandbagged! And you never knew what hit you. The headhunter didn't know either. Maybe he's a very nice guy...perhaps a personal friend. He might even have backed off, rather than jeopardize an opportunity for you.

Too bad you had a price-tag on your head.

There are three circumstances under which you might be submitted "on contingency."

And in all three, you're better off getting to the employer on your own.

Let's take a close look at your self-interest in every possible situation where you might have the alternative of introducing yourself...or being introduced by a recruiter operating "on contingency," whether he or she is normally "contingency" or "retainer."

Possibility One: The employer has NOT listed the position with the recruiter.

Submitted "on contingency," you arrive with an $80,000+ price-tag on your head. Nobody asked for you. And now the company is $80,000 less interested in seeing you than if you'd submitted yourself.

Possibility Two: The employer HAS listed an opening with a fine and highly ethical contingency recruiter.

Now we've got a much closer case. However, I think you'll agree that you're probably better off to reach the employer on your own...having had nothing to do with the contingency recruiter, and not knowing that he had a listing for the same job you hear about and apply for on your own, regardless of whether you find the opening through personal contact, networking, direct mail, a story in a trade journal or a newspaper, or a job listing on the corporation's own Web site...whatever.*

---

*These possibilities for you to discover an opening on your own and "go direct" to the employer do not, of course, include responding to a contingency recruiter's ad on an Internet job site or in the newspaper. The point is to reach the employer without being involved at all with a contingency recruiter.

On the negative side, you won't have the recruiter advocating your candidacy. But is he primarily in touch with Mr. Decisionmaker or with the Human Resources Department? And of course, if you're ever discussed with the recruiter (not likely, because he's biased), he may "faint-praise" you and plug his people.

But you cost *zero*, and the contingency recruiter's people have all got $80,000+ price-tags on their heads. Even without advocacy, you can count on an objective evaluation by the employer.

The situation would have been different several years ago, when you were a recent graduate, or a junior- or middle-manager trying to get a leg up after just a few years' experience. Then you may have needed advocacy, just to be considered. Today you and all the other candidates at your level have track records that can...and will...be objectively compared.

Let's even be a little cynical. Not having to make a capital investment of $80,000+ to acquire you, Mr. Decisionmaker can feel *freer to try you out.* If you don't succeed, he can dump you, without having $80,000 worth of egg on his face. You have a political, as well as an economic, edge.

Possibility Three: The employer has assigned a search to a retainer recruiter. Now another recruiter submits you without a listing from the employer.

This happens much more often than you would think.

Sometimes a contingency recruiter may submit you without knowing that a retainer search has been assigned. You're a nifty candidate, so Mr. Contingency attaches his price-tag, and races to your likeliest employers. Or Mr. C reads in a trade paper about an executive switching companies, thereby creating an opening at the former company. Bang! He's in touch with you, and your resume is on its way.

On the other hand, perhaps the recruiter operating "on contingency" *does* know that a retainer recruiter has been engaged...and chooses to involve himself anyway. Consider the following examples:

Perhaps a contingency recruiter regularly gets lower- and middle-management listings from a company. He "hits" well, but the company assigns its highest-level openings to retainer firms. Knowing of an on-going retainer search, Mr. Contingency "lobs one in from the sidelines."

Or perhaps there's a "shoot-out" in which several *retainer* firms compete for a search assignment. Here are two ways I've personally seen unethical retainer firms "go contingency" in an effort to snatch victory from the jaws of defeat:

> 1. Write the company expressing regret at not being chosen, and enclosing resumes of "some great candidates we had lined up for you."

> 2. Call the employer three or four weeks later, ask if the job has been filled (of course it's too early), and offer to do "a computer run, to see if we come up with anyone your other firm isn't showing you."

No retainer arrangement, and no charge unless someone is hired in (1). And in (2), a nominal fee of $3,000 for the "computer run," after which one of the firm's recruiters also spends two weeks on the phone trying to scrape up candidates...something a contingency firm with a non-exclusive "listing" might also do. The "computer run" was just a flimsy excuse for reversion to contingency operation after failure to achieve a retainer.

As a retainer recruiter myself, I can tell you that I and most other retainer firms would never even imagine such unprofessional behavior. Yet, as the "shoot-out" winner, I've personally witnessed both examples (I could never have dreamed them up) as performed by two of America's most famous retainer firms. Incidentally, I'm pleased to report that both failed to make any headway. But they must succeed sometimes, or they wouldn't try such gambits.

Whenever there's an ongoing retainer search, for which the employer is paying the full fee (in both instances above, more than $40,000 per month was being paid over a three-month period), you're at a monumental disadvantage, if you get "lobbed in from the sidelines" on contingency. The $80,000+ price-tag on your head is *in addition* to the $80,000+ being paid to the retainer recruiter. Hiring you will cost over $160,000! You're like a doubly-inflated basketball the headhunter is trying to slap through the hoop.

**The only time you gain from an
introduction by a contingency recruiter is when**

1.   there's a legitimate listing, and
**2.   it's from a company you wouldn't have contacted,
if the contingency recruiter hadn't persuaded you.**

Obviously, you're better off without a price-tag on your head. So you really should develop direct contact with all the companies of potential interest to you. That requires some effort. But your reward is being an unencumbered prospect for employment with the companies you consider most attractive.

Indeed, why not cultivate good professional rapport with all the major competitive companies in your field? Someday you may be interested in working for one of them. Or you may ask some of their people to work for you.

A Proper Contingency Referral...Helpful to You and to the Client

But now let's suppose that "out of the blue" a contingency recruiter who has a definite listing from a company you admire calls about the position and persuades you to pursue it. You didn't know the opening existed. Or if you did, you previously chose not to follow up.

Having (1) had a true listing and (2) persuaded you to pursue it, the contingency recruiter has done both the employer and you a service, and she deserves to be paid.

You must, in good conscience, *pursue the opportunity only through her.* It's too late to contact the employer directly. Indeed, the employer wouldn't respect you if you tried to go around the contingency recruiter at this point.

Moreover, because the contingency recruiter has a bona fide listing, there's a good chance that the employer may receive several candidates from her and discuss them with her, thus generating valuable feedback that the recruiter will share with you...another benefit to both you and the employer.

A good, ethical contingency recruiter, under these circumstances, is doing what a good retainer recruiter would do. This is particularly true if the contingency recruiter has an *exclusive listing* and there are no candidates from other contingency recruiters, and no "no-price-tag" candidates who reached the employer directly. Under such ideal circumstances the contingency recruiter becomes a full and objective participant. She's not kept in the dark about candidates from other sources, because there aren't any. And she's not presumed to be economically biased. Every candidate came from her, and she'll be paid regardless of which one is hired.

But beware of a different fact situation that would look the same to you as a potential candidate.

Now we'll assume that the contingency recruiter...or a retainer recruiter switching into the contingency mode...has not been in touch with the employer before calling you. He's merely following up on an item in this morning's edition of your industry's trade paper. Let's monitor his phone call to you:

CONTINGENCY RECRUITER: "Have you heard that Bob Smith, the Marketing VP at Acme, has resigned and is going over to Zolo as President?"

YOU: "No, that's interesting news."

CONTINGENCY: "Well, I don't think there's a better person in the industry for that job than you, and I'd like you to be a candidate for it. What do you say?"

YOU: "Absolutely! I've always admired Acme and the President over there, Hal Clay...brilliant, and a very nice man. Count me in. I'd love to be considered."

CONTINGENCY: "Great. I knew you'd see it that way. I'll get back to you."

Too bad! You just got a price-tag on your head. Unless Clay has set up a barrier to unsolicited referrals, using his secretary and a simple form letter that begins on the next page, you and any other obvious candidates Contingency can line up are about to have your resumes mailed to Mr. Clay with a pushy letter from Contingency, who has not been asked for his assistance.

Unfortunately for you, Clay has assigned Richard Retainer to do a fee-paid search. Moreover, Clay doesn't yet have his secretarial defense system operating.

So Clay is handed Contingency's letter and the enclosed resumes. He calls HR, and Contingency is identified as "a good resource, who hits pretty well for us on sales jobs and some middle-managers too; really knows our industry and where the bodies are." Rather than offend Contingency, Clay sets up his defense system for the future and writes Contingency a note informing him that Retainer has been engaged to do a search, and that no further candidates should be proposed by Contingency, "although these will be considered."

Then, along with a list of names he's personally thought of as prospects, Clay gives a copy of Contingency's letter and its five enclosed resumes to Retainer, saying:

> "Check these out, if you wish. I'd be willing to pay the double fee if you find that one of them is the best we can do. I don't know any of these people from Contingency except (you!). He'd have been on my list too, but you've got his full resume in this stuff here. He's young...maybe a little brash...but he appears to have lots of drive and

creativity. Also some good common sense, and that's not easy to find. I talked to him at his company's booth at Product Expo last winter. I'd definitely be willing to consider him if you think we should."

Did you ever hear from Retainer?

No? You're not surprised, are you? It's inconceivable that Retainer would want his $80,000 project "completed" by a candidate from Contingency... thus making Retainer's efforts superfluous, and doubling the cost of filling the job to $160,000.

Of course, all this is happening before you and I have finished our look at the "Rites of Passage." You'll be handling things a lot differently after our guided tour through the land of headhunters...especially Chapter 9 on "How to Handle a Recruiter Who Calls You."

You'll never again bend over and let any recruiter...contingency or retainer... paste a price-tag on your head, unless he passes your rigorous testing to make sure he has an appropriate client relationship.

You have no obligation to serve as a lottery ticket just because a recruiter calls you on the phone. If the company hasn't asked him to submit candidates, you and he are on the same footing. It's up to you whether he sends your resume or you send it yourself. Certainly the straightforward approach is more to your advantage, now that you're a recognizable executive earning a very substantial level of compensation.

Here's the letter executives use to fend off unwanted contingency referrals and maintain their right to see and talk to whomever they wish, without having an uninvited outsider try to interpose fees of 25% to 35% on what would otherwise be *free speech*:

```
Dear _____:

I am Mr./Ms. _____'s secretary, and
I open his/her mail.

I opened your letter recommending a person
(or people) to Mr./Ms. _____.  I'm
not passing it on to him/her or to anyone
else in our organization, because* we have
an executive recruiter on paid retainer to
handle the project you refer to.  We have
not listed our opening with agents and are
not accepting agent referrals.

So I'm returning your letter.  I have not
```

```
passed it or its contents to anyone else in
the organization, and have not kept a copy
of it.
```

```
Thank you for your interest.
```

```
                    Sincerely,
```

```
        Secretary to _____
```

```
*Omit "because" clause, if inapplicable.
```

Don't fall for the old "let me represent you" line.

There was a time when "headhunters" did represent potential employees, but they no longer do. As we discussed in the previous chapter, prior to the early '60s, the people who today are contingency recruiters and are paid by the employer, used to label themselves "personnel agencies" and were paid (usually 6% to 12%) by the people for whom they found work...just like the Hollywood agent who, for a 10% to 15% fee, represents Tom Cruise or Julia Roberts.

A person who represents someone else is called an "agent" and the person represented (called "principal" or "client") is *always the one who pays*. And the fee, of course, has to be affordable. You wouldn't even consider paying 25% to 35% of your first year's compensation to be "represented," and Tom and Julia wouldn't either!

True representation is intended to help get a person hired, not discourage it. Only if you were paying would you be "represented." Otherwise, any "push" you get from a recruiter is more than offset by the drag of the $80,000+ price-tag she applies. Neither the dictionary and legal definition of "representation," nor common sense, allow any recruiter...contingency or retainer...to imply that she "represents" you. Don't you let her imply it either.

So, when a contingency recruiter calls, you must find out unequivocally, that he or she already has a firm agreement to *represent the employer*, who's promised to pay if and when one of the recruiter's candidates is hired. Notice that the agreement must apply to *the specific job being discussed*. Previous deals with the same employer are irrelevant. Remember, *if the recruiter had been able to obtain a legitimate listing before contacting you, he would surely have done so.* "I didn't have time" or, even worse, "I came to you first" is no excuse.

If you learn...and you'll probably have to dig to get a straight answer...that the recruiter does *not* have a specific agreement with the employer about the specific job he calls and asks to "represent" you on, then there is only one answer:

"No, thank you, I'd prefer to represent myself!"

The recruiter you know may give you more trouble than the one you don't.

Just as crime statistics show you're more likely to be murdered by a family member or an acquaintance than by a stranger, you're also more likely to be hurt by a recruiter you know well than by one you don't know.

Opportunistic handling of the people they know tends to become a habit pattern among some of the recruiters who specialize in a certain industry. They watch the trade press with eagle's eyes, and have the ears of a bat when it comes to the rumor mill. And in incestuous industries and job categories with lots of movement from company to company,* it's not surprising that recruiters come to regard almost every "match" as one they should have made.

It's just a short step from reading with disappointment in the trade press about job changes made without any recruiter involvement where the recruiter happened to know the new employees...and by name at least, the employers...to the point where the recruiter feels that:

1. This industry is my domain, where I know the people. They are my inventory...built up through the years.

2. Therefore, whenever people I know move, whatever companies they go to owe me a fee. I'm entitled!

3. I must act aggressively to make sure I don't lose out on any of the fees I'm entitled to.

4. Therefore, whenever an obvious opening occurs, I must line up and "submit" all of the people most likely to wind up in that spot.

---

*Exactly the types that tend to be served by contingency recruiters...the retailing, consumer product, advertising, hospitality, transportation, hi-tech, health care, e-commerce, and publishing industries; and the marketing, sales, financial, EDP, engineering, and legal categories, regardless of industry, are typical.

Earnestly feeling approximately as described, industry-specific contingency recruiting firms...or more often today hybrid contingency-and-retainer firms...seem almost innocently oblivious to the disadvantageous position in which they put unasked-for "candidates" in relation to others with no price-tags on their heads.

Self-Interest: The Bottom Line on Contingency Recruiters for the Executive Above...or Even Just Reaching for...$100,000+

When it comes to referrals involving yourself as the candidate, the situation is clear. You're always better off getting to the employer entirely on your own, unless the contingency recruiter has:

1.   A *valid listing* from the employer (not obvious),

2.   which is *exclusive* (no other recruiters...retainer or contingency...are involved; also not easy to know), and

3.   the job is one which you wouldn't have pursued if it weren't for the contingency recruiter's persuasion.

On the other hand, if the contingency recruiter alerts you to a fine opportunity you wouldn't otherwise have found out about...or persuades you to pursue one you were aware of but otherwise would have ignored...then he's done you and the employer a very valuable service. You owe him your full cooperation...and your thanks.

Above all, don't fall for the "let me represent you" line. Unless *you're* paying the more than $80,000 fee on a $250,000 position—and proportionately more on a bigger one—and therefore are not put at a disadvantage relative to the "no-price-tag" candidates, you're in the best possible position when you get to the employer on your own. This is usually true too, although less obvious, with respect to *retainer recruiters*, whom you and I will look at next.

Chapter 7

Retainer Recruiters:
Look Out for Yourself

Welcome to the posh and prestigious realm of the retainer executive recruiters.

These are the headhunters whose efforts and expertise are valuable enough that they must be paid regardless of whether anyone they introduce is hired.

These are the recruiters who usually...but not always...get the assignments to find executives at $100,000+...and + + + !

And these are the executive search consultants you can almost...but not entirely...be certain will never slap a price-tag on your head and race you to your most likely employers.

**Yes, even some of the most prominent retainer recruiters may occasion-
ally shift into the contingency mode...for their benefit, not yours. Then
everything I told you in the previous chapter applies. Consider yourself
forewarned.**

**But now let's take a look at your self-interest in dealing with a retainer
recruiter who's operating strictly as a retainer recruiter should.**

Getting to the employer before she engages the retainer recruiter is very much to your advantage.

With the retainer recruiter, just as with the contingency recruiter, you're way
ahead if you get to the employer before he does. Consider these advantages:

The employer saves time and lots of money...$80,000 if the job pays,
for example, $240,000, and proportionately more as you move up. No
employer will hire you just to avoid a fee. But if you're right for the
job, she's glad not to wait three months for somebody to find you. And
not spending $80,000 on a retainer recruiter pleases her just as much
as not spending $80,000 on a contingency recruiter.

You're a class of *one*. The retainer recruiter would present several
candidates. You're good. But don't be overconfident. The employer
just might hire one of the others.

There's no risk that the recruiter won't present you. We'll soon
discuss six reasons a retainer recruiter may not present you. By getting
to the employer before he does, you've bypassed all six roadblocks.

The employer is more open-minded and flexible. You may not
have precisely the background the employer insists on getting in return
for an $80,000 or a $150,000 search fee. But whatever you have that's
not ideal may look quite attractive before firm specifications are written and lots of money is being spent to pursue them.

The job may be tailored for you. If you arrive when the employer is
only beginning to analyze her business problems that require outside
talent, she may include your availability in her thinking.

I can't overemphasize the benefits of reaching an employer *before* he or she is committed to either kind of search...retainer or contingency. By the time a search is assigned, a specific job is being filled. Detailed specifications have been written. Potential employees who show up at that late date tend to be thought of as either *relevant* or *irrelevant*. Try to arrive before you're considered a square peg, merely because the opening has been declared a round hole.

**After a retainer search is under way,
you're best off meeting the employer
as one of the retainer recruiter's "finds."**

Unfortunately, that's not easy to accomplish.

With our example of a retainer search in progress, $80,000 is being spent to have a consultant look for you. And with the money already spent, you're best off walking in as living proof that it was well spent. You have these advantages:

You're custom-selected for the job. Meticulous specifications have been drawn up, and you've been found in response to them.

You're expert-recommended. A professional commanding a substantial fee has identified, examined, and proposed you.

You're not challenged by an expert. Despite his or her financial impartiality, the $80,000 expert may still tend to see more merit in candidates he finds than in ones that, being impartial, he evaluates as *"also excellent."* Talk is cheap. It's human nature...and good business...to want the client to feel she got more than an objective discussion for $80,000.

You confirm the employer's wisdom. She decided to hire a consultant. *You prove she was right.*

No question about it. If you can't get to the employer before the retainer recruiter does, then your self-interest is best served if the recruiter "finds" and presents you.

But *will* he?

Not unless you meet a surprisingly restrictive set of six criteria...three of which have nothing to do with your ability to do the job.

When all six of these criteria are present, your self-interest is served by the retainer recruiter.

His introduction is the best possible way to reach the employer in situations that meet the following conditions:

1. When he's searching to fill a job *you could perform exceptionally well*;

2. When he's searching for someone with *exactly your qualifications*;

3. When he's *personally convinced* that you possess those qualifications;

4. When you're *not blocked by the You-work-for-a-client "Off-limits" Rule*;

5. When you're *not blocked by the You're-allocated-to-another-recruiter-within-the-firm "Off-limits" Rule*;

6. When the recruiter *doesn't already have plenty of other fine candidates*.

Don't you wish there were just one criterion? And of course the one you'd cling to would be #1...*a job you could perform exceptionally well*. However, even #1 can be a pain. "Exceptionally well" doesn't mean "competently." Since the retainer recruiter is being paid upwards of $80,000 to "search," what he finds had better be *something special*.

But suppose you are special. And, at least in your opinion, you're absolutely the right choice for a specific position you know is being "searched" by a retainer recruiter. Suppose, too, that you've found out his name and his firm's name. Should you call him? Or should you go directly to the employer instead?

There's a "catch 22" when you know there's a retainer search and you know who's doing it.

You don't want to be overlooked.

But if you go to the recruiter, you're playing "Russian Roulette" with up to 5 bullets in your 6-shooter.

The only one of the six criteria on which you have direct information is #1.

You know that *you could perform exceptionally well*. That's the harmless chamber in your revolver. However, even then you may be wrong...not about your abilities, but about the job content, which may be differently defined for the new person sought than for the former one, and for people with similar-sounding jobs in other companies.

With respect to each of the other five criteria, you don't know if it's "no problem," or possibly a fatal shot.

For you to get to the employer through the retainer recruiter...admittedly the ideal route...you've got to survive all six potentially eliminating criteria. How different from regular "Russian Roulette"! With only one chamber loaded, and only having to pull the trigger once, the traditional game is as safe as badminton when compared with trying to get a retainer recruiter to "present" you on a job you know he's "searching." Then, five of the six chambers *may* be loaded, and you've got to pull the trigger on all six, hoping that *none* of them is.

We've covered #1. Forget about whether or not you can *do the job*. Let's look at the remaining five of these invisible threats to your candidacy. You should have gone directly to the employer, rather than playing with your Retainer-Recruiter-Revolver, if even one of the other five chambers has a hidden surprise for you:

> 2. *If your qualifications and experience aren't EXACTLY as specified.* For $80,000, the recruiter is expected to hit the target. If others match the specifications more closely, he'll present them, not you. On the other hand, if you get to the employer directly, and he meets and likes you, he may observe special abilities, or experience, or fine personal characteristics that outweigh your deficiencies. Even if he merely forwards your mailed-in resume to the retainer recruiter, he's implicity *expanding the specs* to include you.

> 3. *If the recruiter isn't personally convinced* that you've got the right stuff. You may seem more appropriate to the employer than to the recruiter. If so, let's hope you meet them in that order. Meet the employer first and you're in the running. Meet the recruiter first and you're dead.

> 4. *If you're blocked by the You-work-for-a-client "Off-limits" Rule.* Then you must go to the employer. The recruiter's "don't-bite-the-hand-that-feeds" problems mean nothing to the employer.

He'll ship you to the recruiter...or deal with you himself, if the recruiter refuses to touch you.

5. *If you're blocked by the You're-allocated-to-another-recruiter-within-the-firm "Off limits" Rule.* The only way you'll ever hear about two appropriate-for-you jobs simultaneously within the same retainer firm is if *YOU go to Employer #2.* No recruiter will ever tell Client #2 that you're his at a cost of $80,000, but he may have a hard time hiring you, because the firm is also providing you to Client #1.

6. *If the recruiter already has plenty of other fine candidates.* Whenever you're one of a great many people who'd be appropriate, *ordinary statistical odds* will usually kill you. The recruiter doesn't need you, because he already has a full slate.

Two facts are clear:
1. it's nice to be among the retainer recruiter's "finds,"
2. but that's not going to happen very often.

so

There are two things to do:
1. go directly to employers, and
2. get known to lots of retainer recruiters.

How strong is your interest in changing jobs *right now?*

Would you merely like to hear occasionally about career-advancing alternatives to a job you love and would hate to leave? Or are you eager to move? Are you out of work? Your degree of interest in changing jobs will dictate how much you do.

But what to do is obvious.

Go directly to employers.

As we've just seen, you're better off if you get to the employer before the retainer recruiter is brought in. Even when you find out for sure that a retainer recruiter is working on a specific job you'd love, there's a strong likelihood that she won't "present" you for one or more of the six reasons we just looked at. And of course, 99% of the time you won't know the job exists...nor that the recruiter is working on it...nor that one of the six reasons stands in your way.

So, as a general rule, going directly to employers is your smartest move.

When you're not interested in changing jobs, of course, you won't be contacting any employers. But when you're *very* interested in a change, it's in your self-interest to contact as many employers as possible, as effectively as possible. How to do that will be one of the many "Rites of Passage" we'll cover later on.

Know as many retainer firms as possible.

Since it's clear that each retainer firm...no matter how large...is only going to show you a very few opportunities per year that would interest you, the only way you can know about more recruiter-handled opportunities is to *know more firms*. Certainly your self-interest lies in that direction, and how to achieve that goal—both conventionally and on the Internet—is something else we'll look into.

Contingency firms, however, are another matter. If a firm offers *any* contingency services...even though it also offers retainer services...consider it a contingency firm and look out for the potential disadvantages we examined in the previous chapter. You're probably already acquainted with some very fine contingency firms which have agreed never to submit you without first identifying both the employer and the job, and getting your advance approval. I suggest limiting your involvement with contingency firms to the ones where you have this high level of personal rapport.

Reach out to firms you don't know only if they're *exclusively* retainer, and hence unlikely to jeopardize their "pay-me-to-look" status by circulating your resume to any company that hasn't paid.

||| **And now a logical question everyone always asks:** |||

||| **Wouldn't getting in touch with lots of retainer recruiting firms make me seem too readily available?** |||

Absolutely not.

Retainer recruiting firms do not call each other up and compare notes on who's been in touch with them. Neither do employers.

And of course no two retainer firms will ever be "searching" the same job simultaneously, since no employer would ever pay two suppliers to do the same work at the same time.

Therefore, no employer...and no retainer recruiter...will ever find out how many other recruiters and employers you've been in touch with.

Limiting the number of retainer recruiters who know about you doesn't increase your value to anyone. Such "exclusivity" merely reduces the number of attractive positions you'll know about, by reducing the number of firms that know about you.

The only potential problem you could have along these lines would be if you happened to contact both the employer and his retainer recruiter simultaneously. Then the employer might feel that the recruiter didn't have to look very hard to find you. However, the recruiter will also present several other fine candidates who *weren't* obvious, so he's in no trouble for presenting one obvious candidate. Indeed, he might have seemed remiss *not* to identify and check out the obvious one.

Notice that medium-sized and smaller retainer firms are likely to do you just as much good as the largest ones.

Don't neglect medium-sized and smaller firms. After all, no retainer firm— no matter how large, and how many of its jobs would interest you—is likely to show you more than one-at-a-time and two or three a year. Therefore, a firm that annually handles only thirty jobs you'd want may be just as likely to show you three-a-year as a huge company that handles three hundred you'd want.

Incidentally, from the sophisticated employer's point of view, the smaller firms can sometimes be *far more valuable as recruiters* than the largest ones, because they're far less handicapped by the "you-work-for-a-client" and the "allocated-to-another-recruiter-within-the-firm" barriers.

Don't imagine that being well known to a retainer firm will get you exposed to the most attractive opportunity they have in terms of your self-interest.

As you know, the firm will only tell you about one-opportunity-for-you at a time...usually no more than two or three per year. Chances are that "Murphy's Law" will have you allocated to an opportunity in Hog Wallow Bend, when the firm is asked to fill the job you'd love in an ideal company just twelve miles from your home.

If this happens when you're actively "looking," and you fail to reach the nearby employer, don't blame the retainer recruiter handling the Hog Wallow Bend search...nor his colleague doing the Hometown search. And don't blame me. You knew that you should have been in touch with the target employer directly. *You're* the one who failed to watch out for your self-interest.

Contact retainer firms long before you're ready to move. Avoid the "he's-in-trouble-so-we-can-show-him-anything" presumption.

Getting in touch with a recruiter raises an unfortunate presumption. Executives ordinarily do so only when they're out of work, or in trouble and anxious to move. The more recent the contact, the more it looks like the difficulty is *now!*

So if your resume is a recent arrival, you'll probably be earmarked for something relatively unattractive. The firm *won't* feel you have to be lured away from a great situation. And once you're allocated to a recruiter for a search, nobody in her firm can contact you on anything else, until she's finished her project and her administrative assistant has "returned you to the pool." You'll never know if something more attractive is co-pending, or comes along during the weeks and months before you're back in circulation.

Keep in touch as your career progresses.

For all the reasons we've just seen, it's good strategy to have your up-to-date information in the files and/or databases of all the exclusively retainer recruiting firms well *before* you actually want to move. Each time you get a major promotion, use that opportunity to send the announcement memo to the firms you've had contact with.

The implication is that you're continuing to move ahead on the fast track. You're the type of person the retainer firms want to show their clients. You're not in trouble. You're not answering the ads placed by the contingency firms in newspapers and on Internet job sites. So you certainly can't be offered uninteresting, low-salaried, out-of-the-way jobs. Your announcement arrives at a time when you're obviously on a high. And the firm updates its information on you accordingly.

But suppose you're only belatedly contacting retainer firms, and you want to move right now.

Should you try to visit several offices and meet several recruiters in the largest firms?

No. Make contacts that are convenient and time-efficient. But don't waste lots of valuable time that you could devote to other aspects of a well-rounded job search.

Remember that even the largest firms normally allow you to see only one-position-for-you at a time...probably only two or three per year. Once any firm has a file on you and you've met even one of its members, you're about as fully involved as you can possibly be.

Moreover, if any firm is already *actively discussing* any job with you, you know that you won't hear about anything else from them until that search is completed, or you've declared yourself a non-candidate...*and* until the recruiter's administrative assistant has returned you to the "pool."

The only sure way to get strongly involved with any retainer firm, large or small...and with any retainer recruiter, regardless of firm...is to be frank and helpful whenever you're called to solicit your personal interest and/or suggestions. Then *you're* helping the recruiter, not trying to get him to help you. If you sound impressive on the phone...and you genuinely try to help...those facts will be noted and preserved.

Later, when other recruiters in the firm get their hands on your information, the first recruiter's comments will encourage them to call you for suggestions, even when you don't personally look like the solution to their problem. Gradually, over the months and years, you'll meet many of the firm's recruiters by phone, and...when you're appropriate to be interviewed...face-to-face as well.

Just as you can't get a baby in a month by getting nine women pregnant...or if you're a woman, by encouraging nine men to get you pregnant...you also can't become the darling of Korn/Ferry or Russell Reynolds Associates by hustling several of their recruiters simultaneously. Rather than spending lots of time trying to reach more recruiters in the same large firm, you'd be better off contacting additional firms.

Go to the employer
before **you hear about his job from the recruiter**
...not afterward.

You must reach the employer before the retainer recruiter tells you about the employer's position. Once you hear about the job from the recruiter, it's too late for the direct approach.

Of course, if the retainer recruiter is free-within-his-firm to deal with you, and he's likely to decide you're an ideal candidate, you don't want to "go direct." Then you bask in the spotlight of his recommendation. You're part of what the employer paid upwards of $80,000 for...a "finalist candidate."

But suppose you're interviewed by the retainer recruiter...in the office, or just on the phone...and he decides you're *not* a "finalist." Maybe you lack something the employer has clearly asked for. You feel, on the other hand, that what's missing is outweighed by special advantages which, when the client's aware of them, will cause him to widen his specifications to include you...and perhaps others like you.

Now, however, it's too late to do what you easily could have done earlier. Now you *can't* go straight to the employer. If you do, it will be an outrageous affront to the recruiter. And remember that the retainer recruiter, unlike the contingency recruiter, is financially unbiased. Therefore, he usually helps the client evaluate *all candidates from all sources*, not just the ones the recruiter supplies. Someone you've slapped in the face will probably be asked his opinion of you.

On the other hand, if you'd gone to the employer *before* the recruiter turned you down, the employer might have pronounced you a worthy candidate. Or asked the recruiter to check you out...indicating that your deficiency wasn't disabling. Then, the recruiter could have "adopted" you. Indeed, you'd have broadened the specifications and *made his work easier.*

Now, however, you're a pain in the neck! Now you've *defied* the recruiter. And you've *called his judgment into question.* Why didn't he at least see you as a close case? Why didn't he at least *ask* if you were worth considering?

Pursuing a recruiter's client after the recruiter rejects you is unforgivable. Your centrally maintained information will be annotated. No other recruiter in the firm will ever risk a similar experience. *You'll never again be a candidate of that firm.* Yes, Virginia, there *is* a death penalty!

Going to the employer before...
rather than after...talking to the retainer recruiter
not only avoids his wrath; *it may delight him.*

Once you get to an employer and persuade him you're a viable candidate, hidden blockages with the retainer recruiter disappear. Either the employer meets and evaluates you without involving the recruiter; or, more likely, he passes you on to the recruiter, who's forced to follow up.

If you were held back merely because the recruiter had plenty of other fine candidates, he may keep plugging his "finds." But he'll also "adopt" you. And he'll be glad to get the job filled, regardless of who's hired.

If "You-work-for-a-client" was the barrier, the recruiter may reveal it to the employer as his excuse for not "finding" you. Secretly, of course, he'll be delighted that you've innocently helped him complete his search.

If "You're-allocated-to-another-recruiter-in-the-firm" was the problem, the recruiter will never admit it, because this handicap of larger recruiting firms is never publicly exposed. However, he'll be equally pleased to have this roadblock removed.

Whatever the barrier may have been, you've broken through by going straight to the employer. *And the retainer recruiter is probably just as happy as you are with the result.*

By now you may be saying: Wait a minute!
Aren't you telling me two diametrically opposite things?

1. I'm better off as the recruiter's "find" than
just walking in off the street, and yet
2. I should go straight to the companies I want
to work for.

Isn't this inconsistent?

No. Most of the time, your *only choice* is to contact the potential employer directly. Because most of the time you won't know:

      1.   that a suitable position is open, and

2. that a retainer recruiter is filling it, and

3. who the recruiter is.

And unless you know all three facts, you have no choice. Contacting the recruiter is impossible.

Even in the rare instance when you *do* happen to find out all three essentials, you'd better think long and hard before you go to the recruiter, instead of the employer.

Whenever you contact a retainer recruiter on a job you know he or she is handling, you're playing Russian Roulette with potential bangs in five barrels.

Play those odds if you want to.

I wouldn't.

An "advanced technique" with retainer recruiters:

There is one terrific way to get around a retainer firm's rules and learn about the position you'd like best among all those the firm is filling.

This "end run" can only be scored if you've already established a close personal friendship with one of the firm's recruiters...a relationship built over a period of years. Your friend probably first called you as a potential candidate. You weren't interested, but you went out of your way to offer excellent suggestions. Several became "finalists" or valuable "sources" of further ideas. You've made money for the recruiter. You've also been trusted with secrets that never leaked out. Maybe you've even met with him or her on several occasions.

Now you want to move. So you call your friend and ask if there's anything at his firm that might meet your objectives.

> YOU: "Jim, I'd really like to get out of this family-owned business and into a big public company where I can develop a track record with full P&L responsibility for a good-sized subsidiary, and I was wondering if there's any way you could possibly let me know what's going on over at your place that might fill the bill."

If your recruiter friend wants to—and he certainly has no obligation other than friendship to "go around the rules"—he can do the following:

1. *Get your information.* He'll pull you up on his computer screen and identify himself as the person currently authorized to deal with you. And if someone "has you," he'll click "next to use," so he can have you when the current person "drops" you. This will pull you away from searches that don't appeal to you.

2. *Look up the firm's assignments that could interest you.* He'll consult his computer terminal or a weekly printout for this information.

3. *Tell you the relevant searches, and help you select the ONE you like best.* Probably there will be 20 to 60 or more such assignments among the various offices and recruiters of a large retainer firm doing thousands of searches per year. The computer will tell your friend the location, name of company and subsidiary, projected salary range, and name of the firm-member doing the search, for every active project. How far out on a limb he'll go to reveal these facts to you will depend on how much he trusts you to keep the discussion *absolutely confidential.*

When you and he agree on the best opportunity for you that his firm is working on, he'll then call up the recruiter handling it:

YOUR RETAINER RECRUITER FRIEND: "By the way, Dick, I know somebody who'd be terrific for that Ideal Subsidiary project you're working on for Charington Corporation. In fact, he's a personal friend of mine, and he's marked for me on the computer. Not only does he have the perfect background, but I'm sure he'd be interested. Would you like me to turn him over to you?"

DICK: "Is he really good?"

RECRUITER FRIEND: "Outstanding! I've tried several times to get him to be a candidate on general management projects I've been handling. But he works for a family-owned mini-conglomerate and they've kept giving him more money and responsibility, so I've never had anything he was willing to spring for. In fact he's practically running the place now.

"They're about $850 million in everything from consumer products to a grey iron casting company. But he's finally decided that it's time to build his career in a big public company; he's gone about as far as he can where he is.

"Your project makes sense, because his experience is exactly right...and you've got a high enough salary on that job to be able to afford him. Most public companies don't pay as well as Charington does."

DICK: "Well, if you think he's that good, let's go ahead. I've got three fine candidates right now, and I could use a fourth to round out the slate."

RECRUITER FRIEND: "Fine, I'll turn him over to you in the database. He's on my screen right now. I'll tell him to expect a call from you."

But remember, your retainer recruiter friend can only do that if he's sure you're going to play square with him.

If you later contact the employers on some of the other searches your recruiter friend has told you about, *it'll be obvious that you violated his trust.* Every one of the firm's clients that you reach is likely to involve his or her recruiter from the firm in evaluating you. And every recruiter will check the firm's central computer files to get permission to deal with you. Bang! Your deceit is *automatically* exposed! If you cheat, you'll be blacklisted by your friend's firm, and you'll lose one of the most valuable recruiter contacts any executive can ever have.

| | | **Networking Your Way Around the Problem** | | |

When I first wrote *RITES*, I saw the strong personal relationship shown above as your only hope of gaining insight into the many appropriate searches going on simultaneously in the giant retainer firms and making sure you're involved in the one you consider best for you.

Not so! A reader—in the midst of changing jobs—called me with the following suggestion, which I find absolutely diabolical in its insight and effectiveness:

"John, I'm a pretty hot property at the top search firms. Almost every one of them has me meeting one of their clients. But, as you explained, they're only showing me one thing at a time. So, of course, they have lots of good stuff they're *not* showing me.

"But I've found a way around that. In my networking, I'm making it a point to stay tight with just about everyone who's left my company in the past year or so and found a new job. Their backgrounds are just like mine (He'd just left McKinsey.)

"Those folks have all worked hard to become acquainted at the top retainer search firms, and now they're getting lots of calls, either as potential candidates or asking for suggestions. All the jobs fit me perfectly. Immediately, my friends call to let me know what a recruiter has called them about.

"Right now" (one of the very largest firms) "has me as a candidate for a big job at CitiGroup. And yesterday they began looking to fill exactly the same position at Chase. Of course they didn't call me. But by this afternoon, I had six messages on my voice mail from people they *had* called...and *those* people called me.

"What I'll do is mail a letter and resume to the person the job reports to. It's a real power resume...I used your tips and spent a lot of time on it. And what'll happen—in fact it already has, several times—is I'll either get a call directly from the client—in this case the Chase bank—or the headhunter on the Chase search will call and explain that his client is asking for me.

"And of course they" [the search firm] "can't be mad at me. I didn't hear about the job from them and then go behind their back. I'm innocent. I'm just sending out letters like anyone else who's looking for a job."

Wow! He's right. The search firm *can't* object. He hasn't used their information and gone behind their backs. In fact, whoever is handling the Chase search at the giant search firm will probably be delighted to have another fine candidate...and one that, by the rules, he could never even have talked to until CitiGroup had either (1) hired or (2) rejected our savvy job-seeker.

When headhunter #2 calls from the same search firm because his client wants our wise young friend to be a candidate on his search, the firm has become involved in what the very large firms now call "parallel processing." Yes, it's against traditional practice, but flexibility is increasing. (See page 153-55.)

Chapter 8

How to Handle Executive Recruiters
...When You Contact Them

We've come a long way together in exploring the two types of recruiters
...contingency and retainer...and your self-interest with both. I've also
shown you quite a bit about how to handle each type.

But that hasn't been our main thrust. I've raised "how-to-handle" issues
only as they came up in the context of the basic "self-interest" concerns.

Now, as we continue our trek through the land of headhunters, let's
cover all the remaining "how-to-handle" information. This chapter's on
"when-you-call-*them*," and the next two will deal with "when-they-call-
you."

Soon we'll have seen headhunters from every angle, except the inside of their own offices. And that vantage point, too, is available to you in Appendix I. There you'll observe an executive search from start to finish, through the eyes of the recruiter. That account...fictionalized, of course, to protect everyone, and to make sure it covers everything you should know...is your postgraduate course. Do take it. But only after you've read the whole book as background for it.

Meanwhile, back to the matters at hand.

||| Sometimes you won't be content |||
to wait for the recruiter's call.

Obviously, you'd love to have the most respected retainer firms phoning every few months to tempt you with leap-ahead opportunities.

Then, if you happen to feel stymied and frustrated when a call comes in, you can say, "Interesting...tell me more." With very little effort...perhaps not even the preparation of an up-to-date resume...you'll be swerving past the obstacles at your present company, and gaining momentum on the fast track.

But suppose that right now you're known to only a few firms...and not well known. You have no close personal friend at any major firm who'll go out on a limb for you as we saw at the end of the last chapter. You're a stranger to most of the firms. And you want them to know you...as favorably and as soon as possible.

Be careful. Don't go
"cruisin' for a bruisin'."

Whenever you develop a strong determination to seek out recruiters and spark their interest, you're ripe for trouble.

You're in just the right frame of mind to be delighted when a contingency recruiter proposes to put a price-tag on your head and rush to potential employers before you do. And you're equally vulnerable to having that same price-tag applied by a retainer recruiter, who's so impressed by you that she's tempted to slip momentarily into the contingency mode.

With enough of the right bad luck, you can even wind up with a double price on your head...tagged for $80,000 or more by someone lobbing you in on contingency, with respect to an opening that a retainer firm is already being paid over $80,000 to fill.

The first step in handling an executive recruiter is to figure out which type you're dealing with ...contingency or retainer.

You certainly can't tell from the name on the door, since these days both contingency and retainer recruiters call themselves by exactly the same names ..."executive recruiters," "management consultants," "executive search consultants," etc. And you can't tell from the office decor, since both have posh layouts.

Moreover, both types fill $100,000+ and $200,000+ positions, although they're far more frequently handled by retainer firms than by contingency firms. Both may have the utmost polish...*and impeccable integrity.* And to make things even more confusing, both types may switch opportunistically to the opposite payment method.

A warm welcome is a hot clue.

It's only natural, when you're presenting yourself to a recruiter, to want a favorable reaction.

Ironically, it's a contingency recruiter inclined toward the broadest possible distribution of unasked-for resumes, who will be most eager to grant you a courtesy interview. After all, his business is attaching price-tags to people and scattering their resumes to the four winds. He *wants* people coming in.

So if your appointment is easy to get, and the visit itself rushes along very favorably, warning bells should go off in your head. You may be "working with" a recruiter who feels you're "highly marketable"...a lottery ticket to be played with a few dollars worth of postage or a list of e-mail addresses.

Beware of the recruiter who tells you what you want to hear.

Imagine someone arriving for a courtesy interview. After the opening pleasantries, he hands the recruiter his resume. As the recruiter scans it quickly, the executive speaks to reinforce the major points, telling about present responsibilities and outstanding accomplishments. The recruiter looks thoughtful... smiles...and renders a verdict:

> "Well, this is a very impressive resume! And you've also impressed me on a personal basis, Bob, as we've been sitting here talking. I'm really glad you came in. You seem like just the kind of executive who'd do well in several companies I'm thinking of that I could present you to."

> "Just leave a copy of your resume with me. I'm going to see what I can do to get you some interviews."

> *(He stands up and shakes your hand.)*

> "I think I can help you."

An executive who didn't know as much as you already do about recruiters might make a serious error in interpreting what we just saw. He might meet his wife for lunch and say:

> "Just had a great meeting! I saw an executive recruiter who was really impressed, and he said he'd be working to help me."

> *(Time out for a discreet hug to express the good mood.)*

> "Let's pick up a bottle of champagne; I've got a hunch it won't be long now before we're celebrating!"

This guy's interview was certainly no cause for rejoicing. Quite the contrary. *The recruiter just gave his guest fair warning that he intends to begin racing him to the employers most likely to want to hire him.*

It was obvious from a scan of the executive's resume and the fine personal impression he made that he was highly employable, if unemployed...or obviously ready to move up, if currently employed. So the recruiter is about to offer the executive—with price-tag attached, of course—to all the appropriate employers the recruiter can think of.

When a recruiter circulates a resume to various likely employers it's called *"floating"* the resume. I consider it absolutely reprehensible for any recruiter, whether contingency or retainer, to refer the name and background of any individual to any employer without the prior knowledge and consent of the individual.

And *every* recruiter will invariably tell you he would never do such a thing. In fact, however, it seems to happen fairly often...and it may be done by both contingency and retainer people. *"Floating resumes"* is a little like "insider trading." Everyone claims not to do it. And yet it still happens.

What to Tell the Eager Recruiter

Whenever you hear a recruiter say he thinks he can "help," the best thing to do is grab your resume and head for the door. Tell him you don't want to be submitted, unless he contacts you ahead of time and gets your approval to offer you to that particular employer for that particular opening.

Indeed, it wouldn't hurt to write him a letter to the same effect. As we discussed in Chapter 6, you absolutely do not want a recruiter pre-empting contacts you'd be better off making on your own.

The Old "Tell Him, but Don't Let Him Know You Told Him" Technique

The conversation we've just imagined is, after all, a pretty blatant announcement of the recruiter's intention to "float" his visitor's resume. Some approaches are much more subtle. For example, some recruiters actually *obtain your permission* to send your resume to literally scores of prospective employers. The discussion goes something like this:

RECRUITER: "Well, Judith, you look like an outstanding consumer products marketing executive. I think you're ready to become overall vice president of marketing for a diversified consumer products company...or maybe it's about time for you to move up to the presidency of your own division of a very large consumer products company."

YOU: "That all sounds great to me."

RECRUITER: "I'd like to test out some of the types of companies you'd be interested in working for. Now I could see you fitting in beautifully at Bristol-Myers, or Colgate. Or maybe American Home Products or Quaker Oats, or Nabisco Brands, or Carnation out on the Coast."

YOU: (assuming that the conversation is purely speculative) "Well, yes, I think I could fit in at any of those places...and I wouldn't mind moving to California."

RECRUITER: "Or I could see you being successful and enjoying yourself in one of the big cosmetics companies, like Revlon or Estee Lauder."

YOU: "I guess that's a possibility, too."

RECRUITER: "Or you might go all the way to the fashion field with a Warnaco or a Ralph Lauren."

YOU: "Well, I hadn't really thought about it, but I guess if the right thing came up..."

RECRUITER: "Or I could even see you in one of the more advanced and forward-looking industrial companies...they're sometimes interested in grabbing a consumer marketing generalist with an outstanding track record. I'll see if I can come up with any companies like that. And have you ever considered getting into the marketing of financial services, or information products, or..."

The recruiter talks on and on, outlining what seem like nothing more than attractive options for the future development of your career. You think he's merely mentioning some of the types of companies for which he might consider you, if and when they come to him with an appropriate opening to fill.

But he's deliberately taking your nods and smiles as permission to send your resume to all of the companies and industries he's mentioned. If he does a good job of canvassing your interests and mentioning potential employers, you may find that he's outrun you to almost all of the companies you're likely to end up working for.

As times goes on, you may find out by accident that your resume has been submitted to the companies that the contingency recruiter mentioned to you during your courtesy interview. Perhaps you'll see Mr. Decisionmaker at another of your daughter's swim meets. Remember him from Chapter 6? This time he mentions that he happened to notice that your resume is in his company's HR department's files, submitted by Quick Associates.

You call Ralph Quick to protest. His response:

> "Don't you remember when we met in my office? We talked about a number of companies you'd be interested in. So I submitted you to all those companies. As a matter of fact, I kept notes on our visit and jotted down that long *list* of companies we discussed; it's here in your file. I've put in a lot of effort to help you."

What to say when, during a courtesy interview, you run into a recruiter who's preparing to race you to all the employers he mentions, is this:

> "You've talked about a lot of companies. I hope you don't intend to send those companies my resume, when you don't have a specific assignment from them. I've already made contacts myself

with a number of companies, including many of the ones you've just mentioned. And I'm going to be contacting others."

"Therefore, I'm not authorizing you, or anyone else, to submit me to any company without letting me know first what company you've been engaged to represent, and what job that company has asked you to fill. You *must* check with me first...before you submit my name anywhere. You must get my 'go-ahead' for that particular job at that particular company."

Getting in to see an overly-aggressive recruiter is as easy as slipping on a banana peel.

Getting your foot in the door at the best retainer firms can be difficult. Some clout will help.

Getting into a prominent retainer recruiting firm usually isn't easy. After all, every retainer recruiter needs you only if he personally happens to have a search at the moment that calls for someone with exactly your qualifications.

In *Texas Business*, the chief of the Houston office of one of America's largest retainer firms came out with the most forthright statement I've ever seen in print on this subject.

"People are always trying to break through to us, but our secretaries are very well trained. The only time an unsolicited call or a resume will make it through is if a recruiter is searching for someone with that background."

Nonetheless, most retainer firms will, if you persist, arrange for you to receive a courtesy interview...often with one of the most junior members of the firm, who's forced to handle PR duties that the more senior and busier recruiters try to avoid.

If you're a very high-level executive, then just your resume in the mail and a follow-up phone call may get you a courtesy interview. One reason is that you may be someone the firm can use to fill one of its current or future assignments. But a far more likely reason is that the firm wants to get acquainted with you now, so they'll be in a better position to solicit your recruiting business later, when you're building your own team in a new job. And that solicitation will occur, regardless of whether they're involved in your transition.

Even if you're not at quite such a high level, but have a fine track record, well communicated by an impressive resume, you can probably wangle an interview. But if you're just one among many high-potential middle-managers-on-the-way-up, then the *clout of a referral* is essential. And it's always helpful, regardless of how prominent you are.

But whose name should you drop? Whose referral will give you the most clout? I'm continually amazed at how naive many executives are in picking names they think will blast open a reluctant recruiter's door. Here are the people who might refer you...ranked from most to least clout:

1. *Ideally, someone who spends lots of money with the firm you're trying to meet*...the Chief Executive, or the head of Human Resources, or another senior officer of an important client. The recruiter will always shake a hand that has shook a hand that feeds.

2. *Next-best is someone able to provide future recruiting business*...the Chief Executive, or the head of Human Resources of a non-client company. And that's especially true if there's already been a hint that business could be forthcoming.

3. *People who've helped the recruiter in other important ways*... someone the recruiter placed in a job, even though that person hasn't yet spent money with the recruiter. Or a *very-well-thought-of-candidate* on a past search. Or a *valuable "source,"* who's provided much-needed information. Having befriended and profited from these people, it's hard for the recruiter to deny them the favor of seeing you.

4. *The least clout...even negative clout...comes from the mention of a competitive executive recruiter*, proudly referred to as someone you know well and have done lots of business with. It seems bizarre to me that many executives think that invoking a competitive recruiter's name will force a courtesy interview. Why should it?

Every recruiter wants to think of every candidate as a potential future *client*, not just a possible solution to today's search. If you stress your well-established relationship with another recruiting firm, not only will you *not* obligate the unfamiliar recruiter to give you a get-acquainted interview, you'll make him leery of ever proposing you at all. Why should he jeopardize a solid client relationship by bringing in someone who's known to favor another recruiter?

The Limited Goal of a Courtesy Interview: "To Be Continued"

Of course, you *hope* to just walk in and find the retainer recruiter hard at work on a search that represents an exciting next step in your career. Or if she isn't, you hope she'll take you right down the hall to meet another recruiter who is.

Don't you wish!

What you're hoping to gain from an interview that *you* ask for sounds far too much like what you'd be lucky to get, even if you were already well known, thoroughly checked out, and eminently respected by the recruiter you're meeting...not just an attractive "walk-in" making your own unsubstantiated assertions of background and achievement.

Moreover, the recruiter handling your courtesy interview has no authority to declare you a candidate on any search except the few she's personally handling at the moment you're in her office...probably no more than eight to ten. So even if you have her totally convinced, and even if she's with a giant firm handling upwards of 3,000 searches per year, the statistical odds are infinitesimally small that what you're selling is what *she's* buying on the day you walk in.

So keep your goal realistic. Expect only to demonstrate these three points:

1. *Valuable experience*...potentially appropriate for some client someday, but probably not for a current search of the person across the desk from you today;

2. *Excellent track record*...consistent and impressive achievements; and

3. The *personal characteristics* that tend to indicate...but don't guarantee...a fine executive.

Once you've successfully registered these points, a warm *to-be-continued, but later-and-probably-by-someone-else* assumption will suffuse the conversation.

That's it. That's all for today. Take "yes" for an answer! And, like any other good salesman, leave before your "sold" customer begins to have renewed doubts.

Prove you're an effective business communicator, and your courtesy interview is a success.

Prove you're *not*, and you're finished at the firm.

The courtesy interview will be short and superficial enough that you can easily get through it without revealing that you don't do your job very well. Challenging discussion on that subject won't come until you're brought back as a potential candidate on a search.

But the get-acquainted interview *will* reveal whether or not you're potentially *an attractive candidate*. To prove you are, you'll have to demonstrate one attribute that's important for success on the job, and even more important for success as a candidate:

You must be an effective business communicator.

Prove that you have the common sense to figure out what's important for you to cover, and the poise and confidence to put it across in a limited time.

If you don't show these abilities in your courtesy interview, the recruiter will assume you won't in a client interview...or on the job. And he'll mark you as an unlikely candidate for future searches by his firm.

Do unto the retainer recruiter as he'd like to be done unto:

Thoughtfulness and efficiency will win him over.

When you arrive for a courtesy interview with a retainer recruiter, you're getting—free—his most precious resource, the only inventory he has to sell: *his time*.

Format your visit so you don't waste it:

    1. *Express appreciation* for seeing you.

2. *Exchange pleasantries.* Maybe admire something in his office. Probably mention the contact who brought you together. Whatever. A few unhurried but brief pleasantries will make sure that you don't just barge in and take over.

3. *But then, get right down to business.* You'll get plus-points, not demerits, for being organized and efficient. You've asked for this meeting. So it's okay for you to subtly assume some early initiative. Chances are the recruiter aches to say, "Let's get this over with, so I can get back to my search work." By moving along, you give him what he wants, without forcing him to be impolite enough to ask for it.

"How much time do we have?"

As attention turns toward your "sales pitch," try to get a sense of timing:

> "How long do we have? I realize you can't afford to give me the same amount of time you would if this were an interview on one of your searches. So I'll fit my background into the time you have for it."

It won't seem pushy to ask for time parameters, if you do it out of sensitivity to the recruiter's needs. And it'll certainly help you pace yourself. Not overstaying will dazzle and delight the recruiter, because hardly anyone else is ever so considerate and efficient.

The average recruiter spends about one-hour to an-hour-and-a-half interviewing a candidate he's referring on a search. Therefore, you can't expect to get more than one-third as much time...about *thirty minutes maximum*. And, if you can get in and out in 15 or 20 minutes, the recruiter will breathe a sigh of relief, admiration, and gratitude...thinking to himself:

> "Wow! That guy was really on the ball. He knew what he came for, and he got his message across. He was very efficient, yet thoroughly pleasant, attractive, and likable. What an effective executive he must be!"

Bring your resume...and hand it over.

Good business communication is two-fold: written and oral. And the written is indispensable to an effective courtesy interview with a retainer recruiter.

You'd never attempt an important presentation at your company without visual aids, and a persuasive document. If you were presenting a budget review, or requesting money for an acquisition, or proposing a new product introduction, you'd use charts or slides, and a good "leave-behind"...the tools that help a business audience "track" your message, and refer to it later.

Similarly, at the courtesy interview, you must have your resume. You asked for this meeting. So you're obviously selling. This is no time to play coy and say, "Oh, I don't have a resume." Or "It's not in finished form yet." *Of course* you have a resume. And it wasn't difficult...or vastly time-consuming...for you to prepare it. After all, you *are* a highly competent and well-organized person.

Believe it or not, quite a few executives deliberately employ the irksome tactic of showing up for a courtesy interview without a resume...perhaps because there are several how-to-get-a-job books that recommend it. Don't fall for that advice. The premise is that you'll appear "less eager" by not having a resume. Or that you'll get a second shot of the recruiter's time and attention when your resume and follow-up letter arrive in the mail.

Face it. Your eagerness was out of the bag when you asked for the courtesy interview. And the recruiter's lasting impression will be formed while meeting you face-to-face. It won't be something she reads later. Indeed, she may not bother to read anything you send later. Don't be tempted to play the "withhold your resume" game. It's obvious and obnoxious to every experienced recruiter.

Bring in a polished resume and leave it behind. Then immediately after meeting you, the recruiter can conveniently set up a file that states your experience and track record...to which she'll add her fresh-in-mind favorable comments about what an effective communicator you are.

The recruiter's comments will be far less favorable if you have to "wing" your presentation without a visual aid, and if afterward you tell her to wait for a letter in the mail to deliver a clear impression of you.

Four Loathsome Lines...and One Bad Attitude:
Retainer-Recruiter "Pet Peeves"
About Courtesy Interviews

Retainer recruiters consider courtesy interviews a "necessary evil"... whereas contingency recruiters run ads in newspaper and on Internet job sites to encourage them.

So you're "swimming upstream" to even get a courtesy interview with a retainer recruiter. She's busy looking for people who fit several narrowly-specific searches and...no matter how polite and cordial she may be...she's more likely to think of you as an interruption than an opportunity. Therefore, you'll want to avoid several amazingly prevalent mistakes that executives make in seeking and handling courtesy interviews:

1. *"Let me buy you lunch."* Here's the #1 loathsome line, that makes every retainer recruiter cringe. Lunch is too much time, when you're not part of a current search. With only five lunch dates per week, the recruiter can't allocate them to people who...for now at least...aren't the ones she's looking for.

The only situation where you probably *will* have lunch with a retainer recruiter is when you're suggested by somebody who spends lots of money with her. Then *she'll* take *you*, as a display of respect for the person who referred you. Bear in mind, too, that lunch isn't an ideal setting. You may be overheard. Also, it's hard to read and handle papers. They're forbidden at most private clubs, and awkward anywhere, until you're down to the last few minutes over coffee.

"Let me buy you lunch" also has an insulting twang. Is the retainer recruiter so hard up socially and financially that she can be manipulated with a free lunch? Indirectly, of course, the offer also says that the person making it is petty and cheap...vigilantly conscious of who pays at the lunch table.

A truly seductive offer, on the other hand, could be made by changing just one word in the hated "Let me buy you lunch." The retainer recruiter would be thrilled if you could truthfully offer: "Let me buy you *time*." And of course you can, by being considerately well-organized and brief when...at your request...you visit her.

2. *"What do you think of my resume?"* This question wouldn't be so bad if it were asked right up front to indicate that the executive wants to use the session for free counseling, instead of pushing himself as a potential candidate. But it usually comes after having answered all the recruiter's questions, and used up all the interviewing time. Then it demolishes the visitor's image as a secure, decisive executive. It's a loser's question...a departing plea for further attention, from someone obviously frustrated and frightened

because he isn't getting much response to his job-changing efforts.

Polish your resume to your satisfaction. Ask help from anyone who's knowledgeable. *But don't spoil your courtesy interview!* Winding up with a question about your resume is like winding up a chart presentation to your CEO with: "What do you think of my *charts?*"

3. Don't ask for career counseling. Just as bad...and usually delivered at the same wrong time...is a request for career advice. Don't say, "With my background, what do you think I ought to be doing next?" Or, "What level do you think I'm ready for?" Surely, if you know anything, you know that. If you need counseling and psychological testing to figure out what kind of job you're suited for, get it before you reach the retainer recruiter. Don't ask for it at the end of a courtesy interview when your time is up.

4. "How's the job market?" This question should never be asked. The market is always elusive to almost every executive at the moment he wants to change. But ultimately it turns out to be excellent for the outstanding executive. The other types, of course, have difficulty regardless of the economy. So here's another downer that implies you're a fearful, frustrated loser.

5. Don't demonstrate a "God's gift" attitude. Don't be the person who comes in rather pompously, feeling that the retainer recruiter obviously needs grist for her mill, and ought to grovel in gratitude for grist like him. If you take this attitude, you're dead. The underlying assumption, of course, isn't true. There's a *glut* of grist...even in very strong job markets. And plenty of the finest executives have a pleasant, straightforward, cooperative attitude. You'd better, too, or you'll be cancelled out.

Don't be misled by what's said at the end of a courtesy interview: the "pseudo review" of searches in progress.

At the end of your courtesy interview with a retainer recruiter, he'll probably look at a book or a computer screen to check a list of current assignments...

information visible from where he's sitting, but *not* from where you are.

If the firm is a large one, it may handle well over 1,000...and even 4,000... searches per year. You know darn well that there must be several—most likely dozens—that would represent excellent next steps in your career.

Since reading this book you also know, of course, that you'll never hear about more than one at a time. But now that you've been through an exploratory interview, you surely expect to hear about *at least one* that looks like a potential fit.

In fact, however, unless you come very highly recommended, have made an incredibly fine impression, and your interviewer is personally looking for someone exactly like you, that's not what will happen.

Instead, referring to his notebook or terminal, the retainer recruiter will give you a *pseudo-review of current assignments*. He'll summarize several of the firm's searches, in a performance that will seem confusingly like the "ideal relationship" review I showed you at the end of the last chapter. But it will be different in three important ways:

> 1. *There will be something unacceptable to you about every job that's mentioned*...industry, function, compensation, title and reporting relationship, size of business, or calibre of company, etc. And each "fatal flaw" will be one that would be obvious to anyone knowing what you just told the recruiter.

> 2. *The identity of the company will not be revealed*...unless the position has already been filled. "Too bad you weren't here a few weeks ago when we recruited the..."

> 3. *You won't walk away knowing for sure that you'll be a candidate on the job you like best among all those the firm is actually working on.*

Suppose you sense that, in his interview-ending review of current assignments, the retainer recruiter is deliberately overlooking the searches on his list that would be highly attractive to you. Or, if he does read off pertinent searches, you suspect he's ad-libbing into the description of each job a factor that he knows will make it unacceptable to you.

You're probably right!

But don't feel bad. You just received the standard "*pseudo-review of cur-*

rent searches," which most retainer recruiters almost always use to close a courtesy interview.

Why do they do this?

Because turning to a reference, and appearing to check what the firm has underway in your field and at your level implies that:

1. you passed the recruiter's screening, and

2. you'll be called when the firm receives more-appropriate assignments.

The recruiter doesn't have to declare you a non-candidate; *you do that yourself.* Meanwhile, you're quickly on the way out of his office...happy in the knowledge that there are obviously no prejudices against you and no failure to understand and admire your qualifications.

Chances are the retainer recruiter will close your courtesy interview like this:

> "Well, it's always an accident of timing, whether we have anything that fits or not. I'm sorry these jobs today are either in the wrong place or too low paying. Of course, there's that one job that *would* interest you. Unfortunately, I'm not handling that one, and I think I heard that it was filled last week. But I'll check, and if there's still a chance on it, I'll call you. Meanwhile, I'll put your information into our system and we'll wait to see what new assignments we get. Thanks for coming in. We'll keep in touch."

That's what he says. Here's a smorgasbord of possible meanings; take your pick:

> "You look right for a search one of our other recruiters is handling. But she may already have all the candidates she wants for now. I'll tell her about you. But I'll save her the bother of dealing with you if she doesn't want to, by not telling *you* about her."

OR

> "There's a search here that looks perfect for you. I'll pass your material along to the recruiter handling it. He can check out your story with someone else he may know in your company before deciding whether or not to talk to you."

OR

"I see that my colleague down the hall is doing a search you'd be perfect for, and it's exactly what you want. But *I'm* likely to get a similar search within the next month or two. I may as well save you for myself."

OR

"Too bad you're such a vague communicator, and so unattractive to boot. You'll *never* be a candidate on one of our searches."

OR

"Mister, I *had* to be nice to you, because you were referred by a client who spent $750,000 with this firm last year. But I don't buy your act. No way."

Don't place a lot of significance on it...one way or the other...if you get the usual "pseudo-review" of current assignments at the conclusion of your courtesy interview with a retainer recruiter. How favorably and how soon you'll hear from his firm...if at all...may have very little to do with what was said as you walked out.

Chapter 9

How to Handle the Recruiter Who Calls You

You're happily employed...doing an outstanding job for a fine company that recognizes and appreciates your contribution, pays you well, and has you on its fast track toward bigger and better things. You're not dissatisfied. You're not thinking about leaving.

Then the phone rings.

Your caller says he's an executive recruiter filling a major position in your industry at a level you realize you'd have to wait at least two, and maybe five to seven, years...or longer...to achieve in your present company. Are you interested?

Perhaps you should be.

But only if the opportunity stands up to some important questions you can raise over the phone, and only if the recruiter himself passes your savvy scrutiny.

Your caller may be working on a retainer search...or on a legitimate contingency listing...to fill a job that could advance your career. On the other hand, he may be "trolling" for resumes by describing an extremely attractive but nonexistent opening...or an actual and widely publicized opening which he has not been requested to fill.

He may be calling because he's heard great things about you through one of his dependable contacts who knows you. But it's equally possible that he's calling you "cold," just because you're at the right level in a company he's "targeted" to explore, in which case he has no idea whether you're terrific...or just two weeks away from being fired for gross incompetence.

He may even be soliciting you and your company as a possible executive search client under the guise of approaching you personally with some non-existent "opportunity."

**How you react to a recruiter's call depends
entirely on his relationship with the employer.**

**There are only three possibilities:
1. a retainer search assignment,
2. a valid contingency listing,
3. no relationship at all.**

**Figure out what he's up to,
and you'll know how to handle him.**

By now you know where your self-interest lies with respect to all three relationships a recruiter may have with an employer.

And, despite a dizzying dose of doubletalk that may be administered when you try to figure out what the relationship is, there are only three possibilities. Let's review them, and then let's take some phone calls.

1. A Retainer Search

This is the ideal relationship from your point of view. You're too late to reach the employer ahead of the recruiter, and maybe get the job without competition from recruiter-supplied candidates. Now a recruiter is being paid $80,000* to look. Therefore, you're best off as one of his "finds."

If the caller is on a true retainer assignment, you'll want to cooperate.

2. A Valid Contingency Listing

This is a good, but somewhat less-desirable, relationship, as far as you're concerned.

If the caller has a contingency listing directly from the employer on the job he's describing to you, then you may wish to cooperate. Generally speaking, however, you're not obligated to do so.

There is only one narrow set of circumstances in which you're morally obligated to go ahead with a contingency recruiter...or forgo the opportunity. We'll cover this subject later.

3. No Relationship at All

This is a lousy situation from your point of view. The recruiter couldn't get either type of relationship with the employer...retainer or contingency...so now he wants to tie *you* up!

If the caller...whether normally a retainer or a contingency recruiter...has no direct arrangement with the employer on the job he's calling you about, you do not want to cooperate.

So much for the ground rules. Now "Let's go to the phones," as they say on TV. First, an easy one.

> YOUR CALLER: "Hello, I'm Joan Chase from the executive recruiting firm of Randall Radley Associates, and I'm calling because I

---

*The fee on a $240,000 position. Your level may be much higher. If so, the fee—typically one-third of annual compensation—is proportionately more.

have a situation that might be of interest to you or perhaps to someone you might wish to recommend."

YOU: "Oh, I know your organization. It's one of the fine retainer
firms. I've met a man named Stevens in your company; do you
work with him?"

CALLER: "No, Bill's in our Atlanta office, and I'm calling you from
Cleveland. But of course we know each other."

Enough already!

You know the firm and its fine reputation as a retainer recruiting organization.
This woman is obviously with them, because she knew Stevens and volunteered his correct location. So let her go on, and listen open-mindedly. She
appears to be entirely on the up-and-up, and doing exactly what she says
she's doing.

"But," you say, "couldn't she be who she is and still be calling about a job on
which she hasn't been in touch with the client, intending to 'float' my
resume?"

Not likely. She seems to be a rank-and-file recruiter in a well-known retainer
firm, just grinding out one of their regular assignments in the regular way.
Remember that retainer-only firms hardly ever jeopardize their "pay-me-to-
look" status by offering resumes they haven't been paid to find. Let's put your
conversation with Ms. Chase "on hold" for a while, so you can answer a more
challenging call.

This time we'll listen as you smoke out the intentions of someone who really
is planning to "float" your resume. Ironically, this caller is someone you've
known and been friends with for years...a contingency recruiter specializing in
your industry, who helped you find one of your early jobs, and whom you've
used occasionally to recruit subordinates during your rise to $100,000+ and
far beyond.

CARL CONTINGENCY: "I suppose you saw in the trade papers that
Andrea Williams left Colonial to become President of TransWestern.
That means they'll be needing a new President over at Colonial,
and I don't think there's anyone inside who's up to the job. As you
know, Blake Stevens, their new VP - Marketing, was just promoted
to that level from head of the field sales force a few months ago.
He's certainly not ready for the presidency. And they surely won't
give it to some Finance or Manufacturing person in such a market-

ing-driven company. What do you say, Bill? Would you like me to put you in the running for the presidency over there?"

What an easy example!

You're immediately skeptical. You're surprised that Carl would be seeking a President. As far as you know, his mostly contingency practice...while widely and justifiably respected...hasn't been filling positions at quite that high level.

Moreover, Carl is being perfectly straightforward. He isn't saying he's been *requested* to seek candidates for the presidency of Colonial. Indeed, he makes it clear that he's merely reacting to what he's read in the trade papers and drawing his own conclusion. No search has been assigned. Or if one has been, it's obvious that Carl doesn't have it. He hasn't been briefed by the CEO of Colonial. If he had been, he'd have told you so.

Since Carl is referring to an opening publicized in the trade papers, it's a situation that everyone in your industry knows about. Indeed, you've probably already been thinking about writing or calling the Chairman of Colonial. You know her slightly, because you were on a panel she chaired at your industry's trade convention two years ago.

Have you missed your chance to go ahead on your own, just because Carl's phone call reached you before you made your move?

Absolutely not.

Let's see you take it from here:

> YOU: "Thanks for the call, Carl. In fact, I've been thinking along those same lines. I've intended to call up Gloria Wing, the Chairman over there, or send her a letter and a resume...I haven't decided which. I was on a panel she ran at the trade convention in Las Vegas a couple years ago. Now, Carl, I gather that Mrs. Wing hasn't put you on retainer to find her a President, has she?"
>
> CARL: "Well, no she hasn't talked to me specifically about this situation. But I've filled quite a few jobs over there during the past several years. I'm perfectly sure I can present you."
>
> YOU: "Thanks for offering, Carl, but I'd rather not. I'd prefer to be in touch with her on my own. I'd rather handle it myself."

Simple as that! You figured out that Carl has no mandate. So you turned down his offer to interpose himself between you and the employer. He offered. You politely refused. The only explanation you needed to give was:

"I'd rather handle it myself."

Now, you're just as free to get in touch with the Chairman directly as you were before Carl called. If Mrs. Wing hasn't yet engaged a recruiter, she may decide to meet you and perhaps one or two other obvious prospects. Indeed, she may make her choice without ever feeling the need to hire a retainer recruiter, or to put out contingency listings. On the other hand, perhaps she already *has* hired a retainer recruiter. If so, you're still free to be part of that person's project, without the handicap of an extra price-tag applied by your friend Carl.

However, don't become overconfident. Carl wasn't really trying very hard. He helped me help you, by delivering a classic pitch designed to demonstrate the basics.

Now let's take a much more challenging call. This one's from a prominent *retainer* recruiter whom you know and trust. You'll have to be more alert and probing, because Randy's not going to send you the obvious signals Carl and I contrived for you in the previous example. Randy's going to give you the full treatment.

> RANDY RETAINER: "I'm not sure if you're aware of it, but I've done several recruiting projects over the years for Pete Pinnacle, the Chairman over at Acme Consolidated. He's got an opening at the top of his Industrial Products Division, what with Jason Evans leaving to become Chief Executive of Trombley Consolidated. You'd be absolutely perfect for that spot, now that you've got a few years' experience under your belt as number-two in an operation that's almost their size and, if anything, is doing even better than they are. What do you say? Would you like to be a candidate on it?"

> YOU: "Maybe, Randy. I've been thinking it's time for me to take over my own show, and I've been wondering what they'll do to fill Jason's job. I thought maybe they might promote somebody from one of their own divisions. If they stay inside the Industrial Division, I'm afraid I have to agree with you...nobody there would be as good for the top job as I would be. Matter of fact, I was thinking of maybe dropping the Chairman a hint that I might be

interested...possibly through one of his outside Directors I know pretty well, or through another friend of mine, who's one of their biggest distributors.

"Tell me, Randy, has the Chairman definitely made up his mind to go outside to fill that job, and has he put you on retainer to do the search?"

RANDY: "Oh yes; he's got to go outside. It doesn't make any sense at all to take somebody like Nancy Stein...who's doing a great job, by the way...out of their Maritime Division and put her into Industrial Products. And the same goes for Clem Smith, who's Executive Vice President of their Defense Systems Division. He's a great guy and certainly ready to run his own operation. But it ought to be something closer to his field. He's never sold to any customer but the Pentagon. Really they don't have anybody over there who'd be as appropriate as you would, to take charge of Industrial Products.

"Why do you think I called you? Not just because we haven't talked for awhile. Today we're doing business. I want you to be a candidate. In fact, I think you'll be the strongest of all the candidates I'll be presenting. What do you say?"

YOU: "As I said before, I might be interested. But I didn't quite get your answer to the other part of my question. Have you personally got a retainer search assignment to fill this position? Because, if you do, then I'd like you to tell me a lot more about what the Chairman has told you he's looking for. Has he put you on retainer to solve this thing?"

RANDY: "Well, not exactly. Not quite yet. But I'm sure that if I let him see someone as ideally appropriate for his Industrial Division presidency as you are, that'll make it obvious to him that he shouldn't stay inside. What do you say? Would you like to go for it?"

This time you had to work a lot harder. And you were up against a tough adversary...a well-known retainer recruiter, whom you certainly wouldn't have suspected of "floating resumes." Randy knew plenty of detailed information. Moreover, you were well aware that he had previously done high-level recruiting within that company.

But even this retainer recruiter you've known and trusted for years failed to pass your savvy scrutiny, now that you're challenging *every* headhunter who calls you, to find out whether he has a client assignment and what the exact nature of that arrangement is.

Now you're faced with a choice.

Randy has previously worked for the Chairman on retainer. Maybe he'll be asked to do so in this instance, too. If so, he may not be enthusiastic about your candidacy...on this or any future job...if you're uncooperative now. On the other hand, the Chairman doesn't always use a recruiter when he hires a high-profile person from outside. And even if he does assign a retainer search, he may not choose Randy this time.

Indeed, if Randy were confident of getting a retainer search to fill this opening, he'd have waited to get his mandate before contacting you or anyone else. Maybe he suspects the Chairman will promote from within...or "go it alone"...or choose another recruiter. Maybe the Chairman already *has* chosen another recruiter.

(Time out while you decide what to do.)

Congratulations!

You've decided to remain your own person. I thought you would. You didn't get where you are now by allowing people to manipulate you. Now let's see how gracefully and inoffensively...yet firmly...you handle this situation:

> YOU: "Thanks for offering, Randy. But I'd rather not have you bring me up with the Chairman until you've got a firm search assignment from him. Why don't you take the next few days to get in touch with him and see if he wants you to take charge of finding someone on the outside for the presidency of that division?" (You know this won't be easy for Randy...if it were, he'd have done so before calling you; but he can't say that.)

> "Please don't tell him that I might be a candidate. I want to keep my options open. If the Chairman does assign a search, there's nobody I'd rather see get that project than you. But if you don't, I want to still be in a position to go after him through informal connections, or to be contacted by the recruiter he does select, or maybe just to drop the whole thing. I'm going to be away on Wednesday and Thursday. Why don't you call me on Friday and let me know how you made out? I won't do anything until I hear from you."

See...it wasn't all that difficult. You caught Randy proceeding when he didn't have the proper basis to do so. But you didn't make a fuss. You didn't back him into a corner. And you also didn't allow him to corner you, which was the purpose of his call.

Congratulations again. You matched wits with a master...and you came out ahead.

Always qualify the recruiter.

Even if you know him well, you still don't know his connection with the employer.

By now it's easy to see the central truth that you should always keep in mind when answering every headhunter's call: You don't know for sure whether your caller has a definite arrangement with an employer, and you don't know what the exact nature of that arrangement is. Since both points are important, you'd better clear them up before agreeing to anything the recruiter proposes.

And you're *able* to find out...as you've just proved. You caught a prominent retainer recruiter, whom you personally know and respect. He was about to put a price-tag on your head in one of his exceedingly rare departures from his professed way of doing business. Firmly, but gracefully, you stopped him. If you can do that, surely you can figure out what just about everyone else who calls you is up to...and *react strictly according to your own self-interest.*

But before we leave Randy Retainer, let's speculate on his motives. He may have a strong relationship with Pete Pinnacle, the Chairman of Acme Consolidated. Maybe Randy's altruistically concerned that the Chairman will make a less-than-optimum appointment from the inside, if not confronted with unasked-for resumes from outstanding outsiders. It's far more likely, however, that Randy has a weakening, marginal, or defunct connection with Mr. Pinnacle, and suspects or knows that another retainer recruiter will be the one officially looking for the next President of Acme's Industrial Division.

No retainer recruiter will ever attempt to submit you on contingency if he can readily get himself hired on retainer to look for you. And the likeliest reason he can't get hired is that somebody else already has been. If so, you'd better be the other recruiter's "find"...or the employer's. Otherwise, you probably won't be hired.

**Ironically, when you're a high-level executive,
your resume is much more likely to be "floated"
by a recruiter you know well, than by a stranger.**

It's no accident that the two people you've caught intending to forward your resume without a proper employer-mandate have both been people who know you well...not strangers. If you're a senior executive, that will usually be so.

And *when a true retainer recruiter is involved*, that will *virtually always* be so. The reason, once again, harks back to his normal fee arrangement...to get paid *for the act of looking*, regardless of whether anyone is hired. Therefore he normally never offers resumes without first being paid to find them. If he did, the employer would think, "Why pay him just to look, when he'll submit candidates without being paid, just like a contingency recruiter does?"

Therefore, a true retainer recruiter breaks his operating pattern...if at all...only on very rare occasions when he has no shot at a fee unless he does something drastic. And even then he won't, unless he knows the potential "candidate" on a personal basis well enough to hide behind this excuse:

> "She's *someone I've known very well for a long time*,
> and she'd be perfect!"

The retainer recruiter can never admit he *actually looked for new people* that he's sending over on a contingency basis, because to do so would destroy his claim to be strictly a retainer recruiter.

The *contingency* recruiter, on the other hand, has a different problem. He isn't usually asked to fill extremely high-level positions. Therefore, he lacks credibility when he claims to have a high-level executive tied up and accessible only through him. He almost *has* to say:

> "This is *someone I know very, very well*."

**If you're a middle- or lower-level executive, my tip
that the headhunter likeliest to float your resume
is probably someone you know well does not apply.**

The further down you are from President, General Manager, or head of function such as Finance, Manufacturing, Marketing, R&D, etc., the more numerous are the positions in which every organization can use your talents, and the more frequently...perhaps even continuously...the organization has an opening at your level that urgently needs to be filled.

Under such circumstances, suggestions of potential candidates tend to be much more welcome, regardless of source. Contingency listings may be handed out to virtually any headhunter who asks. And resumes may be cheerfully accepted and kept on file, even though the headhunters submitting them haven't bothered to secure a listing in advance.

Indeed, as I pointed out in Chapter 6, when you're seeking a foothold at the bottom- and middle-levels of the corporate pyramid, being pushed by an aggressive contingency recruiter may be very helpful. It may get you noticed, when you wouldn't be otherwise. And the contingent price-tag on your head may not matter much, because it's a low fee at your low salary level; and paying agency fees is pretty much standard practice when lots of openings have to be filled and a busy personnel department doesn't have time to pick over hoards of applicants.

Don't fall for the "you should be represented" comeback.

Whenever you respectfully, but firmly, refuse to be introduced by any headhunter who lacks an employer mandate...or by a contingency recruiter who has one...you'll invariably be socked with the usual high-pressure pitch:

> "Surely you don't want to be *unrepresented*!"

Just say:

> "Yes, thank you, in this particular instance that's
> what I prefer."

Only if you're a glutton for futility will you try to get the recruiter to admit that being your "representative"...your agent...would require that *you* be the one paying him and not the employer, as you and I discussed in Chapter 6.

Unfinished business with caller #1...

Once you established that Joan Chase was from a well-known retainer recruiting firm, you gave her the benefit of the doubt and let her complete her pitch. Chances are...999 out of 1,000...that she's working on a regular retainer assignment. Since she's a rank-and-file member of the firm, and since she didn't previously know you and have a cordial relationship with you...nothing outside the ordinary character of the firm appears to be involved in her routine call to you.

Nonetheless, it won't hurt to ask:

YOU: "Who's your contact on this assignment? Are you working directly with the Chairman?"

CALLER: "Yes, I had a meeting with him and with their Vice President of Personnel last Wednesday."

Stop beating a dead horse. Clearly, she's doing a retainer assignment. You're just as well off to deal with her as with the client himself.

But now let's take another call.

YOUR CALLER: "Hello, this is Mae Findham from Seekim Associates. We're management consultants specializing in the field of executive search, and I'm calling you about a very attractive position that might be of interest to you...or if not to you, to someone you might wish to recommend."

YOU: "I'm sorry, I didn't quite get the name of your firm. Did you say, Seekim Associates? How is that spelled?" (She tells you.) "And you're located here in Chicago? Or where are you calling from?" (She tells you.) "Let me have your phone number, in case we get interrupted, so I'll be able to call you back. I'd like to hear what you have to say, but I may not be able to stay on the phone any longer than just a very few minutes right now. But go ahead."

CALLER: "Well, of course I can't be specific as to the actual identity of the company, because this is a highly confidential assignment, but there's a..."

YOU: (Here's your opening; jump on it.) "Oh, why is that? Are they firing the person who has the job now, and he doesn't yet know about it?"

CALLER: (slipping away) "Well, you might say it's something like that, although not exactly. All I can tell you for right now is simply that I'm not at liberty to disclose the identity of the client."

YOU: (interjecting again) "Well, I certainly don't want to press too hard for the client's name, if you're not in a position to give it. Are you working on retainer? Or is this a contingency assignment?...In which case I can perfectly understand why you aren't comfortable in being specific about the client."

CALLER: "Rather than concern ourselves any further at this point about who the client is and why I can't give you that information, let me just tell you this...it's a client we have served many times over the years, and one I personally know very well. But right now let me tell you a little more about the job so we can see whether it's an attractive one for you to consider, or whether you would prefer to recommend someone else."

You now let the recruiter drone on, and you pursue the full line of questioning we'll look at in the next chapter for screening any "opportunity" that's pitched to you over the phone. However, the tone of this conversation so far has been sufficiently mysterious and evasive to let you know that you may well be dealing with a headhunter who, at best, has a nonexclusive job listing, and indeed may not have any direct commitment from any employer. *You will proceed with caution*!

If Ms. Findham had been a retainer recruiter with an assignment conferred directly by the employer, she would have immediately told you so, explaining that her secrecy was not because of a tentative mandate, but rather because of specific reasons why it would hurt the employer if his search became known.

Does a headhunter's calling you about a job force you...legally or morally...to pursue the job only through him?

Have you lost your right to contact the employer directly?

Usually not.

Of course, if he's a retainer recruiter being paid to look for you, you want to be one of his "finds." You hope he will introduce you. If he refuses, you can ignore his "wet blanket" and go directly to the employer. He'll resent your action, and "blackball" you for all future searches by his firm. But he can't stop you.

With the contingency recruiter, the shoe is on the other foot. He'll seldom say no to you. He *wants* to submit you...with his price-tag attached, of course. But you may prefer to go directly to the employer without his tag. Can you?

Usually you can.

If the contingency recruiter *hasn't* identified the specific employer and job to you, you have no obligation whatever to let him apply his tag and send you onward to an undisclosed recipient. You're just as free after his call as you

were before it, to canvass any and all employers you wish and offer your services.

Even if he *did* tell you precisely the employer and the job on which he wants
you to be his candidate, and even if he has a valid listing, you're still at liberty
to contact the employer directly if some other source of information... apart
from his phone call...has also made you aware that the job is open and likely
to be filled from the outside.

But be forthright; otherwise the recruiter will think you took advantage of his
call and sneaked around behind his back. Just tell him that you already know
of the opening through other sources, and that you may or may not wish to
follow up on your own. The contingency recruiter won't be pleased with your
decision, but there's nothing he can do about it. You have every right to refuse
his offer to make an introduction that you prefer to make yourself.

Suppose the contingency recruiter just happens to be someone you don't like
or respect. You don't want him to know whether you're willing to be a candidate or not, and you don't *ever* want to be submitted to any employer by him.
Just say:

> "George, I'm not sure whether I want to be a candidate over
> there, or that I want to go there through you. Please do not sub-
> mit me. I think I'll wait a while and read about the situation in
> the trade papers. Then, if I decide afterward that I want to go
> ahead on my own, I won't feel I've taken unfair advantage of
> this phone call from you."

Needless to say, you must *really* dislike the contingency recruiter to take this
approach. But it's your prerogative. Any recruiter...contingency or retainer...
merely *offers* to introduce you. He doesn't own you.

**The only situation in which you're morally obligated
...and possibly legally too...to go ahead with the
contingency recruiter, or not at all, is when he:**

1. has a valid listing from the employer and

**2. has revealed a situation that you wouldn't
have known about, or wouldn't have pursued, if he hadn't caused you to do so.**

You know what's fair and what's not. Let your conscience be your guide.

When the opening is not public knowledge, and you learn about it only from the recruiter, then you *are* morally obligated...and perhaps legally, too...to pursue the opportunity only through an introduction made by him.

Similarly, if the existence of the job was known to you through other channels, but the recruiter told you about attractive hidden features which caused you to go ahead when you wouldn't have otherwise, then too, fairness demands that you pursue the position only through the recruiter.

When a contingency recruiter has a valid listing, the employer has agreed to pay the recruiter if he hires someone the recruiter places before him. So, if the reason you know enough to contact the employer is because the recruiter has contacted you, then the recruiter has done his job and has earned his fee.

Moreover, in my opinion, that's true even if the recruiter doesn't specifically identify the employer, but drops clues enabling you to *guess* the employer, or presents the job so tantalizingly that you canvass *all* the employers in your industry attempting to hit the job the recruiter has told you about.

It would be highly improper for you to "go around" the contingency recruiter under any of those circumstances, in an attempt to make yourself less expensive for the employer to hire. If you were to do so, any ethical employer would consider your behavior sleazy in the extreme. He should forgo hiring you on the basis of low moral character. And if, by chance, the employer were to be sufficiently devious himself to applaud your actions, his own moral character would be such that you'd be better off not working for him. Or, perhaps, you'd deserve each other.

Here's a question a lot of people ask:

"Is there any sure and easy way to tell whether a headhunter who calls is from a contingency or a retainer firm?"

There's no simple "litmus test."

But the calls you've taken throughout this chapter have all helped sensitize you to "contingency vibes" and "retainer vibes."

An aura of secrecy is one of the strongest clues that your caller may be approaching you from the contingency direction. Often a contingency recruiter will be highly vigilant that you not figure out who her employer/client is unless and until you agree to be a candidate...and maybe even then, not until just before you go to see the employer.

That's because your knowing creates several hazards to her earning a fee: You may go directly to the employer. You may start grapevine rumors that send *other candidates* to the employer. And those same rumors may send *competing contingency recruiters* to the employer. Your call from Mae Findham was a classic example of "contingency vibes," telegraphed by a secretive manner.

So, as early as possible in any phone call from a headhunter, you may as well ask the ultimate question:

> "Are you *on retainer* to submit candidates for this job, or are you working *on contingency*?"

The recruiter on the other end of the line may be a bit shaken by your highly aware and direct question. If so, that momentary discomfort may be your answer.

On the other hand, if he's glib and experienced, chances are he'll give you a side-stepping answer:

> "Oh, I *regularly* send this client outstanding people."

> OR

> "We have a long-term relationship with them, going back to 1998, when we recruited the person who's now General Manager of their Catalog Marketing Division."

> OR

> "We have a *standing order* to send them people we feel would be right for the businesses they have."

The variations are endless. But the theme is consistent. *Previous* contact is invoked to suggest a definite arrangement to fill the job the recruiter is phoning about. Unfortunately, in the words of the immortal Gershwin tune: "It Ain't Necessarily So."

If in doubt, call "time out."

Another thing you can do to "qualify" the recruiter on the other end of the line is to interrupt your conversation, offering to call back later. Meanwhile you have time to do a little investigating.

One strong indication that a U.S. recruiting firm *doesn't* operate on contingency is membership in the Association of Executive Search Consultants

(AESC), the professional association founded and supported by retainer firms. You can call them at their New York headquarters, (212) 398-9556.

Unfortunately, the AESC has slightly over 100 members out of an estimated 1,000 or more qualified U.S. retainer firms. However, many of the largest and best-known firms *do* belong to the association. Not being in AESC says nothing negative about the firm you're trying to check on. But membership can be a favorable indication, because there is a peer review procedure prior to entry.

A more expedient way to check on a larger number of recruiting firms is to see if the firm is shown in Appendix II of this book or listed on *Rite*Site.com as a *Rites*-honored recruiting firm. Both of these resources identify the same list of outstanding search firms.

The most expedient technique you can use to determine whether a recruiting firm operates on contingency...or more often contingency *and* retainer...is simply to call the firm's switchboard and ask what kind of arrangements it offers an employer interested in using that firm to find an employee. Ask the receptionist or secretary who answers:

> "With your firm, is it necessary to pay even if nobody you supply is hired? I know some firms operate that way...'on retainer,' they call it...but that's not the kind of arrangement I have in mind."

The telephone-answerer may conceivably give you a more straightforward response than you'll get from an executive of the firm, who'll be trying to size you up and will speak much more cautiously. The receptionist may say:

> "Well, I know we *prefer* to work on retainer, but we also work the way you have in mind. Let me put you through to someone who can tell you more."

Note: The next several pages discuss relatively arcane (and in some cases, perhaps transitory) wrinkles in the retainer recruiting business. Logically they belong in Chapter 7. They're here because this is where *you* will find them more interesting and relevant.

A trend toward subtle revision of traditional ethics in the search business is being pioneered by some of the very largest and most prestigious firms.

Know what's happening. Use it to your advantage.

Two main ethical rules have governed the retainer-compensated executive search business ever since it began in the '50s. Indeed, they're based on common sense principles that govern every business that has customers.

You already know what they are: (1) you can't bite the hand that feeds, and (2) you can't sell a single item to two customers simultaneously and charge both of them the full price.

Surprise! Even these verities are being challenged. This is a fact you should know...and one you may be able to take advantage of.

First . . .

The We-won't-take-your-people-for-at-least-2-years Off-Limits Rule (employer's viewpoint)

...which is also the

You're Off-Limits for 2 years after the retainer firm has been paid to assist your employer (potential candidate's viewpoint)

Don't injure or offend a customer who's just spent money with you. That's the main reason for the "Two Years" rule.

There's also a second practical reason. In doing a retained search, the recruiter acquires deeply confidential information. Coming in as a trusted consultant, he or she is told about the strengths and weaknesses of executives currently on staff: Who's excellent and slated for promotion? Who's merely adequate at current level or—although promising—newly proving himself? And who will probably have to be replaced in a future search?

Would a client "tell all" if he thought the recruiter interviewing him about the current search would conduct a well-informed raid on his organization just as soon as the final retainer check hits the bank?

Hardly!

Which is why the "Two Years" rule was born and why, even today, it is proudly and enthusiastically observed by virtually all small and medium—and most large—retainer search firms. However, the "Two Years" rule has proved increasingly inconvenient for the *very largest* firms, because it tends to limit their growth. The more companies they've recently worked for, the fewer whose people they can solicit. And with fewer places to look and fewer people to choose from . . .

Well, you get the idea. And so do the Wall Street analysts, now that several of the very largest firms are public companies!

Therefore, the time-honored rule—once religiously upheld by the largest firms as ethical arbiters of the industry—is no longer merely inconvenient. It now jeopardizes the business plan. Therefore, it's got to be made more flexible...and, if possible, *nonexistent*.

That's a tall order. Clients and potential clients are resisting. Competitors—nearly all of whom can now claim to be "holier than thou"—are shouting. And the controversy is about to heat up!

Nonetheless, the less-than-a-handful of largest public firms are making some progress in attempting to temper the ethical precepts they led the industry in establishing. Off-limits protection is no longer standard for all clients of those top two or three or four publicly traded firms. It's no longer specifically described in their selling literature. And the duration of the protection, when granted, may now be 18 or even 12 months or less. Sophisticated clients now realize that they must specifically negotiate this issue prior to start of a search and get it written into the engagement letter.

Unsophisticated clients, of course, fail to raise the issue. Sophisticated ones awarding **lots** of business, of course, **do** insist on the traditional "Two Year" protection. And, having plenty of economic power, **they can usually get it**. Other clients—notably HR professionals—may be sophisticated enough to realize they must ask in order to receive. But they may intentionally pursue a "Don't ask; don't tell" policy. Reason: they want to hire the big name search firm. Their CEO expects them to. But their occasional search assignment won't be sufficient volume to force strong off-limits protection. And of course, they don't want to be faulted for **not** securing protection if the current *recruit-in* is discovered to be soon followed by a *recruit-out*. By not raising at the outset an issue they did not have enough economic power to win, they leave themselves room to save face later. If and when trouble surfaces, they can say to the CEO...and maybe even to the search firm too: "I had every right to **assume** that the traditional rules applied."

Meanwhile, of course, the vast majority of less-than-giant firms aggressively flout their righteous adherence to traditional values. It becomes a central marketing argument. Their brochures, engagement letters, and "shoot out" sales pitches all aggressively promote the "protection" issue.

So what does all this controversy mean to you as a potential candidate?

Certainly nothing bad!

For one thing, you'll probably see a few more opportunities from the largest firms your employer uses than you would have seen just a few years ago. And that's *great* from your standpoint!

Moreover, knowing about the escalating ambiguity on this issue, you may be emboldened to sketch out your career desires to the recruiters who are now searching for your subordinates. And they may tap your shoulder a lot sooner than you'd ever have expected.

Similarly, of course, while you're cautiously talking *more* about yourself, you'll talk *less* about your own best subordinates. You're smart. You know what to do.

And secondly the . . .

You-Paid-for-These-Candidates-/-They're-Yours-Alone
Off-Limits Rule (employer's viewpoint)

...which is also the

You're-Allocated-to-Another-Recruiter-in-the-Firm
Off-Limits Rule (potential candidate's viewpoint)

The common sense of this rule is that no vendor should be able to sell the same work to two customers simultaneously and get fully paid for it by both. The client pays a stiff fee for candidates. At the traditional one-third of annual compensation, the fee on just a $240,000 job is $80,000. Even if as many as 5 candidates are presented, they each cost over $16,000 for the recruiter's work in finding them. If only 3 are presented, each costs over $26,000.

At that rate, how do you imagine the employer will feel if his or her candidates are simultaneously provided to another client of the same retainer search firm?

Not happy!

Client employer #1 is now under time pressure to hurry up and select the best candidate before client #2 hires her away. Client #1 may also have to overpay, in order to out-bid client #2. And all this difficulty is being created by the recruiter who's being paid to *solve* the problem, not *compound* it!

Not a happy situation!

Since the dawn of retainer recruiting, presenting the same candidates to two retainer-paying clients simultaneously has been unthinkable. Indeed, *not* doing so has been one of the main points of difference and superiority in contrast to the employment agencies (contingency recruiters), who—being paid nothing for their efforts until a transaction occurs—present all the candidates they have to every employer willing to meet them.

Up until now, it's always been assumed that a consultant fully paid on retainer for his work in finding candidates will deliver that work only to the client who has paid for doing it. Only after *that* client has chosen one of the candidates to fill the position, is the consultant free to offer his remaining "finds" to another retainer-paying client.

But here again, when the economy is booming and excellent candidates are scarce and hard to move, we have an inconvenient limitation on the giant publicly owned search firm's ability to be the growth stock Wall Street wants it to be.

So what to do?

The solution is obvious. Dump the rule when it's inconvenient. All that was needed to facilitate that radical change was a euphemistically bland and benign term for doing so. And in the surprisingly vibrant economy of 1999 the necessary term was invented:

"Parallel Processing"

That's now what the recruiter—paid on retainer by client X—is said to be doing in simultaneously presenting the same candidates to clients Y and Z, who simultaneously are paying the same full fee for the identical work.

In *The Wall Street Journal*, the CEO of one of the two largest publicly owned retainer search firms is quoted as saying that in September '99 his firm:

> "began to permit 'parallel processing' of candidates for as many as four e-commerce assignments as long as clients and search consultants agree. 'We tell client companies that we are going to parallel-process and even triple-process,'" said the CEO. The article continued, "The approach makes sense, 'given the time

limits involved and the fact that there are a lot more openings than there are good candidates,' he adds."

The article continues, "Rival executive recruiters oppose the shift because client companies could end up vying for the same executive. 'Clients would be very distressed that they would be competing with their own search firm for a candidate,'" a spokesman for a competitor was quoted as saying. Then the WSJ went on to state that the remaining two of the three largest retainer firms— both publicly traded—"also prohibit the practice." But the article wound up saying, "Despite such public pronouncements, search-industry watchers say, parallel processing is widespread."

Amen!

Again, what does all this mean to you?

Merely that you—as a presumably hard-to-find "good candidate"—may have more bargaining power than you would imagine...especially if you're a proven hot shot plying the "new economy."

Above all you now know the buzz words—"parallel processing"— to use when you want to be presented on a second job you find out is being filled by the same search firm that already has you as a candidate on another position.

However, unless the same recruiter you're already working with is also filling the second position, I think you'd be better off pursuing the second job directly with the hiring company which, of course, may gracefully return you for "processing" by *their* recruiter at the same search firm. Recruiters tend to support most warmly the candidates they feel sure will actually accept their job if offered. Telling recruiter #1 that you're more interested in another job being filled by recruiter #2 in the same firm may diminish the first recruiter's enthusiasm for you as his preferred candidate, while not necessarily getting you very far with recruiter #2. On the other hand, if the first recruiter also is handling the second job, he'll close one or the other of his two searches with you, no matter which job you take. That, he'll figure, is a "win-win" deal.

There's another new wrinkle in Off-Limits policy. However, its impact is more important when you're hiring than when you're hoping to be hired.

Many of the largest retainer search firms are accepting stock warrants or options in return for filling positions with "new economy" startups and promising young companies.

According to *The Wall Street Journal*, in March 2000, America's largest retainer-compensated search firm had warrants or outright stock at "more than 360 companies"...all of it acquired in full or partial payments for searches.

Which brings up an interesting question: If a firm owns a substantial equity stake in a company for which it has previously done search work, when is that company *not* off limits?

A young company can ill afford to lose a key manager. Will a search firm that has a major financial interest in their success penetrate them in behalf of its other clients? Will it *tell* its other clients if it will not?

These are interesting questions currently being discussed by industry insiders. But are there any practical implications that you can take advantage of?

Probably not. Except that, when engaging a recruiter to help you find a subordinate, don't just listen to a search firm extolling its experience in finding a key manager for a hot young company and assume it can do similar work for you. It will not recruit out anyone it has put in. But can it take out any of the firm's *other* employees?

Now more than ever before, it pays to submit to any recruiter you are considering hiring a written list of the companies you want searched. And of course, to get in return a written list of any and all companies on your "hit list" that the search firm cannot enter in your behalf.

Observers who don't understand the business sometimes report that the leading retainer firms are doing contingency recruiting.

It's not true.

And what they *do* occasionally do has no effect on your self-interest at all.

The recession of the early '90s hit the retainer search industry fully as hard as any other part of the economy. Even some of the largest and most prestigious firms took steps to cut overhead and to compete far more aggressively than they would even have considered doing during the booming, '80s. The result is a quirky development that has survived unabated into the 21st century. It began as survivalist price-cutting. Today it's an effective competitive weapon.

"Preferred Supplier" Deals

The survivalist strategy during the early-'90s recession was to negotiate "preferred supplier" deals with the large corporations that were still doing quite a few searches per year (down from *lots* of searches in the boom years). If a company would guarantee X number of searches or Y dollars of fees during the year, the search firm would reduce its fee from the traditional 33% to a lesser percentage. This "cheaper-by-the-dozen" approach (1) undercut competitive firms on price and (2) put all or most of the client's search budget beyond the reach of competitive firms.

A True Retainer...With
Some Contingency Added

At the same time, some companies with multiple searches to give out, even during those lean times, used their "clout" to drive a very hard bargain with the retainer firms. After squeezing the fee percentage as much as possible, they applied this coup de grace: "We'll pay the first 2/3 or 3/4 of your fee as a retainer regardless of whether we hire any of your candidates, *but we won't pay the last third or quarter unless we hire.*"

In the sunshine of the '80s, the giant retainer firms would have said "get lost" to any prospective client making such a demand. And that's what they say today. Indeed, it's what they *always* say when there's a thriving market for search work. But when approached by a mega-client with a fist full of searches during the devastating early-'90s recession they said, "What an interesting and creative idea; let's try it."

Born of necessity, "preferred supplier" lives on. The huge search firms realized that their price-cutting deals negotiated corporation-wide at the parent company/headquarters level were tying up much of the mega-client's total search budget and cutting it off from the smaller, hungrier, or more specialized firms that had been nibbling up lots of that money by forging tight relationships with the corporation's various subsidiaries and business units.

Watch the economic barometer. The cheaper-by-the-dozen idea now survives in good times and bad. But in good times the hold-something-back-'til-we-hire feature is disdainfully shunned. Whenever less prosperous times come along, however, expect even the most prestigious firms to become surprisingly innovative.

Whether those slightly-contingent retainer deals are "in" or "out" at the moment makes no difference to you as a candidate.

So what, if all 100%...or merely 75% or 66%...of the traditional fee is paid regardless of whether anyone is hired? Still the employer is paying the retainer recruiter as a consultant, not merely a broker. Any client powerful enough to impose super-onerous terms on a retainer recruiter will certainly continue to enforce the "don't-take-my-people-for-at-least-two-years" and the "don't-present-my-candidates-to-anyone-else" rules. So as far as you as a potential candidate are concerned, the contingency vs. retainer distinction is unaffected by making the last third or quarter of the fee contingent.

Do you want a price-tag on your head? When and why should you go straight to the employer and steer clear of the recruiter? How do you play the recruiter game to win? These are the questions you care about. And they depend on the 2/3 or 3/4 of the fee that's nailed down...not the third or quarter that may be flapping in the breeze.

Chapter 10

Doing Business with the Recruiter...
on the Phone, and in His or Her Office

Okay. When a recruiter calls, your first reaction is to find out exactly who that recruiter is and...even if you know the person well...the exact nature of his or her mandate, if any. How appropriately the recruiter is tied to the employer and the job may be far more important than how attractive the job is.

From here on, we'll assume that you've examined the recruiter and his or her client relationship, both of which are fine indeed.

You've accepted the recruiter. Now let's do business.

Interestingly, whereas your first few minutes of the recruiter's call were somewhat adversarial...you brought up something *not* on the recruiter's agenda...now that you're getting down to business, your interests and the recruiter's are almost identical.

Of course, the recruiter is still trying to sell you something which you may be wise not to buy. That will be true up to the moment you accept the employer's job and resign your present one. But during this initial phone call, you and the recruiter both want to know the same things... although in opposite order of priority:

Recruiter's Priorities	Your Priorities
1. Are you qualified?	*1. Are you interested?*
2. Are you interested?	*2. Are you qualified?*

You want to find out whether the *job* is right for you...and whether the recruiter knows enough about it to actually have a proper assignment to fill it. The recruiter, on the other hand, wants to know whether *you're* right for the job. And if not, he or she doesn't care how interested you are.

| | | ## Let's do it *your* way. | | |

Let's indulge your priorities. First, are you "interested"? And only secondly, are you "qualified"?

If you've got a job and the recruiter's trying to get you to consider a different one, then *you're the buyer* and *he's the seller*. He'll have to follow your agenda, if you just assert it:

> YOUR CALLER: "I'm in the process of filling an exceptionally attractive position for a management information executive in your industry, and I've heard some very good things about you. But I'm not entirely sure that your background is a 'fit.' Tell me, first of all, are you in charge of systems-development throughout the entire corporation, including those business-to business e-commerce initiatives?"

> YOU: "Yes, I am. But I'm in very good shape here at Outstanding Corporation. Before we go into my background, why don't we just see if the situation you have is something that I ought to think

about. And if it's not for me, I'll try to suggest some other people who'd be more appropriate."

Right at the outset you've got things rolling in the direction that's best for you. You've conveyed a pleasant, receptive, helpful attitude. But you haven't given up your superior bargaining position. You've politely asserted your obvious advantage.

Already the recruiter is sizing you up. On a subliminal level...and probably on a conscious level, too...he's now alert to the fact that, on this call, he's dealing with a highly aware and competent person. Maybe you're the one he's looking for.

Of course, if you were out of work and the recruiter were calling in response to your letter and resume, your buyer/seller roles would be reversed. You'd be willing to answer all his questions about your background and track record prior to hearing the specifics of the job he's filling. He'd be the buyer.

Ask probing questions about the opportunity.

They will:
1. further qualify the recruiter;
2. rule out a no-benefit opportunity;
3. at the same time, demonstrate you're the calibre of person the recruiter wants.

If there's some reason for you not to deal with the recruiter, or not to be interested in the job, you want to find out right away. Then you don't waste your time or hers.

Ask probing questions. Simultaneously you'll find out whether the position is worth considering, and whether the recruiter is well-informed enough to really be on retainer to fill it. Sometimes, *although far less often than most people think*, even a retainer recruiter may not be at liberty to identify the employer. But if she's tied in, she can describe the *job* in detail.

So ask everything that will help you see whether you should spend any time beyond the initial phone call to explore the opportunity:

What are the specific responsibilities?

What's the title?

What position would you report to?

How many subordinates? With what functions?

Is it chief executive, reporting to an outside board? If it's president or general manager of a subsidiary, does it report to the CEO, or to the COO, of the parent? Or is there a group officer in between?

If it's a top marketing job, does the sales force report to it? How large is the sales force? How many product managers? Are manufacturers' reps and distributors used? Which ad agencies? Budget? Media mix?

If it's chief financial officer, does the position have responsibility for administration, management information services, internal auditing, subsidiary controllerships (straight or dotted line), etc.?

If it's a top manufacturing job, does manufacturing engineering report to it? Quality control? Purchasing? Physical distribution? How about off-shore operations and plants? Plants within the subsidiaries?

If it's a top engineering job, does it just include work on new products? What about quality control and manufacturing engineering?

Don't trust the title to describe the job. Whatever your specialty, ask, ask, ask! And then go further:

What's the boss like? What characteristics does he value most in his employees? What's his preferred working style...lots of documentation or very little paperwork...lots of autonomy or close supervision?

What's the location? Would you have to move?

What about compensation? Will it include an incentive program? Stock options?

What's the structure, momentum, and atmosphere of the company or division? Highly centralized, or decentralized? Growing.... plateaued...in trouble? What are the short-term, intermediate, and long-range goals of the business? What's its share-of-market and its reputation for quality and customer satisfaction?

Why is the job open? What specific business problem is supposed to be solved...or opportunity exploited...by going outside to fill this position? What happened to the person who's had it up to now? And the person before?

I could go on and on. And you have every right to do so too. Find out whether it's worthwhile for you and the recruiter to go to the trouble of a face-to-face interview.

Fortunately, the same questions that will convince you to proceed will simultaneously show the recruiter that you're the right calibre of person...an alert, analytical executive, who can quickly ferret out key issues and come to an informed decision.

Indeed, the more your questions show an awareness of the problems and opportunities facing your industry and specific companies in it, the more he'll be sure that you're someone his client wants to meet.

If the opportunity is wrong for you, it will probably be for one of three reasons:
1. wrong responsibility,
2. wrong location,
3. wrong money.

Save your time...and the recruiter's.
Dispose of all three in the initial phone call.

Chances are you can't be certain, just from the recruiter's call, that the job definitely is for you. That will take in-person, in-depth meetings with the client, not just the recruiter. But you can quickly find out why the situation is *not* for you.

All of the top-three turnoffs can be smoked out in the initial phone call. And they'll eliminate 90% of the "wild goose chases" you might otherwise be subjected to:

1.   Wrong Responsibility. Question the recruiter. The job had better be considerably more attractive than the one you have now. A same-echelon job in a much larger and finer company can be an excellent reason to move. So can a higher job in a same-level company. But money alone usually isn't enough. And if you're on the brink of a breakthrough where you are, say so. There's no reason to withhold information at the outset which, in the end, will cause you to say "no thanks."

2.   *Wrong Location*. If the job isn't commutable from your home, you can certainly decide

    a.   whether you're willing to relocate at all, and
    b.   if so, whether the proposed location is acceptable.

If either answer is no, or if you have to poll and persuade your family, say so. If your husband's or wife's career isn't portable, or if your children are in special schools, or if you want your daughter to keep that swim coach who has her almost ready for Olympic tryouts, or if you can't desert an ailing parent, then you can immediately...or after an evening or a weekend to think it over...rule out a job that requires relocation.

Don't waste your time, the recruiter's, and possibly even the employer's, on an interview, when your personal life prevents your taking the job. If you do, you'll prove you're a lousy decision-maker. And then the recruiter won't call when he gets another fine opportunity that *doesn't* require relocation.

3.   *Wrong Money*. The recruiter almost certainly will not tell you upfront exactly how much the client prefers to pay. And of course, until the job is filled, nobody knows what will be negotiated.

However, the recruiter has a very good idea what the *upper limits* are. He's undoubtedly found out what peer-level jobs in the client company pay. And a smart recruiter always asks the compensation of the position directly above the one being filled. So even if he doesn't want to "go public" by telling you, the recruiter does know "how much is too much."

So how do you uncover too-low money?

Simple. Just give the recruiter a clear idea of what you're making now, and what improvement you expect within the next year. If the recruiter is someone you already know and trust, or appears to be a first-class professional from a respected firm, you may decide to be forthright:

> "The responsibility is very attractive. I'd certainly like to be running my own show. But I'm not sure this situation would make sense for me *financially*. My base is going up to $250,000 on August 1, and I'll earn about a 40% bonus on top of that. So we've got to be talking close to $450,000 for me to come out with any real improvement in money."

If you're less confident about the recruiter's integrity and confidentiality, just give the bottom line without saying anything specific he can repeat to others about your compensation:

> "I like it here and I'm very well compensated. However, I *would*
> be willing to listen if you're talking upwards of $450,000.
> Otherwise, I'm really not interested in changing."

Knowing where you stand on money, and knowing there's a ceiling at $290,000 in base-plus-bonus, the recruiter will immediately pull back and ask you for suggestions of other able people in your field. Best of all, he'll regard you as smart and decisive. You haven't wasted his time. Expect to hear from him again, when there's a higher-paying job.

"Sounds like a lateral move."

Quite a few executives...almost routinely...react to every new situation they're phoned about with an irritatingly common cliché:

> "Sounds to me like a *lateral move.*"

Using these precise words is a bad idea, because they're a formula response. Hardly ever will any new situation be exactly on a par with what you have.

So skip the cliché. But use the same approach. Latch on to the specifics the recruiter mentions, and point out all the ways the proposed job doesn't appear to be an advancement:

> "Of course I already have my own profit center, and we've been
> doing well since I took over three years ago. We're already larger
> in sales...and I'll bet a lot stronger in profits...than the company
> you're proposing, even though they've been around longer and lots
> of people probably still think they're bigger than we are."

OR

> "Of course I'd love to have a 150-person sales force, because so far
> we've had to use manufacturers' representatives, and I'm only just
> now getting a few of our own people into the field. But here I have
> total responsibility for all Marketing, reporting to the President.
> And if I understand you right, in the situation you're describing I'd
> be reporting to a Vice President of Marketing, who also has a
> Product Management group that I wouldn't be involved with. I
> think I'm better off to stay here and keep building this

business...and wait for you to call me again in a couple years when we've made even more progress. Then you may have a job like his for me to consider."

OR

"They're a big outfit, and I believe you when you say that I can probably make a nice improvement in salary by going with them. But money isn't everything, by any means. Increased responsibility and long-term career progress are what really interest me. Tell me what this opportunity might do for me in those terms."

See what you've done? You've virtually forced the recruiter to give you more information right there on the telephone.

If you're going to say "No," do so as soon as possible.

Move the conversation quickly to your key decision points. These are issues that only you know about, since they have to do with your current situation and your career objectives.

And as soon as you know you'll ultimately say "no," by all means do so. Then offer to suggest more appropriate candidates. You'll not only save time; you'll enhance your image in the eyes of the recruiter. Seeing how efficiently you handle her inquiry, she'll figure you're equally adept at your job. Expect to be called again!

If you don't find any disqualifying negatives, let the recruiter "sell" you by phone ...and then ask for more information by mail.

If your caller does have an attractive opportunity, hear her out. Let her sell you.

Then ask for a little homework. Have the recruiter send you an annual report, a 10K, a proxy statement, a product catalog and price list, a description of the position...whatever will supplement your telephone impressions. If the recruiter doesn't have such materials, chances are she's not on retainer.

Suggest a time when you'll call the recruiter...or she'll call you...to continue the discussion, after you've studied those items. A retainer recruiter...highly paid to serve her clients' interests...will gladly call you in the evening or on the weekend, if that's what you prefer.

Never pretend to be interested if you're really not.

Some executives, unaware of the behind-the-scenes workings of a recruiting firm, will pretend to be interested in a job, just to get to know the recruiter... in the hope of discovering more-appropriate openings than the one being described.

As you can see, this strategy is way off base. If you express interest in the search you're called about, the recruiter's firm *won't show you any other job* until that project is finished and all the prospective candidates on it are returned to the central talent pool...which may take several months. It's a guaranteed method for staying *out* of the action at that firm for a substantial time.

If you say "No," try to offer helpful suggestions ...even hook the recruiter into your network.

If you're not interested, always try to suggest people who'd be more appropriate. Also suggest people the recruiter should talk to as "sources." They wouldn't want the job, but probably can suggest potential candidates.

Indeed, if you're highly impressed with the recruiter, offer to *let him use your name*. Help him get through to the people who know you, but don't know him. He'll be grateful...and will chalk up another reason why you should be one of the first people called when he or someone else in his firm undertakes a search that could interest you.

In closing the phone conversation, also be sure to let the recruiter know what sort of an opportunity *would* excite your interest. Might as well plant a seed for the future. If you've been competent, warm, and helpful, the climate is right.

Beware of the recruiter who wants to meet you after you've said "No."

If you've clearly pointed out mismatches between the recruiter's proposal and your situation, and he still urges you to come in for an interview, you should suspect him of wanting...above all...to apply his tag to your head and see that your resume is widely circulated. Chances are he won't merely be wanting, as he'll say, "to know you better for the future when the right thing *does* come across my desk."

Generally speaking, true retainer recruiters are extremely busy finding the people clients are paying them to look for today, this week, this month. The successful ones have very little time or inclination to interrupt their ongoing searches to meet anyone...no matter how able and attractive...who doesn't fit a current search.

The odds are overwhelmingly against any retainer recruiter...no matter how large the firm he or she works for...ever personally getting the exact project that's right for you at the exact time when it's appropriate for you to move. Expect the recruiter to behave accordingly. *And be wary of one who doesn't.*

How much manipulation are you willing to put up with?

Lots of recruiters...sometimes encouraged by employers who'd like them to operate that way...will try to get you to come in for an interview without telling you the identity of the employer you're being considered to work for.

After you've expressed potential interest in their proposition, they go on to say something like this:

> YOUR CALLER: "Naturally, of course, I can't give you the identity of the employer *on the telephone.* We can talk much more frankly in my office, if you'd like to come in and explore this situation further. And do bring your resume. We can look it over as we talk, and we'll have it in case we decide to go ahead."

What baloney!

Is the recruiter's phone bugged...or yours? Conceivably, a switchboard operator might overhear *yours* if you're at work. But *his* shouldn't be a problem. And he raised the point...you didn't. Any legitimate concern—and only you will have it—can be eliminated by continuing this call via your home phone tonight, or on the weekend. And all first-class recruiters—retainer and contingency—will gladly do so.

Re-read what the recruiter said. Did he promise to identify the employer, even if you *do* go to all the trouble of visiting his office, and you hand him your resume, *and* you submit to an interview? No, he didn't! And don't expect him to, if you meekly go ahead as he suggests.

Obviously the recruiter wants the option of knowing everything about you and conveying nothing specific to you about the identity of the employer...if indeed he's actually been engaged by one.

Plenty of recruiters would like to proceed that way. But no employed executive has to accept such ground rules. Indeed, the unemployed executive who objects to them will be considered a lot more formidable than the one who doesn't. Let's hear how you pick up the conversation:

> YOU: "Oh, I have no problem with the phone; we're perfectly free to go ahead.
>
> "Also, I can't tell you whether I'm interested in interviewing for a job unless I know what the job is, and of course that includes knowing what company I'd be working for. I'm doing very well here, and haven't been thinking at all about making a change. On the other hand, what you're suggesting does sound interesting...at least on the surface. Is there something more you'd like to know about me, in order to see whether you think we should go any further?"

The ball's back in his court. If he wants you for a candidate, he'll just have to be more forthcoming now, while he has you on the phone. You're warmly open and cooperative...offering to address any potential shortcomings.

If the recruiter doesn't come forward now and ask his key questions which might disqualify *you*...and let you ask your key questions that might disqualify the *job*...he knows he'll lose you. Then he'll have to go to the trouble of finding someone else with your qualifications...and with your interest in the opportunity. Someone who, unlike you, is willing to submit to a highly one-sided procedure. That means someone more insecure in his or her job...or as a person...than you are. And unfortunately, the employer probably won't be as interested in that person as he would be in you.

So even if you're sitting at the other end of the wire absolutely quivering with delight at the prospect of having a shot at the position the recruiter has described, *you have clout.* Use it.

What will the recruiter do now? One thing's absolutely certain. He won't think less of you just because you're not a pushover. His next move will depend on the actual motives behind this call to you:

> 1. If he's trying to tag your head prior to nailing down a proper client assignment, he'll forget that idea...meanwhile telling you, "Too bad; you're missing out on a great opportunity!"
>
> 2. If he was going to befriend you, and later pitch for your executive recruiting business, after this nonexistent "search" is... alas... "cancelled," he'll forget that idea.
>
> 3. If he has a retainer search, and is merely proceeding with approach #1 of his standard "M.O.," he'll shift very smoothly into

approach #2. In return for your telling him what he needs to know, he'll tell you what you need to know...including employer identity, which he'll request you to "keep confidential." *Expect this result 80% of the time.*

4.   If he has a retainer search and also a legitimate mandate for secrecy *from the employer*, he'll come out with a specific and plausible reason for not being able to name the employer:

> YOUR CALLER: "I'm sorry, but I really can't identify the company. The person in the job is going to be fired, and we're lining up a slate of candidates who'll be all set to go when that happens."

> YOU: "Well, I guess I won't be standing there all interviewed and waiting, when the other person gets the axe. But do call me when you're in a position to be more specific. I definitely might be interested, depending on who the company is. Meanwhile, I appreciate your thinking of me. Thanks for the call."

Only in possibility #4 was there any legitimate employer-dictated need for confidentiality. And I'm being very generous in estimating that such a need may actually exist in as many as 10% to 20% of the instances when a recruiter calls you. Then, of course, he can't back down.

But what will he do? By holding out, have you lost your shot at the job he called you about?

Probably not. Chances are, you've made yourself more desirable.

In all likelihood, when the recruiter briefs the employer on the executives who were willing to be interviewed without knowing whom they'd be presented to, he'll also describe the two or three *even more impressive ones*...like you... who wouldn't go along with that procedure. He'll explain that he can re-contact these, as soon as the employer lifts the secrecy. Chances are ten-to-one that the employer will immediately say:

> "Don't wait. Open up to them right away, so that we can meet any of those who are willing to talk to us, right along with the candidates you've already interviewed."

So, even in this rare instance where there was an employer-imposed mandate to interview without disclosing company identity, you came out just as well by standing firm as you would have by caving in. In fact, you probably look stronger and will be more sought after than the people who jumped at the chance for a "blind" interview.

Of course, if you'd been out of work when the recruiter called, your reaction might have been different.

If your caller had been from a *retainer* firm where you'd been trying for weeks to get a courtesy interview, you'd instantly have accepted the invitation. However, you'd have known that interviewing on this job would have assigned you to this search, even if you weren't told the employer's identity. Therefore, you probably wouldn't have been returned to the firm's talent pool for consideration on anything else, until after the "mystery" search was completed.

Of course, you'd *never* have submitted to interviewing by a contingency recruiter without being told to whom you were being offered, unless you were sure that the firm is totally ethical. Otherwise, they might have taken your willingness to be offered to one undisclosed employer as permission to covertly submit you to any company that might hire you.

The furthest I'd be willing to compromise, if I were you...

If I were happily employed, I'd never agree to be interviewed for any "opportunity," no matter how attractively described, unless I knew in advance the employer's identity. However, if I were eager to move, I might propose the following:

> YOU: "I'd be pleased to meet you and discuss my background, which seems to be exactly what you're looking for. The only thing I ask is that you not submit me to any employer without telling me whom I'm being offered to.
>
> "You can tell me who it is after the interview, if you decide to present me. Or tell me that you have other candidates that you prefer, and therefore you *won't* submit me. Or tell me you *don't know yet* whether I'll be submitted, and you'll get back to me later if I *am* to be submitted.
>
> "I just don't want my name and information submitted to anyone without knowing who it is. Is that OK with you?"

Even employment agencies for clericals accept the proposition that "applicants" have the right to say in advance what companies they are and are not willing to be presented to. When you state your position in this way, *no legitimate executive recruiter can refuse.* But do so on the phone prior to your interview...when you'll have more clout, and you'll get a clearer answer.

You can push the recruiter toward frankness
by being frank yourself.

To encourage a "let's get down to it" telephone discussion, volunteer a thumbnail review of the points...pro and con...that should spell "go" or "no go" to the recruiter:

> YOU: "Look, I'm in charge of all marketing and sales over here, reporting to the President. I moved up to this job three years ago from head of product management. Since then we've been making very strong gains in market share, volume, and profitability. Here are a few things you should also know, however: I'm 54 years old and I don't have an MBA. In fact, I don't quite have my BS. My only college has been at night at NYU, and I've let that program slide since my promotion to this job. I'm about 15 credits shy of a BS in Marketing. Also, you've got to be talking *over $300,000* or you can't reach me on money."

It's all there!

That took you less than a minute to say. Yet it summarizes the key points the recruiter would have tried to draw out in a face-to-face meeting.

If the recruiter knows his client will never accept a non-college graduate (and in my opinion, that's very shortsighted), or won't want somebody in his 50s when the search has already turned up several outstanding candidates in their late 30s, then both you and the recruiter will be spared a useless interview.

On the other hand, if the prejudicial factors you raise are not disabling, then you've undoubtedly "sold" yourself to the recruiter with your 60-second summary...a virtuoso display of cutting through to the heart of a matter. The employer will be identified, and you'll be invited to meet the recruiter.

If the recruiter is uncertain about the employer's attitude toward the factors you've laid on the table, he'll:

> 1. say that his client is a wonderfully broad-minded person who'd never break the "equal-opportunity" laws, and

> 2. promise to get back to you with "further information," once he's "ready to go ahead."

Meanwhile he'll find out what his client really does feel about the points you've raised. If and when the recruiter calls back, you'll know you're not wasting your time by exploring a job you'll never, in the end, be hired for.

Special Note for Employers Using Executive Recruiters:

Your first impulse...particularly if you haven't been served and coached by top professionals in the recruiting field...will be to request your recruiter to keep your project "highly confidential," and perhaps not to reveal your identity until after he's interviewed the executive and "confirmed that the person is really a strong candidate."

The less competent your recruiter is...and the less honest, as he competes for your business by telling you what you want to hear...the more likely he'll imply that he can provide such "confidentiality" and still get you the strongest possible candidates. Don't imagine for one minute that this is true.

The executives most willing to go along with such treatment are out of work (which these days doesn't mean they're not good)...or in difficulty...or so marginally qualified for your job that they're thrilled to pursue it, regardless of the overbearing procedure.

Executives who are already at the right level for your job, and are currently employed by companies that think they're excellent and reward them accordingly, will not be clogging their calendars with interviews by recruiters who won't tell them who they're being solicited to work for.

Face-to-Face with a Recruiter: Your Interview for the Job She Called About

You and a recruiter have accomplished about as much as possible over the telephone. You tried to disqualify the opportunity, and you couldn't. You're not "sold." But you *are* interested. So you're going to go see the recruiter...or possibly she's coming to see you. Now what?

Now you prepare for the meeting!

That's right. Even though the recruiter called you; you didn't call her. Even though you agreed to the meeting only after she drowned you in charming persuasion. Still you *prepare*. This meeting is far more important to you than to her. It's just part of one day's work to the recruiter. But it could change...for better or worse...your entire career.

So take some time to figure out what you want to accomplish. What questions do you want answered? And what do you want to communicate, so that the recruiter will rank you among her finalists and will accurately convey your best features to her client?

Your Two-Fold Agenda: Selling and Inquiring
...with Emphasis on Selling

One objective must be virtually in-the-bag by the end of the meeting. The other can be pursued later by phone, if necessary.

If time runs out on your interview and you haven't asked quite all of your questions...or if new ones occur to you afterward...you can always phone for answers. Is there anything wrong with this?

> YOU: "A few important questions occur to me that we didn't get a chance to cover when we were together..."

No, nothing at all out of line. But imagine this call:

> NOT YOU: "Unfortunately, Paula, I was so busy asking questions during my interview, that I got home and realized I hadn't told you some additional...and very impressive...things you should know about me. Make yourself comfortable, and I'll begin reciting my further virtues to you now..."

You get the point. You had plenty of chance to challenge the job during one or more phone calls before your interview. And you can phone with more questions later. The interview is your chance to let the recruiter find out how ideal you'd be for the position. Don't wind up with you convinced that the job's right for you, and the recruiter not convinced that you're right for the job.

Of course you can try to fill in omitted selling points with a follow-up letter. Indeed, that's your only shot. But the recruiter's impression will overwhelmingly be based on your face-to-face interview. It's almost impossible to raise your ranking by anything you mail in afterward.

So ask and sell. But don't fail to sell.

At the outset:
1.   determine how much time you have, and
2.   reconfirm the ground rules, if necessary.

As in the courtesy interview, you'll be wise to ask:

> "How much time do we have?"

And if you've got to leave within a limited time, let the recruiter know right away:

> "I hope I've scheduled enough time for this, and I'll be glad to come back if you want me to. But I couldn't avoid setting up another meeting at four o'clock. So I'll have to leave here by three-thirty."

Forewarned, both you and the recruiter can modify your agendas to fit the pre-acknowledged time slot. Such a statement isn't discourteous; it's the mark of a thoughtful and efficient executive.

Candidate interviews by recruiters usually range from an hour to an hour and a half. I personally devote far more time to them, but I also pre-screen more restrictively and invite only a few exceptional people to interview. Each recruiter has his or her own personal style. Achieve your objectives by adapting to the recruiter's game plan.

Another point. If you agreed to this meeting without knowing in advance the identity of the employer, you should also reconfirm, right upfront, the ground rules that were negotiated earlier:

> "You know, Paula, you still haven't told me who the employer is. Your feeling was that at the end of this meeting, you'd know whether or not you'll be presenting me. Then you can tell me *who it is*...if we're going ahead...or that I'm *not a finalist* if we won't be going further. That's just fine with me. What I really want to be sure of is that we're agreed that I won't be presented anywhere, unless I know in advance where that will be."

Beginning with a recapitulation of points agreed on earlier over the phone is merely appropriate businesslike procedure. But if you delay them to the end of the interview, the same points will seem nagging and distrustful.

Set up an informal agenda.

Once timing is established, it's not offensive...and can be helpful...to send up another trial balloon:

> YOU: "I don't know where you want to start. I do have some potential reservations about the job...especially since reading the 10K and proxy statement you sent me. Or do you want to start by talking about me? I just know that before I can agree to be a candidate, I'll have to have answers to a few key questions."

Your concerns aren't such "show-stoppers" that you should have phoned and possibly cancelled your interview. But they do have to be addressed. The recruiter can now decide whether to tackle them right away, or to go ahead and talk about your qualifications, with the understanding that she can't sign off until your questions are answered. Indeed, your down-to-business approach may encourage her to proceed just as frankly:

> "Let's take a look at *our main questions* first, and cover whatever else we have time for at the end. My two basic questions about you are: How much experience have you had in acquisitions and divestitures? And what happened at Yesterday Corporation?"

Or the recruiter may even say:

> "Look, I'm already convinced that you're one of the best candidates in America for this position; let's get your questions out of the way first, and then let me tell you some further things I've learned about the job."

The better you and the recruiter know how much time you both have, and the issues of greatest interest to the opposite party, the more useful...and persuasive...the meeting will be.

Do you have a resume? And do you hand it over?

Yes! You never come to a recruiter interview without a resume. And once you're satisfied that you're dealing with a professional you respect, you don't hesitate to hand it to her.

As a successful executive at and far beyond $100,000+, you know about visual aids and leave-behinds. A resume is both. Even if you're more concerned about getting information than communicating it, the resume will still be helpful. It will speed the recruiter's inquiry...and make more time available for *your* questions.

If you're being courted by the recruiter, and the job seems only marginally attractive, just bring in the last resume you made...even if it's ten years old. Update your home address and phone number. Also jot down on a sheet of yellow pad the dates and titles of your more recent jobs. Your early career will be thoroughly covered, and you can talk your way forward from there. First-class recruiters always type up their own version of candidate information. So informality won't count against you, even if you wind up meeting the employer.

On the other hand, if the position could be a major career breakthrough, it's certainly worth the time and effort to prepare a highly persuasive resume, stressing your most recent...and presumably your greatest...accomplishments. Not only will it help the recruiter understand and communicate what you've done, the very act of creating it will prepare you to meet the recruiter *and* the employer. You'll be in command of facts-and-figures...not only on what you're doing now, but on what you've done in the past.

If you just bring an old resume, be sure to *read it over*. I'm amazed how many people hand out papers they seem totally unfamiliar with. Time is wasted as the recruiter, who's freshly read your information, seems to know more about your early career than you do. You're a dud as a business communicator when that happens.

Also, be prepared to *talk* your way through your work history. Some recruiters will read your resume carefully, asking questions and making notes. Others will set it aside and ask you what happened. You won't score points with a "tell-me" recruiter if you clam up and say, "It's all there in the resume."

Bring along any supplementary information you may need.

If you don't have an encyclopedic memory, bring a few sheets of statistics, so that you can refer to them when a performance question arises.

A recruiter's interview has two purposes:

1. to obtain information, and

2. to see how well you handle yourself and how thoroughly you seem to understand what you're in charge of.

Short answers are better than long ones. And specifics are far better than vague generalizations. You may not want to hand over confidential charts. But have them handy, to remind you of the numbers you've achieved. Vague, nonspecific communication will count against you.

Be honest about negatives.

Be frank up front about major negatives that referencing will highlight. Expect the recruiter to check you out before he passes you along to his client. If you've been fired, or if profits have evaporated under your management, he's probably going to find out. And it will be a strike against you that you tried to conceal the information. No one has a record of perfect achievement. And many very able people have been fired. Offer a brief explanation that establishes your version of the matter, but don't highlight it, and don't be defensive.

Don't view the recruiter as your "advocate."

Bear in mind that the retainer recruiter is paid to represent the corporation's best interests, not yours. Don't expect him to conspire with you about the best way to present your qualifications. It would be a breach of professional ethics to try to convince the client that you're a strong candidate when you're really not.

Are there any special considerations associated with your candidacy?

If so, bring them up.

Anything that could make you more costly or inconvenient to hire than other candidates should be brought out during...or prior to...your interview. Then the recruiter can forewarn the employer, and you'll be considered from the beginning with your "disadvantages" in full view.

If you're the best person, then simultaneously with his growing interest in you, the employer can think of ways to deal with your special needs. Above all, there won't be "unpleasant surprises" later, to throw cold water on your candidacy and raise doubts about your candor.

For example:

> You have a low-interest mortgage, and without a "mortgage-differential" from your new employer, you'll lose $90,000 to $120,000 in after-tax out-of-pocket costs.

> You'll lose $125,000 in profits on stock options which won't vest for another ten months.

> You have a child with a costly medical problem, and you can't afford to move unless the illness won't be excluded as a "pre-existing condition" under the new company's insurance.

> You're in the midst of renovating your house, which could be tough to sell right now at its proper value. You'll have to stay where you are, unless you can have the services of a home relocation company that will price it fairly and take it off your hands.

> You have a pension that vests, all-or-nothing, in seven months, and you'll move prior to that only if you can negotiate a settlement with your present employer or receive special treatment from your new one.

Tell the recruiter about any problem that may require modification of the way her client normally handles a new hire.

Prepare yourself for a later client interview.

If it looks like the recruiter is "sold," and you're going to be a "finalist," ask questions that will get you ready to meet the employer. Take advantage of the recruiter's knowledge of his client's situation...either at the end of the interview if there's time left, or in a later phone call. Find out exactly what the employer is looking for, and get a sense of what to expect at the interview.

The Ideal Result: "To Be Continued"

Just as with the courtesy interview, a positive ending to this session is the sense that exploration of your candidacy is "to be continued." If and when it becomes clear that you're a "finalist," accept "yes" for an answer, and leave. And if there are questions in your mind about whether you should be a candidate, resolve them with the recruiter and either decide to go ahead or withdraw.

Executive recruiters can be frustrating.
Grin and bear it.

From the job-changing executive's point of view, retainer recruiting firms seem dismayingly inefficient. When you deal with a large and respected firm, you know that, at that very moment, they're handling hundreds or even thousands of searches...many of them almost certainly an ideal "next step" for your career. Yet you only hear about one at a time. And which one is largely accidental, depending on which recruiter in the firm happens to be in a position to deal with you, what jobs he's trying to fill, and what success he's had with each of them.

For example, he may show you something in Distant Falls, a place that doesn't particularly appeal to you, because that's his most urgent search at the moment. Meanwhile, he says nothing about the job that's even more attractive, and located only twenty minutes from your front door...simply because he already has more candidates than he needs on that one.

There's very little you can do about the haphazard way your involvement with a retainer search firm unfolds. It's simply the way those recruiters work...a method that's not designed to favor *your* interests as a job-changing executive.

Still, a good, ethical retainer recruiter does know of jobs that can advance your career. Under the right conditions, he or she and others in the firm may show you at least one opportunity...possibly even two or three...within the year or so that you may be seriously thinking about a move. And you can know more opportunities handled by retainer firms if more firms know you.

Consider the highly professional retainer recruiters as *one conduit* to career opportunity...and the highly ethical contingency firms as another.

But now that you know how executive recruiters really work, you can clearly see why they shouldn't be the only way you seek to advance your career. At least not when you want to move fairly quickly. And not when you want the widest possible knowledge of what's available in the marketplace.

Chapter 11

Being Where You Can't Be
...and Selling When You're Not There

Isn't it too bad that you can't be everywhere at once, and find out about every major career opportunity that might interest you?

Wouldn't it be great to have your own equivalent of a spy-in-the-sky satellite that could survey a forty-mile radius of your house...or the entire USA...or the world...to identify all the situations you'd like to know about, whether current openings, soon-to-be openings, or searches underway at recruiting firms?

Then you'd be sure not to miss any situation that could foster your career.

Of course there's always the likelihood that you'll learn of career-enhancing job possibilities through personal contacts and networking...talking to old business friends and associates, meeting lots of new people, and picking the brains of everyone you reach.

Unfortunately, although face-to-face communication is the most power-ful form of contact, your time is limited. No matter how diligent you are, you simply can't be everywhere at once. You'll make your networking contacts one at a time, maybe two or three a day, a dozen or so a week. That's not exactly a speed-of-light satellite reconnaissance. And it's likely to miss *most* of the jobs available "out there somewhere," which your contacts don't happen to know about.

You've also clearly seen that retainer executive recruiting firms aren't going to show you everything they know of. They'll reveal only one job at a time, and probably no more than two or three per year.

In fact, there are only *two ways* by which you can even attempt to find out about *all* the available or soon-to-be-available jobs that may be the right "next step" for you. Those ways were numbers 4 and 5 on our list of five main methods:

1.   Personal Contacts...getting in touch with people you
     already know.

2.   Networking...getting in touch with a series of people
     others refer you to.

3.   Executive Recruiters...dealing with the various species
     of "headhunters."

4.   Direct Mail...letting the Postal Service take your
     message more places than you can visit and phone.

5.   The Internet...taking advantage of modern technology in
     job-hunting and career management.

What do 4 and 5 have in common? They're ways to get yourself known to far more people than you'll ever be able to meet face to face.

||| One Message. Two Different Distribution Methods. |||

Your message, obviously, is:

"Here I am. And here's what I can do."

To find out about all the jobs that might interest you, you'd have to get that message to (1) every employer currently needing to hire someone exactly like you, and (2) every recruiter now being paid to search for such a person.

Up until several years ago there was only one way to simultaneously reach such a vast number of employers and search firms that statistical odds would guarantee you'd surely hit a few who were actually seeking you when your message arrived.

Direct Mail was the only way to dispatch your message to more people than you could meet face-to-face through networking. Indeed, it still is the only way to make a dignified and appropriate—rather than an obnoxious and self-defeating—overture to a CEO or to the head of a division or a department who might right now want to hire someone exactly like you as a subordinate.

The Internet, however, is now an alternative way to reach many other recipients. E-mail is lightning-fast It's also convenient and appropriate in many situations. It defeats "snail mail" in every speed contest, and it also has an appealing informality and even intimacy that can sometimes be very desirable. But it is absolutely *not* the way to send an unsolicited self-introduction and an accompanying resume to any never-heard-of-you senior executive you're hoping to impress favorably.

First of all, you probably can't get his or her personal e-mail address. But even if you had it, would you use it?

Ask yourself: Are you pleased when unexpected e-mails are spammed into your list of incoming messages? Do you read those e-mails? Are you grateful that someone has sent them your way? Does your assistant open them, glance at their content and appearance, and select a rare few that might actually be of interest to you?

You answers: No, No, No and No. Of course. So don't even dream that someone at the right level to hire you as a subordinate is going to react any more eagerly to your spammed e-mail than you would if you received something similar from someone else.

> **Forget the Internet—method #5—for what it *can't* do.**
> **It's quite wonderful in what it *can* do,**
> **and we'll explore all of its exciting possibilities.**
>
> **But first let's examine Direct Mail—method #4—which**
> **(1) succeeds where the Internet fails and**
> **(2) is the fine art of mass communication**
> **on which all *skillful* use of the Internet is based.**

Clearly, barging onto the incoming e-mail list of a person you might want to work for is far too pushy and obnoxious to do you any good at all. If someone *invites* you to send a resume by e-mail, that's a wonderfully fast and efficient way to do so. But when you merely invite yourself to do the same thing, it's about the dumbest move you could possibly make. Either you get deleted and not remembered at all...or you get noticed as impolite and obnoxious and you're shunned when you later arrive in a more polite and appropriate fashion. Heads...you lose. Tails...you lose.

However, there's nothing impolite or too pushy about sending an elegant and persuasive *letter* to someone you don't know and want to reach with a message that might be of interest. That's been a common and effective practice for at least two hundred years. Indeed one of the most prized possessions of a friend of mine is a letter handwritten by Abraham Lincoln, who is graciously responding—albeit in the negative—to a person he's obviously never heard of, who wrote to the President about wanting to become his personal assistant.

| | | **But isn't direct mail a weak method?** | | |

Many people think direct mail is a weak technique, particularly for a job search. I've had lots of senior executives...even top marketing executives (who should know better)...say to me:

> "John, I don't believe in direct mail. It's not effective. Nearly all the letters you send are either thrown away or relegated to the Personnel Department for a polite 'no-thank-you.' Therefore, you just don't get anywhere with a direct mail campaign. It doesn't have the punch that personal contact does."

Mostly true. But whenever I meet people who criticize direct mail as weak and ineffective, I remind them of their own reactions where they've needed to hire someone they were having a tough time finding:

> "When you had a really difficult hiring problem, and you urgently needed someone with a particular background to fill an important spot, didn't you *then* follow up by contacting *everyone* whose resume came to your attention and seemed to show exactly what you were looking for?"

Invariably they reply:

> "Well, of course *then* I did. *Anyone* would."

So I press the point:

> "What if, instead of the Postal Service bringing that resume, it just blew in through the window...all tattered and dirty, along with a bunch of autumn leaves? Wouldn't you still call up the person if he or she looked like the possible solution to your problem?"

You know their answer. It would be yours too.

My firsthand experience as a retainer executive recruiter doing searches at the $100,000+ level—and much higher—for the past 30 years has proven beyond doubt that mailed-in employment inquiries do get attention.

In about one out of every two searches I conduct, the ultimate decision-maker who hires me hands over at least one...and more often several...resumes he or she has collected before calling me in. Approximately a third of those have been forwarded by outside directors, employees, customers, suppliers, lawyers, accountants, etc. (the product of personal contact and networking). The majority, however, were merely delivered by mail. And of course I'm not called—and never see the resume—when anyone is so tempting that there's an interview, offer, and acceptance without any need for me.

It's all a matter of timing.

The key advantage of direct mail is not how strong a medium it is, but the fact that it's strong enough, if it reaches a decision-maker *at exactly his or her moment of need.*

Moreover, it doesn't matter what method you use, if you reach the decision-maker when he or she has *no* need. Even you-in-person...with all your persuasive logic, charm, wit, elegant grooming, and both your new shiny shoes... won't achieve a sale if your host isn't seeking what you're selling. That's always the problem...with most networking calls, and with most mailed-in resumes, too.

On the other hand, your resume, dog-eared and folded, that a CEO happens to find protruding from the pocket on the seat ahead of him when he flies the Concorde to Paris could net you an exciting phone call. The same lucky break might also occur if you happen to sit next to him on the flight...assuming of course that he talks to seat-mates.

The value of direct mail is not in how it's delivered, but rather in the great number of potential buyers it can reach simultaneously, in order to stimulate one or two of the rare few who happen to have the right need at the right moment.

Use direct mail to reach the whole universe of potential buyers.

That way, you should hit some of the very few who are actually ready to buy.

Consider what corporations do. The President and the Chief Marketing or Sales Officer may personally contact key accounts that provide enormous volumes of business. Customers who buy fairly often will be handled by the direct salespeople...perhaps 150 to 300 people spread across the country. And finally, to reach customers in out-of-the-way places or who order only once-in-a-while—customers it isn't feasible to serve with salespeople—companies rely on direct mail, or telephone marketing, or a combination of both.

But even telephone calls have serious limitations. You can only call so many people per day. Your listener will seldom stay on the wire long enough to hear a comprehensive sales pitch for a complex product. And afterward there's nothing left behind on paper to refresh his memory and encourage follow-up.

So the method companies turn to when they want to cover the whole market at once, to get where they can't send a salesperson, and yet deliver their entire selling message and have it remain afterward in writing...is a wide-ranging direct mail campaign.

Indeed, direct mail *is* effective, or it wouldn't be so widely used. The proof is in your mailbox every day. If direct mail weren't effective, the companies who send it would soon be out of business, having thrown their money away on something that doesn't work.

You're surprisingly similar to the other products direct mail sells very effectively.

What kinds of products are sold through direct mail? Not the inexpensive, uncomplicated things that everyone needs every day. Soap, corn flakes, diet cola, floor wax, and nationwide "fast food" chains are best advertised in TV commercials aimed at the entire population. Such products are easily understood. Just about everybody is a potential purchaser. And the whole story can be boiled down to 30 seconds or a minute. Forget the "cents-off" coupons. The long letters in your mailbox are not about cake mix and laundry detergent.

What *are* those long letters about? Seldom-purchased products and services that:

1. only a few people out of the vast population are likely to need and be able to afford at the moment they get the advertisement, and

2. require more explanation and persuasion than can be crammed into a 30-second or one-minute TV spot, or even into a one-page magazine ad.

Examples: professional-development seminars; building lots and time-share condominiums; insurance plans; expensive "limited-edition" books, porcelains, and store-of-value collectibles; tax planning and investment services; special-interest magazines; economic newsletters...those sorts of things.

You see the analogy. An executive is a seldom-acquired item...very costly, unique, and relatively complicated to understand and evaluate. One of the best ways that the marketing geniuses of the 20th century figured out to spread the news about such an item was by direct mail advertising. And the fact that—despite the advent of the Internet—you're still receiving plenty of direct mail in the 21st century, is dollars-and-cents proof that it's still highly effective.

The Networking vs. Direct Mail Trade-Off

If you reach someone when he or she has no need and knows of nobody else who has a need, there's no sale. And it doesn't matter whether you get there in person or in writing.

The advantage of a personal visit...networking...is its human interaction. Your host may not have or know of a job that could advance your career. But seeing and befriending you...and wanting to do a favor for the person who referred you...she can usually be persuaded to pass you along to several others. Your contacts will, indeed, *"increase geometrically."* But "geometrically" *only* until you have more people to see than you have hours to go see them. After that, you've got strictly a linear progression of appointments to make, two or three a day...probably ten to fifteen a week.

The advantage of direct mail, on the other hand, is that you can reach an unlimited number of people simultaneously. Therefore, *you can inflate that number to the point of very high probability* that you'll reach some of the rare few who actually do need what you're selling at the very moment you happen to make your contact. And when you finally do reach someone with an immediate need for what you're offering, that person is likely to be interested...even though no mutual acquaintance made the introduction.

Is there a downside to direct mail?
Will reaching the potential decision-makers in
lots of companies make you seem:

    a. too available?

    b. too eager?

    c. unwanted and unloved?

    d. desperate?

    e. none of the above?

The answer, of course is E, "none of the above." And the reasons why, when you think about them, are pretty obvious.

No chief executive nor anyone else in control of a job that might represent a valuable career advancement for you is sitting at his desk wishing a letter and resume from you would arrive...that is, unless he's one of the infinitesimally rare few who right then happens to have that job wide open, urgently needing someone like you to fill it.

The person who doesn't need what you're offering will merely throw away your mailing, or pass it along for filing and a courteous "no thank you." He's *not* going to pick up the phone and ask his peers in other companies and his contacts in the leading executive recruiting firms if they also got your mailing, and what did they think of it, and what are they going to do about it, and weren't you stupid not to have known in advance that he and they didn't need anyone like you right now.

The fact is, either he'll do you *some good*, or he'll do you *no harm*. And in the "some good" department, you may be pleasantly surprised. If a colleague in his own organization, or a friend, or an executive recruiter calling him for suggestions happens to mention a need for someone like you, the person who's just received your resume and doesn't need you himself will probably pass your resume along, just as one of your networking contacts would.

And if your mailing is so impressive that the recipient or his HR department saves a copy for a few weeks or months, he might wind up referring several inquirers to you. When extremely well done, direct mail can, with luck, take on a bit of the same "geometric" dimension networking has.

"But," you ask, "will I diminish my luster and usefulness to the prestigious retainer recruiting firms if I conduct a direct mail campaign?"

No. A lot of people worry needlessly about this possibility, so let's examine it.

Retainer recruiters actually *expect* you to send your mailing to the decision-makers in a wide range of companies, because it's in your best interest to do so. They realize too, that you'll contact other retainer search firms. Since no two retainer firms are ever working simultaneously on the same project, you simply *must* send to additional firms to reach additional projects.

Of course, it's unthinkable that you would simultaneously be presented...

"sold" at the rate of $8,000 to $30,000 and more per candidate...to more than one client of the *same* retainer recruiting firm for the reasons we looked at earlier. But there's no client PR damage to either firm when two different retainer firms present you to two different companies. If either or both of these companies should find out, they can't blame their own retainer firm for what a different one has done.

Moreover, the idea that you may have written to her client company won't scare away the one-and-only recruiter in a sizable retainer firm who, for the moment, has the right to deal with you. She always expects you to have taken that perfectly logical step. And she has no reason...or method...to reward you if you haven't. Indeed, going directly to companies is the only way you can possibly break through the barrier that confines you to this recruiter and her client company, while putting you "off-limits" to all the other recruiters in her firm and to all their client companies.

Believe it or not, if you're really a good candidate, a retainer recruiter is less worried that his client won't be amazed when he identifies you, than he is that the client will think he's a dope for not finding you when you've already made yourself obvious to the client company.

The bottom line on trying to be more attractive by being less known:

It doesn't work!

Known is like pregnant; you're known or you're not known...by each person individually. The way the relationships we're interested in work, each player in the game either knows of you or he doesn't; they're never going to gang up on you and take a poll to see *how many* know about you.

What will *make you less attractive is being unemployed a long time, and the fewer people who know about your fine background and your availability, the more likely that might happen.*

The only circumstance where being widely known is dangerous to your economic health is when a recruiter *operating on contingency* submits you... price-tag attached...to companies who never specifically engaged him to do so.

Getting around on your own is altogether different. It's great. Circulate!

Enough about the "why" of direct mail; let's take a look at the "how." And in the process, we'll add the persuasiveness of direct mail copywriting to your resume.

You may never need to conduct a direct mail campaign to advance your career, although it is one of the "Rites of Passage" you should be aware of.

But you and every other executive should always have a persuasive sales-representative-on-paper standing by, ready to go anywhere...by hand or by mail... to do the best possible job of communicating your abilities and achievements to people who haven't witnessed them firsthand. That's a resume. And its purpose is *to be where you can't be and sell when you're not there.* Direct mail marketing is the *science* of doing just that...the most thoroughly understood and quantifiably proven of all the marketing techniques.

In Chapter 13, I'll tell you how to conduct an effective direct mail campaign for purposes of your own career development.

First, however, I want to show you in Chapter 12 exactly how to use proven direct mail copywriting techniques to make your "sales representative"... your resume...as compelling as it can possibly be, regardless of how it's delivered.

Your Personal Sales Representative

As an upwardly-mobile executive, you need a really good personal sales representative...one that can be where you can't be, and sell when you're not there.

You need a resume.

And it should be as persuasive as you can possibly make it. Indeed, it should be compelling enough to take on the hardest selling challenge of all: to make "cold calls" on complete strangers...and get results.

That's what a resume has to do as the core of a direct mail campaign. It arrives uninvited and unexpected. And usually it's assisted by nothing more than a brief covering letter. If it can convince someone who's never before met or heard about you to call you up or to write you a letter, then surely it can do everything else you could ask a resume to do.

You can trust such a resume to be your spokesman whenever you can't be present. Whether you leave it behind after a successful interview, or send it ahead hoping to get an appointment, it will give every recipient the same persuasive, ungarbled message you'd convey in person. Effective all by itself, your resume will also be an indispensable aid to anybody who wants to "sell" you to someone else...from the recruiter telling his client about you, to your potential boss telling her boss, to the CEO telling his Board.

Before we start creating your optimum "Sales Representative" resume, let's discuss why it's worth the effort, and dispose of your excuses for not making it.

It'$ your most valuable credential.

How long did you spend in undergraduate college...four years? And maybe in grad school after that...two to five years? And besides the time...the money? And for what?

Alphabet soup. Credentials! Stuff on paper that you hoped—and to some extent you've found—could enhance your earning power and career achievement, in addition to culturally enriching your life.

Suppose it takes you a month, at the outside, working every spare moment nights and weekends, to compile a succinct but compellingly information-packed recounting of what you've learned and achieved since college...the only things a potential employer really cares about and pays you big money for. The resume you wind up with is the most valuable credential you can have today. Again it's symbols on paper, but this time far more negotiable at the bank.

"I don't need a resume right now, since I'm not considering a change."

Great! Now's the ideal time to examine your career and demonstrate its value. Now...when you have the leisure and the objectivity to do a really thoughtful, comprehensive job.

Tomorrow's paper may bring news of an unexpected opening at a leading company in your industry...one that's likely to be filled from outside, and one where you could easily reach the decision-maker through networking, or maybe just by picking up the phone. He'll probably ask for your resume. Is it ready?

And shouldn't you also have your most persuasive possible resume in the hands of your friends at the top retainer search firms? Even if you're permanently on file electronically, they'll be glad to have your "formal" resume handy whenever they actually present you as a candidate.

The "total immersion" study of your career and its accomplishments that's necessary to produce the ultimate "sales representative" resume will help—indeed force—you to size up (1) where you stand now relative to your long-range goals, and (2) how special you really are—or aren't—relative to your peers. Maybe you're already gaining momentum in the passing lane on the fast track. But maybe you're just cruising along an access road. There's no speed limit on your career, so why not step on the gas?

"I don't need a resume because it's classier not to have one."

Well, as least it's less work.

"I don't need a resume because I'm not looking. And when the prestigious retainer recruiter comes after me, he'll create my resume."

That's true; at least so it will seem to his client. Even if you hand him an excellent resume, his assistant will retype it so that it will appear consistent with the papers he presents on his other candidates.

But suppose he's got a really terrific opportunity for you...*and five other people*. Do you want to rest your case on what he'll write from memory after an hour or so of conversation? If you hand him a highly persuasive resume, he won't make it worse to match the rest. And if he has to write it, chances are he can't make it good enough to match the best.

"Fortunately, I don't have to bother writing my own resume; the people who fired me have paid for outplacement services."

Some things are more important to you and to your future than they are to anyone else. The document that positions you in the employment world is one of them.

Incidentally, three chapters from now (in Chapter 15) we'll look at outplacement...another of the "Rites of Passage."

Okay, we've got the "why's" and "why not's" out of the way. Now let's talk about your ultimate credential, the true "Sales Representative" resume... strong enough for use in direct mail, and therefore best for every other use, too.

Direct mail selling is the hardest test persuasive writing can be put to. By mailing to large numbers of potential purchasers, it's possible to blanket so many that you'll surely hit a few who have a need at the exact moment your envelope arrives. But grabbing attention, engaging interest, and convincing strongly enough to stimulate action...that's still a lot to ask of mere words on paper. You'd better send something powerful. And the core of your package is your resume.

The only reason that a resume blown in through the window...or abandoned on an airliner...or delivered by the Postal Service...prods any recipient into action is that it's an effective sales rep. It's *a persuasive piece of writing* that communicates enticingly and fully enough to convince the reader that the person behind the resume might be the solution to the reader's problem.

That's what your resume is: your "Sales Representative" on paper, who'll speak for you when you can't be there. And that's true regardless of whether your resume:

1.   *arrives "cold"* in the mail, or by accident, or

2. *is hand delivered...*by you yourself, or by someone who's met you, and wants another person to know you as fully and favorably as she does.

Indeed, as we shall see, a resume effective enough to perform in this situation will also be effective when:

3. *you offer it as an orientation aid at an interview.*

...And now for the shocker.
What's the number-one principle of direct mail copywriting?

In almost every industry, there's a bedrock principle discovered years ago... and reconfirmed again and again through the experience of everyone in the field...until it becomes the rule that all know and follow. In real estate, for example, it's:

"Location is everything."

Or, stated another way...

"The three principles of real estate are:
(1) Location, (2) location, and (3) location."

In direct mail copywriting, as in real estate, success or failure is proven in dollars and cents. Before any company sends a mailing to 5 million or 15 million households, several different versions are tested, ranging from short to long copy, and trying new gimmicks, such as envelopes that look like bank statements, bills, telegrams, etc. Objective: to see which variation pulls most orders per thousand dollars of cost.

Some of the new gimmicks test well and are used. Others are forgotten. But, like real estate, direct mail copywriting has one bedrock principle that everyone respects...proven during sixty years of testing and reconfirmed by test after test today:

"Long copy sells."

Proof of this honored axiom is delivered to your home every day. If shortness worked, brevity would be in your mailbox. And all the companies now using long-copy direct mail could achieve multi-million dollar savings in paper, printing, and postage...everything that makes a fat letter more expensive than a thin one. Those companies aren't stupid. They test. They don't spend more money unless the results *more* than justify the extra cost.

However, this proven axiom might, as advertising guru David Ogilvy pointed out, be more accurately stated:

"Factual copy sells."

Famous for his "long-copy" ads, Mr. Ogilvy was also a crusader for very clear and *succinct* writing. He conveyed each fact with arresting clarity and *brevity*, and then piled up a wealth of these impressive facts to prove his client's product superior to competitive brands. Master of the concise well-turned phrase, Ogilvy summed up the principle this way: *"The more you tell, the more you sell."*

Incidentally, the experts I've talked to tell me that the only exceptions to the "long copy sells" rule occur with simple products that every recipient is already thoroughly familiar with before the mailing arrives. In such cases, explanation of the *product* is unnecessary, because only the briefly stated *offer* is new.

For example, you can sell someone a half-price subscription to *Time* or *Fortune* with a postcard or a little self-mailer envelope, whereas it will take several pages of facts and pictures to persuade the same person to sign up for a "four-months-free, cancel-and-pay-nothing" offer on a new publication.

When you get in touch with a prospective employer, you're always an unknown new publication. You're not *Business Week*, *Forbes*, or *The Wall Street Journal*, and don't you forget it!

There are always, of course, a few "celebrity" executives in any field who... at least during their transitory heyday...could get by with brevity instead of a convincing dose of long copy. Remember when just this sort of note from one of the "Steves"—Jobs or Case—would have produced a flood of inquiries?

```
          I've pretty much finished what
          I set out to do here.

          If you think I could be helpful
          to your company, please give me
          a call.

                  Sincerely,
```

John's Fire-in-the-Forest Analogy

I had a very successful career as a consumer products marketing executive before I got into executive recruiting 30 years ago, and I've thought many times about the question of *why* long copy—or as I prefer to describe it, *adequately specific* copy—invariably sells complicated, expensive items by direct mail much better than short copy does.

The experts either say:

"People need a certain amount of *convincing* to break down their barriers."

Or they say:

"Who *cares* why? Experience proves that long copy works!"

Well, over the years I've come up with a little analogy which has helped satisfy my need for a "why," and it may strike a responsive chord with you, too.

Hitting people "cold" with a written sales pitch and taking them all the way from no-such-thought-anywhere-in-their-heads to the point of picking up the phone or a pen and taking action requires quite a process of change to take place step-by-step in their minds.

Think of the process as a chain reaction analogous to building a fire in the forest when you have just one match. Before you strike that match, you must have the entire makings of your fire all laid out. First you find some tinder... maybe an old Kleenex®, or some dry leaves. Then you add dry twigs and small dry sticks. Then some bigger sticks and branches...as dry as you can find. And on top of everything else some big branches and logs...dry, if possible, but if not, the other stuff burning under them will get them ready to burn. What you've assembled will keep the fire going all night, or at least long enough for you to round up more fuel.

You wouldn't dream of wasting your match by starting the chain reaction with only part of your fuel in place. You'd have everything ready. Otherwise, your fire might get off to a promising start...and then go out.

Something similar, I submit, must happen when a mailing convinces its reader to buy a complicated, expensive, seldom-purchased item. The letter must take him from complete unawareness and indifference...to first spark of interest...to casual but somewhat more interested reading...to avid devouring of all the information provided...to phoning or writing the sender. Since we know for a fact that short, sketchy copy doesn't perform as well as longer, more informative copy, I submit that the reason may be too little fuel.

The reader may have a first flicker of interest...which may grow into casual, and even attentive, reading. He's not yet convinced to make a phone call or write a letter. But he *is* willing to read further.

Suddenly the fuel runs out. The reader would have considered more information...*but it wasn't there!* And not deeply involved, he doesn't bother to send out for more facts.

You've got just one match. Don't waste it!

You have your reader's attention when she first glances at your resume... whether it blows in through the window or it comes in the mail. Your match is lit and burning. It ignites the dried leaves. But if you haven't laid out enough persuasive factors to fuel the chain reaction, your match is wasted. You've sparked attention. But there's no bonfire. And your phone doesn't ring.

Q: What happens when you apply direct mail copywriting to your resume?

A: It goes from 2 pages to 3 or 4 pages... and it contains 3 or 5 times as much of the persuasive information employers are interested in.

"Look, John," I'll bet you're saying, "forgetting for the moment the fact that everyone has always told me resumes should be brief, not long...and maybe conceding that the direct mail people do know about stimulating action through a written sales presentation...still I can't let you get away with saying that *doubling* the pages from two to four will provide *five times* as much persuasive information."

I knew I'd grab you with that idea.

But think about it for a minute. On two pages you're barely able to list your name, address, office and home phone numbers, college degrees, a couple personal facts, and lay out a reverse-chronological listing of all the companies you've worked for and the progression of titles and responsibilities from college to now...all requisites of a good resume. Certainly that's true if you create a nice clean layout with lots of white space separating all the elements, so that where you've been and what you've done is easy to scan...a point we'll get back to later.

So in two pages, you *are* able to list all the job titles you've held and give a skimpy description of responsibilities for the more recent and important ones. Unfortunately, you haven't got room to say much, if anything, about what you *achieved* when you held those responsibilities. And achievements proving you're special are what a prospective employer is looking for.

Everyone has been given responsibility. Only a special few—you among them, I hope—have given back anything really substantial in the way of achievement.

Let's say that in a nice, open, quick-to-scan layout, with your chronological units floating in a decent amount of white space, you get 400 to 500 words on a page, 800 to 1,000 on two pages...and 75% of them are devoted to covering the mandatory data. That leaves about 200 to 250 words for accomplishments that could make you stand out as interesting—and hopefully special—in the eyes of a potential employer.

Now go from two pages to four. You've got room for 1,600 to 2,000 words... 800 to 1,000 more than before. And *every additional word* can be devoted to achievements, because the basics were already covered in the two-page version. Add your original 200 to 250 words on achievements, and the box score looks like this:

	TOTAL WORDS	BASIC DATA (WORDS)	ACHIEVEMENTS (WORDS)	HOW MANY TIMES AS MANY ACHIEVEMENT WORDS?
2 Pages	800-1000	600-750	200-250	1
3 Pages	1200-1500	600-750	600-750	3
4 Pages	1600-2000	600-750	1000-1250	5

**But now let's go back to the point about
everyone telling you to keep your resume brief.
Who told you? And when? And why?**

Who and When?

Was it your "Counselor" at the contingency firm that helped you get your first job out of college or graduate school? Was it someone who "worked with" you or "headhunted" you as you moved into middle management with your second or third job?

Face it: in those days you hadn't done anything really significant yet. At that stage no one has. Or if they have, nobody is prepared to believe they have.

From entry level up through middle management you're somewhere from a "GI Joe" to a first lieutenant in the army of industry. What an employer wants to know is where you've been...how fast you're moving up...and how closely your experience matches what she wants done. That information fits neatly on one page...certainly no more than two. Indeed, if you're bright, attractive, and ambitious, it won't matter if your entire early career has been working on a string of corporate *flops!* You won't be blamed. You didn't commit the corporation to those misadventures. And you weren't so centrally responsible for implementation that anyone will figure you made a good idea fail.

Today, however, you're in an altogether different situation. You're at or far beyond $100,000+. Now you're at least a "field commander." You legitimately *can* claim some victories. And you can be held responsible for some defeats. *Your resume must deliver more factual information.*

Also consider the "why" behind the advice you're given.

If you're now well above $100,000+, and *"when"* you were told to "keep it brief" was yesterday, and *"who"* told you was a prestigious retainer recruiter...then maybe we should consider *"why"* he said that.

The most obvious reason is that you only have a fleeting moment of your reader's time and attention before he'll give up on your resume as too tedious to figure out, and toss it aside. *This reason I totally agree with.* However, I don't agree that the solution to the problem is to strip away your persuasive factual information.

The other reason could be that the retainer recruiter has orally "pre-sold" you to his client, so your resume doesn't have to be persuasive. My reaction to this reason from your standpoint is "OK...*but.*" The recruiter is introducing several other candidates besides you, and if you have some impressive achievements, you want them clearly known to the employer as she chooses between you and the others.

| | | **Your resume must perform two functions.** | | |
Brevity suits one...and defeats the other.

Your resume absolutely must do two things. Unfortunately, while brevity achieves one, it defeats the other. Therefore, unless your exploits were the cover story in Monday's *Fortune*, brevity isn't your answer.

1.   Quick Orientation

Your reader will allow your resume only about thirty seconds...no more than a minute...to orient him to who you are, and whether you might be relevant to his needs right now. Certainly that's true if it arrives "cold" in the mail or is blown in through the window; he'll spend *more* time with it, not less, if he's paid a retainer recruiter over $80,000 to look for it.

Most of the time your resume will reach the reader when he doesn't need you. Your "one match" will burn less than a minute. By then, if you've done a poor orientation job, he'll have dumped you for being too tedious and confusing. And even if you've done a good job, he'll almost always have dumped you for not being needed right now.

2.   Thorough Convincing

But in the rare, rare instance when you do happen to hit a reader at the moment she has a need you might fill, and you quickly orient her to that fact, then she's willing to extend her attention span a bit further.

She didn't find you irrelevant. Now she's looking to find you ordinary. But, wait a minute; you've been involved in several things that were impressively successful...another "turn off" bypassed. Okay, but probably these programs were conceived, planned, and strategically implemented by others, and you were merely a supporting player. No, wait another minute; your clear, succinct explanation of the reasons underlying the actions that were taken certainly sounds like you were the strategist, not just the "gofer." Your reader decides:

"This guy is *interesting*. I'll read to the end. And then I'll go back over this whole thing again. If he still looks okay, maybe I'll even call him up."

As you see, a very brief resume could have performed the quick orientation and helped your reader turn off. Unfortunately, it probably couldn't have turned her on...and on...and on...to the point of picking up the phone and calling you.

Fortunately, a resume written according to the "long copy sells" principle of direct mail copywriting is capable of walking and chewing gum at the same time.

Right away you're probably saying, "I can see, John, where long copy will be great at 'Thorough Convincing,' but won't it interfere with 'Quick Orientation'?"

No. Not if you're careful to make your resume *visually accessible*. Format and layout become extremely important. Just make your resume:

Scannable!

Your reader will glance at 3, 4, 5, or 6 pages if it's instantly evident with just one glance what's on each of those pages. If you arrange your resume right, the recipient will probably glance through *all* of the pages before reading *any* of them. That's everyone's normal impulse as a reader anyway. You probably flipped through this book before you began reading it page-by-page. Fortunately, with resumes in particular, it's easy to help that normal human tendency along.

Don't you just hate topically-oriented resumes?
Don't you wish everyone did?

I have never yet met anyone who likes to receive a topically-oriented resume.

You know the kind...where practically the whole thing is a list of claimed accomplishments, presented entirely out of context of when they happened... who the executive was working for...what his title, responsibilities, reporting relationships, and staff were...and what the size and nature of the businesses were. Finally, if you're lucky...and it's not always there...you find a deliberately sketchy little "Chronology of Employment" buried at the end, from which...if you're not already too turned off...you try to guess when and for whom and from what position of how much authority those previously claimed management miracles were achieved.

You and I are in the overwhelming majority in disliking topically-oriented resumes (also sometimes euphemistically referred to as "achievement-oriented"). When on the receiving end, virtually everybody prefers the good, honest, comfortable, easy-to-read old-fashioned kind, where name, address, and business and home phone numbers are at the top, and work history proceeds backwards from current job on the first page to earliest on the last page.

Everyone's recognition of...and preference for... the standard-format resume solves your "scannability" problem, without getting you into the brevity trap.

If you don't go out of your way to confuse your reader, you've got the scannability problem solved...no matter how long you choose to make your resume.

Everyone in a position to hire an executive earning over $100,000 has read hundreds of resumes before. If yours is in standard reverse-chronology format, and each employer/time/position copyblock floats in enough white space to make it clear where one segment ends and the earlier one begins, *your reader will go on automatic pilot*...scanning through any number of pages in just a very few seconds.

One page or five, he quickly sees that you're *not* somebody he can use right now. But if by stroke of lightning you happen to have dropped into his hands at precisely the time he *does* need someone with a background even remotely like yours, he'll read on...and on. Having your entire "fire" laid out, you've got an excellent chance that your reader will proceed all the way from flicker-of-interest to action. Expect a phone call or a letter!

Not only does the standard reverse-chronology resume solve the scannability problem; it's also more convincing, because it's more straightforward.

Forget about "long copy sells." Assume that two resumes, one reverse-chronological and the other topical, are *the same length...any length*.

The one that deliberately strips away the employment context from the claimed accomplishments not only frustrates the reader's comprehension, *it also raises the presumption that there must have been some very good reason for doing so*. "This woman obviously has something to hide," thinks the reader. "I wonder what it is."

Usually it's too-brief tenure at the latest or two latest jobs...and maybe at lots of jobs along the way. That's what the reader immediately suspects. And readily confirms, if a truthful "chronology" is included anywhere in the resume. And assumes if it's not.

Wanting to de-emphasize their latest job and not put it at the top of a reverse-chronological list is overwhelmingly the reason executives turn to a topically-oriented resume...even though when they're personally hiring, they hate to receive one. That's a mistake. It's better to deal with the problem straight-forwardly.

Below I've shown a successful lead-off entry for a reverse-chronological resume. This person wisely stuck to the traditional format.

2001 (9 months)

FLY-BY-NIGHT SCHLOCK ELECTRONICS CORP.

Vice President - Engineering

> After seven years of increasing responsibility at Lucent Technologies and its predecessor, Bell Labs Div. of AT&T, I was recruited as Chief Engineering Officer of this fast-growing four-year-old maker of video games and electronic gambling devices (2000 sales, $132.5 million), by the Founder/CEO, who'd been his own chief engineer.
>
> Six months later, I still hadn't received the equity stake which was a primary incentive to join, and still hadn't been allowed to install any of the operating changes I felt could benefit the company. So I proposed and the Chairman agreed that I should re-distribute my duties to subordinates and seek a situation where I can assume a more assertive role.

1994 - 2001

BELL LABORATORIES DIVISION
(LUCENT TECHNOLOGIES AND PREDECESSOR AT&T)

Group Director - Laser Engineering Department

As you see, by the third paragraph on the top page of her resume, the writer is back to telling the Bell Labs story she loves to tell. Above all, she hasn't been forced into a topical resume...a cure far worse than her mild disease.

If you're right, John, that almost everyone prefers to read standard-format resumes, why do people write the other kind? And do the executives who write them also dislike receiving them?

Questions I've always been curious about, too. So I've checked into them with the people who've handed me topical resumes over the past 30 years.

Invariably, once we got down to talking frankly, these people pointed out problems similar to the one I just dealt with, which made me feel they were forced to give up the standard reverse-chronological format. I can't recall a single person maintaining that he went to the topical format because that's the type he preferred to receive.

And now, maestro...an appropriate drum roll and cymbal crash as we unveil a sample resume written according to the "long copy sells" principle of direct mail copywriting.

It's from Sam Sage, one of the many executives you'll meet when you view an executive search through the eyes of a retainer recruiter in Appendix I.

As you look at Sam's resume...begin by doing what everyone always does with a resume. *Scan* it for a few seconds.

What function does Sam perform?

Who's he done it for?

How long has he been at it?

See if Sam's someone you might need right now. Chances are he's not. And you'll see that at a glance.

Next...before you actually read the resume...do me a favor. Ask yourself:

Could a shorter resume have turned you off any faster?

Would Sam be any further ahead if it had?

Having scanned the resume, do me another favor. Change the facts. Pretend that you now have even the slightest...the weakest possible...glimmer of interest in someone even remotely like Sam. For that reason, you're inclined to begin *reading* the resume.

Are you interested enough to continue from page 1 to page 2?

From page 2 to 3? All the way to the end?

Face it. If you're not interested enough to spend the two or three extra minutes it'll take you to finish reading about Sam, you're certainly not interested enough to call him up and kill an hour or two meeting him face-to-face.

Finally, after you *have* read all the way to the end, ask yourself:

Could Sam have "sold" you better with a shorter resume?

Would knowing less about Sam have made you like him more?

What information could he have withheld in order to *really* turn you on?

And is that information anything that even the briefest one-page resume *could* conceal?

Note...

The resume we're developing here is the classic high quality document you should always have ready and up-to-date. It's your best possible representative, whether delivered by mail, handed over at an interview, or passed along by people wanting others to appreciate you.

This resume will be attractively formatted and easy to scan, with contrasting typography and elegant use of white space to guide the eye and encourage reading. When faxed, even though fuzzy, it will still retain its basic communicating prowess.

Sadly, these days you also need an unstyled, generic *electronic* resume that can be e-mailed...and possibly also stored on and transmitted from various Web sites. Later when we explore the many wonderful opportunities the Internet opens up for executive-level career management we'll help you do the best you can with a resume that meets the styling constraints of the Web.

SAMUEL P. SAGE
219 Waring Drive
Denton, New Jersey 07299

Home: (201) 719-0932
Office: (212) 121-3000
ssage@aota.com

1996 - Present

FARRINGTON LABORATORIES
(Merged into Pan Global Pharmaceuticals Ltd. in October '01)
New York, New York

Vice President - Chief Marketing Officer

Recruited to this privately-owned $1.3 billion maker of prescription drugs as Vice President - Chief Marketing Officer by Blair Farrington, Founder/Owner/CEO in 1996, when sales were $592 million.

Mr. Farrington doubled what I'd been making in the same position at the much larger (then $1.2 billion) Swiss-owned Medica Suisse USA Ltd. But the primary incentive was this 72-year-old gentleman's plan to take the business public with me as his successor, after we worked a few years together to increase volume and improve profitability. Instead, the company has been purchased by...and merged into...Pan Global Pharmaceuticals (October '01). With their acquiescence, I'm seeking a new challenge...hopefully a Presidency; otherwise Chief Marketing Officer joined in '96 and 3 years prior:

	Sales ($millions)	% Change	Pre-Tax Net ($millions)	% Change	% ROI
'01	1,342.6	+31.5	223.0	+62.4	28.1
'00	1,021.0	+24.9	137.3	+52.3	24.6
'99	817.5	+36.1	90.2	+43.1	17.2
'98	600.6	+23.2	62.9	+39.8	12.7
'97	487.5	-17.7	45.0	+81.9	9.4
'96	592.4	-2.4	24.8	-16.8	3.6
'95	606.9	+4.5	29.8	+6.6	4.9
'94	580.8	+7.2	27.9	+8.2	5.7
'93	541.8	+6.1	25.8	-1.1	9.1

The product line was reduced from 618 SKUs in '96 to 309 profitable items in '99 (expanded with new products to 384 by '01). The 109-person sales force was reorganized into 11 regions in '97 and expanded to 225 people by '01.

Nine profitable new drugs were introduced via cross-licensing agreements with other manufacturers ('01 sales, $258 million; $62 million pre-tax net), and $23.4 million pre-tax was generated by granting licenses to other companies.

SAMUEL P. SAGE - 2

Physicians' top-of-mind brand-name awareness of our three largest-selling drugs was raised from 18% in '96 to 62% in '01 by a massive sampling, detailing, and professional advertising campaign (budget tripled from $18.8 million in '96 to $58.2 million in '01).

As a result of Farrington Labs' excellent growth trend and high profitability, Pan Global paid 30 times estimated '01 earnings in a 50%-cash/50%-stock transaction.

1993 - 1996

MEDICA SUISSE USA LTD.
Marshall Plains, New Jersey

Vice President - Pharmaceutical Marketing

Rejoined this $3.6 billion Zurich-based maker of prescription drugs, veterinary biologicals, and fine chemicals as Director of Pharmaceutical Marketing, reporting to the Managing Director - USA, and heading all marketing and sales for all North American pharmaceutical lines (total '93 sales, $630 million) after a two-year hiatus to aid my family's automobile business in Ohio.

By 1996 sales were nearly double ($1.2 billion) 1993 volume, and ROI had increased from 17% ('93) to 24% ('96). Market share of U.S. prescription tranquilizer market rose from 11.6% in '93 to 19.2% in '96, and veterinary products gained 1.3 share points to 7.2% in '96.

...y earlier recommendation (in '91) that the company's consumer pet-health lines be sold to generate cash for acquisition of young growth companies in the higher-margined ethical drug field was implemented while I was away ('92), and I helped identify and purchase in '93 and '94 three small companies...BioTRITON, Radio-Tra-Chem, and Synestial Laboratories...which have all grown and prospered under Medica Suisse ownership. One of these, BioTRITON, was publicly reported as having worldwide sales of $560 million in '00, with the highest ROI of any Medica Suisse business anywhere in the world.

'94   Vice President - Pharmaceutical Marketing.   Promotion in title, no change in duties.

'93   Director - Pharmaceutical Marketing.   Rejoined Medica Suisse in charge of corporate Marketing, Market Research, Telemarketing, and Sales Promotion departments (total of 41 people); plus two sales forces...Ethical Drug (135-person) and Veterinary (32-person).

1991 - 1993

SAGE CHRYSLER / TOYOTA, INC.
Kensington, Ohio

Upon my father's sudden death (2/91), I took charge of the family business ($2.8 million sales

SAMUEL P. SAGE - 3

in '91, $4.4 million in '93), holding it together until my younger brother could finish his MBA at Wharton ('91) and join my mother in running the company.

Increased TV advertising, and diversified by building two Taco Bell fast food franchises (since expanded to seven). Profits nearly doubled in two years.

1989 - 1991

MEDICA SUISSE USA LTD.
Marshall Plains, New Jersey

Group Product Director

Invited to join my client from New World Advertising Agency as Group Product Director (with 4 Product Managers and 5 Assistant PMs), in charge of:

(1)   Marketing existing U.S. lines...$68 million consumer (Krueger's flea-and-tick collars and home remedies for pets) and $96 million professional ($42 million veterinary and $54 million human prescription drugs); and

(2)   Introducing new family of prescription tranquilizers (Dopatreem) for Rx sales in the

... is a major new Rx drug is impossible without a large field force (and Medica Suisse had only 22 salesmen carrying both Rx and veterinary lines), I cut off advertising on all lines for 10 months; used the cash flow to build a 100-person field force calling only on MDs; and launched a $20 million sampling and ad campaign for the Dopatreem line.

Result: 14 months after introduction, Dopatreem and Dopatreem X were #2 and #5 tranquilizers in the U.S., with $440 million combined annualized rate of sales. Profit from Rx lines was then temporarily diverted to help rebuild other lines to all-time high share levels.

1985 - 1989

NEW WORLD ADVERTISING AGENCY
New York, New York

Vice President - Account Group Supervisor

Joined as Account Executive on $38 million Whiskers cat food account when the AE on my P&G business moved to New World as Account Supervisor and asked me to join him. Through growth of Whiskers and acquiring new accounts, became VP - Account Group Supervisor in charge of $102 million in billings (4 AEs and 3 Assistant AEs) from Megopolitan Foods ($76 million on Whiskers and Arf! brands) and Medica Suisse ($14 million on consumer items and $12 million on veterinary and Rx human drugs).

SAMUEL P. SAGE - 4

As AE in '85, led the task force that "re-staged" Whiskers brand with CLIO-winning "Caesar-the-Cat" TV commercials and portion-control packaging that doubled Whiskers' market share from 5% ('85) to 11.2% ('89). Factory sales rose from $106 million ('85) to $298 million ('89); and advertising rose from $18 million to $52 million. Led successful solicitation of $14 million Arf! dog food account ('86), which billed $24 million in '89 (sales rose from $64 million to $158 million). Personally brought in Krueger's flea-and-tick collars ($8 million in '87) from Medica Suisse, which consolidated all their North American business with us in '88.

'87 Vice President - Account Group Supervisor. A 26% 12-month sales increase in Krueger's flea collars, etc. from Medica Suisse enabled us to win their veterinary and prescription drug accounts…the first medical advertising handled by New World. Promoted for building of Megopolitan and Medica Suisse accounts.

'86 Account Supervisor. Turnaround on Whiskers enabled us to land $14 million Arf! dog food billings ('86) and Krueger's consumer pet items ('87).

'85 Account Executive. Entered on the Whiskers account with assignment to stem share

PROMOTE & GAMBOL COMPANY
Cincinnati, Ohio

'84   Assistant Brand Manager. Handled $52 million TV & print media and $16 million sales promotion budget on GLOSS-X floor cleaner. Promoted to head successful test marketing and regional expansion of new GLOSS-O floor wax.

'82   Brand Assistant. Traditional P&G home office and field sales training assignments; handled TV copy testing for Soft-Ah! paper products.

EDUCATION: MBA, Harvard Business School, 1982
BA, University of Michigan, 1979

PERSONAL: Born June 1, 1957
Married, 3 children.
6' 1", 185 lbs.

Editor's Note…

This model resume by John Lucht in RITES OF PASSAGE has raised the prevailing standards for proving one's superiority to the others seeking a desirable position. To master these breakthroughs, use pages 41 to 135 in his EXECUTIVE JOB-CHANGING WORKBOOK, which provide (1) "real life examples" and (2) templates for creating your personal job-winning resume.

Could Sam have made you like him better by omitting something you just read?

And if so, could even the shortest one-page resume have concealed that *particular* "something"?

You scanned Sam's resume in seconds.

You saw at a glance that he's a *marketing* executive. And a very *high-level* one.

Is there any kind of resume, no matter how brief—or any kind of letter, no matter how vague and misleading—that could have hidden Sam's basic information from you? And could he have benefited from the concealment, even if it were possible?

I don't think so.

If you didn't need what Sam was selling, merely limiting your knowledge couldn't have increased your need.

But if you'd had even the slightest interest in anyone even remotely like Sam, then seeing how very special he is would have made you more...not less... interested.

Indeed, Sam even managed to tell you that he believes he's ready to be a president; to imply that he's recently been functioning almost like one; and to demonstrate over and over that he certainly thinks like one.

You saw, too, that Sam's been transplanted several times and has succeeded in each new context...even running the family car dealership. He's versatile. And his sense of loyalty...as extended to his mother and brother...is also admirable.

About the only thing you could imagine Sam wanting to hide is the fact that he's spent the most-recent and highest-level part of his career marketing *drugs*...a fact which, if known, might turn off a CEO looking for someone to market anti-aircraft missiles or panty hose.

But Sam can't even *name* his employers without letting his "drug experience" out of the bag. And no CEO...indeed, no reader...is going to be turned on by self-praise in mere "percentage" terms by someone who refuses to reveal who he's worked for until *after* he's been granted an interview. Straight to the wastebasket with a letter or resume like that!

After reading Sam's resume, you and I suspect that he could market just about anything...missiles and stockings included. Nonetheless, no retainer recruiter being paid, let's say $150,000, to find a "defense" or a "soft goods" person can get by with just offering Sam plus a "he-could-do-it" pitch...even though Sam might make a good "wild card," tucked in among several "on-target" candidates.

On the other hand, if Sam can somehow get the resume we've just read into the hands of the CEO of an armaments or a hosiery company *before* he's paying somebody $150,000+ to find exactly what he wants, the CEO may think:

> "What the hell? It won't cost anything just to meet this Sam Sage.
> He's done some very impressive things. And frankly, most of the
> marketing people in our industry don't impress me at all.
> Marketing is *marketing!* A smart outsider like Sage might just
> show us a few tricks we never thought of."

Face it. Despite any kooky advice to the contrary, there's no way Sam can "package" himself differently for different employers. So he's being straight-forward. And he's right! Just like you and me, others will also admire Sam's achievements...their diversity...and *the thinking behind them.* They too will envision him doing an outstanding job, no matter where he ends up.

No question about it. Sam's taken the best possible approach with his resume. He's told the *truth* openly, voluntarily, and impressively.

David Ogilvy knew what he was talking about when he said:

> "The more you tell, the more you sell!"

Notice that Sam used narrative paragraphs, rather than "bullets" to tell his story.

There are two common approaches to presenting a work history. One is to use paragraphs, with each job written up as a mini-essay. The other is to use "bullets"...sentence fragments preceded by a raised dot. Commonly used by advertising copywriters, the "bullet" format attempts to make every single point seem like a highlight.

Either style is acceptable. But, for several reasons, I strongly prefer paragraphs...very tightly and specifically written. Sentences in paragraphs are easier for the reader to comprehend and believe, because they closely resemble what he sees in newspapers, magazines, books, memos, and other informational writing. Bullets, on the other hand, resemble advertising copy... subliminally *not* an aid to believability.

Also, sentences in paragraphs enable you to use transition phrases and conjunctions that *connect* the various statements in ways that serve your purposes better than a series of unrelated exclamations. It helps to be able to say: "In recognition, I was promoted to..." "When my report was accepted by the Board, I was asked to assemble a team..." "After consolidating these three acquisitions..." You get the idea.

Sam also made his resume factual and concrete...something many people have trouble doing. Here are a few tips:

Orient your reader with specifics.

For each management-level job, orient your reader to the size, nature, and trend of (1) the larger unit in which you participated and (2) the part of it you were responsible for. What was the size of your operation in people, sales, and profit? What was its mandate? The general business climate around it? The problems and opportunities you identified? The strategies you came up with? And the results you achieved?

Use numbers wherever possible.

Focus on quantifiable data. Give dollar figures for sales, profits, ROI, costs, inventories, etc. before and after your programs were implemented. When you use percentages, you'll usually want to give the *base*...plus any comparative figures on the rest of the industry or another part of your company that will show your numbers are special.

Avoid empty words and statements.

Omit the self-praising adjectives that losers wallow in..."major," "significant," "substantial," and "outstanding." Wherever such a word is justified, a number will be far more persuasive. And never make meaningless over-generalized statements like this:

> "Responsible for managing the strategic technical issues impacting the company's ongoing core businesses."

What does this person do all day? What's his budget? Whom does he report to and who reports to him? Has his employer gained anything from having him around?

Create a mosaic.

You've seen those pictures made out of lots of little colored stones. Imagine that each promotion to a new job, each numerical improvement, each specific point of analysis and strategy is a stone. When put together in the right order, these fragments will be connected by your reader into an image of you. Don't assert what the shape of it is. Just lay out enough specific facts...stone by stone...so she'll see for herself the favorable patterns they imply. Let her create her own picture in her own mind.

If you'd like to change industries or career fields, consider making a second version of your resume... but even then, don't switch to topical organization.

Maybe you're in a declining field and you'd like to move into a growth industry. Or you're re-entering the commercial sector after a sojourn in the military, government, or academia. If so, make a special version of your resume that drains off industry-specific buzz-words and explains your exploits in terms everyone can appreciate. But resist the temptation to "go topical" and try to hide "where" while emphasizing "what."

Your reader will never quite be able to believe your claimed achievements unless he has a mental picture of you located at some specific place and time in the real world actually doing them. Withdraw orientation, and he drops belief...and probably attention, too.

Rather than resort to a topical resume, you should:

1.   Write a covering letter that says what *specific need* your reader may have that you from another field can fill for him in his field. Don't say, "Here I am; guess what I can do for you."

2.   And be realistic. If you're stumped when you try to write a persuasive covering letter explaining how you can fill a specific need of an employer in an unrelated field, then stop. Think of someone else in a different field for whom you *do* have a persuasive message. Don't pursue a hopeless mismatch. If *you're* not persuaded, you can be absolutely certain that no one else will be either.

Should you include a "Career Objective"?

Many resumes begin with a statement of what-kind-of-job-I-want labeled *"Career Objective,"* or simply *"Objective."*

This is a good idea when you're fresh out of college or grad school and you want to orient the "Counselor" at an employment agency, or the personnel department of a corporation, to what you're looking for. But it's seldom necessary after your career is well underway. By then, what you're prepared to do next should be pretty evident from what you've already done.

If you're retiring from the military or the diplomatic corps, or leaving academia or the priesthood, then maybe your resume should begin with a statement of what you seek in the business world. Otherwise, let your resume be a clear and self-confident statement of where you've been and what you've achieved. Say what you're looking for in your covering letter and through personal contact.

Instead of an "Objective," a very brief summary can be effective. But don't label it "Summary." *Don't label it at all!*

If you want a *very few* words of orientation at the top of your resume, make them a strong and succinct statement of what you've proven you can do. Now you're *not* talking about what *you want*—a job, of course—but what you deliver that an *employer* wants. However, if you use a strong assertion as, in effect, the headline of your resume, the rest of your resume had damned well better prove you deliver what you've so boldly claimed on top.

Examples:

1.   CEO with a Track Record of Turn Arounds

2.   Chief Financial Officer or Chief Operating Officer
Successful in Improving, Building and Restructuring Companies

3.   Chief Marketing Officer - Consumer Products Company

4.   Senior Human Resources Executive
Comprehensive Policy and Operational Leadership...Domestic and International

5.   Operations Executive or Chief Information Officer
...Successful at Improving Business Operations

6.   Chief Executive / Chief Technology Officer
Performance. Economy. Solving Problems. Making Profit.
From "Fortune 50" to IPO, I've made technology pay.

7. (Nothing but the name/address/phone preceded the following at the top of resume page 1)
   I get results:

   As General Manager, I've just finished saving a failing business...increasing its net worth from zero in 1998 to more than $200 million today.

   As Chief of Corporate Planning, I brought strategic business planning to one of the world's largest manufacturing companies, helping many of its businesses in many ways.

   As Manager of Engineering Departments, I always delivered on time and on budget.

Those are not hypothetical examples. Each headed the resume of an executive I personally assisted. The prior employer (not the individual) paid 15% of annual compensation ranging from a minimum of $50,000 to a maximum (cap) of $75,000. As you can imagine, at those rates I put in lots of effort—often 20 to 30 hours at my computer—helping create a resume that's (1) 100% true and (2) fully supportive of its bold thematic summary.

Results? Every one of these people got a more attractive job than the one he or she had just left. Number 6, for example, got $175,000 higher base salary than in his prior job and made close to $1.5 million in option profits in his first year. Number 4 went from #2 in HR in a very large company to #1 in an even bigger one. Number 7 sent out 500 letters to CEOs of Fortune 500 companies and, just from his mailing, was immediately hired as Chief Technology Officer of one of them. And Number 5 met his goal of moving from consulting to line management at equal or better income without relocating from his medium-sized midwestern city.

The Most Important Ingredients of a Resume: Time and Thought

Above all, you must devote plenty of time and thought to (1) deciding which facts will prove you get great results...and (2) stating those facts in a distilled, clear way. You'll face competing candidates. To defeat them, you must appear on paper and in interviews to be the one person who can be counted on to turn in the #1 best performance of everyone being considered.

When I provide assistance, the person spends two days one-on-one with me in New York (plus another day with a psychologist if they're willing). At least 4 hours are my taped interview probing accomplishments, which my staff transcribes. The person then goes home and, using the transcript, works hard on the resume (ideal preparation for future interviews). We continue by fax and phone. Finally the person has done his or her best. Depending on the result, I may still spend further hours polishing to remove words and sharpen meaning (see page 69 of my *EXECUTIVE JOB-CHANGING WORKBOOK* for a before-and-after example). Usually I can cut at least one full page without dropping a single fact. So can you. But only if you work hard to edit what you've written. The tightened result is quicker and easier to read...and far more convincing.

Lots of people will tell you that resumes don't really matter. True! The generic *this-could-be-said-about-everyone-in-the-industry* resumes those folks would have you write *do not matter*. But a resume that truthfully shows by past performance that you're likely to outperform everyone else being considered *does* matter. If you have the right stuff, be sure to put in sufficient time and effort to display it well.

Reasons for Moving

Your resume may look like you've had too many recent jobs to really be a star performer. Yet the opposite may be true. If you joined Company X, made a great impression, and were soon asked to follow your boss to Co. Y. Say so! Don't let having been a star make you look like a dog. And if you were one of 2,000 sluffed off in a merger—or one of 6-out-of-8 senior officers dumped by a new CEO who brought in a team from his former company—why not say so? Don't be defensive. And don't give a reason for *every* move. Then, says Shakespeare, "Me thinks thou doth protest too much!" But if at a few pivotal times you'd otherwise take a bum rap, set the record straight.

Creative Use of Avocational Interests in Your Resume

In general, never mention your hobbies and other outside interests.

If you had time to be assistant pastor of your church, chair the United Fund drive, coach a Little League team, do petit point, build an extension on your home, train for and run a marathon, and groom and show poodles in the U.S. and three foreign countries last year, when did you have time to work?

But if you're 58 years old, it might be good to mention your marathon running, and the fact that you're an avid scuba diver and an instructor for Outward Bound. Your stamp collection, of course, will remain in the closet.

And if you're a paraplegic, your competitive sports car driving and skeet shooting might just be a worthwhile inclusion. So might building that wing on your house, if you're only missing one arm or one leg.

If you just have a high school diploma, the fact that you're an amateur writer who's published stories in *Harper's* and *The New Yorker*...or even a trade journal or the business section of your daily newspaper...could help show you have a mature, cultivated mind others respect. So might your appointment to the Mayor's Commission for the Arts, your being on the board of the Inner City Improvement District, or your playing duplicate bridge.

And if you're in a racial or ethnic minority and have the stomach for such a gambit, you may feel like listing your memberships in exclusive social and athletic clubs that haven't always had people with names or faces like yours. Everyone else should maintain a discreet silence on all clubs.

Now, as we wind up on resumes, let's look at several other items of purely personal information and how to handle them.

Age

Don't fall into the trendy trap of leaving age off your resume and omitting years from college degrees so it can't be calculated. True, employers can't ask. But voluntarily listing year, month, and day of birth subliminally shouts "forthright and self-confident," whereas concealing age just because the law permits you to do so sends out the opposite "vibes"...and raises a presumption that *you* think you may be over the hill.

Incidentally, employers who, in the late '60s and early '70s, considered 30 to 35 the ideal age now seem to feel that way regarding mid-to-late-40s, and have virtually no qualms about dynamic people in their 50s. They still find a young hotshot attractive. But they no longer insist on one. I absolutely refuse to discriminate on the basis of age, and have recently had candidates in their late 50s win out over excellent candidates ten and twenty years younger.

Education

List college degrees, *with years*...highest and latest degree first. Forget about Class President, and Varsity Letters. You've moved on to more recent and bigger achievements.

If you have several years but no sheepskin, say: "Completed three years toward B.A. at Syracuse University." And if you flunked out of several fine schools, say: "Two years of college, intermittently at Carleton, Dartmouth, and the University of Virginia." With no college, you may want to say, "Self-educated during an uninterrupted career," and then bail yourself out under the heading "Other Interests," with some suitably cerebral and cultural avocations.

Marital Status

Say "Married," "Divorced," or "Single," whichever applies and, if you wish, number of children (not names, ages, or with how many and which mates).

Gender

If you're a woman with a name like Lindsay or Leslie, or a man with a name like Carroll or Kelley, use a middle name to be more specific...or just let your reader be surprised when he or she meets you.

Height and Weight

Nice to put in if it's favorable; although women usually omit weight because it seems sexist to raise the subject. Overweight men and women might consider listing an optimistic weight toward which they're dieting, as a way of cushioning the inevitable visual shock with some advance notice.

Religion, Politics, and National Origin

Silence!   If the reader has a prejudice, you may stimulate it.

Race

Probably silence. For all minorities but African American, surnames dispel any impending visual surprise...hardly a major consideration anyway. For the person of color who wants to dispel surprise, mentioning support of any obviously African-American institution...possibly along with similar non-racially-defined institutions...will do the trick.

Health

Don't mention. It's fine, or you should be writing a will instead of a resume.

Picture

Never, *NEVER, NEVER!* Nobody could possibly be attractive enough to justify the narcissism implied by attaching a picture.

Chapter 13

The Classic Direct Mail Campaign
...still the #1 way to reach the many
decision-makers who might want to hire you

When I first wrote *RITES OF PASSAGE* **there was only one way to get your resume into the hands—and hopefully the minds—of people who were too distant or too numerous for you to reach face-to-face.**

The only alternative was to distribute your resume and cover letter by direct mail. And of course there were two types of recipients:

**(1) decision-makers who might want to hire you for
their own organization, and**
(2) recruiters who help them search for executives.

For reasons we've already discussed, classic direct mail is *still* **the only polite and practical way to reach the decision-makers themselves.**

Even if you could smoke out their e-mail addresses at the office and at home, you wouldn't spam them with your resume at either place. You're smart enough to realize how irked they'd be by that treatment...as you'd be too, if you were in their position.

Recruiters are a different matter. They make their livings by finding out about executives who might fit the openings they've been hired to fill. They now have channels specifically designed to receive and sort electronically submitted resumes. Using those channels—as we'll discuss in the chapter after this one—is exactly what you ought to do.

But for now, let's cover the skillful use of direct mail to reach and persuade the decision-makers who directly have the power (1) to hire you themselves...or (2) to instruct others—subordinates and recruiters—to give you very serious consideration.

Orbiting Your Spy-in-the-Sky Satellite

Now that your resume has been strengthened by direct mail copywriting, let's use it to launch a direct mail campaign...the nearest thing to scanning the globe via spy-in-the-sky satellite to find the opportunities you should know about.

Delivered by mail, a powerful resume can truly "be where you can't be and sell when you're not there."

And unlike every other method, direct mail can be almost limitlessly increased in power, when you're eager to change jobs. It can also be targeted toward exactly what you want, in terms of industry, size of company, location, or any other set of criteria.

Moreover, a direct mail campaign can be modified to perform its unique functions *secretly*. Believe it or not, you can use this powerful medium without letting your current employer discover you're "looking."

This chapter will tell you everything you need to know to make sophisticated use of direct mail: how many letters to send, whom to send them to, what to say in your covering note...and how to keep your current employer from finding out, if you want to look for a better job without risking the one you have.

| | | **The Accident of Timing** | | |

Timing is the problem.

Don't you wish we could crack open every job that might advance your career...and do so at precisely the time you're considering a move? We'd schedule all the retirements, firings, and additions-to-staff just when they'd create ideal options for you. Then, with just a few calls to your personal contacts, a few networking visits, and a handful of letters, you'd be exploring plenty of exciting opportunities.

Regrettably, Murphy's Law of Career Opportunity works the opposite way. Virtually all the jobs you'd be most interested in will be *filled* at the moment you decide to make a change.

Every company needs you at least once in fourteen years.

Unfortunately, the overwhelming odds are that they won't need you within the four to fourteen weeks that your inquiry will be considered current.

Face it. No matter how appropriate you are for a particular company, how much you'd like to work for them, and whom you're able to talk to inside that company...when they don't need you, they won't hire you. Appropriateness and desire don't count, if timing is off.

In the rare instance when the right need does exist, a compelling resume and covering letter sent to just the right person at just the right time will usually get you considered.

Unfortunately, the concepts of using direct mail to reach corporate decision-makers in a well-thought-out executive job-changing campaign have become widely known and understood. RITES OF PASSAGE has been a major contributor to that trend. As a result, the standards by which executive resumes and cover letters are judged have risen very high. Today a mediocre career presented in a mediocre resume-and-letter—*indeed, even a superb one in a mediocre resume-and-letter*—won't even get you a nibble! Don't waste time and money on direct mail when it's hopeless (beginning on page 257 we'll discuss when that is).

But for now let's assume your career *and* writing skills are strong enough for direct mail. Even so, timing is critical. What you send must arrive at *exactly* the right time. For three or four months your inquiry may be considered current. After that, you'll be presumed to have found your job, if you're really good. Otherwise, you'll be presumed *not* to be as good as you seemed. And if you've relocated, but are still willing to "talk," you'll seem unstable, unethical, or both.

Harsh and unfair presumptions! But they're almost universal. Might as well face them...and work around them.

Now for the bad...and good...news:

"Playing the numbers game" with direct mail is lots of work.

However, if you're willing and able to do it right, you're very likely to succeed.

The beauty of direct mail is that, depending on how hard you're willing to work, you can infinitely increase the number of contacts you make until you reach enough decision makers to be virtually certain that at least a few will actually need someone like you at the time you write them.

Everyone's odds are different, of course. Some folks at some times shouldn't even play. But typical odds these days are about *3 to 1 in favor* of an aggressive direct mail campaign generating a few attractive job leads for the very able person who makes an unstinting effort.

On the other hand, the odds are at least *199 to 1 against* the possibility that any one *letter* will arrive at the moment someone like the sender is actually needed. And the way the laws of probability work, you can't be sure that by sending only 200 letters you'll actually hit one recipient who has a need. To have a statistical shot at hitting on 1 out of 200 letters, *you must send at least 1,000 letters*. A few years ago, that number should have yielded 5 or 6 interested replies...an average of about 1 for each 200 letters sent out. Today, most companies have downsized. Their management pyramids are much flatter. And most CEOs and high-level executives are far less impulsive about hiring. Therefore, you may need several times as many letters to hit even fewer decision-makers at an opportune time.

Here's the classic formula. This effort...and more...will be needed:

Send at least 1,000 letters...not less.

Expect to receive 3 to 5 affirmative replies...not more.

**But *if you do it right*, those 3 to 5 meaningful replies
should lead to 2 or 3 interviews
and 1 or 2 offers of almost exactly what you want.**

When I lay out these numbers, most people say:

"But, John, can't I get by with *less than* 1,000 letters?"

And my answer is always the same:

"Absolutely! You only need five letters. But *which five?*"

You could be very lucky and have your first four or five letters bring encouragement. On the other hand, the last five might be the ones that pay off. And if you get less than five interested responses, you might get the two or three that lead to offers...or you might get the two or three where you interview but *don't* receive an offer.

Success is likely...if you enter the realm of *statistics*. But if you insist on merely *gambling*, then just send one letter. Or five, or 600, or 900. Only at (or much better *above*) 1,000 do you begin to play the odds. Don't complain if you get disappointing results from fewer letters. You haven't bypassed mere chance and grabbed statistical probability.

And of course the odds I'm quoting assume you're seeking a position for which you'll seem obviously relevant. If you're attempting a drastic switch of career fields, or if you're trying to overcome an apparent deficiency in your background or a glaring failure in your track record, you should probably double or triple the threshold number of 1,000 letters, in order to be realistic about the response you're likely to get. Or maybe you should ignore direct mail at *this* unfortunate juncture.

"John, I hate the idea of 1,000 letters just to get in the game."

"On the other hand, I love the idea of 2 or 3 interviews and 1 or 2 offers out of just 5 affirmative replies."

"Why such good odds after such poor ones?"

The reason you do so well after having done so poorly is that, although only a very few decision-makers will need what you're offering at the time you write, those few who *respond* will be the ones who *do* have a need. The only reason they reply is that they feel they may want to hire you.

And if you've done a good job on your mailing, the openings you'll be called about will be ones you prefer and are qualified for. And, of course, those are precisely the jobs you're likely to interview successfully for and wind up getting.

Also, since you're taking the initiative, rather than waiting for a recruiter to contact you, there's a good chance that your mailing may arrive before a search has been assigned. If so, you won't face the usual stiff competition from five or six additional recruiter-supplied candidates. Not only do you find out about the job; you're early enough to have a better-than-usual shot at getting it.

Whether by phone or letter, your positive reply will say, "Let's meet." Anything else is a negative reply.

Typical "positives":

> "I'm going to Europe for two weeks. Call me after the 15th so we can arrange to get together."

OR

> "I'm turning your material over to Jane Cole, President of our Keystone Division. You should be hearing from her within the next couple weeks. If not, give me a call."

Typical "negative":

> "You sound wonderful! We'll remember you forever, and call you as soon as anything arises here that might interest you."

Unless there's an appropriate opening within about three months after your mailing is received, you won't hear anything further. You'll be sandbagged by the twin presumptions that (1) if you're very good you'll have been hired by then and (2) if you're not hired by then, you probably weren't very good. Moreover, there'll be little reason to dig deeper than 12 to 14 weeks into the files, because similarly attractive and more recent mailings will have arrived since yours came in.

"But how can I possibly find decision-makers in 1,000 companies I might want to work for?"

Don't worry, you can.

Thanks to the Internet, that's a lot easier and less time-consuming to do today than ever before.

For years my advice on this subject was pretty grim. And if you're not yet hooked up to the Internet you'll still have to do things...

The Old Fashioned Way

I used to say, "the procedure, though arduous is simple," and continue with this advice:

> Make friends with the reference librarian at your nearest large public, university, or corporate library and ask to see all the directories listing companies you might want to work for. Appendix III of this book will familiarize you with the leading on-paper references your library may have. Narrow your choice to the two or three volumes that interest you most, and settle down with the one you consider first-priority.

> Glance at its entries from "A" to "Z," noting size of company, location, product line, number of employees, etc. If a company interests you, copy the information you need, and move on through that book...and others...until you've got upwards of 1,000 companies to write to.

> You'll use some of the same books we saw earlier as aids in "targeted networking." For general information, look at *Standard & Poor's Register* from McGraw-Hill; *Million Dollar Directory* from Dun & Bradstreet; and *Directory of Corporate Affiliations* and *Standard Directory of Advertisers* from National Register Publishing.

Check the industry-specific references listed in Appendix III. And contact the trade association of your industry, which probably publishes a directory.

I even suggested you buy favorite reference books so you could...

"scribble on it, or otherwise abuse it in any way that speeds your work."

Today's Way

Fire up your computer.

Go online.

Check out the wealth of information on companies that you can bring up on your own screen in your own home at any time of the day or night. Forget about going to the library during its limited hours, waiting for an always-checked-out-to-somebody-else reference book and, when you finally get your hands on it, laboriously copying its data in longhand or typing it into your notebook PC. What a pain!

Fortunately all that is history. Today it's *almost easy* to compile a mailing list. New sources of information—much of it no- or low-cost—are appearing on the Web nearly every month. See page 338 for sites that supply information on corporations. Look, too, at the search engines (p. 334-35), directories (p. 335), metasearch engines (an especially interesting group on p. 336), and the sure-to-expand category of search tool locator(s) on p. 337. Sources of information on associations (p. 339) will point you toward groups whose membership lists may identify potential employers you otherwise wouldn't have thought of.

Research has never been so easy!

Accurate copying of names and addresses is now quite simple. Just apply the "cut-and-paste" method to your online resources. Sure, you still have to edit. And yes, you still have to phone check. Moreover, if you want to concentrate on a certain geographic area, you may even pay for a mailing list of nearby companies and other institutions that—even after paying—you still have to refine and upgrade through phone calling.

Even so, compiling a job-change mailing list is a walk in the park, as compared to what it used to be.

Before you embark on a direct mail campaign, please be sure to read pages 480-86. I've put information there that could just as logically go here.

Why? That's my "Summing Up" chapter. I don't want you or anyone else to leave our time together and wind up in the situation of the fellow described on pages 480 and 481. You'll see what I mean.

**Once you've lined up your information resources, start
making your mailing list. Begin with the
most obvious companies you should contact
...and keep broadening until you have 1,000 or more
that really interest you. Once you get rolling,
they're not hard to find.**

Most people begin their mailing list with companies in their current industry. The top ten or twenty leap to mind. But you may be surprised to discover 100 or 200 smaller firms. Although probably offering less prestige and perhaps a lower salary, these companies may also offer advantages, such as less bureaucratic red tape, and even a major equity opportunity...things you may not get from the giants.

Also, you'll undoubtedly want to send *several* letters to each of the largest corporations. Those near the top of *Fortune*'s 1,000 list have many subsidiaries that are larger than entire companies lower on the list. And each has its own CEO, CFO, head of manufacturing, head of R&D, head of marketing and sales, etc. Look up the parent in National Register's *Directory of Corporate Affiliations*, and you'll probably wind up sending letters to five or ten separate business units in each of *Fortune*'s top 100 corporations.

Moreover, don't feel that you must arrive at your minimum of 1,000 letters by staying within your current field. If you're a financial or an MIS manager, your skills can be used in almost any industry. Might as well write to every one of the *Fortune* 1,000 and most of their subsidiaries. As head of manufacturing you're more specialized, but the processes you know are used for many other products than the ones you're making right now. If you're in marketing and sales, look for industries selling to the same customers, or through the same channels of distribution. Whatever your job, you have relevance to many industries including those from which your current company buys its components, raw materials, and supplies...and to which it sells its goods and services.

Don't worry, you'll soon have your list of 1,000 companies...and, if you're really aggressive, 2,000 or more.

One of the great advantages of direct mail is that it can be concentrated on a very specific target, in order to achieve objectives you might not accomplish any other way.

Remember, as you look at online information and/or peruse directories, that one of the main advantages of direct mail is that it can be *targeted*.

If, for example, you want to move to a different location...for later retirement in a warmer climate, or for putting your children through college, or for aiding your aging parents...you can make geography a key criterion (and there may be a state or a "metro" Web site or directory to help). If you want to move from a technologically obsolescent industry into one that you feel will be on the leading edge of technical and market growth for the next decade, you can look up the companies in your favorite fields and mail only to them.

If you're sick of dealing with products you find boring and of little real value to society, you can write only to companies which provide products or services you find interesting and intrinsically beneficial. And if it's big-company bureaucracy and politics you'd like to leave behind, you can mail only to companies with no more than 500 employees...or 100, for that matter, because you can readily identify companies that small and smaller.

You get the idea. The beauty of direct mail is that the choice of each corporate mailbox is entirely up to you. The industries, companies, and locations that recruiters present to you will be chosen at random, *except for a strong bias toward offering you more of exactly what you have right now*. On the other hand, the companies...and nonprofit organizations...you decide to mail to will be the ones you really want to explore.

"Making a list of 1,000 companies seems like so much work! Can't I have someone else do it?"

It's true that selecting a mailing list of more than 1,000 potential employers is a time-consuming project. So you may be tempted to delegate it to someone else...a secretary, a professional researcher, or an outplacement firm which, to save itself effort, may try to discourage you from conducting an extensive tailored-for-you direct mail campaign. *Resist the temptation!*

There's no substitute for your own decision-making. Only *you* can decide how you feel about various companies: products that interest you vs. ones that don't; large vs. small company; high vs. low prestige; preferred vs. unattractive location; entrepreneurial and fast-growing vs. stable and well-established organization; regional vs. national or global operation; risk-taking vs. conservative environment; etc.

Would you be willing to work for a casket company if it were in your preferred location...or if you could be its president? Would you work for a struggling company in real danger of going under if you could have the number-one or number-two spot? Would you leave your industry in order to stay in your present location? Which seemingly unlikely companies might actually appeal to you? No one else can answer these questions. This research...tedious though it may seem...must be done by you.

Moreover, the process of considering and deciding these potential trade-offs is a valid, creative exercise which will help you come to grips with your own talents, desires, and goals. No two people viewing the same information resources—even people with similar backgrounds—will come up with the same list. Each person makes his or her own subjective judgments...and gains new self-knowledge.

One thing I can assure you. I have never seen a dynamic, creative executive set out to develop a mailing list of 1,000...or even 2,000 or 3,000...companies and fail to do so. And never has such a person failed to comment enthusiastically afterward about what a valuable self-assessment process compiling his or her list turned out to be.

Write to the CEO
...or a person two levels above your target job.

At the same time you're scanning directories and deciding what companies you'll write to, you must also decide *what position* on their organization chart is your ideal point of contact. When you're writing about a top-level executive position, you certainly can't send out letters addressed "Dear Sir/Madam" or "To Whom It May Concern."

Who should you write to?

If you're expecting to be president and chief operating officer of an entire company, of course you'll direct your letter to the chairman/CEO; or if it's a subsidiary of a holding company, you'll address the HC's group officer responsible for that subsidiary or, better yet, the chief operating officer of the overall corporation.

My general suggestion is to address your letter *two levels above the job you want*...to the person who supervises the boss of the job you're aiming at.

Since titles can be misleading and lines of responsibility aren't always clear, it's much better to aim too high than too low.

There are several advantages of aiming high:

> First, the person just one level above your target job...your potential boss...may be in trouble. If so, he's certainly not going to invite you in and show you around...only to become his future competition. If you'd written to his boss or his boss's boss, you might even have been considered for *his* job, a level higher than you'd have guessed.

> Moreover, your letter gains "clout" by being passed downward. If your potential boss merely gets your letter in the mail, she can dispose of it casually. If it comes from a superior, she's far more likely to follow up.

> And the higher the person who receives your letter, the more likely he or she is to know of potentially appropriate positions in additional business units, subsidiaries and affiliates.

> Indeed, your letter may even spur a CEO or division-leader into taking action to replace a shaky manager...and you may be a candidate to fill the opening. Or the senior executive may want to talk to you because he knows that a whole department will be restaffed as soon as the head of it (as yet unaware) is let go.

Therefore, write to a real, living person—addressed by name and title—who has the function you think appropriate to control the boss of the job you've got your eye on.

Directories are approximately 35% out-of-date when they arrive...and go downhill from there.

Believe it or not, even corporations' own Web sites are surprisingly obsolete.

Someone should phone to check each name, title, and address. Fortunately, this is a job you can delegate.

The main reason a directory is marked "2002" is to get everyone to buy it, even though they already have one with "2001" on it.

Publishers, both on-paper and on the Internet, do make an effort to update, by sending out questionnaires and computer-accessing published announcements. But an incomplete effort at best. Worse yet, when a book is involved, it goes to the printer several months prior to the date on the cover. And chances are, you won't use it until several months after publication. Meanwhile, corporations continually reorganize. The average senior executive remains in any specific position only about one to three years (a few more if CEO), so you can see why more than a third of all on-paper published information is inaccurate.

Surprisingly, many corporations—including even some of the very largest—are sometimes several months behind in updating the senior executive rosters displayed on their Web sites. News releases of staff changes appear on the site at the same moment they're sent to the press. But bios and pics of the top brass are not tended to as promptly. Glance at a year of press releases (the topic headings scan quickly), before you accept the Web site roster as gospel.

Sending your mailing to the wrong person in the organization...or to someone no longer there...won't achieve your purpose. Therefore, someone should check by phone to see that each person an information source has indicated for your mailing actually has the title, function, and name-spelling listed. Unless you phone to confirm, about 350 of your 1,000 mailings will be wrongly addressed and probably worthless. In effect, you'll only be sending 650...not enough to escape chance and launch into statistical orbit.

Enlist any competent help you can get...secretary, temp, college student, spouse, mother, teenage daughter or son. Whoever calls should ask for the person's secretary...bypassing the operator/receptionist...and follow approximately this script:

> "I'm sending a letter and want to be sure I have the right information. He's Chief Executive?" (or some other title you seek). "And the exact spelling of his name...and the office address?"

Then probe for reassurance on other key points:

> "Executive Vice President...is that for the entire corporation, or for a specific subsidiary or division?"

> "Vice President of Operations...does that include responsibility for the Management Information Systems function?"

> "You say she's gone? Who took over her duties?"

> "Oh, *he's* not? Then who *would* be in charge?"

Unfortunately, the automatic activities of the outplacement industry have altered forever what you must do, and how effective you can be.

Recognize today's facts of life ...and work around them.

Fifteen years ago, you could have written to the Chief Executive of a *"Fortune* 500" company, and a secretary might have brought in your letter and resume along with the rest of the opened mail. And that might have happened even if your letterhead, letter, resume, and envelope were all obviously mass-produced...automatically run off using identical equipment, type face and pale-ivory paper.

But today that same CEO routinely receives dozens of such letters per week. Indeed some high-profile CEOs get that many per *day*. Not surprising, when you realize that these people are programmed into the word-processing equipment of scores of outplacement firms "counseling" thousands of executives. Here's what the secretary to one of those CEOs told me:

> "We get a big pile of outplacement letters every day. Usually they're the assembly-line kind, where everything matches. But sometimes they're disguised as personal letters with no resume enclosed. Those are easy to spot too, because a real personal letter doesn't begin 'Dear Mr.,' and the applicant wouldn't dare write 'Dear Harry.'

> "So on every employment letter, my assistant who opens the mail runs off a form response and sends the letter down to Human Resources for filing. Mr. _____ can't spend his time reading that stuff or he'd never get any work done. However, sometimes, if an extremely impressive letter and resume come along, and I know he might be looking for that kind of person, I put it into a folder he does glance at. 'Cream-of-the-crop,' we call it."

You see the problem.

Automatic mailings by the outplacement firms have virtually destroyed the receptivity of all their standard targets...the CEOs of America's leading companies. We'll design a letter for you that will stand out from the crowd. Even so, it may not escape the standardized handling of such letters in the offices that get bushels of them.

The only solution is to write at least 1,000 of your letters to senior executives who are **not** likely to be on the outplacement "hit lists." Send to Presidents of the appropriate *subsidiaries* of the largest companies. Send to heads of functional departments. Send to the CEOs of *smaller* companies that, although interesting to you, are not at the top of everyone else's list. And in *"Fortune 500"* companies, be especially careful to restrict yourself to the person *only two or three levels above* the job you want...probably not the CEO.

Don't feel you must ignore the most obvious targets. Do let your outplacement firm send your mailing to them...or send to them on your own. But supplement any mailing to these high-profile executives with at least 1,000 letters to others who aren't being deluged. That way you won't be counting on a normal reaction to your mailing among people whose circumstances are not at all normal.

Now let's design a covering letter that will do the best possible job of making whoever receives it want to look at your resume.

To get any attention at all for your resume, your covering letter absolutely must convey two essential messages regarding you as a human being, and you as the potential solution to an immediate business problem:

  1. This is a *fine person*, obviously desirable as an employee.

  2. He or she might be *for me*, possibly the executive I need right now.

If your papers in the reader's hand don't shout "fine person," then there's no point in reading them to see if your background might be what's needed right now.

So first of all we'll make sure your covering letter conveys the right personal impression.
Then we'll perfect the story it tells.

Right away and above all, your covering note must—at a glance—label you as a first-class individual, regardless of background.

You must instantly be perceived as an intelligent, well-educated, socially poised, tasteful person...dynamic not passive, self-confident and cordial but not obnoxiously pushy, oriented toward delivering what others are interested in, an effective communicator, basically competent and commonsensical, and maybe even *interesting!*

Now I'm not saying that you, I, or anyone else can instantly prove for sure that we have all those fine characteristics in 300 words or less. But we'd better not give off even the slightest subliminal hint that we *don't* have them. Your reader won't even consider the contribution you could make to the organization, if you don't seem like the right sort of person to bring into it.

There's a double standard. Employers will tolerate employees with less than ideal human characteristics if they're outstanding performers on the job. But they won't go out of their way to bring in anyone who doesn't "feel" right to begin with. And face it...perusing your resume is going out of the way. The easiest reaction is just to throw it in the wastebasket. *Your covering note must not give off any negative "vibes."* And in that regard I submit the following:

Don't seem insensitive, bumbling, and not customer-oriented.

You've already avoided the biggest pitfall in this direction by phoning ahead to make sure you've got your reader's name-spelling, function, and title right. Your letter has come to the right person, and has approached him or her with impeccable courtesy.

Avoid looking tasteless and cheap.

Recent college graduates can get by with plain typing paper for their covering letter. You can't. Good quality stationery with your name, home address, and phone number, steel-engraved at the top, is ideal. Monarch size (7 1/4" x 10 1/2") looks especially nice clipped to a standard-size (8 1/2" x 11") resume, and if you boil your message down to attention-grabbing brevity, it'll fit on a Monarch page. Paper should be crisp, with rag/cotton fiber, in classic white or a *very* pale tint of grey or ivory. Ink should be black (or possibly grey, navy, or deep maroon).

Get both Monarch and standard-size stationery...mostly Monarch, because you'll use it for the "cover letter" that accompanies your resume (also for "thank yous," etc.). Envelopes, on the other hand, should be mostly #10 (business-size), because they will hold your resume, in addition to your Monarch letter. Put your return address on the envelope-flap, rather than the front (on both sizes), because that looks more like truly "personal" stationery. And before you buy, check the Yellow Pages for "Engravers"...not "Stationery, Retail." Buy proper quantities for a direct mail campaign, and you'll get the same low prices accountants, lawyers, and businesses enjoy.

Unfortunately about eight weeks' lead time is required for true steel engraving. If you're rushed, or short on cash (see p. 473-74), substitute ordinary printing. *Or use plain but rich paper and a laser printer, applying a letterhead in contrasting type as you print your letters.* Keep the design understated...three or four lines, each no more than 2 1/4" long...with your phone and fax numbers and your Internet address much smaller but legible on the bottom line.

Unless your covering letter describes unusual circumstances that make it appropriate, never use your current employer's stationery.

Don't appear pretentious.

Veer toward modesty and matter-of-factness in name, address...and stationery. Imagine a letterhead from "Cottsworth O.M. Kensington-Smithers IV," saying he lives at "Nine Chimneys," followed by street number, etc. What fun it would be to throw *his* resume into the waste basket! Moreover, since you're sending a business letter, avoid all gimmicks on the stationery... family crest, house-picture, yachting flags, crossed polo mallets, colored or shaggy borders, etc.

Avoid looking like the passively-packaged product of an outplacement firm.

Today so many fired executives are being processed by outplacement firms, that every retainer recruiter and almost every senior executive knows the #1 tell-tale sign: perfectly matching paper and electronic typesetting used for stationery, covering-letter, resume, and envelope.

Following the theory that "colored papers stand out on an executive's desk," most of these firms eschew classic white and turn instead to a distinctive shade I call *"Outplacement Ivory."* And of course everything matches, because it's all produced at the same time on the same paper by the same equipment.

"What's wrong," someone might say, "if my mailing openly proclaims that the people who let me go nonetheless cared enough to buy me outplacement services?"

Only this, in my opinion: Your reader will be more interested in what you have to say if he or she feels it's been written and sent solely by you, rather than by someone else who's been paid to get you out of one office and into another. There's absolutely nothing wrong with accepting outplacement help.

But you'll seem much more confident and creative...far less hapless and passive...if you appear to be preparing and sending your own correspondence.

Therefore, make sure your covering note and resume *don't* match. A Monarch-size note is especially helpful. The smaller paper forces impressive brevity; reveals at a glance that your resume *doesn't* match; is consistent with genuine personal stationery (*never* 8½" x 11"); and is inconsistent with outplacement cover letters, (*always* 8½" x 11"). Your note can be run on a quality laser-printer, and your resume can be done the same way. However, if you're printing a large quantity of resumes—say 500 or more—it probably won't cost you much more to have them done by true offset printing, rather than laser printing. That way, your resume, when mailed, will arrive looking immaculately sharp and clean. Laser printing, especially on textured paper often arrives looking smudged. Use classic white paper for your resume, and a different texture or shade of white, or else *pale* ivory or grey, for your cover letter.

So much for appearances.
Now let's get to the content of your covering letter.

This is your "free sample."
It demonstrates that you're a "fine person"
in terms of thinking and communication skills.

Only after evaluating "how you say it"
will your reader weigh "what you say."

To succeed, your covering letter must be pleasantly businesslike in tone, and conjure up the image of a competent, self-confident executive who's letting a colleague know that he or she is available to help, if there's a need. Somehow, a letter from such a person is never a jarring intrusion, whereas a letter from the typical "job applicant" always is.

The difference is dramatic. So few people are able to write a really good covering letter that, when one arrives, it stands out like a beacon. Its author is immediately given "plus points" for outstanding executive communication skills, and the resume is almost always scanned, in the hope that it offers something the recipient...corporate officer or recruiter...can take advantage of.

Fortunately, creating such an impressive covering letter isn't difficult, if you incorporate the four central attributes that outstanding ones have and poor ones don't. Be sure your covering letter:

1. is not too long. Brevity is essential! Get right to the point, and leave out all the useless and obnoxious things that "job applicants" put in their letters.

2. has a central theme. Your message must be arrestingly clear...not diffuse and blurred.

3. offers benefit to the reader, rather than merely harping on what *you* want.

4. deals with compensation.

Later on I'll cover point 1 by giving you a list of stuff to get rid of, so your letter won't be cluttered with the unproductive statements "job applicants" put in theirs. And after that, I'll show you in detail how to handle compensation to your advantage. But first let me cover points 2 and 3 by showing you a covering letter that has a clear central theme (point 2) of benefit to the reader (point 3).

The following letter is from Sam Sage, whose resume we've already reviewed. Sam's an exceptionally competent executive. And from the minute we first glance at his covering letter, we begin to see how very special he is. No nonsense. No wasted words. And no claims that aren't fully backed up by his accompanying resume.

Samuel P. Sage
219 Waring Drive
Denton, New Jersey 07299
Phone (201) 719-0932 Fax (201) 719-0933
spsage@aota.com

(Date)

Mr. Sherman J. Summit
Chairman and Chief Executive
Integrated Standard Corporation
4225 Scenic Parkway
Lovelytown, New York 10591

Dear Mr. Summit:

Could I help you as a divisional president...or corporate chief marketing officer?

The $1.3 billion company I've helped build over the past five years as Chief Marketing Officer has more than doubled sales, increased profits nine-fold, and raised ROI from 3.6% in '96 to over 28% in '01.

We've done so well, in fact, that we've just been bought out at 30 times our estimated '02 earnings by a company that's absorbing us into their own operations.

Although I'm far more interested in a fine company and an intriguing challenge than merely in money, you should know that in recent years my total compensation has been in the range of $420,000 to $550,000.

May we talk?

Sincerely,

Sam Sage

Samuel P. Sage

SPS:mj

Editor's Note...

For John Lucht's in-depth help with your own personal job-winning cover letter use pages 136 to 163 of EXECUTIVE JOB-CHANGING WORKBOOK.

Sam rang all the bells!

Sam's central theme is sure to dilate the pupils and speed the pulse of any red-blooded CEO...impressive advances in sales, profit, and ROI.

For many letter-writers those claims would be too bold. They'd be mom-pie-'n-flag *clichés* that the accompanying resume couldn't possibly live up to. But Sam's got the stuff. So he flaunts it.

Notice too, that Sam didn't waste words on anything that's obvious. His resume *is* enclosed...no need to say so. And *of course* Sam would like Mr. Summit to get in touch with him...or Sam may call Mr. S. No need to talk about that either.

Moreover, Sam didn't invoke self-praising adjectives and adverbs. Rather, by making numerical claims, he directed attention to his resume, which is packed with specific facts and figures that *demonstrate* what he can do. Sam also treated compensation in an advantageous way that we'll discuss later.

Above all, the sparseness and directness of Sam's letter tell us a lot about him. He's an exceptionally dynamic, clear-thinking person. On the rare occasions when a letter from someone like Sam comes in, the reader will always glance at the attached resume. Indeed Mr. Summit became quite interested, as you'll see later in Appendix I.

||| **Changing Your Letter for Recruiters** |||

These examples are addressed to employers. For recruiters, merely change your opening question from "Do *you* need...?" to "Does *one of your clients* need...?" or "Are you looking for...?" Replacing just a few words in the first one or two sentences will neatly reposition any letter, without destroying the brevity and directness that are just as attractive to recruiters as they are to employers.

Note, however, that the next chapter will show you new technology that can bring you to the attention of every top retainer recruiter with incredible ease. You'll still send your elegant mailing to recruiters you know personally and to any stellar ones you're introduced to by personal contacts and through networking. But you probably won't bother with personally addressed letters to the hundreds of others who thus far are nothing to you but names on a list.

Karen S. Kash
12 Countinghouse Road
Pittsburgh, Pennsylvania 15213
Phone (412) 999-1814 Fax (412) 999-2816
kskash@apremidia.com

(Date)

Mr. Peter R. Pinnacle
Chairman
Acme Consolidated Corporation
6902 Postal Turnpike
Pittsburgh, Pennsylvania 15224

Dear Mr. Pinnacle:

Could Acme Consolidated...or one of your largest divisions...
benefit from a strong chief financial officer?

Having been continually challenged and rapidly promoted at
U.S. Heavy Industries...last year I became our youngest CFO
since USHI was founded in 1869...I've never before thought
about joining any other employer.

But now we're shutting down our steel mills and home office
here in Pittsburgh, and headquartering at our insurance
company in Hartford. Relocation would be a hardship for my
family. So I'm contacting a few outstanding Pittsburgh area
companies before committing to a move.

If you have a need, I could do an excellent job for you.

Sincerely,

Karen Kash

Karen Kash

P.S. Money is <u>not</u> my main consideration, but in recent years
my total compensation has been in the range of $240,000 to
$360,000.

Editor's Note...

For John Lucht's in-depth help with your own personal job-
winning cover letter use pages 136 to 163 of EXECUTIVE
JOB-CHANGING WORKBOOK. Available at all booksellers.

Matt Ginyus
146 College Point Drive
Skilton, Massachusetts 01128
Phone (413) 112-2465 Fax (413) 112-2466
mattgin@trionet.com

(Date)

Mr. Gerrard Global, Chairman
International Interchemicals, Inc.
1202 Industrial Beltline
Wilmington, Delaware 19808

Dear Mr. Global:

Could any of your laboratories...corporate or divisional...be more innovative?

If so, perhaps I can help.

Within the spending limits of a young fast-growing $196 million company, and with only a 26-person laboratory, my staff and I during the past five years have produced 14 commercially exploitable new compounds...6 of which are already on the market, providing 72% of current revenue. During that time I've personally received 8 patents, and my staff have received 46.

Having proven what I can produce for a small company, I'd like to do a lot more for a much larger organization.

An exciting challenge will be the main reason, if and when I move. But you should know that in recent years my total compensation has been in the range of $190,000 to $270,000.

Please keep my inquiry confidential, Mr. Global. The published rumors that we may be acquired have prompted me to think about the world outside DrexelChem. Nevertheless, I don't want to disturb either my staff or the rest of the company just by considering alternatives.

Thank you.

Sincerely,

Matt Ginyus

Matt Ginyus

Different Pokes from Different Folks!

Different as they were, all three of the letters you just read would have stimulated the interest of any reader who needed what they offered.

Why? Because each:

1. was **not too long,** and

2. had a **central theme**

3. of **benefit to the reader.**

Sam Sage presented his outstanding track record as a marketing virtuoso-cum-general-manager. Matt Ginyus amply demonstrated his ability to get results in the laboratory. And Karen Kash showed that she was an outstanding employee, who'd never have been available, if not for exceptional circumstances. Her letter said, "Help yourself to someone else's superstar."

Of course, the very best thing about each of these letters is that only one person in all the world could have written it. Each person came to life through mere words on paper, because those words were clear and specific, and *applied only to him or her.* There were none of the vague generalities that give most such letters a boring fill-in-any-job-applicant similarity.

So before we move on to point **4, dealing with compensation,** let's list some things you'll make sure to *leave out*, which litter the letters of "job applicants."

OMIT...OMIT...OMIT!

Everything obvious, and all clichés. Letters from "job applicants" always state the obvious, and lean heavily on clichés: "Enclosed please find..." "I would like to take this opportunity to..." "This letter will serve to..." "Here is a copy of my resume for your review and consideration." "If my background and accomplishments are of interest, I would appreciate hearing from you." "Thank you in advance for your interest."

Self-evaluations. Don't bother describing your personality or your performance. You're biased, so we can't take your word for it. And if you enclose or quote something from a psychologist, we'll *know* you're on the defensive. Don't say, "I'm a results-oriented executive with a proven track record," or that you're "intelligent," "analytical," "profit-minded," "honest," "hardworking," "loyal," "reliable," or any of that stuff. "Job applicants" use those words.

Willingness to relocate. "Ho hum," if you're willing to move for a great opportunity. So is everyone else. Don't bring up relocation unless the fact that you won't relocate is the reason a lucky local employer has received your letter. If your employer...or your specific job...is leaving town and you don't want to, you've got a good believable reason for writing your letter. Exploit it. Otherwise say nothing about relocation. And don't give personal hardship details. Just say, "My family and I prefer to stay in Indianapolis." The fact that your spouse's real estate practice brings in twice what you do, or that your mother has a health problem doesn't make you any more attractive as a potential employee.

"Further information and references." Every "job applicant" is "pleased to supply further information and a list of references." But you're smart enough not to say so, and thus you further differentiate your letter from theirs. Besides, your "sales representative" resume...unlike theirs...has "further information" built right in. The next thing your reader will need or want is to see you.

The Mafia approach. Don't end your letter with a warning that you intend to make a follow-up phone call. "Job applicants," salespeople, and Cosa Nostra do that. If your reader is a prospective "buyer," he or she will probably take the next step. The "foot-in-the-door" approach needlessly makes you look pushy, because without the warning you are just as free to call as with it. Indeed, including it may prompt the reader to give orders to block your call.

And now "point 4"...current compensation. Rightly or wrongly, it's the #1 screening criterion.

Every employer wants to know that "money is right" before "wasting time" on any candidate.

The ideal covering letter gives that assurance ...and rushes the reader right into your resume.

One of the most important factors in establishing the "this-person-might-be-***for-me***" reaction on the part of your reader...and indeed any employer... is your level of compensation.

Yet most executives omit any mention of money...either current or desired. They worry that some employers may be frightened off because the figure is too high, and others may lose interest because it's too low. And any employer who winds up making an offer, they fear, may propose less than he otherwise would, if he knows what they're accustomed to.

What these wary executives don't realize is that by *not* mentioning salary, they've created a situation that's even *more* limiting. Compensation is the *single most important factor* in categorizing people as appropriate or inappropriate for a particular job. For employers...and executive recruiters as well...it provides a quick and easy way to figure out whether a candidate is "the right size." Titles can be misleading, and the importance of a given position can vary considerably from one organization to the next. Salary remains the most reliable index, since it's determined by the marketplace.

So the challenge is to mention compensation in a way that encourages consideration. You want every potential employer to look at your money and think:

> "Well, that's in the ballpark. He might be *for me*."

Obviously, if your money is above what the position pays, she'll figure she can't attract or hold you. And if you're earning far less, that's a pretty good indication that you're not yet ready for the responsibility the position entails.

So how do you handle compensation?

Here's a magic sentence that will do the best possible job of getting you considered:

> "Although other factors such as (fill in your own non-financial 'turn-ons') are of primary importance to me, you should know that in recent years, my total compensation has been in the range of _____ to _____."

To appreciate what that disclosure accomplishes, you must first:

Meet the weasels.

In consumer-products marketing, there's a term for wordings that state the truth precisely enough to wiggle through the narrow openings defined by company attorneys and government regulators. They're called *"weasels,"* after the squirmy little animals that are almost impossible to catch.

The three key phrases..."weasels"...in your compensation statement are: *"in recent years,"* *"total compensation,"* and *"in the range of."* Used together, they open the way for you to state, *perfectly truthfully*, a broad range that will make you seem "right *for me*" in the mind of every reader who controls a position you could possibly be interested in and qualified for.

The *"low-end"* figure will be the least take-home pay you'd consider, assuming the job offers major advantages beyond immediate compensation. After all, the preface to your "three-weasel" sentence said, in effect, "money isn't everything to me." For this bottom figure, use a round number that approximates your tax-return "income-from-employment" for a recent lean year.

For the *"high-end"* figure, start with your top base salary within the past few years. Then add everything else you're getting:

> performance bonuses (use the figures that...combined with base... represent your best year);

> the amount of your employer's contribution to FICA;

> the value of medical, dental, and life insurance provided by your employer;

> money paid by the firm into pension and profit-sharing accounts in your name (whether or not fully vested);

> any other tax-deferred compensation, such as annualized incremental value of your stock options, and your employer's matching contribution to thrift and stock-purchase plans;

> and the pre-tax value of miscellaneous perks, such as a company car (less your pay-back for personal use), city and country club memberships, the right to use the company condo in Nassau for two weeks vacation per year, and the college scholarship your child receives under a competitive company-wide program.

You can even estimate this year's raise, and include that in the base of your "high-end" figure.

Thus, using the three "weasels," you can truthfully state a wide range. You'll probably end up with numbers that are $50,000 to $90,000 or $150,000 apart...maybe even more. *It's perfectly reasonable for the second figure to be 50% larger than the first:* $150,000 to $230,000 for example, or $390,000 to $520,000.

Let's imagine that you've specified a range of $180,000 to $250,000.

First we'll picture your letter reaching the CEO of a young growth company with great prospects, but with venture capitalists on its Board who don't want Management draining its life blood with high salaries. This CEO looks at your low number, $180,000, and figures she can realistically reach *up* to you. She can't offer more than $115,000 in cash compensation. But you'll have the opportunity to purchase at 50 cents per share 50,000 shares of treasury stock the company expects to take public at about $20 per share within 18 to 24 months; and as an officer, you'll have a company car. She's pretty sure she can grab your attention. So she calls to suggest a get-acquainted lunch.

Now picture the CEO of a large multi-national corporation who must fill a job he thinks is worth a little over $300,000. He sees your top figure of $250,000...assumes it represents your most recent year...and reaches *down* to you. After all, you're probably expecting an increase of at least 10% or 20% for making a move. Obviously, your next job should be in the neighborhood of $300,000...just what he expects to pay. So he asks his assistant to give you a call.

As you see, your "three-weasel" range of $180,000 to $250,000 has actually triggered a *"for me"* response in the minds of two very differently situated employers. You're being considered for jobs paying anywhere from about $125,000 (with car—plus stock) to a bit over $300,000 a year. Cash compensation on one job is more than 100% above the other.

Moreover, you haven't given up any negotiating flexibility. You've got a shot at a job that pays even more than the top figure you mentioned. And of course you can always settle for less, depending on the job's advantages that extend beyond immediate in-pocket cash.

Mentioning money...and having it "right" for your reader...encourages him or her to consider your resume. And using a "three-weaseled" range lets you be "right" for every reader whose job could possibly be right for you.

||| **And now a word of warning...** |||

**Don't fritter away the #1 advantage of direct mail.
Avoid the hill-beyond-the-hill-beyond-the-hill dilemma.**

Just about everybody refuses to believe they can be as good as they are, send out lots of letters describing how good that is, and not be swamped with phone calls, appointments, and interviews. Worrying that they can't cope with too many responses, they hold back on their mailing, sending only a portion of their ultimate total per day or per week.

Don't make their mistake!

Don't drop your spy-in-the-sky satellite back to earth. Don't forgo the instant reconnaissance that only direct mail can give you. Instead, send your letters everywhere at once, so you'll look everywhere at once. Do an *aerial scan of the entire desert.* Survey every oasis. See all three, four, or five of them... simultaneously. Then you'll be able to pick the greenest.

Sending only a few letters, when you could have sent them all, puts you back on the ground, where you can only see as far as the horizon.

You're still looking for water in the desert. But now you're riding a camel. Suddenly you spot a brackish little watering hole in the valley below. Should you head for it? Or should you keep to the high ground and peer into the valley beyond the next hill? Maybe that's where you'll find the main outflow of the underground stream this little trickle merely foretells. If so, the water will be cool, sweet, and abundant. There'll be plants, fruit trees, and maybe even a comfortable bed for the night. And if not beyond the next hill...then surely beyond the one after that. But what if there's only sand? Then you'll fervently wish you hadn't passed up the meager security of this little spot.

You see my point.

Believe me when I say that 1,000 letters won't bring more than 3 to 5 interested responses...2 or 3 interviews...and 1 or 2 offers. *And that's **not** too much "action" to handle all at once.*

No matter how good you are, *timing* will be wrong at almost every company you contact. So send all your letters at once and get all your offers simultaneously. Then you can choose the best the market has for you at any moment in time. What's more, you'll *know* it's the best, and not a compromise you feel forced into, because you can't risk waiting to see what's behind the hill behind the hill.

Another mistake is to neglect direct mail until very late in an all-out job-changing campaign.

Ideally, it comes right up front.

For some reason many people think direct mail should only come *after* personal contact, networking, and reaching out to executive recruiters, in an aggressive job search.

There's only one logical reason I can think of to justify this view, and it's because direct mail is a lot of work. So most people don't bother with it, until after the other methods have been tried and seem to be failing.

That's really shortsighted. The *first* thing needed is an ideal resume...one written so persuasively that it could be effective when merely delivered by mail. This document is your best possible "leave-behind" in personal contact, networking, and dealing with recruiters. And when it's prepared, you've already done about half the work of your direct mail campaign.

Moreover, just as preparing your "sales representative" resume forces you to study your achievements and determine what you'll say about them, preparing your mailing list forces you to survey prospective employers and determine where you're most likely to do well and gain satisfaction. Shouldn't this strategic analysis come at the beginning, rather than the end, of your job-changing efforts?

Bear in mind that:

1. Your personal and networking contacts will only know a very few of the possibilities that exist for you in the world of work, and

2. The retainer recruiters will only show you a very few of the opportunities they're working to fill.

So hurry up and get the five or six leads your 1,000-letter direct mail campaign can generate.

Also take advantage of the 200 or 300 rejection letters you'll get. Sift them carefully to find the unusually cordial ones...perhaps 10 or 20...from people who were so impressed by your mailing that they really *did* wish they had a place for you. Since they're at high levels in industries and companies that appeal to you, they're ideal early contacts for your networking campaign, which would otherwise be narrowly based on the people you already know.

Begin your "search" by skimming your best personal contacts and alerting the retainer recruiters you're already acquainted with..and also by alerting the executive search community in the quick and easy ways we'll discuss in the next chapter. If that doesn't solve your problem within the first month you're "looking," then chances are you're in for a full-scale effort. If so, you may save many months in the long run, by devoting two or three weeks to direct mail right at the outset.

|| | **We've looked at the sunny side of direct mail.** |||
    Now let's examine its dark side.

Some products can be sold by direct mail and some can't. Same with people. It works for some and not for others.

Moreover, the requirements for direct mail success are exactly the same for both people and products. So let's talk only products for a moment, and bypass the ego and emotion that make it nearly impossible to talk about ourselves as people. Here are the make-or-break questions:

1. Is the product special? Exceptionally high quality? Uniquely useful? Then we're interested. But if it's ordinary...something we see in every store all over town...we'll pay no attention at all, when we get a letter about it.

2. How many potential purchasers? Is this something nobody has and everyone wants? Something everyone has and nobody needs two of? Something nobody has and nobody wants? There are some things a letter can't *fail* to sell; and others it can *never* sell.

3. Is the description enticing? Maybe the product is truly wonderful...surpassing everything else. But if the description makes it seem like something we see in every store all over town, we yawn, and throw the letter into the wastebasket.

You, I, and everyone else have no difficulty accepting and dealing with such tough, obvious facts about products. But seeing ourselves....our own backgrounds, achievements, and persuasive writing skills...with such merciless objectivity is an entirely different matter.

That's why I'm glad we're not face-to-face right now. I can deliver some harsh facts and—even if your gun is loaded—you can't shoot the messenger.

For most people during most of their career, direct mail is one of the four components of an all-out job search. But for some of us at certain times, direct mail cannot possibly work Even the Internet activities we'll discuss in Chapter 14—although worth doing because they are so easy—are likely to fail when a person's employment facts are unappealing or poorly presented.

Then methods 1 and 2...skillful handling of personal contacts and unrelenting networking among strangers...are the only really good bets. At such an unfortunate moment, whatever the Postal Service delivers cannot be both truthful and persuasive. And the respectable retainer recruiters will not risk their credibility by pleading the job seeker's currently weakened case.

Direct mail plays the odds.

And for some people at some times, those odds are almost unplayable.

Here are five surprisingly prevalent situations in which sending out your letter and resume probably won't pay back your mailing expense:

1. Too many too-brief jobs. It's very difficult to seem special...exceptionally high quality, or uniquely useful...when you haven't been in place long enough to generate impressive recent accomplishments to include in your letter and resume.

Sometimes, of course, brief jobs *can* be favorably written up. For example, the boss who recruited you to a new company may have been so impressed with your first six months' achievements (describe them!) that he took you with him to a more exciting company. But then a takeover swept you both into a third company, where you were both forced out. Written up as a three-year segment of great work for the same superior, those three short jobs may look okay.

Remember, however, that employers all realize that it takes the better part of a year for you to dig in and get established. During that time you're more pain and drain, than gain. So even if you do wonderful things for a few months afterward, but then walk out, it's right back to pain and drain with someone new. Your former employers are *not* thrilled. And readers of your mailing probably won't be either.

Face-to-face...preferably with supportive friends and acquaintances..is the only effective way to convince a potential employer that "this time it will be different." For direct mail to work, the premise has to be "more of the same."

2. Not special enough. What if you've been a good, honest, kind, congenial, competent, zestfully healthy employee, with an engaging sense of humor, a great home life, outstanding kids, a wide and devoted coterie of friends, and lots of commendable civic involvement? And what if, at work, you were never absent, never late, never given a poor performance review, and never unwilling to sacrifice an evening or a weekend to cope with a crisis?

But now you're looking for a new job.

Can even the finest direct mail copywriter make you as tantalizing as that dastardly, driven, and devious workaholic with the string of remarkable accomplishments that even those of us who detest him are forced to applaud?

No. I like you a lot better than I like him. And I'd much rather have you as a friend, a neighbor, or an in-law. But in job-hunting, you'll do far better face-to-face with the many people you already know and the strangers they'll enthusiastically introduce you to, than you will if you ask the Postal Service or even the Internet to do your communicating.

And besides, with your fine connections in your community, you're likely to find a fulfilling job right where you are. One of the great advantages of direct mail is that it can extend your search to unfamiliar companies in far-off places. But are they where you want to go?

And what do the nay-sayers mean, "Not special enough"? You're plenty special...among the people you're special to. So make absolutely the best resume you can. Develop it into a "sales representative" on paper. And then put it into circulation *in person*. Don't dump it in the mail box!

3. Changing field or function. Suppose you've toiled for years in a certain field or performing a specific function. You're exceedingly proficient. You've racked up enviable accomplishments, and in the process you've become quite well paid.

But now you've had it. You're *bored, BORED, BORED!*

Or the handwriting is on the wall. Your field or function is a downer. And you want to get into something more promising.

Or maybe you're retiring from the military or the diplomatic corps, leaving the clergy or teaching, walking out on your family's business, or ending an ill-fated entrepreneurial venture.

I could go on and on. But you get the idea. You've been something significant for quite a while, and you're very good at it. You have an expert's accomplishments and, hopefully, you're earning an expert's pay. If you decide to continue, you can probably write a great "sales representative" resume and get a similar or better job for the same or better money.

But no! You want to do something different. Something in which you're *not* yet an expert, something other people know a lot more about than you do. And you'd like to keep right on making your usual or better money, while somebody gives you on-the-job training, or patiently waits for you to bring yourself up to speed...somebody who could just as easily hire an already-established expert with lots of experience and a string of achievements that are just as impressive in the matching field or function as yours are in a foreign one.

Isn't that too much to expect from just a letter and a resume—no matter how elegant—merely dropped into the mail by a complete stranger interested only in his or her preferences, and not the recipient's needs? Usually it is.

Generally speaking, when you're trying to stretch-fit yourself into an entirely new situation, direct mail is *not* a realistic option. Nor is the executive recruiter who, to earn his pay, is slavishly working to "fulfill the specifications."

When a "leap of faith" is required, you're much more likely to achieve it face-to-face through your already-supportive personal contacts and the open-minded strangers you meet and impress through networking.

4. Special, but you can't, or refuse to, communicate. You may be very special indeed. But if you can't look shrewdly into your career and choose as the theme of your letter and the show-pieces of your resume the things you've done that will best recommend you to a new employer...and if, having chosen, you can't distill them into a very few clear, simple, straightforward, and non-self-praising words...then you'd better not waste your time and money on a direct mail campaign.

Direct mail is merely another form of advertising. And with all advertising, success or failure depends on whether or not it identifies the most strongly-felt consumer need the product can satisfy, and then persuades the consumer that the product *will* meet that need.

If you insist on writing a cover letter centered on what you want, rather than what the employer wants that you provide (based strictly on specific past accomplishments that are likely to be repeated, rather than self-praising adjectives and evaluations)...and if your resume is nothing but the usual recitation of times, titles, and responsibilities...then don't take it to the mail box. It won't do you any good at all, unless you hand it over in person, concealing the self-centeredness and insensitivity your cover letter would otherwise have revealed, and unless you're right there extolling the achievements your resume leaves out.

If you can't, or refuse to, create a direct mail resume...then by all means, don't undertake a direct mail campaign.

5. Not very good and your mailing proves it. Remember, whatever you send in the mail is a free sample of your intellect and your performance. If it's obviously inferior, nobody will respond. Nobody will invite you in for an interview. And you'll never know why.

Just one example will illustrate:

A couple years ago, I heard of a man who sent out 5,000 letters and resumes and didn't receive a single affirmative response. Intrigued, I invited him to come in and bring me a sample of his mailing. He sounded great on the phone. And in person he was a perfect "10" in executive looks, tailoring, and personality.

The resume was on two pages in reverse chrono format with latest jobs on page one, dwindling to personal data at the bottom of two. I noticed right away that his four latest jobs were within the past 5 years. And virtually no accomplishments were stated (not surprising, since there was no *room* for any, and probably little *time* for any in such brief jobs).

Why, I wondered, would a top marketing executive spend his own money on such an unpersuasive advertisement? But then I *glanced again.* *"Forget the brief jobs,"* I thought. *"Look at the **words!"*** Condensed, here's his first page...the most important 50% of his resume:

Name/Address/Phone

Objective
(lengthy)

To do great marketing for a marketing-oriented company.

Summary
(lengthy)

A Marketing executive experienced in all phases of marketing.

Work History

Company A	Vice President, Marketing and Sales
Company Y	Senior Vice President, Marketing
Company X	Vice President, Marketing and Sales
Company W	Vice President, Marketing

What's wrong with it?

This fellow is spending lots of his own money on an ad campaign with *no advertising!* Over and over it says, "I am a marketing person looking for a marketing job"...not "I am a *good* marketing person, as these accomplishments prove." Just the four titles on page one tell us he does marketing. And mailing his resume says he's job-hunting. The "Objective" and "Summary" take up the top half of page one, 50% of his best space...25% of his total space...and yet they tell us absolutely nothing that isn't obvious!

Should we hire this Senior VP to make sure our corporation gets maximum effectiveness from every dollar it spends on advertising? No way! Forget the dark cloud of four jobs in five years. Here's a total eclipse of marketing judgment, as *demonstrated* by his resume. He has sent you, me, and 4,998 other people a free sample of his work. And not one of us has liked it enough to want more!

The same thing happens when an educator's resume displays poor grammar (hazardous to the rest of us too); a lawyer's isn't logical; a CFO's leaves us wondering whether some of his figures are pre- or post-tax; a President's or General Manager's speaks only of sales and not profits, and confuses ROI. You get the idea.

Your resume is always scrutinized as a sample of your work, whether you mail it, or walk in with it. But the risk is greater when you mail, because you're not there to distract attention. If you're not very good and your resume proves it, don't go near the Post Office!

A bit more, before we leave this fellow. You're probably thinking, "Yes, John, but doesn't he also represent fault #4, 'Can't, or refuses to, communicate'"? Yes, that too. His merely saying "Marketing, marketing" rather than "Good marketing" is also a #4 failing. But since communication is the very *essence* of marketing, he proves he's no good at his *job*. Failure or refusal to communicate under #4 could be accomplished by someone who told us "Manufacturing, manufacturing" rather than "Good manufacturing," but we wouldn't know from just his resume that he can't do his job. Obviously too, this man displays fault #1, "too many, too short jobs." Recommendation: Non-stop networking (ultimately successful for this fellow).

How Many vs. How Good?

Just 20 outstanding letters and resumes...or even one or two...are far more likely to get you an interview than tons of mediocre ones. Statistical odds are overwhelmingly against a few succeeding. But tons of unimpressive...or as we've seen, *negatively* impressive...letters and resumes won't do any good at all. And mailing them does a lot of harm, because it wastes precious time and money.

So I warn you against this very real danger. If and when you're ever unemployed, you'll be under lots of stress, and you'll tend to become the panicky soldier in the old cliché:

"Ready...fire...aim!"

Please be careful. Try to get back into the same objective frame of mind I insisted on as we began this section by talking about *products*, rather than people. Your letter and resume are a small free sample of *you*. The sample had better be good...or don't send it.

Knowing the terrible statistics of direct mail...only three to five out of 1,000 companies having the right job open right now...lots of people panic and think only "How many?" They forget that success is even more dependent on "How good?"

||| **Hiding Behind the Post Office** |||

Most of us are shy.

Probably you're like me. You love a big party, if you know everyone there. But you hate going to the same affair if you only know the host or hostess. Because after a couple minutes with them, you'll be on your own...an embarrassed wallflower, or a pushy nerd, accosting unintrigued strangers.

And if you have to make phone calls for your church, temple, or trade association, you don't mind rescheduling a picnic. But like me, you're a lot less comfortable asking for money.

Unfortunately, networking by its very nature demands we do both unpleasant things...plunge in among strangers, and request help. No wonder most of us would rather avoid it if we can.

But sadly, we can't. Reaching out to our personal contacts and networking among strangers are the most powerful of all job-hunting techniques. Face-to-face communication *does* have more oomph than a letter. But what direct mail does—and very effectively—is to lengthen our reach beyond the relatively few and nearby people we can visit face-to-face. Direct mail *expands* networking; it doesn't replace it.

So here's the single biggest danger and downside of direct mail:

Hiding behind the Post Office.

Lots of basically shy folks like you and me are tempted to avoid massaging our personal contacts and networking strangers, merely because we don't enjoy that sort of activity. If we did, we'd be VP of Sales, instead of CFO. So quite understandably, we'd rather stay home and do nothing but send out letters. That's dumb...cowardly...and lazy! If it becomes your idea of an all-out job campaign, don't say I suggested it.

||| The Trade-Off: Follow-Up vs. Get-'Em-Out |||

Obviously, there's potential benefit in calling up the people you write to, and trying to see them for a networking visit. Or perhaps phoning them long-distance to network.

Some people I know have even succeeded in making friends with the secretaries of their direct mail targets. They call to ask if their letter arrived; what's being done with it; whether it's realistic to try for a few moments of the boss's time in person or on an aptly-timed phone call; who else might be more appropriate to receive such an approach; and so on.

Unfortunately, aggressive follow-up takes lots of time. If that's your strategy, you can't handle more than 50 or 100 per week. At that rate, it will take you 10 or 20 weeks...two and a half to five months...to send out 1,000 letters (and preferably today a lot more) in the hope of hitting just three to five recipients who, according to statistical odds, ought to have the right job for you *open* or soon-to-open.

Of course, if your letter and resume do a fine job of selling your impressive accomplishments (and they'd better *be* impressive), then just the mild stimulus of your mailing without follow-up should trigger a call from those few recipients who have a screaming need for someone like you right now. Wouldn't it be sad if a delay-for-follow-up strategy made your mailing too late for the one or two most attractive jobs that will open up while you're unemployed?

I can't tell you how to balance this trade off. Should you risk under-exploiting your mailing? Or should you risk missing current opportunities? And, of course, also missing the looked-everywhere-before-I-had-to-decide bene-fit of a direct mail spy-in-the-sky satellite.

Maybe you should divide your mailing into two categories:

1. Highest-priority are the most attractive employers, and the ones where you're already so well-connected that they merit maximum follow-up.

2. Lesser-priority are the far larger number that are less attractive, or where you're less well acquainted.

How long can you afford to stretch out the release of your highest-priority letters? A month? Two months? How many letters can be aggressively followed-up in that time? Skim that number and schedule them accordingly.

The remainder might as well go into the mailbox right away, because even the best mailing will generate only about three interested replies...certainly not enough to disrupt your high-priority activities. Moreover, any unusually warm "no thank yous" will arrive in time to be "networked" when you finish processing your high-priority letters.

There's no pat answer to the follow-up vs. send-'em-out dilemma. But at least there's an organized way to deal with it.

The Proof is in the Proofing

Here's a tip from the exceptionally sharp-eyed woman who opens and sorts my mail:

"Tell them not to trust their own proofreading."

She spies a typo in "about a third" of the letters and resumes she looks over. And quite often it's in a spot Murphy himself would have chosen...like an early paragraph of the letter or the first title in the resume. Her theory on why:

"I'll bet these people work so hard on *thoughts* that they almost stop seeing *words*. Give 'em a week to cool off, and they'll spot their flubs just like I do."

Be forewarned. Show your mailing to two or three completely fresh-eyed people before you push the mass-production button.

Also, don't count on the computer's "spell check" function. It's no substitute for careful human proofreading. If you typed "or" instead of "of" or left out the word "not"—the sort of thing I do all the time—the computer won't catch your goof.

So much for the basics.
Now let's take direct mail to its ultimate extreme.

Let's mount a wide-ranging campaign
right under your current employer's nose,
and never let him suspect you're "looking."

First of all, you'll need an anonymous version of your "sales representative" resume. And secondly you'll need a "sponsor" to send it out for you...and to receive the five or six interested responses you're likely to get from a 1,000-letter mailing.

Your Anonymous Resume

It's easy to omit your name, address, and phone number from your "sales representative" resume. And it's not hard to describe your current and recent employers "generically," rather than identify them by name. Employers that are "ancient history" can be left "as is."

Please thoughtfully consider this resume transformation. Doing so will help prepare you for Chapter 14, where we'll look closely at the Internet and how to navigate it safely.

Assume, for example, that your "regular" resume has headings like the ones shown on the next page.

As you see, it's possible to substitute information about the corporation and what it does, for the name of the company. In effect, you're merely moving facts you'd otherwise provide in the first sentence of the following paragraph up into the line that normally identifies your employer.

Try to give concrete orientation to your reader, even though you can't "name names." Leave out specific trademarks. But state all the same numerical comparisons you'd include in an "open" version of your resume. Also, give your actual college degrees (with dates), and your marital status. After all, you're not the only married person who graduated from Stanford in 1985.

1998 - Present
DIAMOND/ACME COMPANY
(Subsidiary of Multi-Continent Industries)
Bucolic, Vermont

<u>Vice President & General Manager</u>

1992 - 1998
NEW-MOTION CONTROLS LTD.
Sunbelt, Arizona

'96   <u>Vice President - Marketing</u>

'94   <u>Director - Product Management</u>

Restate your headings like this:

1998 - Present
<u>$190 Million Manufacturer of Flow-Control Devices</u>
(Subsidiary of Conglomerate)

Vice President & General Manager

1992 - 1998
<u>$450 Million Manufacturer of OEM Control Assemblies</u>
(Privately owned)

'96   Vice President - Marketing

'94   Director - Product Management

Editor's Note...

For John Lucht's in-depth help with your resume and cover letter use pages 40 to 134 and 136 to 163 of the EXECUTIVE JOB-CHANGING WORKBOOK.

Your Sponsor

You're doing something difficult. And this time you can't do it without help. You must have a "sponsor" who's willing to "front" for you...distributing the anonymous version of your resume and accepting replies from employers who are interested in meeting you.

Of course, you might instead try to be a "Lone Ranger." You *could* send out your own identity-concealed resume. And you could ask that responses be addressed to a post office box, explaining your need for secrecy, and hoping that mystery and novelty might make up for your lack of straightforwardness.

Unfortunately, this approach has already been tried many times. And as far as I know, it has always failed. Considering candidates for management positions is no joke. And people in a position to do so are too busy to fool around. Your resume won't be taken seriously unless it comes from an obviously credible source.

Therefore, since *you* can't send the resume—and you certainly don't want it circulated by some headhunter who's attached a price-tag—you need someone else who can submit it almost as straightforwardly as if it came directly from you.

You need a *"sponsor"*...a real live respectable person who'll openly send your name-omitted resume, say why she's doing so, and forward to you any interested responses she receives. Moreover, it will be a big help if the person is rather prominent in the business world...someone obviously capable of knowing a fine executive when she sees one. Then her mailing out your resume will more than make up for your anonymity. Indeed, *it will enhance your image*.

"Sounds great, John," you say, "but who am I going to get to do that for me?"

Well, it can't be Ricky Martin, Sandra Day O'Connor, Bill Cosby, or Dr. Ruth Westheimer. Prominent they are. But experts on who would make an ideal chief manufacturing officer for a large metal-bending business they're not. Better for your purposes—and easier to enlist—would be someone who could begin this letter knowledgeably:

> "As president of a $550 million division of Innovative All-Steel Products Corporation, I know the importance of having a Vice President of Manufacturing who can really be depended on."

Here's someone you and I never heard of...yet a perfect "sponsor." Lining up someone like that probably isn't beyond your reach.

Since your spokesperson should claim to have firsthand knowledge of your outstanding on-the-job performance, chances are he or she is a former boss or subordinate. She's probably *not* just a prominent businessperson you know socially or as a fellow board-member of a nonprofit institution...although "any port in a storm," as they say.

However, you don't want a sponsor who's *too* high on the corporate totem pole relative to the position you should occupy, because one essential element of his letter must be a believable statement of why—despite your being so special—he can't use you himself. If your sponsor is Chief Executive of IBM, it's hard to believe he can't fit you in somewhere. Therefore, the reader will suspect he doesn't want to.

**Here are the essential elements of a "sponsor's" letter
sending out your identity-concealed resume:**

1. His *credentials* that make him a valid judge of executives like you;

2. His *vantage point* that enables him to endorse your on-the-job effectiveness;

3. His *recommendation*;

4. His *reason for not employing you himself*;

5. His *explanation of your need for secrecy*; and

6. His *offer* to put the interested reader in touch with you.

Now let's look at a "sponsoring" letter that meets all these criteria.

TRILOVANCE ELECTRONICS CORPORATION
1010 Solder Circle, Verdant Valley, California 95014

Monique Micreaux
President

(Date)

Mr. Donald Drive
President
Peripheron Corporation
18 Silver Saddle Road
Diva Del Sol, California 95038

Dear Mr. Drive:

As Founder/CEO of a publicly-held young high-tech growth company...we started four years ago and will hit $390 million this year...I know the importance of a Chief Financial Officer who can provide absolutely reliable information without needlessly cumbersome procedures that stifle momentum.

Those people are rare and difficult to identify. Which is why I'm writing to you.

Last week I learned that the financial executive I respect most after 12 years with IBM and North American Dauntless Corporation—and tried hardest to recruit as CFO when I founded this company—is now willing to explore outside opportunities.

However, since he's very solidly employed, he can't afford to "go public" with his intentions. And, since I can't capitalize on his availability without doing an injustice to the person who took the plunge with me four years ago, I'm sending his identity-omitted resume to you and several other CEOs of high-tech growth companies.

If there's any chance that you may have a need, just let me know, and I'll put you in touch with one of the very best financial executives you could possibly consider.

                    Sincerely,

                    Monique Micreaux

                    Monique Micreaux

MM:gr
Enclosure

P.S. Although growth environment and equity opportunity will be primary concerns, you should know that his total compensation in recent years has been in the $255,000 to $340,000 range.

What an endorsement!

The "sponsored" mailing not only provides "cover," it also heightens impact.

Someone introducing a colleague can say things that modesty prevents the individual from saying about himself.

And such a plug is far more believable coming from a senior executive with no economic axe to grind than from a headhunter filing for $80,000 or $120,000 or more. Moreover, a "no-price-tag" introduction is much more likely to be followed-up.

"Sponsored" direct mail is often "the only alternative" in a ticklishly sensitive situation. Fortunately, when handled well, it also becomes a highly persuasive marketing campaign.

The Dual Standard on Stationery

Notice that the "sponsor" uses her corporate stationery when recommending someone else, whereas she normally would *not* do so when proposing herself.

The reason for this dual standard is purely psychological. Corporate stationery is virtually essential to prove that the sponsor is indeed a substantial, knowledgeable person in the business world. And fortunately, the reader has no negative reaction to the use of office paper to help a colleague.

But the "vibes" are totally different when the writer offers himself. Then using his employer's paper triggers a negative reaction. His reader says, "Wow, at the same time he's trying to get me to hire him, he's ripping off his current company's stationery and postage meter."

"I know a couple people, John, who'd be ideal to send out a mailing like that, and they respect me enough to do it."

"But they're extremely busy. I could never ask them to take on so much work."

Absolutely right! You couldn't. And you *won't*.

You're requesting a huge favor, just to have them lend you their name, mailing address, and phone number. So you've got to get virtually all the work done without burdening either your sponsor or his personal assistant.

Here's what *you* do:

1.   Get your sponsor's general agreement to help.

2.   Show him a letter you've drafted (to save him work), stressing that he may change it as he sees fit, since it's his letter.

3.   Establish agreed-upon wording for the letter, and walk away with at least two reams of office stationery and 1,000 #10 envelopes (enough for 1,000 letters).

4.   Create your mailing list, check it by phone, and have "his" letter word-processed. But first, show him a sample to make doubly sure he's satisfied. Also offer to let him see your mailing list, in case he wants to make sure you haven't accidentally hit anyone he'd rather not be "writing" to.

5.   Sign, stuff, stamp, and mail the letters yourself. That's right, I said sign them...with *his* signature. Unless he feels like signing 1,000 letters, he'll gladly leave this chore up to you. But ask before you barge ahead; this point is inconsequential to some people and an emotional issue with others.

Here's what your sponsor and his assistant do:

1.   Almost nothing else. After he approves your letter and list, he's just about finished. *Remember, a 1,000-letter mailing will produce only 3 to 5 interested replies*...hardly enough to create a traffic problem.

2.   Letter replies will be opened by your sponsor's assistant with the rest of his mail, and merely forwarded to you every couple days in a large envelope. These could be a slight nuisance for a week or two, because 200 to 300 recipients will send polite "no thank yous."

3.   The 3 to 5 phone callers who inquire about you will be cordially dealt with by your sponsor. He'll say he doesn't know the exact status of your explorations at the moment, but will gladly forward their name and number to you. Then, if you're not already in your new job, you'll call their office, giving your sponsor's name as well as your own, so they'll know you're the person they inquired about.

That's it. Nothing more.

But look what you've accomplished. While keeping yourself completely hidden, you've probed 1,000 (or more) companies to find the *rare* 3 to 5 who right now are interested in what you have to offer. And you've done so without tipping-off your current employer!

True, you've put a lot of work into the project. But, except for checking a few times with your sponsor, *no more work than sending the same mailing under your own name.* Your sponsor has also contributed some time. But not much. You've done everything, except sat in his office and been him when three to five people called to ask about you.

"Sponsored" direct mail can do more than keep a secret.

It's also a problem-solver.

Joyce is in a tough spot.

She needn't be secretive. But she does face a high hurdle. Someone almost has to "speak the unspeakable," and it's a matter Joyce can't very well bring up for herself.

See how a "sponsored" mailing can come to the rescue.

MONOLITHIC FOODS CORPORATION
White Plains, New York 11618

MAURICE MARKETIER
Vice President - Marketing

(Date)

Mr. Cabot Carson
President
Family-Owned Candies, Inc.
10 Ginger Road
Scottsdale, Arizona 09099

Dear Mr. Carson:

As Vice President - Marketing of Monolithic Foods, I've seen hundreds of fine marketing executives over the years, and one of the very best is my former boss at MegaFoods, Joyce McKee, who taught me most of what I know.

Recently the company where she's been Vice President - Marketing, Yumm Foods, was acquired through an unfriendly tender offer. And now at an amazingly youthful age 59—Joyce ran the New York Marathon again this year—she's available for another assignment.

Although company and opportunity will be Joyce's main concerns, you should know that in recent years her total compensation has been in the range of $240,000 to $320,000.

Joyce is the calibre of person there's hardly ever a shot at hiring, and nothing would please me more than to bring her in here. Unfortunately, I can't do that without dealing an undeserved blow to one of the two executives who head my Marketing Department...or by giving up my own job.

So, on the chance that you may have need for an exceptionally dynamic, creative, and versatile marketing executive, I thought I'd bring Joyce to your attention.

Sincerely,

Maurice Marketier

Maurice Marketier

MM:jc
Enclosure

P.S. With Joyce's exceptional knack for training and recruiting, you can count on her building a strong department, with excellent people to take over whenever it's time for Joyce to retire.

Think of "sponsored" direct mail as your "SWAT team," to be called in when the going gets really tough!

You catch the concept. The more tendency to discriminate against an executive, the more helpful "sponsored" direct mail becomes.

With direct mail, the number of employers contacted can be infinitely expanded. Maybe 2,000 or 3,000 will have to be reached in order to find 5 to 8 with an immediate need, because only one-in-three or one-in-five will consider a disadvantaged candidate. Fortunately, a "sponsor's" letter can deal with the prejudicial factor far more frankly and successfully than one from the candidate herself...or from a headhunter or an outplacement firm with a fee on the line.

Whenever there's a severe problem, consider sponsored direct mail. A successful business executive who's a retired military officer can make a strong case for a former subordinate just mustering out. A former top-echelon businessperson who's now an ambassador or a college president can knowledgeably extol a current subordinate who wants to enter business from the diplomatic corps or academia. And any high-level executive can sponsor a former subordinate or boss with an attribute most employers will shun—lawfully or not—such as age, physical handicap, obesity...even, perhaps, return to work after a jail sentence for "white-collar-crime."

Direct mail, with or without a "boost" from a sponsor, may turn out to be the only viable "Rite of Passage" when you're looking for the exceptionally rare employer who must have—in addition to need, which is always rare anyway—broadmindedness, compassion, or firsthand knowledge that an apparent disadvantage isn't disabling.

Try it. For yourself...or for a friend.

**And there you have direct mail
...the ultimate career-development weapon.**

Results are limited only by how hard you're willing to work.

Direct mail *is* hard work.

When you're fully challenged and well rewarded where you are—and you're also being tempted by retainer recruiters—you won't bother reaching for the unlimited power of direct mail.

Indeed, direct mail as a job-changing method is rather like the police, the fire department, and the hospital. Drastic! But great to have around when needed.

Whenever more casual methods aren't enough, you know what to do.

Chapter 14

You've Got Exciting New OnLine Tools for
Executive Job-Changing and Career Management

Be adventurous!

"Space," said President Kennedy, "is the new ocean; we must sail upon it!"

Almost as soon as "cyberspace" emerged, the Internet had its commercial navigators. Among the earliest to put up sites were the ad agencies and newspapers already publishing traditional classified employment advertising. They saw the online format as incredibly cheap (no paper, no presses, and far less labor) and far-reaching...global, rather than just city- or country-wide.

Not surprisingly, these sailors of the old ad ocean became the first ship owners on the World Wide Web. They launched Monster.com and a fleet of others. And all the contingency recruiters and corporations buying "help wanted" ads in conventional media hopped aboard.

Next, the largest retainer search firms hoisted sail to the winds of low-cost advertising. Korn/Ferry launched FutureStep.com in partnership with THE WALL STREET JOURNAL and Heidrick and Struggles launched LeadersOnLine.com. With names and logos that separate them from their sponsoring parents, those sites can advertise for candidates just as the contingency firms do, and yet not imply that their prestigious parents have changed their highly personalized and thus labor-intensive candidate-finding methods.

Those high-profile sites were quickly followed by dozens, then hundreds, and now thousands more, put up by retainer and contingency concerns to publicize their firms and to gather potential candidates. Meanwhile, even more sites were being put up by entrepreneurs, the media, educational and governmental entities, trade associations, charitable and religious organizations...the list is endless. And, of course, most sizeable corporations now have their own employment sites as key areas of their overall corporate site. Today there are estimated to be over 80,000 employment sites on the World Wide Web...and more appear every day.

What does all this mean to you?

Read on. We'll clarify the confusion and relentlessly pursue your self-interest.

We'll also look at a largely noncommercial Web site I've designed to make that far easier to do.

||| **It's All About Advertising** |||

Whenever something valuable is being given away free, there will always be plenty of takers to grab it and figure out how to use it.

So it's not surprising that, when Internet technology provided nearly cost-free communications, the print advertising industry was among the earliest to see its advantages. No presses, no paper, and virtually no delivery expense...coupled with the reaching of every person on the planet, not just local readers. Here was an opportunity too good to pass up!

But what form of advertising to sell?

Classified, of course...those simple, generic listings of cars, houses, boats, used furniture, collectibles and, yes, *help wanted* opportunities, that we all see in every newspaper every day.

Helping employers find employees and helping employment agencies (contingency headhunters) find applicants has always been one of the main categories of classified advertising.

Posting...an Old Term That
Perfectly Fits the New Technology

You *buy* a classified ad. Or you *place* it. You don't *post* it.

The idea of *posting* goes way back in time...and it doesn't involve payment.
Posting merely means putting your message where people can see it. Think
of the posters at the theater. Toulouse-Lautrec's lithos for the Moulin Rouge.
American colonists' freedom tracts on fence posts. Luther's paper nailed to
the church door.

Internet employment site entrepreneurs needed a narrow and neutral word
meaning merely "to put your message where people can see it"...a word that
didn't specify whether or not you had to *pay* to do so. The venerable term
post was dusted off to provide it.

Fast-Forward to *Posting* on an Internet Site

Most Internet sites make employers and recruiting firms pay to post their needs
where potential employees can see them...just as if they were buying an ad in
the paper. The same is true of flashing banners and bold logos that—with a
click—zap the visitor to an employer's site.

But remember, publishing ads on the Internet costs the site's owners a small
fraction of what it would cost to operate a newspaper.

Therefore, the Internet employment sites have been able to bring back a form
of advertising that, although frequently tried in the past, never succeeded
commercially...ads placed by individuals looking for work. Called "positions
wanted"—in contrast to "help wanted"—these ads have been around since the
earliest days of newspaper classifieds. However, "positions wanted" never
brought in the vast advertising revenues that "help wanted" did.

Why?

Not because of any lack of jobseekers willing to run such ads. The problem
was economic. The newspapers had to charge enough to cover costs and
make a profit. Employers could afford those rates. Employees could not.
And, because few employees were advertising, employers didn't bother reading the "positions wanted" ads. A vicious circle of unaffordable cost and few
employer eye balls doomed "position wanted" newspaper ads.

But now, on the Internet where operating costs are miniscule, employee self-
advertising has returned. The Internet sites can easily afford to run these
ads—indeed they *post entire resumes free of charge*—because the cost of

doing so is virtually nil. And because individuals pay nothing or almost noth-ing to post their resume, thousands upon thousands are doing so. Now that vast numbers are posting, employers and recruiters *are* casting their eyeballs on the resumes conveniently available and indexed on the various Internet employment sites. Again there's a vicious circle. But now it *favors* advertis-ing by individuals.

| | | ## "Findability"...the Digital Advantage | | |

Your resume zapped into a database—any database—usually won't be as eye-catching as it is on paper (more about this later). You'll still want an impres-sive on-paper version to hand to an important decision-maker.

But as words in a computer—hopefully with a "profile" of sorting criteria and plenty of "keywords" included—your resume's digital version will be far more *findable*. When in a database and properly classified, it will come up without fail whenever the computer is asked for someone exactly like you. Through modern technology you can make yourself *unforgettable* and *unoverlookable*.

**Obviously, you've got a lot to gain from making
yourself and your accomplishments widely known
...if you don't jeopardize your current situation.**

Does every employer with an open position that would be an ideal next step in your career know about you? Does every recruiter filling such an opening know about you?

Of course not. But you wish they did!

If your resume were posted where every one of these people would be sure to look...and if they *did* look...and if your resume were properly persuasive... then you could be sure your career would fulfill its finest destiny.

Sadly, there's no way to achieve that utopian dream. But through modern Internet technology you can edge closer to it. You can post your resume where *many*—though obviously not all—of the right people are likely to look for it.

In effect, you can use posting on the Internet as a substitute—and in certain circumstances even a superior substitute—for direct mail.

Posting *might* work with high-powered decision-makers.

As we saw in Chapter 13 on direct mail, you can't make a favorable impression on CEOs and other top decision-making officers by spamming your resume into their e-mail...even if you could get its address. That would be obnoxious and likely to backfire. The only proper way to reach out to those people is by a letter and resume as we discussed.

On the other hand, if you put yourself on record—conveniently indexed and downloadable—where they might *voluntarily* choose to browse, there's nothing impolite or too pushy about that. They could discover you and maybe even be amused to do themselves what their HR people and outside recruiters were failing to do. Unfortunately, not many top decision-makers will ever take this do-it-yourself approach to staffing (except, perhaps, CEOs of startups, who'll hand you pre-IPO stock). But a rare few sometimes will. Do you feel lucky?

Posting definitely *does* work
with recruiters and HR departments.

Unlike CEOs and other top decision-makers, these people are *supposed* to do the grunt work of filling open positions:

1. Executive recruiters

2. HR departments of companies

Those people *are* at their computers and/or have subordinates at computers combing databases for candidates who meet certain specifications.

So for those folks, your presence in a digital rather than an impressive on-paper format is an advantage, not a liability. With a few keystrokes they'll sort the database. Which people meet the criteria? Some will look ordinary (maybe just due to a generic resume) and be ignored. But not all will. Face it. It's a lot quicker and easier to cull a group of people identified by a few key strokes than to discover and cull an equal-sized pool of prospects by conventional headhunter networking methods.

"Fool's names and fool's faces
are often found in public places."

But there's a dangerous downside to being readily findable by the right people.

You may also be found by the wrong people! Your current employer may discover that you're willing to leave for an exciting opportunity. So what?

So is just about everyone else! Although unfair and shortsighted, your current company may feel, as folks used to say where I grew up:

"Here's your hat; what's your hurry?"

Your boss might browse the Web and find your resume. Or his/her boss. Or a subordinate or coworker who'd gain from your downfall. Or the person assigned to monitoring employee e-mails, which the law says is a management prerogative and not a violation of privacy. Or perhaps worst of all, your resume might be scooped up by an unscrupulous headhunter and spammed to every company in your field, including your current employer.

Therefore, as we dive into the maelstrom of possible posting sites, we'll be continually on the lookout for potential risks and safeguards.

"But John, with an estimated 80,000 employment sites already operating and more appearing every day, how can I figure out what use I should make of this phenomenon?"

Relax.

The bad news is that there are 80,000 sites, and all have different formats and sponsorships. The scene is bewildering.

The good news is that when you look really closely, all of the sites fall into *five* easily identified classifications. Within each of the categories there are advantages and hazards, which we will examine. Once you figure out what type of site you're dealing with—and how it matches or varies from a central theme—you can judge the risks you face if you participate.

I can't lay out rules that will fit you at every moment. Your needs, goals, and circumstances are always changing. So are the benefits and dangers of dealing with any particular employment site. You've got to be alert and think for yourself. But your analysis—and the self-interested actions you choose—will soon be nearly as clear to you on the Internet as they were when we examined the headhunting business.

To cut through the clutter and confusion, we'll identify and analyze the 5 different types of Internet employment sites.

The 80,000 sites currently estimated will grow into several times that many worldwide. Even so, they'll still all fit into just five categories, depending on (1) what they do and (2) who they do or don't charge for their services. Here are the five types of sites:

1. *Commercial Service Sites*

2. *Proprietary Headhunter Sites*

3. *Proprietary Corporate Sites*

4. *Executive Interface Sites*

5. *Altruistic Sites*

And here are the basic considerations you should apply in deciding whether or not to participate in any employment site you encounter on the Internet. There are only three:

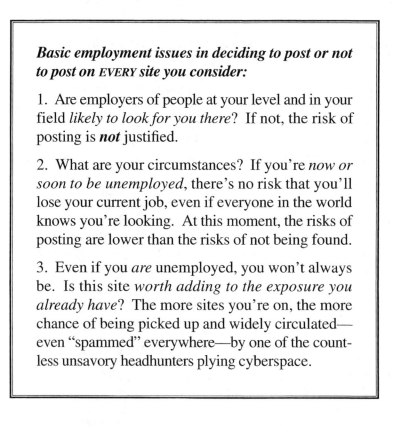

> ***Basic employment issues in deciding to post or not to post on*** EVERY ***site you consider:***
>
> 1. Are employers of people at your level and in your field *likely to look for you there*? If not, the risk of posting is ***not*** justified.
>
> 2. What are your circumstances? If you're *now or soon to be unemployed*, there's no risk that you'll lose your current job, even if everyone in the world knows you're looking. At this moment, the risks of posting are lower than the risks of not being found.
>
> 3. Even if you *are* unemployed, you won't always be. Is this site *worth adding to the exposure you already have*? The more sites you're on, the more chance of being picked up and widely circulated—even "spammed" everywhere—by one of the countless unsavory headhunters plying cyberspace.

The three basic issues as to whether and to what extent you should participate in any particular employment site will vary from time to time depending on your circumstances, needs and interests at the moment.

The characteristics of the five types of site, however, are clear and constant. Once we've sorted them out, you'll find it very easy to decide what to do with each, depending on your current circumstances and objectives:

1. Commercial Service Sites
(the overwhelmingly predominant category)

These sites *sell their services to employers and headhunters*, who pay the site (1) to publicize their job descriptions and/or (2) to view the database(s) of resumes collected on the site, whether in response to specific job postings... or to an open invitation for everyone to post...or (though they may not say so) from *both sources* combined. Some may allow their database of posted resumes to be looked at without paying, although most do not. Virtually all of these sites sell banner and other display advertising and earn "per-click" revenue by channeling their visitors to other sites.

Sites based on some variation of this employers-and-headhunters-pay-to-advertise-jobs-and/or-view-the-database model are the vast majority of the employment sites you'll see on the Internet. With only a very few exceptions, these are the huge sites that advertise on TV and in newspapers and magazines. Monster.com is overwhelmingly #1. Other examples are: HotJobs.com, CareerPath.com, Headhunter.net, CareerMosaic.com, etc.

General Advice:

These sites may have the job you want. Look and see!

But be careful.

No matter what they tell you, do not believe that all their postings are from recruiters and/or companies you can trust. No site, no matter how well-meaning, can avoid shifty operators and outright scam artists. The law of averages guarantees that the larger the site, the more unsavory—as well as excellent—headhunters it will lead you to.

No matter what they tell you, do not believe that they will keep your resume from being seen by people you do not want to see it. Assume that everything you post anywhere on the Internet will be seen by your boss and your worst enemy. Word it—and time it—accordingly.

(More about that later.) Realize that you usually must take some risk to play any sort of an Internet job-hunting game.

Hype and Misinformation to watch out for:

"*Your own company won't see your resume on this site.*" or **"*Tell us which companies should not see your resume.*"** This misrepresentation is based on having software on the site that prevents sending a particular resume to computers linked to the Net through a specified company's known domain name. Does anyone even dream that a corporation hiring someone to look for employee resumes on the Net wouldn't get that person hooked up through an outside vendor? And if your boss and/or a rival is checking, they'll snoop from home.

"*We are strictly for high-paid executives. Only our exclusive list of America's finest search firms will see your resume.*" On a typical site aggressively making this type of claim, the fact is that every headhunter willing to pay the fee to look will see your resume (true of every site I'm aware of). And the annual fee is miniscule...far less than even the smallest contingency firms are paying to run just a few newspaper ads. Moreover, everyone who signs up and pays is automatically listed on the site as one of America's outstanding search firms. On any such site, compare the firms they list with the list of top retainer-compensated search firms honored in *RITES OF PASSAGE* (see p. 579-98). Virtually all firms shown on such a list will not be the ones this book honors.

2. Proprietary Headhunter Sites

There are thousands of these sites...each owned and operated by a single headhunter firm or a franchised chain. Their purpose is to publicize the firm and/or collect resumes for the firm's own database. Several thousand firms—contingency and retainer—have their own sites and most accept resumes. The site may or may not describe positions it is filling. Many top-drawer retainer firms merely indicate the *types* of jobs they fill, not specific current searches. *If you know and respect the firm, post.* They'll treat your digital submission as ethically as they do your paperwork.

There's also a variation. Huge retainer firms, including the two largest, not only have parent firm sites (which accept resumes online), they also have highly advertised subsidiaries...for example, *FutureStep* from Korn/Ferry and The Wall Street Journal and *LeadersOnLine* from Heidrick & Struggles. These subs collect resumes to feed separate groups of computer-assisted head-hunters. Highly automated, the subs are designed to handle search assignments under $200,000 annual compensation (K/F) and $150,000 (H&S), whereas their parents do searches above those levels in the traditional way. The arm's length distance between parent and subsidiary provides the opportunity for differences in off-limits policy and operating methods that would be harder to promulgate without the separation.

Do post on these sites if you're below $200,000 a year. Integrity should be fine. "But," you ask, "will posting with the subsidiary also put me in the parent's database?" No. These firms claim there's a "Chinese Wall" between the two. Therefore, if your money's on the borderline, post on both.

General Advice:

Posting on a search firm's own site is an ideal way to get firmly into the consciousness of the firm. The digital format makes you unforgettable and unoverlookable (see p. 281). However, insuring you'll be considered doesn't guarantee you'll be contacted. If your resume is generic and unimpressive, it'll be glanced at...and ignored or even deleted. Today as Internet submissions vastly inflate a search firm's database, you'll encounter a continually rising threshold for being (1) relevant and (2) outstanding as shown by your resume.

With vastly more people readily "findable" in search firm databanks, you've got to spend more effort—not less—in making sure that your self-presentation—your resume—is as outstanding as you are. Otherwise you'll lose out to folks who do understand that simple, harsh fact.

Don't fail also to use your impressive on-paper resume if you have one. It has its own special advantages, which we've discussed. Send it to any recruiter in the firm you already know personally. Hand it or mail it to any of the firm's recruiters you're introduced to by personal contacts and/or through networking. There is absolutely no harm in using both your online and your on-paper resumes in dealing with the same search firm. Just make sure your facts on both are consistent.

But be careful.

On these individual search firm sites, the ethical conduct you will or won't encounter depends on the ethics of the firm presenting the site. If a firm honored in *RITES OF PASSAGE* (see p. 579-98) has a Web site that accepts resumes, take advantage of the opportunity to post on it.

***Don't post your resume on the sites of search firms you know nothing
about.*** If you accidentally post your resume with a highly aggressive
and not-very-ethical headhunting firm, it's likely to wind up in far
more places than you'd ever want it to. It's also likely to be shared
with lots of similarly aggressive—if not down right sleazy—additional firms, all of which can be expected to be just like the first bad
apple. You'd love it if the finest retainer-compensated firms would
share you with their peers. Sadly, they don't. But at the opposite end
of the market, many contingency firms—and often the most aggressive and unsavory of the lot—like to widely share their databases,
hoping to score split fees from as many co-users as possible.

Hype and Misinformation to watch out for:

***Here's a misimpression many folks are jumping to, even though
absolutely nothing improper is being done to create it.*** Sites as
widely advertised as FutureStep and LeadersOnLine that are put up by
eminently respected retainer search firms are being expected by many
executives to expose them to far more opportunities than any site
influenced by retainer compensation practices possibly can.
Operationally these sites resemble contingency firms because (1) they
advertise and (2) they seek their candidates in a much more mecha-
nized manner than the highly personalized solicitations of their elegant parent firms. However, they usually charge on a retainer basis,
just as their parents do. Therefore, they are similarly limited as to how
many jobs they can show you simultaneously and whether you may be
off-limits because they're doing lots of business with your employer.
In fact, they may be almost as limited in the number of positions they
can show you simultaneously or per year as their parent. So don't
relax after posting on these sites and think that you've harnessed the
monolithic giants and won't need any further exposure. You've made
a couple very worthwhile and nonrisky postings. But that's all you've
done. Now get busy and do something more!

3. Proprietary Corporate Sites

These sites are the employment areas on a corporation's own Web site. Logically, they should display only the company's own openings, gather resumes
of people applying for them, and circulate the resumes—if at all—only inside
the company. The company should also save resumes for reconsideration
when other appropriate positions open up.

However, some of the commercial sites (#1 above) have persuaded corporations to outsource to them the employment part of the corporate site...in which case, when you browse for jobs on the corporation's site, you may be steered beyond the company's own jobs into the commercial site's full list of jobs. Moreover, your submitted resume may go into the commercial site's database, not just the company's.

General Advice:

By all means make it a point to figure out which are the firms you'd most like to work for, visit their Web sites, and if they give you an opportunity to submit your resume online, do so. It's great to be able to make yourself unforgettable and unoverlookable for current and future consideration by the employers you'd most like to work for.

But be careful.

Security on a corporation's own employment site should be ideal. They're in the widget business or the cheese business. They're not running a commercial resume database on the Internet and charging companies and headhunters—no matter how disreputable—to look at it. There should be virtually no chance at all of your resume being seen or circulated outside the company.

Unfortunately, as pointed out earlier, quite a few corporations have been persuaded by the operators of commercial databases to outsource running the corporation's job site...in which case the resume that you think you are submitting only to X Corp. is actually entering the pay-us-to-look database of a huge operation that is aggressively soliciting lookers and *may already have signed up your employer!*

A sure giveaway is if, when you peruse a fairly wide variety of job listings on X Corp.'s site, you suddenly find yourself viewing jobs that appear to have been posted by headhunters or by companies other than X Corp. If that happens, ask yourself this question: "Is my current situation such that I should be posting on every large commercial employment site?" If you're a beginner or an unemployed middle manager seeking all the publicity you can get, then proceed to broadcast your resume online. If not, pursue any X Corp. openings through the non-Internet methods discussed in other parts of this book.

Hype and Misinformation to watch out for:

If the employment site isn't outsourced, participate! The only exception to this advice— and it's worth considering—is that entering the

***company online submits you to the jurisdiction of the HR depart-
ment.*** That's great when they know someone like you is needed and
they're advertising for you on the company's Web site. Then, as a first
step in finding you, they will consult their database. And it's better to
have them introducing and supporting your candidacy than challenging it.

But what if HR has not yet been informed by the decision-maker?
What if referral by an enthusiastic personal contact, or classic networking, or even an elegant and persuasive mailing from you might
have gotten the ball rolling with the decision-maker even before he or
she informed HR or an outside search firm? Then you'd have had a
chance of being considered before those sources provided strong competition for your candidacy. Also, putting your resume in the corporate database does define you. If you subsequently walk in the front
door, the information you submitted at the back door probably will
wind up being looked at and compared with your latest paperwork.

4. Executive Interface Sites
(sites that really <u>do</u> serve executives)

There are thousands of the prior three types of job sites, but less than a handful
of these...notably, Exec-U-Net.com, NetShare.com, and SearchBase.com.
Also called "executive networking sites," these Internet employment sites
make their money by ***charging their executive "members" to inform them of
various searches being conducted by retainer search firms*** which, as you're
aware, normally (1) *never advertise for candidates in the media* and (2) *never
post their jobs on the commercial Internet employment sites*...even the ones
claiming to have high-paying jobs or to be "for executives."

Executive interface sites obtain the information they sell to their members by
soliciting retainer-compensated search firms to tell them about the openings
those firms are filling. The site then puts that information into its database,
which its members—using personal identification codes—can access over the
Internet. The site publishes only as much information as each cooperating
recruiter is willing to allow...usually only a description of the job, without the
identity of either the employer or the search firm.

If the member sees a search on which he or she would like to be a candidate,
he/she instructs the site's computer to submit his/her resume to the anonymous recruiter, who remains unidentified to the member and therefore is free
to contact or ignore the member, as the recruiter prefers.

What does each party get out of this arrangement?

The executive, in return for a membership fee of approximately $300 to $450 annually, finds out that searches to fill positions he/she would like to be considered for are being conducted. Since the retainer firms doing these searches normally never advertise their projects—not even on the sites claiming to be for "high-paying" or "executive" jobs—the member would have no other way of finding out that such searches are under way unless actually called by the recruiter. The executive usually isn't told the employer's or the recruiter's identity. But, the site's computer *does* know the *recruiter's* identity. So the executive instructs the computer to send his or her resume and cover letter to the recruiter. By paying the annual fee, the executive makes sure that his or her information reaches some—though of course not all—recruiters actually doing appropriate searches.

The recruiter, in return for revealing what searches he or she is conducting, gets a number of resumes, some of which may come from attractive candidates. Many of the executives buying annual memberships are ***not*** currently unemployed. Many purchase their memberships just to "continually shop the market." Since they already have good jobs, they respond only when something they really like shows up.

Recruiters prefer employed candidates. Finding some who are all revved up and eager to go is the "payment" the recruiter gets for bothering to tell the site what he or she is looking for. Best of all, the recruiter can choose to remain totally anonymous. That way, he or she has absolutely no obligation to spend any time on any applicant who doesn't perfectly hit the spot.

"But," you ask, "isn't this recruiter who 'never advertises' actually advertising when he or she posts a job description on this site?"

Indeed, you sly fox! You figured that out!

But notice: he or she is merely accepting *free* advertising, not *paying* to advertise. That's because he or she doesn't really *need* to advertise. Merely starting with the retainer firm's database and making phone calls to "sources" (people who won't want the job but know the field and will have good suggestions) and "prospects" (people who might be ideal candidates) normally yields a fine result without advertising. Indeed, it's usually less trouble to ask people known to be outstanding in a field for their suggestions than it is to sort through a pile of resumes and figure out who's outstanding and who's ordinary.

The operators of the interface site, of course, are winners too. They make money on the membership fees, which compensate them for their efforts in soliciting information from "we-never-advertise" retainer recruiters and publishing it to the site's "members."

General Advice:

These sites enable you to have your online resume sent to a retainer recruiter at the very moment you know for sure that he or she is working to fill a job you'd like to be considered for. Your timing goes from unavoidably haphazard to absolutely perfect. That's the central benefit you're paying for. However, these sites also provide secondary benefits...many of which are provided to nonmembers too, in order to attract them to the site, where they can be told the advantages of buying a membership. For example the site may publish a newsletter on job-hunting techniques and provide links to it—and to other articles—which can be read by non-members and members alike. The sites may also sponsor talks at various locations around the country by authors of job-hunting and resume-writing books (I did a few of these when *RITES* first appeared), which cost x for members and x+ for nonmembers.

There are differences among these sites. So, if you're considering purchasing, do spend considerable time on each and check out all of its features before you commit. Which site seems to have the most jobs that might interest you? Can you "paste" in your entire existing resume, or must you create a standardized and/or abbreviated version by filling in a questionnaire or a series of type boxes? Can you see what jobs are posted on the site and trigger the sending of your information in response to certain ones, or do you passively await recruiter inquiry? Are there publications and social events? Check out the features.

But be careful.

You will be spending a substantial amount of money just to be able to have your resume sent—along with who knows how many others— to an anonymous recruiter who has expressed a willingness to receive them. Please, please spend the major time and effort it takes to make a first-class "sales representative" resume that will be visually scannable at a glance and—after that glance stimulates interest—factually communicative enough to persuade the recruiter that you are one of the dozen or so who's an outstanding performer...as contrasted with the 50 or 100 or 500 more who will seem too pedestrian to pursue.

Hype and Misinformation to watch out for:

Reading the promotional descriptions of these sites, you could imagine that a very substantial proportion of all retainer-compensated searches will be drawn to your attention on the site you're reading about. Don't imagine for one minute that all retainer recruiters are posting all of their searches on any of these sites. Only a relatively few bother to post any of their projects, and quite a few of those tend to post only their difficult-to-fill jobs. When a highly attractive opening arises, they just make a very few phone calls to people they already know are (1) outstanding and (2) interested in a change. And why not? When a search can be completed that easily, why bother inviting any strangers to apply?

The bottom line is that only a small proportion of the searches being carried on every day of the year by the retainer firms will find their way onto the executive interface sites. However, some is more than none, and many executives have been very pleased that they paid for the reconnaissance that this type of site provides.

5. Altruistic Sites

The four previous categories of sites have all involved making—or at least saving—money. The commercial employment sites—Category 1—are surely among the most crassly overloaded with fees and advertising of all the addresses on the Internet. Although individuals can post their resumes on most of those sites at no charge, companies and search firms almost always must pay to post jobs and/or to look at the site's database of resumes. A very few sites may also extract a hiring fee.

The headhunters' own sites and the employment areas of corporate sites—categories 2 & 3—help the headhunters to earn fees and the corporations to save on fees. And the executive interface sites—category #4—as we've just seen, are also about money.

A few years ago, when the Internet was just beginning to catch on, its "early adopters"—mostly twenty-something techies and even techi-teens—were outraged when they saw advertising sprout on the Net. Today those same techies are planting and IPOing vast fields of green.

However, there are still a great many sites that can be thought of as ***altruistic***...

set up mainly as a public service, rather than as a money-making activity. They allow the posting of both jobs and resumes at low- or no-charge and, with rare exceptions, they don't extract payment when employee and employer find each other and strike a deal.

Governmental & Civic

One enormous example is America's Job Bank (www.ajb.org). Sponsored by the federal and state governments, it publishes over a million job postings from throughout the 50 states. You can also create and post your resume online (several million people have done this). Functionally this site used to be primitive, but now it's impressive...and *improving!*

As you would expect, there are few executive-level jobs and an avalanche of lower level positions. But take a look. Posting jobs on this site is one way that giant companies can demonstrate how open and nondiscriminatory they are, even though—in the end—they may have to engage a search firm to find the needed executive. For small local companies and shoestring startups hoping to grow and IPO, this site may be a valid tool for hiring people while avoiding recruiter fees. There are also state (reachable on wwwajb.org) and city employment sites. Other geographic sites are sponsored by regional and local booster groups and Chambers of Commerce.

Industry & Professional Groups

Many industry and professional associations operate employment sites for the benefit of their members. Obviously, in industry associations where *corporations* pay the fees, there's no desire to help employees depart for a better deal elsewhere. That would disrupt staffing and raise compensation industry-wide. Companies don't pay to help bring *that* about!

On the other hand, a professional association supported by the dues of *individuals* has the opposite perspective. If it can promote a free market in talent and raise the levels of personal fulfillment and compensation among its members, it's doing exactly what they want it to do.

For an excellent example, take a look at *shrm.org*, the site maintained by SHRM, the Society for Human Resources Management, a professional association supported by the fees of over 100,000 individual members.

The point is that many industry and professional associations already have employment sites. More are being created every day. Some merely post job opportunities. Some post both jobs and resumes. Either way, these sites can be thought of as being *altruistically motivated.* Look at their job postings.

Consider posting your resume. Some employers are far more likely to look for you on a professional site than on the huge commercial sites. You may be "between jobs" and—not needing secrecy—decide to post openly. Or you may be happy to find that the site will allow you to post anonymously.

Colleges & Universities

Most institutions of higher education have some sort of job and resume posting service for their alumni. Check to see what your alma mater offers. Also, check to see if jobs are openly listed on the sites of prestigious schools in your field that you did *not* attend. If the employer's identity is revealed, there's no reason why you can't follow up with your impressive direct mail package or even using an e-mail link if one is provided. Often, both the jobs and the resumes on educational institution sites are weighted toward recent graduates...and thus not much help to an executive vastly exceeding $100,000+. That's especially true of liberal arts college sites. But if you have an MBA or an advanced degree in any technical field you may be very pleasantly surprised at what you'll find on your grad school's site.

Fraternity & Sorority

Does your college fraternity or sorority have an alumni job-and-resume bulletin board? Many do. As with the sites put up by colleges and universities, emphasis will be on helping new and recent grads. Even so, a visit to your organization's site might reveal some warm-spirited individuals you can contact as part of your networking activity.

General Advice:

Altruistic sites are self-explanatory. My best suggestion: If your field has a professional association supported by individual memberships, get involved. Help build up a respected and widely used know-our-members Internet site. Try to make it a standard and virtually routine matter for every member to put their business biography and professional achievements on the society's open-to-the-public membership list. Recruiters will be grateful to have this information openly disclosed, rather than hidden, as usually occurs where corporations pay the dues. If you and other individuals are paying, you can encourage the organization to keep the long-term career advantages of its members in mind.

Now that we've surveyed the field, let's look at

*RITE*Site.com

...my effort to help you benefit from the Internet.

*RITE*Site.com
...the Executive Level Career Information Exchange

The purpose is to help you discover what high-level positions are being filled and—simultaneously—to help the world discover you. Here's the nearest thing to an Altruistic Site I can provide to readers of *RITES OF PASSAGE*.

Ever since the Internet first appeared, I've been investigating the best ways to use it to help *RITES* readers and the outstanding retainer recruiters honored in Appendix II, as well as other recruiters who are willing to clearly identify themselves, and also employers who are equally straightforward.

The idea is to bring you information and services not available elsewhere and not repeat anything already on the Net, unless the prior service can be greatly improved and delivered at far lower cost...or even free, if possible.

*RITE*Site's two-way flow of Executive Level Information:

1. Positions being filled.

Top recruiters—and especially those honored in Appendix II—are filling positions you should know about. *RITE*Site's *Free Service* meets your needs and the recruiters' in a much improved way. It brings you at no charge the same category of information that others now pay over $300 a year to receive. Moreover, as *RITE*Site matures, it can bring you this information in far more comprehensive *quantities* than other sources, regardless of how much they charge.

2. Executives worthy of consideration.

You'd like to be "findable" on the Net whenever an ideal position to advance your career is being filled, regardless of who's filling it. Yet you're realistically concerned about being so openly posted. On the other hand, you'd love to have your full information openly and continually available to the most *respected* search firms. That way, they can call to offer jobs and get suggestions when working in your field, and you can begin now to cultivate the valuable career-long recruiter relationships that every upwardly mobile executive should develop. *RITE*Site's *Custom Career Service* achieves *both these goals and more*.

3. Computerized Career and Search Management.

You can benefit from sophisticated computerized career management. Indeed, far more than you'd expect, until you see what Custom Career Service actually *does* to aid your career. For CCS there's a modest $94 annual fee, which will never be raised to *RITE*Site's early members.

4. No Advertising.

Are you as fed up as I am with the ads on Internet sites? Welcome to *RITE*Site...a career tool, not an advertising medium.

*RITE*Site is concerned above all with confidentiality and integrity issues. They are the #1 problem in dealing with *executive level* careers on the Web, and they're at the core of *RITE*Site's approach to letting you know about positions being filled.

||| **_RITE_Site.com: Where You'll Find Out About** |||
||| **Retainer Recruiters' Unadvertised Searches** |||

All of the recruiters in the 356 firms honored in Appendix II (p. 579) work only on retainer. Therefore, as we've discussed, they don't send out anyone's resume without first being paid by an employer to do a search for such a person...and, assuming they follow proper procedure, talking with the person to get their approval to be submitted. Normally the vast majority of these recruiters *never advertise* the jobs they're filling...not even on the Commercial (Type 1) Internet sites claiming to be "for executives" or for high-paying jobs. Instead, these search firms either present outstanding executives already in their databases, or they phone those people to get suggestions.

The nearest thing to *advertising* that retainer recruiters normally ever do is that some of them sometimes post some of their searches on the Executive Interface sites (Type 4). Reasons: (1) posting costs them nothing and (2) those sites do not—unless the recruiter requests—reveal the recruiter's identity. There's only upside and no downside. The recruiter might discover a candidate...and—being anonymous—never has to deal with anyone he or she is not interested in.

Unfortunately, the number of executives who'll *see* the anonymously posted job description on such a site is limited to the site's few thousand fee-paying "members." *RITE*Site—being for all readers of *RITES* and indeed for all executives everywhere—exposes the job description to the entire universe of potential candidates. Because it reaches far more executives, *RITE*Site is much more likely to attract enough valid candidates to justify the bother of posting.

*RITE*Site is a purely *Altruistic* (Type 5) site in this service. It charges *RITES*-Honored recruiters nothing to post their searches, and it charges *RITES* readers—and other executives as well—absolutely nothing to view the postings.

|| | ## *RITE*Site.com: Where You'll Know
Whom You're Dealing With ||| |

*RITE*Site.com is highly concerned about lessening the danger of unethical recruiter behavior that abounds on the Internet. This site wants its users to know whom they're dealing with. The Internet, with its low fees to post jobs and view databases, is the preferred base-of-operations for the wildest of headhunters and, thanks to modern technology, their unauthorized circulating ("floating") of resumes is now flashing worldwide at the speed of light.

"*RITES*-Honored" Recruiters

The list in Appendix II (p. 579) is carefully screened to present outstanding U.S. and Canadian recruiters who've stated that they work only on retainer. Members of those firms—and only those firms—are allowed to post their jobs on *RITE*Site (1) anonymously and (2) free of charge. The *RITES*-Honored list on *RITE*Site is continually updated and therefore is even more current than the one in this book.

When you look at *RITE*Site, you'll clearly see which postings are by *RITES*-Honored recruiters. What you will *not* know is *who* posted *which* job. *RITE*Site's computer will send your response to the recruiter who posted.

Recruiters who are not *RITES*-Honored must provide identification...and it's passed along to you.

It is estimated that the Rites-Honored firms do about 80 to 85% of all searches done on retainer by firms that refuse to do any work on contingency. The reason that figure will never be 100% is that not everyone who deserves *RITES OF PASSAGE* recognition will (1) come to our attention or (2) ask to be considered. There will always be some fine 100% retainer firms we do not know.

Today there are also contingency firms that fill executive-level jobs. They will never qualify for Appendix II and thus *RITES*-Honored status. But some will be filling jobs that merit your attention. Therefore, *RITE*Site allows non-*RITES*-Honored recruiters to post. They cannot, however, post anonymously. In securing the right to post, they must provide personal name, firm name, address (which cannot be a P.O. box), e-mail address, and telephone number. If any of these items is absent, their application is rejected.

Moreover, every time anything they post is shown on the screen or made available for printout, their entire sign-up information is automatically added to whatever they later say in their posting. That way, you can do some checking before you give them any confidential information.

Call a telephone information operator. Ask for the number of a firm with their name in their city. Are they listed? At the right address? Call and see how they answer. Do they sound like a professional outfit? If they're in your city, consider their address. Are you impressed? Even doing everything I'm suggesting won't guarantee that the firm is proficient...or honest...or anything else you'd want them to be. *Be cautious!* On *Rite*Site you always have information on which to exercise your caution...information that you usually *don't* receive on the Commercial sites.

Why have I included Contingency Recruiters?

I've had a very tough time—personally—figuring out what to do about contingency recruiters on *Rite*Site. Should they be included? Should they not?

As I told you earlier, I got my first big career break through the efforts of an incredibly fine woman—a contingency recruiter named Verché French—who moved me from J. Walter Thompson to Bristol-Myers in 1964. No one I've ever known in retainer recruiting is more admirable or trustworthy than Verché was. (She died several years ago.) And today there are contingency recruiters—just as there are retainer recruiters—buying and giving away copies of *Rites* to educate candidates and clients on how their scrupulously ethical practices differ from those of their unsavory competitors.

So what could I do—originally with *Rites* and now with *Rite*Site—to identify and reward the truly fine contingency firms? Frankly, I'm perplexed. I haven't wanted to give absolutely no free service to contingency recruiters. Yet I have no way to tell the Verchés from the worst offenders. Stressing identification and reminding you to do your own checking on non-*Rites*-Honored firms is the best solution I've been able to come up with.

*Rite*Site's job postings are an Altruistic Site
bringing you the information you need at no charge.

*Rite*Site brings the searches of America's most prestigious retainer recruiters to your attention as an *Altruistic* site. (1) *Rites*-Honored recruiters are charged nothing to post. And (2) you don't have to spend the several hundred dollars a year you'd spend for a membership in an Executive Interface Site to view their postings. Elsewhere that information is sold. On *Rite*Site it's free.

There's more that's free. To encourage posting by recruiters *not* honored in *RITES*, so that you'll also have jobs from them to consider, *RITE*Site gives away free a limited amount of the advertising that they must pay for elsewhere. On *RITE*Site, any firm willing to thoroughly identify itself can post up to two positions in any 12-month period *free of charge*. Expect them to come to *RITE*Site with at least their two highest-level jobs.

Inviting those firms to post two jobs free is as far as altruism toward them can be extended. To post more, they pay a modest fee. Yet paying does *not* allow them to escape *RITE*Site's stringent identity requirements. However, if they can prove they're eligible to be a *RITES*-Honored firm, *RITE*Site will raise their status and *eliminate* their payments! Now that *is* altruistic!

In fact, *RITE*Site is the exact opposite of the Commercial sites (Type 1). Paying money does **not** earn *RITE*Site's highest recognition. Instead, qualifying for the top recognition *eliminates* all payments. On the Commercial sites most notable for claiming to specialize in high-paying jobs, paying to post jobs and/or view the database earns a prestigious ranking indicating that the customer is an elite firm. On *RITE*Site only the less prestigious and/or nonretainer firms ever pay to post. Moreover, when they pay, their label says, in effect, "Watch-this-firm-closely; it's not *RITES*-Honored." On a Commercial site it would say, in effect, "This is one of the very finest firms."

"Who's on the list?" is crucially important. Look at any site that says it deals only with the finest search firms or with high paying jobs. See that site's list of outstanding firms. Compare it with the firms in Appendix II, which are also the firms "*RITES*-Honored" on *RITE*Site. You will find few—if any— *RITES*-Honored firms on the other list, no matter how loaded it is with paying customers it obligingly praises.

No Advertising

Another kinship with the altruistic sites is *RITE*Site's complete absence of advertising. No banner ads, no flashing logos. It's a professional tool, not a "dot com money machine." Indeed it's my gift to *RITES* readers and *RITES*-Honored and other highly ethical recruiters and employers...a place where we can all go to look...and find...and help each other.

I've put over $400,000 into *RITE*Site. But in just a few years of *using RITE*Site free of charge I, and every other *RITES*-Honored retainer recruiter, should be able to earn that much and far more in extra profit just from faster and more efficient search work using this comprehensive and technically advanced Executive Career Information Exchange.

Time Out!

Here's a topic I wish did not exist. But it *does* exist, and it's likely to become as widely talked about in the next few years as it currently is *not* talked about and is even covered up.

So far, in discussing risk, we've only dealt with the possibility of losing your job if your employer finds out you're interested in outside opportunities. The precautions we've discussed—and others that begin on page 312—deal only with that possibility.

Theft of Identity

There is another problem that worries me and many others who closely observe the Internet employment sites.

Resume information can aid con artists engaged in the growth area of crime known as "theft of identity." These people don't just make a few phony credit card purchases. Instead, they pass large checks, make sizeable cash withdrawals and transfers, open and close bank accounts, manipulate brokerage accounts, collect deposits on false real estate transactions, etc. And if you're their victim, cleaning up the mess and clearing your credit record can be incredibly time consuming.

True, merely having a person's resume does **not** make such a crime feasible. But, for the criminal who has—or gets—bank or brokerage account numbers, a social security number, or credit card numbers, the resume can provide very helpful supplementary information.

Therefore, I will not personally have any involvement with any application on the Internet unless it (1) admits that everyone in the world can, with minimal effort, see what's posted and (2) enables 100% of its career-building users to present themselves anonymously.

On *Rite*Site, you can post your achievements while concealing your identity. If you wish, you can open up to *Rites*-Honored recruiters. But the rest of the world cannot find out your identity if you do not post it...unless and until (1) they reveal themselves and (2) you choose to respond. The tools to protect yourself are in *your* hands.

Introducing *RITE*Site's Custom Career Service: the Inexpensive Way to Make Yourself Known While...

Controlling Your Exposure

You want everyone filling a position that could be a great career opportunity for you to be able to find out (1) that you exist and (2) what impressive career accomplishments you've achieved. But you hesitate to post your resume on the Commercial Sites which sell the viewing of their databases to every head-hunter willing to purchase the privilege. You'd rather not risk having your resume "floated" through cyberspace by an aggressive contingency recruiter. And you most assuredly don't want to be a target for con artists who buy database viewing privileges.

On the other hand, you'd like to make your resume available to the widest possible list of highly respected retainer recruiters, because you know they normally never submit anyone without being paid to fill a specific position and without meeting and interviewing the person. They usually have the best opportunities...some of which you'd like to hear about. Even if almost nothing could persuade you to leave your current job right now, you'd like to begin to hear from prominent retainer recruiters, assist them with suggestions, and start now to develop career-enhancing relationships with recruiters in the prominent firms.

*RITE*Site can help you fulfill both objectives and do much more as well.

Make yourself known to the World: Post your *Identity-Concealed Resume*.

Make yourself known to Rites-Honored Recruiters: Select the *Rites-Honored Option*.

As you see, there are two entirely different ways of publicizing yourself on *RITE*Site. Most people most of the time will want to take advantage of both simultaneously. But you can choose to use or not use either or both.

Post your Identity-Concealed Resume.
Make yourself known to the World.

Your basic *RITE*Site presentation is your identity-*concealed* resume posted and findable by anyone in the world...retainer and contingency recruiters (and these days top contingency recruiters handle some very major jobs), corporate recruiters, entrepreneurs and founding staff members of exciting young companies and startups, and perhaps even angel capitalists with an inventor and a dream. Those are the good folks, and they're scattered everywhere. But there are bad ones too...the hazardously over-aggressive contingency recruiters who subscribe to the Commercial Sites and snoop through the Altruistic Sites, your worrisome rival in your current company, and occasional con artists of every description.

*RITE*Site—like every other site—cannot welcome the first-class *many* without also letting in the undesirable *few*. *RITE*Site's solution to that problem is that nobody—from best to worst—will know who you are unless you choose to tell them. After viewing your identity-concealed resume, they must contact you via *RITE*Site's computer, indicating their identity and proposal. If you're impressed, you respond. If not, you stay hidden. And if you're intrigued, but they've provided too little information, you simply demand more specifics before you open up to them.

*RITE*Site "levels the playing field." You may be scoring your accomplishments at a little-known company recruiters don't raid. Or toiling unseen in the belly of a beast-sized corporation. Or in the shadow of a credit-thieving boss. Written up skillfully and truthfully—though anonymously—on *RITE*Site (see pp. 325 - 333 for help), you'll be as easily found, understood, and appreciated as anyone else on the planet. Indeed far more so, because you're findable with digital ease in the most logical place to look.

Select the *RITES*-Honored Option.

Make your full information available to recruiters in 356 highly respected retainer search firms.

Besides making yourself visible to the entire world—which your identity-concealed resume can do with relative safety—you can also achieve an entirely different and more powerful visibility with *RITE*Site's 356 *RITES*-Honored recruiters.

Merely select the *RITES*-Honored Option when you register. Automatically your contact information—name, postal and e-mail addresses, and phone and fax numbers—*will be added at the top of your resume when viewed or printed by a RITES-Honored recruiter.*

Moreover, when you elect to add the *RITES*-Honored Option to your service, a window is provided for you to add either (1) an addendum to your identity-concealed resume that fills in specific employer names and any other data you've left out or disguised. Or, easier and better still, (2) *merely paste in your regular resume...the one you'd normally e-mail to prominent firms.* That way, any *RITES*-Honored recruiter can make an immediate phone call to you...or click a link and send you an e-mail...or tell an assistant to send you a letter. He or she can even put your resume into the firm's own database, a very favorable result from your point of view.

Regardless of whether you're interested in what the *RITES*-honored recruiter proposes, if you handle yourself well, you've probably taken the first steps toward a career-long relationship with one of the top firms. Eventually you will develop several relationships like the example shown on pages 113-15.

In a hurry? Enter *RITE*Site's Custom Career Service immediately via the *RITES*-Honored Option.

It will take you awhile to convert your regular resume to an effective identity-concealed resume (see pp. 325 - 333 for help). If your regular version is ready now, don't delay. Make it available to *RITES*-honored recruiters immediately. Reach out to the rest of the world with your identity-*concealed* resume later on, when you get it ready.

Just one posting on *RITE*Site, and you're accessible to all *RITES*-Honored recruiters in Appendix II. This is *not* true when you post on any of the commercial (Type 1) sites claiming to be for executives or for high-paying jobs. They *charge* recruiters and employers to view resumes...proudly naming the ones that pay to look. As we've discussed, those firms are almost *never* the trusted retainer-only firms selected for *RITES*-Honored status.

Custom Career Service: the Total Program...

Continually and secretly hear of career breakthroughs when you're employed.

Get a new and better job faster when you're unemployed.

Use RiteSite's computer to manage your career as you'd never have the time to do in any other way.

If you want your background and achievements continually "findable" by recruiters and employers filling jobs you should consider, but you must be secretive to protect your current situation, Custom Career Service solves that problem. With CCS, you can have 24-hour 7-day computerized career management tailored to your exact needs and career strategies:

1. **Keep your *identity-concealed* resume anonymously posted year-round on *Rite*Site.** In its most rudimentary form, CCS enables recruiters and employers to continually find you in the most logical place they could possibly look for you...on *Rite*Site's easily sortable database.

   Display your successful career in a persuasive resume, but eliminate latest employer names, your name and address, and any other information that might embarrassingly identify you. Recruiters and employers can reach you through *Rite*Site's computer, which will e-mail their proposal to you (or you may choose a more secretive communication method than e-mail).

   But why limit yourself to just one career development strategy when you have so many additional sophisticated tools at your disposal?

2. **Post specialized *identity-concealed* resumes for various functions and industries.** Are you qualified for more than one type of position? More than one industry? Showcase different aspects of your talent and experience. With your identity concealed, you can make multiple presentations of yourself if you choose to do so.

   Post your resume anonymously in as many of *Rite*Site's 49 industries as you consider appropriate and in up to 4 different versions. Can't decide between (1) a multi-page fact-filled resume with lots of specifics to prove your superiority or (2) a 1-pager that's quick to read but makes you seem generic? Post both. Are you qualified for two different positions...perhaps CEO of a small to medium sized company and/or CFO of a very large one? Post two truthful but different resumes.

3. **Reach out to *Rites*-Honored Recruiters. Select the *Rites-Honored Option* and post on *Rite*Site the same *identity-revealed* resume you'd submit in a direct mail campaign to those outstanding firms.** Now recruiters in the 356 *Rites*-Honored firms are permitted to search, find, read, print and download your complete resume. It's almost like placing it in each firm's database. Indeed, it may be a lot more readily "findable," because *Rite*Site's indexing and sorting methods are more advanced than the internal systems of the vast majority of search firms.

4. **Respond to positions posted on *Rite*Site and elsewhere without revealing your identity.** Tell the computer to forward your *identity-concealed* message and/or resume in response to job postings on *Rite*Site and elsewhere. If the recruiter or employer wants to talk to you, he or she will have to identify himself/herself in a response to you via *Rite*Site's computer. Reply if interested; otherwise remain con-

cealed. Or respond by asking for clearer information, and identify yourself only if you get it.

5. **Put the computer on 24-hour 7-day "Opportunity Alert" for searches that might interest you.** Tell it specifically what you want. It will continually compare your criteria with all of *Rite*Site's newly posted job descriptions, and e-mail you every new submission by a recruiter or a company that meets your requirements. Or, if you're nervous about receiving this sort of information by e-mail, *Rite*Site's computer will compile and save the information for you, so you can access and print it online without ever having it transmitted in an e-mail.

6. **Screen recruiters and deal only with the finest.** Unscrupulous operators use multiple names and post jobs they don't have in order to attract resumes they can scatter. Unfamiliar ones you see on the Internet are among the worst offenders. Many even imply they're corporate employers when they're not. Each time *Rite*Site's computer contacts you it will either (1) reassure you that the headhunter has demonstrated that he or she is from a *Rites of Passage*-honored firm or (2) caution you to the contrary.

7. **If you wish to take an even more aggressive approach to *Rites*-honored recruiters than simply opening your identity-revealed resume to all of them on *Rite*Site, take advantage of the *Rites-Honored Download*.** *Rite*Site's entire database of *Rites*-Honored Recruiters is continually updated to contain e-mail and postal addresses and fax numbers of all the firms, plus instructions on how they prefer to receive unsolicited resumes. There's even a "maximum-efficiency list," which includes (1) all firms accepting by e-mail, (2) all accepting by fax but not e-mail, and (3) the remainder who accept only on-paper submissions or who insist on input via their Web sites. Instantly download the latest data for your own personal use. When sending electronically, you'll be using the exact e-mail address and/or other instruction the firm has specified for unsolicited resume submissions, and you'll be *sending from your own PC*. That way you're obviously operating independently. You are *not* part of the mass spamming (unwelcome to many of the finest firms) now being automatically "blasted" (for a fee) by commercial services to long lists of recruiters (many of whom *you* do *not* want to receive your resume).

8. **Review your Career Management Summary Report.** *Rite*Site's computer will work behind the scenes to make sure you're (1) informed when your desired jobs appear on *Rite*Site and (2) found when recruiters search the database using criteria that match the background and objectives you've indicated. *Your membership includes a continually updated status report on your entire customized program.* Check it periodically at your leisure.

9. **Customize a program that fosters your personal career strategies day and night, year after year.** (1) Put persuasive identity-*concealed* information about yourself on *Rite*Site, where recruiters and employers are sure to find it. (2) Pursue multiple career development scenarios simultaneously using different but entirely truthful identity-*concealed* resumes. (3) Make your identity-*revealed* information available to *Rites*-Honored recruiters using the *Rites*-Honored Option. (4) Keep *Rite*Site's computer scanning for the exact combinations of industry, function, compensation, and location that might interest you. (5) Meanwhile, **concentrate on your current job**. Give it 100%. Move up where you are. As you do, (6) ask *Rite*Site's computer to pursue even higher goals for you in the outside world.

10. **The cost of all these Custom Career Services is just $94 per year**, and that rate is permanently protected against future price increases because you're an early *Rite*Site member.

At last! Say Goodbye to Direct Mail Drudgery in dealing with Executive Recruiters.

Finally!

Using *Rite*Site, it's easy to make yourself findable by the search industry.

Frankly, I wouldn't bother with direct mail to reach *recruiters* these days, even though employer decision-makers *should* be approached by mail (see Chapter 13). Of course, you *will* send your elegant on-paper mailing to any first-class recruiters you already know personally.

However, if you're a CCS member and you do want to send your on-paper mailing to a broad list of *Rites*-Honored recruiters, you can remove most of the work from that process by using the *Rites*-Honored Download. CCS can't stuff and seal envelopes. But it can effortlessly send you the names and addresses you'll feed into your PC's mail merge program.

Super-Advanced Technology ...at Your Disposal and the Recruiter's

The point is that now you have a convenient tool to make yourself known to every person on the planet who might want to hire someone into a position that you consider the ideal next step for your career. He or she pays nothing to probe *Rite*Site's database, and it's unique sorting systems are—by a wide margin—the most sophisticated anywhere in the industry today.

No matter how large and/or excellent the search firm, chances are that its candidate-sorting and search-management software are notably less sophisticated and helpful than *RITE*Site's database, with its 49 industry categories, its comprehensive array of 1,374 corresponding industry-specific job categories, and its artificial intelligence-like sifting of people from related industries and functions to find many highly appropriate matches above and beyond the ones that are logically obvious.

Will the recruiters you prefer find you on *RITE*Site? I can't guarantee it. But I've done everything possible to make that the easiest and most logical thing for them to do.

If *RITE*Site is so good, why is it so inexpensive?

There are several reasons.

First, the main thing executives pay over $300 a year for on Executive Interface Sites is reconnaissance on searches being conducted by retainer executive recruiters. *RITE*Site unbundles that benefit and gives it away free.

All that *RITE*Site *does* charge for is computer service actually rendered to the executive. Yes, the service is unusually comprehensive and technically advanced. On the other hand, *RITE*Site does *not* provide any publications or social events. Those are frills I'm not interested in providing.

My enthusiasm lies in an entirely different direction. Today, as never before, the tools exist to greatly improve the world's utilization of human talent. And I'd love to provide any little nudge I can toward that objective. The reason for pricing Custom Career Service at approximately the cost of providing it— rather than at its value, which would be many times higher—is to encourage wide participation. With more executives participating, more recruiters and employers will visit to see who's available. And best of all, with large numbers of executives participating, employers will find it less and less reasonable to take offense if an individual is discovered to have indulged in the very modest and reasonable expression of self-interest *RITE*Site represents.

I believe that everyone deserves to achieve his or her "highest and best use," as the real estate industry would say. And if their current company—or their current boss within their current company—doesn't think that way, then I believe the employee deserves to be discovered and put to more professionally and personally rewarding use elsewhere.

So if you decide to use *RITE*Site, you'll not only be helping yourself, you'll be helping a long and growing line of others too.

So Much for RiteSite and Its Position among the Major Employment Sites

...except This One Last Difference:

There is no legal "fine print."

So there's no need to hunt for it...and no danger of overlooking it.

In designing *Rite*Site, I've tried to make it as unhazardous and user friendly as possible. I've told the computer wizards to make the site state-of-the-art in service, strength and security.

But let's be realistic. I can't guarantee that you can't have any problems.

Please don't imagine that you can participate in *Rite*Site or *any* Internet site without taking on personal risk. You can't. But if the site hands you the tools to do so—and *Rite*Site is designed to do just that—you can take steps to limit your risk to the point that you feel the rewards of using the site exceed the risks of doing so. The best analogy I can think of is air travel. Planes crash. We know that. Yet you and I *do* fly.

*Rite*Site does not have the usual explosion of lawyer-worded "Terms and Conditions" tucked onto an obscure page. Instead, common sense prevails... and it's stated right up front:

NOTE ——Computers and people, including both you and us, are fallible and make mistakes. In providing this free and/or low cost service, we can't and don't promise that you will not be harmed by computer malfunction or vandalism or by intended, negligent or stupid acts by yourself, ourselves, or anyone else who may reach you through *Rite*Site.

Do not proceed if you are not willing to go ahead alertly and at your own risk. By proceeding, you are telling us that you accept these terms.

Sail on brave mariner. Cyberspace awaits!

I hope you find RITESite.com as helpful as I've tried to make it.

Now let's go back to covering topics that apply to every site on the Internet.

||| **Posting in cyberspace is fundamentally** |||
risky as well as rewarding.
Let's talk about strategies to minimize that risk.

Whether you post your *identity-revealed* resume on a commercial site or an altruistic one, you've put your identity and your achievements where the whole world can see them.

You've taken a risk that your current employer may someday be handed a copy of the resume you posted and speak the dreaded words:

"What's going on here? Are you looking for another job?"

If you proceed wisely when you do the actual posting, you can deflect that challenge with a rebuttal you developed when you posted. Or you can, in effect, put information about you where recruiters can easily find it, without actually "posting" it at all. Here are some suggestions:

1. **Post at an innocent time.** Nobody can fault you for posting—or otherwise distributing your resume—when (1) you're out of work and aggressively looking for a position or (2) your company is the subject of a tender offer or (3) your business unit is for sale. Self-preservation is an OK motive. So even if you feel a looming change may *not* end up hurting you, seize the moment to publicize yourself and your accomplishments. Action taken then is justified and—unless you've been warned otherwise— can't be faulted later.

   Incidentally, if there's a "stay bonus" which you must stick around X months to collect, check carefully what the specific terms of it are. Normally you are *not* prohibited from making yourself known. You *can't walk* before payday, but you *can talk.*

2. *Mark* **the innocent time you posted.** If you're posting an identity-revealed resume at an innocent time, make sure it's dated. A header at the top of page 2 and every following page should do the trick:

   Page 2 - Carl T. Covert - 9/12/02

   Because everyone's browser and computer programs handle online words differently, your page/name/date notation will probably *not* be printed, as you intended, at the top of the recipient's pages. Who cares? Your date-mark will be just as effective if it interrupts a page as if it's above. The important thing is to have it included, so that you can use it as a defense, if you're ever challenged later on.

3. **Conform the information to an innocent time.** Maybe you must launch your information at a hazardous time. If so, perhaps you should end your resume just *prior* to your current title or current employer. That would keep your paperwork absolutely truthful—which it *must* be—yet place it at an innocent time. If you ever need to do this, do not use the dating technique in #2. Everything you ever say in a resume must be true. Note, incidentally that most sites date their postings...an embarrassment that will show up on the screen, even if not on your paperwork.

4. **Post anonymously.** Need we say more?

5. **Become findable without actually posting.** Get involved in industry affairs. Recruiters and their researchers are constantly on the Internet looking for people who are outstanding in their field. They've always looked for the authors of appropriate trade journal articles. But today the Internet provides lots more information...biographies of nominees for offices in industry associations (you don't have to win to *win!*), and announcements and agendas for industry meetings, conferences, conventions and seminars. And not only the elections and meetings that will occur later this year, but also ones that occurred one, two, three, and four years ago. Also copies of the prepared remarks various speakers presented. That sort of information used to disappear after the event. Now it seems to be archived forever on the Internet. *Nobody's emptying the trash in cyberspace!* Headhunters are continually sifting through it for people each industry considers outstanding.

6. **Encourage your company to publicize you.** Today more and more companies proudly post brief biographies of their senior officers on corporate Web sites. Departments are also putting get-to-know-us information on their sites...rosters of their sales and marketing teams, distinguished members of their scientific staff, etc. Information that used to be jealously hidden in don't-let-any-outsider-see-it directories now glows on the Web. Trendy movements are afoot and the corporation exhibits them on the Internet. For example: Let's-get-close-to-our-customers-and-suppliers. See-what-eminent-people-work-here. And so forth. Great! If you don't want to be overlooked by recruiters filling jobs that might be your big career breakthrough, this is the kind of PR you should encourage.

7. **Encourage your professional association to publicize you.** We discussed this on pages 294-95.

These days you need two resumes: Electronic and On-Paper

Let's get busy on the electronic side.

With the computers and printers we all have these days, we can easily create documents that look as handsome and communicate as well as any book, magazine, or newspaper. When you hand someone your on-paper resume, it must make a first-class visual impression. It must rise to the standard that everyone now can easily produce.

However, the standard is different—and lower—when you're sending a resume electronically. First of all, you want it to arrive and be readable. And secondly, you want it to slide effortlessly into the recipient's database, so you'll be found when there's a search for someone exactly like you. Your aesthetics are no help if your functionality fails.

Submit your resume in the body of an e-mail.

Why bore you with technical jargon? Here's the bottom line. To submit your resume electronically, *send it in the body of an e-mail*. Not as a file attached to an e-mail. It must be sent as readable words *in the message*. If you do that, everyone can read your paperwork when they get it. Moreover, your resume can be inserted effortlessly into everyone's database. Then, whenever there's a search for someone like you, you'll be found...and your information will be easy to read, process, and forward.

Sure, you'd like your online resume to have all the typographic features of your handsome hand-delivered paperwork, with bold type for headlines, Italics in a few places, charts with neat columns of figures, etc. Well it ain't gonna happen! At least not until Internet technology has advanced far beyond its current capabilities. Here are some helpful observations and tips:

If your recipient supplies instructions, take advantage of them. On some sites you *can* submit your information in a way that retains, displays, and prints most of the handsome formatting of your hand-it-out resume *for that recipient,* because they tell you exactly how to conform to their requirements. But don't try to apply one site's specified methods when dealing with any other site. They probably won't work!

Never, *NEVER* send your resume as an appended file unless specifically instructed to do so. This point is worth repeating and explaining. There are two controlling reasons: (1) Many search firms and companies will not open any file from a stranger for fear of getting a virus.

Forget why you're sure your file cannot be anything but safe. They have a *policy!* And it says *trash your submission.* (2) There are so many possible mis-matches among even the most popular brands and versions of software, and inside-the-company systems that whatever you send *isn't likely to open on the first click.* Sadly, nobody has the time or inclination to experiment with any alternative method that might open an unsolicited resume. There are hundreds more waiting in line after that one. So trash it and move *on!* These are harsh facts, but you'd better face them.

Make a generic electronic resume, formatted so that you can cut-and-paste it into an e-mail or the resume input area of virtually any Internet employment site. Here are a few step-by-step instructions for converting your beautifully formatted on-paper resume into a form that will e-mail smoothly and be easily digested into the recipient's database when it arrives:

1. **Open a new document** in your word-processing program...Compose your e-mailable resume in this new document or merely import an already created resume.

2. **Set your margins** for a 6.5 inch line.

3. **Select a type face that does not involve proportional spacing.** Courier is the classic...used on most of the old IBM Selectric typewriters.

4. **Emphasize your name and topic headings...***simply.* Probably you'll merely type them in capital letters. (All caps are OK for emphasis within your resume, but not in your cover letter where they would be considered impolite "shouting," as they are in Internet chat rooms, etc.)

5. **Use parentheses around the area code of your phone number** if you are submitting your resume to a *RITES*-Honored recruiter or to a company employment sector not outsourced to a commercial site. These recipients are likely to have resume reading and storage software that looks for phone numbers presented in that way.

   However, if you are posting your resume on *RITE*Site.com or on any other site that aims at confidentiality, *do not include your phone number in your resume unless it is unlisted.* Listed numbers can easily be reverse-queried to get your name and address...thus exposing you to theft-of-identity possibilities.

   Indeed, with *RITE*Site's confidentiality options you will probably choose not to display even an unlisted number. You cannot be anonymous in postings to the public and/or to various recruiters (who for a nominal fee can access almost any Internet resume database) if you include a phone number that is listed or an e-mail address that leads to your actual ISP, both of which can be easily investigated to find your identity. *RITE*Site provides alternative e-mail addresses, or you can get one from a provider such as HotMail, Fiberia, Excite, AltaVista, Yahoo, Email, etc.

6. **Use the space bar to indent; do not use tabs.** If tabs have been used, delete them and replace them with space bar-created spacings. Even taking that precaution, I personally have never been able to successfully communicate a complex chart such as the one on page 211. It looks OK when I send. It does ***not*** when it arrives at many of its destinations. Maybe the state of the art will have improved by the time you read this. But my best advice at the moment of writing these words is to forget about achieving perfect-looking charts in your e-resume. They'll communicate, even if they look ragged.

7. **Run your spell-check. Also proofread very carefully.** "To" instead of "or" and a missing "not" won't be caught by the spell-check. Mistakes abound in resumes...and especially in electronic ones, because those often are not run and checked on paper prior to transmission. This is a hazard you can easily avoid.

8. **Do a "Save As"...name...and keep a permanent copy on your hard drive.** When you save, choose the most basic and generic option...ASCII (pronounced "Askee" and short for American Standard Code for Information Interchange). You will probably have 3 types of ASCII to choose from, possibly without the ASCII acronym even being mentioned. They are Plain Text.txt, Rich Text.rtf, and Hypertext.html. Use Plain Text, unless a specific site has suggested you use Rich Text (which preserves some formatting if your recipient can cope with it, but causes problems if not). Hypertext.html, of course is the language of Internet sites—and a whole other subject—but it's inappropriate for the simple e-mailing we're talking about here. If you're using a Macintosh choose Simpletext.

9. **Test your handiwork. Send your resume as an e-mail to several friends.** They will have different computers and software, and may note problems you can correct. You'll have many future opportunities to cut-and-paste your carefully perfected electronic resume—or a variation—into e-mails and resume solicitation pages of recruiter and employer Internet sites. It pays to make your self-representation tool as good as you possibly can.

Destined for a Database

In the late '80s and early '90s the largest corporations and search firms bought software from companies like Restrac, Resumix, Personics and others that enabled scanning resumes into databases and retrieval through keyword searches. Now those vendors and many new ones have made scanning—with its vast labor and many errors—obsolete. Every word you submit in the body of an e-mail can be vacuumed almost effortlessly into any database using such a system.

Nouns have never been so important!

Insert plenty of the right "keywords," so that the computer will find your resume.

Virtually every database your electronic resume will enter is able to sort its resumes by "keywords." When looking for a resume, the inquirer thinks of wording—usually a noun—that ought to appear in the resume of the sort of person being looked for, and the computer selects all the resumes containing that word or phrase. Unfortunately, some programs—perhaps a third—search for keywords in just the first 100 or 200 words of each resume, not the entire document.

Therefore, you should (1) make sure your overall resume contains a wide spectrum of the words you'd expect someone looking for a person like you to think of, and (2) make sure that the likeliest words are used within the first half or so of the first page.

The best way to do that is to create an introductory summary paragraph that says what you do and briefly mentions the successes you've had. This succinct telling of your story is worth doing well because it serves several purposes:

1. It orients the reader to who you are and sparks interest in reading further.

2. It uses all your most important keywords where they are sure to be found even by the computer that doesn't scan the whole document.

3. If you're filing an identity-concealed resume, this summary at the top of page one replaces your name, address, and phone (otherwise the summary is just under that information). Therefore, it substitutes for your identification. Making it crisp, clear, and enticing helps

give you tangibility. Even without a name and a city you seem like a formidable person worth clicking an e-mail button to reach.

Some Sample Keywords and Phrases to Get You Thinking about that Introductory Paragraph

For a CEO, COO, or CFO: Chief Executive, CEO, Chief Operating Officer, Chief Financial Officer, CFO, Chairman, President, Executive Vice President, shareholder value, Board of Directors, Management Committee, earnings per share, EPS, mergers and acquisitions, M&A, (*do* use more than one wording for the same thing), restructuring, recapitalize, divest, divestiture, Chapter 11, debenture, bonds, equity, tender offer, pre-tax profit, return on investment, ROI, EBIT, EBITDA, EVA, dividend, higher margin, strategic planning...you get the idea.

For a Marketing Executive: Chief Marketing Officer, Director of Brand Management, Product Manager, Vice President, EVP, National Sales Manager, Region Manager, (people seeking a certain level of candidate will often use titles as keyword queries), share of market, market share, market research, advertising, sales promotion, packaged goods, pizza, franchisees, premiums, shampoo, routes, pre-packs, conventions, etc.

For a Manufacturing Executive: Chief Manufacturing Officer, Plant Manager, purchasing, procurement, supply chain, JIT, just in time, outsource, engineering, quality control, quality assurance, QC, maintenance, international, overseas, Baldridge Award, union, collective bargaining, strike, teams, injection molding, grey iron casting, valve, pipe, recycle,waste management, nuclear, hydroelectric, wafers, etc.

For an HR Executive: Chief Human Resources Officer, Senior Vice President, compensation and benefits, comp & benefits, recruitment, organizational development, succession planning, diversity, collective bargaining, strike, non-exempt, diversity, acquisition, integration, subsidiaries, divisions, executive coaching, CEO (as in report to the CEO), etc.

For Everyone: Titles of *lots of earlier positions*, with several that show any *specialties that preceded your current function*. People looking for a President or a Division Manager with a prior orientation in Marketing, Manufacturing, or Finance will probe the database with key words to identify such people...Product Manager, Plant Manager, Controller, etc.

More than Enough Examples!
What do they tell us?

Please go back and *consider those examples, even if none of the functional categories applied to you*.

Notice the value of being very concrete and specific in naming what you've been called and what you've dealt with. You might be tempted to describe your activities in vague generalities, because you feel that doing so would be "less limiting." Don't make that mistake!

Resume databases *are*—by definition—loaded with people. The user of the database will choose narrowly specific keywords to sort them. Reasons: (1) the vast number of people is overwhelming, and using vague general terms is **not** the way to cut a total of 2,000 down to the 5 or 6 who are most appropriate. Conversely, (2) the vast number of people is an opportunity. "Surely," thinks the user of the database, "in that huge group there must be at least 5 or 6 who'd be *precisely* what I want. Therefore, I must be very specific in probing the database."

Please read the above examples several times. Imagine *yourself* seeking a person of each type shown. See why you'd instinctively try each of those words in an effort to nail precisely the right person. Now change places. Become a seeker of talent *at your own level in your own industry*. What words would pull *you* out of the crowd? What are the buzz words, the trendy issues, problems, opportunities, equipment, etc. that an outstanding person in your field should have dealt with? Okay. Now think of the likeliest words to describe them. Those are the keywords to be sure to include in your resume.

| | |Now Let's Modify Sam Sage's Resume for Electronic Use. | | |

You remember Sam's on-paper resume from page 210. Look at it again.

It's not too hard to think up a good keyword summary paragraph for Sam.

What *is* hard to accomplish is the outstanding impression made by the chart at the beginning of Sam's on-paper version. Sadly, e-mail's lack of formatting (tabs don't work) means he'll have to use spacebar spaces to approximate columns. The result will be serviceable, but not beautiful.

Notice, however, that the overall look of the electronic version is actually quite neat and inviting. Realize too, that nobody else's resume is going to look any better than Sam's. *Dependably* constructed electronic resumes are dull to look at...truly a *"level playing field."*

Therefore, the realm of competition is *keywords*. I cannot begin to emphasize adequately the importance of the strategic thinking and word-choosing described on the prior page. The trick is to get the database user—recruiter or employer—to keyword you and not someone else as his or her needle-in-a-haystack. Good luck!

SAMUEL P. SAGE
219 Waring Drive
Denton, New Jersey 07299
Home: (201) 719-0932
Office: (212) 121-3000

As Sent ①

②

Dear Recruiters:

Do you seek a division president ... or a corporate chief
marketing officer ... with an exceptional record? ③

The $1.3 billion company I've helped build for five years as
Chief Marketing Officer has doubled sales, increased profits
nine-fold, and raised ROI from 3.6% in '96 to over 28% in '01.

As a result, we've been acquired at 30 times earnings. Success
is the reason I'm available.

Compensation in recent years has ranged from $420,000 to
$550,000.

Resume follows. Thank you.

④

CHIEF EXECUTIVE OR CHIEF MARKETING OFFICER

As Vice President - Chief Marketing Officer preparing to take
over from the CEO, I've led the marketing-oriented turnaround of
a $1.3 billion privately owned pharmaceutical company,
Farrington Labs, from slow growth and low profit ... '96 sales
$592 million with $25 million pre-tax profit and 3.6% ROI to
high growth, high profit, and high ROI ... '01 sales $1.3
billion, $223 million pre-tax, and 28% ROI.

⑤

Recruited to restructure and reorganize marketing, advertising,
and sales force, and to spur new product development. On track
to succeed the owner as CEO. Instead we've been acquired. My
strategic planning of acquisitions and divestitures for an
international pharmaceutical company were equally successful.
Earlier, as VP Account Supervisor, headed their account at New
World Advertising Agency, and earlier was Assistant Brand
Manager at P&G. Experienced with TV advertising, consumer
packaged goods, prescription and veterinary drugs, pet foods,
household products, etc. Have BA and Harvard MBA.

⑥

1996 - Present
FARRINGTON LABORATORIES
(Merged into Pan Global Pharmaceuticals Ltd. in October '01)
New York, New York
VICE PRESIDENT - CHIEF MARKETING OFFICER ⑦

Recruited as VP - Chief Marketing Officer by Blair Farrington,
Founder/Owner/CEO in '96, when sales were $592 million.

Mr. Farrington doubled what I'd been making in the same position
at the much larger (then $1.2 billion) Swiss-owned Medica Suisse

SAMUEL P. SAGE
219 Waring Drive
Denton, New Jersey 07299
Home: (201) 719-0932
Office: (212) 121-3000

> **As Received**   ①

②

Dear Recruiters:

Do you seek a division president ... or a corporate chief marketing officer ... with an exceptional record? ③

The $1.3 billion company I've helped build for five years as Chief Marketing Officer has doubled sales, increased profits nine-fold, and raised ROI from 3.6% in '96 to over 28% in '01.

As a result, we've been acquired at 30 times earnings. Success is the reason I'm available.

Compensation in recent years has ranged from $420,000 to $550,000.

Resume follows. Thank you.

CHIEF EXECUTIVE OR CHIEF MARKETING OFFICER ④

As Vice President - Chief Marketing Officer preparing to take over from the CEO, I've led the marketing-oriented turnaround of a $1.3 billion privately owned pharmaceutical company, Farrington Labs, from slow growth and low profit ... '96 sales $592 million with $25 million pre-tax profit and 3.6% ROI to high growth, high profit, and high ROI ... '01 sales $1.3 billion, $223 million pre-tax, and 28% ROI.

⑤

Recruited to restructure and reorganize marketing, advertising, and sales force, and to spur new product development. On track to succeed the owner as CEO. Instead we've been acquired. My strategic planning of acquisitions and divestitures for an international pharmaceutical company were equally successful. Earlier, as VP Account Supervisor, headed their account at New World Advertising Agency, and earlier was Assistant Brand Manager at P&G. Experienced with TV advertising, consumer packaged goods, prescription and veterinary drugs, pet foods, household products, etc. Have BA and Harvard MBA.

⑥

1996 - Present
FARRINGTON LABORATORIES
(Merged into Pan Global Pharmaceuticals Ltd. in October '01)
New York, New York
VICE PRESIDENT - CHIEF MARKETING OFFICER

⑦

Recruited as VP - Chief Marketing Officer by Blair Farrington, Founder/Owner/CEO in '96, when sales were $592 million.

Mr. Farrington doubled what I'd been making in the same position at the much larger (then $1.2 billion) Swiss-owned Medica Suisse USA Ltd. Primary incentive was this 72 year old gentleman's plan to go public with me as his successor, after we worked a few years together to increase volume and profit. Instead, the company has been purchased by ... and merged into ... Pan Global Pharmaceuticals (October '01). With their acquiescence, I'm seeking a new challenge ... hopefully a Presidency; otherwise Chief Marketing Officer with early transition to general management.

Following (with Mr. Farrington's permission) is our performance since I joined in '96 and 3 years prior:

	Sales($M)	%Change	Pre-Tax Net($M)	%Change	ROI	%Change
'01	$1,342.6	+31.5%	$223.0	+62.4%	ROI 28.1%	
'00	1,021.0	+24.9%	137.3	+52.3%;	24.6%	
'99	817.5	+36.1%	90.2	+43.1%;	17.2%	
'98	600.6	+23.2%	62.9	+39.8%;	12.7%	
'97	487.5	-17.7%	45.0	+81.9%;	9.4%	
'96	592.4	-2.4%	24.8	-16.8%;	3.6%	
'95	606.9	+4.5%	29.8	+6.6%;	4.9%	

⑧

Sam Sage did a lot of what we've been talking about.

Look at it from two viewpoints on pages 320 & 321.

As you see, Sam submitted his cover letter followed by his resume directly to a highly respected retainer search firm with an outstanding reputation...one of the firms listed in Appendix II. He visited their Web site to get the precise e-mail address they use to receive unsolicited cover-letters-and-resumes directly into their database. Or perhaps he downloaded this resume-submission address along with upwards of 300 others from *RITE*Site, as a member of its Custom Career Service.

Either way, Sam didn't hesitate to clearly identify himself. He trusts this firm to work only on retainer and not to share its internal database with other firms he might not know about. Indeed, he's delighted to have his information in their computer, so that he'll come to their attention every time they go to their database looking for someone like him.

Looking Better Later

Page 320 is how Sam's resume looked when he sent it. Page 321 is how it looked when a recruiter in the firm read it. As we discussed, Sam set his margins at 6.5 inches and used 12 point type in a font (Courier) with no proportional spacing. And of course, he had to use all caps to achieve emphasis, which he applied to his name, company names, and major job titles. As a result, the pages of copy he pasted into the body of the e-mail message looked depressingly bloated from his end. However, his letter and resume actually looked quite nice when they were printed out from the firm's database by one of the recruiting firm's members, as shown on page 321. The reason is that, by the time Sam's material had been delivered by e-mail, absorbed into the search firm's database, and printed out for the recruiter according to his default preference (similar to most defaults), what Sam sent had been transformed into different and smaller 10 point type. The recruiter saw what you see on page 321.

Tips and Comments Marked by Numbers on Pages 320 & 321

These comments match the numbers on either page, except that only page 321 goes far enough down to reveal number 8.

1. **All caps on name. Full identification right up front.** Also **every line begins at the left margin...***the safest possible way to zap information* into the wild blue yonder so it'll show up mostly unscrambled everywhere.

2. **Two blank lines** precede the salutation of the cover letter, which is *short!* There's *no need to name a person* when zapping an e-mail into a database. The letter hits the main *one or two central selling ideas*—which the resume *proves*—and signs off. Making Sam's letter longer would have made it *worse*, not better. The same is true of yours.

3. **One blank line between every paragraph** (two "hard returns" in word-processing talk). Also, note the ellipses (...). For electronic use these must have a space on either side of the 3 dots, or adjoining words won't wrap.

4. **Three blank lines** precede the *all-cap first line of the resume*, which *labels the person*. This is the "Position Desired," but Sam's smart enough never to state the obvious with an unnecessary label.

5. **These two paragraphs are the contemptible toxic waste dump of potential keywords someone might use to look for Sam.** *They're great!* He cut a single huge dump into two parts to make it less of a visual barrier. Almost every word in the second paragraph is a keyword he wants upfront, even P&G, an icon for some in his field. Count. There are *over 40 keywords and keyword phrases* in those two paragraphs that someone wanting someone with Sam's experience might intuitively use to pull a few needles out of a hay stack of very similar people. Sam's embarrassed by these two cliché-ridden and logically unnecessary paragraphs. He'd rather go straight from the letter...to the single all-caps line...to "1996 - Present." But this is an *electronic resume* and he's done a great job of making his "Keyword Summary" (unlabeled of course) relatively palatable.

6. **Two blank lines prior to the current—and every prior—employer**.

7. **All caps on company *and* position** after two-blank-lines-above *highlight the transition and invite reading*. Include *cities* you wouldn't mind working in again; they're keywords that may be used to locate you.

8. **Charts are powerful eye-catchers in executive-level resumes**. Executive eyes zoom to charts when they otherwise wouldn't look at a page. Sadly, in electronic form you *cannot use tabs to make perfect columns*. Using 12-point type in a 6.5 inch line and equal numbers of spacebar spaces between entries with each line starting at the left margin, Sam did the best he could. He couldn't have gone one space further without violating the 6.5 inch limit on what he sent. When he sent those columns they were evenly spread across the entire width of the page. However, even as distortedly as the recruiter sees the chart at the bottom of page 321, it's still a highlight of Sam's resume. It will get him hired!

'94　580.8　+7.2%　27.9　+8.2%;　5.7%
'93　541.8　+6.1%　25.8　-1.1%;　9.1%

Cut the product line from 618 SKU's in '96 to 309 profitable items in '99 (expanded with new products to 384 by '01). Reorganized the 109-person sales force into 11 regions in '97 and expanded it to 225 people by '01.

Introduced 9 profitable new drugs via cross-licensing agreements with other manufacturers ('01 sales, $258 million; $62 million pre-tax net). Generated additional $23.4 million pre-tax by granting licenses to other companies.

Physicians' top-of-mind brand awareness of our three largest-selling drugs was raised from 18% in '96 to 62% in '01 by a massive sampling, detailing, and professional advertising campaign (budget tripled from $18.8 million in '96 to $58.2 million in '01).

As a result of Farrington Labs' excellent growth trend and high profitability, Pan Global paid 30 times estimated '01 earnings in a 50%-cash/50%-stock transaction.

1993 - 1996
MEDICA SUISSE USA LTD.
Marshall Plains, New Jersey
VICE PRESIDENT - PHARMACEUTICAL MARKETING

Rejoined this $3.6 billion Zurich-based maker of prescription drugs, veterinary biologicals, and fine chemicals as Director of Pharmaceutical Marketing, reporting to the Managing Director - USA, and heading all marketing and sales for all North American pharmaceutical lines (total '93 sales, $630 million) after a two-year hiatus to aid my family's automobile business in Ohio.

By 1996 sales were nearly double ($1.2 billion) 1993 volume, and ROI had increased from 17% ('93) to 24% ('96). Market share of U.S. prescription tranquilizer market rose from 11.6% in '93 to 19.2% in '96, and veterinary products gained 1.3 share points to 7.2% in '96.

My earlier recommendation (in '91) that the company's consumer pet-health lines be sold to generate cash for acquisition of young growth companies in the higher-margined ethical drug field was implemented while I was away ('92), and I helped identify and purchase in '93 and '94 three small companies...BioTRITON, Radio-Tra-Chem, and Synestial Laboratories...which have all grown and prospered under Medica Suisse ownership. One of these, BioTRITON, was publicly reported as having worldwide sales of $560 million in '00, with the highest ROI of any Medica Suisse business anywhere in the world.

Promoted '94 to Vice President - Pharmaceutical Marketing.
Higher title, no change in duties.

Joined '93 as Director - Pharmaceutical Marketing. Rejoined Medica Suisse in charge of corporate Marketing, Market Research, Telemarketing, and Sales Promotion departments (total of 41 people); plus two sales forces...Ethical Drug (135-person) and Veterinary (32-person).

1991 - 1993
SAGE CHRYSLER / TOYOTA, INC.
Kensington, Ohio
INTERIM CEO

Upon my father's sudden death (2/91), I took charge of the family business ($2.8 million sales in '91, $4.4 million in '93), holding it together until my younger brother could finish his MBA at Wharton ('91) and join my mother in running the company.

Increased TV advertising, and diversified by building two Taco Bell fast food franchises (since expanded to seven). Profits nearly doubled in two years.

1989 - 1991
MEDICA SUISSE USA LTD.

< Look to your left!

Most of the remainder of Sam Sage's electronic resume is shown on the opposite page—not as Sam submitted it (see p. 320)—but rather as it is viewed by a recruiter in a major search firm (see p. 321). Notice that, with the formatting suggestions on pages 322-23, the primitive but *reliable* body-of-an-e-mail submission method has delivered a very nice looking presentation. Most importantly, the vast majority of intended recipients will actually *see* it.

On the other hand, if Sam had used an appended file or had retained the formatting of even the #1 market-leading word-processing program, his e-mailing might have been thrown away by who-knows-how-many recipients. Worst of all, he'd never have had any way of knowing that— although received—his submission fizzled.

Look to the Future!>

Concealing your identity while publishing your resume is the greatest challenge... and opportunity...of the Cyberspace Era.

Think of it!

We are now at the threshold of something the world has never seen before... truly a free market in human talent. Make that *executive* talent, and you see the potential benefit to your own career.

If you could be exposed—advertised—so that every recruiter and employer filling a position that could be your ideal career breakthrough could easily find you, *and* if simultaneously you could keep your identity concealed and reveal yourself only after you know with whom you'd be dealing and what they're offering, you could truly maximize your career progress and meet important life-style goals as well.

But to do that, you'd have to make yourself and your achievements—essentially your resume—open to the world, while keeping your identity concealed. And that's more easily said than done...especially at the executive level. Executives are not as interchangeable as Wal-Mart clerks. Executives are unique and can only be understood and selected on the basis of specific factual information.

Publishing is no problem.

Among the 80,000 career sites on the Internet an increasing number let you post anonymously. That's a *trend*. Someday—and it's not far off—many sites hoping to deal with executives will offer you this option. The question is, how do you take advantage of it?

CONFIDENTIALITY

The problem is staying truthful and specific enough to encourage contact, while also staying anonymous.

Face it. No recruiter and no employer will intentionally spend even one minute reading a resume that is a work of fiction.

Face it. Every recruiter and every employer will feel frustrated, angry and abused whenever he or she finds the person behind an identity-concealed resume is not in every way up to par with what the resume has implied.

People hate it when you mislead them and waste their time!

Moreover, recruiters can easily penalize you. They have computers. Even if they smile as they smoke out the truth during your interview, afterward they'll mark you permanently for "NO FURTHER ATTENTION." You may be able to get an interview or a phone call by over-claiming in your identity-concealed resume. But the end result will be to put you permanently off-limits at a search firm that might have greatly helped you in the future. Back in the '70s when I was an officer of one of the largest search firms we chose our words less sensitively. In those days you'd have been marked "DESTROY." That meant dump your file and—as our computer would remind everyone in the firm—never deal with you again.

Rules of Concealment:
1. Conceal *as little as possible.*
2. Disguise *down.*

Your objective is to tell everything that could possibly help you get pulled out of a vast database of executives. And then, as your identity-concealed resume is read, you want to stimulate "good vibes" that will have your reader thinking something like this: "I realize this person couldn't be specific about his/her current situation. But he/she tried hard to give me as much specific information as possible." People who supply only vague generalizations and disguise several of their jobs do ***not*** get that reaction.

Only you can decide what's too sensitive for you to reveal. But consider the following tips. Then turn the page to see Sam Sage's identity-concealed resume. His secrecy problem in working directly for the owner of a private company is probably far worse than yours. Even so, he tries for openness and he takes some calculated risks.

Think courageously in hiding your identity. Think of the #1 person you're most afraid might discover you've posted an identity-concealed resume. What's the worst he/she could *do?* How likely is that to happen? How might you defend if it did? Chances are, you'll see more opportunity than danger... especially if you plan ahead to mitigate the danger. Read Sam Sage's resume beginning on page 328 and its numbered suggestions very carefully.

Reveal *harmless* specifics. Think of ways to present facts that don't spill sensitive numbers but are specific, nonetheless. And don't fail to realize that information that was confidential a while ago is no longer a problem today. Sam's methods will spark your own personal creativity and common sense.

Get specific as near the top of your resume as possible. Sam now works for a shrewd CEO who owns the company. Worse, Medica Suisse, Sam's prior employer is one he worked for earlier. Being invited back proves how good Sam is, and he wants to include that fact. So he has several employers to conceal. Your situation is easier. You probably just want to conceal your current job...and possibly also the one before that.

Reveal your current job and all previous ones if you have no major reason not to. Just because you're permitted to conceal doesn't mean you should if you don't need to. If no retribution is likely—perhaps you're unemployed or the company is for sale—tell everything but your name, address and phone number. You've got good performance and a good reason to investigate leaving. Flaunt them!

Brand names and company names are *keywords*. So are cities. People accessing databases often use them to look for experience they want. Some names might be too sensitive for you to reveal. But others will get you pulled up and looked at, even when 1,000 other people in the database equally match the criteria.

Above all, disguise down. Make your descriptions modest, not exaggerated. Round figures to be slightly *less* favorable, not more. Never disguise yourself in any way that could let anyone feel disappointed or misled when your full facts come out in your actual resume (which you'll hand over as soon as possible) or in a phone call, or an interview, or a reference check. ***The fully revealed truth should be a welcome and impressive clarification, not a downer.***

CHIEF EXECUTIVE   OR   CHIEF MARKETING OFFICER

> *Sam's Identity-*
> *Concealed Resume*   ①

(Currently employed - highly successful)

②

As VICE PRESIDENT - CHIEF MARKETING OFFICER of an OVER $1 BILLION COMPANY, I've led a marketing-oriented turnaround. In 5+ years, sales have more than doubled. Pre-tax profit is up 900%. ROI is up from low single digits far into double digits.

I was recruited to restructure and reorganize marketing, advertising, and the sales force, and to spur new product development. All objectives have been met and far exceeded. I'm now recognized as a logical CANDIDATE FOR CEO when our CEO retires.

Previously my marketing leadership and strategic planning of acquisitions and divestitures for a foreign-   ③ owned international pharmaceutical company were equally successful. Earlier, as VP Account Supervisor, I headed that company's account at New World Advertising Agency. I started out as an Assistant Brand Manager at P&G. Experienced with TV advertising, consumer packaged goods and, prescription, proprietary, and veterinary drugs. Also, pet foods, household products, etc. I Have a BA and a Harvard MBA.

5+ Years with current employer
> PROPRIETARY & PRESCRIPTION PHARMACEUTICALS COMPANY   ④
> VICE PRESIDENT - MARKETING, SALES & STRATEGIC PLANNING

Since I took over sales, marketing, and strategic planning reporting directly to the CEO, we've focused on selling fewer but higher-potential and more profitable products. Every year our profit has grown. We've had just one year of intentional volume decline (due to culling the product line in my first year). Since then we've consistently hit new highs in sales and earnings. Here are the latest three years compared with the three just before I got here (numbers rounded for confidentiality):

SALES
> up more than 120% in past 3 years
> up about 30% in each of the past three years.

PROFITS
> up more than 700% in past 3 years (900% in 5 years)   ⑤
> up about 50% in each of the past three years.

ROI
> up by more than 15 points in past 3 years.

In the 3 years prior to my arrival (which were followed by two years of reorganizing and restaging) the company's performance shows quite a different picture:

SALES
> rose no more than 7% in any of those three years.

PROFITS
> rose no more than slightly over 8% in any of those three years.

HOW WERE THESE RESULTS ACHIEVED?

We cut the product line from over 600 SKU's in '96 to half that number ... all profitable ...in '99 (expanded   ⑥ with new products to nearly 400 by '01). The sales force was reorganized regionally in '97 and nearly doubled in size to 200+ people by '01.

We also introduced several profitable new products via cross-licensing agreements with other manufacturers ('01 sales in the $100s of millions; with pre-tax net in the mid-$10s of millions) and generated additional $10s of millions pre-tax by granting licenses to other companies.

Top-of-mind brand awareness of our three largest-selling products rose from upper teen percentages in '96 to upwards of 50% in '01. Our advertising and promotion budget ... funded by the rising strength of the overall company ... has tripled from '96 to '01.

As a result of our excellent growth trend and high profitability, there are beginning to be RUMORS OF INTEREST IN ACQUIRING THE COMPANY. I'm delighted to help continue our exciting progress and increasing momentum. Therefore the appeal of any outside opportunity would depend on further developments in my current company and, of course, the nature of the opportunity.

(7)

1993 until joining Current Employer
    FOREIGN-OWNED INTERNATIONAL PHARMACEUTICAL COMPANY
    VICE PRESIDENT - MARKETING

(8)

Rejoined this $3+ billion maker of prescription drugs and related products as Director of Pharmaceutical Marketing, reporting to the CEO Director - USA, and heading all marketing and sales for all North American pharmaceutical lines (total '93 sales, $600+ million) after a two-year hiatus to aid my family's business in Ohio.

By 1996 sales were nearly double (well over $1 billion) 1993 volume, and ROI had increased from 17% ('93) to 24% ('96). Market share of U.S. prescription tranquilizer market rose from 11.6% in '93 to 19.2% in '96, and veterinary products gained 1.3 share points to 7.2% in '96.

(9)

My earlier recommendation (in '91) that the company's consumer pet-health lines be sold to generate cash for acquisition of young growth companies in the higher-margined ethical drug field was implemented while I was away ('92), and I helped identify and purchase in '93 and '94 three small companies, which have all grown and prospered. One of these was publicly reported as having worldwide sales of over $500 million in '00, with the highest ROI of any of this global company's businesses anywhere in the world.

(10)

PROMOTED '94   to Vice President - Pharmaceutical Marketing.
Higher title, no change in duties.

JOINED '93   as Director - Pharmaceutical Marketing. Rejoined the company in charge of corporate Marketing, Market Research, Telemarketing, and Sales Promotion departments (total of 41 people); plus two sales forces...Ethical Drug (135-person) and Veterinary (32-person).

1991 - 1993
    FAMILY-OWNED LOCAL BUSINESS
    Kensington, Ohio
    INTERIM CEO

(11)

Upon my father's sudden death (2/91), I took charge of the family business ($2.8 million sales in '91, $4.4 million in '93), holding it together until my younger brother could finish his MBA at Wharton ('91) and join my mother in running the company.

Increased TV advertising, and diversified the company by building two Taco Bell fast food franchises (since expanded to seven). Profits nearly doubled in two years.

1989 - 1991
    FOREIGN-OWNED INTERNATIONAL PHARMACEUTICAL COMPANY
    GROUP PRODUCT DIRECTOR

(12)

Invited to join my client from New World Advertising Agency as Group Product Director (with 4 Product Managers and 5 Assistant PM's), in charge of:

(1)   Marketing existing U.S. lines...$68 million consumer (flea-and-tick collars and home remedies for pets) and $96 million professional ($42 million veterinary and $54 million human prescription drugs); and

(13)

(2)   Introducing new family of prescription tranquilizers for Rx sales in the U.S.

Since introduction of a major new Rx drug is impossible without a large field force (and the company had only 22 salesmen carrying both Rx and veterinary lines), I cut off advertising on all lines for 10 months; used the cash flow to build a 100-person field force calling only on MDs; and launched a $20 million sampling and ad campaign for the new tranquilizer line.

Result: 14 months after introduction, our two new tranquilizers were #2 and #5 tranquilizers in the U.S., with $440 million combined annualized rate of sales. Profit from Rx lines was then temporarily diverted ⑭ to help rebuild other lines to all-time high share levels.

1985 - 1989
    NEW WORLD ADVERTISING AGENCY
    New York, New York   ⑮
    VICE PRESIDENT - ACCOUNT GROUP SUPERVISOR

Joined as Account Executive on $38 million Whiskers cat food account when the AE on my P&G business moved to New World as Account Supervisor and asked me to join him. Through growth of Whiskers and acquiring new accounts, became VP - Account Group Supervisor in charge of $102 million in billings (4 AE's and 3 Assistant AE's) from Megopolitan Foods ($76 million on Whiskers and Arf! brands) and the foreign-owned pharmaceutical company (above) that later hired me away from New World ($14 million on consumer items and $12 million on veterinary and Rx human drugs).

⑯

As AE in '85, led the task force that "re-staged" Whiskers brand with CLIO-winning "Caesar-the-Cat" TV commercials and portion-control packaging that doubled Whiskers' market share from 5% ('85) to 11.2% ('89). Factory sales rose from $106 million ('85) to $298 million ('89); and advertising rose from $18 million to $52 million. Led successful solicitation of $14 million Arf! dog food account ('86), which billed $24 million in '89 (sales rose from $64 million to $158 million). Personally brought in Krueger's flea-and-tick collars ($8 million in '87) from the foreign pharmaceutical company, which consolidated all their North American business with us in '88.

PROMOTED '87   to Vice President - Account Group Supervisor. A 26% 12-month sales increase in Krueger's flea collars, etc. enabled us to win this client's veterinary and prescription drug accounts ... the first medical advertising handled by New World. Promoted for building of Megopolitan and foreign-owned pharmaceutical accounts.

PROMOTED '86   to Account Supervisor. Turnaround on Whiskers enabled us to land $14 million Arf! ⑰ dog food billings ('86) and Krueger's consumer pet items ('87).

JOINED '85   as Account Executive. Entered on the Whiskers account with assignment to stem share decline (averaging 0.9 point per year since '80).

1982 - 1985
    PROMOTE & GAMBOL COMPANY
    Cincinnati, Ohio   ⑱
    ASSISTANT BRAND MANAGER

PROMOTED '84   to Assistant Brand Manager. Handled $52 million TV & print media and $16 million sales promotion budget on GLOSS-X floor cleaner. Promoted to head successful test marketing and regional expansion of new GLOSS-O floor wax.

JOINED '82   as Brand Assistant. Traditional P&G home office and field sales training assignments; handled TV copy testing for Soft-Ah! paper products.

EDUCATION:
    MBA, Harvard Business School, 1982   ⑲
    BA, University of Michigan, 1979

PERSONAL:
    Age 44, married, 3 children.   ⑳
    6' 1", 185 lbs.

NOTE: Sam's Identity-Concealed Resume is shown above as it will be viewed by a recruiter, not as it looked when he sent it. Sam used proper body-of-an-e-mail format (see pages 314-316). When he dispatched the resume it looked like the one on page 320.

Now let's scoop up some tips on identity-concealed resumes from Sam Sage's example on pages 328 to 330.

(Numbers are circled in the resume's right-hand margin)

1. If Sam had needed a cover letter, he would have begun "Dear Recruiters" and adapted the one on p. 320 by eliminating his name, address, phones, etc. and changing the figures to the sketchy ones he's using here.

2. Every line begins from the left margin and only the space bar is used to move the start of new lines inward. Remember that space bar indents only work at the beginning of a new line (they must follow a hard or soft return created by hitting the "Return" key). Note the extra spaces on either side of the "OR" in the top line. White space is your main tool to achieve visual clarity and emphasis. Use it wherever it helps...even in the middle of a line.

3. These first three paragraphs serve "double duty" as Sam's "keyword summary" by putting words that might be tried by a user to sort the database up near the top of the document. This is an irksome requirement, but Sam has made it into a serviceable summary. Note that in using *RITE*Site, there's no need for a keyword summary near the top; the entire document is always scanned for keywords.

4. Note how Sam's made the exact distribution of time between the prior and current employer intentionally vague. There was so much publicity about his leaving Medica Suisse for the much smaller Farrington in '96, that he prefers to keep this date vague. You'll probably never want to do anything similar, but Sam has shown us we can be creative in communicating very specific information, while still staying vague. We know (1) he's still employed and (2) he's been where he is now for more than 5 years. Note that Sam adds space bar indents on each line under the date line in every new employment entry. *Irregularity of the left-hand margin with space bar-added white space at major transitions is the #1 way to add visual style to an electronic resume.*

5. Here's a powerful substitute for the chart of actual numbers Sam used so effectively when he had Mr. Farrington's permission to do so. Now, of course, he *can't* use the chart, because he's proceeding behind Mr. Farrington's back. Note that the sales and profit comparisons here are *not* bullets. Instead, they're specific information in a specific context... and thus, far more interesting and persuasive than bullets.

6. *See all the specific facts. They lend a sense of reality and believability.* Yet they don't identify Sam's company, and they're no help to any competitor who might discover them. ***Note too, the use of "$10s" and "$100s" of millions. These handy approximations enable you to be adequately specific when you can't be precise.***

7. *Here Sam has planted his excuse in case he gets caught by Mr. Farrington. Indeed, Sam has even declared his continuing loyalty,* despite what Mr. F—if he finds out—is likely to consider a disloyal move. "I was just looking ahead," Sam will say in his defense. "In fact, as you see, I pointed out that I *wouldn't* move if I continued to be needed here." That's ***not*** quite what Sam said. But it comes close enough for Mr. F. to reconcile with Sam. After all, Sam's doing a fabulous job for Mr. F, who'd really hate to lose Sam.

8. *Leaving and being rehired is powerful proof of Sam's ability. Therefore he resists any temptation to make the employer shown here seem different from the one shown at #12.* If any of Sam's peers in the industry—or Mr. F—wind up reading this resume, they'll probably guess Sam's identity. He's taking a calculated risk by allowing that possibility. However, he has ***eliminated the most serious risk by never mentioning the words Medica or Suisse.*** Anyone probing a database looking for Sam would surely try those words.

9. *These numbers would have been highly confidential several years earlier. Now they're entirely harmless*...and doubly so, because Sam no longer works for Medica Suisse.

10. *Here again Sam shrewdly avoids naming names.* If he had mentioned the specific companies he suggested for purchase, their names if tried as keywords in probing the database, would instantly have "fingered" Sam out of the many thousands of people in even the largest imaginable database.

11. *Here Sam strategically chooses two more names to avoid*...the car brands his family dealership (another word he avoided) sells. Everyone who knows Sam, including Mr. F, has heard him tell stories of selling Chryslers and Toyotas. Looking for those car names in combination with "pharmaceutical" and "marketing" would have been another quick way to pull Sam's resume out of 10s of 1000s. Note, however, that he maintained a feeling of specificity by naming the town in Ohio. That's a detail he feels hardly anyone would remember.

12. *Even before this early date Sam would—and you should—have been naming every name.* We're talking about way over a decade ago! However, we know why Sam doesn't use the words Medica or Suisse anywhere in his identity-concealed resume.

13. ***Notice how a little extra white space*** after the (1) and (2) gave special emphasis and brightened the page. If Sam had done this often the effect would have been detrimental, not positive.

14. ***These impressive facts could identify Medica Suisse to industry experts... and point to Sam.*** He took a calculated risk here.

15. ***At last Sam can name an employer. Note that he also names cities*** whenever he can...New York, and Kensington and Cincinnati, OH. Cities are often used as keywords to probe a database. Be sure you include any that are not confidentiality problems. Recruiters and employers habitually use cities as keywords to probe databases in the hope of finding candidates who won't require relocation, or at least are familiar with the area and might not mind going back.

16. ***Including this "ancient" history may do Sam a lot of good in an electronic database.*** About one-third of databases won't scan this deeply into a resume for keywords (hence, the "keyword summary" at the outset). But a great many, including *RITE*Site, will. Sam's been out of the consumer products realm for a long time, but he wouldn't mind going back. The names of the agency, the brands, and P&G might get Sam pulled out of the pile. Once that happens, his terrific performance—albeit in pharmaceuticals—will take over and show he's a world-class person.

17. ***Note the all-caps, the year, and the extra white space after PROMOTED and JOINED*** (also seen at #10). A nice touch that gives emphasis where Sam could not indent, as he does in his on-paper resume (see pp. 213-17).

18. ***Many people should be combining brief early jobs at this remote point in their resumes***. But Sam didn't have a long messy string of beginner jobs, and P&G is *the blue chip name* in his field. Also, he gets to mention a different type of consumer product. Note "household products" in the third paragraph of his keyword summary at the top of the resume.

19 and 20. ***Sam wisely includes the years of his college degrees (he's not the only person to graduate in those years), plus his age and some sketchy personal information.*** True, the law says you don't *have* to provide such information and no one can ask you for it. But the law does not require anyone to disqualify you, just because you've volunteered facts that cannot be requested. Databases are huge and cough up vast numbers of similarly credentialed people. Including information that can't hurt and might help is not a bad idea. At least that is the opinion—although not for attribution—of one of America's leading employment law firms, with whom I checked Sam's common sense approach to this issue.

Now let's stay *2* extra minutes in Cyberspace.

Please just *glance* at the next few headlines. Don't bother reading. You won't use the tools immediately. But you'll be glad they're handy when you need them!

Today your computer at home can deliver almost all of the same information previously available only at the library and only in books that are far too expensive to purchase for home use. Moreover online information is often much more up-to-date. You short-cut the several months for printing, selling, and shipping that precede you to the reference desk.

Helping You Navigate

First we'll take a look at tools you can use to hunt for information on the Internet. Then we'll classify the kinds of information you might want to find and give you some sites to look at. The Internet keeps growing so fast that any book about it is obsolete by the time it's printed. So consider our references a good starting point. There will never be a "last word."

Search Engines—————————————————

Search Engines are services based on computer programs sometimes called 'spiders' or 'robots' which scan various parts of Web pages and create indices of data. When you enter a query, the engine searches its indices and returns a list of sites which contain the keyword(s) you specify.—————————————

alltheweb.com - Very fast. Try "advanced search," which easily lets you customize your search. Rule out some words, insist on others, omit foreign language sites, etc. Try it!

altavista.com - Simple or advanced searches of the Web, news and discussion groups. Tips pages help you search effectively.

northernlight.com - Very sophisticated and customizable. Returns huge specific number of hits fast. Separates them into folders representing different aspects of the subject.

hotbot.lycos.com - Customize your search using pulldown menus. Database index of over 110 million Web documents is updated every 3-4 weeks.

excite.com - Search levels range from basic to advanced. Yellow pages & people finder are available.

infoseek.go.com - Search engine Infoseek and Web guide Go.com combined in one site. Simple and optimized searches include 'search within these results'. Results sortable by date or relevance.

lycos.com - 2 search levels, people and yellow pages links.

search.msn.com - Simple and advanced searches, white and yellow pages. Customizable to limit or sort results.

thunderstone.go2net.com - Web site catalog excels at locating firms and associations by product, locale, function, or subject.

webcrawler.com - Simple search version of Excite includes people finder, e-mail lookup and yellow pages. Display results with or without summaries.

Web Directories

Web Directories; also called Guides. Although sometimes mistakenly referred to as "search engines," Web directories are different in that each site they list has been chosen and classified by a human editor, not by a computer program. Some even introduce you to their editors! Directories usually display their lists by category, allowing the user to search both general and more specific topics. Most directories/guides are searchable by keyword.

google.com - Presents results it deems most relevant first. Relevancy is determined by the number of pages linked to the page in question.

goto.com - Simple, efficient interface with high percentage of relevant results. No annoying banner ads; instead it shows what it is being paid to position certain replies high-on-list.

about.com - Names and pictures its guides and allows you to e-mail them. Great to have guides who live in cities you ask about. Others are experts in their fields.

looksmart.com - "Connecting" section includes Chat, E-mail, Find People, forums and HomePages searches.

magellan.mckinley.com - Searches over 50 million sites in its database. Ranks results by relevancy. Search tips and help onsite.

dmoz.org - Directory of over 1.5 million web sites selected by volunteer editors. Also provides data for Alta Vista, Netscape, and Lycos.

snap.com - Features include "Top Web Sites" which have been reviewed, "Live Directory" which allows site owners to add their site to the list without the review process, and "All the Web" which includes, well...sites from all the Web. Power search available.

yahoo.com - Among the largest of the Web subject indices. Basic and advanced search options. Yellow pages and people search features.

mdchoice.com - Has respected medical people on its "Editorial Board." Claims to service both the public and professionals.

Metasearch Engines

These sites allow you to launch your query to several different search tools simultaneously. Many send your work to both search engines and directories. Be sure to try these. They can be a real timesaver.

savvysearch.com - A customizable search interface which interacts with hundreds of search tools. Specific e-mail search.

c4.com - (formerly Cyber411) Simultaneous query of up to 12 Web search tools. Can be customized as to time spent on any one search, number of hits per search engine, and number of hits listed per browser page. Can also choose to search newsgroups, company names, and more.

queryserver.dataware.com - Customize the search time, number of returns, and organization of results from this set of 10 search tools. Returns are categorized and ranked according to your criteria.

dogpile.com - Customizable to query up to 18 web search tools, usenet, or newscrawler. Results are categorized by search engine. Also search white or yellow pages.

highway61.com - An entertaining site which sprinkles humor in amongst the search criteria and even provides inspiring quotes while you wait for your results. Searches can be customized as to length of time spent searching and number of hits.

infind.com - Allows you to select various maximum search durations up to 60 seconds. Longer searches yield more answers.

infozoid.com - Employs up to 12 Web search tools at once. Allows some customization of results display. Can also search usenet.

ixquick.com - Fast and powerful interface submits queries to 14 search engines or 6 news services and ranks the returns as to relevancy. Translates queries into appropriate syntax for each search engine.

metacrawler.com - Incorporates results from the top search engines and directories, scores results, and produces a comprehensive list of relevant sites. White and Yellow Pages included in resources section.

profusion.com - Customize your search by type of phrasing, number of results shown, and which of 9 search engines to use. Will also check links if you choose that option.

redesearch.com - Submits query to your choice of up to 10 search tools simultaneously. Returns are grouped by search engine, resulting in some duplication. However, duplicates are noted.

supercrawler.com - Searches Lycos, Infoseek, Altavista, Excite, and Yahoo! Amuse yourself looking at the 15 most recently searched topics (screen refreshes every 15 seconds).

search.com - Offers a specialized group of engines for locating people.

zworks.com - Customizable submission to up to 12 search tools. Translates queries into appropriate syntax for each search tool. Cumulative ranking of results.

Search Tool Locators

Entrepreneurs are continually creating new kinds of sites that put themselves above several others in the info-searching food chain. They want you to enter the process at their top-layer site, where they get paid to run ads and/or to link you downward toward where the work is actually done. First came the Search Engines and Directories, which still do your work. Then came the Metasites, which send the work simultaneously to several search engines and directories. This latest wrinkle—Search Tool Locators—links you to a wide choice of Metasites and other resources. Shown below is one pioneer. There will be more. At a minimum, sites like this show you additional search tools you wouldn't otherwise think of. With this and every other tool, test to see which site you prefer for a particular task. Don't assume that something higher on a chain necessarily gives you a better or faster result. It may not.

langenberg.com - A portal to multiple search tools. Categorizes and groups tools applicable to type of search, e.g. white pages, yellow pages, person finder and business and personal reverse directories and business address cross reference. Yellow pages grouping includes tutorial on most effective ways to search.

People and Business Finders

Many tools specialize in locating people. Some look for names and addresses, some for phone numbers, some for e-mail addresses, and some for more than one result simultaneously. Obviously individuals are searched for mainly in white page phone directories and businesses in the yellow pages.

bigyellow.com - Very efficient in finding people, business, e-mail addresses. Supplies a map and driving directions to the person or business found.

411locate.com - Search by person's name (you must indicate which US state), business name, yellow pages, or reverse phone number.

555-1212.com - Directory includes white and yellow pages, reverse lookup, e-mail, and metasearch functions.

anywho.com - Directory of white pages, yellow pages, toll free, e-mail and Web sites. Basic and advanced search options.

bigfoot.com - Yellow & white pages and e-mail searches. Can search white pages and e-mail simultaneously.

infospace.com - Yellow and white pages, e-mail, reverse lookup, business finder and international search functions.

iaf.net - Internet @ddress Finder. White pages directory with over 6 million listings. Name and e-mail searches.

switchboard.com - Search for a business, person, or e-mail address.

uswestdex.com - Find a business, person, or toll-free number using basic or advanced search options.

whowhere.lycos.com - E-mail, white and yellow pages. Part of the Lycos network.

people.yahoo.com - Telephone and basic and advanced e-mail searches.

UseNet

Usenet, commonly called "NewsGroups," is a distributed bulletin board system. One of the oldest areas of the Internet, it is international in scope and among the largest decentralized information utilities in existence. Here are its two leading search tools.

deja.com - Front page search is for 'products', not 'discussions'. Click on the "Looking for Usenet? Click on DISCUSSIONS" link to conduct your usenet search.

remarq.com - Search by message board, messages, or author. Quick and easy access and tips for new users.

Company Information

Information on companies, their businesses, and officers is available on many sites...indeed, so many that we'll merely get you started here with some of the best and most used. New sites with business information are continually being put online. You will soon find your own favorites among these and the large number of new ones currently in development. Our emphasis below is on sites that assist you free or at modest cost. We do not cite sources that charge, say, $1000 per year and/or sell you four paperback books at that price and include online access free. For that sort of resource refer to Appendix III.

corporateinformation.com - Over 300,000 profiles of companies worldwide (some in French and Spanish). Search by company name, industry, state or country for profiles with key officers, headquarters address, URL links, business description, stock charts, and earnings/dividends. Links to their profiles (research reports; analysis summary; sales, price, and earnings analyses), plus links to other profiles of the company on the Internet. Population, GDP, inflation, and unemployment data and links to resources in over 100 countries. A wealth of information geared toward business and market analysts. (free)

hoovers.com - Company summaries with key officers, headquarters address, description, financials, and URL links for free. Membership ($109.00 per year) required to view expanded profiles and use extensive search tools. Many links to business resources. Books, CD-ROMs, and targeted mailing lists are for sale on the site.

comfind.com - A global business directory with unique search features lets you search business category, product or service; then displays related subcategories to narrow the search, followed by geographic options. Results contain company name, address, phone, map and URL link to company. (free)

www.companiesonline.com - Database of over 900,000 public & private companies. Search by keyword, name, state, ticker symbol, industry, city, URL or browse category. Displays name, address, phone, URL, annual sales, and number of employees. (free)

businesswire.com/cnn.shtml - Browse alphabetically, by industry, name or keyword for news articles and URL links, profile, stock quotes. (free)

www.jobsafari.com - Index of links to company home and employment pages searchable alphabetically or by location. (free)

Business Publication Sites: *BusinessWeek* businessweek.com, *Forbes* forbes.com. *Fortune* fortune.com and *The Wall Street Journal* wsj.com all maintain very rich, diverse sites that are continually upgraded and expanded. The famous lists of companies compiled by *Fortune* and *Forbes* are particularly notable, because they conveniently provide company address, name of the CEO, links to its Web site and much more. *INC.* magazine at inc.com similarly documents its list of fastest growing companies. Spend time with these!

SEC Filings by Companies————————————————
This is a major convenience as you research a particular company in depth.————————

www.sec.gov- Securities and Exchange Commission. Links to EDGAR database of SEC filings **www.sec.gov/edgarhp.htm**. Since May 1996 companies are required to make electronic filings with EDGAR. Information is posted within 24 hours of receipt.

Association Information————————————————
Information on Associations, both business and non-profit, is widely available on the Web. Here too, we point you toward a few of the best resources. You will find others you like.————————

To Find Business and Professional Associations...

www.ipl.org/ref/AON - Browse links alphabetically or by category for professional, trade, cultural, political, academic and research associations. This impressive collection is provided by the **Internet Public Library, www.ipl.org**, a great general resource, created at the University of Michigan School of Information in 1995, and staffed by professional librarians and volunteers worldwide.(free)

marketingsource.com/associations - Directory of 2,500 national and international business associations. Directory contains association name, address, phone, fax and sometimes e-mail, URL, contact name & number of members. Search free online, or purchase the database on disk for $75.

trainingforum.com/assoc.html - Database of 10,000 U.S. business associations hosted by Interactive Training (sells soft skills and information technology courses, seminars, and conferences). Search by keyword phrases for name, address and phone number of the organization. (free)

dir.yahoo.com/Business_and_Economy/Organizations - Links to over 8,000 organizations categorized by subject. (free)

To find Nonprofit Associations...

www.idealist.org - Search 20,000 nonprofit and community organizations in 140 countries, by name, location or mission. International volunteer and employment opportunities in the nonprofit sector are posted here. The site also has links to resources for working abroad, salary surveys, academic programs, funding and managing nonprofit, and a directory of consultants and businesses that provide products and services to nonprofit organizations.(free)

ncna.org - The National Council of Nonprofit Associations is a national support network for state nonprofit organizations. Members are listed alphabetically by state and represent small and large organizations within their state. Listing includes the association name, contact person, address, phone, e-mail, URL, and mission statement. (free)

Supplementary Job-hunting Resource Locators————

Some of the following sites are mentioned—not because of their content—but because of their links to a vast array of valuable factual information.

Beware! *They may also link you to dubious advice on job hunting, resumes, and other career topics and/or encourage you to send your resume into databases you should avoid for reasons covered earlier in this chapter.*

You must use your own good judgment to extract the benefits of these sites and avoid their pitfalls.

Typical topics: Relocation information, compensation ranges, cost-of-living data, information on cities, schools, climate, local crime rates and more.————

Miscellaneous Sites Offering Links to Informational Resources

rileyguide.com - Portal to hundreds of other online sites and services helpful to the job hunter. Topics like "what am I worth" "where is my job going" "maybe I need more education" "tell me about this employer"and "I'm considering moving."

careers.wsj.com - The Wall Street Journal's collection of links to articles and sites for the job seeker. 'Toolkit' provides links to lots of resources covering everything from salary comparisons to starting your own business.

jobweb.org/catapult - Collection of job related links from The National Association of Colleges and Employers.

General Relocation Guides

bizjournals.com - American City Business Journals. In addition to 41 city business journals, the site also presents industry-specific journals and information as well as miscellaneous resources pertinent to business.

relo-usa.com - American Relocation Network. City info, school info, crime reports, Internet access, weather, local maps, real estate & rental info, insurance & moving & storage. Online mortgage calculators & order relocation packets.

homefair.com - Interactive site has salary calculator, crime rates, school and city reports.

relocationcentral.com - Searchable site. Also select by state or category of service. Climate, top employers, unemployment, income, taxes, crime, schools, government, city guides.

virtualrelocation.com - Search by city, state or service or select a category. Calculate moving costs, home affordability. Links to salary comparison calculators.

City Guides

citysearch.com - US, Canadian, international. Select city, then browse or search by neighborhood or zip code for more info.

infospace.com - The City Guides link presents a comprehensive portal to sites about the city you choose.

olcg.com - OnlineCityGuide.com Choose the state and city, and you'll get a list of links varying from attractions to transportation.

verticals.yahoo.com/cities/ - Yahoo! Over 20 city comparison categories in areas such as education, economic, weather, and quality of life.

Schools

www.asd.com - American School Directory. Interactive portal to 108,000 K-12 public and private schools.

schoolmatch.com - Directory of US K-12 schools is searchable by metro area, zip, school district or school name.

theschoolreport.com - Select state and city for a grid showing student population, student/teacher ratios, average class size and information about computer availability in classrooms.

Salary & Cost of Living Comparisons

verticals.yahoo.com/cities/salary.html - Yahoo! Real Estate

datamasters.com - Site relates mostly to the IT profession, but has cost of living comparisons for nearly 400 US cities and metro areas.

Workplace Humor

dilbert.com - The Dilbert Zone by Scott Adams, daily comic strip, trivia games, and weekly polls.

hardatwork.com - Read or send comments on day-to-day workplace drama, organizational behavior and career crisis case studies.

Employment Sites—Commercial

You continually see advertising for the most famous sites, such as Monster, Headhunter.net, and HotJobs. An estimated 80,000 of these sites already exist. New ones continually sprout up and promote heavily. Scan our long alphabetical list that illustrates this vast category. It barely scratches the surface. See category 1 on p. 285-86.

Accounting.com - Accounting & Finance Jobs

ActiJob.com - Canadian; in both English & French

AdRecruiter.com - Advertising, marketing & graphic design

Aecjobbank.com - for building industry

Alumni-network.com - ERP, E-Commerce and Engineering

AmericanJobs.com - General

AvJobs.com - Airline Employment

BestJobsUSA.com - General

Bio.com - For Biotech industry

www.Bloomberg.com/careers - mostly senior financial jobs

www.Career.com - General

www.CarDealerJobs.com - Automotive Retail

CareerBoard.com - Ohio emphasis

CareerBridge.com - Jobs in Canada

CareerBuilder.com - General

CareerBuzz.com - General

CareerCast.com - General

CareerCity.com - From Adams Media, who put out city job directories

CareerClick.com - General

CareerEngine.com - General

CareerExchange.com - General

CareerExposure.com - Internationally Oriented

CareerIndia.com - Employment in India

CareerInvestors.com - Minnesota Jobs

CareerKey.com - General

CareerLinkUSA.com - General

CareerMag.com - General

CareerMarketplace.com - General

CareerMart.com - General

CareerMosaic.com - General

CareerNet.com - General

Careers.altavista.com - Altavista's career center, no fee to see or post job/resumes

Careers.eharvest.com - Agribusiness industry

Careers.wsj.com - Mid/Senior Executives

CareerSite.com - General

CareerPath.com - General

CareerWomen.com - for women in all industries

CasinoCareers.com - Gaming Industry

CastingDaily.com - Acting Career Resource

CollegeCentral.com - For recent graduates

ColoradoCareers.com - Colorado jobs

ComputerWork.com - Hi-tech jobs

CoolWorks.com - Jobs in resorts, outdoors, on cruise ships, etc.

Cruelworld.com - General

Cweb.com - General

daVinciTimes.org - Trys to lure engineers to Syracuse

Dice.com - Hi-tech jobs

DiversityLink.com - Women and minorities

4work.com - General

FinCareer.com - Entirely financial

FloridaCareerLink.com - Florida Jobs

FreeLancers.com - Illustrators, writers, editors, photographers, etc.

ggrweb.com - GeoWeb Interactive (technical jobs)

GlobalCareers.com - International focus

GoJobs.com - General

www.gvpub.com - Allied health industry

Hcjobsonline.com - Health Care Jobs

Headhunter.net - General

HealthCareerWeb.com - Health Care Jobs

Hisp.com - for Hispanic community

HotJobs.com - General

www.iminorities-jb.com/landing.html - Minorities Job Bank

IT123.com - Information Technology

JavaWorld.com - for Java Programmers

JobBankUSA.com - General

JobCircle.com - IT professionals in Tri-state Area

JobDirect.com - College Students

www.JobEasy.com - International Entry-level

JobExchange.com - General

JobFind.com - General

JobIsland.com - General

JobLaunch.com - General

JobLocator.com - General

JobNet.com - Delaware Valley emphasis

JobNet.com.au - IT Jobs in Australia

JobOptions.com - General

Jobsadverts.co.th - Europe and Asia

Jobs.cell.com - Job in Biological Science

Jobs.com - General

www.JobServe.com -IT Jobs in the U.K.

JobStreet.com - International emphasis

JobTrak - Recruits college students

JobWarehouse.com - Information Technology

www.Latinoweb.com/jobs.html - For Latinos

www.LawJobs.com - from National Law Journal

LATimes.com/class/employ - from Los Angeles Times

www.Manpower.com - Temporary & Full-time jobs

MBAFreeAgents.com - Short term assignments for MBAs

Medzilla.com - BioTech & Medical

Monster.com - General

NationJob.com   General / Heavy Midwest

NewsJobs.com - Diversity Newspaper Job Bank

www.Netjobs.com - Canadian

Net-Temps.com - Temp Jobs

NJJobs.com - New Jersey jobs

Online.hkstandard.com - Hong Kong Standard newspaper's site

Optics.org/employment - Photo-Optical professionals

OraSearch.com - Oracle programming specialists

OrlandoSentinel.com - Jobs in Orlando

OverseasJobs.com -International

PassportAccess.com - Technical

PharmaJobs.com - Pharmaceutical Industry

PositionWatch.com - Canadian

PrivateSchoolJobs.com - Education

RehabOptions.com - Rehabilitation oriented medical workers

RetailJobNet.com - Retailing jobs

Saludos.com - For Hispanics

www.SelectJobs.com - Information Technology & Hi-Tech

ShowBizJobs.com - Entertainment Industry

SixFigureJobs.com - High Paying Jobs

www.SJMercury.com - San Jose Mercury News

www.Sorkins.com - Midwest

Taps.com - U.K and Europe

www.TCM.com - Human Resources jobs

TeacherJobs.com - Education

TopJobsUSA.com - General

Virtual-Fdge.net - Virtual Job Fairs

WebJobsUSA.com - Internet jobs

VJF.com - Technology Information

WorkAvenue.com - Local jobs

Employment Sites—Executive Interface

There are only four of these sites (see p. 290-93). Although they are a limited category, they differ substantially in concept, function and cost. Take a look at all four.

ExecuNet.com

NetShare.com

RiteSite.com

SearchBase.com

Employment Sites—Proprietary Headhunter

Please note and visit the Web sites of the outstanding search firms honored in Appendix II. Their Web sites are listed with their other information. A few Rites-Honored search firms have launched online search subsidiaries that operate from different sites than those shown for their parent companies. These too are highly recommended (see p. 286-87).

FutureStep.com

LAICompass.com

LeadersOnLine.com

PeopleScape.com

Employment Sites—Proprietary Corporate

Virtually every company has a site and on it almost every company lists current openings (see p. 288-90). Visit the site of every company you'd like to work for. If you find an attractive opening, proceed according to the suggestions made throughout Rites of Passage, which have been designed to foster the sophisticated pursuit of your own self-interest, which may or may not be to merely follow instructions provided on the corporate Web site. Good Luck!

Employment Sites—Altruistic

Only you will know which of the trade and professional associations, college alumni, religious, etc. sites may have career sections you should look at (pp. 293-95). Please don't neglect these sites, which may pay off handsomely because others also tend to overlook them. Obviously we can't even attempt to cover the vast noncommercial realm. However, you should know that RITESite.com is altruistic in every function except its modestly priced Custom Career Service to Executives. You will not be subjected to advertising and will receive at no charge information you'd pay hundreds of dollars for elsewhere.

...And there you have executive-level job changing and career management on the Internet.

Yes, there are hazards. But also vast opportunity, tremendous flexibility, and unlimited possibilities for personal creativity in achieving the status and recognition you deserve.

Match your career use of cyberspace to your own personal needs, circumstances, tolerance for risk, and sense of adventure.

Yes, cyberspace is *the next great ocean. Set sail!*

Chapter 15

References, Newspaper Ads, Barbed Wire,
Busy Signals, Trick-or-Treat Letters,
Transmission Trade-Offs
Getting Personal, Outplacement, Franchises,
"Search," "Selection," & "The Hidden Job Market"

This chapter picks up loose ends.

We've got five remaining topics that require separate chapters. But now let's take a break, and cover some matters that also merit discussion...but not a lot of it.

| | | **References** | | |

For most people most of the time, references are no problem.

Indeed, bosses, subordinates, and peers are your greatest source of career opportunity. Your current boss may promote you. Coworkers' comments may help move you ahead. And former associates may lead you to outside opportunities.

It's nice to be well spoken of. And I'll bet you are...almost all of the time, by almost everyone. But when you're being "referenced," you want to make doubly sure the right impression is given. Here are some suggestions:

Your first step in job-changing is to get in touch with your references.

Begin any job campaign by reaching out to your work-related personal contacts, past and present. Ask for a reference rather than a job, and achieve all the advantages we discussed in Chapter 3.

With a little effort you'll soon have plenty of pertinent people whose enthusiasm you've tested—and re-stimulated—either face-to-face, or by long-distance phone. Interviewing potential references advertises your availability. It also lets you know who's enthusiastic, and who's lukewarm.

Don't "wear out" your references.

Even though you know from the start precisely who you want potential employers to talk to, do *not* accompany your resume with a list of references. Neither recruiters nor employers expect such information until you're about to get a job offer. And you're better off not providing it.

Your references feel most enthusiastic and least imposed upon the first time they're asked about you. If they have to respond several times, fatigue and boredom set in. Their answers become perfunctory. And after a while they begin to wonder why lots of people have investigated you, and nobody has hired you.

Whose names do you give?

Since you're being considered for employment, almost all of your references must be *work-related*. Moreover, your potential employer wants to know how good you are today...not how special you were a long time ago.

So if you're employed, you must open a window on your current reputation in your present company. And if you're "between jobs," you've got to show how you were regarded in the job you've just left. The number-one person your potential employer wants to talk to is your current boss, if you're employed. Or your most recent boss if you're not.

Normally, of course, you can't deliver your present boss as a reference on an outside job. And no one will expect you to. But do try to come up with two or three people whose confidentiality you can rely on, and who know first-hand how well you're doing *now*. Perhaps a trusted subordinate. Maybe a peer. Possibly the head of a department or function who works closely with you...and ideally, with your superiors and subordinates too.

Anyone discreet who's recently left your company is a good bet to maintain confidentiality. She doesn't care whether you leave or stay, and chances are she won't be in touch with the people who do. An outside supplier or customer who works closely with your organization is another possibility. He, too, observes your situation. He isn't quite as knowledgeable, but can be helpful nonetheless.

If you're employed you can, of course, refuse to allow contacting of anyone in your current company. But "stonewalling" will raise doubts. Every competent and commendable human being makes at least a few friends among the people he or she works with. If there's *nobody* you can trust, your potential employer will surely wonder why.

On the other hand, when you're out of work, there's no logical reason why your would-be employer can't talk to your most recent boss. So even if you parted on the worst of terms, you'd better prepare for the inevitable. Much as you'd like to, you probably can't substitute your favorite boss for your most recent one.

There's safety in numbers.

The more open and helpful you are in allowing yourself to be checked out, the stronger you look right from the start...even before a single person is contacted.

So when you're about to be hired and the time for serious referencing has finally arrived, either hand over, or volunteer to prepare, a comprehensive list. Say something like this:

> "When I'm hiring, I like to learn as much as possible about the person I'm considering. I'll put together a list of names and phone numbers, and you can call anyone you want to."

Then, taking the confident "my-life's-an-open-book" approach, supply a list that covers all of your recent jobs and includes a generous sampling of bosses, subordinates, peers, and maybe even customers and suppliers, if appropriate. Provide home as well as office phone numbers, if your references are willing to receive calls at home.

Since your list is fairly extensive, you can *edit*. You must include the person for whom you've done most of your most recent work, even if the parting was unfriendly and the evaluation is likely to be negative. Omitting him or her would sound a warning. But you can make sure that person's opinion is in context of others who will be objective.

Maybe, if you're lucky, the person you're worried about won't be called. Or won't be available. "Negative" references tend to avoid returning calls. Moreover, today most companies have policies restricting commentaries to nothing more than dates of employment. Potentially "negative" references tend to cite the policy and clam up, whereas "positive" references often ignore it and enthuse at length.

With a "safety-in-numbers" long list of references, even if the worst occurs... your nemesis is called *and* treats you unfairly...your potential employer has right at his or her fingertips the names and numbers of additional people who will balance the bad words with a far more fair and favorable account.

Consistency is the key.

When an employer or a recruiter talks to a reference, he wants to hear the same story he heard from you. Suppose you say:

> "I've always got along well with all my bosses, and Sharon was no exception."

But when Sharon's called about you, she says:

> "Frankly, the chemistry wasn't good, and the constant bickering got to be a drag after a while."

Now you've got a problem. Much better to have provided a safety-in-numbers list of references and *forewarned*:

> "I've always gotten along well with all my bosses, and all my co-workers too. Sharon was the only exception."

Don't go overboard anticipating problems and raising negatives that may not come up. Most people like to be gracious and upbeat when called as references. Indeed they're often fearful of being otherwise. Even the boss who just fired you will probably feel guilty and want you to find a new job quickly and to think and speak well of him in the future.

But don't fail to lay a little groundwork, if there's a negative you're *absolutely sure* is coming. Above all, referencing probes the consistency of your story. Are things really the way you presented them?

But suppose you were fired for cause. There *was* a problem. Then control damage by using the "reference statement."

If you've been fired and the pertinent people have good reason to take a dim view of you, then the outplacement firms urge you to move in quickly with a *reference statement.*

Within the first day or two after you're fired, they say you should draft a concise statement...no more than one page...stating your tenure and performance in terms as favorable as possible to your future employment. Present it to your former boss. Will he or she go along with it? If not, negotiate until you have a written statement you can both live with. Then line up two or three additional references who are pertinent and hopefully more favorable to you. Negotiate written statements they, too, can live with. And make sure a consistent theme links all versions.

These statements become the "party line" when anyone inquires about your departure...former co-workers, customers, suppliers, *and potential employers*. The actual written statement is never handed to anyone; it merely becomes the agreed-on script for conversations about you. Here's an example:

> "Dale Jones was with us eleven years, and rose from Plant Superintendent, to head of Quality Control, to chief of Plant Engineering, to Vice President of Manufacturing, his job for the past three years. As Vice President, he was responsible for three plants employing 1,800 people, and he reported directly to me as President. He left because he saw the company pursuing one course and we saw a different one, and he felt his career would be better fulfilled elsewhere."

That's not a terrific reference. But at least it leaves out the fact that your employers were scared to death that the bigoted and boorish behavior they continually warned you about would eventually provoke a law suit charging the company with discrimination and/or sexual harassment.

You can survive this reference and find another job. The main thing is to have a consistent and not *too* damaging story told by all three or four of your current-company references. If what we've just seen is what the person who fired you will say, and you've managed to line up some other observers who will be more expansive and generous, you'll probably do fine.

If you're in enough trouble to need a "reference statement"—and most people never are—the important tactic is to move quickly and take personal charge of the story that will be told about you. Don't wait passively until weeks later, when a prospective employer is about to phone your references. By then the situation will be out of control. The rumor mill will have filled the vacuum. And the word on you may be a lot worse than the consistent and only-slightly-negative story you could have negotiated earlier.

Frankly, as an experienced recruiter, I'd smell fish immediately, if I called even a couple references and got nothing beyond strategically brief, consistent remarks. But this *is* the prescribed method for damage control. I'd be very surprised—and disappointed—if you should ever need such a strategy. But if you do, at least you know the defensive steps to take.

What about purely personal references?

If some of your most admiring friends are also friends of your prospective employer, you may want to drop their names into your interviewing conversations. But don't list non-business acquaintances as business references.

And don't suggest your pastor, priest, or rabbi. He doesn't observe you in the office. Moreover, people who are truly moral or religious feel no compulsion to prove their virtue. And experience teaches us to suspect anyone who does.

Also, don't bring up that college or military friend you've kept in touch with for 25 years. He or she is not an on-the-job observer. Moreover, friendship has destroyed any objectivity.

Who else should I talk to?

Before we drop the subject of references, here's my best tip for checking someone *else's* references. After you finish talking to each person whose name you've been given, ask if there's anyone else who would also know about the person you're checking. Who would have an even closer vantage point?

Unless you're on the phone with the reference's direct boss for the past several years, you'll surely get additional names that are even more pertinent. If the candidate has already provided those same names, you know that she's open and self-confident. The unflinching relevance of her list is, in itself, an excellent reference.

If, on the other hand, the names you've been given are rather off-target, call them anyway, to compile a list of bull's-eyes. Don't phone the more-relevant people you've identified...especially if you've agreed not to go beyond a specific list. Instead, merely go back to the candidate and ask permission to contact the further people you've found. Now the whole story will spill out:

> "As a matter of fact, I *purposely* didn't list Herb and Paula because there was a situation I felt they might not be completely objective about."

There's your thread. Pull on it!

||| **Should you reply to newspaper ads?** |||

This is a more interesting question than it might seem at first glance. And the answer is:

It depends on who placed the ad.

If it's *signed by a corporate employer* attempting to fill its own opening, go right ahead. Employer-signed ads are always authentic. And the attractiveness of the opportunity often stems from the prestige of the company that's asking you to consider working for it.

But be careful if the ad is *signed by a recruiting firm.* Retainer firms almost never advertise. On the other hand, contingency firms always do. Indeed, advertising attractive jobs that may or may not exist is the main way they get new people for their database. If you're an entry-level or middle manager seeking a toehold, the contingency firms are very helpful. And these days, they may have surprisingly high-level listings. You will, however, be self-interestedly vigilant.

The recruiter-signed ad to really steer clear of is the one with *only a newspaper or post office box number* for replies...no address and no phone number.

A relatively few corporate personnel departments sometimes place ads under phony names designed to look like executive recruiter partnerships, in newspapers and on Internet employment sites. The purpose is "to find out what's available in the marketplace," without revealing that the company has openings. Answer one of these little beauties, and you may be communicating with your own employer. They're just one more reason why, if you're beyond $100,000, you should approach newspaper ads with extreme caution, *unless they're straight-forwardly signed by corporate employers, or by reputable recruiting firms that include their address and/or phone number.*

What to submit, if anything, is easy. Use the same thing you'd use for a direct mail campaign or for posting yourself online. But *who* you send it to may be a different story...

In answering newspaper ads, never do as you're told!

When Mega-Merger Corp. advertises that they are looking for an executive to take charge of their XYZ function, that's a solid gold job lead.

Found gold, as a matter of fact, because the nugget is right out in plain sight. You don't have to network for it, or cultivate recruiters, or mail letters. Just open the paper!

However, if you're going to be successful in picking it up, you'd better *not* bend over as instructed in the ad. Do *not* send "a complete resume and salary history" to "Box 2996" or to the "Corporate Director of Recruitment and Staffing."

Instead, find out where the job is and who it reports to. Suppose it's Director of Laser Engineering. By networking and phoning directly into Mega-Merger, you can readily determine that all of their laser development activity is handled in their West Coast R&D lab in Sunnyvale, California, which is headed by Shirley Steele, VP - Electronic Technologies.

Now your task is simple. Is there anyone who knows both you and your professional abilities *and* Shirley Steele well enough to introduce you? If so, great!

If not, merely address your standard mailing to Ms. Steele, and bypass the entire screening procedure in the Personnel Department. Now they get no chance to decide you don't meet specifications...and, even if they think you're right-on-target, to shuffle your papers into a big stack of "qualified applicants."

You've reached the decision-maker days and perhaps weeks ahead of the deluge through proper channels. If you're excellent, as demonstrated by a "sales representative" resume, yours will be the achievements that later arrivals are measured against. Maybe you'll even be met and hired before the responses to the advertisement have been culled and forwarded.

"But," you ask, "don't I risk offending the HR Department by going over their heads?"

Not if you don't refer to the ad in your letter. And of course, you'll never *volunteer* that you've seen it. Let it be an accident that what you're sending to all the likeliest companies happened to hit Shirley Steele at just the right moment.

A Case that Proves the Point

I give lots of speeches and seminars. And during Q&As at one of them, a young woman told us:

> "You're right! That's how I got the job I have now. For weeks, I answered ads, including the blind ones. And, of course, I networked my head off, and I also waged a direct mail campaign.

> "My current boss called me up right after he got my mailing—he was desperate to find somebody—and we had a great interview. At the end of it, he hired me. And then he showed me a huge blind ad the Personnel Department had been running. Hadn't I seen it? And if so, why didn't I answer?

> "Seen it! I'd answered weeks before, with exactly what I mailed him. So he grabbed the phone and called Personnel. Why hadn't they sent him my reply?

> "They *hadn't wanted to bother him.* He was insisting on an MBA, and I didn't have one. I had a PhD!

> "Incidentally," she added, "my resume clearly showed that, besides heading market research for a competitive company, I was also an Adjunct Professor in a Business School."

Sound familiar? Whether the position is advertised or "headhunted," the winning strategy is usually to go straight to the decision maker.

||| Bending the Barbed Wire to Get Beyond the Directories |||

Suppose you know that a company is looking for someone like you. Perhaps they're running an ad. Or you've heard on TV that they've won a major contract, or taken over a poorly managed company, or announced an expansion into your area of the country.

Whatever. You know they might have a new position you could fill. But where would that position be? Who would it report to? And how do you find out?

Let's retrace your steps through the corporate barbed wire to Shirley Steele, VP-Electronic Technologies, in Sunnyvale, California. You reached her with no map beyond an ad for a Director of Laser Engineering signed by "Mega-Merger Corp., P.O. Box 2996, Rye, New York, 10914, an equal-opportunity employer."

First, you got on the Internet and found Mega-Merger's corporate site. It described the various businesses they own and indicated the headquarters address of each. There were at least four divisions at various locations that could require "Advanced Laser Engineering." The site also had pictures and personal profiles of its top officers, including the corporation's Senior VP-Research & Development, Selwyn Circuit.

When you called headquarters you were told Dr. Circuit is at a 201 area code number in New Jersey. But when you asked his administrative assistant whether laser engineering is handled corporately or divisionally, at what location, and who it reports to, you were asked why you wanted to know:

> "I'm writing a letter and want to direct it to the proper person."

You gave the right answer. It was truthful and should have elicited the information, if the assistant were inclined or permitted to cooperate. Unfortunately he said:

> "I'm sorry, but we don't give out that information on the telephone. If your letter concerns employment, I can give you the name of the Director of Recruitment. If you're selling something, I can refer you to our Purchasing Director. And if it's anything else, just send your letter to Dr. Circuit and he or I will direct it to the proper person."

Stonewalled! Here's a senior executive's assistant who does his job. Fortunately, however, the citadel has less alert sentries. Here are seven techniques, any of which might have led you from Dr. Circuit to Ms. Steele:

1. Call again. Try at lunch time, when a pinch hitter who doesn't know Dr. Circuit's "Don'ts" but does know the organization may help you.

2. Call the switchboard. Phone company information will give you your target company's number in the location you're probing. Ask the switchboard operator for "someone a bit lower than Dr. Circuit, but in his area." Let the operator select a person who's also inside the barbed wire, but whose assistant may be more forthcoming.

3. Call unrelated departments. Phone and ask for the #2 or #3 people in other areas (assistants to #1 might be as guarded as Dr. Circuit's was). Try Accounting, Manufacturing, Quality Control, the Computer Center (often a font of organizational information), Marketing, PR, etc. Explain to the answerer that you've obviously reached the wrong person, but could they refer you to someone at such-and-such level in the target department. Chances are, they will.

4. Call sister subsidiaries. To identify your person in Subsidiary X, call Subsidiary Y. Choose one with related products, markets, suppliers, etc. The person you reach will probably know and name his counterpart.

5. Call "Customer Service." Don't ask for the people who deal with the public. Get to the ones who expedite orders for major customers. They usually know who does what to whom and cheerfully share their knowledge.

6. Call the working people. To find a biggie in headquarters marketing or sales, ask a product manager. Or the Assistant West Coast Sales Manager 1000 miles from headquarters. Or call a Plant Manager to find out the hierarchy in Manufacturing.

7. Call after hours. If all else fails, call one, two, and three hours after quitting time. Use the same numbers that yielded no cooperation during the day. Less wary workaholics may pick up at night. Also try the switchboard. Probably you'll get a recording. But if you're lucky, you may reach a night receptionist or even a watchman, who'll dial several numbers "up there" trying to find one that will *answer*.

And now the most obvious suggestion in this book:

People responding to your resume must never call your home...and get a busy signal.

This suggestion, of course, applies only to those rare times when you're conducting an all-out job campaign. Then you're knocking yourself out on personal contact, recruiter liaison, networking, direct mail, and very well-thought-out Internet activity. You're doing everything possible to get a few people to dial that number at the top of your resume.

And when someone does call, what happens? Your line is busy!

He calls back 15 minutes later...still busy. Then 20 minutes later he calls again...and no answer.

Frustrated, he *may* try tomorrow. Or never again. The impulse to call after reading a resume is fragile and fleeting. If your reader has an urgent need and if yours is the only plausible resume he's seen in weeks, he'll surely keep trying. But if you've merely reminded him to think about a potential replacement for someone who'll retire three years from now, your reader probably won't attempt another three calls tomorrow.

What almost all unemployed executives fail to appreciate is that the calls they want to receive at their homes will be placed by executives who are accustomed to calling employed people in *offices*. Every single call to such a person is answered...if not by the person herself, by her secretary or a receptionist, or by an automated "voice mail" unit.

One call always works for your reader...until she tries to reach you. If she can't at least leave word on voice mail, your image nose dives. She starts out trying to phone an impressively-credentialed executive. After just one or two aborted calls, she gives up trying to reach a hapless out-of-work person, who probably shares the family phone, and isn't even resourceful enough to establish reliable telephone linkage with the outside world!

In fact, however, *you're* the one causing most of the congestion, by making outgoing calls. But somehow that's not how the situation is interpreted. When we call a home we envision what's on the other end of the wire in terms of our own homes...not an office.

So here's an appropriate telephone policy for a typical family when Dad's—or Mom's—all-out job campaign is in progress:

1. Get an additional telephone line installed in your home. It becomes

your "business" line, and its number is printed on your personal stationery and at the top of your resume.

2. Insure against anyone ever being thwarted by a "busy signal" on that line by purchasing (1) "Call Waiting," the system that warns you an incoming call is being attempted and (2) "Voice Mail," the system that takes messages of any length and can be phoned for playback when you're away. Your phone service will fully match the impersonal service that most executives are putting up with these days. And, by calling your unit three or four times a day, you can respond to business-hours phone calls about as promptly as any busily employed executive. Indeed, even if you *are* employed, you can use this set-up for a secretive job campaign.

3. Better still, get two new lines. Hook a fax machine or an old PC with fax software to the second line and put your "fax number," along with your e-mail address, on your stationery and resume. Then you can make outgoing calls on your fax line and, if you wish, simultaneously screen incoming "business line" calls with your Voice Mail and perhaps also Caller ID. A fax machine can hand someone your resume almost anywhere in the world in a couple minutes...and hand you job specs just as fast. E-mail is essential these days. So is fax.

4. Make sure every family member knows *who should answer* your "business line"...you, your spouse, and poised, responsible teenagers...no one else under penalty of early bed and no supper! With Voice Mail service from the phone company your "business line" will be answered in a professional manner *24 hours per day*. That's important. The call you're hoping for may be placed by an executive in another time zone, or stuck some night in an airport or a hotel room, or at home some evening or on a weekend.

Trick-or-Treat Letters... the Direct Mail You Can Do Without

I wouldn't use our limited time together to discuss these odd concepts, if it weren't for the fact that successful books have been written about them, and they're always handicapping a considerable number of people. Hence, this digression.

The "Tease-'Em-and-Spoof-'Em" Method ...a Short Letter, and No Resume Until Later

This direct mail technique was the subject of a very successful book about executive job hunting that flourished in the '60s and early '70s, then went out of print for many years, and now has been reintroduced...helped along by a strong plug in a popular paperback job-hunting book.

What it says, basically, is:

1.   Send out a very brief letter that makes *one or two exciting claims,* which will surely get you an interview. *Do not enclose a resume.*

2.   Go to your interview. *Do not bring a resume.* Find out what sort of person and what background the employer wants.

3.   Go home and *write a special resume* proving you have exactly the right stuff. Mail it with your "thank you" note.

4.   Enjoy your new job, for which only you...among all the people the employer has seen and talked to...seem pre-eminently qualified.

This method has a nice clear logic to it. If you accept *three* very doubtful premises, then the scenario will unfold exactly as promised. Otherwise, maybe you should forget this ploy. Let's consider each assumption separately.

Premise #1:

That anyone...short of the "Steves"—Jobs and Case—who included *no claim whatsoever* in the hypothetical note that we saw earlier...can create a short letter with *one or two claims so compelling that he or she will be granted an interview* on the strength of it.

You've undoubtedly received one- or two-claim "teaser" letters from people trying this method. And, like me, you probably questioned their sanity or at least their business sophistication. This will refresh your memory:

Dear _____:

As Director of Marketing, I increased sales 30% per year during each of the past three years.

If that's the kind of performance you'd like to see in one of your divisions, perhaps we should meet.

Sincerely,

Sidney Surface

Maybe this guy did a terrific job...and maybe he did a rotten one...we can't tell. However, since he's obviously looking for work, we suspect it was the latter and not the former. How fast were sales of competitive products in his market rising...50% or 200% per year? What happened to profits? Did they plummet as he hyped sales with too-rich deals; filled the pipeline with unsuccessful new products now being returned for credit; and failed to weed unprofitable low-volume items from the line which, streamlined by his successor, is now highly profitable and poised for solid growth?

The fact that this guy obviously thought we'd be jumping up and down to meet him after reading his "teaser" letter confirms that either he thinks in a very unsophisticated manner, or he figures we do. Too bad. Heads...he loses. Tails...he loses.

Premise #2:

> That anyone can go through an interview with either you or me and not have us make her say what she's done in her career so far...even if she does claim not to have a resume, or to have left it home.

Maybe she can keep us talking and answering her questions during most of the interview, and thereby keep us from figuring her out while she's in our office...although I doubt it.

But afterward, will our impression be so favorable that we'll eagerly await her resume—whether e-mailed or snail mailed—proving she's exactly what we're looking for? Of course, maybe she'll have been so wonderfully glib that we're left with an oral preview of her "perfect-for-us" resume. If so, and we don't hire her, she'll probably land a starring role in the Second City improvisational theatre group.

Premise #3:

> That it's fundamentally possible, even after hearing what we want, for anyone to write a "custom" resume proving they have what we seek, when a more straightforward version would have revealed they don't.

Here we have the fatal flaw of every "withhold-your-resume-so-you-can-doctor-it" scheme. This concept doesn't have to be tied to a "teaser" letter mailing, just because a widely read book links these two ideas. If it worked, the same thing could be done in every interview, regardless of how the interview is obtained. Unfortunately, it doesn't work.

Frankly, my advice is to check out a great many potential employers until you find one...or hopefully a choice among several...where you're right for the job and the job is right for you. Then your straightforward "sales representative" resume will be your ideal aid in getting the job.

You'll be a lot better off trying to *find a fit* than, through distortion and misrepresentation, trying to *fit a find*.

The "Spoof-'Em-Only Method"
...a Long Letter and Never a Resume

Here's another deviant form of direct mail, which you've undoubtedly received and may even have considered sending. This one omits the "tease-'em" lead-in and skips all the way to the "spoof-'em" ending. The trick here is to avoid having a resume altogether, by writing a long letter, which will say just what you want to about your career...*and no more.*

Like the topically organized resume, this long letter lets you escape from the revealing contours of a chronological work history, so you can spotlight whatever you wish, and leave out whatever you want to conceal. Indeed, because it isn't labeled "Resume" at all, you're not even obliged to make a bow in the direction of chronology somewhere near the end, as most people feel they must in a topically organized resume.

If you're really desperate to bury your work history...which includes short jobs, bad references, and maybe a jail sentence...this is undoubtedly the best way to do it. Your reader will surely hanker for a revealing straightforward resume, and will presume that there must be a good reason why you've gone out of your way not to provide one. Nonetheless, you may get a long way into your "sale" before the demand for a specific chronology of prior employment comes up...especially if you send the long letter prior to your interview and handle yourself very smoothly during your visit.

An astute employer should very pointedly ask for your resume during the interview and...failing to get it...should ask you to take home and fill out one of those "Application for Employment" forms normally required only from lower-echelon people, which will smoke out your chronology. But if she doesn't, "Caveat emptor," as they say. "Let the buyer beware."

But now let's assume you have nothing to hide. Let's look at the long letter as a communication device, in comparison to a brief covering note and a "sales representative" resume. There's no contest. The two-, three-, or four-page-long letter lacks the crisp introduction a brief covering letter provides, and is *not* scannable the way a traditionally blocked-out resume would be. Because the long letter lacks visual organization and isn't broken up into familiar segments, it's more bothersome to the reader. It's less inviting to enter, harder to plow through, and raises naggingly negative presumptions as well. If you don't need it, don't use it.

| | | **"Personal and Confidential"** | | |

Puh-leeeez!

Don't put "Personal and Confidential" on any envelope you mail to a stranger when you're job-hunting. People often try to attract attention that way, and it's always a dumb idea. (On the other hand, "Personal and Confidential" on your blackmail and extortion notes may be appreciated.)

If there's anything an assistant is trusted to do, it's open the mail. So, regardless of how your envelope is marked, it will be handled in the usual way. That's what happens in *your* office, isn't it? Attempting to bypass an assistant with such a warning just makes you look naive, even silly. And that's *not* what you had in mind.

There's only one way to get your mailing looked at when others are not. Make it more impressive. Write a shorter, clearer, more elegant cover note. Enclose a very succinctly worded, yet logical and factually persuasive, resume. And don't let whatever you send merely be the 50th of a common thing and no better than the 49 that preceded it.

| | | **Signing Letters** | | |

Remember when you and the other kids used to write your signatures every which way, trying to make them impressive? Girls dotted *i*'s with circles. Boys swooped up to cross *t*'s. Swiss bankers, I'm told, are *required* to have an illegible signature. U.S. physicians too?

How you sign does make a difference.

Surely there's no harm in a confident, legible signature. (In Europe handwriting is often analyzed; here it's not.) But even more important than *how* you write is *what* you write. And judging by the mail I get, at least a third of all executives give no thought to the impression their signature makes.

They write, hoping for a friendly reaction...ideally a phone call. Indeed, they may even imply friendship or at least warmth by starting out, "Dear John." But look at their signature! It's "Wendleton P. Wellington III." Or "W. P. Wellington." Or "WPW." And maybe even with their secretary's initials added, to further stress that the reader is utterly insignificant.

Maybe these folks are not as arrogant as they appear. But it's obvious who they think is the lesser party in an as-yet-unformed relationship. Is that because I'm a headhunter? No, they probably write to CEOs the same way.

Please don't make their mistake. You're too nice a person to behave like that.

The One Best Way to Sign

Here's a simple rule for signing job-hunting letters to strangers: Sign informally, using the first name you'd like the recipient to call you.

If you sign Richard P. Smith, how can anyone know whether you go by Richard, Dick, Rich, Richie, Rick, RP, Bud, or Pete? Same with Katherine, Kathy, Kate, or Kay. Signing your preferred conversational name lets your reader become friendly and informal at the slightest impulse. And isn't that what you want?

But go back up to the top of the letter. What about the salutation when you write a stranger? This is strictly "feel" and judgment, and yours is as good as mine. But I veer toward caution. I hesitate to use a stranger's conversational name, even if I know it. Many folks aren't offended. I'm not. You're probably not. But what's the harm in extending a respectful Ms. or Mr. at the top of the letter, and then signing an unpretentious and friendly Jim Jones or Shirley Smith at the bottom?

There's No Harm in Asking

When you're phoning to check name-spellings, title, address, etc., there's absolutely no harm in asking what the person likes to be called:

"Does she prefer Suzannah, or Sue, or what *does* she prefer?"

"I notice his name is William. Does he go by Bill or Will, or something else?"

The answer you get may surprise you.

"He's the finest dearest person you can imagine, and we all love him. But he's from the old school. People who don't know better will sometimes call him Bill. He's so polite, he just doesn't say a word. But inside you know he's seething. Nobody here ever calls him anything but Mr. Kennedy...to his face or behind his back."

Now you know something important that others will not know.

||| **Transmission Trade-Offs** |||
Sending Your Resume by Mail vs. Fax vs. E-mail

How should I send my resume?

That's a frequently asked question. And the answer depends on what you want to accomplish.

Mail if you want to deliver a top-flight visual impression. Your on-paper resume has bold-faced, regular, and Italic type...perfectly aligned indentions...charts with perfectly spaced columns...and stylish, precise distribution of white space...all of which guide the eye and the mind through a logical, easy to follow, and impressive telling of your story. No e-mail can match this level of visual organization and no fax can match the crisp, clear look of the "real thing."

Clearly this is the way to approach important strangers when you're hitting them "cold" with a direct mail campaign. You want to make absolutely your strongest, best impression.

Whenever speed as well as appearance is important, use FedEx, UPS, or Postal Overnight Delivery Service.

Fax if you want to get your well-formatted paperwork in the hands of someone who's asking for it on the phone and wants to read it *right now!* The formatting, charts, and other visuals will be there. Crispness, clarity and elegance will not. Small type may even be hard to read. No problem...if the person is already enthusiastic about you and merely wants information. However, if he'll be forwarding your materials, you may want to offer copies by FedEx for that purpose.

If a search firm is willing to receive unsolicited resumes by fax (many are not), and if your only objective is to get your paperwork glanced at by an assistant to see if you match a current search, faxing can save you time, effort, and money in doing a fast distribution of your resume.

E-mail if you want to get your resume into the database of a firm that has technology enabling you to do so. In these days of stylish desk-top publishing, it's frustrating to voluntarily retreat to the stylistic limits of the old IBM Selectric typewriter of 30 years ago. However, as you saw on pages 320 and 321, if you use enough white space and stay tightly anchored to the left margin you *can* get an attractive and communicative visual effect.

The important thing about e-mail is that it is *not merely an image,* as the other two communication alternatives are. E-mail arrives as a *computerized file of data.* It can be printed like the other two. More importantly, it can be stored in a database and accessed by keyword searching. It *can make your background—and therefore you—findable!* At the same time, it can also act as a word processing document. If a recruiter wants to write a "presentation" about you—as most retainer recruiters do—he or his assistant can "cut and paste" sections of your resume stored in the database into a detailed write-up about you without the added effort of retyping them. This may help get clearer information into the hands of the recruiter's client. Indeed, it may even put you ahead of another candidate when time is short and staff support is minimal.

However, to successfully deposit your resume by e-mail, you must *exactly follow each firm's specific instructions for e-mail resume submission*. Visit the search firm's or corporate employer's Web site. They may have a form you can paste your resume into that will send it to their database for unsolicited resumes. Or maybe you can click on a link that opens an e-mail window in your browser addressed to send your e-mail directly into that database. Merely finding and using a general office e-mail address or the e-mail address of a certain person who has requested your resume will not necessarily get it into the database.

Indeed, sending an unsolicited resume by e-mail to any address that has *not* been designated to receive unsolicited resumes is a very bad idea. Few things are more irritating than junk e-mail. And anything that comes to an e-mail address not intended to receive it *is* junk. *Infuriating junk!* The *Delete* button awaits! Meanwhile, of course, you'll think you've communicated when, in fact, your transmission was received but discarded.

There's a trend, but preferences are still diverse.

The larger and more technically oriented search firms are increasingly accepting and preferring e-mailed submissions. Yet many firms refuse e-mail submissions. Some of those accept resumes by fax. All accept resumes by mail. *RITE*Site.com's Custom Career Service, as mentioned earlier, monitors this changing scene and provides downloadable e-mail addresses, fax numbers and, of course, mailing addresses matched to the preferred submission methods of the *RITES*-honored search firms shown in Appendix II.

Try To Get Up Close and Personal

...as Soon as You Can, but *Not Too Soon*

Your objective every time you reach out to a potentially helpful stranger is to establish communication, congeniality, respect, trust...perhaps even a relationship as customer, mentor, employer, friend.

But be careful. Don't go too fast. Everyone is surrounded by zones of privacy...their own space, ringed by invisible barriers at inner distances known only to them.

As they gradually accept you, they drop one barrier after another, *inviting* you each time to come a bit closer. Unfortunately they relax—and stiffen—those barriers *subconsciously*. And even more unfortunately, they expect (again subconsciously) that you'll recognize each new freedom to come closer without offending. *And if you don't proceed, you seem like a wimp!*

But beware. There's another barrier right inside the one that just went down. If you barge through the next one prematurely, *you're an insensitive, pushy boor!*

Become a wimp *or* a boor, and your progress with this person—potential customer, mentor, employer, friend—is set back, maybe ended. I'd love to write a whole book about that. But for now, these tips:

Get on a First Name Basis Right Away

Be alert. Go "first name" as soon as you politely can. Suppose you're entering Mr. or Ms. Big's office. He or she is very prominent and powerful...and perhaps the key to a major new job or customer relationship. With warm handshake and sparkling eye-contact, the Great One says:

"Hi, Bill, I'm delighted to meet you. Sit down."

Surprise! You expected formality, standoffishness. You expected you'd always have to call him *Mr.* Big. Instead, here's your chance to go right onto a first-name basis. Seize it:

"Thank you. I'm delighted to meet you, Mr. Big; may I call you Ken?"

If he hadn't been so spontaneous and warm, you couldn't have done this. But at this moment, it's hard for him *not* to grant you first-name permission, after so buoyantly using *your* first name. Awkwardness and ambiguity are ended. To you he's "Ken," today and forever.

Notice how much weaker your position becomes with the passage of time. Suppose Mr. Big *never again* uses your first name during the entire meeting. Now try to look him in the eyes and ask, "May I call you Ken?" How pushy...and even weird!

Suppose on the other hand that he goes on to use your first name several more times, and you continue calling him "Mr. Big." Your subservient role becomes etched in stone. Now you can only hope he'll voluntarily pull you up off your knees, saying "Please, call me Ken." Will he?

Suppose instead that he keeps using your name, and you self-consciously avoid calling him anything. *Now* you pipe up and ask for equality. It'd be a devastating put-down to refuse, and Big's not a sadist. But surely he'll think, "What a Milktoast! I never gave any indication that he couldn't treat me as an equal, and *now* he asks permission. I doubt he's got the guts to take over that division."

Who Are You Dealing With?

Mr. Big was a convenient example, because he's clearly more powerful and prestigious than you are. But don't get me wrong. Just because someone has the power to hire you or to sponsor your progress does *not* mean you must ask permission to use his or her first name.

With someone anywhere nearly equivalent to you, use their nickname without asking. Indeed, you'll look like a wimp if you don't. On the other hand, if you want to do a subtly flattering and respectful genuflect, just leave out the preliminary "Mr." or "Ms." and still ask permission:

> "I'm very pleased to meet you; may I call you Ellen?"

First-Naming on the Phone

Never is it easier...nor more important...to get onto a first-name basis than when your initial conversation with a stranger occurs on the phone.

Why? Because, there'll be follow-up. Whether it's your new-business proposal or a letter-and-resume, chances are you'll put something in the mail almost as soon as you hang up. Handle yourself right, and your letter begins, "Dear Lisa" or "Dear Adam." Fumble, and you wind up feeling and looking far less confident as you write to "Ms." or "Mr."

Actually, first-naming is easy over the phone. If there's no need to be deferential, you just start using the person's preferred name if you know it, and inquire if you don't. If that feels awkward, you'll get another chance when you wind up the call and offer to mail something:

> "Now, your address is"...(get it or confirm it). "And may I call you Fred...or what do you prefer?"...(ANSWER). "Thanks, Fred, I'll get that to you by overnight mail."

Find Out and Remember Names...and More

Before you head off to any important business or social event...and especially to any series of job interviews...always find out and commit to memory the names and backgrounds of the key participants.

Names, above all, you must nail down. Personally I'm no good at those "have-an-amazing-memory" courses that tell you to sear the letters of "George" into your brain by picturing a *G*iraffe *E*ating an *OR*an*GE*. But whatever works for you, do it. Nothing else so simple is so pleasing to people as knowing their names.

But Please Don't OD on First-Naming

Have you had formal sales training? If so, you're in danger of becoming one of the many people who've overdosed on the instructor's exhortation to repeatedly say the other person's first name. That gambit is now so common—and so obviously phony—that it's deeply offensive to almost everyone. You know the script:

> "Well, John, that's another achievement I'm very proud of. You see, John, folks have always told me that I have great people skills. And beyond that, John, I was fortunate enough to have been sent to this sales training course—you know the type, John—the kind that not only makes you a great persuader, John, but also a truly wonderful warm, caring person. And that, John, is another reason I've been so successful."

Ugh! Bring in the next candidate, *please!*

Hang Up "Sir" & "Ma'am" with Your Uniform

Here's some advice I've had to give again and again to men and women who've spent a long while in military service...or who grew up attending one of those otherwise superb military prep schools. Please, PLEASE, *PLEASE* stop calling people Sir and Ma'am. Affirming with every utterance that "you're-above-me" is not necessary in the outside world. Until you break that ingrained habit, you'll never be accepted at the executive level in business.

||| Outplacement: Welcome Help When You Need It |||
...But Don't Remove Your Common Sense at the Door

For over a decade *RITES OF PASSAGE* devoted an entire 30-page chapter to outplacement. Much of that information has become self-evident with the passage of time. The remainder is condensed and included here.

Economic History

In the late 80s and early 90s outplacement was a growth industry...and enormously profitable. Pricing was 15% of the annual compensation of the outplacee, and all of the leading firms pretty much held the line on price.

Inevitably, overcapacity and price competition arrived. Even the largest and proudest firms began to offer flat fees at less than the traditional rate. Indeed, it was the giant firms who started and sustained a downward spiral.

> ***Central economic fact:*** In outplacement the entire fee is paid by the firing company before service begins. If you're ever "in outplacement," all of the money the outplacer gets for helping you will already be in the bank by the time you show up for service.

In the mid-90s a new weapon in the industry's price war was invented...one that you—if you're ever an outplacee—should know about. Some of the shrewdest fee-slashing outplacers approached cost-conscious HR VPs with an even better deal: "We can't go lower on fees," they said. "However the departing employee *may not need a full year of service.* So why don't we just bill you 50% of our usual fee. If he/she finds work within 6 months, half is all you pay. We won't bill the rest unless we're still working with the person 6 months from now."

HR VP reaction? *"Wow! Heads I win 50%; tails I lose nothing!"* The deal was an instant success, and it's still pushed by aggressively competitive outplacement firms today. Meanwhile the individual who's the subject of this commercial transaction has no clue it exists. The clever outplacer—unless he/she relishes 50% less income—has an obvious conflict of interest and perhaps a dubious agenda.

Therefore, this word to the wise: If you're anywhere near outplacement, try to find out the basis on which the firm serving you is being paid. View the relationship and the advice you're getting through the prism of that insight.

Take the initiative in choosing your outplacer.

Often an employer paying for outplacement will allow you to investigate more than one firm and choose the one you prefer. If this option is offered, be sure to take advantage of it. And if it's not offered, you may still be able to get it if you just ask for it. Say something like this:

> "Oh, I've heard quite a bit about outplacement...some of it very good, and some of it not so good. I guess it makes a lot of difference what *firm* you get, and even which *counselor* within the firm. Would it be okay with you if I interviewed more than one firm and chose the one I'd feel most comfortable with?

> "Of course I'll give first preference to the firms you recommend. And I'll stay within the right price range, if you'll just tell me what that is. But I'd also like to check out a couple firms where I've heard of people getting really good help. I don't know the names offhand, but I can find out...maybe they'll be the same ones you have in mind. Would it be okay for me to shop around a bit?"

Chances are, you'll be told that the company is way ahead of you in this line of reasoning, and you'll be handed an already-prepared list. Or one may be jotted down for you. Since a main purpose of outplacement is employee PR, your request, when presented in this rational, dispassionate fashion, will probably be cheerfully granted.

On the other hand, if you fail to express interest in selecting your outplacer, you may merely get the next one on a rotation schedule...or the least expensive one...or in a large layoff with several firms or counselors operating at full-capacity, the one the choosier folks *aren't* choosing.

Visit every firm you're permitted to consider. Ask what you'll receive. But also be realistic.

Respect openness, honesty, and practicality in your outplacer.

Outplacers are like everyone else. To stay in business they have to cover expenses and make a profit.

What might an outplacer provide? How much of what sort of assistance do you feel you need? Here are aids you might receive from an outplacer. Which ones are most important to you?

Counseling: Your counselor must be someone whose experience, judgment, insight, common sense and humanity you sense will be genuinely valuable. At a crucial time, here's your chance to engage an ideal paid helper and friend. Can the firm deliver such a person?

Desk Space: Do you need workspace away from home during the limited hours it would be provided? Would the facilities be equal to your own computer at home? Would you be strengthened or depressed by being with other unemployed executives?

Secretarial Service/Word Processing: Not much of this is provided. Moreover, most executives now are computer literate and don't need or want it. Do you?

Mailing: Does the firm discourage the sending of letters and/or have a specific limit on the number allowed per day or week? Amazingly, some large and famous firms do. What about FedEx? The issue is ***money***, and it might as well be discussed up front.

Telephone: What are the limits on long distance calls from the firm's office? Can you call from elsewhere and bill to the outplacer?

Reference Materials: Today on-paper reference books are far less important than online resources, and much of what you'll use is available from your home at low or no cost. What do you need?

Stationery/Resume Printing: Most outplacement firms provide nothing beyond simple laser printing for stationery and resumes. Do any of the firms you're talking to?

Bear in mind that, at least as far as I know, no outplacer anywhere delivers all of those services to the maximum possible extent. Give "plus points" for honesty to the ones who clearly and voluntarily reveal their limits on each item. Being careful what they promise is a good indication that they intend to do what they say, and therefore may perform a lot better than the ones who affirmatively gloss over everything you ask.

I personally do three or four outplacement "cases" per year...partly because I greatly enjoy the work...and also because I want to be state-of-the-art current with the field. My fee—negotiated case-by-case—is the traditional 15% of prior annual compensation, but is capped at $75,000, regardless of how high the compensation may have been. The minimum fee is $50,000. Regardless of fee, 20% of the money becomes an "escrow account" for out-of-pocket spending to support the person's transition.

I provide steel engraved stationery in a variety of sizes plus business cards (the same stuff you get at Tiffany or Cartier), styled to the individual's own unique taste. He or she comes to New York for three days and stays at a first-class hotel. Two full days are spent working one-on-one with me in my office. If the person is willing, a third day is spent in the office of an eminent psychologist probing interests and talents to make sure that any new job the individual and I pursue together is as interesting and fulfilling as possible (the person, the psychologist, and I spend the following morning working out strategy on these issues). Needless to say there's plenty of money to reimburse postage, FedEx, and long distance phone, and to provide offset-printed (not laser printed) resumes. If money is left over after these "mandatories," it goes toward otherwise unreimbursed travel expenses the individual may have.

Needless to say, that kind of support—the escrow account ranges from $10,000 to $15,000—cannot possibly be provided by an outplacer your company has squeezed into accepting a total fee of only $10,000. Note too, that my program, deluxe though it may be, does not provide even one minute of come-in-and-sit-here-with-the-others-we're-helping. The offset, of course, is my being available by phone and fax 7 days a week from 9 am to 9 pm Eastern time.

The important point in negotiating your outplacement is to find out where you stand on each item of service up-front. That way, you may be able to negotiate giving up something you don't need, in return for additional help with something else. Or, if you otherwise prefer the firm and the counselor, you may negotiate to pay personally for an enhancement. Whatever you do, don't expect to wheedle and charm your outplacer out of something later on that she's reluctant to promise at the outset.

Your First and Most Important Question:
"Do you have various classes of service?"

Each place you visit, start out by asking whether the firm offers more than one level of service...what the differences are...and which level your employer has you ear-marked for. There may be a VIP service featuring a better seating arrangement and/or unrestricted sending of letters. You may never know about it if you don't ask up-front. And knowing, you may be able to get your employer to spring for it.

Even if your employer refuses to upgrade you, you'll be better off knowing where you stand. And the outplacer won't be in the awkward position later on of having to encourage you to do only a minimal program, just because that's all your former employer is paying for.

Referencing an Outplacement Firm:

**Don't be content with the names the firm gives you.
And don't just find out whether the counselee
liked the firm or happened to get work quickly.**

What did the firm actually *do*?

Outplacement companies are in the business of being friendly, sympathetic, and concerned. Hence, their counselees usually like them.

However, if the firm has mainly been dispensing coffee, sympathy, and dubious advice, it may not have been really helpful...even though its counselees may have a favorable impression. Find out about specific recommendations and concrete help.

When outplacers are suggested by your personnel department, ask for a list of folks they've been sent. Call several. And when you visit a firm where you don't have an independent list, try to shake hands with users of the facilities on the day you visit. Remember names and phone later, using the privacy of your call to encourage more frankness than you'll achieve in front of the counselor showing you around.

Investigate as if you were spending your own money. Outplacement is a major nontaxable economic benefit. Try to make the most of it.

||| **Today's outplacement is almost always a good value,
because your former employer pays for it.** |||

But should *you* purchase job-hunting help?

Frankly, I'm skeptical.

Corporations get three benefits from outplacement: (1) removal of the ex-employee from the premises, (2) avoidance of hard feelings that might prompt litigation, and (3) a tangible demonstration of concern. And, of course, a corporation has vastly deeper pockets than you do. The company's readily affordable dollars always purchase 100% performance of all three objectives.

Your situation is totally different. Removal and avoiding litigation aren't what you're seeking. Neither is a demonstration of *concern* for your re-employment. You must find *actual* re-employment. And that is never promised by anyone who proposes, for a fee, to help with your job search.

Whether it's an outplacer who works only for employers, never individuals...or a "career counselor" who works mainly for individuals, advertising to them on the Internet or in the "Help Wanted" sections of newspapers...or a firm that solicits both corporate and individual "clients"...all contracts are the same. Stripped of hype and lawyer-language, they boil down to this:

> *"Only you can find a job for you. We'll help with your resume, and show you how to seek a position, but you'll have to find it on your own."*

Despite the thousands of dollars you'll pay, you're still left with a do-it-yourself project. You'll get education and encouragement. Plus letter and resume suggestions (although who knows how *good* they will be?). Also, probably, some over-priced clerical service. But you're still left with total personal responsibility for the end result.

Could that ever be a good deal? A few years ago I would have said, "No, never!" More recently, however, I've heard of empathic and corporately-knowledgeable people who *do* provide valuable career assistance, ranging from just being a "sounding board" on ticklish political problems, to helping with resumes and cover letters. But these people are seldom the ones you see advertising in the papers; they get their clients through enthusiastic personal recommendations from others they've served. And they are expensive! One woman I know, a Ph.D. industrial psychologist with lots of common sense and general business know-how, gets $3,000 for just a single all-morning start-up consultation.

On the other hand are some highly promotional outfits that advertise in the newspapers. Self-labeled "Career Counselors," "Career Development Specialists," and even flagrantly *mislabeled* "Outplacement Counselors" or "Executive Search Specialists," outfits like these have been around for the past 40 years, promising to help unemployed executives find jobs, and to help dissatisfied ones find better jobs...a very appealing concept to sell, but a difficult one to deliver.

Therefore, these outfits have perennially been in hot water with Better Business Bureaus, District Attorneys, State Attorneys General and...when these came along later...Consumer Affairs Departments and investigative TV shows including *60 Minutes* on CBS. Their advertising and high-pressure sales pitches often implied that they represented employers looking for executives...a channel which would be opened after job-seekers signed fine-print contracts and paid hefty fees. Or there was an implication that these firms would actually *achieve* employment for those who signed and paid.

Indeed, even the remarkably large sums these firms charge tend to be implicit promises of great things to come. "How could I have known they would do so little, when they were charging so much?" say the executives who sign contracts, and later complain to the authorities and to the media.

In the early '60s these firms were charging executives in excess of $1,000. Today's fees often run above $5,000. And at least one firm asks over $15,000 plus a second fee that's often even higher than the first, because it's based on X weeks of salary if and when a job is found. Here's a tip, in case you're ever tempted by such a 2-payment deal: The person pitching you probably earns *a lot* on the "Part 1" fee. Nonetheless, you'll hear: "We're in this together. I hardly break-even on the front-end; for me to make a profit, you *have* to get a great job and pay your 'Part 2' fee." Believe that, and I've got a famous bridge you may be interested in purchasing!

What usually gets these firms off the hook is the very limited commitment in their carefully worded contracts (paraphrased on the prior page) as to what they are actually going to do. BEWARE! *If you let yourself get clipped by one of these outfits, don't say I didn't warn you!*

All of which brings me to the main point I'd like to leave with you on out-placement...

Above all remember this:

Outplacement is a safety net,
not a hammock.

The finest outplacement assistance your employer's money can buy... even the VIP program with maximum support services...will never put you in your next job.

Finding your job is *your job*.

||| **Should you consider buying a franchise?** |||

Here's an idea that many outplacement firms will bring to your attention by holding franchise fairs, inviting in franchise salespeople, and distributing sales brochures for franchises.

Frankly, I'm not keen on that tactic. There's nothing inherently wrong in telling you franchises exist, or in suggesting you think about buying one. But is that helping you find a job? Is that what your employer paid to have done for you? How is that better than the newspaper ads the franchisers are always running to lure you to the same spiel they'll give you in the outplacement office? As one national sales manager told me:

> "Whenever we get into an outplacement office full of panicky unemployed executives with severance money in their pockets, it's like shooting fish in a barrel."

Of course. Far easier than corralling and pressuring the idly curious who stroll the franchise fair at the Coliseum on Sunday afternoon.

Maybe a franchise is life's perfect fulfillment for you. Maybe. But please, always be careful with your life's savings. And especially when you're uniquely vulnerable...out of work and bracketed between an outplacer emptying an office and a salesperson filling a quota.

Here are two rules for when folks yell, "Invest in yourself!" and then suggest franchises:

> 1. *Don't risk your savings* when you're unemployed, on something you wouldn't even look at if you had a good job.

> 2. *Do work at least one week* in a unit of the franchise without anyone knowing you might be a purchaser. Put on old clothes... drive 200 miles...stay in a motel...do anything necessary...to wiggle your way into a $7.90 an hour job behind the counter or desk of the very same outfit you're about to risk your savings and sanity on.

In at least one local office of one national outplacement firm, more than half the executives who "found their jobs" during a 90s recession year bought franchises. That is *not* a statistic to be proud of. Nor is the follow-up survey, which revealed that two years after buying their franchises, two-thirds of all the outplaced purchasers were unhappy with their businesses, or had gone belly-up, or had unloaded them (usually at very severe losses).

||| "Search," "Selection," and ||| "The Hidden Job Market"

This is a book of plain talk.

So I've purposely avoided using two terms that are often misused and misleading..."*search*" and "*the hidden job market.*" But you'll confront them almost every day. Hence, these explanations:

"Search"

"Search" shouldn't be a problem. It has a plain meaning everybody understands...*looking for something when you don't know where it is.*

If people in the recruiting business would use "search" to mean what you and I assume it means, there'd be no confusion. Unfortunately they don't. Even worse, they treat the word as if it has a *special* meaning. And, worse yet, that special meaning is different, depending on who you talk to.

So far, you and I have avoided confusion by using only one word, which has only one obvious meaning, for bringing people into an employer's organization: "*recruiting.*" And when it comes to different ways of performing that function, and of getting paid for it, we've been specific about the distinctions. Therefore, you now know everything necessary to unravel the meaning of "search," no matter who uses the term and what they mean by it.

At one end of the market, you have the *contingency* recruiter who tells you:

"We also do *search.*"

She means that, besides submitting resumes and getting paid only if and when one of those people is hired, she's also willing to accept a retainer and be paid for her efforts while she attempts to fill the job. And since she's assured of payment, she's presumably going to look harder and longer...hopefully right up to the point of finding the desired person.

However, it's nothing new or remarkable for a contingency firm to "do search." For over 30 years, the agencies have stopped calling themselves agencies and have stopped waiting for people to come in and "register." They still advertise attractive "come-on" jobs in the newspapers and on Internet sites. But they also call up employed executives the very same way the retainer firms do.

So in the sense of looking-for-something-when-you-don't-know-where-it-is, the contingency recruiter has long been "doing search," and today he does it on both his contingency and his "search" assignments. Of course the first place she "looks," regardless of payment method, is her database and a number of the commercial and other databases on the Internet. And if the answer is there, it's not necessary to look further.

On the other side of the market, you have the *retainer* firms. They pioneered the idea of looking for happily employed executives rather than waiting for the unhappy and unemployed ones to "register." They, too, have enormous databases...both from people they've already interviewed and from unsolicited resumes coming in every day by e-mail and snail mail. Sizable retainer firms boast of having anywhere from 50,000 to 500,000 resumes. And the first place they "look" is their files. They, too, may find it unnecessary to look further.

The ultimate irony occurred in 1982, when the professional association of retainer recruiters changed its name from Association of Executive *Recruiting* Consultants, Inc. (AERC), to Association of Executive *Search* Consultants, Inc. (AESC)...thus abandoning the "recruiter" terminology which originally differentiated them from the employment agencies. The idea was to separate the Association by name from the contingency firms. Impossible! There have always been—and there still are today—about an equal number of contingency and retainer firms. And almost twice as many contingency firms are using "search" in their names as are retainer firms. Moreover, among the contingency firms using either word, "search" leads "recruiting" by a 2-to-1 margin.

So what does the word "*search*" mean, when applied to the people business? Your guess is as good as mine. Contingency recruiters use it when they want to be *paid* on retainer. But they also use it—justifiably—to describe what they *do* when working on contingency. Both contingency and retainer recruiters *may* do it when they look for executives. But then again neither may do it if, by "search," you mean looking for new people they don't already have in their database.

And of course individuals, and outplacement and executive marketing companies, also use "search" to mean the seeking of *employment*, rather than the seeking of employees.

So if you tell me you want to go "search" for gold, or oil, or buried treasure, I'll say that's a good idea. I may even come along. But if it's "search" that involves employment, "Thanks, but no thanks." It's too much bother to figure out what you mean.

| | **"Selection"** | |

Selection is a term, newly popular in the U.S., for doing executive recruiting through the use of advertising. So what? That's how it's always been done in Europe, the U.K., Canada, Latin America, and elsewhere. It's also the way contingency recruiters have always operated here in the U.S.

In traditional U.S.-style retained "search," the recruiter identifies, approaches, and persuades potential candidates. In "selection," the opposite occurs. The recruiter runs advertising. Potential candidates see it. They approach the recruiter, claiming to be valid candidates. The recruiter merely "selects" among potential candidates the advertising has pulled in.

That assumes, of course that the advertising *does* bring in good candidates. If not, the recruiter calls up any appropriate people already in his/her firm's database or in commercial databases the firm subscribes to. If that doesn't solve the problem, he/she may do traditional on-the-phone sourcing to find and persuade candidates who *aren't* answering ads and posting themselves on Internet employment sites.

The U.S. retained search industry has always prided itself on seeking *ideal* candidates, not merely *available* ones...claiming that executives whose presence at one company rather than another can shift an industry's competitive balance of power are usually *not* unemployed *nor* so dissatisfied or fearful that they're responding to employment ads.

It's impossible to fault that logic!

However, it can make sense commercially to abandon any pretense of looking for *absolutely the best* candidates and, instead, serve up only the best who are currently "in the market." The major retained search firms learned to operate this way when they expanded internationally. So it's no surprise that the two largest—Korn/Ferry and Heidrick & Struggles—were the very first to jump on the Internet's essentially no-cost advertising to launch FutureStep and LeadersOnLine. To describe their new advertising-centered services they chose the term "selection," because it emphasizes *how the work is done*, rather than "contingency," which denotes the same operating methods but also indicates a payment method which those firms do *not* prefer.

Because "selection" methods are quicker and easier than retained search, payment terms can be more lenient and flexible. I attended a search industry meeting in March 2000 at which the New York Client Development Executive of LeadersOnLine openly told the audience of its—at least then—highly flexible "performance based" terms, which he specifically went on to describe as partially "contingency based"...taking advantage of the shock value of the "C word" among the up-scale audience he was addressing.

The Client Development Executive hastened to point out, however, that he demands an up-front payment to embark on any new project. That money goes right in the bank. Further payments—depending on what specifically is negotiated—may then depend on actually filling the positions involved.

| | | **"The Hidden Job Market"** | | |

This intriguing phrase—obviously invented by a copywriter, rather than merely plucked from the dictionary like "search"—is likewise used by people to mean different things.

The most prevalent and legitimate meaning is the shadowy world of job openings not yet referred to recruiters or advertised in newspapers or on the Web. However, some users expand the expression to include jobs-that-aren't-jobs-yet...situations where there's nagging dissatisfaction with the incumbent, but not yet a firm decision to fire. Also, where a need to add a new position is felt, but not yet formalized as an empty box on the organization chart.

Obviously, it's a good idea to discover such situations before others have beaten a path to them. And as long as "The Hidden Job Market" is merely a sexy way of saying "go-straight-to-the-employer-and-quickly" through direct mail and networking, it's certainly a valid concept, even if overly hyped.

The problem comes when executive-marketing and outplacement companies try to extract big money from you or your employer because they propose to "Introduce You to the Hidden Job Market." The clear implication is that there's an undisclosed supply of real jobs which they know about and you don't. And you'll never find those jobs unless they tell you. And they won't tell you unless they're paid a stiff fee.

After all that build-up, "The Hidden Job Market," being such a little idea with such a big bold name, becomes deceptive...or at least very disappointing. You feel "ripped off," when your "introduction" inevitably turns out to be nothing more than a description of networking and direct mail techniques.

Chapter 16

The Interview...
Making a Sales Call and
Demonstrating the Product

Face it. When you go to an interview, a purchase decision is being made.
The employer is seeing you and others to determine who she'll acquire
and who she won't.

Chances are she's read your resume, which you or a recruiter sent her.
Now a salesman is coming over with the actual product. Get ready. She
won't just look at the paint job and kick the tires. She'll take a test drive!

You're the salesman. And you're also the product.

Moreover, because it's an interview...not just a social call...your host has
permission to probe deeply. She can ask tougher and more personal
questions than she'd ask at any other time. And she can examine your

analysis and strategy in solving business problems...yours and hers...far more frankly than she would under any other circumstances.

You've got to be prepared for a really penetrating inquiry, if your interviewer takes that approach. If she doesn't, you've got to reveal yourself to her. And if the interview fails to display your merits, that's your problem, not hers.

Ideally, your potential employer will wind up wanting to buy the car...or at least to drive it again, after she's seen and tried some others. If so, you'll be offered the job...or at least invited back for another round of interviews.

In the end, you may decide that this employer and her opportunity are not for you. But what you and I will work on in this chapter is making sure that she doesn't conclude you're not for her.

Bear in mind that you're proving yourself
on two levels:

1.   as a fine person, and
2.   as someone obviously able to do the job.

Your behavior and appearance will be scrutinized far more critically when you show up for an interview than on any ordinary work day in the next ten years.

The person who's thinking of hiring you wants to be sure that you're someone he'll enjoy working with. And also someone who can walk around inside and outside the organization as a favorable reflection on the company and on him. Only if he's satisfied on these *"fine person"* points, will he concern himself with whether he thinks you can handle the job, as indicated by your experience and track record. He's hoping to find you:

Intelligent, and also "street smart," with abundant common sense;

Analytical, logical, goal-oriented, and a planner;

A skilled communicator...good at listening, speaking, and writing;

Unmistakably a leader...but also a "team player," cooperative, and congenial;

Healthful, attractive, and well-groomed;

Tasteful in dress and decorum;

Poised, courteous, and cultured;

Sensitive to the feelings of others...not pushy, pigheaded, or obnoxious;

Honest, loyal, and straightforward;

Politically aware, but not a political operator;

Committed, responsible, and diligent;

Cheerful and optimistic, with a "can-do" attitude;

And overall, an *interesting person*, with curiosity, enthusiasm...and maybe even a sense of humor!

Virtually all of the attributes listed above will help you to do the job, once you land it. But in interviewing to get the job, don't underestimate the seemingly superficial aspects that are more "image" than "essence." Appearance and behavior are first to be noticed. And if they're deficient, you may flunk the *"fine person"* test, even though you score plenty of "but-he-could-probably-do-the-job" points.

Interviewing is a time of maximum scrutiny. Make sure you arrive feeling and looking your very best. Get a good night's sleep. Have a fresh haircut or hairdo. Get your shoes shined. Tend to your grooming in every way. Don't wear a noticeable amount of fragrance. Dress as you would for any other daytime matter that you take very seriously. Even if you've heard from the grapevine that you're arriving on a "casual Friday," wear your first-class business attire. That is, of course, unless you've been specifically instructed otherwise by the person who invited you.

So much for "good-impression." You've been making one or we wouldn't be discussing a $100,000+ or $400,000+ interview. The bottom line is that you'll never get "points taken off" because you show respect for someone by polishing your appearance to meet him or her. Any danger that you'll be perceived as a "stuffed shirt" (or blouse), if that worries you, is easily dispelled by a warm, open, unpretentious manner...which I hope you always have anyway.

So let's forget "image" and go straight to "essence." You're about to make a sales call. And, like any other salesperson, you've got to deliver *enough persuasive information to convince the prospect that your product can **do the job***.

Interviewing is a difficult form of selling for two reasons:

1. **It's a "package deal," where the salesperson comes with the product; and**

2. **The customer, not the salesperson, controls the unfolding of the sales presentation.**

Ordinarily a customer can take the product...and leave the salesperson. Unfortunately, you're a "package deal." Therefore you must sell with great finesse. Much as you'd like to, you can't just make a well-organized presentation and afterward deal with questions and objections.

The interview is a unique ritual drama, in which a sales call is played as if it's a social call.

Which it's not. One of the two parties is totally in command. He's the buyer. He's the decision-maker at the end. And he's in charge all along the way. By controlling the use of time and the choice of topic in a Q-and-A format, he determines which features are brought up, and in what order, and how thoroughly or superficially each one is discussed.

And the fact that *your* sociability is part of what's being sold prevents you from saying what a regular salesperson would say:

> "That's a very good question. But *let's hold it* until I've finished explaining how the machine works."

> "No, that's really not a problem with this machine. *Ours is the only one* which doesn't have that disadvantage."

Politeness, modesty, loyalty, confidentiality. You must display these and many other attributes, because you're "the product." Unfortunately, having to do so handicaps your sales presentation.

||| **The first principle of interview salesmanship:** |||
forgo the monologue
...at the outset, and all the way to the end.

Because the format of the interview is ritualistically conversational, you can't give a too-long answer to any question. You can't sell yourself as socially-polished, if you monopolize the conversation.

So don't use any question...no matter how broad...as a springboard for a monologue. Instead, give a concise answer that hits the highlights in clear and specific terms, including numbers ("a little under $15 million in sales and about 150 employees") and approximate dates ("as I recall, that was in late '98").

Don't ever talk longer than one or two minutes. Finished or not, wind up your sentence, shut your mouth, and look at your interviewer to see if she wants more on the same topic...or would rather switch to something else. If she wants elaboration, she'll say so. What's more, she'll point you in the right direction:

> "Interesting, and I certainly agree with your strategy. But when we tried something along those lines, we ran into trouble with the unions. How'd you make out on that score?"

Now you've got her eating out of your hand! How much better than if you'd bored her with a full explanation before "coming up for air."

Learn "newspaper style."
Written and oral, it will make you an outstanding communicator.

...And it's a lifesaver in the interview format.

Do me a favor. Next time you pick up a newspaper, notice the way every item is written:

1.   The headline sums up the article.

2.   The first paragraph lays out the entire story.

3.   The first sentence of every paragraph tells what the whole paragraph is about.

4.   And the major facts of every story always come earliest. Lesser, more detailed points come later, and the most trivial are at the end.

There's good reason for this "big-picture"-first format. It allows you, the reader, to get what you want out of the paper very quickly and efficiently. You can stop reading any article after a paragraph or two and still know the gist of the story. And when an article really interests you, you can dig deeper and deeper into the details, by reading further.

See the analogy to what you're trying to achieve in an interview? Just like you reading the paper, your interviewer always has the prerogative to dig deeper, or switch to a different topic. You can drop any article after just a headline or a paragraph. And he can divert you to a different subject, just by asking another question.

Therefore, all of your answers must be organized in "newspaper style." You've got to state your main point in the first sentence or two of each answer. You can't wallow in detail, "setting the stage" for your main point. Because if you do, a new question may cut you off before you *get* to your main point. Then you'll appear petty, illogical, and detail-oriented...even if you're not.

Surprisingly few people—even senior executives—have learned what their newspapers show them every day. Study and master newspaper style. Use it orally and in writing. Every bit of your business communication will improve...not just interviews, but memos and presentations, too.

**Just because you can't deliver a salesman's monologue
is no reason not to prepare one.**

**Analyze your product and your customer's needs,
and develop the sales message you *wish* you could
deliver in a 15-minute monologue.**

**Then divide it into brief topical capsules.
Believe it or not, almost every interviewer...
no matter how inept...will ask questions that allow you
to present everything you have clearly in mind.**

That's right. The questions you receive *will* relate to what you want to say, if you *know* what you want to say. That's because your interviewer really does want to find out how your background and achievements fit his needs, and how they guarantee you'll perform as well for him as you have for others.

Fundamentally, he wants to hear what you want to communicate. Not necessarily, however, in the order you'd like to present it. And, of course, with more attention devoted to your failures and gaps in background than you'd prefer.

So prepare as if you could deliver a salesperson's monologue. If you've figured out what you should present, then you'll hear it asked for. And when each "appropriate" query comes along, you can drop in the right one- or two-minute capsule. Unprepared, you'd have found those same questions "irrelevant," and "not leading anywhere." But knowing where the conversation *should* be going, you'll more readily see the interviewer's questions as a path to get there.

How often have you been asked a question in an important meeting and given a "so-so" answer, only to realize afterward that you had a perfect opening to say something really favorable? That's an experience we all have almost every day. Prepare yourself. Don't let it happen in a potentially career-making job interview.

What about questions specifically designed to give you trouble?

The possibilities are endless...too many to discuss. But almost all such zingers aim for a relatively few slips and wrong answers. Those I can identify for you.

As I said before, your interviewer is on your side. She wants to find out that you are the person she's looking for. If so, her staffing problem is solved. But if you're not as good as you appear to be, hiring you could cause far more difficulty than it resolves.

Therefore, she'll ask lots of questions aimed at revealing your flaws. Even your answers to the most bland and casual queries will be scrutinized for damaging admissions. And chances are, those revelations won't have much to do with your resume-stated background. Instead, they'll relate to your personality and your management techniques...the kinds of shortcomings behavioral psychologists probe. So here are some wrong answers to watch out for...both with the employer, and with the company's psychologist, if you consent to meet him:

WRONG ANSWER: **No, I haven't got around to visiting your Web site yet.**

This answer is so wrong that you should kick yourself *really hard* if you're ever asked any question that could possibly lead to such an answer. Maybe the site is so innovative that the interviewer is merely proud and wants to brag. More likely, she's thinking something like this:

> "You seem so pitifully uninformed about us that you must have made absolutely no effort whatsoever to prepare for this interview. I wonder if you've even gone to our Web site?"

Never *ever* go to an interview with an employer or a recruiter without knowing everything a competent and intellectually curious executive should have wanted to find out in preparation for such a meeting. What kind of person are you if you haven't done this? Clearly not the sort the company wants to hire.

Today's corporate Web sites make it easier than ever before in the history of the world to find out about a company. There are descriptions of all their businesses, profiles of their senior officers, annual and quarterly reports and proxy statements (most recent and prior years), stock performance tables and charts...and more. Plus a treasure trove of news releases neatly filed from latest to earlier. Those will prompt you to look on the Web for related articles in the media. Today, at the executive level, ignorance has no excuse.

WRONG ANSWER: There's more bad than good.

Of all the "wrong answers," this one fits more questions than any other. So many, in fact, that I can't even begin to think up enough examples to suggest its vast possibilities. However, the minute you're about to list attributes of anyone, anything, or any situation, be sure to ask yourself:

"How many good ones should I mention and how many bad ones?"

Decide shrewdly. Sometimes there should be lots of bad ones and hardly any good ones, as in the list of probable results you mention when your interviewer gets your reaction to an operating policy that verges on the unethical and illegal.

But suppose he asks how you feel about your current job. Obviously, it fails to utilize your prodigious talents and energy level. But don't slip. There's more good than bad; otherwise, the interviewer will expect you to be malcontent in his job, too. And in describing your current boss, there's probably a lot that's admirable, not just shortcomings; otherwise your interviewer envisions you talking negatively about him. Same with your reaction to the overall management of your current company. Some policies and approaches (which you will list) make lots of sense. However, certain *key* ones have serious disadvantages (obvious to any thinking person, including your interviewer).

Needless to say, you also see far more advantages relative to disadvantages when asked how the job you're interviewing for fits your talents and aspirations, and how you fit the job. Same, too, when it comes to balancing the opportunities in contrast to the obvious problems facing the industry and company you're being interviewed for. Same goes for the U.S. and its industrial and other institutions, and on and on.

You're no Pollyanna. You can see defects and problems, analyze them accurately, and conceive and execute realistic and creative strategies for dealing with them. However, you're absolutely not one of those "nattering nabobs of negativism" Spiro T. Agnew warned us about.

WRONG ANSWER: You'd live your life differently if you could.

This is the wrong answer to all those "if" questions. If you could be anyone other than yourself, who would you be? If you could go back and change an earlier career decision, what would you be doing today? Don't accept any offer to rewrite your personal history. You're basically a happy and highly functional person, who has high self-esteem and is busy producing and enjoying...not fretting and regretting.

Also bear this "wrong answer" in mind when faced with "if" questions about the future. If you can be anything you wish five years from now, it will be something that represents fine progress along the path you're on right now.

With respect to your current and past marriages, outstanding or difficult children, and other highly personal facets of your life, probably the less said the better...at least until you're sure that your values and circumstances clearly correspond to those of your interviewer. You can't possibly gain anything by being either ahead of, or behind, him on these points.

And of course if you're asked whether you "consider yourself successful," the answer is "Yes" and briefly why...not, "Well, sort of, and I'd have been more so, if it weren't for..."

WRONG ANSWERS: Illustrations of your greatest talents and achievements that:
      1.   don't relate to the job you're interviewing for, and/or
      2.   happened long ago.

Not surprisingly, your strongest attributes and the achievements you're proudest of are work-related and correlate amazingly well with the requirements of the job you're interviewing for. The fact that, after eighteen years of avid competition, you recently bred, trained, and groomed a Dalmatian that won Best-In-Show at the Grand National Competition of the American Kennel Club is hardly worth mentioning. Especially when compared with the fact that last month your Division's hemorrhoid remedy scored the highest market share in the 64-year history of the brand.

Don't be confused. When asked for your "best" achievements, always give your latest ones. Only when specifically asked about early phases of your career will you trot out the corresponding long-ago achievements...thus demonstrating that you've always been an over-achiever. The greatest days of your career are now and in the future, not in the past.

A variation on this theme has to do with what you like most and least in your current job or the one under discussion. Your preferences will match the job you're interviewing for just as neatly as your talents do.

WRONG ANSWERS: **You've failed to develop nonbusiness interests.**
AND
You spend time on nonbusiness interests.

These wrong answers are bookends; they come as a matched pair. You're apt to be asked what your avocational interests are. Better have some ready to mention. Active sports are always good. Intellectual and artistic interests begin to look respectable when you get comfortably over $100,000 or $200,000...and they take on great luster when you get over $400,000. Charitable and "cause" interests also gain respectability and ultimately cache, as you soar into the corporate stratosphere.

However, until you're being considered for a position high enough to be corporately ornamental as well as useful, don't let on that your wide-ranging interests take any significant amount of time away from work. Chances are your potential boss wants you "hungrier" for performance bonuses than for intellectual and humanitarian nourishment.

By the way, there's a chance you may be asked what interesting books you've read lately. Anyone who asks won't worry about your time, since reading is usually done when and where you can't work. Don't bring up the subject. But do prepare. If you seldom read, you should pick up a critically praised *non*business volume...perhaps a biography or a spy novel... from the current bestseller list. Comment knowledgeably. And if pressed further, mention a couple other books you'd like to read but haven't had time for. That's enough. You're joining a business, not a literary society.

WRONG ANSWER: **Your aspirations for the future don't springboard from the job you're discussing.**

"What-would-you-like-to-be-when-you-grow-up?" questions are just a variation of the "if" questions we discussed earlier. Make sure your stated objectives are consistent with getting the job you're interviewing for and pursuing it as wholeheartedly as the company could wish.

WRONG ANSWER: Anything but the frank truth about when and why you're leaving.

If you were FIRED, say so. Reference checking will surely reveal the fact, even if you still have an office and phone message service at your former company. Any attempt at cover-up will seem dishonest, unintelligent, and emotionally immature. Give a short, simple explanation, objectively avoiding bitterness and complaint. Show you can rise above temporary setbacks. Your forthrightness and maturity in comparison with most people, who fidget, fiddle, and fume, will come off favorably. More about this later.

WRONG ANSWER: The too-vague answer.

For every job you've held, know and be able to state without hesitation your title, whom you reported to, what size and type unit you commanded (in people, facilities, budgets, sales, profit, market share, etc). Know too in approximate numbers the size and situation of the overall organization of which your unit was a part. You absolutely must know what you're doing now...and you should also know what you've done in the past.

Remember JFK? Most of the nation became convinced he could cope with our problems...in large part because he could speak about them so succinctly, and yet so specifically in facts and figures. It takes no more time to say "a $55 million division in Akron" than it does to say "a medium-sized division located in the Midwest." Yet the former avoids raising several unnecessary questions in the interviewer's mind:

"I wonder what she means by 'medium-sized.' "

"*Where* in the Midwest?"

"Why didn't she just give me the specifics? Maybe she's afraid I'll know somebody who was there when she was."

WRONG ANSWER: "Confidentiality prevents me..."

Use common sense when it comes to confidentiality. Don't be a blabbermouth. But if the competitor who's interviewing you frankly discusses his business with you, then reciprocate. Knowing the other person's figures won't make them your figures, and vice versa. If you've been responsible for something very brilliant and very recent, which must be screened from your competitor, just give a definite but nonspecific comparison he's undoubtedly already guessed:

> "With the new line included, sales for the first quarter are
> more than double what they were in the same period last
> year. *Much* more than double."

The sparkle in your eyes and your smile of pride and achievement will communicate your accomplishment just as well as if you'd stated the exact figure for the new line standing alone.

Remember: A lot of people who've done a poor job use confidentiality as a cover-up, which is what you'll be suspected of if you "take the Fifth Amendment." People who've done a great job are eager to tell about it.

WRONG ANSWER: More than was asked for.

One rather tricky question is to ask for your "four greatest achievements"...or your "three strongest talents"...or some other number of something favorable. Give exactly the number asked for, *and no more*. The test is to see if you'll plunge right past the requested number, piling on achievement after achievement, in a binge of self-praise. If so, you'll be revealed as a braggart, psychologically suffering from low self-esteem. At the very minimum, you'll seem to be someone who doesn't listen and follow instructions alertly.

WRONG ANSWER: A too-long answer.

This wrong answer is asked for by every agonizingly open-ended question...one of the commonest headaches of the interviewing process. Here the remedy is one of those *capsules* that I suggested you create out of the fifteen-minute salesperson's monologue you're not being allowed to deliver. That highly refined quarter-hour of mandatory product description and product advantages nicely fills anywhere from seven to ten 1½- to 2-minute capsules, which can be administered as requested throughout the interview.

Suppose you're zapped with this frequently thrown open-ender:

"Tell me about yourself."

Don't be wimpy and grasp for help:

"Well, what particular aspect would you like to know about?"

Instead, just plunge in and *cope!* Take no more than one to two minutes and hit the highlights, covering everything from childhood to now. Include a few words about where you grew up, because this question is usually asked to evoke a broad-brush personal portrait. To prove it can be done, I'll give you my own:

> "I was born and grew up in Reedsburg, Wisconsin, a small town of 5,000 people, where my father was a partner in the Ford car and tractor business. Worked my way through the University of Wisconsin and the University of Wisconsin Law School as a radio announcer and taught Legal Writing at the Law School for a year. Came to New York City in 1960 as Radio-TV Contract Administrator at J. Walter Thompson Advertising Agency and later became an Account Executive on various consumer products. Joined Bristol-Myers Products in '65 as a Product Manager and ultimately became Director of New Product Marketing. Next I was Director of Marketing for the Sheaffer Pen Company, and then General Manager of the Tetley Tea Division of Squibb-BeechNut. In '71 I got into executive recruiting with Heidrick & Struggles, where I became a Vice President and one of the firm's top producers of fee income. And in 1977 I started The John Lucht Consultancy Inc., specializing in the selection of high-level executives for major corporations...the same firm I operate today. I also continually update RITES OF PASSAGE, take on about three high-level outplacement cases per year, do some executive coaching, am an expert legal witness on lost earnings in major personal injury cases, and have recently launched RITESite.com on the Internet as a career aid to readers of RITES OF PASSAGE.

That's under two minutes, and yet it certainly covers "Tell me about yourself." If this were an interview, anything else of interest could be asked about.

| | | **Capsules: The Interview Pain-Reliever** | | |

Gapingly *open-ended questions* are one of the worst headaches of the interviewing process. They're painful as you grope for an answer that's appropriate, clear, and succinct. And if not handled well, they can lead to the serious complication of bogged-down monologuing, which can demonstrate that you're innately a poor communicator, disorganized, less-than-candid...and more. Indeed, open-ended questions are asked, in part, because they *are* troublesome to insecure, fuzzy-thinking people, who don't communicate well under pressure...people the interviewer wants to weed out.

I just administered a capsule for "Tell me about yourself." You may not need yours, but be sure you take it with you to your interview. Indeed, take along plenty of capsules. Like the Lomotil®, Dramamine®, Tetracycline®, Alka-Seltzer®, and Pepto-Bismol® you take on your foreign travels, you'll feel better knowing they're on hand, whether you wind up using them or not.

Your interview pharmacopoeia should include:

A "Tell-Me-About-Yourself" Orientation   (CAPSULE)

Already prescribed.

Key Segments of Experience and Achievement   (CAPSULE)

These are the topically organized segments of the fifteen-minute "salesperson's monologue" you'd love to deliver but can't in the conversational format of an interview. Have your selling points of experience and achievement clearly in mind, with specific figures stapled into your memory. Nothing minimizes an achievement more than failing to remember precisely what it was.

Achievements in Rank Order   (CAPSULE)

This one prepares you for any "Top Three" or "Top Five" question. Since your greatest achievements should also tend to be your most recent, you'll ponder the importance/time trade-offs in preparing this list. If there's nothing major to report from your most recent briefly held job, don't feel you have to make something up, just to "represent" the ill-fated career move.

Maybe you have one monumentally large achievement sure to command awe and respect...and clearly attributable to your being there as the instigator and not merely one soldier in the platoon; but it happened too long ago to be one of your "latest-and-greatest." Prepare it succinctly, and deliver it *last*...third out of three, or fifth out of five, depending on how many you're asked for.

Strengths and Weaknesses   (CAPSULE)

Give this one some real thought. Your strengths are at the heart of your sales pitch, and they ought to be the right ones for this job...or you'll be better off not getting it. Be ready to name and—if asked—illustrate several. Include your high energy level.

Come up with a proper "more-good-ones-than-bad-ones" answer; the ratio should be overwhelming...maybe 4 to 1. But, within the boundaries of enlightened self-interest, also try to be honest. The standard formula for an interview-confessed "weakness" is "*A strength carried to a fault.*"

Examples:

> "Sometimes I may drive my people a little *too* hard. Since I'm a bit of a workaholic, I tend to expect others are, too."

> "Sometimes I can be *too* supportive of my people...hanging on to them, still trying to train and coach, when perhaps I should just pull the plug a few months sooner."

And how's this for a reverse-spin on a weakness?

> "I'm the broad overall conceptualist...the strategist, the planner, the schemer...and also the enthusiastic motivator of the team. But I'm not the down-to-the-nitty-gritty implementer. I always make sure to have an operations officer I can absolutely depend on to see that things don't slip between the cracks...and also a meticulous controller, to make sure that there are no financial surprises. Without both of those people doing their jobs, I couldn't do mine."

Obviously, this approach will work only if you're discussing a big job in a big company. But you get the idea and can adapt it to many situations.

Reason for Leaving   (CAPSULE)

It's not enough just to avoid the "wrong answer" of saying you quit—or worse yet that you're still doing your job—when everyone who's likely to be asked knows you've been fired. Prepare an accurate capsule on what happened and what your current status is. And *keep it brief and simple!*

If the new CEO brought along his own person for your job, no harm in saying so. Add, if true, that you too might have brought along someone you knew and trusted if you were in the CEO's shoes and had such a limited time to effect such a major turnaround. Indeed, you went out of your way to cooperate with the woman who's now your successor, during those first awkward weeks when you were both on the payroll and she hadn't yet been named to your job. As you see it, what she has to do to be successful is to finish installing this-and-this program which you were putting into place when the upheaval occurred, and she seems to be taking basically that approach (if true).

There wouldn't be room in this entire book for the enormous smorgasbord of familiar firing scenarios...one of which may one day happen to you. A great many, like the one above and all sorts of consolidation and staff-cutting measures, can be frankly stated and endorsed. "Personality clash" with your boss, however, normally should *not* be the diagnosis. Say instead, "Fundamental policy differences," and cite some concrete examples. You simply can't afford to be categorized as someone who can't get along with people.

The trick in discussing firing is to take an open-minded dispassionate, managerial stance. Observe, comment, and react as an informed, objective observer, who's also a very skilled manager...not as someone subjectively involved, wronged, and wounded. You're willing to stand and be judged on the wisdom of your programs and the next administration may have to continue them. On the other hand, if you tried something that failed and you were in the process of changing course, say so. You'll be judged far more on the calibre and comprehension you demonstrate, than on the fact that you were fired. Chances are, your interviewer has also been fired at least once in his career.

Your Management Style   (CAPSULE)

For your answer to ring the bells on this issue, you'd better know what style the company feels *it* has. When you visited the company's Web site you may have noticed a few words about "our corporate values" or "our culture." Above all, be sensitive to clues dropped by your interviewer. The "participative" style is usually in vogue, whereby your door is open to your subordinates and their ideas, and you get results through motivation and delegation.

But for some companies you should hedge your bet..."On the other hand, nobody wonders who the boss is or where the buck stops." Other possibilities include: "Problem solving"..."I enjoy analyzing what's wrong, figuring out a solution, and implementing it." And "results-oriented"..."My decisions are highly concerned with how the result will impact the bottom line." You might add, "On the other hand, I also care a lot about my people; training and developing them and seeing they're fairly treated is extremely important." A pragmatic pastiche, plus taking the pulse of your interviewer, will you get you safely past this issue.

What Appeals to You About Our Job and Our Company? (CAPSULE)

Capsule or no capsule, you will have thoroughly studied the company prior to your interview. When you devour the company's Internet site, be sure to make notes with this question in mind. Nothing warms the heart of a tough, hard-to-convince interviewer quite like an immediate, enthusiastic, and well-informed answer to this question.

Current Status and Long-Range Trends of Your Speciality and the Overall Industry (CAPSULE)

If you know anything at all about your present field, you certainly have some good ideas on where the action is now and where the future may lead. Marshal them. Don't just pull them together on the way *home* from an interview where the CEO of a diversified corporation had more thought-provoking insights into your specialty than you did.

What Would You Like To Know About Us? (CAPSULE)

The easiest or the hardest of questions. Ironically, the more you want the job, the tougher the question is. If you're skeptical about whether the job will advance your career, you're loaded with questions that have to be resolved to your satisfaction.

But suppose you're thrilled to be considered for the job. It's with an impeccable company, and represents a career breakthrough in responsibility. Then what do you ask? Certainly not about benefits and retirement. Maybe about what they see as the key problems and opportunities to be addressed by the person who gets the job, willingness to invest in the business, and whether it's central to the company's future growth or a candidate for "harvest" and possible divestment. But be careful. Shouldn't you *know* what the problems and opportunities are? Check for a *common view* of such issues; but don't imply you can't see without being told what some of the key ones probably are.

The invitation to ask questions is inevitable. Be prepared for it.

Reading...and Writing...Between the Lines

You know darn well that your interviewer will be trying to "read between the lines" of your answers...looking for accidental unspoken nuances that may be even more revealing than your statements.

So, since he's *reading*, you may as well make sure you're *writing*.

For example, when you're asked about your creativity, give some instances where you thought up a great idea that worked out well. But also give some samples of outstanding creativity within the unit you're responsible for, but which you personally did *not* think up. Give credit to the lower-echelon research subordinate whose "far-out" idea you backed with some money from your "Venture Fund," and to your CEO whose unpopular idea worked out sensationally well after you and your subordinates removed the kinks from it, and to the advertising agency that came up with the winning campaign after you asked them to give it "just one last try."

Incidentally, that until-recently junior scientist now has her own sizable section of the laboratory to run. And, far from being fired, you were able to help that ad agency win a client relationship with another division of the company you work for.

We see, of course, that you're creative. But we also read what you've written between the lines. You care about, and listen to, what others around you are thinking...*even your boss*! With you in charge, the company isn't limited to your own personal creativity. You recognize anyone's good idea when you see it. Moreover, you probably get along well with others, commanding their respect and loyalty, because you reward them for a job well done.

You get the idea. When answering questions about talents and triumphs, you have a perfect opportunity to write between-the-lines messages about your other fine characteristics and management techniques.

The "Pregnant Pause"...and How to Deal with It

The "pregnant pause" is a gimmick some interviewers use to unnerve candidates, and to force them to reveal personal insecurity, and hopefully to voice unguarded statements.

Here's how it works. After you've finished answering his question, the interviewer says absolutely nothing to move his side of the conversation forward. Dead silence. No question, no comment. He just looks you in the eye, waiting for you to panic and rush in to fill the awkward pause.

This startling stoppage may come at random...or possibly when the interviewer suspects, or wants you to *worry* that he suspects, that you're not telling the truth, or at least not the whole story. One recruiter I know loves this gimmick so much, he tries to use it on his co-workers at lunch.

The only way to deal with this behavior is to nip it in the bud. The first time your interviewer breaks the rhythm of the conversation this way, pause with him long enough to make absolutely sure he's "pregnant pausing" and to make sure he knows that *you* know that's what he's doing...maybe 20 seconds or more. Then say, kindly and helpfully, as if perhaps he seems to have lost track of the rather complex discussion you've been having:

> "Is there anything else you'd like to know about...(the question you just finished answering)?"

Treating the pregnant pause as a lapse of attention by the interviewer is the only way to deal with it. If you knuckle under to even one "cross-examination by silence," you'll signify that you're the insecure sort of person who submits to interrogation in this arch, smug fashion. If so, you're in for a tense, defensive interview. On the other hand, by kindly and inoffensively calling the interviewer's bluff, you create unspoken recognition and respect. If, by chance, your interviewer decides to try again, repeat the treatment.

Coping with the "Stress Interview"

Let's hope you never run into it, but there is a really bad idea in interviewing that still hasn't completely died out...the "stress interview." Pioneered long ago by an executive recruiter who'd been a prisoner in one of the Nazi death camps, the idea was to discover what he called the "counterfeit executive"... the one who can't take pressure...by applying great pressure and tension during the interview. Seat the candidate with the sun in his eyes; put him in a very low or soft-cushioned chair so that he realizes he is obviously beneath you; quickly interrupt his answers, telling him he obviously didn't understand the question; "pregnant pause;" imply knowledge of information contrary to his statements. The possibilities for rude, challenging, inhospitable behavior are endless.

You'll almost certainly never get the full treatment. Even the guy who invented the process quit operating that way after achieving a few years of notoriety. But you may run into someone who kicks off the interview by throwing down the gauntlet:

"I can't see how you're qualified for this job!"

He goes on from there with argumentative, demeaning, and perhaps embarrassingly personal questions. Maybe he deliberately misinterprets your answers. And probably he avoids looking at you...gazing over your head, thumbing through his calendar, and shuffling papers. You're getting an updated version of the stress interview.

What to do? You have to call his bluff. That may be all he wants. Say:

"I'd appreciate it if you'd look at me when I'm talking to you. If we can get this conversation on a more cordial basis, we'll communicate much better."

Maybe just saying something like that will pass his "test." If not, I suggest you get up to leave, turning back as you get to the door:

"I'd still be willing to have a good conversation with you, but this session doesn't really seem worthwhile."

Chances are, he'll call you back, say you passed his "test," and continue the interview on a new and more cordial footing. By then, however, you wonder whether you should even consider working for this guy or the company he represents. So do I.

Who's in Charge of the Interview
...You or the Interviewer?

No question who's responsible for the outcome of the interview. You are. You've got to get your message across. If your appropriateness, your ability, and what a fine person you are fail to register, it's your loss. And it's your fault, not the interviewer's.

But who's *in charge*? Now that's a different question. Believe it or not, some people think that you should take charge. Go in, say "Hello," and see if the interviewer asks the questions that draw out the information you want to convey. If not, begin answering different questions from the ones she asks, and twist and lengthen your answers to make sure you cover all the important points that support your candidacy. Be poised and pleasant, but don't be afraid to demonstrate aggressiveness and leadership...crucial qualities in an executive.

If you're interviewing for Vice President - Marketing of a company that sells vacuum cleaners door-to-door, that's probably good advice. Barge in and take over. But for any other job, in my opinion, a much more polite and sensitive approach is absolutely mandatory.

First of all, you're selling yourself as a *"fine person"*...polite, socially poised, and someone who, if hired, will wear well as a co-worker over the years. Somehow, the pushy vacuum cleaner salesman doesn't fit that description.

Secondly, and equally important, if you try to take charge and control what information is covered, you may not convey what your interviewer wants to know. You may bore her with a persuasive pitch on points she was willing to concede...meanwhile, failing to address the doubts and concerns you would have discovered if you'd sensitively followed her lead.

Moreover, since the interview is a *demonstration* of how you think and operate, there's a good chance your interviewer may conclude that you're a "hip-shooter"...a superficial thinker, who plunges ahead before gathering information, and checking preconceived assumptions. After all, that's the way you behaved in your interview.

Therefore, all things considered, *don't try to grab control*. In terms of personal image, you can't afford to dominate the interview. And in terms of accomplishing your objectives, you don't really want to.

Steering the Interview with Questions
and "Red-Flagged" Answers

Only your own good judgment during the actual interview can determine to what extent you can and should try to influence the direction it takes.

If you're willing to become overtly pushy and aggressive, you can cover whatever you wish. But if you want to stay within the ritual boundaries of a social conversation in which the employer has the prerogative of asking most of the questions, there are really only two techniques by which you can gently guide him toward matters you'd like covered.

Questions

You can always ask a question to see if he's interested in a subject you want to talk about:

> "Is the development and marketing of internally generated new products a major factor in your growth plans? That's an area where I've had a lot of successful experience."

Nothing impolite or too pushy about that approach.

He may say:

> "Absolutely! Tell me about it."

Or he may say:

> "We're not entirely opposed to internally-generated new products. But over the years we've become skeptical. We find we get a lot more for our money by acquiring underdeveloped products someone else has pioneered. Have you ever tried that approach?"

Well, now you know where he stands. Maybe you've also got success stories of the type he's more interested in. In any event, you didn't waste time and suggest future philosophical differences by giving a long recitation of exploits he's not looking for.

Red-Flagged Answers

Sometimes you can wave a red flag at the bull and he'll run for it... sometimes not. Even professional TV interviewers are often unbelievably nearsighted. The famous actress winds up her answer:

"Of course, that was back when I was stealing cars for a living..."

And the oblivious interviewer moves right along with:

"Tell me...looking back on all the films you've made...which hair-dresser has influenced you most?"

Nonetheless, a valuable technique for attempting to steer an interview along more promising lines is to wind up an answer with a provocative statement that cries out for a follow-up question, if the interviewer is interested:

"...which is why, of course, I then completely changed our approach to incentive compensation."

Your interviewer ought to be tempted to ask what kinds of changes you made and what resulted. But if he's not, at least you haven't been rude or boring, and you haven't wasted time on a topic he's apparently not interested in. The bull doesn't always run after the red flag.

And that's it. Questions and flagged answers are the two polite ways you can attempt to steer an interview toward topics you'd like to discuss. The advantage of both is that they merely suggest...they don't force...a change of direction. They both leave control of the interview in the hands of the interviewer, which is what you will normally want anyway.

Out of Town Tryouts

Most people find that, in interviewing, "practice makes perfect." By the time they're in their third or fourth interview, they're very effective. But what if you haven't interviewed for quite awhile and you suddenly face an unexpected "biggie"? Or if you look forward to a series of interviews and don't want to waste the first one or two? Then try your show in Philadelphia and Boston prior to opening night on Broadway.

"Role playing," of course, is the answer. A social friend or your spouse can sit in for the interviewer, perhaps asking questions from a random list you've prepared. Better yet, try to set up a real grilling by a business friend from the right industry. Choose someone who can come up with his own tough questions, and who will give you a clear-eyed critique afterward.

The Danger of Being Prepared

There's no such thing as being over-prepared. There always is, however, the danger of being over-eager to play back what you've worked on. And by recommending "capsules," I certainly don't mean to encourage that tendency.

Occasionally I come across people so anxious to deliver the thinking they've developed that they don't listen carefully to the question and conform their answer to it. These people are extremely rare...only one of them for every 50 or 75 who fail to come up with clearly focused, brief, and factually explicit answers to questions they certainly should have anticipated.

You're too alert to make either mistake.

| | | **Engines Ready...Contact!** | | |

Prepared as you are, you have absolutely nothing to fear as you take off into the sunrise. If you've got anything close to the right stuff, your interview will demonstrate it.

However, let's run through a preflight checklist of practical tips:

Check the forecast. If your interview has been arranged by a recruiter, call her in the morning or the afternoon before. She may have new information since you saw her last, regarding job content, what's looked for, how long other interviews have lasted, what line of questioning was pursued, and what mistakes other candidates made. Don't betray nervousness by asking about all these items. Just say: "Anything I should know before I go over there tomorrow morning?"

Pack your flight case. Into your elegant attachée go extra copies of your resume (just in case your host has misplaced his or wants to pass some along), a yellow pad and a *quality* pen, any charts of figures you may need to refresh your memory if questioning gets detailed, and a *Wall Street Journal* to pull out and read if your host is interrupted or you have to wait a few minutes.

Arrive early and check the equipment. Get there five minutes ahead of time and ask to use the lavatory before being announced. That way you can check for lint on your collar and parsley on your teeth. You'll perform best knowing you feel and look perfect.

Return your salute from the crew. The interview begins in the corridor as your host's secretary greets you and maybe offers to shake hands (be alert for this). He, and through him possibly the receptionist too, will probably be consulted for a report on your poise and personality. Your down-the-corridor conversation with him...cordial but not presumptuous...is the start of your interview.

Don't land prematurely. After your *firm* handshake, I hope your host doesn't feign a landing and then pull up, leaving you discourteously plopped for an awkward minute or two. But he might. It's a fairly common maneuver. Circle gracefully until you get landing instructions, or you clearly see where he's landing.

Warning. There's advice going around...maybe via a book or a psychologically oriented outplacement firm...not to sit where the interviewer first suggests and, wherever you land, to *move your chair*. This odd behavior is supposed to connote an aggressive personality. I merely find it obnoxious. Unless you've got a bad back, or the sun's in your eyes, why not just sit down where indicated, and relax?

Five-minute warning. Don't go all-business all at once. Get off to a positive, upbeat start on a relatively personal note. Admire something in the office, or the company's convenient location, or the fine weather. Do *not* start off with the lousy weather, a bad commute, or any other "downer."

Hazardous terrain. Enter the Bermuda Triangle with extreme caution, if at all. Avoid such obviously hazardous topics as politics, religion, and sexually- and racially-oriented issues. Beware of trick questions aimed at exposing your negative attitudes on these matters by implying in advance that the interviewer has such feelings. Even sports can be a hazardous topic until you know your host's opinions. Believe it or not, some interviewers will see your failure to share their views on player trades as an indication that you're probably not a very shrewd analyst in the world of business either.

Keep an eye on the radar. Read the interviewer's body language. Leaning back signals a smooth leisurely ride; tapping fingers, fidgeting, and checking the clock call for crisper answers. "Closed position" (tightly crossed arms and legs) says you're meeting resistance, whereas open, loose limbs say "all clear." And hand-to-face says he...and you...are uncertain, possibly untruthful. Body language can be overrated, but shouldn't be ignored. If you haven't read a book on the subject, you ought to.

Don't go on autopilot. No matter how well things seem to be going, don't let your guard down. The most skilled and subtle interviewer is never the one who treats you roughly. The one who puts you totally at ease is the one who'll find out even more than you'd prefer to tell her.

Debrief promptly. If a recruiter is involved, call soon afterward to debrief. The client will also call, and if the recruiter can play back your favorable comments, they will reinforce the client's good feelings about you. Don't be a sappy sycophant. But don't be coy, either. People tend to like people who obviously like them. And recruiters are more inclined to support candidates who probably will accept, than those who might not.

File your flight report. Why not send a brief "thank you"...two to four paragraphs, using "Monarch" ($7^{1/4}$" x $10^{1/2}$") personal stationery if you have it, otherwise "regular size." While you may refer in some way to what was discussed, this note is *not* a parting salvo of hard sell. Instead, it's a courtesy that says *fine person*...and differentiates you from the vast majority of candidates, who don't bother with amenities. Even more importantly, write down for future reference everything you found out at your interview. Most candidates won't do this either. Therefore, you'll be more on the employer's wave length than they will, at "second round" interviews three or four weeks later.

||| **Answering the Unasked Questions** |||

No interviewer these days is going to invite legal action by asking:

"Do you really think a woman can handle this job?"

"Aren't you a little too old for a grueling position like this?"

"Do people respond to you just like everyone else, even though you only have one eye?"

"With that brace on your leg, I don't suppose you get out to visit the companies in your group very often, do you?"

In an ideal world, these questions would not only be unasked, they would also be unthought. But our present world is far from ideal. If you vary much from the norm...if you're an ethnic or racial minority, physically handicapped, noticeably younger or older than most executives, considerably heavier or shorter...there may be unspoken questions in the mind of the interviewer about your ability to handle the job because of your "difference." The best course is to rebut these objections, even though they're not voiced.

But you must communicate *indirectly*. You can't simply pipe up and say, "Don't worry about my age; I'm more effective at 59 than I ever was at 30 or 40." If by chance the interviewer *wasn't* thinking of your age as a problem, he'll wonder why you're being so defensive. And if he *was* thinking about it: (1) he'll be offended that you caught him, (2) he'll be unconvinced by your self-serving assertion, and (3) he'll worry that you may already be hinting at legal action if he doesn't give you the job.

Just as in writing your resume, you can answer such unspoken questions with offsetting information. If you're probably a lot older than the other candidates, casually mention spending your vacation as an instructor for Outward Bound...or that you're leaving in August for two weeks of mountain climbing in Nepal. Or maybe just mention your interest in finding a challenging partner for a few good sets of tennis while you're in town. Make the interviewer think of you as healthy, vigorous, and in your prime. Don't talk about something you watched on television, or how hard you were hit by the flu that's going around. Everyone watches TV and gets sick occasionally, but you can't afford to raise image problems with someone who doesn't know you.

Shatter your stereotype.

Offset *youth* with civic and business responsibilities normally reserved for someone more mature...president of a stodgy country club, trustee of a college, outside director of a bank. (For this purpose, forget "when-do-you-have-time-for-it?" concerns.) Fight the *age* problem with evidence of vigorous physical activity and a fast-paced schedule. And if you're a *woman*, stress the fact that you're accustomed to extensive travel, to making difficult decisions, to operating independently. And throw in an anecdote that makes it clear that your household is organized accordingly.

If you belong to a racial or ethnic *minority*, be warm, self-confident, friendly and informal...thus demonstrating (1) that you'll fit right in, and (2) that you don't have any doubt or insecurity about fitting in. And if you're *physically handicapped*, stress your ability to function effectively in the mainstream of everyday life; mention a party you went to recently, grumble about a speeding ticket, talk about your participation in active sports. And if you're *overweight*, stress the fact that you lead a highly disciplined and energetic life...that you adhere to demanding self-imposed schedules...that you work for long-term goals.

What the Interview *Can't* Do for You

For years one of the leading literary agents has been trying to get me to write a book which ought to be called *How to Package and Pretend Your Way Into a Big Job You're Not Qualified For.* Naturally that's not the title he proposes, but it perfectly describes his premise.

Such a concept is not only dishonest, it's ridiculous. No combination of slick resume and glib interviewing can enable you to defeat an array of really excellent candidates and win a job you're not qualified for.

And you shouldn't want such a job. Get it, and your life will be miserable until you lose it...and even more miserable afterward!

However, armed with the information in this book, and the willingness to work as hard as necessary to obtain the position you do deserve, you should be able to fight off the other fine candidates competing against you for any job you fully deserve and can perform.

Good luck. I hope you do.

Chapter 17

Negotiating Your Employment Contract...
Getting Plenty, and Making Sure

So you're giving up a fine job where you're comfortably settled, well respected, generously paid, and on a fast track toward bigger and better things. You're seizing an even greater opportunity.

Or maybe you're just winding up an agonizing period of unemployment you feared might never end. You're grasping a lifeline.

Either way, the question now is: What are you going to *get*?

The single most important...and the easiest...way to win a very good deal from a new employer is to make him or her fully aware of what a good deal you have where you are. Then the initial offer should be something

you can graciously accept. Bargaining can be minimized or avoided altogether.

Protection is another problem. Probably you're thinking:

> *"I'd like to have an employment contract.*
> *But most companies refuse to give them."*

You're right, of course. Most companies don't want to hand you a document marked "Contract." Nevertheless, these days more and more corporations are putting more and more in writing.

And believe it or not, every time you start a new job, you *can* have an *employment contract*...even if you *don't* receive a paper with that title on it. You and I will make sure that your terms-of-employment are solidly nailed down...and as favorable as they can possibly be.

We'll also define the jargon you may be confronted with. And we'll review how you can pleasantly and reasonably speak up for what you want.

||| **Before we talk about anything else, let's pause for** |||
a few words about the nature of compensation.

Just a few years ago—it seems only yesterday—we began reading about scores of twenty-somethings getting an idea, writing a business plan, getting "angel" and/or venture funding, working outrageous hours to spark an operation, doing an IPO, and—after a 1-year SEC curb on selling restricted shares and a 6-month lockup imposed by the underwriter—cashing in for millions of dollars.

And weren't we envious!

These kids had—*still* have—youth, good looks, and boundless energy. Plus, now they also have astonishing wealth. True, they worked unbelievably hard day and night to get it. But for how long? A year, two, maybe three. Max!

I hope you didn't buy *RITES OF PASSAGE* expecting I could lead you to a similar result. I can't. For that kind of lightning to strike, you have to be standing in the just the right place at the just the right time with just the right people who are all willing to risk all the traditional wealth and status they have, which—conveniently for a beginner—is almost none.

The Nature and Stages of Compensation in Young Companies

At startup, the only employees of a business may be just an entrepreneur with a dream and a circle of pitch-in-and-do-whatever-is-needed associates. The entrepreneur can't pay much to these people. Even if the business has some income, it's not enough for market-level salaries.

Cash pay is subsistence at best. The real pay is the highly uncertain chance of a huge windfall through stock options, plus far more responsible and interesting work and a higher title than an inexperienced person could command elsewhere.

At intermediate stage, the business is up, operating, and generating sales. Maybe there's even a slightly positive cash flow. Or venture capitalists may have injected funding and there's lots of positive publicity. The potential of the business is more apparent. Risk seems lower. Therefore, less equity is now needed as bait. And more experience is demanded. Indeed, the company now *needs* some sophistication in its key managers. Newcomers are still sacrificing current cash. But less so than the earliest employees. By now we clearly see the nature of compensation...in a young *or* a mature company. There are three components:

1. *Cash*,

2. *Career opportunity*...a more interesting and challenging job with a higher title than one could obtain in a larger, more mature and stable company, and

3. *Equity opportunity*...options or warrants that *might* create great wealth.

At IPO stage, experienced professional managers are needed to impress Wall Street analysts and the investing public. The company needs credentialed "been-there-and-done-that" people. Cash compensation for these people is still lower than they'd make in an established company, and options are still the main reward. Maybe a $500,000-a-year person will accept $200,000, plus options. But by now cash is at least credible.

My point in all of this is that there's no free lunch. If you want to go for the *MegaMoney*, you've got to be willing to be grossly underpaid in cash at every stage of a company's development. In fact, you're really *purchasing* your stock participation...and paying for it in cash! In the earliest stages, you're also being paid to a high degree in career opportunity. Maybe you're just a Financial Analyst in a large company. Now you leap to CFO of a risky startup. If you can mature to the point that your title is merited by your performance, you'll have been paid handsomely for your time, even though not in dollars.

Yes, lots of people have made killings that make us envious. More folks will in the future. But there are trade-offs and enormous risks. Wherever you choose to position yourself on the risk/reward continuum, I wish you good fortune.

||| ## Now let's look at the difference between employment negotiations and every other kind. |||

When you negotiate to buy a house, or a boat, or a car, the object itself stays the same in your eyes, while you haggle over price. Your liking and respect for the seller can drop to zero. But what you're trying to buy remains just as enticing as it was the first moment you saw it.

Unfortunately, when you negotiate for your own employment...and even if someone else "fronts" for you (which I don't recommend)...you're not just selling yourself. You're *being* yourself. You were a "class act" during your interviews. Don't figure it's now safe to turn into a ruthless...or a petty... sleaze, just because the employer has chosen you and begun discussing your terms of employment. As my Granny used to say:

"There's many a slip, twixt the cup and the lip."

If you demonstrate any undesirable characteristics at this point, the whole deal may be off. Anything that seems overreaching or underhanded will be held against you.

So stand by everything you promised, stated, or implied. If you described your current compensation as X, don't suddenly claim it's X plus 35%, just because four friends tell you that's what they're getting for almost exactly the same job you have. And if you initially implied that it would be easy for you to relocate, don't later raise all sorts of costly problems you want your potential employer to throw money at.

She just may decide that you've been less than forthright...or at the very minimum that you're a drag to deal with. And on either basis, you could still lose out to another candidate.

||| **The trick in negotiations is to indicate** |||
what a good deal you have where you are.

In the end, you won't move unless you score a significant improvement.

And nobody's going to ask you to. At least *not if they fully appreciate your current circumstances and compensation.*

Responsibility, growth opportunity, and possibly a chance to build long-term net worth...not just a boost in current income...will be the main reasons for you to consider any move. But you *do* expect financial improvement, both immediate and long-term. And the only way your prospective employer can know the full extent of what you're getting now is if you tell him.

As an executive recruiter, I always make sure to find out every facet of current compensation, plus any expected changes within the next 12 months. And I communicate all of this information to my client in a detailed written summary *before he meets the candidate.* That way he realizes right from the start that Candidate X will have to get upwards of $490,000, whereas Candidate Y can probably be hired for $370,000 and possibly less.

Face it. Cost/value assessment works exactly the same in hiring executives as in buying merchandise. There will be no reluctance to pay what you obviously cost...a reasonable incentive over what you're making now...if you're evaluated and proven "the one we want" during realistic shopping for alternatives.

But if you allow yourself to be thought of as a $250,000 candidate, when it will really take more than $360,000 to move you, then don't be surprised to receive an "underwhelming" offer. And don't be surprised either, if subsequent disclosure and bargaining can never quite build the financial platform you should have stood on from day one.

Prepare a written summary of current compensation. It's as helpful as your resume in orienting recruiters and employers.

Take a look at the financial summary I prepare on the candidates I present. I've laid out the information as if you were preparing the chart for yourself.

Unfortunately, many recruiters don't bother to dig into current compensation. Moreover, you may be on your own, with no recruiter involved. So, unless you work up a financial review, chances are your proper figures won't be registered in the early stages when they'll do you the most good.

Indeed, you've probably got to do some figuring, just to find out for yourself where you stand. Nine out of ten executives I meet don't fully appreciate their current compensation until I prompt them to think about it in detail. In the end, of course, everyone always figures out to-the-penny what she's now making, in order to weigh the financial offer that accompanies an enticing opportunity. But by then it may be far too late to get the employer to think of you in the right price range.

The summary is *informal* (even though precise), so you won't put a title on it.

	X Year (Current fiscal/ ends in 4 mos.)	Y Year (Next fiscal)
Base Salary	$302,250	$385,000 [a]
Bonus	93,000 [b]	155,000 [c]
Short-Term Incentive (Cash)	62,000 [d]	84,000 [e]
Long-Term Incentive (Deferred)	77,500 [f]	103,500 [g]
Company Car Allowance	24,640	24,640
County & City Club Dues	7,130	7,130
Approximate Annualized Value of Stock Options	65,800 [h]	65,800 [h]
Daughter's Tuition Scholarship	18,600 [i]	18,600 [i]
	$650,920	$843,670 [j]

[a] Assumes promotion to EVP/COO in June, and mid-point of $350m to $420m salary bracket for that job. If not promoted, my base will probably rise 8% to $326,430.
[b] Assured; could go to ceiling of $110,000.
[c] Estimate assumes promotion; otherwise $110,000 to $125,000.
[d] Based on achieving personal goals (100% earned in past five years).
[e] Assumes promotion; otherwise approximately $72,000.
[f] Based on Corporation achieving four-year profit goal. Paid past three years, currently on-target.
[g] Assumes promotion; otherwise $84,000.
[h] Difficult to predict; however, this is the actual average of the past three years.
[i] Linda is one of five winners of a company-wide academic high school scholarship competition, granting full tuition to four-year college. Next year is the second-last year of her scholarship.
[j] Assumes promotion; if no promotion, I expect $714,670, based on these figures in Y year: $325,000[a], $116,500[c], $72,000[e], and $85,000[g].

Keep your summary as simple and objective as possible. Only discuss cash. Don't bring up FICA, insurance, medical, and other ordinary employee benefits that are likely to be comparable, wherever you go. That makes you look petty. If you get $328,000 straight salary and nothing else, say so.

But if you've got money coming at you from several directions, point out and add up *everything*. If you expect a raise or a promotion within the next several months, be sure the recruiter and the employer know what's coming. Your incentive to move must be figured on top of what you'll soon get where you are...not just on top of what you have at this very minute.

Even if you're unemployed, you want your prospective employer to realize what you're *accustomed* to getting. If she's sensitive and smart, she won't want you to feel that your duress has been taken advantage of. And, since you'll be nervous about asking more than she offers, you'll want to make doubly sure that her initial offer is as high as possible.

When do you hand over
your compensation summary?

Maybe never.

The recruiter or the employer will surely ask, "What's your current compensation?" Answer with an approximate figure justified by your summary. At that point he may say:

> "Well, that's in our ballpark. We can certainly come up with an
> attractive incentive."

If so, don't go further. Keep your summary in your attache. Obviously you're going to get a tempting offer.

On the other hand, your current compensation may spark a reaction like this:

> "Wow! That's certainly more than I would have thought. How
> do you come up with that number?"

If so, you're prepared to handle compensation in the strongest, yet least disruptive, possible way:

> "Well, I did a little figuring before I came over here. I didn't want
> to waste your time, if what I already have is close to what you'll be
> offering. When you have a few minutes, you can look this over

and see if it's something you can see fit to improve upon."

(Hand over your paper.)

"By the way, are you having any problem with the new emission standards?"

See what your paper does? It lets you register...without being at all boastful, obnoxious, or tedious...all facets of the good deal you already have. And you do so without skipping a beat in the central conversation that is convincing your host that you're the person who best understands his business and can do the most to build it...the person he needs, regardless of cost.

Today executive compensation packages are hardly ever simple and straightforward. They have to be studied to be understood. How anyone will fare in years one, two, three, and beyond in leaving X Company to join Y Corp., which has different programs, requires careful analysis.

Chances are, the person you hand your "summary" to won't even attempt to evaluate it himself. He'll have it looked at by his compensation expert, who can authoritatively analyze what you have, compared to various proposals he might make.

The result will be an offer your prospective employer is comfortably sure will be attractive to you. Moreover, it will probably be accompanied by a visual aid that clearly showed him...and now proves to you...what the advantages of his offer are.

The best way to negotiate is to avoid having to do much negotiating at all. Do your homework right away. And let your would-be employer know as quickly and clearly as possible what you're already getting. He's a lot more likely to make you an offer you can't refuse if he's thoroughly aware of what you *can* refuse.

Now let's discuss contracts.

Can you get one?

Yes!

Play your cards right and you can almost certainly put your new employer under a written obligation. And if you're smart, you'll surely try to do so.

As you may recall from your Business Law course in college, a verbal contract is just as enforceable as a written one. *But only if, by its terms, it's to be performed within one year.* This, of course, becomes important if you are looking for a firm agreement of employment to last more than a year.

Indeed, if you only have an oral agreement, it had better not promise anything that can't be performed in a year. Otherwise, the *whole agreement can't be enforced*...even the parts that can be performed within a year.

And of course "time protection" for more than a year is usually the main thing an employee tries to negotiate. When she tells her would-be employer, "I want a contract," she's saying:

"I want to be sure, before I give up the secure job I have, that you can't casually dump me on the street in no time at all, and for no good reason."

And in his traditional reluctance to provide a written "contract," the employer is saying:

"That's exactly what I want to be sure I *can* do. I can't *manage* my business unless I'm completely free to pick and change my team at any time and for any reason."

How do these seemingly irreconcilable views get resolved?

By compromise. The executive asks for a four- or five-year "contract," and the employer comes up with two-years, or less. Seldom will a company commit itself for five years to an executive who isn't already on its payroll.

Consider the "Termination Agreement."
It's better than an X-year "Contract"...and easier to get.

The employee wants firing to be permissible only for criminal acts...and maybe also insanity, wanton negligence, or gross incompetence. The employer, on the other hand, wants just about any reason to suffice, as long as time parameters are respected. In the end, the employer will usually get plenty of leeway as to *cause* for firing. The employee will hold out for...and achieve...*time* protection, which is basically all he ever hoped for anyway.

Which brings us to the advantages of a "termination agreement" over a straight X-year "contract." Employers who are unwilling to grant two- and three-year contracts will usually be more amenable to an 18-month...or if you can't do better a 12-month...termination agreement which says, in effect:

"You can fire me at any time for any reason. But you must give me 18-months' notice, or at least keep me on the payroll for 18 months afterward."

This arrangement doesn't tie the employer's hands, and it doesn't box him in for an exceedingly long time. So he's more willing to go along with it.

And for all practical purposes, you receive even better protection than under a two- or three-year "contract." Security under those deals soon elapses to zero. But with an 18-month termination agreement, there's always a year-and-a-half of future paychecks. Even if you become CEO at $1.4 million per year, you can still whip out the termination agreement you got when you joined the company as a zone manager at $102,000 ten years earlier. You'll collect $2.1 million during the next 18 months...thanks very much!

There are contracts...
and there are C·O·N·T·R·A·C·T·S!

On the one hand, there are handshake agreements,
written into an "offer letter."

And then there are "employment contracts,"
hammered out by opposing lawyers.

If you can get ideal protection from something simple
and friendly, don't hold out for "big deal" paperwork.

I've known lots of prominent and highly paid New York lawyers...business-controlling partners in the famous law firms, and General Counsels of America's largest corporations.

Standing head-and-shoulders above them all is the smartest human I've ever met...about 5' 2" and hardly 100 lbs. (mostly brain)...who attended law school over 60 years ago and since then has been doing post-graduate work in common sense. He's always practiced independently of the huge law firms. Many corporations use them for routine matters...but bring him in on very important and difficult issues. Moreover, the CEOs of those corporations insist on getting his slant on their personal legal matters.

Interestingly, this legal ninja has a devastating secret weapon that many of the other "super-lawyers" seem almost unaware of:

Simplicity!

Phil (not his real name...but close) would much rather have an agreement embodied in a plainly worded letter or an exchange of letters than in a 27-page document full of convoluted clauses.

It's not at all unusual to go to Phil asking that a contract be drawn up to formalize an agreement along the lines of a simple letter or an exchange of letters you show him, only to be told:

"No way! You've got 'em flat-footed on the basis of this *letter.* If they don't perform, we can sue them and get everything you're looking for, plus punitive damages as well. But if we go in and try to negotiate a formal contract with their legal department involved, there's no way in the world we can get language like this.

"Just write them a friendly reply, saying you're pleased to go ahead as they've suggested, except for that one little change in the schedule that you've both agreed to.

"And for heaven's sake, don't misplace the letters. They prove what your agreement is, and you could be mighty thankful to have them later on."

You get the idea.

It may be comforting to have a long and explicit document spelling out every conceivable facet and contingency of your arrangement with your employer. But it's not necessary. She and her company are just as bound by what she writes in her offer letter...assuming you accept her offer and go to work relying on it...as if there's a fancy paper marked "contract," which you both sign. And she's equally bound whether she asks you to countersign her "offer letter" or not.

Today almost every company provides offer letters.

So don't quit your job until you have something in writing.

You have clout.

You may not have enough leverage to get all the money or all the protection you want. But whatever you do get, you certainly have the power to get into writing.

Just say:

> "Well, Herb, I guess we're agreed on all the really important points. The title will be Senior Vice President - Manufacturing. I'll report directly to you as President, and I'll be on the Management Committee. Besides all factories in the U.S. and abroad, I'll have responsibility for Purchasing, Manufacturing Engineering, and Quality Control...but not New-Product Engineering.
>
> "My base salary will be $450,000, and I'll participate in the officer-level short- and long-term management incentive programs— and receive options—as you outlined them to me. I'll also get that $160,000 upfront to make up for not coming under your bonus plan this year, and to help with any moving expenses not covered by your most comprehensive moving package, as described in this booklet. And I'll receive a $1,700 monthly car allowance.
>
> "In terms of job security, I'll be getting 18 months' termination protection. You can discharge me at any time for any reason. But unless I've done something criminal against the company, you must either give me 18 months' notice, or pay me for 18 months after you let me go. And if you give me some notice but less than 18 months, you'll continue to pay me up to a total of 18 months from the time you give me notice.
>
> *"As soon as I have your offer letter putting all of this in writing, I'll go in and resign."*

That's the way.

Just *assume* Herb will be putting what you and he have agreed on into an offer letter. When he does, you'll resign. And, of course, not before.

How can he refuse? He'd have to say:

> "Well, you've accurately summarized what I'm going to do for you if you join us. But I'm certainly not willing to confirm in writing what I've just been telling you. Why, that would help you hold me and the company to it later on!"

No, he can't say that. And when you have your "offer letter," you have your "contract." The essence of your agreement with him is in writing.

About the only resistance he could put up would have to go something like this:

> "We do things here on a handshake. There's mutual trust. It's almost like a family. You have my word. That ought to be good enough. And if it isn't, then maybe you and I don't have the right relationship to go ahead on anyway."

Your obvious rejoinder would be:

> "Herb, there's no question that *you and I* have exactly the right relationship. I know you'd never break your word to me. But, God forbid, something might happen to you...or me...on the way home tonight, or next month, or a year from now. I know of an instance where that's exactly what did happen. So before I resign, I'd really appreciate a note from you."

If Herb refuses, no matter what reason he gives, you're better off not going to work for him.

Virtually no employer will refuse you an "offer letter."

But many will deny you a "contract."

Yet the two papers amount to the same thing!

Ironic...but true. Ask for an "offer letter" and you'll almost never be refused.

But ask for a "contract," and you'll be refused more than half the time:

> "No way, George. We just don't *have* written contracts here. Why, I don't have one myself. I can't...and I won't...do for you what nobody's ever done for me. We're not one of those shifty outfits where that sort of thing is necessary. I trust my boss completely to do what he promises me. And he's never let me down. If you can't think of me the same way, then maybe I'm not right for you...or maybe our company isn't right for you."

Now you've confronted yourself with a tough argument to overcome. You've asked for a "contract." You haven't merely *assumed* you'll get an "offer letter"...something virtually every company gives, and something your prospective boss *did* get when she came aboard.

Lots of luck!

Why should your would-be boss try to achieve for you, an unproven new-comer, something she's never received during nine years of loyal service and outstanding performance?

Seen through her eyes, your asking for a "contract" seems presumptuous, if not downright unreasonable. Fortunately, there are several rejoinders you can make, and I'll lay them out for you.

But don't blunder into arguing for a "contract," when an "offer letter" will work equally well, and be vastly easier to get. The trick is to find out in one of your earliest discussions...long before you begin "negotiations"...whether the company uses "employment contracts," and whether they're willing to give you one. If not, don't even bring up the subject later on. Just *assume* your way into an "offer letter" that covers the same ground.

But suppose...for whatever reason...you want to get a mutually signed document labeled "Employment Contract" out of a company that traditionally refuses to give them. Here are the arguments you can use:

1. "It's a logical, businesslike approach to a business matter. People die and move on, and memories fade. A written agreement is the obvious safeguard."

2. "More and more companies *are* writing 'employment contracts' for senior managers these days." Some estimates and surveys suggest that over 50% of America's largest corporations now enter into formal written agreements with a substantial number of their executives.

3. "I have an 'employment contract' at my current company, and I appreciate the security it provides. It's just one of many advantages, and I don't feel like moving to another company and getting *less* on any score than I've got now."

4. "With today's business uncertainties, all executives are more reluctant to move than ever before. I believe that it's important for your company to rethink its policy against giving contracts. Not only do I want one. But I'll also be trying to recruit other outstanding and well-situated executives to work for me here. Being able to give them the reassurance of a contract will be very helpful."

5. "Moreover the company can extract some important concessions from the executives it has under contract. We can put reason-

able restrictions on their ability to walk out and leave us in the lurch...to join our direct competitors...to reveal our trade secrets...to be paid for work other than ours in their spare time...and so forth. Besides helping us get people, our contracts can help us get *what we want out of them.*"

There you have your strongest pro-contract arguments. Use them as you see fit.

> # If you do wind up negotiating a formal employment contract, lawyers will be involved on both sides.
>
> # Don't underestimate their prodigious ability to destroy a good deal for you.

I've seen it over and over. An executive gets a once-in-a-lifetime opportunity. In a love-feast of seeing eye-to-eye on absolutely everything, the prospective employer and employee "let the lawyers take over from here." Far from merely "getting things down on paper" or "tying up loose ends," as the happily mated principals expect, the result is total destruction of the deal.

Here are a couple of examples. Names, of course, are changed to protect the foolish.

> Len was President of a $350 million group of companies owned by a $18 billion conglomerate. I recruited him to join a far more prestigious $8 billion corporation as President of its $1.2 billion group of similar companies. He wasn't and never would be a corporate officer of the $18 billion company, because his businesses were insignificant to its volume. At the $8 billion company, on the other hand, he'd head one of just four "Groups," and he'd be a corporate officer and a Director.
>
> Len and the CEO readily agreed on everything...salary, duties, directorship, generous participation in incentive programs, and a fistful of stock options. So the CEO supplied a contract, which Len had a week to check out with his lawyer.
>
> On the second-last day, Len phoned me. He was at the office of a prominent attorney used by his sister, a world-famous entertainer. "I don't know what to do, John. I'm getting way more than at X corpo-

ration, but this guy points out that it's quite a bit less than the other three Group Officers make. He wants me to ask for more."

I told Len it was too late. The CEO would tear up the contract, if Len went back on his word. And besides, Len was becoming one of five top officers and a board member. Any inequity would be corrected as Len proved himself through performance, and increased the relative size of his group through internal growth and acquisitions. "Attack any other wording of the contract on advice of counsel, but don't let him make you look sleazy and indecisive," I told Len.

"You're right, of course," said Len. "But would you mind coming over here and saying the same thing? This fellow is a close friend of our family. He's an expert, and he's charging me far less than he normally gets. So I don't want to just casually dump on the advice he's giving me."

Shocked...and concerned that the CEO and I had both made a mistake in selecting this otherwise brilliant and successful executive...I walked four blocks and took an elevator 38 stories to the intimidating opulence of the great lawyer's office. The guy was a sleaze! And he was encouraging Len to be one, too. Nevertheless, I spoke diplomatically.

Len did not return his contract as he should have the following day. Nor did he call. After the weekend and two days of the next week rolled by, the CEO and I agreed that I should call Len...hear a good excuse if he had one...and if not, tell him the deal was off. Len may have been advised to await a panicky call from us offering more money. That did not happen. And the deal was off.

Less than a year later, Len's conglomerate divested his unit to a company that didn't need his services. He's had other jobs in the several years since. But none as good as the one he was forced out of. And none even remotely as good as the chance-of-a-lifetime job on which he gave his hand-shake acceptance...and then asked his lawyer to check his contract.

Another example is equally pathetic.

I recruited an executive we'll call Bill, who had built the fastest-growing business in its field for Conglomerate X. The CEO of Conglomerate Y wanted him to take over an operation of equal size and much greater potential.

The attraction...besides an exciting challenge...was a contract, which gave Bill a percentage of increased-profit. Moreover, Bill couldn't be fired except "for cause." Salary was well above Bill's current base-plus-bonus, and the deal was designed to more-than-double his pay after a couple years of his dependably excellent management. Within five years Bill...who was enthusiastic about the opportunity...should have earned about $1.2 million per year, three times his current compensation.

This time the employer's and the candidate's lawyers both helped queer the deal. The CEO of Conglomerate Y wanted Bill's contract signed within 72 hours, to provide extra news at a previously scheduled Monday afternoon meeting of securities analysts. A contract was hastily prepared by company lawyers who, unfortunately, included a clause they use with executives who don't get Bill's deal.

The flawed document was zapped to Bill by facsimile late Friday afternoon. His lawyer pointed out the offending phrase as "bad faith" by the over-eager CEO, who could legitimately be accused of "applying time pressure" toward hasty acceptance. Bill had been invited to call the CEO at home over the weekend with any questions. He didn't. And meanwhile, Bill's current CEO called Bill and pressured him to stay.

Result: Instead of calling his new employer on Monday morning, as agreed, to confirm he'd signed the contract, Bill called to say he was backing out. Shocked, the CEO offered to let Bill's lawyer revise the wording as he saw fit. He also offered to forgo the announcement in favor of any more leisurely schedule Bill preferred. Too late. Bill had been wrongly convinced that his prospective employer was looking forward to breaking the contract.

Percent-of-profit deals with no cap and no time limit are exceedingly rare. Bill will almost certainly never be offered another one. Indeed, almost no executive ever gets such an opportunity.

But there's a bit more to this story. Although Bill was thrilled with the opportunity, he and his family disliked moving from the "Sun Belt" to the residential suburb of New York, where the business is located. So his lawyer's advice reinforced other qualms. Ironically, Bill's current company soon promoted him to their Manhattan headquarters. Now he lives in a town very near to where his once-in-a-lifetime opportunity is located. But instead of a five-minute drive to the office, he has an arduous daily train ride.

Meanwhile, a more junior executive has completed his first year in the job Bill could have had. Sales are up nearly 50% and profits are up about 70%. This young man receives only ordinary compensation. Bill, on the other hand, would be earning twice what he does with his current company, even after a big raise that accompanied his promotion and relocation.

In both incidents, lawyers served as "sounding boards" and "counsiglieri," when excellent executives were emotionally vulnerable. It's one thing to be coldly analytical and decisive when dealing with business problems...and quite another when weighing an irreversible change in your personal circumstances. Then you reach out for...and cling to...the advice of your lawyer. More than at any other time, you're likely to let someone else *help* you decide, rather than merely provide further input for your *own* objective decision.

Interestingly, the lawyers engaged by both executives were personal friends... supposedly eminent attorneys, and supposedly working for far less than their customary fees. How easy it is to give undue weight to the comments of a lawyer who's your friend, and confirms that friendship through a low fee.

I bring all of this to your attention for a reason. *If and when you negotiate an employment contract, chances are you'll turn to a personal friend who's a lawyer for advice.* From experience I know that's what almost every executive does.

Please be careful.

You've experienced the universal tendency of lawyers to screw up every kind of deal. Know right here and now that they...your friends included... will have just as much tendency to screw up your break-through employment opportunity.

**So much for general advice on
negotiating your employment contract.**

**Now let's quickly look at the topics to cover,
and how to handle them.**

**Re-read this section for ideas,
whenever you're hammering out a formal contract.**

Despite its seeming complexity and its importance to you, your "Employment Contract" will cover only a relatively few matters:

1. Duration of the Contract

2. Your Duties

3. Getting Rid of You

4. Tying You Down

5. Your Compensation, Including Salary, Bonus, Various Stock Options and Grants, Golden Handcuffs, and Golden Parachute.

We'll look at all of these in relation to your self-interest. What would *you* prefer? And what is the employer trying to accomplish?

As you negotiate a formal employment contract, bear this happy thought in mind: Virtually all experts agree that such contracts benefit employees more than employers. You gain more in job security, compensation, and bargaining clout if and when the relationship goes sour, than the employer does in terms of actually preventing you from leaving at an inopportune time and taking your competitively-significant skills elsewhere.

Duration of the Contract

When a new employee is brought in under contract, the agreement is likely to run only two or three years. Key employees already on payroll...and sought-after superstars from outside...are usually tied down for three to five years. The more sure the employer is that he wants you, the longer the commitment he proposes.

Automatic renewal can extend the contract indefinitely:

> "This contract shall be extended for additional three-year periods, unless either party notifies the other in writing prior to one year from the end of any such three-year renewal."

Very nice protection if you can get it. A more common provision would be an automatic one-year renewal. Consider, however, how favorably an 18-month termination provision may compare with whatever automatic renewal you're offered.

Your Duties

The statement of duties is extremely important, because it opens the door to the two main ways employers try to get out of their commitment. They either:

1. force you to leave by changing your duties, or

2. fire you, claiming you haven't performed them.

It's tough to defend against these twin assaults. But you've got to try. Can you accept a drastic demotion or an onerous relocation? Can you perform to the full extent of a vague and arbitrary standard? If not, keep a sharp eye on the language that goes into your contract.

Nail down specifics. Title? Location? Reporting to whom? With what operations reporting to you? Are you a member of the Management Committee? The Board of Directors? Try to get a statement that you can't be given a lesser title, lower-level reporting relationship, less responsibility, or relocation away from corporate headquarters.

Watch out for these phrases: "*such duties as may be assigned,*" and "*full time and best efforts.*" If you agree to perform whatever duties you're assigned, stand by for some pretty demeaning ones when your boss wants to get rid of you. Try for a modifying phrase such as "of comparable or higher responsibility and status." And if you pledge your "full time and best efforts," look for an attempt to break your contract if you try to do any outside consulting, writing, or speaking in the evening or on weekends. A better promise would be not to do any consulting or other work for any competitor of your employer during nonbusiness hours while on the employer's payroll.

Getting Rid of You

You'd like to tie up your employer so he can only fire you "*for cause,*" as the lawyers say. And very good cause, such as committing a felony against the company. Otherwise, you'd like to force him to employ you to the end of your contract, or at least pay whatever severance is specified.

Your boss, on the other hand, would rather employ you "*at will,*" so he can dispense with you at any time, without a reason, and with no financial consequences, just as he could if there were no contract (although these days age-discrimination legislation and sympathetic courts may provide some protection, even without a written contract).

In the end, you'll get a provision that says you can only be fired "*for cause.*" But you'll have a tough time getting the statement of what constitutes adequate "cause" worded narrowly enough to give you any real protection. You'll want a lawyer to ponder the exact language. But here are a couple particularly troublesome "cause" statements that you should beware of:

"Violations of law and company policy." Will traffic violations suffice? Taking home pencils and pads to do office work at night and on weekends? Failure to get your expense report in on time? Failing to prevent your teenage son from taking the company car for a spin? Failing to obey any order of a superior officer, no matter how frivolous or demeaning?

"Failure to perform duties as assigned from time to time by the employer." Which duties? Newly-assigned, frivolous and demeaning? Requiring relocation to the island of Elba? Failure to meet unrealistic goals, budgets, and forecasts?

Obviously you should try to get permissible firing "for cause" as clearly worded and as limited in scope as possible. "Illegality" might be tagged "except for misdemeanors not directed toward the employer." And, if possible, try to require *"prior written warning"* before you can be fired for "violation of company policy" or "poor performance." Might as well get a shot at correcting your deficiency.

And try to insist that your firing "for cause" be done in writing, and accompanied by a *"written statement of the reasons"* for firing. If the reasons are flimsy, the company may hate to put them in writing, and may either be less quick to fire, or more willing to pay reasonable severance.

Also insist on an *"arbitration clause"* providing that conflicts under the contract shall be settled by binding arbitration. Court calendars are backlogged for years and trials are prohibitively expensive...at least from your point of view. Quicker, cheaper justice helps you a lot more than it helps your employer.

And finally, try to get a clause continuing your company-provided *medical and life insurance* until you're employed full-time by your next employer. If you fail, federal law [COBRA] may give you the right to continue your medical insurance for 18 months, but you will pay 102% of your former employer's cost.

Tying You Down

Obviously one of the main advantages the employer receives is your agreement to work for her during the contractual time period. Since she has you signed up for X years, you'll presumably turn a deaf ear to executive recruiters. And certainly none of the time she's paying you for will go into looking for a better job.

Right up front the contract will say that "the Company employs" and that "the Employee agrees to be employed" from X until Y.

Does that mean you can't possibly leave?

No. As court decisions on these matters often point out, "slavery" ended generations ago. No matter what the paper says, you can't be chained to your desk. The contract gives you various compensation guarantees and some measure of security. But it can't *force* you to work for the employer.

About the best the contract can do for the employer is to try to discourage you from working for any of his competitors. However, that can hurt you. After all, they're more likely than anyone else to want you, and to pay big money to get you. If you're performing brilliantly for your employer, you're able to do the same thing just as well for them.

Two clauses..."*noncompete*" and "*confidentiality*"...will try to keep you away from your most likely alternative employers. Fortunately, both clauses are hard to enforce by suing you for breach of contract, because the employer must *prove damages* in order to get money from you. And most of the time that's not easy. If you leave and take major customers or clients with you, she probably can prove she's lost profits. But if you merely withdraw your management brilliance and the operation doesn't fall apart the minute you walk out, she's got a very weak case.

The "*noncompete*" clause pledging you not to join a competitor during the term of the contract...and possibly for several years afterward...is particularly interesting because there's a logical "Catch 22," which you can use in bargaining with your employer. If you're so valuable that he has to isolate you from all his competitors, then he should be paying you plenty for your work...*and* for your vow of competitive celibacy. Conversely, if your agreement to stay away from your likeliest future employers isn't costing your employer very much, then it shouldn't be very stringent.

Hard as it may be for your employer to recover damages if you join a competitor when prohibited by your contract, the noncompete clause still has some nasty implications. The employer can sue you. And legal costs and time-consuming aggravation will cause you real pain. To your corporate employer they're not burdensome. Moreover, your appeal to other employers may fade if they know you're being sued by your former employer. Indeed, *they* may even be sued...rightly or wrongly doesn't matter...for "inducing" you to breach your contract.

Even though your employer may not be able to win a cent of damages from you in the long run, he can certainly give you trouble when you try to walk out. And in the end he may make you buy your freedom. He may offer to give up his "rights" under the contract if, in return, you give up some of your deferred compensation, a retirement benefit, or your latest earned-but-not-yet-paid bonus.

On the other hand, if you're a really hot property, you may be able to get protection from the company that's trying to hire you. They may be willing to provide the legal defense necessitated by breaking your contract, and to pay any judgment (unlikely) that's entered against you. Now your former employer has to pick on someone his own size. Chances are, he'll drop his sure-to-fail law suit.

So the bottom line is that you can walk out. But you may not be whistling.

In writing the noncompete clause, the employer will try to make the prohibition as broad and long-term as possible...perhaps shielding you from "any company or organization having any activities or interests competitive to the Employer, during this contract, and for X years afterward." You, of course, will want to minimize the prohibition. Try to:

   1. *Eliminate the clause.* Say you aren't being paid enough to curtail your most likely employment opportunities.

   2. *Void the clause if you're fired*, or if your contract *isn't renewed.* Why should your employer be able to tell you what to do after she stops paying you? Moreover, if discarding you is correct and fair, you'll handicap her competitor. She should cheer you on!

   3. *Limit the clause to **full-time** work for a competitor.* Try to preserve your chance to do consulting in your industry after retirement or firing.

   4. *Narrow the coverage to business units that are directly competitive.* When only one subsidiary of a conglomerate competes with your employer, the rest of it shouldn't be off-limits. Try to get her to name the two or three competitors she's most concerned about, leaving you a chance to make a future living with the rest of the industry.

The *"confidentiality"* clause pledging you not to reveal your employer's trade secrets is the Siamese twin of your promise not to work for competitors.

Every business has some information it doesn't want outsiders to know... product formulae or diagrams; R&D, manufacturing, marketing, advertising, and e-commerce plans, methods, and breakthroughs; customer identities and buying patterns; incentive compensation schemes; acquisition and divestiture strategy and plans. The list could go further.

The need for confidentiality is legitimate. Unfortunately, the wording of the clause probably *won't* be. It may prohibit you from revealing anything at all about the company while you work there and perhaps long afterward. Indeed, the clause may be so broad that you virtually can't help but run afoul of it. Then whenever the company wants to get rid of you, breach of confidentiality will come in handy as one among several trumped-up reasons.

The employer's strategy is strictly legal harassment. Damages could never be proven for divulging unimportant information that was probably already widely known. But the lawyers could try to claim a "cause" for your firing, as they chip away at your protection under the contract.

Your strategy, on the other hand, is to whittle down the outrageously broad language. Try to *eliminate* the clause. And, failing that, try to have it cover only:

1. intentional (not accidental) disclosures that

2. could be harmful to the company.

In the long run you needn't fear this clause much. But you know why the employer wants it worded to take in the whole blue sky. So do your best to get it worded sensibly.

Your Compensation

You'll try to get everything you possibly can, and you'll make sure it's all written into your contract: substantial base salary, maximum bonus opportunity, and maximum participation in all of the company's most lucrative stock-related and deferred-compensation programs.

Go for it!

If you'll report just one or two layers below the Chief Executive, be sure to study the company's 10-K and its Notice of Annual Meeting/Proxy Statement, listing compensation arrangements at the top of the pyramid. And do it *before* your compensation is discussed. The best indication of what you can try for now...and work toward in the future...is to find out what your boss is making, or failing that, what her boss is making.

Chances are, the biggest biggies are covered by programs that don't extend much lower. But you might as well ask whether you're in on a lesser share of the same deals they get. If not, the deal just below theirs? Or a third-level deal? How many people qualify for the highest-echelon incentive compensation program you will participate in? The top 15...or 50? Or the top 5,000?

Despite all the glowing words about how important you'll be, nothing is a clearer indication of where you *really* rank than the echelon of the compensation programs you do-and-don't qualify for. Moreover, some polite pre-employment curiosity may get you included in higher programs, if the goodies your prospective employer is planning for you don't quite match the flattery he's handing out.

When it finally comes to writing your compensation into your formal "Employment Contract," there are virtually no pitfalls. *Without your having to argue and push, the document will fully and firmly state what you're getting.*

Why not? After all, the spotlight is on your compensation. It's the star of the show! It's your inducement to sign the rest of the document. It's what the magician *wants* you to see; whereas up to now we've been on the lookout for what he might be doing with his *other* hand...possibly tying a slip-knot on the contractual straightjacket you're lacing him into.

Since your compensation will slide effortlessly into the contract, the best I can do at this point is to give you a hand with the jargon you may encounter. Plus a few comments, wherever I think they might be helpful:

> **Base Salary.** You want it to be upwardly open-ended..."at least X" and "to be reviewed annually," if escalations aren't prenegotiated.

> **Bonus.** In general, you'd like any bonuses to depend to a reasonable extent on your performance, or on a smaller unit you'll influence in a major way... not just a huge entity you won't make much difference to.

> **First-Year Guarantee.** Make sure that—at least during the first year—you're assured of making 25% to 30% more than if you stay where you are. Maybe your new salary alone will cover the incentive to move. If not, you can probably get the first-year's bonus "guaranteed" by pointing out that, after years of experience, you know almost-to-the-penny what your bonus will be where you are. Obviously, you're far less certain of the new situation. In

the second year, of course, you're happy to be treated just like everyone else.

"Signing," "One-Time," or "Special" Bonus. To make up for not immediately coming under intermediate- and long-range compensation programs and to make your relocation more painless than under standard policy—while still not putting your base-and-bonus out of line with other executives at your level—you may be given a "signing bonus," which occurs only "one-time." It's a sensible solution that's used to take care of a variety of problems, and these days very substantial amounts of money may be involved.

Short-Term Bonus Plan. This is the traditional annual bonus, and it is the most universally used incentive compensation device. You may have to meet goals to get paid, and the amount may vary with performance. But normally, whatever you get is paid in cash and subject to income tax.

Long-Term Bonus Plan. This bonus is paid years after it is earned as if it were deferred compensation and usually depends on your individual performance, rather than the success of the overall company.   Payment may even await the time you exit the company, retire, or die.

Stock Option Plans differ from company to company, and the same company may have more than one plan operating simultaneously.

Incentive Stock Options. Often referred to as "ISOs," these options are highly attractive to employees because the profit they generate is treated as a capital gain, rather than ordinary income. There's no tax due when you buy your shares at the less-than-market option price. The only tax occurs when you sell the shares at a profit, and capital gains rules apply.

To enjoy this advantage, however, you will not be permitted to exercise the options until two years after they were granted, and the price-per-share at which your options are pegged must be 100% of fair market value on the day they were granted. Moreover, you can only exercise options worth up to $100,000 (valued at *grant*) per year.

Non-Statutory Stock Options. These options are called "non-statutory," because there are essentially no legal requirements as to their issuance other than those resulting from state and security laws. You pay income tax on your profits when the options are exercised. Nonstatutory stock options are, however, attractive in other ways. Price needn't be 100% of market value, so they can be granted at below-market prices...for example, at or below book value, at some fraction of market value, or even at $1 (or less) per share. There's also no limit on how many options may be granted; exercise can be sooner than two years after granting; and there's no need to hold the stock for any particular period after exercise. However, unlike ISOs, you pay income tax on your profits...the difference between what you pay and the fair market value of the stock on the day you exercise your option and buy the stock.

Stock Grants. You don't buy the stock. The company gives it to you...usually as a reward for having been with them awhile and/or for having done outstanding work. The purpose is to give you an immediate sense of owning a stake in the company. Normally grants are *not* made to attract a new unproven person, but rather to reward and encourage a valued employee. The stock may be provided at no charge, or you may have to pay a less-than-market price for it. When you get the stock, you pay income taxes on the difference between what you're paying and the fair market value.

Restricted Stock Grants. Here the company "gives" you stock, but you have to stay a certain period and/or meet certain performance goals; otherwise, you won't actually *get* it. The tax law calls what they've granted you "substantially nonvested"...oh so true! This device is used to attract and/or retain employees. When you get a grant of restricted stock, you have a 30 day period during which you may elect to pay income taxes on the then fair market value of the stock...either the full market value if you pay nothing for the stock, or market value less what you pay, if you *are* asked to pay.

If you don't elect to pay income taxes at the time of grant, none are due at that time. But if you do elect to pay taxes then, the increasing value of the stock in the future will be subject to capital gains tax rules, rather than ordinary income tax rules. Moreover, when the restrictions have been fulfilled and you gain ownership of the stock (it "vests"), there is no tax consequence. You're taxed only under capital gains tax rules and only at the time you actually dispose of the stock. However, there's a downside to all this. If the stock becomes worthless before you're scheduled to actually get it, or if you fail to meet the restrictions and never do get it, there's no refund of the income tax you voluntarily paid at the time of the grant.

If you do not elect to pay income tax during the first 30 days after the grant, then income tax must be paid on the difference between fair market value of the stock and what—if anything—you are paying for it *when it vests*.

Regardless of your decision on the tax issue, you may—or you may not—receive the dividends on the unvested shares and/or be able to vote those shares, depending on the terms of the grant. However, if you don't elect to pay the tax, then any dividends paid to you before you actually own the stock are treated as compensation income and can be deducted as an expense by your employer. If you do elect to pay income taxes at the time of grant, then the dividends to you are considered dividend income and your employer cannot deduct them as an expense.

Company Stock with Non-Lapse Restrictions. The company can also grant you stock with a restriction that states that it never lapses, and that you or your estate have to sell the stock back to the company whenever you leave at a price calculated according to a formula established when the stock is granted to you. The formula for the repurchase price must be reasonable...perhaps, for example, book value, plus a multiple of earnings. Here again we have an arrangement that can be used to attract a new employee, who hasn't yet proven how valuable he or she may turn out to be. We also have an arrangement—often used by privately owned companies—that will assure that the current owners of the company will remain forever in control. Obviously, under this sort of an arrangement you are never going to get capital gains tax treatment on the money you get when "your" stock is "repurchased." However, this can be an excellent way to make you legitimately feel—for the time you're there— a "part owner" of what is and may always be a family company.

Phantom Stock Options. This is another device nonpublic companies may use as incentive compensation. Unlike restricted stock with restrictions that never lapse (stock which the company can "buy back" from you), phantom stock options technically aren't stock and aren't options. They are merely the grant of a promise to pay you money in the future according to a formula based on the increasing value of the underlying stock, which you do not and never will own. Although the amount of money you may get is defined by growth in the value of the underlying stock, you personally may have to meet time and performance criteria to get it. This is an unfunded and unsecured obligation, which does not escape creditors if the company goes bankrupt. Any money you get on this arrangement will be taxed as ordinary income when you get the cash.

Stock Appreciation Rights (SARs). The SAR is a hypothetical unit linked in value to the rising value of the company's stock (if public) or a formula (if the company is privately owned). Value can decrease with the declining value of the stock, but not below the value of the stock (or formula) at the time of grant. The granting of nonstatutory stock options may be accompanied with the granting of SARs—called a *tandem grant*—in which case the SARs mature simultaneously with the exercise of the accompanying stock options and provide an amount of cash that pays or helps pay the income tax due upon the exercise of the options. There's more complexity here than we can cover together. However, as you would expect, money you get from SARs is subject to income tax...and indeed FICA as well.

Phantom Stock Plan. The stock is hypothetical "shares," not actual shares, and the actual value of the dollar amount originally granted goes up and down with the value of the underlying stock. If the underlying stock splits or dividends are paid, the dollar account is credited with any incremental value, and the actual total value is paid when the individual is terminated, retires or dies. There's no tax consequence at the time of the grant, but when the distribution occurs it is subject to income tax and FICA.

Performance Units / Performance Shares. Here a program is devised to encourage the meeting of long-term performance goals by the overall company. Measurements can be in *units* (a dollar amount) or tied to the value of a *share* of stock. Programs can be whatever the company designs them to be, but to earn 100% of the amount targeted to be paid at the end of the program the compounded growth performance during the period has to be X%. Performance at 90% of goal might earn a lesser amount at the end of the period. Lower performance might earn correspondingly even less at the end...or perhaps nothing, depending on the plan's terms. Payment at the end can be in dollars or stock or a combination or as chosen by the employee according to whatever leeway was written into the plan when it was established. But—no surprise—when payment is due, ordinary income and FICA taxes apply.

Performance Cash Plan. Similar to Performance Unit and Performance Share plans, but often with a shorter duration until the proceeds are paid. Since performance of the company's shares doesn't have any roll in determining how much will be paid, the company knows it will not have to pay more than a certain amount at the end of the term. Taxed, of course, as income when paid.

Deferred Compensation. Many highly paid executives have historically preferred to defer some of their current pretax income for payment after retirement...or on some other agreed-upon date. These arrangements, called "nonqualified deferred compensation plans," allow you to defer payment of taxes until the income is actually received, when you may be in a lower bracket. However, income tax rates fluctuate. Recognize that, if you participate in your new employer's deferral plan, you may actually be moving income into a higher future tax bracket than the one you're deferring it out of now.

Also, if you're participating *now* in your *current* employer's plan, be careful to find out what happens to your deferred compensation accounts when you quit. These plans almost invariably change the payout rules upon termination, and the amount of interest you receive often changes, too. Also keep in mind that the amounts you receive from a nonqualified plan are subject to current income tax at ordinary rates, and cannot be rolled over to an IRA or to another company's plan.

Interest-Free or Low-Interest Loans. If you get a loan from your employer at a considerably lower rate than any other lender would provide, the IRS will want to tax you on what you're saving. And your employer may insist that the loan becomes due if you try to leave...a form of "Golden Handcuff." You're probably better off getting her to strong-arm a bank into loaning you the money.

"Golden Handcuffs." This term covers any compensation program that makes it costly for you to leave the company. Various options, stock appreciation, and incentive compensation schemes make you stick around in future years to get the benefit of what's "granted" now. Click go the handcuffs!

"Golden Parachute." Any compensation arrangement that generously takes care of you, if you're thrown out or demoted because of a corporate merger or takeover is covered by this broad and colorful term. You have to be a very senior corporate officer to get a "parachute." But you'll probably land ever so softly in the lap of luxury, with one to five years of your highest-ever base-plus-bonus annual compensation (your choice of lump-sum or continuation payments), immediate vesting of all "granted" stock, immediate exercisability of all options, immediate payment of all performance-contingent sums under incentive programs, immediate vesting of your pension benefits, and continuation of your company-paid medical and life insurance for the same duration as your compensation, or until you join another corporation full-time.

Notice that you immediately get your hands on lots of stock. Letting the jackals have it at their inflated takeover price will be sweet revenge. And even if you're not high enough on the pyramid to enjoy a "parachute," you'll probably get control of a lot of your "granted" and "optioned" stock, when the corporation that promised it to you goes out of existence. You, too, will probably enjoy immediate payment at what will surely be a near-term, and maybe an all-time, high price.

And there you have the jargon of compensation, as it relates to your employment contract. Please understand that the above definitions and suggestions are not intended to provide legal or tax advice. For that, you must engage a competent professional and make him or her aware of all the specifics of your documents and situation.

Unless you're headed for the very apex of the corporate pyramid, you'll have to content yourself with the compensation programs that serve you among many other executives. But make it a point to find out what programs the company *has*, and try to get yourself included in the highest-level ones you can possibly qualify for.

At this point, I've done all I can to help you reach for a wide slice of the corporate pie. Knowing the terms and techniques we've discussed will help you press for the best possible deal...and to document that deal as firmly and cordially as possible.

We've wound up by talking about what you may encounter in negotiating and drafting a formal "Employment Contract." But don't forget that you can also get good written evidence of your employer's commitments in your "offer letter," and in various other letters and memos that will pop up over the years. Save everything in writing that makes a promise to you.

Corporations forget.

To protect your interests, it's up to you to remember.

Special thanks to Ted Carlson, Houston, TX and Steve Weisen, Great Neck, NY for their comments and suggestions.

Chapter 18

Consulting...
You may find your ideal job by not looking for one.

Believe it or not, one good way to find an excellent job working for someone else has always been to try as effectively as you can to become a self-
employed consultant.

Ironic? Indeed, but true.

The prospective clients you must solicit to establish a consulting practice, are some of the same people you'd reach through job-hunting
involvement with your personal contacts and networking among
strangers.

Moreover, these influential people are likely to react far more favorably
when called about a meeting to discuss an intriguing consulting proposal, than when hit for the 500th time with the dreary "I'm in the

process of making a career change and would like to have the benefit of your thoughts and advice."

As a consultant, you meet and interact with people who have an ideal opportunity to evaluate you, your thinking, and your work. Eventually there's a good chance that one of your clients will decide that he or she would rather "own the cow than keep on buying the milk." You'll be offered an on-payroll position.

However, by the time that happens you may be doing so well that you value your independence far too much to give it up.

Who knows which option—in the end—you'll prefer? Fortunately, it's "heads you win...tails you win."

||| **Should you try to be a consultant?** |||

Let's be very clear on what we're talking about. We're not discussing the common resume cover-up of a gap between jobs with an entry that says "Self-employed Consultant," even though the writer didn't aggressively seek assignments, and didn't handle any worth mentioning. We're talking about actually trying to sell consulting engagements, with the intention of doing a fine job and, hopefully, building a lucrative practice.

Only if you really *want* to become a consultant, will your solicitations have any credibility. If you ask for an appointment to discuss consulting and then come in and try to wheedle your way onto the payroll, you'll have zero credibility...both as a consultant and as a potential employee.

So don't even consider the consulting option unless you:

1.　have *expertise* that would benefit clients;

2.　have the *skills and personal characteristics* to be a
　　consultant; and

3.　are willing to *accept the advantages and disadvantages*
　　of a consulting career.

We'll consider these three issues separately. Then if "all systems are go," we'll take a look at how trying to become a consultant not only won't encumber your search for a salaried position, but may in the end lead to the happy dilemma of self-employment *and* tempting on-payroll offers.

What expertise do you have that can lead to successful consulting engagements?

Almost every $100,000+...or $400,000+...executive has knowledge that could be valuable to clients. Analyzing problems and opportunities, and figuring out what actions to take, are what every executive does. Consulting merely applies those processes to someone else's problems.

However, the most successful consultants...especially *individuals*, in contrast to the huge generalist outfits like McKinsey, A. T. Kearney, Cresap McCormick & Paget, and Booz Allen & Hamilton...generally have a *personal specialty*, which they obviously know more about than a crew of MBAs from one of the giants.

To illustrate, here are four enormously successful individuals who now consult for a living, after leaving the payrolls of large corporations:

1.　Mr. W headed Marketing for one of America's leading mag-
　　azine-publishing and direct-marketing companies. Deposed
　　along with his boss, the Chief Operating Officer, in a political
　　upheaval more than 25 years ago, Mr. W immediately offered
　　himself as a consultant to all the other major print media and
　　direct marketing companies. Then only in his 30s and already
　　making an impressive mid-six-figure salary, he immediately

earned more money consulting than he ever made on payroll... and his earnings have more than kept up with inflation Today he still works out of his home with no secretary and only voice mail to take his calls. Over all the years—and still today—many of his former competitors have been the consulting clients who support his handsome lifestyle.

2.   Mr. X was Chief Executive of a medium-sized public company (10-figure sales), which he led through a very successful decade of growth, both by internally generated new products and through acquisitions. Deposed by his Board, not for poor performance but allegedly for a drinking problem, Mr. X became a consultant to a competitive corporation with the sole mission of scouting small companies for acquisition. Operating on an annual retainer discountable against brokerage fees on the deals he arranged, for several later years he earned "double what I did as CEO."

3.   Ms. Y, a brilliant and widely traveled international marketing executive with one of America's largest corporations lost her job when the unit she worked for was divested and the acquirer already had someone in her role. Her global networking to find employment uncovered an opportunity to barter huge quantities of two basic commodities. "I knew lots of people all over the world," she says, "but nothing about bartering or about those products." She put her first deal together, "with wall-to-wall help from my friends." Now she makes her living (and what a living!) as "an international finder and trader."

4.   Mr. Z retired as a senior scientist with a major chemical company while still too youthful to become inactive. Today he helps foreign chemical companies avoid transgressing U.S. patents, and advises them on whether technology they have developed may be patentable in the U.S. He does no work that requires an expensive laboratory or a research staff. He merely draws on his personal expertise and the resources of a public patent library.

Notice that each of these successful consultants offers a personalized specialty. None is a jack-of-all-trades in competition with the large national consulting firms. What comparably special contribution could you make...and to whom? Only you can say. But here are some possibilities:

1.　CEOs and Division heads of companies in your field might value a "second opinion" on basic issues. Or they might welcome "take charge" handling of special projects.

2.　Perhaps there are companies in fields *related* to yours, that should consider diversification into categories you know more about than they do.

3.　If you're from a large company, you may have sophistication that smaller firms can't afford to keep on payroll. Offer project assistance. Or perhaps several days per month on a continuing retainer.

4.　Foreign companies wanting to penetrate the U.S. market might need your help.

5.　Conversely, domestic companies might benefit from your international experience.

6.　If you're on the leading edge of any specialty, there are always "trailing" edge companies, who are potential clients.

7.　And all around us are Internet-related startups of all sorts that need experienced counsel and do not yet have enough capitalization to fill every key slot on the organization chart.

Do you have the skills and personal traits to be an independent consultant?

Okay, let's assume you've figured out how your expertise *could* help corporate clients. There's still the question of whether you have the right *personal attributes*. Working for Cresap, Booz, McKinsey, or A. T. Kearney is another major-company job. To succeed independently you need everything "large-firm" consultants have...and more:

Salesmanship. Except for "repeats" and referrals from current clients...and starting out you won't have any...every assignment will be one you've had to sell. If you can't approach new people, and can't tolerate rejection, don't go into consulting.

Analytical, Bright, Logical Mind. Clear, insightful thinking is...along with your special expertise...what you're selling.

Written and Oral Communication. Sometimes you'll present informally. But expect to deliver written reports and chart/slide presentations. If your pen and platform skills aren't good, don't enter consulting.

Self-Start and Self-Discipline. Performing *what* you promise *when* you promise is mandatory. And no supervisor will check your progress toward deadlines.

Creativity, Open-Mindedness, Resourcefulness, Versatility, and Adaptability. Being able to invent, improvise, ad lib, and generally deal with the unexpected and unfamiliar is essential. "By-the-book" people have little to offer as consultants.

Common Sense, Practicality, and Pragmatism. Down-to-earth, easy-to-implement recommendations are the best kind.

Service Attitude. Unfortunately, consulting is a service business. If you'd much rather be accommodated than accommodate, consulting is not for you.

Ability to Cope with Financial Insecurity. There's feast and famine...no regular payday.

|||　　　**Fortunately, traits that may handicap you**　　　|||
in large organizations are tolerated...and
even desired...in an independent consultant.

Do you have these characteristics? If so, you may be more welcome on retainer than on payroll.

Obvious Personal Brilliance. The same superior who feels threatened by a subordinate with an off-the-chart IQ is delighted to find such brain-power in an outside consultant.

Strong Self-Assurance and Matching Ego. Same goes for a strong, sure touch and lack of self-doubt...scary in a subordinate or a peer, but excellent in a consultant who can be summoned and dismissed at will.

Task Orientation and Political Aloofness. A consultant must be politically sensitive. But he or she can concentrate on the work, safely ignoring the day-to-day skirmishes that can undermine the too-task-oriented corporate employee.

If you're not average, not a team player, don't care about petty politics, don't suffer fools (other than paying clients) gladly, and tend to challenge authority and to be outspoken...then perhaps you can do the corporation, and yourself, more good as a paid observer than as a salaried participant.

Indeed, even if you have patently undesirable characteristics from a corporate point of view, you may be able to get by with them as an outside consultant. Maybe you like to work three 18-hour days and take a week off. Maybe you have a drinking problem but can discipline yourself to keep critically important commitments. Maybe you're brilliant, but have a loathsome personality and are insufferable as both a boss and a subordinate; yet you're capable of exquisite charm when you choose to display it. Show your clients only the good side of your Jekyll & Hyde personality, and you can succeed as a consultant.

||| **Don't get into consulting unless you can endure** |||
||| **some very negative aspects.** |||

The withdrawal pangs are excruciating!

As a $100,000+ or a $600,000+ executive, you're used to having power. People at your beck and call. The prerogative to decide. Even when you have to seek higher endorsement, *you* determine what is or isn't considered.

Every executive who's had power and suddenly becomes a consultant is shocked by the role reversal. Nothing I say can adequately prepare you.

As an executive, you can call meetings to which any number of people must come...some of them perhaps far more prominent and wealthy than you are. And you preside. One by one the participants tell what they've done to further your objectives since the last meeting, and what they propose to do in the future. Finally, you assess their contributions, and you assign further work in preparation for the next meeting.

How different when you become a consultant.

You can still call a meeting. But this time it's probably a fact-finding session, at which *you* take notes. And if a report has to be written, *you* write it.

Maybe, on the other hand, your meeting is a "progress report" to your client. Elapsed-time-pressure was building up, and you called her before she called you. But now you're the supplier. What have *you* accomplished since the last meeting? And what will *you* do prior to the next one? The shoe's on the other foot. And until you get used to it, it *pinches!*

Moreover, what you produce will be analysis and recommendations. You don't control whether...nor how well...your advice will be carried out. And you may become very frustrated that lots of your time and hard work produces minimal benefit. *Welcome to the world of consulting.* You merely study and suggest. You no longer decide.

Another pain will be the lack of big-company support services. Your computer and laser printer, plus online informational resources, will substitute for personal assistants at the outset. But you'll miss the research department, and the reproduction and mailing people...not to mention all your other capable subordinates. Indeed, you'll even miss the social interaction and the sounding board for ideas that were afforded by the sheer numbers of people around you.

And of course there's the fundamental insecurity of not having a predictable paycheck. Every dollar you get is for a consulting engagement you've sold, and for work you've done...or as general contractor farmed out to others, verified, and submitted to your client. No selling? Then no engagement... no money. Poor performance? Then no repeat business...no referrals...no money. The marketplace is a stern and objective judge. Submitting yourself to it is a gutsy move that shouldn't be taken lightly and, indeed, shouldn't be taken at all by some people.

On the other hand, there are very real advantages to being a self-employed consultant.

True, you don't have a scheduled paycheck. But then you can't be fired. You can lose clients and you can go broke. But through lush and lean, you have a job. There's some security and self-confidence in having even that much control over your life.

And when you make money, only you and the IRS decide what to do with it. Moreover, since you and your accountant will set up an advantageous corporate vehicle and tax-deferral programs, you'll build net worth faster on your own than on a corporate payroll, if your gross profit matches your former salary.

You will, of course, be wallowing in trivia as you set up your office and begin to generate paperwork. On the other hand, your contacts as a consultant will tend to be at *very high levels*, probably CEOs and heads of divisions and functions. And you'll mainly be dealing with major issues.

Also, for some unfathomable reason, outside consultants seem to be treated with more courtesy and respect than subordinates and peers on the corporate payroll. If you're successful and can revel in prestige-without-power, you won't feel you've gone down in the world.

The freedom and flexibility of a consulting lifestyle is another "plus." You can probably do much of your work at home, or at your place in the country or at the shore. And working hours are entirely up to you.

Moreover, consulting is the one form of self-employment that won't risk your life savings. Your first office will probably be at home, and you can equip it with first-class computerized word-processing and copy/fax equipment, stationery, and cards, for $12,000...maybe less.

||| **If you've ever wanted to be a consultant, the time to "go for it" is immediately after you become unemployed.** |||

To the $100,000+ or $500,000+ executive, loss of job—regardless of reason— is a crushing blow. He feels worse if his boss simply wants to replace him, than if his company is acquired and there's no need for *two* Chief Financial Officers. But not much worse. Either way he's devastated.

Even if he's protected by a generous severance, the worst of the situation is the uncertainty. What next? He does everything possible as fast as possible. Yet he still worries, "How long until my next job?"

But suppose that our former CFO has thought about services he might offer as an independent consultant, if he ever gets an opportunity to become one. He has some intriguing ideas that should appeal to CEOs and CFOs of mega-companies at the top of *Fortune*'s list. And he also has some concepts that might interest the CEOs of relatively unsophisticated companies in the $20 to $50 million range...maybe even the entrepreneurs of promising pre-IPO "dot coms."

In walks the grim reaper, just as before. But this time our hero is ready. Even before negotiating his final severance arrangement, he visits the printer to order stationery, cards, and a simple but elegant, triple-folded 8½" x 11" brochure. Day one of his "unemployment" becomes the first day of his consulting practice.

"Death, where is thy sting? Grave, where is thy victory?" Far from being traumatized and immobilized, our new consultant is *busy*. He may still be receiving money from various sources as a result of his "unemployment." But he's also developing a new income stream. Today he's his own boss... hard at work for a sensible, pragmatic taskmaster. Yes, he feels pain, disappointment, and self-doubt. But far less of it than most other people in his circumstances, because *he hasn't taken time out to be unemployed!*

If you're going to try consulting, don't waste your "personal contact" and "networking" opportunities on ordinary job-hunting.

Some people solicit consulting assignments only as a desperate "stop gap" measure *after* they've tried several weeks of personal contact and networking in an effort to get another job. This is entirely the wrong sequence for two reasons:

1. Their approach has been *unnecessarily weak and vague.*

2. Having labeled themselves job-seekers, they have *destroyed their credibility* as consultants.

Let's look at the "job-applicant-first" scenario. Here's what's said to the *personal contact* by the applicant who *hasn't* read Chapter 4:

"Have you got a job for me, Barbara? I'm leaving X Corp."

If the applicant *has* read Chapter 4:

"Barbara, I'm leaving X Corp., and I wonder if you might be a reference for me on our years together at Y Corp."

And to the *networking contact*, following the classic script:

"Mr. Kindly, I'm in the process of considering a career move, and I wonder if I might have just a few minutes of your time to get the benefit of your thoughts and suggestions."

Now imagine going back to these same people weeks or months later and professing to be a consultant. Whether they'll bluntly state it or not, people you've previously contacted as a job-seeker will think:

> "So nobody would hire you. And now you're down to seeking part-time work!"

Failure to find full-time employment doesn't enhance anyone's credentials. Why even *consider* someone who's a consultant only because she couldn't get a regular job?

A timely consulting proposal shows you off as a potential employee.

Generally speaking, a sales call as a consultant is a much better "show-case" for your abilities, experience, and achievements than an ordinary "personal contact" or "networking" call as a job-seeker. Consider these advantages:

High level contact. Your consulting targets will be CEO, Division President, Group Officer, or VP-Chief-of-Function. Networking, unfortunately, takes you randomly to whomever your preceding contacts happen to know...maybe the ideal people to evaluate and "sponsor" you, and maybe far from ideal.

Something meaningful to talk about. The most pathetic aspect of a networking appointment from the job-seeker's point of view... and the most irritating from his host's...is the flimsiness of purpose: "a chance to get your insights and suggestions." People worth seeing are busy. Probably your half-hour no-agenda meeting—if you can get it—will cause your host an extra half-hour of homework. How much better to discuss a consulting proposal geared to his needs. He'll feel more interested and receptive...less manipulated and imposed upon.

You MUST show your credentials. When offering to do consulting, you have to hand out and discuss something on paper that states your services and qualifications. Your expertise is what's being sold. And after presenting your consultant's "puff" piece, you can also provide your chronological "sales representative" resume, as a more forthright disclosure than most consultants are willing to make. But be sure there's no "Position Desired" or "Descriptive Summary" that implies ordinary job hunting.

You operate in a "selling" format. Moreover, on a sales call you're *much more in charge* of your presentation than you are in the "social conversation" of an interview, and the "brain picking" of a networking call.

You have greater opportunity to "sample" yourself. Provide a specific proposal that's written as well as oral. If well done, it's a persuasive *free sample* of your work. You submit it as a consultant. But it also demonstrates what a good conceptualist you'd be as an employee.

You don't have to be said "no" to. "Personal contact" and "networking" visits cry out for a disclaimer from your host:

> "I wish, Sandra, that we had a position for you here. Unfortunately, there isn't anything right now."

On the other hand, your consulting presentation tends to get the standard reaction we always give to salespeople...a courteous hearing and a noncommittal answer:

> "Well, I don't know. *Let me think about it.*"

The psychology is just like asking a personal contact for a reference instead of a job. He's left with a matter that's still *somewhat open in his mind*. And you have *an opportunity to come back* with another proposal, based on what you learned at your meeting.

You're easy to say "yes" to. Hiring you as a consultant is low-risk, compared with putting you on payroll. Your assignment is like a *"budget-priced trial size"* of a consumer product. There's enough to measure performance, but no big investment to lose if the product is disappointing.

Without disrupting his current organization, your client can evaluate your performance, and how he enjoys working with you.

He may "make you an offer you can't refuse." Or he may pay for your project—which has probably been worthwhile in any event—and say goodbye.

Pitch, Performance, and Payment ...Getting Started as a Consultant.

In all earlier editions of *Rites* I mentioned briefly how consultants—from individuals to giant firms—traditionally solicit and bill clients.

The Usual Way

Regardless of whether the client company or the consultant thinks up the project, it's usually done in segments, with a separate fee or estimate for each "phase." Phase I may be a preliminary study of the issues. Phase II, if warranted by I, expands the investigation or begins to implement the findings of I. And Phase III (plus perhaps others) completes the project. This is the way you will probably be structuring your consulting proposals.

The Selling vs. Doing Dilemma

However, there's a classic problem when any individual tries to function alone as a consultant: "When you're selling, you can't be doing, and when you're doing, you can't be selling." To thrive you must do superb work. Unfortunately, that may leave too little time to go out seeking new clients and projects to keep you busy after your current projects are finished.

Crandall's Way

The first of the four consultants I described earlier was one of my executive recruiting clients 25 years ago, when he and his boss were suddenly ousted in a corporate political war. The next day my client-and-friend, whom we'll call Crandall, hooked an answering machine—voice mail didn't exist then—to a phone in his den. With no secretarial support beyond his personal computer (he was among the first to have one), he was soon advising almost every competitive company in his industry. Right from the start, he made more money on his own than he'd made on payroll. And today, 25 years later, he's still going strong, even though he's so financially secure that he surely wouldn't *need* to work.

A few years ago, I asked "Crandall's" permission to tell you the secret of his success and he agreed. Notice how radically he departs from the traditional formula:

> "I never quote on a 'per-project' or a 'per-phase' basis. Instead I negotiate a low monthly billing rate...one the client is extremely comfortable with and will never consider excessive or wasteful. And for that I gladly do whatever they want. If they demand too much, I can ask for a higher monthly rate. And if I'm no longer useful, they can fire me. My low price and flexibility make for an easy sale.

> "But notice the advantages: Once a client is signed up, I never have to resell them or convince them to proceed. The 'can't-sell-while-you're-doing' problem disappears. And my monthly bill becomes a fixed part of their overhead. It's always in the budget.

> "Also, because my bill arrives every month whether they use me or not, the young people in the company feel free to call for advice. There's no bill to defend. Senior management people are usually too busy to call; so if I were uppity and only dealt with them, they'd cut me off because of infrequent use. But they like to have me training their young folks. The young people know that. So they cite me in their proposals to senior management. That keeps my name alive in the company. And pretty soon senior management is asking the more junior people, 'Have you checked this out with Crandall?' I become part of the team. As you know, I've got clients who've been with me for 25 years."

How's that for a different and absolutely brilliant approach! Thank you, "Crandall," for sharing it.

||| **When do you get your job offer...**
when you "pitch" your consulting proposal
or after you've performed? |||

Obviously, an offer could come at either time.

However, I can't caution you strongly enough not to go in with a phony offer of consulting services, which is really a thinly disguised request for employment. If that becomes your game, it's dishonest; it's transparently obvious; it deserves to fail; and it almost certainly will fail.

Frankly, if a prospective client is going to offer you a job, you're better off if the marriage comes *after* a successful consulting engagement, not before. By then your prospective boss knows you and your work. There's less chance that he or she will preempt your independence, only to become disillusioned and discard you later.

Meanwhile, you've also found out some beneficial information. You know lots more about the client company. You know whether you enjoy consulting. And, after your "firm's" pension and profit-sharing plans are in place, you know how much more you're salting away when working for yourself, rather than a large corporation. This is probably your one-and-only shot at independence. Don't toss it away casually.

On the other hand, your earnest pitch for a consulting assignment will show you off to advantage. Therefore, it very possibly may lead to an excellent employment offer, instead of a consulting contract. If so...and if you accept...congratulations and best wishes! You've found a job by not looking for one.

But suppose you don't get an employment offer. You just keep on working for several employers.

Is that so bad...if you make good money and enjoy your work?

Consider two statistical facts:

1. America's largest corporations are cutting the number of executives they employ (and other employees too).

2. America's small- and medium-sized companies are creating most of the new jobs at all levels.

That's right. More jobs—at all levels—are ending than are being created by our biggest corporations. Fortunately for the nation, and for you if you're seeking employment, our smaller companies are creating more new jobs at every level, including executive, than the largest corporations are ending. Unfortunately, smaller companies struggling to grow can't afford—at their stage of development—to pay high salaries.

So the good news is that smaller companies may have employment for you when the biggest ones don't. The bad news is that, being smaller, they can't afford to pay you as much as you've been making with MegaCorp.

However, with luck, you may get equity participation in a smaller company that can make you far, far richer than if you'd stayed at MegaCorp earning three times the salary for a few more years, while watching your MC options sink under water.

Which brings me to the wise words of my friend Paul, 59 years old, who was tossed out of his Senior VP - Marketing & Sales job after 29 years with the same company:

> "I discovered two things, John: It's true that there aren't always that many *jobs*. But there's always plenty of *work!*"

Acting on this insight, Paul, who'd led a hundred people at headquarters and a thousand in the field sales force, immediately got in touch with the presidents of smaller companies marketing to the same types of customers he'd dealt with for 29 years. He also contacted the presidents of customer companies he'd sold to. And several of those CEOs realized that Paul had a great deal of knowledge they could use.

As a result, Paul got "Crandall-type" continuing relationships with three smaller companies, working the scattered-day equivalent of one-week-per-month for each. He also secured exclusive distribution rights to a couple product lines within his tri-state area.

The bottom line for Paul is *employment*. The three consulting activities generate about the same money he was making in his corporate job. But now he has much more economic security. He can lose any one of his part-time deals and still have a good solid income. Meanwhile, his personal distributorship business continues to grow, entirely separate from his three relationships with other companies. Paul has found the best of all worlds...a chance to become entrepreneur of his own young business, while retaining an income from other people's established businesses.

Chapter 19

The Rites of Passage:
What, When, and Whether

We've come a long way in examining *Rites of Passage* within the executive subculture.

We've studied the tribal rites of the headhunters. And we've looked beyond those classic rituals, to every other method by which senior executives move from company to company, including the Internet...today's tribal drum of the Global Village.

You know *what* to do.

Now let's consider *when* and *whether* you should take advantage of the techniques we've discussed.

You'll use different methods at different times, depending on your circumstances. And if you're willing to invest some effort when you're not about to change jobs, you can put yourself in an exceptionally favorable position to hear of attractive opportunities throughout all the rest of your career.

You know the saying:

> *"An ounce of prevention is worth a pound of cure."*

No question about it. Consider this corollary:

> *"An ounce of preparation is worth a pound of panic."*

And this one:

> *"An ounce of promotion is worth a pound of patience."*

Most people can agree with the logic of statements like these. Yet few can bring themselves to act on them. If you're one of the exceptional few, you'll gain a lot from this chapter.

> **Knowing the available techniques, let's apply them to the three degrees of job-changing interest you may have throughout the rest of your career:**
>
> 1. **Happy where you are,**
> 2. **Unhappy...but you can't show it,**
> 3. **Unemployed.**

There's no free lunch. Some of the most helpful techniques are also the most work. And the best time for some of them is when you don't have to do them at all.

Sorry about that!

But you're no stranger to hard work. The trouble is you're doing 100% of it for your employer. Divert some to building a career investment in yourself.

If now's the time to move, do everything you can to make the best possible move. Every subsequent job—by promotion or by stepping outside—will build on your next one.

On the other hand, if everything's going great, now's the time to make yourself known. You won't be called and tempted with leap-ahead opportunities, if the most relevant people in the world outside your company don't even know you exist.

1. What to Do Now, When You're Happy and Not Looking

Your objective now, when your current job is extremely satisfying and you're on a fast upward track, is to make yourself and your excellent record known.

You won't leave for another position unless it accelerates your career by at least two to five years in both responsibility and earnings. Otherwise, stay where you are...avoid the risk and hassle of moving...and wait for another opportunity that *does* provide a really major leap ahead.

So how do you get offered opportunities which are much better than the excellent situation you already have?

You're Happy: Make Yourself VISIBLE! to the Finest Search Firms

Consider both the traditional labor-intensive ways...and the new Internet-facilitated ways.

Visibility to the Finest Retainer Executive Recruiters

The traditional way to make yourself known to the top search firms has always been to mail them an on-paper resume for their files. If it's impressive and you're in a field they serve, a few firms will scan it into their database. A *very* few firms—if you seem outstanding—might also transfer your papers to a folder on a shelf, as they index you into their computer.

The vast majority, however, will merely check to see if you match a current

search. If so, you'll go into a pile for consideration. And if not, into the trash.
That's the harsh reality. More fresh new resumes will arrive tomorrow morning!

Electronic shortcuts can make you constantly and easily findable by the top search firms.

A few years ago the fate of unsolicited on-paper resumes wasn't so harsh.
But today the recruiting business is increasingly fast-paced, automated and,
sadly, less meticulous than it was in previous decades.

However, you can use the trend toward automation at even the most prestigious firms to your advantage. Today most firms indicate an e-mail address
for acceptance of unsolicited resumes directly into a database and/or they
have a window on their Web site into which you can paste your resume.
Either way, if you enter electronically you may wind up on a hard drive...
searchable and findable for quite a while into the future; whereas, if you'd
arrived by mail, the odds are far more likely that you'd soon have been discarded.*

To cover the outstanding firms honored in Appendix II and on *RITE*Site, you
can visit their sites, follow each firm's preferred resume-submission method,
and put your electronic resume into each firm's database. That is, however, a
huge amount of work. When you're happily employed and don't *need*
another job, you're not likely to spend much time making the recruiting industry aware of you, even though future events may prove that's exactly what you
should have done.

What you might find time to do is to become a member of *RITE*Site's Custom
Career Service and choose the *RITES*-Honored Option. No need to make an
up-to-the-minute identity-concealed resume. Merely post the one that's now
in your desk drawer. Even if it's not quite up to date, it may be impressive
enough to cause a recruiter to call when he or she has a search in your industry. Then, even if you're not interested in what's offered, if you're alert, pleas-

---

*Also, do register with Korn/Ferry's FutureStep, Heidrick & Struggles' LeadersOnLine,
and any other Internet sites run as subsidiaries by any of the respected retainer firms in
Appendix II. Examples: Peoplescape from Christian & Timbers and LAICompass from
LAI International, etc. Hit *both* the parent and the subsidiary sites. The subsidiary sites
are supposed to be only for jobs under $150,000 or $200,000. But the public hasn't really
caught on to that distinction and recruiters in the parent may—and in at least one of the
largest of those sites *do*—peruse the subsidiary's database. Those sites should be as
dependable in handling your personal information as their corporate sponsors.

ant, and make an obvious effort to provide helpful information, you will be absorbed into the search firm's database and marked as a valuable contact in your field. Over the years you'll hear from recruiters in that firm again. If you continue to be helpful and always mention what type and level of job *would* turn your head, there's a good chance that the miniscule amount of time you'll spend cultivating prestigious recruiters over the next few years will pay off someday with an extraordinary opportunity you'd never have seen otherwise. Or, if not your ideal job, at least a satisfactory opportunity that you can grab when you unexpectedly need it. (See pp. 113-15).

Under this strategy, you just relax and "go with the flow." But you *do* make at least a minimal and timely effort to get the flow started.

A sign in the garden supply store my Dad used to go to said:

> *The best time to plant a tree is 20 years ago.*
> *The second-best time is now.*

Notice the identical verb in both sentences. The horticultural situation *was* no better 20 years ago than it *is* today. Don't fail to take at least some small action for the future right now. You may be glad you did!

You're Happy: Make Yourself Visible to the WORLD!

Today the Internet makes it possible to publicize yourself and your achievements to everyone everywhere. Review Chapter 14 and consider to what extent you'd like to be "findable."

Consider investing the extra effort involved in creating a truthful and impressive *identity-concealed* resume and then posting it through Custom Career Service on *Rite*Site and/or on any other sites that reliably facilitate anonymous posting (as I believe more will do in the future). Become findable by everyone on the planet...recruiters, corporate employment departments, entrepreneurs staffing startups and, of course, also the scoundrels plying the Internet. On *Rite*Site, *all* can discover your background and achievements. However, they can't find *you*. Since you've concealed your identity, they must *reveal themselves to you*. Respond if you like what they propose...or remain hidden if you do not.

Why, you ask, would you want to post your identity concealed resume for all the world to see when you're happily employed? And especially why, when *RITE*Site provides immediate exposure of your identity-***revealed*** resume to the recruiters of all 356 *RITES*-Honored search firms?

The answer is that the most exceptional situation may not come from a traditional search firm. You may hear from an entrepreneur staffing an exciting startup who doesn't yet have money for stiff employment fees. Or you may hear from fast-growth companies that do their own recruiting in-house. For example, the Vice President - HR and Administration of a hot technology company with sales of over $200 million, whom I know personally, checks for needed management talent on *RITE*Site, In fact, I'm one of the recruiters who may miss out on a search when he connects in this way!

Another reason for posting your identity-concealed resume when you're happily employed and don't *need* another job is that you can be entirely frank—and even downright greedy—in stating right at the top of the resume your minimum requirements to even consider a move. Make them stiff and forthright. You can't do *that* if you wait until you're unhappy and need another job. In essence say, "Don't bother me unless you've got at least this to offer." Your identity-concealed resume begins:

CHIEF FINANCIAL OFFICER / VICE PRESIDENT - FINANCE

Now Controller of Fortune 100 Company. In line for CFO. Prior blue chip Investment Bank / VC experience. Deep M&A experience.

EQUITY STAKE IN EXCITING YOUNG COMPANY ESSENTIAL.
WILL NOT CONSIDER ANYTHING ELSE.

That certainly lays it on the line! But why not? You're happily employed and will not consider anything less than ideal. Say so!

Note that you can comfortably say something quite blunt in an identity-concealed resume posted on the Internet, when you'd never even think of doing so in an identity-***revealed*** resume e-mailed into the database of a prestigious retainer search firm. There, you'd be more concerned about image...and want to set a more gracious and appealing tone.

The point is: Seize the day when you're strong. Don't lie. Don't exaggerate. If a recruiter contacts you because of your identity-concealed resume and finds you in any way less than you implied, you will be permanently branded untrustworthy on the firm's computer and you'll ***never*** be presented by that firm...even for jobs you're clearly qualified to do. But—within the boundaries of truth—be bold, when bold is easy and might pay off handsomely.

You're Happy: Test the market for potential career and lifestyle changes you might want to make.

When you urgently need a new position or face any kind of employment problem—from an obnoxious boss to the rumored sale of your division—it's no time to try to be creative and seek the position you'd love instead of the one you're likeliest to get.

Now, when you're employed and happy, is the time to experiment and see how far you can push the boundaries. Call your personal contacts who could hire you to work for them in the field you desire. Say, as in Chapter 3, that you're thinking of a career change into something closer to their field than yours. They know *your ability* and *their field*. Would they be willing to be a reference for you...indicating to others their knowledge of you that suggests you can succeed in their field?

The online equivalent of this strategy is to marshall the best resume you can truthfully create using your experience and successes in unrelated fields to support your stated objective. Post it as *one* of your four *identity-concealed* Custom Career Service resumes on *RITE*Site. Retainer search firms normally will ***not*** endose your outreach in a new direction. But creative, self-confident employers—and especially entrepreneurs—seeking subordinates might.

The point is: When you're securely and happily employed, you have the time, optimism, and creativity to pursue self fulfillment, rather than mere survival.

You're Happy: Set a Trap for Your Ideal Opportunity

Happily employed, you're busy doing your work and gaining more responsibility and higher rewards in your current company. You don't have time to continually scan the Internet for potential outside opportunities to investigate.

Fortunately, many Internet sites these days provide "agents" that let you identify the type of situation that interests you. They then inform you by e-mail whenever a position of the type you've indicated appears. The nature of the opportunities and the precision with which they're sorted will, of course, be only as good as the site itself.

*RITE*Site's Custom Career Service has, as you would imagine, a highly individualized service. You can define up to 16 "Opportunity Alert" profiles. These can be very specific combinations of industry, position, location, and money. Indeed, even the process of choosing such scenarios is a helpful exercise in examining preferences and setting goals. Put *RITE*Site's computer on

24-hour 7-day "Opportunity Alert" for *exactly* the situations that might interest you. Tell it what you want. Not only will *RITE*Site's computer continually compare your up-to-16 sets of criteria with all of *RITE*Site's newly-posted job descriptions and e-mail you every time there's a new submission by a recruiter or a company that meets your requirements, it will also bring your resume to the attention of any recruiter that looks for a person matching any of your up-to-16 sets of target criteria. And that will happen even when the recruiter does *not* post a job on *RITE*Site.

You're Happy: Prepare a "sales representative" resume.

Every executive should take time out to develop an outstanding on-paper resume. You never know when you'll have an opportunity to use it. Breakthrough opportunities pop up unexpectedly. And then there usually isn't enough time to create a resume that accurately conveys your far-above-ordinary performance.

Follow all the suggestions in Chapter 12. Try 3 to 5 pages which, because of crisp formatting with plenty of white space, can be scanned in 20 or 30 seconds and then—in the rare instance when interest develops—can be devoured by the newly-intrigued "reader," who wants to know more.

You'll probably spend several weekends and evenings developing this compelling *credential*. Figure at least 30 to 60 hours to create those very few pages which—with irreducible succinctness—factually demonstrate how very special you are. Consider the effort a "dirt cheap" investment, in comparison to any other self-advancement program you can undertake. Prepared to perfection, your resume can be used immediately for distribution—either electronic or by mail—to the retainer recruiting industry. Do the hard work now. Updating in the future will be quick and easy.

Even if you have no intention to submit this resume directly to search firms or to post it on *RITE*Site, you should create this most important of all career weapons and keep it tucked safely away in a drawer.

You're Happy: Take your once-in-a-career risk
of publicizing yourself *now*,
while it's minimal and you can afford it.

The risk of disclosure when you submit your background to the top retainer firms—whether by e-mail or snail mail—is very small. And the earlier in your career you distribute your information, the less risk there is.

Even if several recruiters in the retainer firms are close friends of your boss, your nastiest rival, or your company's president, it would be highly unethical for them to call and say, "Guess who just submitted her resume?" Or guess who we just contacted because he has his very impressive resume on *RITE*Site?

Loose talk like that is just as verboten as "floating resumes" among the finest search firms.   And it's even less likely, because there's no money in it. Presenting your resume to a potential employer during a search might net $50,000 or $100,000 or more.   Disclosing mere *receipt* of it to your current employer would earn no fee.   All that would produce is a reputation as a gossip...deadly in the search business.   (See the exception to this rule on pp. 472-73.)

Several years ago a contingency recruiter serving the advertising industry offered, for an annual fee, to inform subscribing employers whenever she received a resume from one of their employees.   Public outcry forced her to withdraw the new "service" a few days later.   Employers, interestingly, expressed as much outrage as employees.

Face it.   You *do* want to start career-long "awareness" relationships with a wide cross-section of retainer search firms.   Sooner is better than later.   Even if word should accidentally leak out of one firm, wouldn't you rather deal with that now, when you're "riding high," than in the future when you might be in jeopardy?   Wouldn't you rather "explain" to your current boss who's just promoted you, than to his replacement who may be looking for an excuse to fire you?

You're Happy: Get the unattractive job suggestions out of the way now.

Regardless of what you say in your covering note, every retainer firm that directly receives your resume will assume you're either out of work, or afraid you soon will be.   That's when—and why—people submit resumes.

Inevitably, therefore, the first opportunity you hear about from each retainer firm you've contacted will probably be no better than lateral in responsibility...and possibly unattractive in other ways, too, such as compensation, location, and/or the prestige and stability of the company involved.

Indeed, whenever a particularly unattractive assignment comes in, the recruiter handling it always alerts the research staff to *"comb the new submissions"* looking for someone unemployed who might want the position, since nobody happy and secure in a comparable job at higher compensation, in a nicer location, or with a better company would even consider it.

Time and refusal are the only rebuttals to the "out-of-work-or-in-trouble" presumption that dogs every submission. If the firm doesn't call you until a year or two after getting your resume, and you're still at the same company with the same title or better, they'll know you're secure. Your letter stated the truth. Similarly if, on their initial call, you refuse a position comparable to your current one, that too will confirm you're "solid."

The recruiter's phone conversation with you will be duly noted in your computerized file. And even though you "submitted" instead of waiting to be "discovered," you'll henceforth be regarded as a secure executive who can't be tempted with anything that isn't a substantial advancement. Let's see what a recruiter types into your information after such a "first conversation":

> "Called him" (date) "to propose VP - R&D of Tacky Technology Corp. Not interested, since he already heads 150-person section of the corporate lab, and is moving up fast, at Blue Chip Corp. *Very impressive* on the phone. Sent in his resume 'just to get acquainted.' So he's ambitious and probably will move for the right thing—*but it better be good!*"

The next suggestion you receive from this search firm will be far more interesting.

You're Happy: Help the impressive recruiter.

At the same time the recruiter was sizing you up, you were evaluating him. He quickly understood that you're secure and won't move laterally. Then he agreed with your realistic assessment of the job he presented, and asked you for recommendations. He wasn't dense. He didn't try "high pressure." Indeed, he seemed professional, pleasant, straightforward, and down-to-earth.

As a result, you went out of your way to be helpful. You listened carefully and came up with several potential candidates, plus another person who wouldn't be interested personally, but might identify candidates. Accordingly, the recruiter made an additional notation that becomes a permanent part of the firm's information on you in their database:

> "Helpful source"   WP

Congratulations! You're well on the way to becoming what they call in the business a "hot file"...someone every recruiter in the firm tries to get access to the minute he or she undertakes something relevant. You'd be a great candidate...and if not, a great help.

Do not, however, help all recruiters equally. If the person sounds like a dope—and some may, even from the most prestigious firms—don't open up to him or her. Any firm may have new and/or inadequate recruiters on payroll, who will ultimately flunk out. No point in going out of your way to help them.

Be most helpful to the most impressive. In each firm, they're the ones you want to have knowing how good you are, and fighting for the right to call you up. They'll be the most discreet with the information you give them. They'll appreciate it most. And they're the most likely to be handling the bigger and better jobs that will interest you in the future.

You're Happy: How much help is too much?
Should you identify people in your own company?

First let's consider prospects who are above you. If you're in a relatively small firm which might be hurt by the loss of a potential candidate, keep quiet. The company would be hurt, and you would also be hurt.

But if the company has several layers of good management, it probably won't be hurt, and a promotion to fill a vacancy above you may "domino" into a promotion for you, too. Figure that a really good recruiter will dig to find out what she needs to know. If you won't tell her, she'll just keep asking until someone else does.

Even when the recruiter's opportunity could be a career breakthrough for one of your subordinates, you may decide to identify your person and let him know that you're his benefactor. One of the most senior and respected executives at General Electric (now retired) always recommended his best subordinates to me. Several became candidates. But every single one that wound up getting an offer from one of my clients ultimately refused to leave GE. They just couldn't walk out on a boss—and because of him a company, too—with such obvious concern for their welfare.

Of course, the best way to shield your subordinates and others in your organization is to suggest lots of ideal candidates from other companies. That way, the recruiter has less need to probe your place. If you're extremely helpful and she likes you, she'd rather not cause you grief, even though circumstances will sometimes force her to do so.

You're Happy: Keep records on recruiters.

The recruiter isn't the only one with a PC. You've got one too!

Start your own file on every retainer recruiter—and his or her firm—that you have any contact with. Begin by noting any submissions you make. Then update each firm's information whenever one of its recruiters calls. And, of course, start a new file whenever someone calls from a firm you haven't contacted.

Years go by and memory fades. Computers don't forget. You want to know who called from each firm, when, what position was discussed, who you recommended if you weren't interested, and *your evaluation of the caller*. Armed with this information, you'll always know who is at least vaguely aware of you at each firm. If more than one person from the firm has called, you know who sounded the most competent and with whom you had the best rapport. And if you suggested people who filled the recruiter's jobs, you can later remind him who they were.

Let's see your notation after the conversation on Tacky Technology. It's the first entry in your file marked "Gordon, Rossi & Boodles":

> Will Pickham, VP, called to suggest VP - Engineering job at Tacky Technology. Shaky-sounding company. Only 55 engineers. Seemed to think I was in trouble. But then became interested in how well I'm doing, and what it would take to move me.

> Told him *"no way"* on Tacky, and recommended Dan Daring and Renata Ready at Intel and Fred Fearless at Xerox. Also Sally Smart and Peter Plunge. Loved the idea of Sally—said, "Mr. Tacky would flip for someone from Bell Labs." Will was fascinated that 5 years after leaving, I'm keeping current with their people to staff my department here, and could name a young risk-taker over there. Also surprised I'd name one of my own best subordinates, and he let *me* tell Pete to call him about Tacky, so I could stress having Pete's interests at heart. I also told Will to use my name and call Erna Entrepreneur for ideas, because Erna's company is in the same field as Tacky.

Liked Will! Very professional, yet down-to-earth. Restoring a Model A roadster. *Excellent GR&B contact.*

Your conversation with Will Pickham has been well documented on both sides. Before we move on, let's look again at the last couple words in Will's notation about you:

"Helpful source"   WP

That modest description hardly conveys Will's full enthusiasm for you. In one phone call, you've gone from "just a submission" to someone Will won't forget when he has another search in your field. Meanwhile, of course, you may be hearing from other recruiters at Gordon, Rossi & Boodles...some of whom you'll like, and help, as much as you did Will. But until someone else comes along that you like even better, Will's your key to GR&B.

**You're Happy: Update the records
that recruiters are keeping on you.**

**Switch to on-paper and voice mail
contact with recruiters you know.**

From now on, whenever you receive a promotion or change companies, send a brief personal note to the recruiter with whom you have the best relationship at each retainer recruiting firm.

Or maybe just write something like this across the top of a copy of the official announcement:

*Will —
An exciting challenge?
Is the roadster finished?
Regards,
Paul*

Will's assistant will probably see that your improved title and duties get into the firm's information on you. However, you won't rely on perfect staff work inside Will's firm. If it's large enough to have several recruiters besides Will—and it does, as you'll see in Appendix I—you'll also submit your news via an impersonal "Dear Recruiters" e-mail to the overall firm at the same time you send your personal on-paper note to Will. Either way, Will's firm stays continually up-to-date on you without your ever reassuming the "out-of-work-or-in-trouble" presumption.

Chances are, by the time you're announcing your next promotion two or three years after doing your initial round of submissions—or using the *RITES*-Honored Option on *RITE*Site—you still won't have heard anything from three-fifths of the firms who've had access to your information. They:

1.   Haven't yet needed anyone with your background;

2.   Didn't get around to calling you when they did have a need;

3.   Or if you submitted directly to them rather than posting on *RITE*Site, they automatically purged your resume from their database because there had been no contact for X years or months after submission.

If you're dealing directly with these firms, "update" the nonresponding ones with a brief "Dear Recruiters" note announcing your promotion—or move to a new company—just as you do Will at his firm. Sure, these outfits have probably thrown your resume out of their computer or weren't equipped to gobble it into their database when you first submitted it to them. But that's no reason why you should go back to zero with them and reaccept the "out-or-in-trouble" presumption. Instead, refer to your original submission and include a copy of your current resume updated to show the happy new development. Say something like you see on the opposite page.

Many, but not all, of the fine retainer-compensated search firms will be set up to receive resumes by e-mail. Prior to an important update like this, check to see how each firm currently prefers to receive resumes. If you're using *RITE*Site's Custom Career Service, be sure to get a fresh *RITES*-Honored Download (see page 307), which will provide (1) e-mail addresses of the firms that accept resumes directly into their databases, so you can zap your information to all these firms in a single "Dear Recruiters" transmission from your

(Use current date.)

RITA R. READER
638 North Webb Avenue
Milwaukee, WI 53959
Home: (608) 524-3093
Office: (608) 524-9800

RE: PROMOTION TO   SR. V.P. - GLOBAL MARKETING & CORPORATE STRATEGY

Dear Recruiters:

This is to update my information submitted December 4, 1999.

I was then V.P. - U.S. Marketing of Sterling Steel U.S.A., the central domestic business unit of Sterling Steel Industries Inc., and also chair of our Global Expansion Task Force.

On April 7, 2001 I was promoted to Sr. V.P. Global Marketing, Sales & Strategic Partnerships, reporting to the CEO, in other words, corporate Chief Marketing Officer. In part, this promotion rewards my work as strategist and lead negotiator on nine major international acquisitions and/or joint ventures during the past 27 months.

Sterling Steel is a $9 Billion diversified basic industries company with mining, smelting, fabrication and power generation operations in 18 countries.

For your convenience, my updated resume completes this e-mail.

Sincerely,

Rita Reader

CHIEF MARKETING OFFICER OF FORTUNE 500 CORPORATION

QUALIFIED FOR CHIEF EXECUTIVE OR CHIEF OPERATING OFFICER

As Vice President - Chief Marketing Officer of this $9 Billion diversified basic industries company I supervise the Marketing, Sales, and Strategic Planning functions in 35 autonomous

---

NOTE: The entire updated resume continues from here in the body of the same e-mail (see pages 314-316). We see the note and top of the resume as it would look when seen by a recruiter. When dispatched, the appearance was as shown on page 320.

---

own computer, (2) fax numbers of firms willing to accept resumes by fax, (3) recruiter names and postal addresses to use with a Microsoft Word or an Excel (or any other) mail merge to do an on-paper mailing to any and all *RITES*-Honored firms, or (4) a *Maximum Efficiency Selection* that covers the total *RITES*-Honored list with (a) all firms that accept by e-mail, supplemented by (b) any that don't accept by e-mail but do accept by fax, supplemented as a remainder by (c) mail merge names and addresses for an on-paper distribution to firms not covered by (a) and (b).

If you're doing an on-paper distribution, here's a promotion announcement letter that also encloses an updated resume:

(Use personal letterhead)

(Date)

Mr. Powers Prominent
President
Prominent Associates, Inc.
925 Park Avenue
New York, New York 10025

Dear Mr. Prominent:

Since I originally submitted my confidential resume for your records in November 1997, I've continued to receive additional responsibility at Blue Chip Corporation, which last month promoted me to Vice President - Engineering.

Sincerely,

Paul

Paul Crane

Enclosures: Announcement
Resume

And there you have it...a program designed to bring you maximum personal advantage from the retainer executive recruiting industry, throughout the rest of your career.

Rejoice! If you've fully taken advantage of today's computer technology, you have a better chance than ever before in the history of the world of not being overlooked—although not necessarily *called*—when your ideal opportunity pops up, whether inside a leading search firm or in the vast employment universe beyond.

A modest investment of effort now, while you're happy, may pay an incredible dividend in future years. It could be as valuable as a lottery win, if it lets you know about a breakthrough career opportunity you wouldn't have had a shot at otherwise. Even if it only reveals a sporadic series of lateral moves you might make, it could be as good as a lottery win...if it comes at the right time to spare you the unforeseeable future pain of job-hunting while unemployed.

**One more thing to do right now
if you can *easily* afford to:
Buy some elegant personal stationery.**

Every executive should have *engraved* (not thermographed) stationery listing home address, and (despite "high society" tradition) phone and fax numbers and e-mail address in *discretely tiny type* (for future job-hunting). In the office and at home, personal stationery enhances congratulations, condolences, gift enclosures, RSVPs, and correspondence in support of charitable and cultural causes. Bringing traditional personal stationery into the 21st century isn't easy, so here's an example for your consideration:

Rhett A. Butler
1175 Tara Plantation Drive
Charleston, SC 29041
Phone: 803.977.1357 Fax: 803.977.3827
e-mail: rhettb@southern.net

Order now, and get the 10-week production period out of the way. Ignore stationery and jewelry stores, and shop the "Yellow Pages" under "Engravers." Get the prices commercial users enjoy. You may not want to store enough for an emergency job campaign...at least 1,000 Monarch ($7^{1/4}$" x $10^{1/2}$") and 500 standard ($8^{1/2}$" x 11") letterheads; plus 500 Monarch and 2,000 standard (#10) envelopes. If so, just buy the "minimum"...probably 1,000 Monarch sheets and envelopes. Your "die" will be cut and on file, and additional quantities will only take two or three weeks.

For less than $1000 (including die) your minimum order should provide enough stationery to be a "class act" for the next ten years. And with your die on-file, you'll have an insurance policy against the "production-line look" for as long as you have your current home and phone, and the engraver remains in business. (To get a *really* good price, ask your lawyer and your accountant what engravers their firms use.)

Fine stationery lends a classy executive tone to your correspondence, which more and more these days is likely to be just a quick handwritten Monarch note...alone in its matching envelope or attached to an interesting clipping or announcement. Nice personal stationery is also terrific for lending credibility to your resume's cover letter in an on-paper direct mail campaign to corporate CEOs. Recruiters, except for the ones you've met or talked to on the phone, can best be handled electronically these days.

But look again at the prior headline. It says, ***"If you can easily afford it..."*** Don't delay a school tuition payment or even a family vacation just to indulge in luxury stationery. For most people most of the time it may not be worth what it costs.

2. What to do when you're unhappy... but you can't show it.

Too bad you didn't submit your resume—or at least make yourself available on *Rite*Site—to the recruiters of the 356 *Rites*-Honored firms two or three years ago, when you were well situated. There's no better remedy for "unhappy-but-I-can't-show-it" than an opportune call from a recruiter. Taking action then would ***not*** be bringing a flood of calls now. But a few welcome calls would be trickling in...maybe couple a month...and that might be enough to solve your problem.

But let's drop the "I-told-you-so's." Now we'll swing into action...***but cautiously***.

Secretly Unhappy: You can still contact retainer recruiters. But now you must be far more careful to avoid the ones your employer uses.

If you think your employer may be as unhappy with you as you are with him, then you've got to be especially careful not to send your resume to the recruiters he uses. Ordinarily you could accidentally contact those recruiters and there'd be no problem. Professional ethics would prevent their calling your employer and saying, "Guess who we just got a resume from."

Now, however, circumstances are different. Your employer may have confided his concerns about you to one or more of the firms he uses. Clients usually *do* discuss key managers' strengths, weaknesses, and probable destinies with trusted recruiters. And after that happens, recruiters *will* disclose receipt of a resume from an employee previously described as not up-to-par:

"You mentioned last week that after we finish the Director of Engineering search, you want us to work on the VP - Manufactuing slot. And maybe early next year, if she doesn't get on the team, you may want to think about a replacement for your head of R&D. Well, I feel a little awkward telling you this, but under the circumstances I feel I must. Today we got a resume from your VP - R&D. Maybe we should proceed immediately on that search, too. What do you think?"

Of course you can't be forewarned if your employer is having secret discussions with a recruiter the company hasn't used before. But stay away from any that he and the rest of the company are known to use.

How can you determine which to avoid? Probably only three or four should concern you, and you may already know them. However, before you proceed, make some discreet inquiries. And if your personal assistant is tight-lipped, subtle, and loyal, send him on reconnaissance, too. Provided with a good "cover story," he may get better information than you will.

Also, if you haven't already done so, consider putting your information at the disposal of leading search firms through the *RITES*-Honored Option on *RITE*Site. Merely allowing yourself to be found and contacted on *RITE*Site has a far better chance of not causing notice or repercussion at a dangerously connected search firm than hitting that firm's researchers with an on-paper submission from a current client's employee. That scenario *always* sets off a loud alarm, which is *always* relayed to the person heading the firm's relationship with the client. Whether his or her lips stay sealed may depend on what will generate the highest billings...not on your preferences or safety.

Secretly Unhappy: Talk to your best personal contacts.

Obviously, your personal contacts can be trusted. Explain that everything is "hush, hush," but you're beginning to look around. Will they serve as a *confidential reference*? As we discussed in Chapter 3, this request will announce your availability just as clearly as asking for a job or job leads. Yet it avoids the up-front final negative, "Sorry-I-don't-have-anything-and-don't-know-of-anything."

Approaching personal contacts is your #1 most obvious and potentially productive step to take when you're secretly unhappy and beginning to look around.

This technique is also extremely versatile. Are you ready for a Board membership? Try saying to a CEO whose Board you'd love to be on, "I'm expecting a couple Board inquiries...although nothing's underway so far that I'd really be interested in. But you know me and how I'd behave and be helpful. Would you mind being a reference if and when the time comes?" This strategy has put quite a few of my friends and clients on their first corporate Board. Additional memberships are infinitely easier to achieve than the first and, of course, involve different tactics.

Secretly Unhappy: Consider "targeted networking."

Ordinary networking is obviously out of the question when you're trying to maintain confidentiality. However, if there's a specific target person you want to reach...perhaps a CEO who has a key executive nearing retirement with no obvious successor...you may be able to reach that CEO as suggested in Chapter 4.

A word of warning, however. CEOs and other executives aren't as sensitive to your need for confidentiality as most first-class recruiters are. These executives aren't malicious...just less accustomed to professional caution. Try to reach your "target" with *no more than one trusted intermediary* who knows your "target" personally and will be sure to stress your need for secrecy.

Secretly Unhappy: Log onto the Internet

Visit the sites of all of the *companies in your field that you'd most like to work for*. Are they posting any jobs that interest you? If so, do some investigation. That shouldn't be too difficult, since it's your industry. Find out who the posted job apparently *reports to*. If you already have even the slightest acquaintance with that person, pick up the phone. Accept voice mail if that's all that's offered. Explain you're employed and need utmost confidentiality. Say you've **heard**—not read—that he **may** be looking for someone like you. May you send him your resume? If you don't know him, try for a confidential introduction through a trusted mutual acquaintance. Do *not* meekly apply as instructed through the HR department when you have a more personalized and confidential route.

Spend a couple evenings or a weekend online, checking to see what positions at your level have been posted on the Commercial employment sites, on *RITE*Site, and on any of the Professional and Altruistic sites that may be appropriate.

If you have not yet taken advantage of *RITE*Site's Custom Career Service, now would be an ideal time. Quite apart from your *identity-revealed* exposure to outstanding recruiters through the Rites-Honored Option, you also have the ability to post up to four different *identity-concealed* resumes. *Identity-concealed*, you can still—even now as the dark clouds gather—present yourself in ways that feature different truthful aspects of your background in addition to just "more of the same." Yes, post three of your four CCS *identity-concealed* resumes in pursuit of the position you realistically are most likely to get. But also devote one to an equally truthful resume that pursues your dream.

Secretly Unhappy: Do a
secretive direct mail campaign.

When you absolutely must get into action in a hurry—and do it secretly—you should always consider direct mail, with a "sponsor" signing the letters and getting the replies. The method described in Chapter 13 can reach upwards of 1,000 or 2,000 potential employers within 2 to 4 weeks and locate the approximately 3 to 6 among them who, according to realistic odds, currently may need you. If luck and odds are with you, about 1 to 3 of the 3 to 6 will be sufficiently impressed when they meet you to extend an offer.

But please don't ignore the warnings on pages 257 through 263. If what you have to offer—or what you write—won't be persuasive, then you're not going to be any more successful having someone else send it than if you'd sent it yourself.

3. Unemployed!

**A rough time. But at least there's no need
for secrecy; all options are open to you.**

**And knowing what you do now, you'll find a new job
far more efficiently than you would have before.**

The reason many executives have agonizing difficulty finding another job that fits their talents, background, and compensation requirements is that they don't know what you do.

They're able. And not lazy. Indeed, they work desperately hard.

But they misallocate their efforts, spending huge amounts of time on activities where they've long since passed the point of diminishing returns. Meanwhile they mistakenly neglect other techniques that could be highly productive, because they consider them of little value or even counterproductive.

Unemployed: Approach executive recruiters realistically.

Executive recruiters are the most misunderstood and misused job-hunting resource. Be sure you use them wisely.

Many unemployed executives spend lots of time early in their search hoping to find a recruiter who'll offer to "help." If they're attractive and readily employable, these executives eventually find the harmful "help" they seek... mailing, faxing, or e-mailing of their resumes to their likeliest employers with a price-tag attached.

You'll deal knowledgeably with contingency recruiters, restricting yourself to the fine ethical firms you're confident will never send your resume or refer your name to *anyone* without contacting you first and getting your authorization for that specific referral. You'll also keep a knowing eye peeled for suspiciously "helpful" behavior by retainer recruiters. And, above all, you'll avoid the unfamiliar—and uninvestigatable—recruiters who abound on the Internet.

On the other hand, the commonest and saddest of all errors made by senior executives is wasting precious time by haunting the halls of the largest retainer firms, trying through networking and other cajolery to meet yet another of the firm's recruiters in yet another office. Vainly they hope to find out about more than one-job-at-a-time, among the dozens and even hundreds of appropriate openings a firm of that size is always in the midst of filling. You know that this strategy is impossible, and you know why.

Sadly too, many unemployed executives fail to submit their resume to many reputable retainer recruiters, hoping by such misguided "selectivity" to enhance their appeal and usefulness to the small number of firms they choose.

You're aware of the "selectivity" pitfall. So when you're unemployed, you'll routinely submit your resume to a wide array of retainer firms...knowing that no two such firms will ever be working simultaneously to fill the same opening, nor will they ever ask or care which other *retainer* recruiters you've provided your resume to.

If any retainer firm is already showing you an opportunity, you realize that they're about as involved with you as they ethically can be. You won't try to pressure them further, except perhaps, to inquire if they do *"parallel processing"* after you discover a second search that you'd like to be a candidate on *being done by the same person in the firm*. If the second search is being done by *another* of the firm's recruiters, chances are you're better off pursuing the job on your own, never letting on that you know the firm is involved in search #2. If you do that and the employer on search #2 submits you to his recruiter at the firm, you may *automatically* get parallel processing!

Needless to say, you will call up the one or two most impressive people you already know at each retainer firm where you seem to be dormant. You'll tell them your current circumstances and mail them an updated on-paper resume.

And when you want to push aggressively into the consciousness of retainer firms that don't already know you, you may *encourage an appointment* by using the clout of someone who spends money with them or who's been a candidate or a helpful source. You won't invoke the name of a competitive recruiter. You also won't waste time on more than one "door-busting" visit per firm, and you won't storm multiple offices of the same firm.

Above all, you won't devote the overwhelming preponderance of your time to recruiters, as so many ill-informed executives do. As you fully appreciate, your main mission is to break through to the vast number of jobs the retainer firms are withholding from you, not merely to pursue the one-job-in-3-or-4-months that each firm may actually show you. Even in the less-than-a-handful of the largest firms that now publicly admit to doing some "parallel processing" you're not going to see more than twice that number.

Unemployed: Sign up for *RITE*Site if you havn't already

When you're unemployed, use *RITE*Site to make yourself findable by the entire world, while *withholding* your identity and all of your contact information. Here's instant publicity, with maximum safety. And, of course, choose the *RITES*-Honored Option to make your *identity-revealed* resume available to 356 *RITES*-Honored retainer search firms.

Now that you're unemployed, you have plenty of free time to take full advantage of the *RITES*-Honored Download. Perhaps even use the Maximum Efficiency list to enter directly into the databases of firms accepting resumes by e-mail. And simultaneously, send an impressive on-paper mailing to a specific prominent recruiter in each office of the same firm.

Don't worry. You will not suffer any penalty for your redundancy. Yes, it may seem as if you are currently in an all-out job search. Of course. When true, that's the only impression you can or should convey. Make your communications truthful and impressive and they will be considered. Would you rather be overlooked?

Unemployed: Use personal contacts effectively.

Needless to say, you'll call your closest contacts immediately...and perhaps get together with the best-situated ones. They'll be surprised and pleased when you merely ask them to serve as a reference. Relieved that you haven't asked them for a job, as most unemployed executives do, their long-standing esteem for you will rise even further.

And reminded of what they already know you've done, and apprised of your latest accomplishments, your contacts will think about how they or someone else in their company may be able to use you. Here, too, you've avoided the serious mistake most executives make, by not forcing a closed-issue "unfortunately-we-don't-have-anything" answer.

Unemployed: Use networking. But keep it in perspective.

Now that you're out of work, you can openly indulge in networking. But don't over-emphasize it to the total exclusion of other useful techniques. Lots of executives have that tendency...especially when pointed that way by "single-method" outplacement counselors.

Nowadays I can never see or hear the word "networking" without recalling an offhand remark by one of the legendary cynics of the "people business," as he boasted to me several years ago about how much money he was making since he shifted his firm from recruiting to outplacement. When I asked how he actually helped his outplacees find jobs, he laughed and said:

"I tell them to go *network* themselves!"

A totally different calibre of person in the "people business" is a psychologist in a fine firm that offers outplacement among its many other services and, likewise, endorses networking as the only worthwhile method. When he and I discussed the plight of unemployed executives, he cited one of his close personal friends as a successful example. A very high-level executive of a top company in a huge industry, the psychologist's friend lost his job when two giants in that field merged:

"Fortunately, networking saved him. After being 'out' for more than a year, he finally found a job as executive director of a trade association in a totally different field. He makes a lot less money than he used to. And I don't think he likes his new work very much. At least I know he's unhappy not to be in his regular field. But without networking, he wouldn't even have the job he's got. Networking saved his life!"

Did this man launch a direct mail campaign?

"No, I advised him not to bother. You get very limited response from that."

Did he try to launch a consulting practice in his specialty? As former head of a large portion of one of America's leading companies, he'd be considered an authority.

"I don't know."

What a classic result of networking-and-nothing-else! This person got the kind of job you'd expect him to get eventually, if he continued long enough meeting and questioning kindly people in the large city where he lives...a job uncovered virtually at random, which has nothing to do with his prior background and current preferences.

If this fellow had spent "more than a year" marketing himself to his regular industry, chances are that's where he'd be working today. Random local networking is ideal for lower- and middle-managers, whose non-specific skills and moderate compensation fit a broad spectrum of jobs. It's far less adequate for the $100,000+ or $400,000+ executive who wants to capitalize on years of experience in his specialty.

If you're ever unemployed, you'll certainly use networking. Especially when it serves your purposes better than the other available techniques. For example, *if you strongly want to avoid relocation, and your skills fit well into a wide variety of companies, and your compensation isn't unusually high, then networking may be the only method you'll ever need to look for a hometown job.*

Let's say you're a financial officer who's been CFO, controller, and chief of internal audit in various size companies at various stages of your career, and there are reasons why you must stay in Cleveland. Obviously, you can be useful to a wide range of companies and nonprofit organizations. Meeting business people all over town and getting each of them to refer you to two or three others is a good way to find out about all the potential local opportunities.

However, you can speed up the process by adding a direct mail campaign. A few years ago I could only give you this advice in *RITES OF PASSAGE:*

> However, you can speed up the process by adding direct mail based largely on the *Ohio Directory of Manufacturers* published by Manufacturers News, Inc.. This book lists about 14,000 companies, either headquartered in Ohio, or Ohio-based divisions and subsidiaries of larger corporations headquartered elsewhere. It doesn't include retailing, wholesaling, travel and transportation, communications, financial, media, advertising, construction, maintenance, entertainment, hospitality, hospital/medical/nursing, education, cultural and other nonprofit entities, etc.
>
> Using Commerce Register's *Ohio Directory* you can identify several hundred local Cleveland *manufacturing* companies. After phoning to confirm name and title of their CEO and their address (see Chapter 13), you can have your letter and "sales representative" resume in the hands of all those potential employers within two or three weeks. If companies with sales of less than $10 million...or some other figure...don't interest you, you won't mail to them.

Printed directories, many of which are listed in Appendix III, are still a logical source of information. They're expensive, but libraries have them, and you can sit in the reading room and type any names and addresses you want into your notebook computer. However, if you're willing to spend just a few dollars—a fraction of what just one of these books would cost—you can make a large portion of this sort of task extremely easy.

Sign onto the Internet and go to ***hoovers.com***. Here's a generous source of no-charge information on large companies. For more in-depth information than they give away free, you can buy a membership which, for individuals, is only $14.95 per month or a discounted $109 per year. Whether you buy a membership or not, Hoovers provides database information you can use to compile a mailing list. They say their database has approximately 51,000 companies, most with sales above $2 billion. Hoovers divides the U.S. into 6 regions and sells you their information electronically region-by-region for just $124.95 per region.

To pursue your Ohio job, you'd buy the Great Lakes Region and get "company capsules" including the information you require to do a mail merge—corporate headquarters addresses and the names of senior officers—in 1,524 companies in Illinois, Indiana, Michigan, Ohio, and Wisconsin. You have a choice: either download the data from the Internet or, if you prefer, get a CD-rom by mail.

Since there are 1,524 in five states, at least 305 are probably in Ohio. In any event, you can cherry-pick the ones you want. And, having non-Ohio information at no extra cost, you may decide to send your mailing to CEOs (or other appropriate officers) of a few companies in surrounding states.

Another potential source of automated help with your mailing list is *Infousa.com*. These people are in the business of selling mailing lists and sales leads, and they allow you to define your target list very specifically. Select by industry or location, and then further narrow according to annual sales and/or number of employees. You can also specify which officer you wish to address, but the entire list must select the same officer...CEO or CFO or head of Marketing/Sales, etc. Their handling of titles is crude. They have a list of 25 titles and tag each person with the most appropriate of their 25 descriptions, rather than supply the exact title the company gives the person. But company phone numbers are provided. You could call each company to get a person's accurate title (and confirm their presence). The advantage of this service is discovery of your target companies in the medium to smaller size range and the fact that you'll only have to tweak each entry, not type it entirely. Cost per company ranges downward with volume...for example, $1.00 each for 24 to 100 records and 50 cents for 501 to 1,000 records...cheaper for more.

Another source of local data is *chamber-of-commerce.org*. Search worldwide or by city and state. This site has lots of links to business, education, community and government resources. A nonprofit might also be the answer for a versatile executive who doesn't want to relocate. For information on nonprofits, visit *idealist.org*. On one of its pages, U.S. states are listed alphabetically with links to directories of nonprofit organizations in each. In Ohio the link is to the Ohio Association of Nonprofit Organizations.

Moreover, just by scanning the Yellow Pages, or any other directories your public librarian may suggest, you can probably come up with at least a couple hundred *non*-manufacturing entities large enough to have a role for you within a convenient commute from your present house. These possibilities can be phone-checked for name/title-of-CEO and mailed within the next week or so of your all-out job campaign.

After letting the appropriate person in hundreds of local organizations—as many as you can identify—know about you within just two or three weeks, you can then settle down to the leisurely pace of networking. Two- or three-a-day networking appointments don't seem so creakingly inefficient *after* you've used your spy-in-the-sky satellite to scan the terrain. Now a ground-level search for clues on foot and by taxi is the perfectly logical next step.

Indeed, your fast preliminary direct mail scan will help target your follow-up networking campaign. Chief executives who take the time to send you a cordial letter saying they have nothing for you...and a few will...can be phoned for the usual "a-few-minutes-to-get-your-thoughts-and-suggestions" appointment. Occupying high-level business positions, and having demonstrated kindness and courtesy, these CEOs will be ideal networking contacts to augment the list of people you already know.

No question about it...meeting you and liking you, some networking contacts who minutes before were complete strangers may feel like probing their minds for ideas and their Palm Pilots for contacts.

The CEO who doesn't need you as her CFO or controller may suddenly realize that you'd be the perfect business manager for the symphony...and as a member of its Board, she can propose you. Or she may send you to her multi-millionaire tennis partner who owns 28 McDonald's franchises in Ohio... someone who can use and pay appropriately for your talents, but whom you'd never have identified by looking through directories or on the Internet for large Cleveland businesses.

However, if you're a $100,000+ or a $400,000+ executive with specific background you want to exploit and with a nationwide or global scene to scan, classic networking visits around town aren't quite enough for you.*

Targeted networking, on the other hand, may provide a breakthrough. Perhaps you want to meet a CEO in your industry who just lost a divisional president and has, in your opinion, no suitable internal replacement. Now that you're unemployed and have no fear of disclosure, you can freely forge a chain of personal introductions leading to your "target," according to the suggestions in Chapter 4.

And finally, don't forget that *RITE*Site's Custom Career Service allows you to indicate your geographic preferences, which will be noted and attractive to recruiters and employers filling executive positions in Ohio.

---

*If you're considering a national mail campaign—or even a local one that isn't exhaustive—consider using as data for your PC mail merge, *The Executive Desk Register of Publicly Held Corporations*. For $59.95 you get headquarters mailing info on all of the approximately 7,000 public companies on all 3 exchanges, including the names and titles of the CEO and the CFO. Add $12.95 for each additional Chief Officer category you need: HR, MIS, Mktg. & Sales, Controller, Treas. Mfg., or R&D. With data updated daily from public announcements, and quarterly and annual reports, this is one of the very few services I consider a sufficiently exceptional *value* to link you to it on *RITE*Site.com.

Unemployed: Don't be afraid to use direct mail.

Unemployed...or at least out from under any secrecy restraints...you're free to orbit your spy-in-the-sky satellite. Moreover, it can be as blatantly identified as the Goodyear blimp. Scour the whole country, or the world. No need to hide behind a "sponsor." No danger that you'll lose your bird-in-the-hand job as you check out the bush.

When you think in terms of your ability to work full-time openly seeking the best possible job for the next stage of your career, unemployment almost seems desirable. And indeed it can be, if you use it knowledgeably and creatively. Unfortunately, many people don't.

I often run into excellent executives who've been out of work six months or longer and remain totally frustrated in their search for another job. They've long since given up hope of finding a better job. I ask them if they've conducted a comprehensive direct mail campaign:

"Oh, certainly not. I didn't want to cheapen myself in the marketplace."

These very words come back to me again and again from executives who should know better. I remember a phone call from a former VP - Corporate Controller of a merged-and-purged Fortune 500 company, who'd already been "out" seven months. He answered my question about direct mail with...word-for-word...the #1 cliché on the subject (above). And before I could respond with even a syllable of rebuttal, he plunged right ahead with cliché #2:

"I didn't want to meet myself coming around the corner."

This guy would be unbeatable on TV's *Family Feud*. "The #1 and #2 most popular answers," as the MC says. And...bang...bang...in that order! Both of these classic "reasons" for an unemployed executive not to include direct mail in his job campaign are not only erroneous, they both seem subtly related to a common practice most maturing young adult males and females engage in: going to college.

"I-didn't-want-to-cheapen-myself-in-the-marketplace" clearly relates to Econ IA, and its "Law of Supply and Demand." After they become leaders of American Capitalism, formerly proletarian college students confuse increasing potential *demand* (more would-be purchasers who are aware of the product) with increasing supply (multiple clones of the VP in question).

Erroneously they figure that increasing demand will drive the price down.

What the professor actually told them, of course, was that increasing *supply* would do that. Indeed, the professor suggested advertising as a means of making more potential buyers aware of the product (increasing demand) and thus (or so she claimed) driving the price up.

For years I've wondered how so many American executives arrive at the identical misunderstanding of the "Law of Supply and Demand" when applied to the sale of their own services. After all, these are the same people who spend millions of dollars on advertising to increase demand for commercial products and services.

Moreover, I suspect that even in other personal economic matters these same people would not make the same mistake. Suppose they owned a house or a boat and decided to sell it at auction. Would they try to restrict the number of people aware of their property's advantages and availability, so as "not-to-cheapen-it-in-the-marketplace"? Would they try to suppress news of the auction in order to assure a small crowd and thus higher prices? I don't think so.

Why then do these executives get "Supply and Demand" confused only as it relates to *themselves*...and not with respect to goods and services, both commercial and personal?

My latest theory is still predicated on the pernicious effects of the years in college. However, I've stopped looking for ineffective pedagogy in the Economics Department. The faulty curriculum, I'm now convinced, is not Professor Greybeard's text on "Supply and Demand." It's *Mom's* advice on dating. She's repeatedly quoted as saying, "*If you seem easy to get, they won't want you so much.*"

Mom's advice clearly presages and parallels the "I-didn't-want-to-cheapen-myself-in-the-marketplace" rationale for not getting in touch with any companies, and likewise being careful to reach only a selective few retainer recruiting firms. Moreover, Mom's principle is adhered to even though the executive knows that no two retainer firms will ever be working on the same job; hence, every firm shunned is potentially a job shunned.

Incidentally, Mom's corollary concern about not getting a "too-available-reputation" can readily be seen as the root logic behind the more colorful, yet enigmatic: "I-didn't-want-to-meet-myself-coming-around-the-corner." Admittedly, that spectre is most disturbing. However, like "cheapening-in-the-marketplace," it's impossible. If you have any lingering concern, check the last half of Chapter 11.

Unemployed: Consider the "Underutilized Asset Discussion"
...an ideal door-opener, if you're seriously interested in becoming
an independent consultant in your field.

Absolutely the best way to get an appointment with a chief executive or with any other corporate decision-maker is to have something specific and highly interesting to discuss. Virtually nothing fits that description better than an underutilized asset...a business or other resource he or she has, that could be put to new, better, or additional use, or could be advantageously sold off.

During the years that you've worked in your industry, you've undoubtedly noticed competitors who aren't making the most of something they have. You've probably even noticed similar examples within your own company, but for political reasons, you haven't been able to pipe up.

As an independent consultant—and perhaps a respected former competitor— viewing the matter from outside, you have no such inhibitions. You can go straight to the CEO of any company with a letter and follow-up phone call outlining your thoughts. If you make sense, he or she will probably be interested enough to invite you in for a hearing.

Typical languishing assets you might identify:

> **Division or product line** underperforming for reasons you'll explain. Or appropriate for divestiture or contribution to a joint venture you can visualize.

> **Trademarks** that could be used for quick penetration of new markets, or licensed to other users.

> **Products of overseas subsidiaries** that should be imported. Even as America drowns in imports, U.S. multinationals fail to think of bringing in their own unique overseas lines.

> **Sales forces and distributor networks** that could handle related lines.

> **Patents, technology, and know-how** that could be licensed to users in other industries or spawn advantageous entry into other fields. Or possibly even be shared profitably with competitors.

> Under-exploited **real estate, air rights, timberland, mineral rights, etc.** Also unused **manufacturing** and/or **computer processing capacity** that other companies might need.

Before you blurt out your analysis which, after all, lacks inside knowledge that only the company itself has, make sure you're on firm ground. Ask questions. Confirm your assumptions, and modify your presentation accordingly. Then show that you've thought more deeply and creatively about the asset than the CEO's own people. Perhaps no one has devoted proper time to it. Or maybe it hasn't had the priority you now demonstrate that it merits.

Propose a consulting engagement. Phase I will study the issues you've pointed out. Phase II, if warranted by Phase I, will implement the recommendations of Phase I. You're prepared to handle implementation totally on the outside, or drawing on inside personnel. Or...*stand by for a job offer*. The CEO may prefer implementation by internal personnel...with you leading the team.

I can't even begin to count the number of executives I've come across over the years who've moved from one corporate payroll to the next, by doing a consulting project so impressively that their client hired them as a permanent employee.

On the other hand, if the CEO is *not* interested in more aggressive use of the asset you point out...and if that asset is severable and salable...maybe he or she will entertain an offer from you to purchase it.

If so, you have something tangible to discuss with investment bankers and venture capitalists. Start making appointments with them!

Rites of Passage

Well, that's it. That's everything I wanted to impart on the subject of changing jobs at $100,000 to $1million+.

We've looked at the employment process from every angle. If you really want to accelerate your career, you've got several important steps you can take right now, while you're happy and challenged in your current job. You can even get extremely aggressive while staying under cover.

And if you should ever find yourself out of work, you know everything you can possibly throw into an all-out campaign.

Someday you may face difficult times. Most of us do at least once or twice in a career. But you'll never have to make the pathetic statement we've all heard so often from previously dynamic executives after months of unemployment, with no leads in sight:

"I feel so helpless. I just don't know what to do."

You know what to do. And at a time like that, you'll be busy doing it, not sitting around wishfully waiting for the phone to ring with news that someone else has done it for you.

You also know what not to do. You'll never make the rounds of recruiters until you find one who says:

"Let me see what I can do to help you."

Nobody will price-tag your head and get to your most likely employers before you do, blocking those casual exploratory sessions your own straightforward contact might otherwise have brought about.

Moreover, you won't waste an undue amount of time on naively ardent courtship of retainer recruiters. You'll get to the most jobs you possibly can through them. And you'll also get past them to far more jobs than they're permitted to show you.

From now on, whenever any headhunter calls, you'll deal with him or her in precisely the way that best serves your self-interest. And over the years, you'll build mutually-trusting relationships with the best retainer recruiters... perhaps even to the point that they'll be willing to suspend their rules to assist you when you urgently need help.

How many and which "Rites of Passage" await you in the years ahead? Almost certainly *interviewing*. Definitely *writing a resume*, and maybe a *covering letter* to go with it. And very likely *negotiating an employment contract*, too. Maybe *outplacement*. And without a doubt plenty of *personal contacts*, *networking*, and *dealing with recruiters*.

Moreover, modern computer technology now influences every aspect of executive career development activity. You know how to take advantage of all its aspects, including *RITE*Site.com, which is my effort to help you advance your career with an absolute minimum expenditure of time and money.

Come what may, there'll be more method...and less mystery...in your approach to the potential passages that are always open to you in the world of employment outside your current company.

As a result, I hope you'll feel free to pursue what's best for you...not just what's handed to you.

Chapter 20

Expand Your Career by Expanding Yourself

Rites of Passage has been about your career. I'd never presume to offer advice on anything else.

However, a successful career affects you far beyond the workplace and the workday. Greater self-esteem, more money, and a higher spot on the totem pole perk up the non-work aspects of your life, too.

Conversely, who you are and who you know and socialize with away from your company...both within your industry and within the community-at-large...can foster your career.

Some people ignore the outside world until their career runs into difficulty. Only then do they launch a frantic program of polishing old contacts and networking new ones. **Don't make that mistake. Learn to live your life so that you continually renew and expand relationships outside your company.**

The legitimate claims on your time and attention made by your family and close personal friends, added to what every employer expects from an upwardly-mobile executive, leave very little time for career-enhancing contact with people you don't see at work.

But you do have a few minutes. This chapter suggests ways you can leverage that small fund of time, so that it will pay large dividends in both career progress and personal satisfaction.

| | | Raise your profile.   Know and be known! | | |

Again and again you've heard the cynical old saying:

> "It's not *what* you know, but *who* you know that counts!"

Unfortunately this cliché is usually spoken bitterly by one of the many losers of the world. He or she is simultaneously making an excuse, and framing an accusation, as to why someone better-connected or more widely well-thought-of has just received a promotion or a new job he or she felt entitled to.

How sad!

Not sad that the loser didn't win. But sad that, knowing one of the many perfectly legitimate reasons winners do win, the loser took no steps to foster his or her own valuable network of personal contacts.

The business world...and society in general...is not a meritocracy in which the wisest and most virtuous person will be sought out from obscurity and escorted to a position of leadership.

Far from it. We all tend to give opportunity and responsibility to people we already know and like. We also tend to give consideration to people warmly recommended by others we know and trust. And we give more attention to strangers who are prominent in their field, than to anonymous strangers who may be equally- or perhaps even better-qualified.

Accordingly, these observations and suggestions:

Trade associations provide a wealth of contacts.

Don't pass up the chance to represent your company in trade association activity. In many companies, association functions are looked down upon, and second- and third-echelon people are often sent because higher-ups are "too busy." Resist any status-minded temptation to be "too busy."

Go. You'll come back knowing people who work for your competitors. If they're high-level and highly impressed with you, someday they may be sources of career opportunity. And if they're lower-level, but able, they may be prospective employees you can hire later on. Even if they're lower-level and unimpressive, you may suddenly find that you need information, and they'll be willing to supply it.

You should always be able to check your database of contacts and identify someone you can phone within every competitor. Wherever your contacts aren't yet ideal, keep upgrading whenever the opportunity arises.

Seminars and Conferences

Not only does it make sense to attend seminars and conferences as a means of collecting valuable contacts, you can benefit even more from participating. Accept invitations to appear in forums and panel discussions. That may be the quickest possible way to become well known in your industry.

And don't "hang back" waiting to be invited to be a panelist. When you're still young and have most reason to want the publicity, you're least likely to be asked.

After this year's event, and before work on next year's gets underway, write or phone the president of the association and/or the designated chairman of the next meeting. Say what you thought were this year's highlights. And then describe a unique new subject area, or a new twist for a traditional event, which you feel would greatly interest the membership. If you phone, follow up with a written description, which can be conveniently circulated to gather opinions and support.

Creative ideas for association meetings are extremely hard to find, and few people are willing to help. If your attitude is helpful, rather than pushy, chances are the powers-that-be may like your idea and may ultimately ask you to execute it. Even if they go ahead with someone else in charge, you'll probably be one of the key participants.

If you become the leader, you've got a license to make very high-level contacts in soliciting panelists...possibly even CEOs. Even as a participant, you gain exposure and make fine contacts. No longer just a face in the crowd, you're on your way to prominence.

Consider starting your own association.

An outrageous idea? It's done all the time. People and companies who have something to gain by it start a new association.

When companies do it, they usually promote an organization of users and potential users of their products or services. Once identified by association membership, these prospective customers are easier to reach with direct mail campaigns to the general membership list, with ads in the association's publications, with booths at conventions, etc.

Examples: a leading computer manufacturer has fostered organizations of EDP professionals within various industries, such as insurance and accounting. And an insurance company very successfully launched America's leading national association of retired people, in order to promote its insurance policies for people over 55.

When a group of individuals promotes a new association, there's often a double agenda:

1. They see a valid purpose for the organization...essential, or it won't attract membership, and

2. They see themselves acquiring professional prominence by being the instigators—and probably the initial officers—of an association representing their field. Instantly they appear to be acclaimed by their peers as top-echelon people.

Executives who wouldn't for years be considered industry leaders join together to proclaim a new and differently-focused professional association. As founders, they become President, Executive Vice President, Chairman of the Executive Committee, etc. There are enough impressive titles to let each of the founders have one.

Amazingly, I've never seen a group of reasonably-credentialed executives fail in an effort to start a new association. On the other hand, I've never seen anything but failure when one self-seeking individual tries to start an association, just so he or she can head it. A solo grab for status is too obvious and obnoxious to attract a following.

Frankly, I could list at least a half-dozen thriving associations started by groups of founders who stardusted themselves, while setting up useful organizations that have survived and thrived. How deliberate and how accidental was the personal advantage? No one can say. The fact is that all of these people achieved something valuable for their profession. If they simultaneously gained something for themselves, it was a fitting reward.

Although I can't name the current crop of organization-starters in this context without offending some of them, I'll share one example which is now ancient history.

In the mid-'60s a handful of self-proclaimed "young influentials" in the field of consumer products marketing named themselves "Cabal" and "by invitation only" attracted one or two other such rising "superstars" from each of the most prestigious New York-based consumer products manufacturers and advertising agencies. Purpose: "To meet and hear off-the-record talks" by Chief Executives of leading companies and agencies.

Despite skepticism about both the premise and prospects of the new organization, I accepted my "invitation." What followed were three years of fascinating monthly luncheons at the Harvard Club, as one after another of the CEOs of America's largest corporations and agencies showed up to address less than 40 middle managers. And during that whole time, the same five or six people who conceived the project held the offices of the group, contacted the speakers, greeted and introduced them, and sat with them at the head table.

So if the Trilateralists, the Council on Foreign Relations, and the leading trade association in your industry haven't beckoned, you might consider joining with several congenial co-founders to start a new association.

Investigate the possibility that there may be an online "community" that merits your participation. Or perhaps start one.

Frankly, all I've seen of online "communities" (admittedly *very* little) has been a complete waste of time. Topics have been trivial at best, and participants haven't seemed to contribute much.

As I told you in Chapter 4, that opinion was challenged by a CIO I know (pp. 60-61), who praised a particular for-members-only forum. However, that site, which was originally run very altruistically by a for-profit organization, has been sold to another company; the administrator who built it into a respected entity has left; and the new owners may or may not have different objectives for it. So, with my prime example in transition, I can only suggest that you check with others at your level in your field to see if they participate in an online forum you should consider.

If not, perhaps you—and they—should take the lead in organizing such a venture...possibly in connection with a professional association that either already exists or *should* exist.

Write your way to prominence.

Perhaps you can be one of the lucky few to author an article of interest to the *Harvard Business Review*, or some comparably eminent publication. But even if your expertise is too specialized and your profile as yet too low for such a celebrated journal, you can probably come up with something for a trade paper in your industry.

Once you've seen yourself in print, you'll be hooked. Each time the writing will become easier. Moreover, as a published "authority," you'll be called for your comments by professional writers and reporters who prepare for their articles by reading prior ones. And when recruiters look on the Internet for leaders in your field, they'll find *you*.

Indeed, if you really have something to say, maybe you should write a book. A couple individuals I know wrote books on the principles of their industry while still only upper-middle managers. The books were successful, and helped widen the distance between them and their peers. Today both have the title President. One heads the company he joined fresh out of business school. And the other is a man I recruited as president of a small entrepreneurial company, which he has since built into the number-one company in America in its field.

Outside board memberships provide contacts and prestige.

Obviously, you'd be delighted to be asked to join the board of a major NYSE-listed corporation, and maybe someday you will. Certainly that's more likely if you rise to the top of the company you're working for, and if you continually take steps to broaden your network of personal contacts.

Meanwhile, however, an excellent interim career-development move would be to join the board of a small growth-oriented company. Such an opportunity is well within the reach of virtually every "$100,000 to $1 million+" executive who makes a point to be as widely connected as possible. Chances are, you already know several presidents of smaller and medium-sized companies, who might be inclined to think of you for their boards, if they only had an inkling of your interest (note top of page 476).

And why not a non-profit directorship? There are many relatively young and struggling charitable and cultural organizations which, unlike the venerable institutions, aren't yet dominated by mega-donors and directors from the second and third generations of the same families. Not only can you be a more significant and higher-level supporter of a young institution, you may even find its mission more pertinent and exciting.

Don't shirk fund-raising duty.

The valuable contacts you'll make as a supporter and potentially a board member of a charitable or cultural institution won't be limited to other supporters and officers. In all likelihood, you'll be pressed into service trying to line up contributions from corporations and wealthy individuals. Don't resist.

Awkward as fund-raising may initially seem, it will gradually fill your personal database with some prominent contacts...particularly if you stress the corporate side, and try to get the business leaders you approach to participate in the institution, rather than just add it to their companies' "contributions" list.

Club your anonymity to death!

Probably you already belong to a respected country club and a city luncheon club. If not, you certainly should. But if you're like most of us, you probably spend very little time at either place. And when you do go, you're usually entertaining an outside guest.

From now on, make it a point to participate in the annual golf or tennis tournament, and other general-membership events, as a means of knowing more of your fellow members. And when you don't have any other lunch date, try sitting at the "club table" of your city club. Sure, you'll meet some dullish habitués. But you'll also meet some very interesting people you'd never have become acquainted with any other way.

Also consider moving some of your otherwise solitary, or socially "throwaway," pursuits to an athletic club. Instead of taking a lonely morning jog along the road near home, why not come into the city early and, using the club as your base, run in the park? You'll join lots of other executives in this ritual, and several may turn out to be valuable business and social contacts. Same goes for your thrice-weekly workouts doing aerobics, machines, or weights, and your lap-swimming, which you can readily switch from a strictly commercial gym to a club frequented by lots of folks in your community you really should get to know. And when you're at the club, why not sign up for a team sport or substitute a pick-up game of tennis or some one-on-one basketball for your usual workout, whenever the opportunity presents itself? You'll get to know a lot more people that way.

One very successful and athletically-inclined CEO of a New York-based Fortune 500 corporation can almost always be found both before and after his 9:00 to 5:30 workday at a prestigious athletic club engaged in strenuous competition with other members of his management team. In fact, over the past decade or so of his presidency, his key aides have been winnowed by Darwinian selection into a group of brainy jocks, who can not only challenge him intellectually in the office, but also athletically at "the club." More than one fine athlete from "the club" has found employment in the corporation. And, except for quite a few women (he's long been enlightened), almost all of the top-level executives he's recruited have been men who work out at "the club."

One final suggestion: If you travel to the same city fairly often, consider a non-resident membership in one of its leading clubs. Or maybe your present city club has reciprocal privileges. Your athletic routine can be accommodated better than at a hotel; you'll probably make some valuable contacts; and reservations will be less of a hassle when trade shows and conventions clog the city. Accommodations may be spartan, but certainly not unacceptable.

| | | **Take the initiative in meeting people who interest you.** | | |

At your current level of achievement and prestige, you're already in a position to make overtures toward people you think may share a mutual interest. Don't hesitate. The worst you'll suffer is rejection...something you should learn to accept, if you haven't already.

When you read an article about someone who's just pioneered a new technology that may have future application in areas you deal with, write a note of appreciation and follow it up with an invitation to lunch. Introduce yourself to the conference speaker whose point of view seems so congenial, and suggest meeting later for a drink. Set up an appointment to meet the dean of a nearby business school; perhaps some of your business problems can become his or her graduate students' research projects, with mutual benefit. If you've admired the work of a sculptor, or a novelist, or a conductor, call or write to say so. You may establish an acquaintance that can broaden your horizons and give you a new perspective. If not, what have you lost?

And if there's someone you particularly want to know, don't hesitate to use your skill at networking to make contact. Gaining a personal introduction through networking is a technique that needn't be reserved just for job-changing.

| | | **Personal contacts are one of your** | | |
most valuable resources.

Let's go back to our cliché:

> "It's not what you know, but who you know that counts."

We've all heard that as a rationalization for not getting a promotion or a new job the speaker felt he or she should have had. Totally wrong-headed, in my opinion.

Don't let the career orientation of this book and the usual meaning of the "who-you-know" cliché obscure the greatest value of a strong and constantly-expanding personal contact network. It's not just a set of "connections" that may help get you hired. After all, you'll change jobs only a few times during your career. Meanwhile, your personal contacts are useful to you...and you're useful to them...every single day, and in every facet of your life.

The nearest analogy to a strong and wide-ranging network of personal contacts is a good education. Someone very wise said this about education:

"It's not what you know, but what you can *look up*."

Following that line of reasoning, a good contact network is far better than a good education. For when you have others to whom you freely lend your knowledge and who freely lend you theirs, then you literally have the benefit of hundreds of different educations, career specializations, ethnic and cultural backgrounds, creative insights, and general data banks from experience and life. The limits of your knowledge and ability to cope are infinitely expanded.

Hence, a good contact network operates just like a good education:

"It's not what you know, but who you can *ask*."

Do you want to find out about the performance of a potential supplier or distributor, about the attitude of a governmental agency, or about the most respected authority on an emerging technology? With a good contact network, answers are a phone call away.

Or do you want to know which heart surgeon the best doctors in your city would choose if they were being operated on, or which local contractor has the best reputation for building swimming pools that withstand your area's harsh winters, or where to send your son to college to study international trade? Again, an authoritative answer to each question should be just one or two phone calls away.

In so many ways:

"It's not what you know, but who you know that counts."

Whatever else you do in your career...and in life...don't curse this idea. Be someone who knows others, and whom others consider worth knowing. Have good contacts, and be a good contact.

| | | **The Challenge: To Keep in Touch** | | |

It's not only a pleasure, but also a great benefit, to know more and more people. People you can call on for assistance and expertise, and people who know they can call on you for the same favors.

The great problem is how to keep in touch with so many people, when you hardly have time to see and enjoy your closest friends. Indeed, as a busy and upwardly-mobile executive, you may sometimes be forced to give your own family less time and attention than they deserve. How, then, can you hope to keep in touch with business and social contacts? Must you always approach them like this?

> "Joan, I'm almost ashamed to call. It must be four years since we talked, and then I was phoning to get your ideas on the Peroni acquisition which, incidentally, were very helpful. Gosh, it seems like the only times I ever get in touch are when I want something. But I wonder if you could help me out with some information..."

You can't go on forever, getting in touch only when you want something. Or at least you shouldn't. But what can you do?

Well, one thing's certain. You can't keep in touch with leisurely lunches and long, chatty phone calls. You just don't have the time...nor does the other person, in most cases. And often the connection isn't intimate enough for such a strong dose of togetherness, anyway.

So what's your strategy? Obviously, something thoughtful but less time-consuming. Here are some suggestions:

Make quick, spontaneous phone calls.

When you see something that reminds you favorably of one of your contacts, grab the phone and say "Congratulations," "Bravo," "Well done."

Maybe it's a shrewd acquisition, an ingenious new Internet site, a terrific new commercial, a compelling speech, a scholarly journal article, a quickly-settled labor negotiation, a successful stock offering, a newly-issued patent...or maybe just an unusually handsome new paint job on the house, a rare second-place finish in "Class B" golf at the club, a 12-inning Little League win, or a daughter's acceptance at Yale Law School. The fact that you noticed...and smiled to yourself...is enough reason to call. Give *voice* to the thought!

And when an assistant or a machine answers, your brief "thought-of-you-and-decided-to-call" call can be brief indeed. Chances are you won't get through. That's fine. Just leave your message:

> "No need to have her call me back. Just tell her I called to congratulate her on her son's making All-State. "

Shouldn't that have been your previous call, rather than another request for free legal advice?

For close friends and personal contacts, consider an "Instant Messenger" arrangement on the Internet

Are there some special people you wish you'd bump into every once in a while but—because they've gone to distant companies or places—your paths no longer cross at the office, club, hardware store, or breakfast table?

Instant Messenger services are a convenient way to stay in touch with friends, business associates, and distant family members. Here's the Internet equivalent of passing on the street and stopping for a chat...or longer if you both have time. No matter which IM software you use, you can establish a list of people to "watch for" and set your IM preferences to alert you when they log on. Then, with just a click, you can send an instant message to open a dialog.

You don't intrude on the person's privacy and you don't phone at an awkward time. Courtesy, of course, requires extreme brevity unless the person indicates a desire to do more than just exchange brief greetings.

To communicate, both parties must be using the same service. However, you can run multiple IM services simultaneously on most computers. Each runs "in the background," using very little memory or CPU power, so whatever else you're doing on your computer is unaffected.

As more of the IM services add voice communication capability, predictions are that these "services" will one day offer the equivalent of long distance phone service. If you're interested, check out these leading IM services:

AOL Instant Messenger.com,   MSN Instant Messenger.com,
   http://www.aol.com/aim/   **http://messenger.msn.com/**

ICQ.com (Meaning "I seek you"),   YahooMessenger,
   http://web.icq.com/   **http://pager.yahoo.com/**

Compuserve Instant Messenger.com,
   http://www.compuserve.com/csim/

Let the Postal Service help.

Some of the most successful executives are those who've learned how to use the mails to keep in touch with large numbers of business and personal contacts. This method of renewing acquaintance needn't take a large investment of time, since your personal assistant does most of the work. Nonetheless it's extremely effective, because you can periodically cover your entire list of contacts, to make sure that nobody gets left behind.

Indeed, annually mailing something "first-class" to all your contacts insures you against inadvertently losing anyone you haven't been in touch with recently. If some of your contacts have moved, the Post Office will probably forward your mailing, and you'll provoke up-dates from people you're not current with. And if the time for postal forwarding has elapsed, your envelope "returned-to-sender" will alert your assistant to get on the phone and track the person down.

Send holiday cards.

A lot of people are delighted to see the decline in the custom of sending Christmas and Chanukah or New Year's cards. That's an understandable feeling, if you're an at-home parent with a ten-room house and three children between the ages of 4 weeks and 5 years to take care of. But if you're an upwardly-mobile business executive with a personal assistant, maybe you should think again.

Renewing valued associations at least once a year is a small price to pay in gratitude for past courtesies and in anticipation of possibly asking favors in the future. How many years can legitimately go by without a note or a phone call, before it becomes more awkward to call up a former friend than a complete stranger?

Actually, with fewer cards being sent, your card...if you choose to send one, and I suggest you do...becomes a more meaningful gesture. You took the time when you didn't have to!

If you do decide to carry on this gracious custom, don't make the ridiculous mistake quite a few executives make. Don't have the envelopes hand addressed and stamped, and then merely put an unsigned, printed card inside. That way the recipient's assistant throws the human touch into the wastebasket. What she hands over is a printed folder that's less personalized than your American Express bill. Word-process the envelopes, and put them through the postage meter. But personalize the card. At least sign your name over the place where it's printed. And if the card goes to someone you've really been remiss in not contacting for a whole year, write a few words of greeting.

Distribute your annual report.

Mail copies of your company's report to any business contacts who might be professionally interested. Attach your card, and add a very brief personal message, such as:

Bob —
Hope you had a good year too
Fred

Let your scissors do the talking.

One of America's most prominent and successful businessmen...and also one of the ablest at selling himself and the company he heads... has an extremely gracious habit that sporadically reminds me and his literally hundreds of other friends that we're on his mind and have his good will.

As he does his voracious reading of periodicals on virtually every subject from all over the world, he clips articles that would interest his friends and has his assistant mail each clipping with just a simple typed note, which he signs:

```
John,
Thought of you when I saw this.
Hope all goes well.
                        Tony
```

You can do the same thing...as I try to, when I think of it. When you do your regular reading of newspapers and periodicals, keep an eye out for articles of interest. For example, you may know that one of your business contacts collects original Audubon prints, coaches a Little League team, cross-country skis, restores antique furniture, or toured Alaska with her husband on vacation last fall. When you run across an article on the appropriate subject, clip it and send it, along with a similar short note:

Dave,
Thought this might interest you.
Susan

Don't worry about whether Linda's already seen the article, or has long since known the information in it. The point is that you remembered her interest and you cared enough to clip the article and send it to her.

Interestingly, you can show personal thoughtfulness with this sort of gesture, when almost anything else would seem blatantly presumptuous. Consider this example: You're three levels down from the CEO on the organization chart, so you wouldn't dream of suggesting a lunch date, even though you occasionally have a few moments of conversation with him while waiting for the 10th floor elevator. It would be a gracious and appreciated gesture, however, for you to send him the article on scrimshaw from your latest *Connoisseur* magazine. You know he's a collector, because he has a lighted vitrine full of it in his office. And of course, if you also happen to be a collector, he may even signal a willingness to talk more freely on the interest you both happen to share.

Indeed, some lower-echelon adventurer who didn't know the CEO even remotely as well as you do could also have sent the article to a Chairman whose hobby is so openly displayed to the entire company. Many CEOs like to feel that they have rapport with more of their executives than just the six on their Management Committee. No matter what your current echelon, why *not* be someone the CEO can speak to, when he wants to break an awkward silence in the presence of several employees?

Early in my career, I watched with awe and respect as a newly-recruited MBA from an unpretentious Midwestern university made five years' progress in two, after "discovering" during his first week on the job that he and the CEO of J. Walter Thompson Company "shared" an interest in collecting antique Wedgwood china. As this clever young fellow so aptly put it:

> "I've got nothing to lose but my anonymity."

Incidentally, when people are mentioned in the press, they often appreciate having an extra clipping. And regardless of whether they'll send the item along to Mom for her scrapbook, they're pleased to know that someone *noticed*. I'm occasionally quoted in out-of-town papers and would never even know it, if not for the clippings friends send me.

Respond immediately to any piece of good news you read, or hear on TV or radio, about one of your contacts. If you see in the paper that someone you know has published a book or a journal article, led her company to a record sales year or her partner to victory in the country club doubles tournament, married off his daughter in style, or been invited to dinner at the White House, clip the article. Attach it to a short note of congratulation and put it in the mail. Surprisingly few people comment on such out-of-the-ordinary events, and the ones who do are warmly remembered.

Don't waste any opportunity to be thoughtful.

Be as lavish as possible with every kind of invitation. Put your key business contacts on every guest list for cocktail parties you give at home and at the office. When an organization of which you're a director or trustee has a special event, even if it's just a Sunday afternoon open-house at the local nature center, ask for additional invitations to be sent to business contacts who might be interested.

And never let a pair of tickets for anything, from a hockey game to a fashion show, languish unused on your desk. If you're too busy to attend, send them immediately to someone you think might enjoy the event. He may also be too busy to use the tickets, but you can be sure he'll appreciate your thoughtful gesture.

If you were anywhere near my age, you'd never forget the black-and-white TV image of John F. Kennedy standing hatless and coatless on that cold day in January 1961, saying:

> "Ask not what your country can do for you; ask what
>   you can do for your country!'"

Somehow his exquisite skill with words renewed a logic as old as the Golden Rule.

A lot of people figure they can network their way through life, asking for time, ideas, knowledge, and sponsorship, with no corresponding impulse to do anything in return, except perhaps to say "thank you." Then, without so much as a backward glance, they're off to scavenge from someone else...always with asking and getting clearly in mind. Meanwhile, helping, sharing, and caring are pretty much forgotten and discarded.

That is *not* the way the most influential and successful people I know operate. They treasure the very special values of friendship. And they warmly appreciate their relationships with kind and helpful people they know less well. Their philosophy would parallel JFK's:

> "Ask not what your contacts can do for you; ask what
>   you can do for your contacts."

A Parting Word

Here's where I leave you.

For now at least, I've conveyed everything I can think of that could possibly help you negotiate the inevitable "Passages" of a successful executive career at "$100,000 to $1 million+"...and, let's hope, even beyond.

Over the years I've had the pleasure of knowing and observing many of America's leading executives. You and I both owe them a "thank you," because much of what we've covered has come from them. The rest has come from 30 years on the opposite side of the recruiter's desk from the one you face...a perspective it's my pleasure to share with you.

But now we part company. You go back to being an executive, and I go back to identifying and attracting the most appropriate ones to meet the needs of my clients.

Let's hope that someday I may have reason to call you as one of the four or five best candidates in America for a specific CEO position that I've been engaged to fill. Or that you rise so far above $100,000 or $500,000 or even $1 million that you have very senior executives reporting to you, and I can help in their selection as a means of further helping you.

Until then, thank you for the time we've spent together. And very best wishes for an outstandingly successful career.

Sincerely,

John Lucht

WHAT'S THE MEANING?

We've covered the facts and suggestions.

Now let's observe executives coping with them.

Even after all we've seen, the results may be surprising.

APPENDIX I

Behind the Scenes with the Retainer Executive Recruiter

Up until now, your side of the executive recruiter's desk has never been the one with the drawers on it.

Too bad. Because changing jobs through a search handled by one of the retainer firms is perhaps the single most important "Rite of Passage" for the executive at "$100,000 to $1 million+." And how the process really works will never be entirely clear to you until you've seen it from the recruiter's perspective.

Which is why you and I are now going to take a look at what happens inside a retainer recruiting firm during a search...and also what happens to all the executives who are involved, whether they realize they're involved or not.

The Drama Begins

And now for your amusement and amazement, here's your initiation into the victories and defeats, the passion and pathos, of retainer executive recruiting. Silently and secretly we penetrate the posh New York offices of Gordon, Rossi & Boodles, one of America's very large retainer firms. The nameplate on the mahogany door we're entering says "Will Pickham." As we slip inside, the phone emits a quiet buzz.

Our hero answers promptly. He's a genuinely nice guy...a boyishly handsome former preppie and former executive, with a quick smile. Tanned, and trim, he's aging elegantly into his late forties, and he's pleased with executive recruiting as his second career.

"Will Pickham here."

"Hello, Will, this is Sherm Summit at Integrated Standard Corporation."

Wow! thinks Will to himself, *it's the CEO in person. I've never dealt with him before. I wonder what's up.*

"We've got a great opportunity in proprietary drugs, plus an e-commerce startup venture, out here and I think you can help us," says Summit.

As he and Summit exchange pleasantries, Will quickly recalls his dealings with ISC, a $9.4 billion corporation. About 18 months ago, Will was retained by the then-President of the Foods Division, Bill Beane, to find a replacement for his Marketing VP. Bill hired another food person, Graham Rusk. And since then, Will has stayed close to both Bill and Graham. But so far there's been no new business for Gordon, Rossi & Boodles.

Bill Beane has since been promoted to EVP of the holding company, in charge of five of its eight divisions, including its large and thriving Food Division and its much smaller—and languishing—Proprietary Drug Division. He's thought to have the best shot of anyone in the company at becoming President and COO fairly soon, and CEO when Summit reaches mandatory retirement in five years. Recently, Rusk moved up to replace Beane as head of the Food Division. There've been a couple management openings recently, but they've been filled from inside. So it'll soon be two years with no searches.

This history is fresh in Will's mind. With time running out, and over 1,200 other client companies off-limits to GR&B recruiters, *We'd soon have had to enter ISC*, thinks Will. *I'm glad they've called. If we'd gone in there, my relationship would have been ruined.*

And now the Chairman's on the phone. Fantastic!

"Bill Beane has told me about you," says Mr. Summit, "and your great work in finding Graham Rusk. In fact, Bill partly owes his promotion to you, since Graham did a fine job in marketing, and was ready to take over from Bill as President of Food. This year we're up 40% in that Division, and I give Bill and Graham the credit."

Will murmurs something modest about how it doesn't take a genius to recognize real talent when you see it. And Summit continues as if Will hadn't spoken.

"Now I've got another project I think you can help us with. I'm taking care of this one personally. Partly because Bill's tied up with our tender offer to the KornerKoffee people. And partly because I've lined up an exciting new e-commerce opportunity through some personal contacts. Call that one 'my baby,' and I want it to get underway in that division. So Bill says, "Sherm, since I'm swamped on KornerKoffee, and the new person's going to have to interact with your contacts on the e-commerce deal, why don't you take the lead in picking him or her. That's what I love about Bill. He doesn't protect his turf. I feel like we're almost partners in running this place."

"Well, Bill," thinks Will, *"You've come a long way in these last few months. Congratulations!"*

"And our Senior VP of HR, Al Umans, won't be around much either. He and his number two are coping with a union-organizing drive, which looks like it'll come to a vote in all nine of our Western plants within the next three months. So this is going to be basically you and me."

There's a pause, while Summit swigs Diet Pepsi from a deeply-cut Baccarat glass.

"Now what we want is a new President for our Proprietary Drug Division...the products that sell over-the-counter without a doctor's prescription. I want someone who can walk right in and take charge."

"So it's got to be a fairly senior executive, with strong experience in proprietary drugs, plus—if possible—some successful involvement in e-commerce," muses Will.

"That's right. We need real strength in marketing...and especially the newest trends. We have a great R&D person, and our manufacturing and distribution are the most efficient in the industry. What we need is somebody who can sell the hell out of our stuff. Today that division is nowhere on the Internet. Now I've personally gone out and made us a terrific alliance with some young e-commerce types who want to use *MaturiTeen*, one of our geriatric product trademarks to build a community of older folks on the Internet. In fact, I've agreed to contribute the use of our brand name plus $2 million... Well, I'll tell you about it when you come out here to start up the search," says Summit.

"What do you feel the job should pay?" asks Will nonchalantly. He holds his breath as he waits for the answer...which of course determines what Gordon, Rossi & Boodles' 33% fee will be.

"I'd like to pay $520,000, plus our very lucrative incentive programs and stock options. I want to peg it just under what we're now paying Graham. That means our first year's guarantee will be somewhere over $660,000."

An exultant voice in Will's head begins to shout, *Ohhhkayyy! That's a fee of about $220,000. Not bad at all. In fact, it's damned good!* Without noticing it, Will has jumped to his feet and...phone in hand...is happily pacing back and forth.

Will's thrilled. But there's a cloud forming on his horizon. Summit continues.

"Now I hope you've had some experience in the proprietary drug field." Obviously he expects a positive reply.

"Oh, yes. Less than a year ago, we put in the new President of CompuMedic. You've probably noticed it's been one of the industry's most exciting turnarounds." No false modesty for Will at this point.

"Yes, I know. They've become tough competitors. Your firm did that?" Summit sounds almost accusing.

"I personally handled the search, and recruited the top executive of Better & Best. Another search I handled was the President of Orchid."

Summit replies, "Well, there was a lot of talk about that one." His tone suggests that the talk wasn't entirely favorable. "I hear she came from Alphanetics...not exactly a major force in the drug field! Is it true that she was only a Marketing VP in one of their smallest divisions?" There's an obviously critical note in his voice. "You did that?"

Yes, thinks Will, *and not necessarily by choice. We have so many client relationships that most of the big and successful drug companies were off-limits to me. So when I found this really extraordinary person, even though she was relatively inexperienced and came from a place like Alphanetics... But she is a sensational talent and will surely be a major player in the industry someday.*

Will answers calmly. "You can't really associate her with Alphanetics' record, because she was only there for about eighteen months. She's been moving up like a rocket in the industry, and she went to Alphanetics after four years of heading the Prestige Panacea account at PanGlobal advertising agency. Of course, the jury's still out, but she's already got a lot of things moving over at Orchid. Did you notice the introduction of their new pain reliever aimed specifically at lower-back pain?"

"Oh, that was her?" says Summit, almost admiringly. "Now I see your reasoning in putting her in at Orchid. Those ads on TV are obnoxious. But the product's already got almost a 4% market share of the entire headache-and-pain-relief category. I have to admit I'd much rather have their new product for backs than our 30-year-old remedy for menstrual discomfort. It's been mired at a 2-1/2% share for the past seven years. The thing is, their product's nothing new. It's the ad campaign that's moving it."

"That's right. Her ad background is what Orchid really needed," says Will confidently. "And she headed all the marketing and sales at that division of Alphanetics." *And if she hadn't come from a place like Alphanetics, I'd have had a lot more trouble reaching her, with most of the biggies off-limits to Gordon, Rossi & Boodles*, thinks Will.

"Well, it sounds like you've done some good work in the drug field," concludes Summit more genially. "By the way, any other success stories I should know about?"

Will thinks fast. He's learned to be wary of all questions introduced with a casual "By the way." He must find the right balance. On the one hand, Summit wants the reassurance of prior experience. On the other hand, wily old fox that he is, Summit may also be probing the extent of GR&B's client conflicts. The more drug companies they've worked for recently, the fewer they can go into now to look for candidates.

So Will adds carefully, "Yes, we did a job recently for Biopharm" [a small firm on the fringe of the market]. "And we found the Chairman over at Gastrix...you know, the company that makes nothing but that very successful line of indigestion remedies."

Will does well. He gives Summit the additional assurance he seems to want, without identifying any other major companies as "off-limits." And Summit arranges an appointment the following Wednesday for Will to come to the home offices of ISC in Lustretown, N.Y., thirty miles outside of New York City, to get further details about the position and the type of person ISC is looking for.

Will hangs up and conveys the good news to his personal assistant, Wilma. On a high, he heads down the corridor to tell his buddy, Buddy Young. For months, Buddy has been urging Will to go into ISC himself, and open it up to Buddy and the rest of GR&B. So Will can't wait to let Buddy know how well things have turned out because of his patience. What are friends for, if not to suffer a few "I told you so's"?

Will arrives just as Buddy is saying goodbye to a man he's been interviewing.

"Hi, Will, how're ya doin'? Meet Sam Sage, who's here to talk to me about that Expodex job. Go on into my office and sit down, Will. I'm just seeing Sam out to the elevator."

When Buddy returns, he's duly impressed with Will's news, and suggests a drink after work at the Four Seasons to celebrate.

So Will's day ends on a high note.

We Live in an Imperfect World

Early the following week, Will makes time to start the groundwork for his upcoming meeting with Summit. He asks Gordon, Rossi & Boodles' chief researcher in the

New York office, Gloria Monday, to check out the top ten companies in the proprietary drug field. He might as well find out how many will be off-limits for the ISC search.

Gloria walks into Will's office at quitting time on Wednesday afternoon. Unfortunately, her report is just about what Will expected. Here's what he has to contend with:

Top Ten Firms

(* indicates "off-limits")

*CompuMedic: Off-limits, as Will has already told Summit.

*Parker Laboratories: Off-limits, a fact unknown to Summit.

Better & Best: Open. But after Will took a key person out for the Compu-Medic job, a highly-disliked successor was promoted; other execs have also departed, and now there's no one left that Summit is likely to favor.

*Orchid: Off-Limits, as Summit knows.

Maxi-Medi-Marketing: Open.

*National Anodyne: Off-Limits, which Summit doesn't know.

Right Remedies: Open.

*Prestige Panacea: Off-limits, unbeknownst to Summit.

*Cosa Nostrums: Off-Limits, also unbeknownst to Summit.

BioDynamics: Open.

In other words, six out of the top ten firms are off-limits to all Gordon, Rossi & Boodles recruiters...although Summit has learned about only two of those six. Of the remaining four companies, Will knows that one is extremely unlikely to have anyone that Summit would consider presidential material. So there are really only three of the "top-ten" proprietary drug companies where Will can find ISC's new division head.

Damn! thinks Will. *On top of everything else, the Chairman is probably going to want e-commerce experience. Now who's going to have that in the consumer pharmaceutical industry?* Will hates to think of the sweat and blood this assignment will require.

Still, as an experienced executive recruiter, Will's faced worse before...and he'll cope again this time. He's good at his job.

Nonetheless, Will is pleased to look up and see Buddy...briefcase in hand...poised in the doorway, beckoning.

"Knock it off, Will. If I don't catch the 6:12 tonight, Linda will have a fit. So let's slip over to the Four Seasons while we can still get a seat, and celebrate. You got a new assignment from ISC, and this afternoon I finally completed my PhantaSee! Fashions search, which has really been the pits!"

Two friends...co-workers in a demanding, but also an intellectually stimulating and financially rewarding, business...unwind together at the end of a tough day. They nab two well-placed seats...and inhale the top third of their drinks. Then, they settle down and slowly savor the rest until train time for Buddy. Soon Will brings up a familiar subject. And although Will and Buddy, their searches, and their employer are fictitious, the information they discuss about recruiting firms in the real world is from published sources and authoritative estimates.

"Darn it," says Will, "even though I'm thrilled to get the ISC search, it looks like it's going to be a bitch. Gloria came in this morning with the rundown. Six of the top ten proprietary drug companies are off-limits. It's a presidency, for heaven's sake! Why, practically every VP - Marketing would be willing to consider a presidency. In the end he or she might not move, but they'd certainly be happy to meet the client and talk. *But I can only go into four of the top ten companies.* And a lot of the smaller ones will be off-limits too. I can't remember the last time I was able to go everywhere in my client's industry and look for the *best person.* All I can do is try to find some good people who don't work for one of our other clients. *And we've now got nearly 1,200 clients!*"

"Know how you feel, my lad," says Buddy, who's had eleven years in the business... only two more than Will. "Part of why I came over from Randall Radley Associates eight years ago is that GR&B was only half their size then. So with GR&B I could search in more places for my candidates...and do it much more easily...because there weren't so many companies off-limits. But we've been growing almost every year, and we're now just as big as they were then."

"The real problem," says Will, "is the number of recruiters on staff. Not only do I have to protect my clients...that wouldn't be too bad, because I've only worked for 20 or so clients within the past two years. But I've also got to protect yours too, Buddy. And the clients of 93 other recruiters! *That's* why we've got about 1,200 companies or subsidiaries we can't go into...at GR&B."

"Yeah, but would you be any better off at any of the other large firms? I don't think so," Buddy interjects.

"Right!," Will replies, reaching into his briefcase. "Gloria got me these figures for a business review article I'm thinking of writing. There's always been a problem, but it's very seldom studied or written about. Way back in October '78, *Fortune* did a cover story. Heidrick & Struggles had 75 recruiters, and 2,000 client companies off-limits. *Forbes,* in July '89, found these off-limits numbers at the four largest firms: Korn/Ferry 2,150; Russell Reynolds 1,567; Heidrick and Struggles 1,289; and SpencerStuart 1,250."

"In early '99, as Korn/Ferry prepared to go public, they reported having done 5,870 searches for 3,750 clients worldwide in fiscal '98, including roughly 43% of the *Fortune 500* companies, according to *Executive Recruiter News. Executive Search Review* reported that Korn/Ferry had 392 recruiters worldwide...174 in the U.S. We don't know their number of U.S. clients, but dividing global clients by global recruiters indicates about 10 clients per recruiter—nearly 1,700 client companies off-limits in the U.S.— with each recruiter having to do about 15 searches per year."

"Heidrick & Struggles went public a few months later in '99 and their 4/26/99 S-1A filing with the S.E.C. was reported in the May '99 issue of *Executive Recruiter News* as having stated that the firm "worked for more than 1,800 clients in 1995 and over 3,100 in 1998." That's a really impressive growth trend, and I can't imagine them wanting to slow it down. *Executive Recruiter News* reported that they wound up '99 with about 391 partners and recruiters worldwide, of which about 200 were doing searches in the U.S."

"The Korn/Ferry figures are pretty close to our ratios here at GR&B...12 clients per recruiter and 14 searches per year. So I agree with you, Buddy. We're certainly not the only ones feeling pressure from off-limits problems and a heavy work load."

"Take a look at this chart Gloria made up for me," Will continues. "It shows the sizes of some of the biggest firms according to approximately how many recruiters each has in the U.S. When it comes to the off-limits problem, the number of their recruiters in foreign countries doesn't matter, because most firms are like us...they usually don't protect their overseas clients in the U.S."

APPROXIMATE NUMBER OF RECRUITERS OPERATING IN U.S. WITHIN LARGE RETAINER FIRMS (2000 Estimate)[a]

Heidrick & Struggles, Inc.	200	Egon Zehnder International Inc.	42
Korn/Ferry International	195	Stanton Chase International	33
TMP Worldwide Executive Search (includes LAI International and TASA Worldwide/Johnson Smith & Knisley)	163	Boyden	30
DHR International Inc.	128	Isaacson, Miller	33
SpencerStuart	107	D.E. Foster Partners	30
A. T. Kearney Executive Search	92	Battalia Winston International	23
Christian & Timbers	84	Diversified Search Companies	23
Russell Reynolds Assocs., Inc.	83	The Whitney Group	22
Ray & Berndtson	80	Fairfaxx Corporation	20
Kenzer Corp.	80	Howard Fischer Associates	21
StratfordGroup	48	Heath/Norton Associates	15

[a]Only U.S. recruiters are shown, because overseas clients usually are not off-limits in the U.S. There are several specialized firms (mostly in health care) that have more recruiters than some of the primarily generalist firms listed above. Numbers of Consultants for these firms are from the March 2000 issue of *Executive Recruiter News.*

"Yeah, Will," says Buddy, "it cuts both ways. We've got our client list off-limits. And on top of that, we also have to stay away from every executive that anyone else in GR&B has permission to talk to."

"Exactly," says Will. "I have to stay away from every executive who works for nearly 1,200 client companies. And I also have to stay away from all the non-client executives who are among the 220,000 that we keep tabs on, unless I've checked in advance to make sure that I—and not one of our 93 other recruiters—have exclusive permission to call that person up. *So what it boils down to is that I get one-94th of what's left, after we bypass all the employees of our nearly 1,200 off-limits client companies!*

"It's tough," Buddy agrees, distracted momentarily by the thought that he forgot to write and mail two college tuition checks totalling almost $45,000. *Can't afford to loaf these days!*

"And, Buddy," Will continues, "all firms track lots of executives. Way back in that old *Fortune* article, Heidrick & Struggles and Boyden said their database had 100,000 executives, and Korn/Ferry said they had 145,000. Today even the smallest firms are computerized—better than the giants were back in those days—and the largest firms have several times as much data as they had way back then. In our business the right hand *does* know what the left is doing. And if you're in a retainer search firm, you've damned well got to keep out of its way. Sometimes I feel like I've got both hands tied behind my back."

"Now wait a minute, Will," says Buddy. "I can't let you get away with knocking the database like that. Sure, it's the way we keep track of the people you can and can't call. But it's also the way we keep tabs on people we can use to fill assignments. You love the database when you're looking for a top-flight Controller or a VP - Manufacturing, and Gloria walks in and hands you a couple dozen likely candidates or sources all neatly printed out."

"Yeah, you're right, Buddy. Most of the time I'm damn glad to have the database."

"And you're glad, too, that 93 other recruiters have been contributing to it for the past umpteen years. Quite a few of the profiles Gloria hands you will be on executives that you, or I, or someone else has interviewed and submitted as a candidate...or worked with as a client. Ten percent, and maybe more aren't just unsolicited resumes from people you have to investigate. They're known quantities...all checked out and, if they're interested in your opportunity, all ready to present."

"You're right on that too, Buddy. There's no way in the world that I could handle my heavy load of assignments, if we didn't have our database. It's the beginning-and-the-end on a lot of my searches. In fact, I had lunch Tuesday with Bill Maverick and Allan Shane, who left us last year to start their own firm. They say that the extra speed and freedom they get from being able to call up practically anyone they want to is pretty much offset by the extra grunting and grinding they have to do because they haven't yet built up a database as large as ours.

"However, they told me about something else that's pretty interesting. Because of their fine personal reputations when they were with us, their firm has been named one of the *RITES*-honored search firms—just like GR&B is—in that new *RITE*Site.com Executive Information Exchange on the Internet. That means they can post their positions on the site *without identifying themselves,* and yet executives will know that each position is a search by one of about 350 top-drawer retainer-only search firms honored in *RITES OF PASSAGE.* On the other hand, the executives who respond don't know *which recruiter* posted *which job.* So Bill and Allan don't have to deal with anyone who replies if they don't want to. The site is new and it's growing fast. Bill says it has some new technology that sorts its resumes even better than ours does. He says he and Allan have already filled several of their searches with candidates they got on *RITE*Site.

"Lots of times, Bill says, they don't post their search. If the job is pretty standard and easy to fill, they just look into the database for candidates...same as we do with our

GR&B database. But there's an interesting wrinkle to that. Executives can enter themselves two ways. One way is anonymously—*identity-concealed*—they call it, so the recruiter or employer doesn't know their name or address or e-mail, and can only contact them through the *RITE*Site computer. If the executive likes what's passed on, he or she responds. Otherwise, the person stays concealed. Or if they're intrigued but doubtful, they ask for more information before deciding whether or not to reveal their identity.

"The other way the executive can post on *RITE*Site is to choose what's called the *RITES*-Honored Option. That means that their personal contact information *will* be displayed along with their identity-concealed resume, *but only when one of the RITES-Honored Recruiters consults the database.* To anyone else, the executive is anonymous. On the *RITES*-Honored Option, what most executives do is just post the same resume they'd otherwise send to the 350 or so top firms in a direct mail campaign. It's as if they've automatically inserted themselves into the databases of those 350 firms. That's the feature Bill and Allan really love. It's almost like the people are in Maverick & Shane's own database. To them the executives *aren't* anonymous. There's no tedious back-and-forth with the computer to smoke 'em out. Just call 'em up or send an e-mail."

"So what," says Buddy. "That's nothing on us. We're just as *RITES*-honored as they are. You and I can post jobs and not reveal our identity just like they can."

"Yeah," says Will. We talked about that a couple weeks ago, when you got that letter telling you GR&B is a *RITES*-Honored firm and you're one of the firm members mentioned in the book. Did you ever try out the site?"

"Damn right. Will, I'm way ahead of you on this one. In fact I've been meaning to tell you. I posted one of my toughest searches on *RITE*Site just to see if I'd get anyone we didn't already have. Well, I did. I got a lot of responses, including a really great guy we'd never heard of. Plus, I also dipped into the *RITE*Site database and got a woman whose resume we'd scanned into our system three years ago, before we began accepting unsolicited resumes by e-mail. Apparently our scanning fouled up her name-spelling and her phone number. On *RITE*Site she'd chosen the *RITES*-Honored Option. So, as a *RITES*-Honored recruiter, I was able to see her phone number. I just picked up the phone and called her. She was interested, so I put her into our database *assigned to me*, even though Connie Lyon and someone else had already requested the Research Department to try to locate her and mark her for them in our computer.

"So the point is, Will, I'd never spend any money to post jobs and view resumes on a commercial site like Monster or the others. And certainly GR&B never would! Why should we? With Gloria's research people and our huge database, we're spending plenty on our own information. We've got 220,000 people we already know, and we can call them for leads on plenty of others. But this *RITE*Site's Executive Information Exchange is *neat.* And it's free of charge to recruiters from *RITES*-Honored firms. It hasn't cost me a penny, and it's already about to fill two of my searches. So I agree with Bill and Allan."

"Okay," says Will. "But there's something else going on at that *RITE*Site that may help Bill and Allan catch up closer to where we are in the long run. They have a system hooked up to receive unsolicited resumes by e-mail just like we do. When people purchase the Custom Career Service on *RITE*Site to post their resumes, they can also download the resume-submission e-mail addresses of the *RITES*-Honored firms. Then, with just one click, they can transmit to every *RITES*-honored firm that accepts resumes by e-mail. So, where before those executives might never have bothered to submit to any more than five or six firms—us included—now, with *zero* effort, they include Bill and Allan and over 300 other quality firms right along with us. That won't grow Bill and Allan's database up to the size of ours. But it will give them current information on lots of career-conscious people willing to consider a new or better job...people who'd never have done the necessary work to send resumes to them otherwise. Bill and Allan feel that *RITE*Site is a real benefit to their business. It shores up their weaker side, without taking anything away from their strong side, which is their short off-limits list."

"Well, let me put it this way," Buddy replies with a note of finality, "I'm telling *you* that I'm using this *RITE*Site thing, because we're always helping each other out. But I'm certainly not mentioning it to everyone else around here. Let them figure it out for themselves. The way I see it, if I can fill a few more searches a little quicker using some outside help, that's great. I'll bump up my earnings and maybe free up some time."

"But Will, getting back to the off-limits issue that you brought up, you say that those 93 other recruiters make your life more difficult by ballooning up our client list. You've got to admit that some of them—especially our good friends in the firm—often make it a hell of a lot easier too. You've probably done favors for them...given them candidate ideas when they were stumped...and most of them will try to give you suggestions when the going gets rough. I certainly do. And it was your suggestion of Joan Flannel—thank you very much—that finally wound up my PhantaSee! Fashions search."

"True, ole Buddy," says Will. "I sure as hell wouldn't help everyone the way I do you...and vice versa, as we've discussed many times. But I do have many friends in the firm to exchange ideas with, and that's a great help. Take Bill and Allan. I used to swap suggestions with them all the time. But I probably won't be doing as much of that, now that they've started their own company."

"Yeah, and what about our offices in seven U.S. cities and five overseas? They come in pretty darn handy when you're traveling. No need to interview in a hotel room staring at a bed," says Buddy.

"Or to rent a suite that you've got to bill your client for, if it's a high-level search and you want to make a really good impression," adds Will.

"And speaking of impressions, Will," says Buddy. "I think you're more likely to get a busy executive to return your phone call right away if you're calling from Gordon, Rossi & Boodles, than if you're calling from an unheard-of little firm like Kermit, Piggy & Fudd."

"Certainly potential clients are more likely to call you," says Will. "Name value is very helpful to the Human Resources people. Their jobs are on the line when they recommend a search firm to their CEO or to another top officer. Not every search will run smoothly, no matter *who* does it. But when they recommend one of the largest and most famous firms and there's a poor result, it's because the giant firm screwed up. It's not because they recommended a small outfit that obviously wasn't qualified. The same goes for almost anyone else who chooses a search firm, whether it's a board hiring a CEO, or a division manager going outside for a head of R&D. The decision maker can always claim 'due diligence,' when he or she turns the matter over to a very well-known entity."

"When you get right down to it, Will, the 'off-limits' restrictions...both client and co-worker...are nothing more than a nuisance for you and me on most searches. Normally, we're just looking for a really good person to fill an opening. He or she can come from almost any company...not just a few leading firms in a certain industry. Only in a situation like the one you've got with Summit, where he's trying to shift the competitive balance of power in his field, does it really matter where you can and can't look. And even then, conscientious firms like GR&B can always get someone good, regardless of the obstacles. Three months from now we'll be back here celebrating your completion of the ISC search."

"Just like we're now toasting your new President of PhantaSee! Fashions," adds Will. "Drink up, Buddy, and let's hit the road."

"And all in all, it's a good life, Will. You have to admit that," says Buddy, whose wife will be meeting him at the station in their new Mercedes, which she just picked up from the dealer this afternoon. "They're not holding any benefits these days for Will Pickham, are they?"

That's Buddy's exit line, as he takes off for Grand Central, and Will heads for a pretheater dinner with his wife, a successful pediatrician.

"That's Exactly the Sort of Person You Need."

The show was a hit. Will and Karen are in a great mood the next morning, as they walk out of their elegant condominium on upper Fifth Avenue. Will may be late this evening. He's driving out to see Mr. Summit.

The interview takes place in Summit's luxurious suite of offices at ISC's headquarters near Lustretown, New York, with every window framing a breathtaking view of the Hudson River. As Summit predicted, no Bill Beane or Al Umans. From Will's perspective, things go very well. He easily skirts the issue of off-limits companies without ever having to say anything that isn't literally true.

Summit begins by stressing two points. First that he's not insisting on prior experience as President or General Manager. "Just get me another Graham Rusk," he says. "A brilliant marketing-oriented business generalist will fit my strategy perfectly. And the opportunity to step up to a presidency will make them hungry as hell to come. With that on the table, you should be able to bring me every one of the best marketeers in our industry. And I *do* mean *in our industry*. I want deep experience in proprietary drugs...drugs sold to the consumer, rather than prescribed by doctors."

"Of course, I know that anyone from the consumer products field could learn proprietary drugs. But even someone very sharp might take a year or more to get up to speed, and I just can't wait that long. The truth of the matter is, I waited far too long to get rid of the guy I had in there."

Summit emphasizes his point by flicking an imaginary piece of lint from the sleeve of his navy pinstripe.

"Now it's essential that I have quick results. So the new person absolutely must be experienced in our product lines, and all set to go. That would be true just on the basis of our regular lines and our current R&D. But there's also an exciting e-commerce angle that, ironically, requires that the President be strong in the basic old fashioned fundamentals...especially the federal regulatory issues on what products we can put out and what we can say in our labeling and advertising. That's subtle—and dangerous—stuff."

"Here's what's happening. My daughter's an editor in New York for one of the biggest international publishing companies. Some hot shot young Internet folks she knows have acquired the rights to a lot of material on the health and lifestyle issues of people over 60 and they're setting up a "community" for those folks on the Internet. My daughter says these kids in their 20s are very creative in writing and design, and they've brought in some terrific computer experts who've built amazing sites for others. She's convinced that group that they should use one of our trademarks—*MaturiTeen*—which we use on geriatric vitamins, for the name of the site and for a new line of herbal-based food supplements which we will develop for marketing on the site. I've agreed that ISC will provide $2 million seed money for the venture and, of course, we'll supply the products which, after a year's exclusivity on the site, we'll then be free to sell through drug stores and supermarkets."

"So, for no more money than we'd spend to run three or four network TV spots, we'll wind up owning 20% of *MaturiTeen.com*. We'll also get a lot of publicity for our existing vitamin products among computer-savvy "mature individuals"—a hipper, more upscale segment of the 60-plus set than we have now—and we'll be putting out a whole line of new products on which the margins are quite, *quite* good."

"But the problem in all this is that we have to make sure that a bunch of enthusiastic amateurs don't get us into trouble. For that I need the rare combination of a seasoned pro in the proprietary drug field who is also upbeat, aggressive, and optimistic enough to work with bright young people like these kids and not kill their enthusiasm."

"That's a tall order, I know," says Summit, leveling an appraising gaze at Will. "But it's also a fantastic opportunity for the industry's best marketing person to move up in the world. Here's the perfect turnaround. Our regular product lines have been undermarketed for the past several years. I intend to free up plenty of extra promotional funds for the division. And, if this e-project is successful, it will turn every head in the industry our way. Nobody's ever done anything like it...and I think it has a lot of potential. What do you say, Will? Think you can find our person?"

Will smiles broadly and nods...registering his optimism without making any specific commitment. He realizes that Summit isn't going to be willing to look at anyone who doesn't have the background he's asking for. *Too bad...that makes it even more limiting.*

"Now I understand that you can't go into CompuMedic," Summit continues, "because you found their new superstar. But maybe that isn't such a big loss as it seems. Right now that company is so profitable that they'll probably offer whatever it takes to tie down their management team for the foreseeable future. And I suppose you can't go to Orchid either. But I understand your woman brought in a lot of new people, and to tell you the truth, I'd prefer to wait and see if they can really turn that thing around. They're still untested, as I see it, and not a place we're interested in yet.

"However, while we're on the subject of women, Will, let me toss in something that you might wonder about if I didn't bring it up. We have eight divisions in this company, and not a single one of them has a woman President. Is that because I don't *want* any? No way. But is it my *fault*? Damn right. Our COO who retired last year was a male chauvinist of the first order. And his attitudes just kind of permeated all through the organization. I knew it, and yet I didn't do anything about it. As a result, we lost two or three young women to other companies who by now would be ready to move up to a job like this. But they're gone, and that's our loss. We've got some terrific young women on their way up, particularly in Bill Beane's part of the company. But they're just Group Product Managers and Regional Sales Managers...several more years away from running their own show.

"Will, this is *not* an affirmative action assignment. Just go out and get us the best person you can. If it's a woman, I'd be delighted. But if I think a man is 10% better, he'll get the job. And I think Bill Beane will vote with me on whomever we choose.

"So where do you plan to look?" says Summit.

Will can recognize a hot potato when it's handed to him.

"Well, you tell me. Which companies in the proprietary drug field do you respect? Which ones have the kind of managers you feel would fit what you're trying to accomplish at ISC?"

Will's candid blue eyes look straight at Summit.

"Let's see. Well, of course, Prestige Panacea is probably the best-managed of the big firms in the field...you couldn't go wrong with the Marketing VP from Prestige. And I think National Anodyne does a consistently good job of marketing. Maxi-Medi-Marketing has one of the hottest growth records in the industry, although I believe part of their success is due to their excellent R&D work. Still, one of their people should know what it takes to get the fast growth we want. Now, let me think...Well, of course, there's Parker Labs. They're an outstanding firm. They've built their brands very solidly, and they have an excellent reputation in the business."

Summit pauses for a moment, steepling his fingers as he gazes fearlessly into the middle distance.

"If I were you, I might take an especially close look at BioDynamics. They're moving into some very promising new areas, and that suggests an alert management with good long-range planning, which I'd like to see more of here at ISC. Oh, yes, and Cosa Nostrums. I've heard their management can be a bit ruthless, but they know how to get cooperation from the retailers. They always wind up with more than their share of shelf space. Perhaps a bit of their promotional aggressiveness would serve us well."

"As I think about it now, I really do like the idea of getting someone from BioDynamics. And of course, Parker or Prestige are very likely possibilities..."

As Summit drones on...repeating again the very limited number of obvious companies on his executive shopping list, Will's spirits are sinking. Four of the six companies Summit has mentioned are off-limits to GR&B...unbeknownst, of course, to Summit. *Where am I going to find my candidates?*

But Will copes with his concern as he answers Summit.

"You've listed some outstanding companies. And there are others too. I'm sure we can find a number of able people. Now at BioDynamics," continues Will, selecting one of the companies open to him, "lately I've been hearing from our West Coast office that they've got some excellent marketing-oriented general managers in those decentralized proprietary drug divisions they've set up. In fact, I noticed last week in an investor's newsletter I subscribe to that their stock was being highly recommended because the analyst was impressed by their top management and the entrepreneurship those separate profit centers are supposed to encourage."

"Yes, BioDynamics should be high on your list. And I've always liked the sort of people you see at places like Parker and Prestige and National Anodyne."

"Yes," Will replies. "That's exactly the sort of person you need."

Summit is satisfied. He pictures Will searching in those companies. Will is relieved. He knows he hasn't committed himself to anything but an expression of blanket approval of the quality of the executives those corporations employ. So both men are in a very good mood as they head for the private dining room and an elegant luncheon whipped up by ISC's corporate chef: grilled sole with a fresh tomato and basil sauce, asparagus puree, and sauteed wild mushrooms that the chef personally collected that morning in the woods at the edge of ISC's property. It's not until they finish the chef's special strawberry sorbet that they go back to talking business.

"By the way," says Summit, reaching into his breast pocket, "I wanted to give you this." It's a brief letter, accompanied by a resume. "I got this in the mail just a few days ago. I never heard of the guy, but it seems that he has the sort of experience we're interested in. Why don't you check him out? From his resume, it sounds like he's been in the right places to get the strong marketing background we're looking for. And, if they're true, his accomplishments are very impressive."

Will's initial response is thankfulness. It will be extremely hard to find good candidates for ISC, so he's glad to get one, even from the client. But his feelings change when he scans the resume. It's from Sam Sage...the very same Sam Sage he recently met coming out of Buddy's office...the Sam Sage who's currently assigned within Gordon, Rossi & Boodles to Buddy for his Expodex search. *Oh, damn!*

There's no need for Will to tell Summit the immediate reason he's less than enthusiastic about Sam. As he glances at the resume, Will sees something else. "I'm not sure that this background is really what you want. If you notice, practically all of his work has been in *prescription* drugs, not proprietaries. Most of his marketing campaigns have been aimed at the medical profession, rather than the consumer."

Summit takes a quick look at the resume again.

"I see what you mean. But I'm impressed by the depth of his experience in drugs... and by the apparent success he's had. And, after all, he began his career as a brand manager at Promote & Gambol. You can't get much better consumer marketing experience than P&G. Why don't you just check him out?"

Faced with Summit's instruction, Will has no choice but to comply.

"Sure, I'll see about this guy," he agrees, as he puts the resume into the breast pocket of his grey pinstripe. *Maybe I'll be able to discourage Summit from asking any further about Buddy's star candidate, muses Will. And, of course, if Summit does bring up Sam Sage again, and gets really pushy, that'll be my clout to make Buddy let me also have him. Now that the industry has a bland-sounding name for it—**Parallel Processing**—it's easier to get by with presenting the same person to two clients simultaneously. GR&B would have considered that hopelessly unethical just a year or two ago. Now I can at least ask our management for permission to do it, whenever I'm as blocked for candidates as it looks like I will be on this search.*

Summit goes back to the subject of ISC's needs.

"We've talked about a lot of the big companies in the field. But I don't want you just to pursue the most obvious solutions. I hope you'll look in a few other directions. There are some aggressive young companies coming into the market these days. Some of those little biotech ethical drug companies are doing a good job of marketing straight to the consumer, now that the FDA has relaxed its rules on advertising Rx products on TV and on selling previously Rx products over-the-counter. Also, there are one or two fast growing firms in the health-food field that are expanding into mass-market proprietaries...the converse of what we'll be doing with *MaturiTeen*. You might find somebody at one of those smaller companies."

That may be my answer. It's a darn good idea!

"Yes," says Will, "I'll cover the smaller companies, too. Sometimes they've got a really outstanding manager who'd love to get into a major corporation."

Will smiles inwardly. He enjoys it when a client indicates some flexibility and leaves him room for creativity.

"Of course, I recognize we're probably not as attractive as one of the top ten firms," says Summit frankly. "Still, it's a $640 million division. And with the right person at the helm using all the resources of a corporation like ISC, growth could be very rapid. We hope that within five years we'll be in the top ten ourselves. I'm willing to spring for acquisitions, if they're brought to me by a credible management team that's doing a good job with our current businesses.

"And obviously I know we'll have to make some major changes in what we're doing now," Summit continues. For example, in an effort to make the division profitable, we've done very little advertising in the past few years. That was the policy of the last division head, and I let him get away with it. But I expect us to be much more aggressive in the future. If need be, I'll pour lots of money into that division for the next couple of years, to enable them to do all the marketing that's required. We've got a great opportunity for the new President. I hope you find us the person we really need."

The meeting concludes with reassurances from Will that he'll get right to work, and optimism from Summit that he'll soon see a slate of several appropriate candidates. In Summit's mind, Will can search almost everywhere in the proprietary drug industry. Whereas, in fact, as Will realizes all too clearly, he's severely limited.

Here are the companies that, following his discussion with Will, Summit visualizes being searched:	*Here is where Will actually can search:*
Prestige Panacea	
National Anodyne	
Maxi-Medi-Marketing	**Maxi-Medi-Marketing**
Parker Laboratories	
BioDynamics	**BioDynamics**
Cosa Nostrums	
"Small up-and-coming companies"	**"Small up-and-coming companies"**

The Struggle Begins

The next morning, as soon as he gets to the office, Will plunges into the ISC search. Better get things moving before his other assignments make new demands on his time.

The first item on Will's agenda is another meeting with Gloria Monday, chief researcher in GR&B's New York office. Since they last talked about the ISC position, she's gone through industry directories and GR&B's computerized files. Today she brings Will print-outs on the four top drug companies that he's able to look into for candidates. Two of these—Maxi-Medi-Marketing and BioDynamics—are on Mr. Summit's mental list. And two others...Better & Best and Right Remedies...while not on that list, are at least sizable enough to rank among the top ten in the U.S.

Through dedicated digging, Gloria has also come up with a list of second-tier companies not currently off-limits to Gordon, Rossi & Boodles recruiters. Will knows that his success rate at these smaller firms may not turn out to be very high. Their top managers usually have substantial equity stakes. So, if the companies are fast-growing and profitable, their managers are unreachable. And if the companies aren't doing well, their executives won't have track records that will impress Summit. Still, Will's thankful at least to have somewhere else to look. Maybe in one of those companies he'll find Ms. or Mr. Right...or anyway, Right-Enough-To-Present.

Gloria also brings Will printouts of the computerized files on some proprietary drug company executives known to Gordon, Rossi & Boodles who aren't currently involved in any other recruiter's search...all of whom she has marked for Will's exclusive use on GR&B's central computer. Perhaps one of these people will actually become a candidate for the ISC job. And even the ones who are working for off-limits companies may still be useful as sources of information about good people somewhere else in the field.

Will thanks Gloria for all her help and settles down to do his reading. As he leafs through the pile of folders on his desk, he spots the name of Andrea Applewhite.

Andrea! Of course, I know Andrea Applewhite...she's PERFECT! Will shouts under his breath, whacking his desk so hard that his Cross pen bounces onto his interviewing chair four feet away. *(Expletive deleted.) Andrea's the perfect person for Summit! (Expletive deleted.) The first thought he came up with was to get the Marketing VP of Prestige Panacea...and that's Andrea! (Another expletive.) I'd forgotten that Andrea got promoted to VP - Marketing four years ago when Dan Dawson moved up to Senior VP - Marketing & Sales. Why, Andrea thinks exactly like Bill Beane, only she has a consumer drug background instead of food. The chemistry's perfect! Summit would FLIP...and so would Bill. Andrea's always wanted a shot at running an entire business. And a $640 million proprietary drug company, with strong backing for growth...why Andrea would love the ISC job. It's a gimme! (One last expletive, but less strident, more resigned.) And my hands are tied...*

Unfortunately, as Will's silent tantrum reminds us, Gordon, Rossi & Boodles has a strong client relationship with Prestige Panacea. In fact, Applewhite herself was recruited to Prestige by GR&B several years ago. All Prestige executives are off-limits. And, recruited by GR&B, Andrea is doubly off-limits.

But Andrea is so perfect for the ISC position that Will even briefly considers going to Mr. Rossi and asking if something can be done to release Andrea. Then he remembers that one of the reasons GR&B got Prestige as a client was that Rossi plays golf every Saturday with Prestige's CEO. Will knows he doesn't have a prayer of getting Andrea freed up for ISC.

In fact, if he even so much as called Andrea to ask for suggestions, Will could be in trouble. It wouldn't do for her to learn about the open position...one she'd be as eager to get as ISC would be to get her...because Andrea might then try to go directly after the job herself. The CEO of Prestige certainly wouldn't take it well if his head of Marketing & Sales ended up with a job that GR&B was searching, however it came about. He'd surely complain to Rossi, and Will knows what Rossi would then say to him. And of course the spontaneous appearance of Applewhite on the scene would also create big problems with Summit, who'd either think Will was inept for not identifying Applewhite or less than candid for not stating upfront that he couldn't go into Prestige. No, Will doesn't dare even breathe in Andrea's direction.

Well, so much for Andrea Applewhite. Put her in the "No" pile.

And here's Karol Klasner, over at National Anodyne. Damn, damn, damn!, fumes Will. *Another great person Summit and Beane would love. She's also dying for a shot at general management. But I can't touch National Anodyne. And I'd damn well better not call her for suggestions either. She's a real go-getter. Don't know how she'd manage it, but Karol would be in Summit's office by noon tomorrow. Not quite 31 years old, and she's already had three years as Marketing VP of the sixth largest proprietary drug company. And just look at those new products she's coming out with,* muses Will. *If she doesn't get somebody else's company to run by the time she's 35, she'll probably start her own! A nice person, too. She recycles and develops people; she doesn't just dump them on the street. Well, too bad Will, old boy. On the street is where you'll be if you touch Klasner. Anodyne is Sylvia Gordon's client.*

Next, however, Will discovers the file of the financial vice president at Prestige. Will decides it's safe to call him, even though he can't call Andrea Applewhite, since a finance person is obviously not going to be a candidate for the marketing-oriented division head Will will be inquiring about. This guy's been in the proprietary drug business for a long time, so he might conceivably know of some promising marketing executives who've been at Prestige over the years and then moved on to other companies. Will immediately marks him to be a "Source."

Painstakingly, Will goes through all the profiles, and he downloads onto his notebook PC the contact and background information on each person he intends to phone. There are no obvious candidates, but Will does succeed in compiling a list of possible sources. Next he tries to build a list of prospects. He turns to the laser-printed pages Gloria and her assistants have gleaned by consulting on-line information services and by visiting corporate Web sites and the sites of the few relevant trade associations, looking for marketing people in the three big firms he *can* go into: Maxi-Medi-Marketing, Right Remedies, and BioDynamics. Will also checks out the top managements of some of the smaller companies. Today, these people are totally unfamiliar to Will. But as he calls his sources to ask for recommendations, he can also inquire about the people on his list.

After a few days of making calls, Will begins to feel quite anxious about his ability to put together a decent slate of candidates for Mr. Summit. According to the sources Will's talked to, he'll never be able to put his hands on any but the most junior of the people at Right Remedies, a top-ten firm that's open to him although it wasn't mentioned by Summit as one of his favorites. All of its upper management are beneficiaries of an incredibly generous stock option plan that was set up during a period of crisis four or five years ago. Although the program has since been discontinued, all of the key people will be multi-millionaires...as long as they stay on a few more years. So Right Remedies is unlikely to yield any candidate.

Another disappointment is the fact that Will has heard very little about good marketing-oriented presidents, general managers, and VPs of Marketing in the smaller companies. If those smaller firms do contain a wealth of talent, the people are unknown to Will's informants. Will and Gloria's researchers will simply have to phone into those companies and ask for their key executives by title, without knowing anything about them in advance...tedious and usually unproductive work, but necessary in a tough situation like this.

Meanwhile, it's beginning to look like Will's entire list of candidates will have to be drawn from just two places: BioDynamics and Maxi-Medi-Marketing. It's been quite a while since he faced a prospect so bleak.

One Step Forward

Will becomes so concerned about the ISC search that he decides to go see Herbert ("Red") Tapecutter. Red is a senior member of the firm...and the person charged with working out knotty problems of client conflict. Will recites his tale of woe, and Red is properly sympathetic.

"Can't you find a way to get just one of those companies on the off-limits list unlocked for me? I know I can't go into Prestige, or Orchid, or CompuMedic...our relationships with them are much too close. But what about the others? Maybe Parker Labs or Cosa Nostrums? I tell you, Red, I need help on this one."

Red promises to look into the situation. Will knows that really means he'll talk to Hamilton Rossi, who usually adjudicates such matters...and get back to Will. In fact, the very next day, Red drops by Will's office with good news.

"Will," says Red, smoothing down the hair that long ago lost the color that conferred Tapecutter's nickname, "It's okay to go into Cosa Nostrums. Our relationship with them on the search we just did was really not very satisfactory. They struck us as extremely unrealistic and demanding, and they certainly acted like they weren't satisfied with our work. I doubt that they'll use us again...and even if they did come back, I'm not sure Mr. Rossi would agree to take any assignment from them. Also, they didn't inquire about off-limits protection. So we didn't promise them any...neither the usual two years, nor any other period. And, of course, the 'Code of Ethics' of the AESC (a trade association of about 120 retainer search firms to which GR&B belongs) "is no longer the bother it once was. So, even though the time limit isn't up, you can go into Cosa Nostrums if you need to."

If I need to. That's a laugh!

"Thanks, Red, I really appreciate the help."

"Any time," waves Red as he departs.

That afternoon, Will at last can look with some satisfaction on his developing list of prospects. As he'd suspected, Better & Best yields no possibilities; there was virtually a complete turnover following the departure of the key executive Will recruited, because his replacement has turned out to be an insecure egomaniac. But Will's heard of a couple people at BioDynamics, and a couple more at Maxi-Medi-Marketing, who sound like good possibilities. He's also going to try some names at Right Remedies, although he's rather doubtful about whether or not they can be lured away. Plus, his research has turned up a couple possibilities at Cosa Nostrums, now happily unlocked. All in all, it's not such a bad starting point.

The next morning, things look even better for the ISC search. Will is able to get through to one of his most carefully cultivated contacts, a senior partner in a major public accounting firm. His contact remembers being impressed with the performance of an aggressive little drug company in Phoenix, called Adam Laboratories. Adam was acquired by a foreign concern, which has since switched Adam to a different CPA firm...the same one it uses for the rest of its U.S. subsidiaries. According to Will's informant, a lot of the credit for Adam Labs' performance goes to their Marketing VP, Charlie Comstock. Will's contact hasn't actually met Charlie, but he thinks there's good reason to believe he might be an excellent prospect.

Will rushes to do a little background research on Charlie, and is delighted to discover that Charlie went to Adam from Parker Labs, where for several years he'd been a senior product manager. It looks like the perfect profile of a young man on his way to the top in the proprietary drug industry. Elated, Will asks his secretary to get Charlie on the phone. Yes, Charlie might be interested in making a move...for the right job and salary...

doesn't mind living in the New York area...will send his resume immediately...and can fly in for an interview in the next week or so.

All in all, Will chalks up a good day's work on the ISC job. *I wish I were making as much headway on some of the other things I'm handling,* he says to himself.

But the next day is one that for several weeks hence Will will call "Black Thursday." As soon as he's sitting down with his first cup of strong coffee, Gloria pops into his office. She's bearing news...good for Gordon, Rossi & Boodles, bad for Will and ISC.

BioDynamics is now officially off-limits.

"Off-limits!" Will groans. "But we haven't worked for them in years!"

"That was yesterday," says Gloria firmly. Gloria is a practical woman who refuses to cry over spilled milk. "One of the recruiters in our San Francisco office, Doris DeWitt, has been on a suburban school board with the CEO. And at last night's meeting, he offered her the assignment to fill the job of head of marketing for their consumer health-care products group."

"Oh, no," says Will. "That's even worse. Not only does it mean I can't go into BioDynamics to look for my person; it also means that Doris and I are going to be chasing the same candidates."

Will gets up and starts to pace as he thinks about how he's going to defend his territory against this new incursion.

"Bad luck," says Gloria sympathetically. "But since I realized this new search was going to put you in a hole, I immediately went through the computer and nailed *everyone* I could find who might be of the slightest use to you on your ISC project...before Randy, the researcher in the West Coast office, requested them all for Doris."

Will swivels around and watches in awe as Gloria drops a deep pile of printouts of GR&B executive profiles on his desk.

"There are 26 in all," she announces, "and all are marked for you in the computer."

"Good work, Gloria!" says Will. There is real warmth in his smile. *Thank God for Gloria! Am I glad I remembered to get her that Hermes scarf last Christmas; it's the best investment I ever made. If I didn't have her on my side...*

Gloria leaves Will's office, her ears still ringing with his words of praise for her foresight. Will immediately reaches for the phone and dials Doris out in San Francisco.

"Doris, darn it, what are you trying to do to me?"

"Just trying to earn a living, Will. Them's the breaks."

"That's easy for you to say," rejoins Will. "BioDynamics was my best hope for the ISC search, a real bug of an assignment, and now you've snatched the company away from me."

"If you want to talk about snatching, my friend, I've got a few complaints of my own. What about the files? Randy here tells me you've got most of the people who might be of any use to me on the BioDynamics search."

"So you noticed that, did you?" chuckles Will. "Serves you right, you know."

After a few more minutes of jocular complaining, Doris becomes more serious, and reminds Will she's gone out of her way to help him in the past.

"So Will, the truth of the matter is that I don't even have a place to start on this search... especially since you've got all those files tied up. Can't you at least let me call some of the people you're holding and ask them for suggestions?"

"I don't think I can do that, Doris. Let's face it. You and I are going to be looking for exactly the same person. It's bad enough that I'm going to have to race you to the best prospects, but I simply can't give you a head start."

"How about letting me have just one of those guys Gloria scooped up for you? You've got the file on Walter Alston, and that guy's a personal friend of mine, for god's sake."

"I hate to play hardball with you, Doris, but I need every one of the people I've got. I'm nearly a month into the search already, and right now I have no candidates, and very few solid leads. I've just got to hang on to everything I have."

Doris's sigh is audible on Will's end of the telephone line.

"You think you've got problems. What about me?" says Doris. "I've got exactly the same problem you have, and on top of it, I've lost the few leads open to Gordon, Rossi & Boodles, because of your quick work in getting there first. Come on, Will, let's see you play on the team."

"I know, it's tough," answers Will sympathetically. *I don't want to cause Doris grief,* he thinks to himself. *In fact I'd like to help her...but I can't give her my people.*

"How about this?" suggests Doris. "If you run across any good people that you can't land because they don't want to move to New York, will you let me have a crack at them? I can pitch them on the climate and the other advantages of San Diego for the BioDynamics job, and maybe I can get them for my search, even if they turn you down for ISC."

"Absolutely. You've got a deal!" Will genuinely likes and respects Doris. She has been helpful to him in the past. And Will may need her cooperation in the future. He's happy to agree.

"Depend on it. Anyone who turns me down, Wilma will assign to you at the same time she releases them from me. That way, nobody else can get their hands on them."

"Thanks, Will, I appreciate your help. I'd like to do a really good job with this search, because I think I can get a lot more business from BioDynamics. They're doing some reorganizing, and they have an ambitious acquisition program, so a lot of positions could open up in the next few years."

"What happened to the guy who used to have the job you're filling?" asks Will, who thinks, *Maybe his going somewhere else will stir up the industry in a way that could possibly be helpful to me.*

"They haven't fired him, and they haven't promoted him either. They've moved him into a staff job at the corporate level, something in corporate planning. My guess is that he just wasn't action-oriented and decisive enough for a company that's becoming very aggressive these days. In describing what they want they've kept harping on ability to make timely, independent decisions. Of course, the kick upstairs may just be a graceful way of giving him plenty of time to look around for something else. I think he's been there a long while."

"Hhhhmmmmhh," says Will thoughtfully. "Maybe there's something there for me. Do you think they'd really like to see him go? Maybe they wouldn't mind if I approached him about the ISC job. What do you think?"

"I can't say for sure, but it might be worth a try. I could check it out with the CEO. If it's true that they want to get rid of him, they might even be grateful if we called him up and got him thinking about the outside world."

"It would sure be great for me," says Will eagerly. "It means I'd be able to present someone from BioDynamics, which is one of my CEO's favorite targets for his search. Not that I'd actually put him in if he's a stiff. But at least I could show that I looked into BioDynamics. And you know, it might even work. If your guy's smart and has a deep background in drugs, he'll appeal to ISC. Maybe it won't matter so much to them that he's a little slow to make a decision, since he'll be reporting to Bill Beane, one of the most action-oriented executives I've ever seen...a guy who's also done some great work in developing people. I know of a couple of dead-assed old farts that he's really got up and running. The guy at BioDynamics is probably a hell of a lot better than they were when Bill started working with them."

"I'll check out the situation with the BioDynamics people," promises Doris.

Losing BioDynamics is a real blow to Will. He'd counted on finding one or two good candidates there...and he knows Summit has been counting on the same thing. Of course, if Doris can swing it, Will may yet present someone from BioDynamics...but he fears it will be largely a matter of window dressing. He still needs to find a really strong candidate to head his slate.

Suddenly, Will remembers the resume of Sam Sage that Summit asked him to check out. More than three weeks have gone by; maybe there's a chance that Buddy can now give him up. *I'd better look into that before Summit raises the issue again*, thinks Will, as he strolls down the hall and walks nonchalantly into Buddy's office.

"Hey, Buddy, you know that guy I met in here a while ago? What was his name... Sam Sage? Is he still a hot candidate for your Expodex search?"

"You bet he is. He's got just the right marketing background, and I think he's going to be one of my strongest runners."

"I was afraid of that," says Will glumly.

He explains that Sam has sent his resume to Sherm Summit at ISC, with the result that Summit has expressed interest in checking Sam out.

"Well, you've got to head that one off," mutters Buddy. "He's mine, and I need him."

"I will if I can, but you know it's not always easy. I already tried to point out that his background is wrong...mainly in ethical drugs aimed at the medical profession...but Summit didn't back off an inch."

"So why don't you tell him you know something...without getting specific ...that makes you think he should pass Sam by? You know, say you've got 'mixed reviews' on him, or something like that, and while he might be great in the slower-moving *ethical* drug industry, he wouldn't be the rockem-sockem guy they're looking for to build their consumer business."

"Buddy, that's not the way I operate," Will replies with strong conviction. "Besides, Summit might hear that Sam got the Expodex job, and was recruited there by Gordon, Rossi & Boodles. Then I'd really look like a jerk!" Will shakes his head in concern. "I'm just hoping that if I keep quiet about it, Summit will forget the whole thing."

"By the way, Buddy, Red Tapecutter freed me to go into Cosa Nostrums. But you'll be glad to know that I didn't ask for *parallel processing* on Sam."

"Will, you're not threatening your old pal, are you? Just to be on the safe side," concludes Buddy with a wink and a smile, "I'm going to set up an appointment for Sam to see the guys at Expodex right away...before I have my complete slate lined up. I'm counting on you, Will, to protect me with my clients. They aren't going to like it if we're selling the same guy to two clients...which is the way they'll interpret it."

"I'll do my best, Buddy," promises Will as he heads back to his own office. But the thought of BioDynamics' new status, plus having to try to keep Sam Sage away from Summit, cause Will to say "Yes" when a favorite client calls with a wild idea. It's a beautiful day. Why don't they use his company's tickets for that afternoon at the U.S. Open Tennis Tournament? Why not indeed!

The First Sketchy Slate

Before the week is over, lucky Will adds not one but two candidates to his ISC slate. He hears from Doris on the West Coast, who tells him it's okay to go after the exec who was kicked upstairs. As they had surmised, BioDynamics is pleased at the possibility that Ethan Evans might find other employment. And it comes as no surprise, when Will finally gets Ethan on the phone, that he's equally interested. In fact, on paper he's an excellent candidate: good education, deep experience in the proprietary drug field, long-tenured employment at highly respected companies. Whatever his flaws may be, they're not readily apparent, and Will is sure Summit will be impressed at seeing a candidate of the caliber of Ethan Evans. And of course he'd damn well better see a candidate from one of the three companies that seem to be of greatest interest to him...Prestige, Parker Labs, and BioDynamics.

And then comes a stroke of luck right out of the blue. Will discovers another candidate from the original group Gloria brought him on Black Thursday...an e-mailed letter and resume that had accidentally got shoved under Will's desk calendar.

Terrific! exclaims Will to himself...but this time out loud, and Wilma steps in to see what's up.

"Did you win the New York Lotto?" she says.

"Dan Dawson's been fired!" says Will. "Of course his letter says 'disagreed on policy'...whatever. The point is that he was Andrea Applewhite's boss at Prestige Panacea...Senior VP of both Marketing and Sales. Andrea just had Marketing. Now I'll bet Andrea moves up to head both. Wilma, this is just the break I've needed. Now I can present someone from Summit's favorite company. And Dawson can't be bad...unless something radical has gone wrong lately...because Andrea has always spoken well of him. Of course I can easily get the inside story from her. You know, Wilma, I never wish any executive bad luck, because I've been in the corporate world and I know how tough it is. But this guy's problem is a real break for me. And thank goodness for Gloria. If she hadn't signed me up for him, Doris DeWitt would have him."

Will calls Dan right away, and confirms that he was in charge of both Marketing and Sales at Prestige for nearly four years, and was in charge of Marketing for two years before that...ideal experience for the ISC job. On the phone and in his subsequent interview, Dan freely admits he was fired, as Will had guessed. But he stresses that it was due to a policy conflict: he wanted to be much more aggressive than he was allowed to be... wanted to investment-spend on the introduction of some new products, right after making a product line acquisition that was taking longer to pay out than originally projected to the Board of Directors last year. So he's out. And...yes, Andrea Applewhite did move up to his job.

Will hears Dan out and pitches the ISC proprietary drug division presidency. Dan is delighted to have a shot at running his own show as President, even though the $640 million business is less than a quarter of the size of corporate Prestige, for which Dan controlled both Marketing & Sales. Moreover, Dan is happy to hear about a job that doesn't require relocation, because his wife has a lucrative law practice in New York. *Dan's lucky, too, that Gloria grabbed those files*, thinks Will.

Of course Will immediately does some preliminary reference checking to confirm Dawson's story. After all, he *was* fired. Among Will's reference calls is one to Andrea Applewhite...ostensibly just to congratulate Andrea on her promotion and ask the circumstances surrounding it since, despite the promotion, Andrea would probably give her right arm for the ISC job.

From Andrea and two other sources Will gets the straight story on Dawson, and it's not really damaging. The acquisition is substantially under-performing the projections Dawson and the President made to the Board, but not so badly that, in the long run, it won't prove a sound diversification. But right now Prestige has got itself into a cash crisis. There have also been some foreign currency losses. And the President just put up a very costly new factory...another good long-range investment...but underutilized now, and raising cost-of-goods. So Dawson's heavy investment spending proposals for new marketing programs...and his blunt outspokenness in support of them...couldn't have come at a worse time. Sensing the Board's frustration, the President seems to have "thrown Dan Dawson to the wolves," says Andrea Applewhite, "maybe partly to save his own skin."

Will is satisfied that Dawson is basically a competent executive, has no relevant personal faults, and seems to be someone who could be guided and groomed by Bill Beane and Sherm Summit into a successful marketing-oriented company President. His personality, however, won't appeal to them nearly as much as Andrea Applewhite's would.

But Dawson is a solid citizen. In fact, Will will be very pleased if every other prospective candidate for the ISC job stands up to preliminary referencing as well as Dawson has.

So at this point, Will has put together a fairly sketchy slate of candidates...not perfect, but at least it's a start:

1. **Charlie Comstock:** Even though he's at Adam Labs, a small company, his track record looks good on paper, and he has a stint with a top-ten firm (Parker Labs) on his resume. He may be a promising find.

2. **Ethan Evans:** Another candidate who looks great on paper and, according to Doris who spoke to him briefly in person, is very polished with an air of success about him. As someone from BioDynamics, he should impress ISC.

3. **Dan Dawson:** Although he's just been let go by Prestige Panacea, he has a very good background and seems to be able to handle himself well. Also, his story checks out.

Not bad. Not bad at all, thinks Will. At least he has a few possibilities. In fact, he's beginning to think the ISC search may turn out to be the least of his current problems. He winces as he thinks about the troubles on some of his other searches.

Moreover, Will still has a few more places to look. He and Gloria's researchers have done their homework on the executives at Maxi-Medi-Marketing and Cosa Nostrums, plus some more of the smaller companies, and Will is ready to get in touch with the most likely prospects gleaned from online information services, corporate Web sites, and from researchers' phone calls. Of course the whole process began when one of Gloria's assistants checked the well-organized computer listings of the 220,000 files Gordon, Rossi & Boodles maintains on all the U.S. executives it has had any sort of contact with in recent years...from being a client or a candidate, to merely having submitted a resume.

Fortunately, three of the eight new prospects Will wants to call are people who haven't previously gotten into GR&B's central computer. Wilma has already flagged those three "no-prior-record" people on the computer as Will's property; now no other GR&B recruiter can communicate with them until Will gives them up. Meanwhile, he can contact them or not, as he sees fit. Moreover, a fourth new prospect Will hears about is also available to Will, even though he's been tracked in GR&B's system for years. It seems that he was returned to "available" status in GR&B's central system just a few days after Gloria in New York and Randy in San Francisco scoured the files for Will's and Doris DeWitt's respective searches. Unfortunately, the remaining four new prospects are on file at GR&B and out of Will's reach; three files are assigned to Doris DeWitt, and one is assigned to another GR&B recruiter.

The first name on Will's list of prospects to call is Gerry Glib at Maxi-Medi-Marketing. He's corporate Senior VP in charge of Sales and Marketing, and is apparently a heavy hitter. His name appears in several on-line directories, and Will is surprised and delighted to find that he's not yet in Gordon, Rossi & Boodles' files, and hence not yet off-limits to Will or any other GR&B recruiter. *Eat your heart out, Doris DeWitt, out there in sunny California. Better get to work!*

Gerry turns out to be quite enthusiastic about the idea of a job change...so much so that it does make Will wonder just a bit what Gerry's situation at Maxi-Medi-Marketing might actually be. But Gerry sounds like an outstanding candidate, and a brief breakfast meeting confirms Will's initial impression. Gerry seems to have a lot of ideas for aggressive marketing campaigns for ISC's proprietary drug lines. Without revealing Summit's MaturiTeen plans, Will probes Dawson's familiarity with e-commerce. He hasn't actually done anything in that area—no *proprietary* drug company has—but he seems incredibly well informed on the subject. Dawson looks like he may be exactly the person Will is looking for.

Another candidate from the same company, Phyllis Finley, isn't quite so strong. She's one of two Marketing VPs splitting product line responsibility in their Consumer Division and therefore is actually a whole level below Gerry. She's probably a *little* junior for ISC's position. But she seems very intelligent, creative, and hardworking. And of course, she'd also offer ISC something of a price advantage compared to most of the other candidates. Will decides to put Phyllis on the "B" list; she's not a top candidate, but she can be introduced to Summit if the "A" list turns out to be too short.

Another candidate is Donna Powers, EVP - Marketing of the Proprietary Drugs Division at Cosa Nostrums. She seems to have accomplished miracles in getting distribution for her firm's new products, with extremely aggressive trade promotions...fighting for shelf space chain by chain, and almost store by store. "Cosa's field sales force is the hardest-hitting in the business," Will is told by a prospect in another company, who turns Will down and recommends Powers. Powers, compensation is unusually high for a top marketing executive, and the ISC job would be a lateral move financially. However, Powers says she's interested in making a move for personal reasons. She claims to be happy at Cosa Nostrums and, as far as Will has been able to discover, the firm is also happy with her performance. But Powers, a single parent, wants to move back to the New York area because her daughter has been accepted at the New York City Ballet School. Unfortunately her present employer has nothing to offer her there. So it might turn out that Cosa Nostrum's loss will be ISC's gain.

The combination of Powers' experience and her forceful and enthusiastic handling of Will's phone call makes Will add her to the "A" team. The list now looks like this:

A

Charlie Comstock — Adam Labs

Ethan Evans — Bio-Dynamics

Dan Dawson — formerly Prestige Panacea

Gerry Glib — Maxi-Medi-Marketing

Donna Powers — Cosa Nostrums

B

Phyllis Finley — Maxi-Medi-Marketing

The very next day brings one of those near-misses that makes Will grind his teeth. He gets a call from Kathryn Keane, the Marketing VP at Parker Laboratories...which is off-limits to GR&B recruiters. Kathryn is an ideal candidate for the ISC job. Will, who has called her for suggestions in the past, thought of her when the search began. But, with Parker off-limits, approaching Kathryn was out of the question. Now here's Kathryn on the phone, announcing that she's eager to leave Parker Labs!

"I want to get out of here, Will. They've appointed a new group executive, a guy I've known and disliked for years. When I was just starting out as an Assistant Product Manager, he was Group Product Manager, and he wanted to get a little more familiar than I thought was appropriate, so I put him in his place. Unfortunately, he's been knifing me every chance he's gotten ever since. We've become a lot bigger company since then, and I've been able to stay out of his way. But now the carousel has swung around again. He's not my *direct* boss, but he's *his* boss; and he's already starting to make my life miserable. This turkey doesn't pass up any chance to knock me, or make me look bad. By now, I've done so well that maybe he thinks I'm a threat to him...even though I'm two layers down. Of course, I'd have been promoted to just one layer down, if he hadn't got his promotion. I just know if I don't get out of here soon, he's gonna cause me real trouble. Will, have you got anything for me?"

Will thinks sadly of the ISC job, a perfect match for the experience and capabilities of Kathryn Keane. But of course it would be as much as Will's job is worth to try to bring them together.

"Kathryn," he replies, "you know I think you're an outstanding executive. But we have a client relationship with your employer...and quite specifically with your division, where we put in a head of R&D three months ago. You know the rules. I couldn't possibly show you anything."

"Isn't there some way to make an exception? It's not like you're raiding the place or anything. I've already made up my mind to leave Parker Labs."

"The only time I can make an exception to the rule is when an executive has already told someone in the supervisory line directly above them...their boss, or their boss's boss...that he or she is looking around and wants to leave."

Will begins to feel a surge of excitement. Maybe he *can* get a really outstanding candidate for ISC. Absent-mindedly, he sweeps a pile of pink telephone slips—unanswered, but marked "Not Urgent"—into the wastebasket.

"Could you go to your boss and tell him how you feel about this guy? Explain that you think he's out to ruin your career, and that you intend to start looking around."

"I don't think I can do that, Will," says Kathryn. "My boss and I get along okay, but we're just not close enough on a personal level for me to trust him. And now *he's* also feeling pressure from this guy. If he thought I was going to leave soon, he'd probably run right upstairs and suggest they get me out immediately, just to prove he's beginning to think on his new boss's wave length."

"How about going up another level, to Charley Phipps, your CEO?" asks Will. "One time when Mr. Rossi and I were in talking to Phipps about my possibly doing a search that never materialized, Phipps mentioned you to us among three or four younger people he thought were 'comers' in his organization, but not quite ready yet for what he had in mind."

"I can't do that either," answers Kathryn matter-of-factly. "After all, he's the one who promoted this guy...and you can bet the guy is really in solid with him at this point. There's really no way. I'm stymied. There are only two people to tell, and I can't talk to either one of them."

"I'm sorry to hear that, Kathryn," says Will sympathetically. *Sorrier than you'll ever know, since I have the perfect job for you right here in my hand, and I'm straining to find decent candidates.* "But I have to play by the rules over here if I want to keep my job. Listen, keep in touch, and let me know if anything changes over there."

Will hangs up with a bang. *What a total downer! Here's a great candidate, who's begging for the job, and she'd be excellent and it would be ideal timing for her, and in the long run it wouldn't hurt the company either because they'll eventually lose her; yet I can't get at her for ISC.* Will questions...and not for the first time...the wisdom of his decision to earn a living as a retainer recruiter.

Will's bad mood is soon to grow even worse. Putting on his suit coat and straightening his tie, he strolls down the hall to share a cup of stomach-destroying coffee with Buddy and commiserate about the day-to-day struggles of their work. In the course of telling Buddy how many things have gone wrong with the ISC search, he eventually breaks down and admits he does have a few promising candidates, among them a guy named Gerry Glib.

"Gerry Glib? Gerry Glib! Gerry Glib!! Hahahahaha!!!" Buddy begins to laugh so uncontrollably that he spills coffee on the stack of resumes on his desk.

"Why are you laughing? What's so funny? What do you know about Gerry Glib?" demands Will.

Buddy finally calms down and wipes his eyes.

"So you got taken by Gerry Glib, huh? Don't let it worry you. It's happened to the best of us."

"What do you mean?" Will finds he's talking through clenched teeth.

"Gerry's one of those guys who's all talk and no action. In interviews, he sounds wonderful. He can sell himself, no doubt about it. But once he gets the job, that's the end of it. One of the big foreign drug companies made the mistake of letting him open up a marketing subsidiary on the Coast to try to penetrate the U.S. market with some of their proprietary items that they got FDA approval to sell over here. They had to give him a lot of rope, and two years later all they had to show for it was a huge stack of bills and an exquisitely decorated office. As far as I know, he never brought in a single dollar's worth of business. Didn't you see the entry I made on Gerry in the computer? It's all in there."

"Well, I thought Gloria must have checked. She's always extremely careful about procedure."

"Maybe she missed him because he's filed under Gaspar G. Glib, his actual name... did you know that?...but he always goes by Gerry. Also, I made his file when he was still at Messerschmidt, and they're known for their industrial products...most people here don't realize they're in drugs, too. She probably assumed that Gaspar at Messerschmidt and Gerry at Maxi-Medi-Marketing were two different people."

Will's heart sinks as he recalls the glowing description Gerry gave him of that episode in his career...somehow he managed to make it sound like a smashing success.

"I can't believe it," he says crossly. "You mean he's no good at all?"

"No good at all," emphasizes Buddy. "I'm surprised you didn't hear that from the people you checked him out with. The guy's a laughingstock of the industry."

Will admits that he didn't bother to check Gerry out very thoroughly...he'd seemed so impressive. And Will was in such need of a good candidate, he just jumped at Gerry when he saw him in the corporate Web site page that Gloria printed out. Will was in a hurry, got careless, and made a mistake. He's grateful that he found out *before* he presented Gerry to Mr. Summit...although he wishes he hadn't let Buddy get one up on him. He knows it will be weeks before Buddy lets him forget his gullibility. *What the hell, it happens to all of us every now and then.* Will crumples his styrofoam cup and heads back to his own office. He has calls to make for another search assignment before the day is over.

First Report to Sherm Summit

The next week, Summit...scheduled to be in the city for a meeting with ISC's investment bankers...has drinks with Will after work. They settle down comfortably at a table in the bar of the New York Yacht Club, and Summit gets right down to the business at hand.

"What have you got for me?," he queries.

"In covering the top companies in the drug field," responds Will smoothly, "I've come up with several people I think you'll find interesting."

"Tell me about them," commands Summit.

"I looked into BioDynamics, one of the companies on your list, and I've got you a real heavyweight. His name is Ethan Evans, and he was just recently promoted from Marketing VP to a job on corporate staff."

"Sounds like coming to ISC as division head would be a lateral move for him," says Summit, shrewdly putting his finger on a weakness in the situation at once.

"That's true. But he's interested anyway because it would get him back into the action."

"What about money?" asks Summit shrewdly.

"I think he's making about $670,000 at BioDynamics, with everything included."

"Well, I don't want to pay more than that unless I absolutely have to. Would this guy leave California and come to our area, without some additional monetary incentive?"

"I think so," Will replies, rather tentatively. "I'll talk to him about it. But I have a hunch that if he could be heading a division as President, with a corporation that intends to really back his unit, he'd go for it." *Damned right he'd go for it. It's a lot better than sitting around waiting to be fired.*

"Another company I've already been into is Maxi-Medi-Marketing. There's only one genuine possibility there: Phyllis Finley, one of two Marketing VPs in one of their divisions. She's a relatively young woman, moving rapidly up the ladder, and I've heard some good things about her from other people in the industry."

"Sounds like she might come from the right place for us. What's she making?"

"Her taxable income is about $365,000, but they have an excellent deferred bonus program at Maxi-Medi, and at her level she might be getting as much as $70,000 or so additional."

"So she's about ready to step up to our range...maybe a little bit at the low end." Summit takes another belt of his Chivas and water. "What else have you got for me?"

Tough old bastard, thinks Will.

"I've also looked into Prestige Panacea. I find that their top marketing guy...Senior VP of both Marketing and Sales...left a few weeks ago, and his replacement has only been in the job for that short time. She's supposed to be a good marketing executive, but has never before had any experience with sales...never even served any time in the sales force. But I did locate the guy who left, Dan Dawson. He's a seasoned pro in the proprietary drug field, and he might be just the one to step into your job and start running."

"Why did he leave Prestige?"

"I've checked that out, and he comes up pretty clean. It's a bit of a story, which I can discuss with you now if you..."

"No, we'll get to that later, if he's still around when you present your finalists," says Summit. "Anyone else?"

"One of the most interesting possibilities is a woman from Cosa Nostrums who has personal reasons for wanting to move back to the New York area. I'm still checking her references, but she looks very promising."

"And is that all?" presses Summit.

"There's also a man from a small company, Adam Laboratories, out in Phoenix. He's got a background with Parker Labs, and I hear the company he's with is doing very well now."

"Never heard of the place, but if he seems to be big enough..."

"I'm seeing him this weekend. If I'm satisfied after an interview, I'll pass him on. Sometimes there's real talent in those smaller companies. People are attracted by the autonomy and the chance to build up an equity stake."

"Well, it sounds like you've come up with a few possibilities," says Summit with a small note of satisfaction in his voice.

And you'll never know how hard I worked to do it! Will pauses to consider the companies he's just discussed, and the gap between the way this interim report has impressed Summit and the daunting circumstances Will has dealt with:

"Top Ten" Companies That Appear Searched	*"Top Ten" Companies That Have Been Searched*
BioDynamics	
Maxi-Medi-Marketing	**Maxi-Medi-Marketing**
Prestige Panacea	
Cosa Nostrums	**Cosa Nostrums**

"By the way, what did you find out about that resume I passed along to you?" Summit impales Will with his piercing blue eyes.

Curse the man's memory! Why couldn't he have forgotten?

"I'm checking him out," assures Will. He meets Summit's gaze without the slightest appearance of flinching...but he does call the waiter over to order another glass of Chablis.

"I'll be interested to know what the story is on him," says Summit. Obviously, he's not going to let the subject of Sam Sage die from neglect. Will realizes that he's probably going to have to show Sam the ISC job. *Too bad, Buddy. Stand by for a ram!*

"Now I hope I'm not throwing you a curve," continues Summit with just a hint of malice gleaming in his eye, "but I've got another candidate I'd like you to check out. His name's Jim Johnson, and he's currently a division head at Daisy Foods."

Will looks up with a surprised expression. Summit has been quite specific about wanting nothing other than a drug background...and now here he is proposing someone from the food industry.

"I know I said I wanted someone with a drug background," says Summit, just as if he'd read Will's thoughts. "I was afraid that someone without plenty of drug experience might take too long to get up to speed, and our situation definitely calls for fast action. But Johnson was recommended very strongly to me by someone I respect, someone who's been on my Board for a number of years. He happened to learn that Johnson has just been passed over for the presidency at Daisy Foods. Apparently, there were several good candidates inside the firm, and another guy just happened to win out.

"I understand that the situation is all very friendly...and in fact Daisy wants to keep Johnson if they can," Summit continues. "But he's quietly looking around to see if he can find something with a more open future. I checked Johnson out with Bill Beane, and Bill was delighted to hear he might be available. He told me, 'He's one of the best guys in the industry...why, he may be the only guy who knows more about marketing food than I do!' So with such good recommendations, I think we owe it to ourselves to take a look at Johnson, even though he does come from the food industry."

Will is relieved to hear that Summit's latest enthusiasm comes from Daisy, a company he happens to know is open to Gordon, Rossi & Boodles. This time he can move quickly, and show Summit that he's perfectly willing to act on client-suggested candidates.

"I'll be happy to check him out," answers Will with real warmth. "With any luck, I can get to him tomorrow." *I wish I'd known Summit would take a food person. It might have made my life a lot easier these last few weeks.*

But in fact Will is perfectly aware that if *he* had approached Summit with this Jim Johnson, or someone like him, Summit would have bridled and reminded Will that he asked for drug background only. When clients are paying, they want their preferences respected. Only they can decide to change the parameters of their search.

But all in all, Will leaves the Yacht Club happy. His five preliminary candidates passed muster, and on top of that, he now has a sixth who comes straight from the client. Four weeks ago, it seemed virtually impossible that Will would be able to find even one decent candidate. Now he has a half-dozen that Summit considers appropriate. And the marvel is that four of them come from top firms in the field, the very ones where Summit wanted him to look...a feat Will never thought he'd achieve.

A Recruiter's Work Is Never Done

Wilma locates Al Umans, ISC's Senior VP - Human Resources, in Seattle at the main plant and warehouse of SomeThinThweet, a $90 million subsidiary that produces low-calorie candy, and gets him on the phone for Will. "Would you believe," says Al, "that this whole big union drive got started in this little shop? How's the Drug Division search coming?" Will gives Al the same optimistic report over the phone that he gave to Mr. Summit.

But Will knows that he still needs to look further for ISC. Although the slate he just presented to Summit is plausible, Will is painfully aware that it's not really quite as good as it looks. Ethan Evans, let's face it, does have a problem making decisions...even though not enough to get him fired during 18 years at BioDynamics. Sherm Summit will almost certainly decide against him during interviews. And if by slim chance he doesn't, Will's final referencing will discourage hiring Evans. *I don't want my long-term relationship with ISC riding on how well they like Ethan Evans three years from now*, thinks Will. Dan Dawson was fired, and Will has seen other clients just as decisive as Summit begin to waver when it comes time to sign up someone a competitor has discarded. Phyllis Finley is a little junior for the position. Only Donna Powers and Charlie Comstock seem problem-free.

Too bad, Will! Charlie Comstock's clay feet are immediately obvious, when he comes in from Phoenix for his interview at GR&B. Charlie talks too much and listens too little. He gives long, rambling answers to Will's carefully phrased questions. And, worse yet, he never includes any facts and figures that might let Will objectively assess Charlie's performance. By the time their hour-long interview is concluded, Will finds himself in real doubt as to whether Charlie actually has contributed anything to Adam Labs' fine growth in sales and profitability. But whatever Charlie might or might not have done at Adam, he's simply too poor a personal communicator to present to a sharp Fortune 1000 CEO like Summit. Not only would Charlie be shredded during the interview, but Will would surely feel the repercussions as well. Sadly, Will strikes Charlie's name from his list of candidates.

While Will is looking for new candidates, other executives are looking for Will. Lanny Lawrence, a marketing executive at CompuMedic, whom Will placed about seven years ago at a different company, phones Will. Since he now works at CompuMedic, he is of course off-limits. Lanny, an extremely ambitious careerist, speaks with a note of petulance in his voice.

"Will, Lanny Lawrence here. I hear you've been calling around for someone to go to ISC as President of their proprietary drug division. Why the hell didn't you call me?"

I hate this kind of conversation. "Lanny, I certainly *did* think of you. But you know that CompuMedic is one of our best clients. I can't take you out."

"But surely you can make an exception for a good friend. I mean, I'm not desperate to leave or anything, but that ISC job is an outstanding opportunity that comes at the perfect point in my career. I could be here another three or four years before I get a shot at a job at that level. Come on...it'll be okay. I'll tell them I was the one who approached you, not vice versa."

Will spends a couple seconds imagining what Mr. Rossi would say if he heard GR&B had gone into CompuMedic, and winces. He's going to have to think fast to head Lanny off. Unfortunately, Lanny's just the aggressive sort of person who would go straight to ISC himself, with or without Will's cooperation.

"Lanny, you know that for you I might try to find a way to get around the rules...if I thought the job was really...well..." He lets his voice trail off.

Lanny is obligingly quick to read a meaning into Will's vague remark. "The only thing that might be wrong with that ISC job is that I've heard through the grapevine that in the last few years they've really cut back the advertising budget for their proprietary drug division. It could be a great job. But if the parent company isn't going to back up the marketing effort, well, that's another story."

"What can I tell you?" answers Will thoughtfully. He pauses to let his lack of reassurance sink in. As the silence grows, Will deliberately represses his memory of Summit's crystal clear explanation of how the problem came about and how it's going to be corrected.

Finally Lanny says decisively, "Well, I wouldn't want to be put out on a limb like that. I mean, to make that division grow and become truly profitable, you've got to have lots of advertising support. Without it, you just can't make things happen. And I can't afford to let a no-win situation like that louse up my career."

Will sighs as he hangs up the phone. His strategy, unhelpful as it may have been to Lanny, has obviously succeeded. He didn't lie. And yet there's little chance that Lanny will try to go directly after the ISC job.

But Will still needs to find one or two more really good people who are not off-limits for the ISC search. He goes back to his printouts, back to his notes, back to his sources. And, wonder of wonders, a new name *does* crop up. Roy Ricardo is a highly regarded U.S. marketing executive who's been working for a South American drug firm, heading their proprietary division. Obviously he took the foreign assignment as a stepping-stone career move. Now he's ready to leave Buenos Aires and return to the States, so he's begun getting in touch with his contacts to see what might be available. One of them... the VP - Manufacturing at Better & Best, whom Roy has kept in touch with since they worked together ten years ago...mentioned Roy to Will.

Will is humming to himself as he checks Roy out. His background is comprehensive and his track record is extraordinary. Bilingual, although born, raised, and Princeton-educated in the U.S., Roy had a meteoric rise to Group Product Manager for all pain-relievers, a $760 million business, at Prestige Panacea here in the U.S. by the time he was 30 years old. Then in the hope of getting strong general management experience before age 35, Roy accepted a very lucrative offer to join the Argentinian company as President of a division which he's doubled in size (to $147 million) in just three years. *Wow*, thinks Will, *he'll be gangbusters for ISC!* Optimistically, Will checks out Roy's present employer against his book of client companies that are off-limits at Gordon, Rossi & Boodles. Just as he has surmised, Los Medicamentos is not listed. GR&B has never done business with this South American firm, even though it has a tiny U.S. subsidiary, so it's perfectly okay for Will to recruit its executives.

It's almost as an afterthought that Will asks Wilma to check whether Roy Ricardo belongs to any other GR&B recruiter. So he's stunned by the bad news. It turns out that Roy *is* in the computer, and is currently assigned to Doug Abel, one of Will's colleagues down the long corridor at GR&B. Will is concerned, but he doesn't give up hope. He knows that Doug has no assignment that involves anything in the consumer goods industry, much less proprietary drugs, so he assumes Doug is merely using Roy as a source on something involving South America. He hopes a stroll down the hall will enable him to talk Doug into relinquishing Roy, who's tailor-made for the ISC job.

But Will soon discovers that Doug isn't taking so cooperative a view of the situation. He tells Will that Roy is a prospect for his most urgent search...a corporate Marketing VP for Brute Force, one of America's leading manufacturers of heavy-duty industrial motors.

"Industrial motors! That's insane. Roy Ricardo is a *consumer* marketing guy, who just incidentally happens to be exactly what ISC is looking for. His proprietary drug experience is going to be wasted in industrial motors."

"You know that, Will, and I know that. But the people at Brute Force don't know that. And they're the ones who are paying their money to get their choice. They want someone with a consumer products background to jazz up their marketing approach."

"But surely the poor guy doesn't want to go into industrial motors...and move to Anthracite Valley to do it!"

"You're probably right that he doesn't especially want to go into industrial motors. But he does want to come back to the States, now that his twins will be entering junior high school in the fall. And he'll probably take the first offer he gets, because he can't run a very efficient campaign from Buenos Aires. Brute Force will pay well. And after all, it's probably the only job he's going to know about...at least the only one from GR&B. Will, I'm absolutely going to keep Ricardo. Do you think it's easy to find anyone in any sort of consumer marketing who wants to go into industrial motors? I searched for weeks before I found this guy. And so far he's my only acceptable candidate. I don't want him to know about any other job in the entire universe, and certainly not a presidency in proprietary drugs. No, Roy Ricardo is going to work for Brute Force in Anthracite Valley."

Will can recognize an immovable object when he sees one. Obviously, Doug is not going to give up Roy Ricardo. And to be fair, Will admits that, in Doug's shoes, he'd behave exactly the same way.

Ironically, Will's final candidate for the ISC job comes to him almost effortlessly. He and Buddy are again having a relaxing drink at the Four Seasons when Will begins to recount the Herculean effort of getting together a credible group of candidates on his ISC search.

"The last time we were here," says Buddy, "we talked about Bill and Allan, and you brought up *RITE*Site.com. I told you I got a couple really good candidates just by visiting the site and checking out the database. Now my total's up to eight or ten...about one extra person we didn't know about for each of my searches. It doesn't cost anything to see who's posted their resume. That's totally different from Monster.com and all those other commercial sites. They all charge you. And sorting on *RITE*Site is extremely easy... easier, actually, than on our GR&B system, because *RITE*Site has a different system. You can sort the people by 50 industries and by job categories that fit each different industry. Also, by salary ranges and by geography, etc. If there's nobody there that fits your needs, you'll know *fast!* But if there *is* someone, you've hit the jackpot...especially if we don't already have them in our database.

"If they've chosen to open the R*ites*-Honored Window, you immediately see who they are and they're probably showing you the very same resume they'd send us in a direct mail campaign. Then you just call 'em or e-mail 'em...same as if they were in our own database. If they're only posting an identity-*concealed* resume the whole world can see, it's still quite easy to deal with them. Click, e-mail 'em your job description, and if they like it, they respond. Of course if they aren't interested, they don't respond...and you can't reach them to try to persuade them. Confidentiality is one of the main points of *RITE*Site.

"So with all this trouble you're talking about, didn't you find even one person on *RITE*Site?"

"Buddy, I'm ashamed to say I didn't look. Maybe I was just lazy and was thinking I'd just work off the leads Gloria rounded up from inside the company. But I'll look as soon as I get home tonight. When you click the e-mail to contact someone who's posted an identity-concealed resume that interests you, do you say you're from GR&B?"

"Of course, Will. And I point out that we are one of the *RITES*-Honored search firms. The person I contact can check a pulldown list to see if we are. Also, for a phone number, I always give our switchboard, because that's a number they can also check from a pull-down on the site. Then, when they call and get our receptionist, followed by my assistant or me, they've already built up plenty of reassurance that I'm authentic."

"But remember, Will, we're a *RITES*-Honored firm. Most people choose to use the *RITES*-Honored Option to let us—but not the outside world—know as much about them as possible. They usually show *RITES*-Honored recruiters the very same identity-*revealed* resume they'd send us in a direct mail campaign. If they do that, there's no need to monkey around e-mailing and waiting to see if they respond. For us and other *RITES*-Honored recruiters, their name, street and e-mail addresses, and phone number are right out in plain sight. Just phone 'em...same as if they were in our own database."

Will and Buddy go their separate ways...Will to a leisurely dinner with Karen at a new bistro in their swank upper East Side Manhattan neighborhood. When they get home, Will signs onto the Internet and begins searching *RITE*Site's resumes. One marked *Identity-Concealed* looks especially interesting, because the person who indicates he or she is "Chief of Marketing," describes having "more than doubled dollar volume, market share and profits" in "just the past three years"...for an unidentified current employer and discusses very specifically some excellent accomplishments earlier at Prestige and National Anodyne.

"Well, whoever it is, he or she is not making it easy for me. But if they're as good as they look, I'll do whatever it takes to reach 'em," muses Will. *"I wonder why they didn't take advantage of the RITES-Honored Option?"*

Will identifies himself and GR&B—but not ISC—and includes the position description he supplies to prospective candidates and sources. *Okay,* he thinks. *Let's see if I have the same kind of luck Buddy's been having.*

And he does! Will signs on and checks his personal e-mail first thing in the morning and finds he already has an answer. Hooray! The person, Mark Matthews, has sent Will an outstanding "Sales Representative" resume. Clearly he's qualified. And, equally important, Will checks and finds he's ***not*** on GR&B's central computer. Mark's cover note says, "Please call me at home, not at work."

There's a three-hour time difference, so Will doesn't make his call until after he and Karen have had a lovely evening...dinner out, followed by a wonderful performance at the Metropolitan Opera, where one of the children on stage is a girl who's been Karen's patient since she was an infant. As Will slips the key in the apartment door, he apologetically reveals a familiar agenda. "Not very romantic...being married to a headhunter," says Karen, softly. "Try to keep it brief!" Which Will, being a very focused individual, is easily able to do.

Mark Matthews answers on the first ring. Obviously he's been waiting for Will's call. Mark apologizes for not putting an identity-*revealed* resume on *RITE*Site via the *RITES*-Honored Option, so that respected recruiters like Will can call him directly without going through the secretive identity-concealed-resume-plus-e-mail screening process the rest of the world is subjected to on *RITE*Site.

"I don't want to seem paranoid," says Mark. "But I'm with a third-generation family-owned business, with family members scattered throughout the company. They're nice people and I love working with them. But some of the younger ones are nearly my age and wouldn't mind having my job. So that's why I'm doing only the concealed-identity resume part of *RITE*Site. I respect your profession—especially the top end of it—but you see where I'm coming from."

Will does understand. Moreover, he's delighted to learn that Mark Matthews is the top marketing executive in the relatively small but rapidly growing drug division of the family-owned West Coast conglomerate, and that Mark's achievements are very similar to what ISC hopes to accomplish. Data Drugs is one of the original businesses of this diversified corporation, which is run today by the grandson of its founder. A little over three years ago, Mark Matthews was recruited as Data's VP - Marketing & Sales. Data Drugs had nothing but a couple of old-time small-volume products: a dentifrice for heat- and cold-sensitive teeth recommended by dentists, and an ancient but effective hemorrhoid remedy.

Mark moved decisively into Data's stodgy operation and made some big changes. At his urging, the company took immediate advantage of the newly relaxed FDA regulations to bring out a cough remedy containing a very effective ingredient previously sold by prescription only. He also took the firm's old-fashioned hemorrhoid medication, at the time selling only to a few elderly consumers of longstanding loyalty, and gave it new life with an aggressive advertising campaign that managed to capitalize on the product's long history in a series of television commercials that poked fun at the product, while also selling persuasively and remaining in good taste.

With Mark's help, Data Drugs has tripled sales and quadrupled profits in less than four years. But the company has not rewarded his efforts with commensurate recognition and increased compensation. So he's ready to make a move, and ISC seems like the perfect next step. It would be an astonishing advance in his career, and it would bring him the additional money he's looking for.

Will wonders why, if Mark is as good as he seems to be and if Data Drugs is growing so rapidly, he and Data escaped notice when Gloria's team combed on-line information sources. The answer is that Data Drugs is not only privately owned, it cloaks itself in privacy as a company. Data does not belong to any industry associations, Mark is not allowed to attend or speak at industry meetings, and no financial analysts are following this non-public company. So Mark, being a talented—although an incredibly busy—marketing executive, took a very logical step to market himself by entering into the CCS program on *RITE*Site.

Mark is also an exceedingly energetic and highly motivated person. Will explains that there is some urgency, if Mark wants to be considered, because Will soon has to report to his client on the best people he has found. Immediately Mark offers to fly to New York on Saturday (the very next day) to see Will—getting away during the week would be almost impossible anyway—and gives Will the home phone numbers of three potential references he's sure would be willing to talk to Will on the weekend. Will needs preliminary references, because Mark drew attention to himself...he was not recommended by one of Will's respected industry contacts. Now Will is just as delighted with Mark's enthusiasm, drive, flexibility, and efficiency as he is with his excellent track record.

And Mark in person—although quite young for the success he's achieved—is impressively mature...a logical thinker, a clear and succinct communicator, well dressed and well groomed, and warmly down-to-earth, with an engaging sense of humor.

Mark is an exceptionally attractive candidate. As far as Will is concerned, his slate is now complete.

Will had already done preliminary referencing on all his other candidates. He knows they have the recent job titles, experience, and college degrees they're claiming, and also that current observers consider them competent and morally upright. Moreover, all candidates know they must submit to Will's intensive final referencing prior to actual hiring by Mr. Summit...if and when both he and they are inclined to take that step.

The Final Slate of Candidates

By the end of his search, Will is very pleased. He has seven attractive candidates for Summit. The finalists are:

1. **Ethan Evans**:   a senior executive with BioDynamics, a top-tier firm. Evans merits consideration, no matter what his decision-making problems might be.

2. **Phyllis Finley**:   an impressive young woman on the way up at Maxi-Medi-Marketing, also a top firm. She's definitely a contender, even though her experience is a bit light.

3. **Dan Dawson**:   until recently with Prestige Panacea, a top-tier firm that's one of Mr. Summit's favorites. Even though he's been fired, Dawson definitely gives a good account of himself.

4. **Sam Sage**:   his experience has been mainly with ethical pharmaceuticals rather than proprietary drugs, and he's a leading candidate on Buddy Young's Expodex search. Nonetheless he's become a candidate in whom Summit is interested.

5. **Jim Johnson**:   highly recommended by a Director of ISC and a favorite of Bill Beane, although his background at Daisy Foods is certainly not what Summit originally asked for.

6. **Donna Powers**:   the person at Cosa Nostrums most appropriate for ISC, although more oriented toward field sales management and sales promotion than toward advertising- and image-oriented consumer products marketing.

7. **Mark Matthews**:   last, but not least...Will's latest find and—along with Sage, Powers, and Johnson—one of the most attractive candidates. He's a rapidly rising young marketing superstar who despite being from Data Drugs, a still-small but (thanks to him) explosively growing proprietary drug division, has a brief but proven track record in doing just what Mr. Summit wants accomplished. Sales and earnings of the operation Mark joined three and a half years ago had been flat for seven prior years under the leadership of the family member who's still CEO today. Clearly, it's Mark who's made the difference.

Will allows himself a twinge of pride, as he watches Wilma staple his slightly edited version of each person's resume into its own beige steel-engraved GR&B folio.

Beautiful!, thinks Will. *Some good people, too. Summit's paying $220,000 ...over $30,000 each. He deserves quality and he's getting it.*

The phone rings. Wilma answers, looks up, and announces that Kathryn Keane is calling.

How ironic!, thinks Will. *There's nobody I'd rather show Summit than Kathryn. And with that jerk giving her grief over at Parker Labs, she'd surely love to meet Summit. It could be her once-in-a-lifetime chance not only to get out of Parker, but also to wind up running a proprietary drug company as President...her career goal for all these years. And now she calls!* But Will's delighted with his candidates. So he sinks comfortably into his interviewing chair, instead of returning to his desk, as he picks up the phone.

"We've known each other a long time. May I ask you a favor?" says Kathryn.

"Of course. You've always helped me. I really appreciate your suggestions. Tell me what I can do."

"If I fax you my resume, would you look it over? I updated it in a hurry, and I'd love to have your thoughts, because I'm having dinner tonight with Carl and Cynthia Cato. She's my dearest friend since high school. Her career is in hotel management, and she was running a fabulous place in Singapore, when Carl bought it out. You've heard of him...his father founded Cato-Colossus in Las Vegas, and now Carl's built that into an international chain of resorts and casinos. Well, one thing led to another and now they're married. They have year-old twins and they work together in running the business. Forgive the trivia, Will, but it's why I need the resume.

"Since I called you to say I wanted out of Parker Labs, I've been networking...but only with you and with friends I can trust to keep quiet. Because if the guy I told you about ever found out, he might try to use my looking outside as a reason to get rid of me and not even pay the severance I should get after 17 years over here.

"Well, my first call was to Cynthia, and I used John Lucht's 'ask-for-a-reference-rather-than-a-job' technique. I said 'I'm thinking about leaving Parker Labs ...and maybe even getting into hospitality, as you've suggested so many times. You know me, Cynthia, and what it takes to succeed in the marketing and general management of hotel chains and real estate developments. Would you be a reference for me, if and when there's interest from folks in your field?'

"She said, 'Absolutely! I've always said you'd be a genius at what I do.' You see, Will, I've vacationed—usually at almost no cost—at some of those resorts she's been running all over the world. Every time I left, I handed her my suggestions...on brochures, check-in, decor, menus, room service, special events, tie-ins with local attractions and so on. And always she's said, 'Your bill would have been $5,000 or whatever. But I got more than that in consulting...and for free, because your suite would have been empty.' Well, bottom line, Will, she and Carl are in town, and they want to see me tonight. 'I'm *not* going to be a reference for you,' she said; 'Carl and I are going to offer you a job.'

"Now what they're talking about, as I gather, is for me to head an entirely new venture. It's out near Aspen, where I'd dearly love to be, because I love skiing, horseback riding, and everything about the outdoors. It seems they signed the papers last week to take over an enormous resort being built on an empty mountainside. The place is two-thirds completed, but it ran way over in construction costs, and lost its funding from the banks and insurance companies.

"Carl and Cynthia got it for twelve cents on the dollar. And the main reason is that it's got a terrible marketing problem. That's why they want me. The location is far, far away from any other resort, and nobody's ever heard of where it is at all. They say the skiing will be fabulous. But Aspen is 130 miles away, and the nearest little town is 45.

"Have you got time for all this, Will? I know you're busy."

"Sure Kathryn. I was taking a little break. My next interview is 10 minutes away; I'll relax 'til then."

"Now here's something you don't know about me, Will. My hobby, which I love, is real estate. I've been buying houses, fixing, and reselling them, and I've built up maybe $800,000 in equity that way. So even though I've thoroughly enjoyed raising Parker Labs to #1 in colds and flu brands and almost #1 in headache remedies, I could happily switch to a career in real estate.

"But here's the problem, and why the resume has really got to explain me to Cynthia and Carl. First, I make a lot more money than they may be planning to offer...$590,000, plus options and a car. Cynthia, I know, was only making about $210,000 when she ran that huge hotel in Singapore, although she got a fabulous suite and every conceivable living expense as a freebee within the hotel. The resume has got to show them that I rescued dying brands and built new ones, and made millions and millions of dollars for Parker Labs. My marketing and sales people and I have been eating our competitors' lunch!"

Yes, and I know one you've made very hungry!, thinks Will.

"The second problem is that Carl and Cynthia are probably thinking of me for *VP - Marketing*. I suspect they're *not* thinking of me for President of the whole thing. And that's the only way I'd ever go there. That's the challenge I'd love. Because *everything* needs to be done. Construction has to be finished, and interior design, decorating and landscaping. And what about transportation? Planes, helicopters, buses? Even getting a decent road in there. And should there be a community? Supermarkets, stores, gas stations?

"And the umbrella over everything is *marketing*. What to name it. How to position it. How to target and bring in customers...for vacations, for conferences, for sales of condos and time-shares and on and on. You can see why maybe they wouldn't be willing to bet on a proprietary drug person to do all that. So you see, Will, my resume's got a big job to do. They like me, they respect me, and they want to hire me. But the question is *for what?*"

"Well, Kathryn, fire away. I'll read your fax as soon as it's here." Will phones his stockbroker. When he looks up, Wilma hands him Kathryn's resume.

Wow! She's even better than I realized. Fabulous accomplishments. And all in proprietary drugs...exactly what Summit wants. I only wish I could show her to him. And look at this resume. She's got to be smart! It's so clear and brief. Four concise pages, based mainly on numbers, not self-praising adjectives. Easy to scan. Inviting use of white space. Nothing stated that's obvious. And no jargon. No need to know proprietary drugs, or even consumer products, to see that she's made money *for Parker Labs. In fact,* thinks Will, *this paperwork is just as strong as Sam Sage's* [pp. 210-17]. *And that's saying a lot, because Sam's resume got action from Summit...and it's one of the best* I've ever read.

So Will phones Kathryn and tells her the resume is exceptional. Her friends can't fail to see that her work at Parker Labs—although different—is fully equivalent to what a President will have to do to finish building their resort and make it successful. Sadly, Will still can't tell her that he's filling a job she might like even better.

Will quickly forgets Kathryn, as he devours tomato soup and a tuna-melt at his desk, while perusing a stack of re-typed resumes Wilma has put there for his approval before stapling them into GR&B's chic folders. Will handles about six searches simultaneously, so he can't waste time on lunch dates. Only when an important client or potential candidate is involved does Will go out.

At four o'clock Will is sorting through files allocated to him for a CFO search, when Wilma taps him on the shoulder. Kathryn's on the phone.

"Hi Kathryn. How'd it go?"

"So well, Will, that it's almost scary. They both read the resume right at the table. We had a great talk. And just as we were about to leave Carl pulled out an envelope, scribbled something on the paper and passed it to Cynthia. She nodded and passed it to me. It was an offer letter. And best of all, VP of Marketing was crossed out; President was written over it. Unfortunately, money was only $240,000. But they said they want to know exactly what I'm making, so they can try to create something I'll find financially attractive. Oh, and one more thing. With the letter was a floor plan of the former owner's intended penthouse apartment, with acres of space, walls of glass, fireplaces, and a huge terrace with a heated pool. I'll be *required* to live there if I take the job.

"So I'm flying out this weekend to look the place over. If it's anything like they've presented it, and if I can push up the money, I may be off to Colorado and an exciting new challenge. But Will, could I trouble you for another favor? If I fax it, would you take a look at the letter? See whether you think it would give me adequate protection, if they up the money and I go ahead?"

"Sure Kathryn. Fax it. I'll let you know what I think."

Even before he hangs up the phone, a plan is forming in Will's mind. *I'll take that letter over to Hamilton Rossi. Sure he's tight with Charley Phipps, the Chairman of Parker Labs. And ordinarily he'd have a fit if I pitched Kathryn on Summit's job. But now if we recruited her, there'd be written proof that she was leaving anyway. It wouldn't just be our word and hers that she was determined to go. Don't know if he'll buy it. But it's worth a try.*

Moments later, fax in hand, Will is in Hamilton Rossi's corner suite. "You young turks think you can bend the rules whenever it suits your purpose," says Rossi. "That's why Red" [Tapecutter] "and I are always keeping our eyes peeled. Because every time GR&B gets caught raiding one of our clients, there are always plenty of other firms that have been begging for their business for months—maybe years—who'll say, *'We would never do that!'* Whether they would or not doesn't matter. They've never *had* any business from our client. So at that moment they're saintly pure, and we're prostitutes. I don't want anyone in this firm *ever* to put me in that position!

"But with that said, Will, I think in this instance I *can* be a little flexible. Ordinarily, for us to be in the clear, you'd have had to get this woman to inform someone above her that she was actively looking. She could have lied. And, we could have accepted her word. We wouldn't have had to challenge her honesty by calling the person...although sometimes I've done that when I was suspicious and the client was important.

"But here's this offer letter in black-and-white on Cato World Corp. stationery. Leave this copy with me. I'll deal with Charley Phipps, if your woman winds up getting the job and he finds out we were involved. Have you got other candidates? She may *not* be the one they hire. Anyway, go ahead. Show Summit there's no other search firm even half as good as GR&B!"

Will's elated. He immediately calls Kathryn and asks if she'd like to have a shot at becoming President of a $640 million proprietary drug company with a strong commitment to fund aggressive marketing programs and maybe even to make acquisitions...a company determined to move rapidly into the top ten in the field.

"Would I! Is the Pope Catholic? You have my resume. Get it over there right away!"

Will explains that he'll be presenting several candidates to Summit on Friday ...Kathryn among them. And she reconfirms her intent to fly out to Colorado over the weekend. "Frankly, Will, I have no idea which I'd choose, if I had tempting offers from both. My whole career has been aimed at running my own company in proprietary drugs, toiletries, cosmetics, or some other consumer product. And yet I love real estate, the outdoors, and the mountains. For months I've been down in the dumps. Now I'm on a 'Rocky Mountain High!' Will, you're a good friend. Thank you for your help."

Will *is* a good friend. But notice that throughout all this, he's had to follow his interests, the firm's interests, his client's interests and—except for commenting on her resume and offer letter—*not* Kathryn's. Nice as he is, Will's in business, not social work.

Is Eight Enough?

Will's absolutely thrilled to be headed out to see Mr. Summit with presentations on no less than eight attractive candidates in his sleek Dunhill attache. The last time he was in Summit's office Will wondered how he could ever fulfill the Chairman's high expectations. Now he's introducing not one but eight attractive candidates. Three are from companies strictly off-limits to Will. And he's done this without breaking any of GR&B's ethical client-protection rules. Notice again the first seven beginning on page 546. And now...

8. **Kathryn Keane**: Frosting on the cake. Will already had several candidates of the exceptional calibre a demanding client like Summit pays $220,000 to meet, plus lesser but still impressive ones. Now he can also present the #1 most appropriate candidate from Parker Labs, one of Summit's preferred "source" companies. Two days ago Will could only have muttered vague excuses if asked whether he succeeded in penetrating this "prime-target" company. Today, despite Parker's being off-limits, Will can answer, "Yes; we've got the very best person in their organization for your needs."

"Client meetings *always* go well, when you're superbly prepared," jokes Will in response to Buddy's "How'd it go?" as they both step into the elevator at 8:15 the next morning. Indeed, Will's fine work *was* favorably received by Mr. Summit. "Interesting people," he told Will. I'm going to interview every one of them. I can see why Bill Beane felt we should go back and use you again."

A modest "Thank you" was Will's only reply. But he was moved by the warmth and respect in the Chairman's voice. *Demanding, but appreciative! No wonder Bill Beane enjoys working for him.*

Bill Beane wasn't present, so Will left Bill's set of presentations with Summit's secretary, who promised to pass them along. And while Will was in Lustretown with Summit, Wilma tracked down Al Umans, ISC's Senior VP - Human Resources, at ISC's huge distribution center in Denver. He'll get an identical set by FedEx.

Will *was* surprised—and also delighted—by Summit's decision to meet all eight. The wily Chairman likes to interview outsiders as a "due diligence" check on the quality and thinking of his own people. Having spent $220,000 to have Will identify and evaluate outsiders, Summit opens his door to them. Afterward, he'll be sure he's chosen the best Will could find. And he'll have learned a lot more from these outsiders than if he'd spent equal time with his own employees.

Actually, Will's eight candidates are a very large slate. Four to six would have been Will's usual number. However, Johnson *came* from Summit. Retainer recruiters welcome client-supplied candidates and treat them impartially, but never want them to be the only—or almost the only—attractive choice. So recruiters don't reduce the number of their candidates merely to include client ones.

Kathryn Keane is the second "extra" within the eight. She was a lucky last-minute accident. Will had assumed her to be hopelessly off-limits.

Winding up with *six rather than just four*, however, *wasn't* an accident. Will had never submitted candidates to Summit before. And from experience he knew that people as strong—and therefore as potentially opinionated—as Summit may habitually reject most of anything presented to them. They think, "Whatever anyone brings me can't possibly be as good as if I send them back to look for more."

Having observed Will's struggle to develop his slate, we know how damaging it would have been if Will had presented only his top three or four candidates and Summit had thrown out some of those rarities. That's why smart retainer recruiters like Will never present just their top few. With his slate of six (expanded by accident to eight),

Will was prepared to lose two or three, while still keeping his favorites alive for final interviewing and selection.

You caught the word! Will does have *favorites*. His criteria: (1) Who can do the job so well that the client will return to Will for more people. (2) Whose personality and behavior will fit the organization so well that the client will return to Will for more people, and (3) Who seems to *like* Will enough to come back to him and not go to a different recruiter for more people. The factors are ranked in order of importance. None is unimportant.

Notice, too, that Will has chosen to do "Slate" type recruiting. He's looking over an entire industry and helping his client pick the *one best person* (certainly that's been Summit's goal). When a search is for president, general manager, or a head-of-function, such as marketing or R&D, then recruiting the industry's very best person can often move the business from "also ran" to #1. After all, *some* company has to be #1...and that's what leaders are hired to accomplish! Notice too, that there's a twofold change in the industry's balance-of-power when you grab its #1 best person away from your competitor: (1) You're strengthened. (2) The previously-strongest company is weakened.

Whenever a company wants to move ahead competitively by getting the best players at every position, "Slate" type recruiting is the only choice: Examine *all* the key people in the field; interview the top few; and hire #1 among those.

There is, however, a prevalent alternative to "Slate" recruiting. It has several names: "Sequential," "Process," and "Beauty Parade" are all apt. But I prefer to call it "Dope-a-Week" recruiting. The goal is *not* to get the very best person and change the competitive balance-of-power. But rather, to assure the client that continual activity is going on and he or she is shaping it.

Under "Sequential" or "Dope-a-Week" recruiting, the client is sent one plausible candidate after another—ideally about one per week—until he or she has "looked at enough people to make a decision" or at least has become sufficiently bored or fatigued to allow the Wheel of Fortune to...COME......TO......... A............STOP (read decision). Which is not to say a fine result is never obtained that way. But merely to point out that the method is designed to manipulate the client and smooth out time-demands on the recruiter, who conducts lots of searches simultaneously and can feed most of them from the long-grey-line of candidates in the firm's 200,000- to 400,000-person computerized database. Indeed one of America's largest and finest firms used to (and perhaps still does) tout the superiority of its services by promising potential clients, *"We guarantee that you'll see your first candidate within a week."* And presumably another the week after that. You can, of course, stop whenever you wish.

While Will certainly didn't anticipate the Chairman's decision to interview all eight candidates, he's not in the least unnerved by it. Each is appropriate and several are outstanding. Ordinarily Bill Beane, as Group Executive to whom the new Drug Division President will report, would screen the slate and present one or two to Summit for final endorsement. But Will's just as happy with the opposite scenario. Probably, as Summit has implied, Beane is the busier of the two. And, as Summit told Will, "This way we don't waste Bill's time on anyone we're not really interested in." *Nor mine,* thinks Will, since Beane is unlikely to want to resurrect anyone Summit rejects, nor to reject *all* the people Summit likes.

Will's presentations contain candidate phone numbers, and only Summit's secretary knows his availability. So it's agreed that she'll set up the interview appointments. Will phones the candidates to alert them to her call, and to remind them to let him know in advance the date of their interview and to phone him immediately afterward to debrief.

Down to the Wire

Summit's first decision is to rule out Ethan Evans.

"You know," he says to Will in a follow-up phone call, "I suspect this guy was kicked upstairs. He definitely lacks the fire in the belly you want to see in a division head. Corporate staff seems like the best place for him. He's the kind of guy who can tell you the pros and cons of every situation, but I don't think he can go on and make a decision about which risk to take."

"That's very perceptive," responds Will tactfully. "I've heard some things along those same lines, which I would have wanted you to consider if you were interested in going forward with him."

"No, I don't think he's right for us. I liked him personally, and I could see him as a staff analyst or a consultant; certainly he knows the industry. But I don't think he'll deliver in the crunch."

Summit signs off, letting Will know that he's seeing Sam Sage tomorrow afternoon. Twenty minutes later, however, Mr. S calls back.

"Sage just called and canceled his appointment! Seems he just this morning signed the papers to do a leveraged buyout of the Accura Flavors & Fragrances Division of Medica Suisse. Accura is an 80-year-old company...$96 million...in New Jersey. They'd fallen way behind their competitors by the time the Swiss bought them four years ago, and things haven't improved since. Just scraping along...not losing money, but not making anything much either.

"Sage says he's always wanted to own a company," Summit continues, "and this may be the only chance he'll ever get. Sounds like a very fine fellow. If I were his age again, and had a chance to go it alone, I'd do the same damn thing. Anyway, I wanted you to know. I've re-read your paperwork on all these people and Sage looked like one of the very best. I'm sorry to lose him."

Wow! I knew Sam was working on some deals, thinks Will, *but I never imagined he'd get one to happen. This is bad news for me. But it'll hit Buddy like a ton of bricks. Sam was his front-runner on Expodex. Hope Buddy's finally got some depth on that search...*

Three days later, Summit calls with another status report. Phyllis Finley has also fallen by the wayside. Just as Will suspected, Summit finds her experience a bit too light. "In a few more years, she'd be right for us...or we'd take her today in another position. But for the presidency right now I have to pass.

"Actually, Will, I intend to tell a few folks over here about her. She's just our type... energetic, optimistic, creative...very intelligent and analytical. Also, I suspect, *very* strong and assertive. And with the nicest possible way about her. Somebody, I suspect, who'd get things done without ruffling too many feathers. She's exactly the sort of person we should be grooming for the future.

"Which gives me one idea how we might eventually bring her over here. Bill Beane and Graham Rusk are thinking of splitting off some of their Foods Division product managers and field sales people into a separate unit to handle just their spices, condiments, and herbal teas...giving those products a separate image as high quality almost gourmet items, and raising their prices and margins. I don't know if they have anyone in mind to head that, but I think someone like Phyllis would be superb. And I'm sure she'd like them and they'd like her."

Wow! thinks Will. *Could be a by-product! And the fee'd be over $100,000, maybe as much as $130,000. Am I glad I presented her even though I knew she was light, just so she could be shot down instead of one of my top candidates...if Summit had been in a shooting mood. And now I might make an extra bundle!* There's nothing a retainer recruiter likes better than placing two people from a single search. The second fee is pure profit. And yet it's perfectly proper. Contingency recruiters get paid for each placement; so do retainer recruiters.

Will makes suitable noises, and Summit continues without responding.

"I especially like Kathryn Keane and Mark Matthews. Her personality is as fine as Phyllis.' She's from Parker Labs, a company we prefer. And she's done it all. Every bit of experience we could possibly want she's had.   Also, I love the entrepreneurial spirit she's shown in her private life. Did you know she's made several hundred thousand dollars buying, remodeling and selling houses?

"Now young Matthews isn't as advanced as Kathryn Keane and, until he got there, who'd ever heard of Data Drugs? But he has done *exactly* what we want. You had to turn over a stone to find him, Will," says Summit approvingly. "And I think he's pretty interesting. I'm having Lucy" [Summit's assistant] "bring back Dawson, Powers, Johnson, Keane, and Matthews. This time they'll talk to Bill Beane. If it were my call, I'd have cut two or three more. But I want Bill to feel he's fully in on this decision."

You've got the makings of an executive recruiter, Mr. Chairman, thinks Will; *How'd you like less pay and harder work?* Happily, Will turns to the other five searches he's conducting. *Tough as it was to begin with, the ISC search is now a piece of cake!*

A week passes. All of the candidates contact Will or he calls them. All enjoyed meeting Summit and wish to go further. The one unnerving call is from Kathryn Keane. "I really like Mr. Summit," she says. "He was so charming and informal...and so genuinely interested in what I've done. It was almost more him selling me than me selling him. However, I must tell you, Will, my trip to Denver was even better than I expected. They've got the most beautiful mountainside...easily a match for Aspen or Vail. And we—I should say they—own 30,000 acres, dominating the slopes *and* the access road for nearly 25 miles. We can do whatever we want! And the physical plant is awesome...500 hotel rooms, plus 150 one- and two-bedroom condos."

I don't like that 'we' pronoun one bit, thinks Will, as Kathryn drones on enthusiastically. *If she might drop out, I wish she'd do it now, before Summit and Beane get to thinking that she's the best.* Will has had other clients initially praise his entire slate and later send him out for a whole new group, after their clear-cut favorite slipped away. He considers steering Kathryn into a frank discussion. *But there's danger in that too*, he decides, so he merely exchanges pleasantries and signs off.

On a happier note, Will also hears from Al Umans, ISC's Senior VP of HR, who's now at ISC's West Coast headquarters in L.A. Al reports that "Summit is very pleased with the search so far. He's enjoying meeting those attractive people you've sent him. Of course, you'd have been mud, Will, if any of them had been a dope. As it is, you're riding high. You may even place that Finley woman, in addition to the person we're searching for. The Chairman liked her a lot."

Will's call to Bill Beane offering to discuss the candidates prior to Bill's meeting them goes very well indeed. Beane has read Will's presentations and, of course, already knows and feels enthusiastic about Jim Johnson. "The others sound good too, especially Keanc and Matthews."

Within a week, Will hears from Summit again. "At this point we've eliminated Dan Dawson, although he seems competent. We found him a little rigid...perhaps a bit too insistent on doing things precisely his way. He might not be the team player we need. Frankly, Bill and I could have warmed more to Dawson, if there weren't others we like especially well in terms of personal characteristics. Maybe I shouldn't say *we*, because they haven't yet been in to see Bill. It's just that he and I—quite fortunately—tend to like the same types. And, I guess the converse is true; we tend not to like the same traits in people.

"And on that basis, there's another person that just isn't quite on our wavelength, even though she's also a very fine person. That's Donna Powers. She seems a bit like Dawson, a little rigid, maybe a little autocratic—I have no way of knowing that; I just suspect it. But what really turned me off in her interview was that she seemed very territorial. She clearly didn't like other people encroaching on her turf. I can't imagine her cheerfully letting me carry the ball on this search for someone reporting to her, as Bill's been perfectly happy to do.

"I'm proud to say that we're a very collegial organization over here. I like to walk into any office and ask any question of anyone at any time. There's no standing on ceremony. Donna mentioned a couple times that she wasn't happy when their CEO happened to walk into one of her regional sales offices and start asking questions and making suggestions without clearing them with her first. Well, she certainly has a point. And in theory, at least, she's absolutely right. But the behavior she described is what, unfortunately, I often do. So I suspect she wouldn't be happy here and we wouldn't be happy with her. And with three people remaining who're the sort we like so well, why bother with her?

"Which brings us to our best three finalists in my opinion. Jim Johnson, whom Bill has known a long time and likes a lot. I do too. His personality would definitely fit in. However, if we have people just as good to work with, who come straight out of proprietary drugs and have equally impressive track records, I'll go with them over Johnson.

"And Will, my boy, we do." *Now it's **my boy**, thinks Will. You can't beat that!* "We've got Kathryn Keane and Mark Matthews. I think they're clearly ahead of the others. Frankly, Will, my money's on Kathryn. As I told you, ISC has eight divisions and not one has a woman President. And she's far more experienced than Mark is.

Well maybe, thinks Will, *but Kathryn may be slipping away. Everything may hinge on what's in the offer letter that will arrive by FedEx tomorrow morning. I sure as hell hope it's nothing amazing!*

Summit winds up jovially. *That's a mood I've never seen before, although Bill Beane has described it.* "Bill and Al Umans are seeing Kathryn tomorrow morning and Mark tomorrow afternoon. Then Bill and I are having dinner tomorrow night. Who knows, we may have our new Division President by the time we get to coffee and dessert."

Will's cheerful goodbye matches the Chairman's buoyant humor. But Will's visibly shaken. Wilma asks what's wrong?

"Five minutes ago I had five great candidates on the ISC search. Now I've got no more than two. Summit has dumped Powers and Dawson, thinking he can have his choice of Keane or Matthews. Johnson he says he also likes on a personal basis, but he prefers Kathryn's and Mark's proprietary drug backgrounds. Actually he as much as said Keane is his choice.

"But *I* know that Kathryn's waiting for an offer letter from that real estate thing out in Denver. Ironically, it will arrive at her apartment tomorrow by FedEx, precisely while she's out at ISC with Bill Beane and Al Umans. So she may be convincing Bill to want her—Summit already does—at the same time she's getting another offer she can't and won't refuse. Damn it, Wilma, I've known I might lose her ever since our last phone conversation. Whenever she mentioned that blasted resort it was **our** 30,000 acres and **our** 500 rooms. That's not a good sign!

"Fortunately Summit also likes Matthews. But it's one thing to like him as a runner-up, and entirely different to accept him as #1, after losing the #1 he really wants. Besides, Bill has never met either Kathryn or Mark. It would be just my luck for him to fall for Kathryn, hate Mark, and then not be able to convince Summit to hire Johnson, whom Bill likes a lot. Then I can just hear them both coming back to me and saying, 'Look, we can't agree on either Mark Matthews or Jim Johnson. So why don't you just go back into the marketplace and see if there's anyone we can both get excited about.'"

"Oh come on," says Wilma. "You're figuring everything that can go wrong will go wrong. Don't torture yourself. It probably won't go that way at all."

By 5:30 Will's so concerned that he grabs his coat, goes down in the elevator, whooshes through the revolving door, and *walks* the 36 blocks up Park Avenue to his condo and the one person who'll help him ignore his black thoughts. The apartment is dark. Not a good sign. There's a note for Will on the demilune in the foyer. "Will, don't wait up. The Shelby child has been transferred to intensive care, and what I'm hearing doesn't sound at all good. I'll do my best. Love you!"

"Damn!" says Will out loud, as he scrounges through an empty fridge and finally grabs a can of Campbell's bean soup from the shelf over the broom closet. Without bothering to "add water and heat," he devours the cold, solid mass. When Karen comes in at 2:00 a.m. Will's asleep in a chair. "Happy dreams, Mr. Headhunter," she says as she wearily covers him with an afghan and proceeds to the master bedroom suite alone.

The next morning in the office Will tries to concentrate on his other searches, but time moves slowly. His mind keeps returning to ISC. *I'll bet Kathryn is wowing Bill Beane. Of course she should if she wants the job. But does she?* And later: *Kathryn's probably on her way back to Manhattan. Probably Bill, Al, or even the Chairman took her to lunch, trying to sell her on ISC. Now it's Mark Matthews' turn. I hope he gives the performance of his life. He'll have to, to replace Kathryn, if she's persuaded them and then she walks away.*

Will's nervous reverie is interrupted by a flurry of call-backs on messages he's left with various "sources" (people who might identify others) and "prospects" (potential candidates). At 4:00 o'clock the receptionist buzzes. Kathryn Keane doesn't want to interrupt...but would like to see Will, if he happens to be free. Otherwise she'll drop off an envelope for him. Wilma suggests coffee as she ushers Kathryn in, and is soon back with two steaming cups.

"Look at this," says Kathryn, handing Will a FedEx envelope. He reaches inside and pulls out a letter just like the one Kathryn faxed him earlier, except that the salary figure has been raised from $240,000 to $450,000.

Fantastic! thinks Will. *Summit's expecting to pay $660,000. And for Kathryn I'll bet he'll easily go $700,000, plus ISC's Stock Option and Stock Grant Plans. Also, ISC has a great comp expert, who'll chart out how all the parts of their program kick in at various times in the next few years to produce really big money. The Denver outfit probably doesn't have anyone like that. We'll not only pay more, but it's going to be very evident that we're offering a lot more.*

But there's something else deeper down in the cardboard envelope. "What's this?" asks Will.

"What does it say on the front?"

"Deed."

"Well, Will, that's what it is. A deed for the condo I'll be *required* to occupy if I go there. Remember? It's the place the original developer planned to live in himself. Here's the floor plan. Living room thirty by forty, formal dining room, library, three bedrooms, two more bedrooms and a bath for the help, a huge slate terrace with a small heated pool maybe twenty-by-twenty—and *three* fireplaces. Will, when we make the resort successful, that condo is worth at least six million dollars...maybe more. And after five years, I'll own it free and clear. I get 20% ownership at the end of each year with the company...even if I should go to work in another of their resorts. And while I'm there, they pay all the expenses of the condo. Of course I'll be using it to entertain celebrities. In fact that's part of my marketing strategy...to get big names and trendsetters to leave Aspen and Vail and come with us."

"What about the career in consumer products you've worked so hard to build?" asks Will. "I want to hear about your interviews today. But even before we discuss them, let me say that I'm almost positive you're about to get the opportunity you've always dreamed about. If you play your cards right, you can be President of ISC's Proprietary Drug Division. But your mind's made up, isn't it?"

"It is, Will. I wish it weren't. And Will, I so hate to let down Bill Beane and Sherm Summit. They're brilliant business people. And so nice...both of them. If I were already with them, I'd never have started working my personal contacts and asked Cynthia and Carl for a reference rather than a job."

"What did you tell them?"

"Carl and Cynthia?"

"No Sherm Summit and Bill Beane."

"Nothing, really. We just had a great meeting. Further steps were left up in the air. Bill Beane said he had another person to see this afternoon. So they still haven't made up *their* minds. But I must say, Bill asked me to come back and see him after my meeting with Al Umans, and he then took me in to see Sherm again, and the three of us had lunch in Sherm's dining room."

Will Pickham is too professional—and indeed too decent and sensible—to try high-pressuring Kathryn at this point. Instead, he says, "Why not just sleep on it tonight. I'll find out how things went for you and the other candidate, and get an idea of what they're about to offer you. Then you can make a final decision with a clear head...and with all the facts on the table."

"Thanks, Will. I really feel you want the best for me. And that's amazing, coming from a headhunter. Most are like used car salesmen. You're *so* different."

Will walks Kathryn to the elevator. He stops in the men's room on the way back to his office. Alone, he slams his fist on the red granite sink-counter and lets out a four-letter word...passionately enough to vent his feelings, but quietly enough not to be heard beyond the double mahogany doors.

"You look awful," says Wilma, when Will returns.

"Of course. Everything's going just as I told you yesterday. She's turning the job down, after they've decided she's perfect and nobody else will do. Now they'll throw out Mark Matthews—whom Summit *loved* only yesterday—and ask me to start all over again!"

"What do they think of Matthews?" asks Wilma, practical as always.

"Oh you're right, Wilma. Things could still be okay if they like him better than her," says Will. *Fat chance! It's easy for you to stay cool. You go home at 5:30. You don't give a thought to this craziness 'til morning...and never on weekends. Meanwhile I'm working lots of evenings and Saturdays and Sundays, on the phone or travelling...* Abruptly Will pulls out of his self-indulgent mood. *So what's the worst that can happen? I have to start over. Big deal! I wonder if the Shelby boy lived or died. Other folks have problems bigger than yours, Will Pickham!*

From Will's introspection comes a plan of action: *I'll call Bill Beane at home tonight. I'll never influence what he and the Chairman decide if I don't act fast.* So after Will and Karen enjoy a dinner of Chinese take-out Will brings home, he's on the phone.

"Bill Beane," says Bill, picking up in his den, where he's peering at his computer screen, manipulating models of his businesses according to various acquisition, divestiture, and investment scenarios.

"Bill, it's Will Pickham. How did things go with Kathryn Keane and Mark Matthews today?"

"Great. I hadn't met either of them, although the Chairman had told me about them. I liked them both. As you probably know, Sherm prefers Kathryn. Certainly she's the more advanced of the two. She's headed all marketing and sales for a much larger company, Parker Labs. And she's done a great job. Also her personality is terrific. She has real leadership ability. I happen to know their Southeastern Regional Sales Manager, who worked for me years ago. And he says she met a lot of resistance and prejudice among the old timers in the field and she overcame it beautifully. Now she's firmly in charge all up and down their marketing and sales organization, and she's very well respected.

"Will, Kathryn's the Chairman's choice walking away. But I'll tell you something, absolutely in confidence. I don't like her as well as Mark for our purposes. For this reason..."

*Thank God! Who cares why you don't like her as well. What I desperately need right now is just for you **not** to. With you favoring Mark, I may have a shot at holding this search together!*

"...and this reason only," continues Bill: "Kathryn has always worked in large companies with exceptionally fine resources. First at Pan-Global Advertising agency...one of the world's largest and richest, where she was on the Parker Labs account. Then she was invited over to Parker, America's third-largest proprietary drug company. They've got more budget, and more people than just about any other company in the field. So whenever Kathryn wants something done, she's got hordes of good people to carry out her directions.

"But our situation is nothing like that. We have *very few* people and limited resources. And the crew we have isn't particularly good, because nobody like Kathryn has been picking and pruning them over the years.

"Our situation, on the other hand, is precisely what Mark has had to deal with his whole career. He started out in his dad's local direct mail agency, just a letter shop really, which closed up while Mark was still in Business School. Then he worked for that little ad agency in Detroit. And now he's burning up product category after product category at Data Drugs, that small family-owned outfit on the West Coast. At Data he's only had shoestring money, a local ad agency, and a staff chosen mainly by nepotism; I gather every aunt, uncle, and cousin's on the payroll. Besides—and I feel this is *also* major—he's been selling strictly through brokers. That's how we sell. He doesn't have the huge direct sales force Parker Labs has. So the way I see it, Mark has personally had to be the creative dynamo powering his businesses, whereas Kathryn has merely been doing a very good job in very professional organizations. They're both very good. But, I'd pick Mark."

"That's very insightful," says Will. *Of course Kathryn has loads of independent creativity,* thinks Will. *I know that and the Catos know that. That's why they're so eager to get her. And brokers / schmokers, she can cope with any selling force. But there's no point in contradicting Bill, just to set the record straight. The objective isn't to make ISC appreciate someone they can't get, but rather to make them* want *the person they* can *get.*

Will winds up the call by further complimenting Bill Beane's analysis.

Will's at his desk at GR&B by 8:15 in the morning. No one else answers, so he picks up when his direct line buzzes. It's Sherm Summit. "Will, a quick word on yesterday, when we had our two favorites back here, Kathryn Keane and Mark Matthews. Things went very well. Kathryn is *such* an exciting talent. You've done a fine job in bringing us the head of all sales and marketing for Parker Labs, one of the top three companies. And that Matthews is a promising lad. Bill and I had a great lunch with Kathryn yesterday. We'd have offered her the job then, but Bill hadn't yet met young Matthews. He came in the afternoon."

"What did Bill think of Matthews?" asks Will offhandedly, trying to focus Summit on what he'll hear from Bill Beane.

"Actually, Will, I haven't had a chance to compare notes with Bill. He had a dental appointment at 5:30."

"Bill and I spoke on the phone last night," says Will. "I think he shares your liking for both candidates. And he has some very interesting further observations. But you should hear them from him."

"Fine. I'll be seeing Bill in a little while on another matter. We'll talk then. I mostly called you, Will, just to thank you for your good work and the fine way this search is turning out."

"Thank you Sherm. It's a pleasure to be working for you." *Well, aren't we getting chummy! That's the first time I've felt I could call him Sherm, as Bill does. Hope Bill can swing the Chairman over to Mark. That'll be a lot easier, if Summit stays in this mood and still thinks he's got a choice. We can always get down to Mark as the last-fish-in-the-barrel. That's more scary. Let's see if I can play out this hand with finesse!*

It's 9:00 on the nose, when Wilma, taking off her coat, sticks her head in Will's office and announces that Donna Powers is on the phone. "Just a quick 'What's-going-on?' call, Will. Haven't heard anything from you since our talk the day after I was over to see Summit at ISC. He said they'd be having second-round interviews in a couple weeks. Anything further on that?"

"Donna, I'm sorry, I probably should have called you to say 'Not yet' for the second round. Sherm Summit liked you—and about four other candidates— very much. The only problem has been to get on Bill Beane's calendar. We nailed a couple appointments...and that was it. And at least one of those <u>people</u>..." *I can't say 'her' or 'him' and maintain secrecy in such a small industry,* thinks Will "...will probably turn down the ISC job. So really we've got a long way to go. I hope to have more to report by the end of next week, or at least the following week. So I'll be calling you soon. How's business? Some of my clients in other fields are seeing an upsurge. But I suppose pain relievers and deodorants aren't as much affected by the ups-and-downs of the general economy."

"No, Will. People get headaches and sweat in good times and bad," says Donna, "I'll look forward to your call. Thanks. Bye now." *Well I got through that one all right,* thinks Will. *I knew that little shot of banal at the end would cut off the conversation before we got into the specifics I didn't want to talk about.*

There's no point in killing her enthusiasm; we may have to come back to her, muses Will. When he looks up, Wilma's handing him printouts on another of his searches. It's their first encounter of the day, and Will begins by sincerely complimenting her on having stressed a far more optimistic scenario for the ISC search than the sour one he blurted out yesterday afternoon.

"Will, I've known you now nearly three years. Things seldom turn out as badly as you foresee them. So lots of times you torture yourself needlessly. But that same ability to see disaster a mile off enables you to take steps to prevent it. And no matter what goes wrong, or how depressed or disgusted you get, you hang in there looking for new solutions. In my opinion, that's what makes you so successful."

"Wilma, *you're* one of the reasons I'm successful. Thank you." *Amazing how close we are*, thinks Will.

"Now, Wilma, let's cut this mutual admiration. If you can, please get Dan Dawson on the phone. I don't think I've got a prayer of shoehorning him into ISC. But if Summit gets frustrated by Kathryn's turn-down and hesitates to fall back on Mark, he may at least be willing to bring Donna and Dan in to meet Bill. Which may be enough to remind him he's had a tremendous search and let him settle on Mark. Thank heaven, Bill *prefers* Mark! In any event, I don't think I can possibly go back into the marketplace and get anyone better than Mark, Donna, or Dan...at least not without tearing up our off-limits rules. Remember, I've still got Doris DeWitt going full blast out there on the Coast. I have to keep everyone I've got as interested as possible.

The morning passes. So does the afternoon. *So far so good*, thinks Will. *Maybe I'll luck out. Right about now Bill should be talking to Sherm, telling him why he prefers Mark to Kathryn. Bill's got a reasonable argument. And besides the job reports to Bill. He ought to be able to have whomever he wants!*

It's 6:15 and Will is just outside his office door when his direct line buzzes. Wilma's gone. He answers. "Hi Will, this is Mark Matthews. Sorry to be late getting back to you, but I've been tied up all day. In a small family-owned firm like this, being mysteriously gone as I was yesterday is noticed. So I plunged in busy as hell today, showing myself to absolutely everyone. But luckily I've got you before you leave the office. Just wanted you to know that things went fabulously well yesterday with Bill Beane and Sherm Summit. Bill especially. And Bill'd be my boss. He and I see eye to eye on everything. Believe it or not we even have daughters with the same first name. How's that for being on the same wavelength?

"Sherm was friendly, but I had very little time with him. I spent nearly four hours with Bill. He even drove me to the airport, where I caught my plane with just minutes to spare. I never saw anyone so warm and open as Bill. He flat out said that unless Summit objects—which I see no indication of—I'm his choice for the job. We even talked money. Bill said he was sure he could get me at least $520,000, plus options and benefits, maybe more.

Smart! Bill, thinks Will. *You remembered what I taught you when we recruited Graham. Say "X-minus-10%...**maybe-more.**" Test 'em with something just a little under where you intend to wind up. That launches a trial balloon, and still keeps room to maneuver. If disappointment is written all over their face, you can immediately go to* *your full amount. And having said "maybe more," you can deal with a counteroffer if there is one without seeming to knuckle under, merely by presenting your "actual offer." If there's no further hitch, you can throw in the last bit of money at the end without being pushed for it. That delights the employee, and sparks immediate personal loyalty to you as their new boss. Good work, Bill!*

All in all, Will leaves his office feeling almost as optimistic tonight as he was apprehensive last night. *I just may pull this one through,* he muses, as he grabs the phone at the receptionist's desk, dials Karen, and suggests they meet at a neighborhood bistro. "Let's not even turn on the kitchen light, much less go in there."

Morning dawns especially fresh and bright, and Will's at his desk by 8:00 sharp. Lucky too, because the phone rings, and it's Sherm Summit. "Will, Bill wants Mark Matthews, and not Kathryn Keane! I would *never* have picked him over Kathryn. However, he *is* a promising lad and Bill has his reasons, which make some sense to me. Tell me, you don't have any *other* folks we should be looking at, do you?"

Will's heart skips a beat. But instead of answering he pauses strategically, prompting Summit to continue. "Anyway," says Summit, "I'm not going to overrule him."

Whooopeeeeee! is the silent scream in Will's head, momentarily drowning out Summit's voice on the phone. *No need to start over. Besides, there was nowhere to start anyway!*

"...and that's why I feel kind of sheepish and embarrassed, Will," continues Summit. *Now what did I miss?* "Which is why I'd really appreciate it if you'd call and kind of let her down gracefully. When I implied she was going to be my choice, she really was. So would you take care of that for me, Will? And of course I'm also going to write Kathryn a note. I want to keep in touch. She's exactly the kind of person we need over here...and who knows what the future may bring?"

"Absolutely, I'll take care of it. I'll make sure she understands." *Little do you know how **well** she understands!*

Moments later Bill Beane's on the line announcing that Mark Matthews will be the new President of ISC's Proprietary Drug Division. "But Will," says Beane, "you had a couple absolutely outstanding finalists. And Sherm is right. We really should have more women at the Division President level over here. As soon as Mark gets up and running, I'd like to see a New Vice President of Marketing in that Division...and I'd love someone from a big company like Parker Labs. That would provide a counterpoint to Mark's mainly small-company/entrepreneurial experience.

"Now Will, Kathryn mentioned her Director of Product Management, who's got a strong market research background. She's a woman, and we'd love to have more women in higher jobs over here. And if she can cut it with Kathryn, she's probably very, very good. It would be too hopelessly tacky for me to go after her right after Kathryn's just told me about her. But keep her in mind. We may soon be confirming a VP Marketing search. And you may feel that you can go after her, even if I can't."

No way!, thinks Will. *I'm blocked and can't touch her. But I'm glad to hear there's another search on the way...another $100,000 to maybe $130,000 fee in the pipeline!*

"Well, Bill, I'm excited," says Will. "I think you've made a brilliant choice. Sherm called me just a few minutes ago to say he was letting you have your way on Mark. So in his mind, it's clearly your call. If Mark doesn't turn out exactly right, that could be an embarrassment to you. Which brings us to references. I've already done preliminary checks on both Mark and Kathryn, so there won't be any big surprises. But let me call Mark for still more names. That way, we'll have an in-depth reading, which may even help you in managing him. And if by some long shot there *is* something negative, we'd better know now, not later. Also, I'll write a report that will protect us *both* with Summit as having done plenty of 'due diligence.'

"When I'm through—and I'll make it a point to finish within the next 24 hours— you can call Mark and, unless there's something neither of us expects, you can tell him he's hired, and welcome him aboard. You can also tell him you've got him that extra 100,000—or whatever—bucks. That will put him just about at your target salary. And he'll feel he's joining a company and a boss that really appreciate him. Considering the importance of this upward move to his career, I don't think there's any counteroffer a family outfit like Data Drugs can possibly make to keep him. But let's get him jumping out of his skin with enthusiasm for ISC and for you."

"Right on, Will. You know what you're doing. That's why I like working with you."

Will immediately places a call to Mark Matthews. "Things look really great," says Will. You're right about Bill Beane. He does favor you, although he also likes the other candidate a lot. And the Chairman, too, thinks you're terrific. But he's *just* as enthusiastic about another person, who has lots more experience with much bigger companies than you do. At the wire, references become very important. Have you given any thought to additional people I can call?"

"Yes, I'm all ready for that. You know we're a small privately-held company with family members and in-laws all over the place, so I have to be unbelievably careful. But I read this book called *Rites of Passage at $100,000 to $1 Million+* and it said you wouldn't let me off the hook without in-depth referencing just because I have to maintain confidentiality. So I've identified quite a list. Folks from every one of my former jobs...a few people here that I'd trust with my life...also people I've worked with here who've since left...plus outside suppliers, customers, and others who can give you a clear reading on how I'm regarded here. And to make it easy for you to check, I've put down home as well as office numbers for the folks who don't mind being called about me at home. Want me to fax you the list?"

"How many people?"

"I don't know, maybe fourteen, fifteen...something like that."

"And they're all *business?* I don't want anybody from your church or club, or your doctor or lawyer, or old school friends you've known for 20 years."

"No problem. I'm well aware of that. You'll be talking to former bosses, subordinates, coworkers, and other people who really know how well I do my work."

Wow, here's a guy with nothing to hide, thinks Will. That's even more proof we've got the right person. With almost no effort I'll look like I did a heroic job of referencing, and my report will be one more shot of hard sell to reassure Sherm that they were right to turn down Kathryn and choose Mark. Will completes plenty of calls in just a couple afternoon hours, plus the evening.

At 9:00 the next morning Will calls Bill Beane and enthusiastically relays in detail Mark's outstanding references. "Bill, why don't you call Mark around noon our time, when he's just getting into the office, tell him about his new, higher salary, and welcome him enthusiastically to ISC. I'll wait to call and congratulate him until after he gets home this evening. That way I can find out what happened when he went in to resign, and make sure there's no counter-offer and nothing brewing at home that could cause us a problem."

Reports listing the references Will has spoken to, plus a summary of what the overall group said, go out to Beane, Summit, and Al Umans by FedEx. "When you've got it, flaunt it!," says Will, as he maps follow-up with Wilma.

Will sighs with relief that it's all over...and that both Summit and Bill Beane feel they've had an outstanding search. It will soon be 9:00 a.m. in L.A., so Will tries a long distance call to Al Umans and reaches another very happy man. The 2,400-person facility in Denver...Al's biggest worry...voted "No" on Friday, and that outcome is almost certain to be echoed in the remaining five West Coast locations, which vote tomorrow.

Everything proceeds smoothly. In a couple days, with both Mark and ISC unequivocally committed, Will promptly calls the unsuccessful candidates to tell them the outcome and thank them for their participation. He also calls GR&B's billing department to tell them Mark Matthews' estimated first year's compensation, so that a final bill bringing Gordon, Rossi & Boodles' fee to one-third of that amount can be mailed out. Then he calls Doris DeWitt in GR&B's L.A. office to tell her that Wilma will be transferring to Doris everyone tagged on the computer for the ISC search.

And finally, Will calls Karen to propose a really special celebratory dinner at the restaurant of her choice (she opts for the main dining room at Caneel Bay on the next long weekend). And then he turns his attention back to the real problem of his existence at the moment: the troublesome search for a chief financial officer for a struggling B-to-B e-commerce venture just 39 blocks down Fifth Avenue from GR&B.

Victory...and an unending challenge. They're all in a day's work for Super Recruiter Will Pickham.

The Box Score

Now that it's all over, let's take a look at how each of the principals in our little drama has fared. Who are the winners? Who are the losers? Could any of them have done things differently?

Sherm Summit

Our wily CEO is delighted with the outcome, especially after Will's reference report renews and expands his initial enthusiasm for Mark Matthews. Ever the fine leader, Mr. Summit is also pleased with his decision to let Bill Beane select his own key subordinate.

Moreover, Mr. S is enjoying the good feeling that comes from knowing he got a very professional search and that, as a result, ISC has been strengthened. He heard about a range of appropriate possibilities and interviewed eight attractive candidates...at least three of whom he viewed very positively.

Of course, what the Chairman doesn't know is that Will knew of other outstanding people he couldn't approach, because they worked for other GR&B clients, or were allocated to other GR&B recruiters.

But bear this in mind: although GR&B's two-year off-limits rule worked against Mr. Summit on this search, it operated to his benefit during the two years following GR&B's search to bring in Graham Rusk. And now it'll protect ISC for two more years. Moreover, the rule that kept Will's hands off other GR&B recruiters' candidates also kept theirs off Sherm Summit's candidates.

The most important thing is that Summit justifiably feels Will's services have been worth the $220,000 he paid for them. He'll almost certainly return to Will at Gordon, Rossi & Boodles the next time he's unable to fill a key position on his own.

Will Pickham

On this assignment, as on most others, Will's had his ups and downs.

At the outset, the situation looked bleak. Undaunted, Will threw himself into solving the problem. He had to work hard to come up with his slate of candidates. But after all, that's what he's handsomely paid to do. Will prides himself on his resourcefulness, and not without reason. Now he has brought in a sizable fee for Gordon, Rossi & Boodles, and he'll be getting more business from Integrated Standard Corporation in the future.

Above all, Will has done his very best to serve both his client and his firm. He's happy that he was able to complete the assignment to the eminent satisfaction of Sherm Summit and Bill Beane; glad he was patient about waiting for more work from ISC instead of beginning to take people out; and pleased to have extended a great opportunity to Mark Matthews.

Will has also expanded his circle of well-deserved professional and personal relationships. Mr. Summit—now "Sherm"—has Will clearly in mind for future searches, as do Bill Beane, Mark Matthews and Graham Rusk. Kathryn Keane will use Will to fill three positions in Colorado and will introduce him to Cynthia and Carl, who'll not only use Will to fill several posts in their global organization, but will also recommend him and GR&B to other potential clients in various places around the world.

With respect to the overseas search opportunities that come Will's way, he will either (1) handle them himself, if they're high-paying (hence high-fee) and in locations he'd enjoy visiting or (2) "hand them off" to people in local GR&B offices, meanwhile pocketing substantial income merely for having "brought in the business."

Bill Beane

Bill made the right choice. Right because Mark Matthews will do an exceptionally fine job. And right too, because merely echoing the Chairman's preference for Kathryn Keane would not only have failed to hire her, but might—and we'll never know for sure—have sent Will off on additional weeks or months of searching. For reasons we know, but Bill doesn't, further work would have been unlikely to yield candidates any better than, or even as good as, the original ones.

Decisiveness is a hallmark of a fine executive. So is instinct...the inexplicable ability to often come up with a correct decision without having an entirely correct or complete basis for it. So too are the self-confidence and integrity that lead to independent thought and action. Bill Beane clearly has all those fine traits. They're why the Chairman is grooming Bill to be his successor...COO in 6 months and CEO in 3 years. And why, backed by fine executives like Graham Rusk and Mark Matthews, Bill will help make Summit's final years at ISC resoundingly successful. Moreover, Bill's success after the Chairman leaves will be the culmination of Sherm Summit's success.

Bill's loyalty is another positive trait. Will did fine work for Bill in recruiting Graham Rusk. Therefore Bill recommended Will for the current search. As Will continually re-earns Bill's trust, he'll receive it again and again. Their business relationship will grow into a lasting personal friendship.

Al Umans

Too bad that the labor emergency has kept ISC's Senior VP - Human Resources from being more accessible to Mr. Summit at this time and more directly involved in the search...particularly at the outset. But Al too is properly pleased with the outcome, and with the diligence and speed Will has demonstrated.

Busy as he is, Al needs outside professionals he can depend on. Will's now on Al's short list of preferred recruiters. Al will warmly recommend Will to other ISC executives who need recruiting services and, when the subject of executive search comes up, to Chief HR Officers of other companies, as well.

Andrea Applewhite

Andrea has no idea she was ever involved in the ISC search. And in a sense, she wasn't, since she was never told about the job, and ISC was never told about her. In Will's mind, however, Andrea was...and still is...the prototype of the person Summit wanted.

True, as Will told Summit in presenting Andrea's unemployed ex-boss Dan Dawson as the logical candidate from off-limits Prestige Panacea, Andrea has never directly supervised a field sales force. But Summit had not stipulated that criterion. And Summit didn't know—as Will does—how ideally Andrea's superior personal characteristics (like Kathryn Keane's and Phyllis Finley's) would have fitted into an ISC management team that already includes Bill Beane and Graham Rusk. Indeed, mildly negative personal characteristics were what caused Summit to drop Dan Dawson, the executive he *did* see from Prestige Panacea.

So it's pretty clear that Andrea Applewhite could have been a leading contender for the Proprietary Drug Division presidency...and very likely the winner. But Will's hands were tied.

Nonetheless, Andrea's weren't.

Right now, as she savors her new promotion to Dan Dawson's job, Andrea is making excellent career progress...and without giving any thought to the "Rites of Passage," which should be learned early and well by all high-potential executives. We congratulate Andrea and wish her well.

However, it will be ironic if tomorrow morning as she scans the "Who's News" section of *The Wall Street Journal*, Andrea notes wistfully that someone almost exactly her age is stepping up to the presidency of a sizable proprietary drug operation from a far lesser position than Andrea held even before her recent promotion, and thinks: *What a career-making opportunity...I wish I were in his shoes!* You probably could have been, Andrea, if you'd made up your mind a while ago that you were ready for a presidency, and if you'd joined us in studying how to precipitate opportunity, rather than just waiting for it to happen.

Karol Klasner

As VP - Marketing at National Anodyne, a company high on Mr. Summit's "hit list," Karol is another potentially ideal candidate, who doesn't know what she may have missed. Since she worked for an off-limits firm, Will ruled her out immediately. So Karol continues where she is, without ever realizing she had an excellent shot at becoming president of a sizable proprietary drug company.

That's ironic, because Karol is an unusually able, assertive, and career-centered person. Weeks before Will was phoned by Sherm Summit, Karol had noted in the Trade papers (1) that the previous President of ISC's Proprietary Drug division had been forced out, and (2) that no successor was announced. She could have:

(1) Identified a mutual acquaintance [see "Targeted Networking," p. 54] who could have introduced her to Mr. Summit.

(2) Or if she were afraid to expose her willingness to leave National Anodyne for even the most exceptional opportunity, she could have used "Sponsored Direct Mail" [see pp. 266-71] to get her identity-disguised resume directly into Summit's hands. Summit *does* take note of a superb and timely letter-and-resume, as Sam Sage's experience proves [pages 522-23 and 539].

(3) Or she could have taken the straightforward approach of merely writing to Summit herself. Obviously there'd have been some danger of exposure. But maybe not too much. Even if Summit "spilled the beans"— which we know he's too gentlemanly to do—National Anodyne probably *wouldn't* fire someone as good as Karol, even if they did find out that she attempted to grasp a once-in-a-lifetime opportunity. Indeed, if she trusts her boss and is friends with him or her (which should be but isn't always so), she might even have defused the risk in advance with words like these:

"There may not be two other people in America with enough boss/subordinate friendship and trust to have this conversation. But I got a hare brained idea last night after reading about the President of ISC's Proprietary Drug Division being tossed out. Now of course my ideal way to move up to a presidency would be for you become COO, and hopefully move me into your job; because I *love this company*. In fact, I often get calls from headhunters and *always turn them down*. But here's a long-shot that perhaps I should play. There are only about a dozen major presidencies in the entire industry and maybe only four or five of them will be filled from the outside in this decade. So what do you think? Would you mind if I sent him a letter? I won't do it if you say No."

Now more than ever before, business loyalties tend to be to *people* we know and trust, rather than to the corporation which, in the hands of other people or in the same hands under changed circumstances, has a proven tendency to do surprising and unpleasant things to us. Twenty years ago such a conversation would have been unthinkable. Today it may not be.

Charlie Comstock

For Charlie, from Adam Labs, the ISC search has been a learning experience. He was thrilled to be contacted by Will and flown to New York for an interview. He correctly assumed that Will's call meant he was beginning to make a name for himself. But since he was never introduced to the client, Charlie, no dummy, concluded that he must have fouled up the interview...which was indeed true.

Therefore, Charlie has decided that if he wants to get ahead, he'll have to learn to do better. So he has signed up for a workshop that videotapes executives in mock presentations and interviews. Now he's perfecting the art of crisp, succinct, factual answers, a relaxed presence, and the ability to really listen to his interviewer. When opportunity knocks again, Charlie will be ready.

Dan Dawson

When he got tossed out of Prestige Panacea, Dan took a very logical step. He dispatched his cover letter and resume by e-mail (thus maximizing his likelihood of entering their databases) to a large number of highly respected retainer recruiting firms, including GR&B. His reward there was an interview at ISC, where he was one of five top finalists. He lost out only because others with superior credentials or attributes...and (in Jim Johnson's case) personal recommendations...became his competition.

If Dan had mailed elegant on-paper letters and resumes to his most likely *employers*, he'd have reached Mr. Summit *before* the Chairman paid Will $220,000 to provide a slate of candidates. Dan comes from one of the top-three companies on Mr. Summit's "wish list." Who knows? Dan might have won, if he'd reached Summit directly *and* early.

As an experienced executive, Dan can accept his failure to get the ISC job philosophically. But what he can't understand is why he doesn't hear from anyone at GR&B for nearly a year after Will phoned to report that Mark Matthews was selected. Obviously GR&B thought Dan was good enough to introduce to ISC. But long afterward, GR&B seems to have totally dropped him from consideration.

GR&B notwithstanding, Dan will soon get several attractive offers through introductions by other top search firms that received his resume through the same instant one-click e-mail transmission by which Dan sent it to GR&B after getting the *RITES*-Honored Download from *RITE*Site. Still other *RITES*-Honored recruiters will find Dan's *identity-revealed* resume when searching *RITE*Site's database for candidates (as Will would have found it too, if he'd originally looked). In addition, a couple very intriguing offers will come from entrepreneurs who find Dan's identity-*concealed* resume on *RITE*Site, send him their identity and proposition through *RITE*Site's computer, and get a response from him that opens their dialog.

Dan Dawson may not understand what went wrong at GR&B, but we do. Immediately after Will's ISC search ended, Wilma reassigned Dan on GR&B's computer to Doris DeWitt. Ironically this ideal hand-off *sidelined* Dan. Doris got him just as her search was "put on hold," pending the outcome of a sudden unfriendly tender offer for BioDynamics. Negotiations dragged on. Ten months later the merger went through, and the search was terminated. Only then did Doris's assistant clear Doris's holds on prospects for the BioDynamics search and make them—Dan included—available to other GR&B recruiters.

Ethan Evans

It was a stroke of good luck for Ethan Evans at BioDynamics that Doris DeWitt and Will made their deal, in which Doris got a chance at the people who turned Will down, in return for clearing Ethan Evans for the ISC search. Everybody won: Doris got more prospects. Will got a candidate who represented an off-limits company. And Ethan got an interview. True, he didn't get the job, but Ethan made two very valuable contacts in Sherm Summit and Bill Beane.

Obviously, Ethan is living on borrowed time at Biodynamics. Soon he'll be forced out. Then, packaging his job search within a search for consulting assignments [see p. 449], Ethan will re-contact Sherm Summit. Having been impressed with Evans' broad knowledge, even though doubtful of his decisiveness, the Chairman will assign Ethan a comprehensive review of the proprietary drug industry and ISC's current and future opportunities. "Who cares if he's not decisive," Summit will say to Bill Beane and Mark Matthews. "He certainly knows the industry, and he impresses me as someone who can identify all the options. Let him gather the information. *We'll* know what to do about it!"

Ethan will find—much to his surprise—that he enjoys consulting and is good at it. He's personable and knows most of the industry's top executives. His work will be based more on chatty phone calls than on Internet and/or library research. But he'll bring a wealth of practical information to his clients. Ultimately, Ethan will develop "Crandall's Way" monthly retainers [see pp. 453-54] with six companies. As an outgrowth of his consulting, he'll also publish a successful industry newsletter.

Phyllis Finley

Phyllis was lucky to be working at Maxi-Medi-Marketing, a company open to Will, and she was pleased to be considered for such a high-level position. Since she realized that she was probably a bit too junior, she wasn't unduly disappointed when Will tactfully explained that ISC had chosen someone with more experience. And since Phyllis wasn't actively looking for another job, she didn't notice that nobody at GR&B called her for nearly a year.

But when Doris' assistant eventually returns Phyllis' file to be recirculated in the talent pool, Phyllis will soon be called by another GR&B recruiter who'll have an opening that's just right for Phyllis.

But that's not all she'll get from the episode we've witnessed. Remember how taken Sherm Summit was with Phyllis' personality? One of her great strengths is that she *listens.* She's *interested* in what others say. She *remembers.* And she *stays in touch.*

Phyllis's pleasant hour-and-a-half with Mr. Summit was obviously a contact worth nurturing. Rather than sit awkwardly eavesdropping when Summit took an urgent phone call, Phyllis walked to a window and gazed out. Afterward, she mentioned seeing purple grackles and a scarlet tanager. Birds, it turned out, are also a fascination of Sherm and Joyce Summit.

So, on *appropriately rare* occasions over the next couple years, Phyllis will send Mr. Summit. a few relevant clippings from U.S. and foreign periodicals [see p. 503]. He'll reciprocate with Joyce's article on setting up neighborhood wildlife preserves. And Phyllis' phone call complimenting Mrs. S on her activities will lead to knowing the Summits socially in the narrow context of a shared interest. Five years from now, Phyllis Finley will be invited by Joyce Summit to join the Board of the National Audubon Society. Contacts Phyllis makes there will greatly enrich her business *and* personal life. But that's another story.

Gerry Glib

Gerry has serious problems. His brief involvement with the ISC search merely highlighted them. Gloria's thoroughness (and Will's desperation) led them both to find Gerry on Maxi-Medi-Marketing's corporate Web site and in the various online directories. Luckily, however, Will's talk with Buddy revealed Gerry's shortcomings as, in the end, referencing would also have done. Had Gerry been a truly competent executive, the result might have been very different. But, given Gerry's poor track record, nothing came of his meeting with Will. In fact, Gerry is now on thin ice at Maxi-Medi-Marketing and is quietly beginning to look for something else.

Gerry was neither helped nor harmed.

He'll never recognize or admit it, but his best bet is to abandon the executive suite and get into one-on-one selling of costly items, such as real estate. That doesn't match Gerry's self image, but it does fit his talents. Too bad he will insist on continuing to be a rotten executive, when he could become a superb salesman.

Kathryn Keane

Kathryn seems mighty lucky these days...especially in view of her predicament a few weeks ago. Then, her outstanding success at Parker Labs was in jeopardy. Indeed, it looked as if we might witness a downward spiral...conceivably even to the point of dismissal followed by justified but hard-to-win litigation.

Since then, Kathryn's had her choice of two extremely appealing situations. The ISC job wasn't actually offered to her. But that was only because Will knew she wouldn't accept it. Therefore, he encouraged rather than rebutted Bill Beane's notion that she is less creative than we know she really is.

Is Kathryn's good fortune just luck?

Not at all. She's a lovely person. A true friend, who keeps up relationships that have no obvious business angle. Staying in touch with her dearest high school friend led to free rooms at places Cynthia was running all over the world. But Kathryn didn't merely "eat-and-run." Instead, she wrote those helpful lists of suggestions after each visit. Kathryn didn't expect they'd lead to a pay-off. She just wanted to help. And in the end, her generous spirit was richly rewarded.

Was it luck that led Kathryn to "ask for a reference rather than a job"? [see p. 25]. No, she read that in a book. This book. And I'm delighted to report that that concept was a gift to me from someone I helped 25 years ago. Like Kathryn, he came to take... but didn't leave without giving.

Was it luck that built Kathryn's friendship with Will long before she needed it? No. She went out of her way to provide good suggestions when he asked for them. Again, it was her *basic nature*, not mere self-interest, that motivated her kindness.

Do nice people always finish first? No. Witness Kathryn's problem at Parker Labs. But nice people tend to know people. In times of need, they have more contacts to approach, as Kathryn did.

Needless to say, Kathryn stays in touch. She'll write "thank you" notes to Sherm Summit and Bill Beane, and add them to her holiday card list [p.502]. And—yes, you guessed it— she'll wind up selling both of them condos...merely by clipping little hand-written "here's-how-it-turned-out" notes to the lavish brochures she'll produce for the resort.

Need I say it? The resort will be a huge success, and Kathryn will revel in her new career. The future holds other pleasant surprises too. Who do you think will become the junior U.S. Senator from Colorado nine years from now?

Jim Johnson

Jim has handled himself very well in his secretive search for a more exciting future since being passed over for the presidency at Daisy Foods. By approaching ISC through networking, he got past the executive recruiter. Will would never have presented him to Summit, because Jim lacked the proprietary drug background Summit demanded. By going directly to ISC, Jim got considered...and became a strong finalist.

Today Jim's future looks rosy. Summit, much impressed, will keep him in mind for future openings and will mention him to the CEO of a soft goods conglomerate, which is putting Summit on its Board.

Will was happy to have one of his "finds," rather than Jim, get the ISC job. But he's highly impressed with Jim, and will present him as his own discovery just as soon as he (1) gets an appropriate search, and (2) simultaneously has the right to "use" Jim within GR&B.

Meanwhile, of course, Jim continues his low-profile program of quiet personal con-tact and very discreet networking. Lately he's also been concentrating on the investment and commercial banking community...quietly seeking leads on companies that may be available for purchase. No deal is in the works yet. But Jim's meeting and impressing many highly knowledgeable and widely-connected people. Indeed, one of them is the ISC Board member who brought Jim to Sherm Summit's attention.

However, having lost out on the ISC opportunity, Jim wants to speed up the unavoidably slow pace of his cautious networking. So he's now lining up a "sponsor" for a secretive direct mail campaign [see pp. 266-71]. Within the next four weeks Jim will get his message to virtually every CEO in America who might control an appropriate opportunity. And he'll do that without ever letting Daisy Foods realize that he's determined to get out as soon as possible. We'll be reading exciting news about Jim in *The Wall Street Journal* very soon.

Lanny Lawrence

Lanny is perhaps the only executive in the entire group who really got shafted. He knew about the opening at ISC, and he wanted the job. Moreover, he would have been an extremely strong candidate. But because Will did what he absolutely had to do to protect GR&B's client relationship with CompuMedic, Lanny drew the wrong conclusion about the open position at ISC.

The moral of Lanny's story is that he should have known better than to rely on Will as his sole informant about the ISC job. And he would have known better if he'd fully understood how the executive recruiting business works, and what Will's needs and problems were. Clearly Lanny needs an initiation into the "Rites of Passage."

Mark Matthews

Mark is the obvious winner. He had fine credentials for the ISC job; he was able to alert and impress Will; he worked for a company that had no client relationship with Gordon, Rossi & Boodles; and when Will needed him he was not allocated to any other recruiter at GR&B. So Mark was introduced and, in the end, got the job.

A series of happy accidents?

Hardly. Crushingly busy achieving his remarkable record for Data Drugs, an obscure private company, this young marketing superstar took some time out to adroitly market himself. He used Custom Career Service on *RITE*Site to post at least one version of his resume (there might have been up to four) with the name of his current company (and his identity as well) ***not revealed***.

Will Pickham visited *RITE*Site, found it easy to search, and found that—unlike Monster and all the other commercial sites—it did not charge a fee to view its resumes. Being affiliated with the prestigious GR&B, Will would never even consider paying a fee to view an outside database. But he followed Buddy to *RITE*Site and found the visit well worthwhile. Will was intrigued by Mark's resume, and e-mailed Mark c/o *RITE*Site's computer. Mark answered promptly, turned out to be as impressive as his identity-concealed resume implied, was eagerly interested in Will's position, followed up with speed and enthusiasm...and the rest is history!

Mark was smart to put his background with the identity of his current company safely concealed out in the open where not just Will Pickham, but every recruiter, every employer, and indeed every human on the planet seeking an executive could easily find it. It's a good thing he did. Privately owned, Data Drugs receives almost no coverage in the trade press, belongs to no trade associations, does not allow its executives to make speeches at industry events and probably would not have allowed Mark to publish an article in any trade association publication. Mark, on the other hand didn't want to be overlooked, so he took a relatively easy step to prevent that happening.

The only thing Mark could have done better would have been to choose the *RITES*-Honored Option and make his identity-*revealed* resume available to the recruiters from all 356 *RITES*-Honored firms. Then Will would have been able to contact Mark without having to e-mail him via *RITE*Site's computer and wait for a reply. If Will had not been so hard pressed to find candidates and/or if there had been several enticing resumes identity-*revealed* by the *RITES*-Honored Option, Will might not have bothered to e-mail Mark.

Note that Mark had also defined several Opportunity Alerts on *RITE*Site, which were all set to inform him by e-mail whenever a career breakthrough position like Will's (and quite a number of other very specific situations Mark identified) was posted on *RITE*Site. Unlike Buddy, however, Mark never posted. He just paid a quick visit...and was rewarded with an excellent candidate whom he otherwise would almost certainly not have discovered.

Mark wins. Will wins. We congratulate them both.

Donna Powers

Donna just wasn't destined to join ISC.

Her marketing slant is toward sales promotion and hard-hitting field sales force activity at the grass roots retailer level, in contrast to big-budget TV campaigns aimed at the consumer. In that, she reflects the philosophy and successful operating methods of the company in which she's gained all of her experience. Unfortunately, her orientation...and her personality...weren't quite what Summit and Beane were buying this time around.

Donna's a very fine person. Other employers, with other needs and other personality preferences will have an entirely different reaction. Very soon she'll achieve her desired move to New York. And her daughter's emerging ballet talent will more than justify the job change. Both Donna and her daughter will enter exciting new periods of growth and success.

Donna will never know it, but she owes Will Pickham a debt of gratitude. His appeal to Red Tapecutter has cleared the internal client-protection blockage at GR&B. And now that Cosa Nostrums is no longer off-limits, she'll soon hear about another GR&B search. Wilma will immediately transfer Donna from Will to Doris DeWitt. When Doris calls, Donna will *decisively* turn down Doris's proposal, frankly explaining that she wants to relocate to New York City and nowhere else. Because Donna also makes some helpful suggestions, Doris will make a point of immediately returning Donna to the system...not wanting to delay any further opportunities for Donna through GR&B. By sheer luck, the next job that GR&B shows her will be in New York—not California—and Donna will be the winning candidate.

In a sense, Donna doesn't deserve the success she's about to have. Wanting a quick move to a particular place, she should have mounted an all-out campaign, rather than just waiting for the accidental actions of retainer search firms to solve her problem. Personal contact activity [Chapter 3]; taking fullest advantage of *RITE*Site's CCS; perhaps some cautious networking among strangers [Chapter 4]; plus a secretive direct mail campaign targeted on the New York area [Chapter 13] would have maximized her likelihood of success. In job hunting terms, she hasn't really worked hard enough for the success she's going to have. She's about to win the lottery. On rare occasions long shots *do* come in.

Roy Ricardo

To some extent, Roy's a victim of the way retainer search firms do business...meeting the needs of clients, not candidates. Roy was highly-qualified for the ISC job. And certainly he'd have preferred to stay in the drug industry and live near New York, rather than go into the industrial motor business and wind up in Anthracite Valley. But, "owned" by Doug Abel for the Brute Force search, Roy couldn't be shown the ISC job or any other within GR&B. He'll never know that a far better alternative existed. Eventually Roy will join Brute Force, just to get back to the States. However, he'd have been a lot happier at ISC.

Obviously, Roy should have written directly to the chief executives of all the companies that interested him, just as Sam Sage did. Roy's list would surely have included Sherm Summit, just as Sam's did. Roy could readily have been exposed to both ISC and Brute Force, just as Sam Sage got a shot at both ISC and Expodex. Roy's credentials are superior to Mark Matthews' and Roy's similarly enthusiastic personality is equally engaging. There is every reason to believe that if Roy had taken advantage of *RITE*Site, as Mark did, Roy and not Mark would be entering the exciting new presidency at ISC.

Roy went all the way to Argentina to acquire his impressive experience and track record in general management which, added to his proprietary drug marketing experience in the U.S., would have made him an ideal candidate at ISC. Now, however, he goes back to a marketing-only position, and enters a field he would never have chosen voluntarily. Out-of-the-country executives need the most comprehensive and aggressive job-hunting campaigns they can possibly mount. Sadly, Roy's fell short.

Rita Rosen

We've never met Rita. But she's the Director of Product Management Kathryn mentioned so glowingly to Bill Beane. Bill will forget her. But Will won't. He'll ask Kathryn about Rita, hear the same enthusiastic comments Bill heard, and enter her into GR&B's central computer with a few hastily written—but absolutely glowing—comments. Will won't, however, get in touch with Rita to ask for a resume because Parker Labs, as we well know, is off-limits to GR&B.

Moreover, when Will later undertakes the search Bill Beane alluded to in originally mentioning Rita to Will, Will won't be able to go after Rita. He'll fill his very good slate with candidates from non-off-limits companies.

But from now on, Will and other GR&B recruiters *will* be calling Rita for her suggestions on searches where she would *not* be a logical candidate. Indeed, the help she graciously gives to another GR&B recruiter will mature into the same sort of mutually supportive friendship Kathryn and Will have enjoyed. The details needn't concern us. But one day history will repeat itself...to Rita's considerable benefit.

Sam Sage

Sam's an extremely savvy executive. He bypassed the allocated-to-another-recruiter-in-the-firm obstacle that kept Roy Ricardo from learning about the ISC position. And all it took was a direct mail campaign that included Sherm Summit, CEO of a company that obviously belonged on Sam's list.

Sam's mailing got action from Mr. S for two reasons:

1. It was very impressive, and

2. Summit had an immediate need.

Because of Sherm Summit's insistence, Sam was finally shown the ISC opportunity, in a *rare* exception to the rule that retainer recruiting firms will never show candidates more than one job at a time. Sam got "parallel processing" in the easiest, surest way... not because he demanded it, but because he stimulated the recruiter's *client* to demand it.

In the end, of course, Sam walked away from the ISC opportunity. He didn't even go to his interview. That was another lucky break for Mark Matthews, because both Sherm Summit and Bill Beane would have chosen Sam over Mark, on the basis of Sam's far greater experience...all of it impressively successful.

Fortunately for Sam—and for Mark—Sam has mastered all the "Rites of Passage." Career-long cultivation of executive recruiter relationships led to Sam's exploration, with Buddy, of the Expodex opportunity. A classic direct mail campaign with superb paperwork [see p. 210 & p. 246] broke through to the ISC opportunity. And creative use of personal contacts and networking...coupled with an "underutilized asset" discussion [see p. 487-88] with his old friends at Medica Suisse...led Sam to a "buyable" company and financing for the deal.

A few weeks ago, Sam suffered a severe setback. Today he's happier and more challenged than he ever dreamed of being. Sam's got a once-in-a-lifetime entrepreneurial opportunity. And you can be sure he'll make the most of it.

Let's put the Internet to work for you...

Face it.

There are far less intellectually demanding books on job-changing and career management than the one you've just finished reading. RITES OF PASSAGE *is not for everyone. It was never intended to be.*

There are also far less intellectually demanding—and ethically rigorous—ways of doing executive search than the exclusively retainer-compensated methods of the RITES*-Honored recruiters you are about to meet when you turn the next page.*

Ever since the Internet first appeared, I've been framing thoughts—and collecting ideas and suggestions from many of the finest search professionals I know—trying to put the incredible power of the Internet at the disposal of both sides of the upper level of the recruiting process.

No question about it. The flow of information about excellently performing executives and the positions

and for outstanding executive recruiters.

that—in the real estate industry phrase—represent their "highest and best use" is far from comprehensive and instantaneous. The process CAN be facilitated. And that's what RITESite is set up to do.

When an excellent appointment is made—and quickly— all parties benefit. A career flourishes. And an employer/recruiter client relationship is rewarded and strengthened.

Working with outstanding technical talent, and giving them plenty of time to get the job done right, I've tried to make RITESite a useful tool. Please visit and see what you think.

Thank you.   *John Lucht*

*Note that you can spell the name in three other ways that sound the same. RiteSight, RightSight, and RightSite. Or even use RitesOfPassage. Put a dot com on the end, and they'll all take you to...

RITESite.com

Outstanding
Search Firms

Ever since R ITES OF P ASSAGE *first appeared, it has provided a listing of outstanding exclusively retainer executive recruiting firms, commencing with 90 fine U.S. firms in its first edition.*

In every subsequent printing, this listing has been refined and expanded along with the rest of R ITES *until, in this revision, 356 outstanding search firms throughout the United States & Canada are recognized.*

With over 8,000 firms doing recruiting in North America, the R ITES OF P ASSAGE *listing is widely-known as a unique and valuable service to both individuals and corporations.*

APPENDIX II

Outstanding Retainer Executive Recruiters

Have you decided to cultivate prominent retainer search firms?

Here is a core list of 356 leading U.S. and Canadian firms. Included are North America's largest, plus particularly outstanding medium-sized and smaller firms. Because they work only "on retainer," every one of these firms is filling a completely different list of jobs than any of the others. Therefore, you'll have the best and broadest (and entirely non-overlapping) exposure if you contact many of the listed firms. Note that some specialize (or are generalists with special concentrations), so don't bother contacting ones that don't fit your background and interests.

An increasing number of firms can now accept resumes by e-mail and insert them into a searchable database. Where available, use this option, with a "Dear Recruiters" e-mail cover letter not addressed to any particular person. When submitting by mail, send to the home office and *do* address your cover letter to a specific person. If a firm has multiple offices, the address given *is* the home office.

Cities having branch offices are also listed, each with phone number and the name of the local manager or another prominent local member. Locally and nationally you can, if you wish, phone and ask who specializes in your field. However, unless you're trying to target a personal appointment, there's virtually no advantage. Inside-the-firm procedures will normally redistribute your inquiry appropriately.

Although *unnecessary*, there's no harm in sending an on-paper letter and resume to one person in each of two or three different offices. If only an electronic file is kept, the papers will be superfluous, and if papers are kept, the filer will merely discard the extras. They won't occasion notice, notation, or comment.

Many of these firms (marked by †) are members of the Association of Executive Search Consultants (AESC), a trade association of retainer-compensated recruiters.

Of course, it's beyond the scope of this book to provide any assurances, but all firms selected for this list should deal with you in a first-class manner. To the best of our knowledge, they all work only on retainer, and almost all accept searches for nearly every management function in virtually any industry. A few outstanding specialists are also included, and their specialties are clearly noted.

You may wish to phone-check before mailing to a recruiter. Information on recruiters changes even faster than on companies.

AEGIS GROUP
(SPECIALIZE IN HEALTH CARE)
23875 Novi Road
Novi, MI 48375
(248) 344-1450
www.aegis-group.com
resume@aegis-group.com

Timothy Ignash, President

ALEXANDER ROSS ASSOCIATES, INC.
21 East 40th Street, Suite 1802
New York, NY 10016
(212) 889-9333
www.alexanderross.com
resumes@alexanderross.com

Ben Lichtenstein, President

ALLERTON HENEGHAN & O'NEILL
Three First National Plaza
70 West Madison, Suite 2015
Chicago, IL 60602
(312) 263-1075
fax (312) 263-1450

Donald T. Allerton, Partner
Donald A. Heneghan, Partner

ANDERSON & ASSOCIATES†
112 South Tryon, Suite 800
Charlotte, NC 28284
(704) 347-0090
www.andersonexecsearch.com

Douglas K. Anderson, Chairman

THE ANDRE GROUP INC.
(SPECIALIZE IN HUMAN RESOURCES)
500 North Gulph Road, Suite 210
King of Prussia, PA 19406
(610) 337-0600
fax (610) 337-1333

Richard B. Andre, President (Florida)
Larry Cozzillio, V.P. & Gen. Mgr.
Also:
Palm Beach Gardens, FL
(561) 630-7800
Richard B. Andre, President

ARIAIL & ASSOCIATES
(SPECIALIZE IN FURNITURE MANUFACTURING)

210 West Friendly Ave., Suite 200
Greensboro, NC 27401
(336) 275-2906
fax (336) 273-2309
www.arailassoc.com
Randolph C. Ariail, Principal

WILLIAM B. ARNOLD ASSOCIATES, INC.
Cherry Creek Plaza, Suite 1105
600 South Cherry Street
Denver, CO 80222
(303) 393-6662
(do not accept unsolicited resumes)
Mr. William B. Arnold, President
Ms. Sheridan J. Arnold, Vice President

AST/BRYANT†
(SPECIALIZE IN NONPROFIT)
2716 Ocean Park Blvd., Suite 3001
Santa Monica, CA 90405
(310) 314-2424
www.astbryant.com
(resumes to Web site only)
Chris Bryant, Partner
Also:
Stamford, CT (203) 975-7188
Mr. Steven Ast, Partner

AUBIN INTERNATIONAL INC.†
(SPECIALIZE IN HIGH TECH & COMMUNICATIONS)
30 Rowes Wharf
Boston, MA 02110
(617) 443-9922
www.aubin.com
info@aubin.com
Richard E. Aubin, Chairman & CEO

AVERY JAMES INC.†
6601 Center Drive West, Suite 500
Los Angeles, CA 90045
(310) 342-8224
www.averyjames.com
itsyourmove@averyjames.com
Michele James, President & CEO

THE BADGER GROUP†
(SPECIALIZE IN INFORMATION TECHNOLOGY)
4125 Blackhawk Plaza Cir., Suite 270

Danville, CA 94506
(925) 736-5553
www.badgergroup.com
resumes@badgergroup.com

Fred Badger, President

BAKER, PARKER & ASSOCIATES, INC.
5 Concourse Parkway NE, Suite 2440
Atlanta, GA 30328
(770) 804-1996
www.bpasearch.com

Jerry H. Baker, Partner
Daniel Parker, Partner

BALDWIN ASSOCIATES, LLC
39 Locust Avenue
New Canaan, CT 06840
(203) 966-5355

Max M. Baldwin, President
Robert J. Kammerer, Partner

THE BALDWIN GROUP
550 West Campus Drive
Arlington Heights, IL 60004
(847) 394-4303
fax (847) 394-0576

Keith Baldwin, President

BARGER & SARGEANT, INC.†
131 Windermere Road, Suite A
Post Office Box 1420-F
Center Harbor, NH 03226-1420
(603) 253-4700

H. Carter Barger, President

BARNES DEVELOPMENT GROUP LLC†
1017 West Glen Oaks Lane, Suite 108
Mequon, WI 53092
(414) 241-8468

Richard E. Barnes, President.

JONATHAN C. BARRETT & CO., INC.
Post Office Box 247
Hawthorne, NJ 07507-0247
(201) 933-2228

A. John Gorga, President

PLEASE NOTE: There's a trend toward accepting unsolicited resumes by e-mail. If e-mail and/or fax are shown, they were considered

BARTHOLDI & COMPANY, INC.
(SPECIALIZE IN HIGH TECHNOLOGY)
10040 E. Happy Valley Rd., Suite 244
Scottsdale, AZ 85260
(602) 502-2178
www.bartholdisearch.com
Theodore G. Bartholdi, President

Also:
Denver, CO (303) 383-2130
Ms. Terry Malouf, Vice President
Reston, VA (703) 476-5519
Carol Holt, Partner
San Diego, CA (619) 881-2664
Thomas Courbat, Vice President

BARTON ASSOCIATES, INC.
One Riverway, Suite 2500
Houston, TX 77056
(713) 961-9111
fax (713) 993-9399
www.BartonA.com
Gary R. Barton, Partner
Kathleen Johnson, Partner

BATTALIA WINSTON INT'L, INC.†
(INT'L AFFILIATION - THE ACCORD GROUP)
300 Park Avenue, Suite 23-West
New York, NY 10022
(212) 308-8080
www.battaliawinston.com
(online form to submit resumes)
Ms. Dale Winston, Chairman & CEO
Ms. Jo A. Bennett, Partner & Exec. VP

Also:
Chicago, IL (312) 704-0050
James F. McSherry, Sr.VP -Midwest
Edison, NJ (732) 549-8200
Terry Gallagher, President
Los Angeles, CA (310) 284-8080
Michael McClain, Partner
San Francisco, CA (415) 984-3180
David Thompson, Director - West
Coast Operations
Wellesley Hills, MA (781) 239-1400
Steven M. Garfinkle, Mng. Director

MARTIN H. BAUMAN ASSOCIATES, INC.†
375 Park Avenue, Suite 2002
New York, NY 10152
(212) 752-6580
www.baumanassociates.com
Martin H. Bauman, President

Also:
Chicago, IL (312) 751-5407
Audrey W. Hellinger, Vice President

THE BEDFORD CONSULTING GROUP INC.†
The Bedford House
60 Bedford Road
Toronto, ON M5R 2K2
(416) 963-9000
www.bedfordgroup.com
search@bedfordgroup.com
Steven Pezim, President

BELLE ISLE, DJANDJI, BRUNET INC.

1555 Peel Street
Montreal, PQ H3A 3L8
(514) 844-1012
fax (514) 844-0539
Charles Belle Isle, Partner
Michel Brunet, Partner
Guy N. Djandji, Partner

BENDER EXECUTIVE SEARCH
45 North Station Plaza, Suite 315
Great Neck, NY 11021
(516) 773-4300
Alan Bender, President

BENTE HANSEN ASSOCIATES
1207 High Bluff Drive, Suite 200
San Diego, CA 92130
(858) 350-4331
Ms. Bente Hansen, Mng. Director

THE BERMAN CONSULTING GROUP
Post Office Box 77886
Atlanta, GA 30357
(404) 816-6321
Frederic E. Berman, Principal

BIALECKI INC.†
(SPECIALIZE IN INVESTMENT BANKING)
780 Third Avenue, Suite 4203
New York, NY 10017-2024
(212) 755-1090
www.bialecki.com
(do not accept unsolicited resumes)
Linda Bialecki, President

PAUL J. BIESTEK ASSOCIATES, INC.
PMB 101, 800 East NW Highway,
Suite 700
Palatine, IL 60067
(847) 825-5131
Paul J. Biestek, President

BISHOP PARTNERS, LTD.†
(SPECIALIZE IN ENTERTAINMENT, MEDIA & COMMUNICATIONS)
708 Third Avenue, Suite 2200
New York, NY 10017
(212) 986-3419
www.bishoppartners.com
info@bishopnet.com
Susan K. Bishop, President
Vincent S. Morgan, Vice President

BLAKE / HANSEN, LTD.
(SPECIALIZE IN AVIATION, AEROSPACE & DEFENSE)
1920 Bayshore Drive
Englewood, FL 34223
(941) 475-1300
www.hansengroupltd.com
Ty E. Hansen, President

BLAKSLEE INTERNATIONAL
(SPECIALIZE IN PHARMACEUTICALS, BIOTECHNOLOGY & MEDICAL)
49 Hillside Avenue

Mill Valley, CA 94941
(415) 389-7300
Mr. Jan H. Blakslee, President
Ms. Joyce Mustin, Partner

BOARD ROOM CONSULTANTS / KENNY, KINDLER, THOLKE & HARDY†
530 Fifth Avenue, Suite 2100
New York, NY 10036
(212) 328-0440
fax (212) 328-0440
www.board-search.com
Thomas G. Hardy, Board Director
Roger M. Kenny, Board Director
Peter A. Kindler, Board Director
William E. Tholke, Board Director

BONNELL & ASSOCIATES LTD.
2960 Post Road South, Suite 200
Southport, CT 06490
(203) 319-7214
www.bonnellassociates.com
William R. Bonnell, President

JOHN C. BOONE & COMPANY
1807 Henley Street
Glenview, IL 60025
(847) 998-1905
John C. Boone, President

BOURBONNAIS CONSULTING GROUP
420 McGill Street, Suite 400
Montreal, PQ H2Y 2G1
(514) 397-9655
fax (514) 397 0410
Francois Durand, President

BOWDEN & COMPANY, INC.
Post Office Box 467
Medina, OH 44258
(330) 722-1722
www.bowdenandco.com
bowdenandco@bowdenandco.com
Chester W. Dickey, President & CEO

BOYDEN†
364 Elwood Avenue
Hawthorne, NY 10532-1239
(914) 747-0093
www.boyden.com
Richard Foy, Chief Executive Officer
(Chairman is Karl Lange in Germany)

Also:
Bloomfield Hills, MI (248) 647-4201
John Slosar, President - Boyden U.S.A.
Calgary, AB, (403) 237-6603
Samuel L. Travis, Mng. Director
Chesterfield, MO (636) 565-1300
George B. Zamborsky, Mng. Partner
Chicago, IL (312) 565-1300
Richard A. McCallister, President
Houston, TX (713) 655-0123
Thomas C. Zay, Jr., Partner
Montreal, PQ (514) 935-4560
Paul J. Bourbeau, Managing Director

New York, NY (212) 843-0200
George Lumbsy, Vice President
Pittsburgh, PA (412) 391-3020
E. Wade Close Jr., Mng. Director
San Francisco, CA (415) 981-7900
Frederick J. Greene, Mng. Director
Summit, NJ (973) 267-0980
Peter R. Schmidt, Mng. Director
Vancouver, BC (604) 944-8081
Roger Gurr, Managing Director
Washington, DC (202) 342-7200
Stanley L. Krejci, Mng. Director

THE BRAND COMPANY, INC.
81 Shores Drive
Vero Beach, FL 32963
(561) 231-1807

J. Brand Spangenberg, President

BRENNER EXECUTIVE RESOURCES INC.†
45 Rockefeller Plaza, Suite 2013
New York, NY 10111
(212) 332-1680
www.brennerresources.com
resumes@brennerresources.com

Mr. Michael Brenner, President

BRISSENDEN, MCFARLAND, FUCCELLA & REYNOLDS INC.
(SPECIALIZE IN HEALTH CARE)
1130 Route 202, Suite E7
Raritan, NJ 08869
(908) 704-9100
www.bmfr.com
inquiry@bmfr.com

Hoke Brissenden, Partner
Carl J. Fucella, Partner
John H. Reynolds, Partner

BROOKE CHASE ASSOCIATES, INC.
505 N. Lake Shore Drive
Lake Point Tower, Suite 5507
Chicago, IL 60611
(312) 744-0033
www.brookechase.com
brookechase@brookechase.com

Joseph J. McElmeel, President

Also:
Livingston, NJ (973) 716-0088
Carol O'Brien, Managing Director
Seattle, WA (206) 770-8926
Marlene McElmeel, Managing Director

BROWNSON & ASSOCIATES
5599 San Felipe, Suite 610
Houston, TX 77056
(713) 626-4790
www.brownson.com

Bruce F. E. Brownson, Mng. Director

CHARLES BUCK & ASSOCIATES
400 East 59th Street
New York, NY 10022
(212) 759-2356

Charles A. Buck, President

BULLIS & COMPANY, INC.
120 Quintara Street
San Francisco, CA 94116
(415) 753-6140

Richard J. Bullis, President

BURKE, O'BRIEN & BISHOP ASSOCIATES, INC.
301 N. Harrison Street, Suite 111
Princeton, NJ 08540
(609) 921-3510
fax (609) 683-1578

James F. Bishop, President & CEO

JOSEPH R. BURNS & ASSOCIATES, INC.
2 Shunpike Road
Madison, NJ 07840-2727
(973) 377-1350

Joseph R. Burns, President

BUTTERFASS, PEPE & MACCALLAN, INC.
(SPECIALIZE IN FINANCIAL SERVICES)
Post Office Box 721
Mahwah, NJ 07430
(201) 512-3330
www.bpmi.com
staff@bpmi.com
(online form to submit resumes)

Stanley W. Butterfass, Leonida R. Pepe
& Deirdre MacCallan, Principals

THE CALDWELL PARTNERS INT'L.†
64 Prince Arthur Avenue
Toronto, ON M5R 1B4
(416) 920-7702
www.caldwellpartners.com
resumes@caldwellpartners.com

C. Douglas Caldwell, Chairman, CEO
& Founder
Anne Fawcett, Vice Chairman

Also:
Calgary, AB (403) 265-8780
Robert Sutton, Partner
Halifax, NS (902) 429-5909
Susan Letson, Partner
Montreal, PQ (514) 935-6969
Richard Joly, Partner
Vancouver, BC (604) 669-3550
Donald Prior, Partner

CALLAN & ASSOCIATES, LTD.
2021 Spring Road, Suite 175
Oak Brook, IL 60523
(630) 574-9300
fax (630) 574-3099
www.callanassociates.com

Robert M. Callan, President

CANNY, BOWEN INC.
521 Fifth Avenue, 19th Floor
New York, NY 10175
(212) 949-6611
fax (212) 949-5191

David R. Peasback, CEO & Chairman
Greg Gabel, Senior Vice President

CARLYLE WHITNEY GROUP
625 N. Michigan Ave., Suite 2100
Chicago, IL 60611
(312) 587-3030
www.carlylegroup.com
research@carlylegroup.com

Mitchell Berman, Partner

CARRINGTON & CARRINGTON LTD.†
(SPECIALIZE IN DIVERSITY EXECUTIVE SEARCH)
39 South La Salle Street
Chicago, IL 60603-1557
(312) 606-0015
www.Cclltd.com
cclltd@cclltd.com

Marianne H. Carrington, Principal

CARUTHERS & COMPANY, LLC
(SPECIALIZE IN CORPORATE COMMUNICATIONS, PUBLIC AFFAIRS & MARKETING)
19 Ludlow Road, Suite 302
Westport, CT 06880
(203) 221-3234
fax (203) 454-2310

Robert D. Caruthers, Principal

CEJKA & COMPANY
(SPECIALIZE IN HEALTH CARE)
222 South Central, Suite 400
St. Louis, MO 63105
(314) 726-1603
fax (314) 726-0026
www.Cejka.com

Susan Cejka, President & CEO

DAVID CHAMBERS & ASSOCIATES, INC.
2 Greenwich Plaza, Suite 100
Greenwich, CT 06830
(203) 622-1333
fax (203) 661-3676

David E. Chambers, President

CHRISTENSON, HUTCHISON, MCDOWELL, LLC†
(EMA PARTNERS INTERNATIONAL)
466 Southern Boulevard
Chatham, NJ 07928-1462
(973) 966-1600
www.chmsearch.com
solutions@chmsearch.com

H. Alan Christenson, Founder & Partner
William K. Hutchison, Partner
Robert McDowell, Partner

Also:
Providence, RI (401) 861-2550
John R. Sahagian, Managing Director

CHRISTIAN & TIMBERS, INC.†
25825 Science Park Drive, Suite 400
Cleveland, OH 44122
(216) 464-8710
www.ctnet.com
resumes@ctnet.com

Jeffrey Christian, Chairman & CEO

Also:
Atlanta, GA (770) 754-1198

PLEASE NOTE: There's a trend toward accepting unsolicited resumes by e-mail. If e-mail and/or fax are shown, they were considered

Russell Gray, Mng. Dir,
Telecommunications
Burlington, MA (781) 229-9515
Stephen P. Mader, President & COO
Columbia, MD (410) 872-0200
William Houchins, Mng. Dir. Mid-Atl.
Cupertino, CA (408) 446-5440
David R. Mather, VP & Mng. Director
McLean, VA (703) 448-1700
Paul Unger, Managing Director
New York, NY (212) 588-3500
Mr. Morgan McKeown, Principal
John Daily, Mng. Dir., Info. Technology
San Fransisco, CA (415) 885-8004
Victoria Wayne, Mng. Dir., New Media
Stamford, CT (203) 352-6000
Mark Esposito, Mng. Dir., Finan. Serv.
Toronto, ON (416) 628-5175
David Kinley, Mng. Dir., Canadian Oper.

CLAREY & ANDREWS, INC.†
1200 Shermer Road, Suite 108
Northbrook, IL 60062-4563
(847) 498-2870
www.clarey-andrews.com
ca@clarey-andrews.com
Jack R. Clarey, Partner
J. Douglas Andrews, Partner

COE & COMPANY†
(EMA PARTNERS INTERNATIONAL)
400 3rd Avenue SW, Suite 2600
Calagary, AB T2P 4H2
(403) 232-8833
www.coeandcompany.com
coe@coeandcompany.com
Karen J. Coe, Ph. D., President & CEO

DEAN M. COE ASSOCIATES†
32 Pine Street
Sandwich, MA 02563-2109
(508) 888-8029
www.dmcassociates.com
Dean M. Coe, President

COLE, WARREN AND LONG, INC.
2 Penn Center Plaza, Suite 312
Philadelphia, PA 19102
(215) 563-0701
www.cwl-inc.com
cwlserch@cwl-inc.com
Richard B. Warren, Chairman
Ronald J. Cole, President

COLEMAN LEW & ASSOCIATES, INC.†
Post Office Box 36489
Charlotte, NC 28236
(704) 377-0362
www.colemanlew.com
mail@colemanlew.com
Charles E. Lew, President

COLTON BERNARD INC.
(SPECIALIZE IN APPAREL & RETAIL)
870 Market Street, Suite 822
San Francisco, CA 94102
(415) 399-8700

www.coltonbernard.com
Roy C. Colton, President
Harry Bernard, Executive VP

THE COLTON PARTNERSHIP, INC.
(SPECIALIZE IN FINANCIAL SERVICES)
44 Wall Street, 12th floor
New York, NY 10005
(212) 509-1800
www.colteksearch.com
W. Hoyt Colton, President

COLUMBIA CONSULTING GROUP, INC.†
The Sun Life Building
20 South Charles St., 9th Floor
Baltimore, MD 21201
(410) 385-2525
www.ccgsearch.com
ccgbal@erols.com
Lawrence J. Holmes, President
Also:
Jupiter, FL (561) 748-0232
Larry D. Mingle, Managing Principal
New York, NY (212) 832-2525
Ann McCarthy, Managing Principal
San Francisco, CA (415) 392-2525
Jean Cranefeld, Managing Principal

COMPASS GROUP HEVER†
401 South Old Woodward, Suite 460
Birmingham, MI 48009-6613
(248) 540-9110
www.compassgroup.com
executivesearch@compassgroup.com
Paul W. Czamanske, President & CEO
Also:
Oakbrook Terrace, IL (630) 645-9110
Jerold L. Lipe, Vice President

CONEX, INC./ INTERSEARCH
150 East 52nd Street, 2nd Floor
New York, NY 10022
(212) 371-3737
fax (212) 371-3897
www.intersearch.org
Fred Siegel, President - USA

ROBERT CONNELLY & ASSOCIATES, INC.
Post Office Box 24028
Minneapolis, MN 55424
(612) 925-3039
fax (612) 922-5762
Robert F. Olsen, President

THE CORPORATE SOURCE GROUP, INC.
One Cranberry Hill
Lexington, MA 02173
(617) 862-1900
www.csg-search.com
csglex@csg-search.com
Mr. Dana Willis, President
Also:
Tampa, FL (813) 286-4422
Mark Hausherr, Senior Vice President

THE CORRIGAN GROUP
1333 Ocean Avenue
Santa Monica, CA 90401
(310) 260-9488
Gerald F. Corrigan, President

CORSO, MIZGALA & FRENCH
90 Eglinton Avenue, Suite 404
Toronto, ON M4P 2Y3
(416) 488-4111
www.InterSearchCanada.com
resumes@InterSearchCanada.com
John J. Corso, Guy French &
Tony Mizgala, Partners

CROWE-INNES & ASSOCIATES†
1120 Mar West, Suite D
Tiburon, CA 94920
(415) 435-6211
www.executiverecruit.com
resumes@croweinnes.com
Jenny Crowe-Innes, President

M. J. CURRAN & ASSOCIATES, INC.
(SPECIALIZE IN BIOTECHNOLOGY, INVSTMT.
MGMT., REAL ESTATE, NONPROFIT)
304 Newberry, Suite 509
Boston, MA 02108
(617) 723-7002
Martin J. Curran, President

CURRAN PARTNERS INC.†
One Landmark Square
18th floor
Stamford, CT 06901
(203) 363-5350
www.curranpartners.com
Mr. Michael Curran, President

JUDITH CUSHMAN & ASSOCIATES INC.
(SPECIALIZE IN PUBLIC RELATIONS)
1125 12th Avenue, N.W., Suite B-1A
Issaquah, WA 98027-3271
(425) 392-8660
www.jc-a.com
info@jc-a.com
Judith Cushman, President

THE DALLEY HEWITT COMPANY
1401 Peachtree St., NE, Suite 500
Atlanta, GA 30309-3000
(404) 885-6642
fax (404) 870-0288
www.DalleyHewitt.com
Ms. Rives D. Hewitt, Principal

JOHN J. DAVIS & ASSOCIATES, INC.
(SPECIALIZE IN MIS)
521 Fifth Avenue, Suite 1740
New York, NY 10175
(212) 286-9489
jackdavis@comcastwork.net
John J. Davis, President

THORNDIKE DELAND ASSOCIATES
(SPECIALIZE IN CONSUMER GOODS, RETAILING

& *HIGH TECH*)
275 Madison Avenue, Suite 1300
New York, NY 10016-1101
(212) 661-6200
www.tdeland.com
newyork@tdeland.com

Howard Bratches, Joseph J. Carideo
&William Venable, Partners

DELOITTE & TOUCHE MANAGEMENT CONSULTANTS
1 Place Ville-Marie, Room 3000
Montreal, PQ H3B 4T9
(514) 393-7115

Paul Atrice Simard, Managing Partner

DENNEY & COMPANY, INC.
Gateway Center
Post Office Box 22156
Pittsburgh, PA 15222-0156
(412) 441-9636
fax (412) 441-0335

Thomas L. Denney, President

DHR INTERNATIONAL, INC.
10 South Riverside Plaza, Suite 2220
Chicago, IL 60606
(312) 782-1581
fax (312) 782-2096
www.dhrintl.com
DHRResumes@JobPlex.com

David H. Hoffmann, Chairman & CEO
Robert E. Reilly, Jr., President

Also:
Atlanta, GA (770) 730-5900
Jerry Franzel, EVP & Mng. Director
Boca Raton, FL (561) 447-0561
Conrad Lee, EVP & Mng. Director
Boston, MA (617) 742-5899
Christopher P. Dona, EVP & Mng. Dir.
Brookfield, WI (414) 879-0850
Robert Stanislaw, EVP &Mng. Director
Burbank, CA (818) 729-3803
Bob Kayhs, Executive Vice President
Cincinnati, OH (513) 762-7874
Harry Rolfes, Sr. VP & Mng. Director
Concord, MA (978) 369-1350
John L. Alexanderson, Mng. Director
Costa Mesa, CA (714) 429-5500
Ronald E. LaGrow, Sr. VP & Mng. Dir.
Denver, CO (303) 629-0730
Martin Pocs, EVP & Mng. Director
East Greenwich, RI (401) 884-1695
Stephen P. Bartlett - Sr. VP & Mng. Dir.
Fort Lauderdale, FL (954) 522-4410
Jean M. Bellin, EVP & Mng. Director
Hutchinson, KS (316) 728-1100
Jim Wright, Managing Director
Indianapolis, IN (317) 684-6948
James K. Doan, EVP & Mng. Dir.
Irving, TX (214) 574-4044
Victor Arias, EVP & Mng. Director
Iselin, NJ (732) 767-5325
Robert Anthes, EVP & Mng. Director
Issaquah, WA (425) 557-3681
James L. Black, EVP & Mng. Director
Kansas City, KS (913) 317-1600

Mike Klockenga, EVP & Mng. Dir.
Lansing, MI (517) 487-9586
Gordon S. White, Jr. Sr.Vice President
Lewiston, ME (207) 783-8834
Bill Klouthis, EVP & Mng. Director
Lincoln, NE (402) 464-0566
Ted Balistreri, EVP & Mng. Director
Los Angeles, CA (310) 789-7333
Bruce Babashan, Executive VP
Milwaukee, WI (262) 879-0850
Robert W. Stanislaw, EVP & Mng. Dir.
Minneapolis, MN (612) 337-9587
Curt Hedeen, Senior Vice President
Mount Pleasant, SC (843) 856-3470
Dan Doherty, Managing Director
Nashville, TN (615) 783-1690
David Higgins, EVP & Mng. Dir.
New York, NY (212) 883-6800
Terence J. McCarthy, Mng. Dir.-Global
Frank T. Spencer, Executive VP
Deborah DeMaria, Executive VP
Robert J. Isacco, Managing Director
Okemos, MI (517) 886-9021
Gordon S. White Jr., Sr. Vice President
Overland Park, KS (913) 317-1600
Mike Klockenga, EVP & Mng. Dir.
Philadelphia, PA (215) 665-5683
Michael E. Volpe, EVP & Mng. Dir.
Phoenix, AZ (602) 953-7810
David Bruno, President - Retail Oper.
Susan Schepman, Senior Vice President
Pittsburgh, PA (412) 255-3750
David Smith, Managing Director
Pleasanton, CA (925) 468-4121
David Kurrasch, EVP & Mng. Dir.
Ponte Vedra Beach, FL (904) 273-4656
William S. Elston, EVP & Mng. Dir.
Providence, RI (401) 884-1695
Stephen P. Bartlett, Sr. VP & Mng. Dir.
St. Louis, MO (314) 205-2115
Steven Wood, Sr. VP & Mng. Director
Salt Lake City, UT (801) 350-9101
Richard Hill, Managing Director
San Diego, CA (619) 792-7654
Joel T. Grushkin, EVP & Mng. Dir.
San Francisco, CA (415) 439-5213
Gerald E. Parsons, Sr. VP & Mng. Dir.
Schaumburg, IL (847) 490-6450
Michael Setze, Executive VP
Short Hills, NJ (973) 912-4444
Hayes Reilly, EVP & Mng. Dir.
South Florida, FL (954) 522-4410
Jean M. Bellin, EVP & Mng. Dir.
Southbury, CT (203) 262-8740
Anthony T. DelNegro, EVP & Mng
Director - Northeast Region
Stamford, CT (203) 359-5644
Lawrence Noble, EVP & Mng. Dir.
Tampa, FL (813) 348-0931
John T. Waters, VP. & Mng. Director
Townson, MD (410) 494-6500
Ken Miller, Managing Director
Washington, DC (202) 822-9555
Stephen A. Hayes, EVP & Regional
Managing Director

DIECK MUELLER GROUP

(*SPECIALIZE IN MANUFACTURING*)

1500 N. Casaloma Drive, Suite 409
Appleton, WI 54915
(920) 733-8500
fax (920) 733-8818
www.dieckmueller.com
execsearch@dieckmueller.com

Daniel W. Dieck, President & CEO

DIECKMANN & ASSOCIATES, LTD.†
2 Prudential Plaza, Suite 5555
180 North Stetson Avenue
Chicago, IL 60601-3708
(312) 819-5900
www.dieckmann-associates.com
dieckmann@dieckmann-associates.com
Ralph E. Dieckmann, President

DIMARCHI PARTNERS
7107 LaVista Place, Suite 200
Longmont, CO 80503
(303) 415-9300
www.dimarchi.com
mail@dimarchi.com
Paul M. DiMarchi, President
Patricia A. McKeown, Principal Partner

ROBERT W. DINGMAN COMPANY, INC.†
650 Hampshire Road, Suite 116
Westlake Village, CA 91361-4211
(818) 991-5950
Robert W. Dingman, Chairman
Bruce Dingman, President

DIVERSIFIED SEARCH, INC.†
One Commerce Square
2005 Market St., Suite 3300
Philadelphia, PA 19104
(215) 732-6666
www.divsearch.com
(online form to submit resumes)
Judith M. von Seldeneck, Pres. & CEO
Burton A. MacLean Jr., Mng. Director
Also:
Atlanta, GA (404) 262-1049
Peter Keesom, Managing Director
Boston, MA (617) 523-6870
Joan Lucarelli, Managing Director
Charlotte, NC (704) 331-0006
Jeffrey Siegrist, Managing Director
New York, NY (212) 972-2800
Elaine Burfield, Managing Director

DMG MAXIMUS
(*HEALTH CARE, EDUCATION, PUBLIC SECTOR, UTILITIES & TRANSPORTATION*)
1800 Century Park East, Suite 430
Los Angeles, CA 90067-1507
(310) 552-1112
fax (310) 552-1113
www.dmgmaximus.com
Mr. Norman C. Roberts, Vice President

DOUGAN & ASSOCIATES
(*EMA PARTNERS INTERNATIONAL*)
333 N. Sam Houston Pkwy. E., Suite 400
Houston, TX 77060-2403
(281) 999-7209

PLEASE NOTE: There's a trend toward accepting unsolicited resumes by e-mail. If e-mail and/or fax are shown, they were considered

dougansearch@pdq.net
Mr. David Dougan, President

DROMESHAUSER & ASSOCIATES
(*SPECIALIZE IN HIGH TECH*)
70 Walnut Street
Wellesley Hills, MA 02181
(508) 358-9600

Peter Dromeshauser, President

J. H. DUGAN & ASSOCIATES, INC.
(*SPECIALIZE IN THE PLASTICS INDUSTRY*)
225 Crossroads Boulevard, Suite 416
Carmel, CA 93923
(831) 625-5880
www.jhdugan.com
resumes@jhdugan.com
(online form to submit resumes)
John H. Dugan, President

EARLEY KIELTY & ASSOCIATES, INC.
Two Pennsylvania Plaza, Suite 1990
New York, NY 10121
(212) 736-5626
fax (212) 643-0409
John L. Kielty III, Chairman
Eugene J. Herman, President
John C. Sterling, Sr. Vice President

EARLY COCHRAN & OLSON
(*SPECIALIZE IN LAWYERS*)
401 North Michigan Ave., Suite 515
Chicago, IL 60611-4205
(312) 595-4200
fax (312) 595-4209
Bert H. Early, Corinne Cochran &
B. Tucker Olson, Principals

EASTMAN & BEAUDINE, INC.
5700 West Plano Pkwy, Suite 2800
Plano, TX 75093
www.eastman-beaudine.com
Robert E. Beaudine, President
Also:
Atlanta, GA (770) 390-0875
Frank R. Beaudine Jr., Senior VP &
Managing Director

EFL ASSOCIATES / TRANSEARCH
7101 College Boulevard, Suite 550
Overland Park, KS 66210-1891
(913) 451-8866
fax (913) 451-3219
www.transearch.com
eflinfo@eflkc.com
Peter K. Lemke, President & CEO
Also:
Englewood, CO (303) 779-1724
Jeffrey K. Riley, Sr. VP & Mng. Partner

EFL INTERNATIONAL
8777 East Via de Ventura, Suite 300
Scottsdale, AZ 85258
(480) 483-0496
www.eflinternational.com
William R. Franquemont, President

Jeffrey D. Franquemont, Senior VP

ELWELL & ASSOCIATES, INC.
301 West Liberty Street, Suite E
Ann Arbor, MI 48103
(734) 662-8775
www.elwellassociates.com
elwellas@elwellassociates.com
Richard F. Elwell, President
David Gilmore, Vice President
Steve Elwell, Vice President

ENNS HEVER INC.†
70 University Avenue, Suite 410
Post Office Box 14
Toronto, ON M5J 2M4
(416) 598-0012
fax (416) 598-4328
George R. Enns, President

EVANS SEARCH GROUP
One Darling Drive
Avon, CT 06001
(860) 677-6770
www.esearchgroup.com
Ronald R. Evans, Managing Director

EXECUCOUNSEL, INC.†
1200 Bay Street, Suite 400
Toronto, ON M5R 3K4
(416) 928-3025
Richard Marty, Managing Director

EXECUTIVE MANNING CORPORATION
3000 N.E. 30th Place, Suite 402
Fort Lauderdale, FL 33306
(954) 561-5100
www.exmanning.com
emc@exmannig.com
Richard L. Hertan, Chairman & CEO

EXECUTIVE RESOURCE GROUP INC.
(*SPECIALIZE IN THE PUBLISHING INDUSTRY*)
29 Oakhurst Road
Cape Elizabeth, ME 04107
(207) 871-5527
fax (207) 799-8624
www.mediahunter.com
Ms. Sibyl Masquelier, President

FAIRFAXX CORPORATION
17 High Street
Norwalk, CT 06851
(203) 833-8300
fairfaxxct@aol.com
Jeffrey Thomas, President
Joseph Tucci, Executive Senior VP

LEON A. FARLEY ASSOCIATES
468 Jackson Street, 3rd Floor
San Francisco, CA 94111
(415) 989-0989
fax (415) 989-5908
Leon A. Farley, Managing Partner
Patricia L. Wilson, Partner

FERNEBORG & ASSOCIATES, INC.†
1450 Fashion Island Blvd., Suite 650
San Mateo, CA 94404
(415) 577-0100
www.execsearch.com
resume@execsearch.com
John R. Ferneborg, President
Jay W. Ferneborg, Partner

FINNEGAN & ASSOCIATES
Post Office Box 1183
Palos Verdes Estates, CA 90274
(310) 375-8555
Richard G. Finnegan, President & CEO

HOWARD FISCHER ASSOCIATES, INC.
1800 Kennedy Boulevard, 7th Floor
Philadelphia, PA 19103
(215) 568-8363
Howard M. Fischer, President

FISHER PERSONNEL MANAGEMENT SERVICES
1219 Morningside Drive
Manhattan Beach, CA 90266
(310) 546-7507
fax (310) 546-7574
Neal Fisher, Principal

THE FLAGSHIP GROUP
(*SPECIALIZE IN FINANCIAL SERVICES*)
C-8 Shipway Place, 13th Street
Boston, MA 02129
(617) 242-1170
Anna Coppola, President

ROBERT M. FLANAGAN & ASSOCS., LTD
39 Fields Road
North Salem, NY 10560
(914) 277-7210
Robert M. Flanagan, President

FLEMING ASSOCIATES OF NEW ORLEANS
3900 N. Causeway Blvd., Suite 770
Metairie, LA 70002
(504) 836-7090
David W. McClung, Managing Partner

FOLEY PROCTOR YOSKOWITZ
(*SPECIALIZE IN HEALTH CARE*)
One Cattano Ave.
Morristown, NJ 07960-6820
(973) 605-1000
fax (973) 605-1020
www.fpysearch.com
fpy@fpysearch.com
Thomas J. Foley, Richard Proctor
& Ms. Reggie Yoskowitz, Partners

L. W. FOOTE COMPANY†
110 110th Avenue N.E., Suite 603
Bellevue, WA 98004-5840
(425) 451-1660
www.lwfoote.com
email@lwfoote.com
Leland W. Foote, President

acceptable when this list was compiled. Regardless of what is shown, preference and/or other information may since have changed.

THE FORD GROUP, INC.
485 Devon Park Drive, Suite 110
Wayne, PA 19087
(610) 975-9007
www.thefordgroup.com
Info@thefordgroup.com

Sandra D. Ford, CEO & Mng. Director

D. E. FOSTER PARTNERS
570 Lexington Avenue, 14th Floor
New York, NY 10022
(212) 872-6232

Dwight E. Foster, Exec. Mng. Director

Also:
Dallas, TX (214) 754-2241
William D. Rowe, Exec. Mng. Director
Stamford, CT (203) 356-9800
Robert Hart, Director
Washington, DC (202) 467-3093
Dann P. Stringer, Ptnr. & Sr. Mng. Dir.

FOY, SCHNEID & DANIEL, INC.
555 Madison Avenue, 12th Floor
New York, NY 10022
(212) 980-2525

Beverly R. Daniel, Partner
James Foy, Partner

FRANCIS & ASSOCIATES†
6923 Vista Drive
West Des Moines, IA 50266
(515) 221-9800
FranSearch@aol.com

Dwaine Francis, Managing Partner
Kay Francis, Partner

KS FRARY & ASSOCIATES
One Salem Green, Suite 403
Salem, MA 01970
(978) 741-5201
fax (978) 741-5203
www.ksfrary.com

Kevin S. Frary, President

FURST GROUP/MPI
(SPECIALIZE IN HEALTH CARE)
555 S. Perryville Road
Rockford, IL 61108-2509
(815) 229-9111
fax (815) 229-8926
www.furstgroup.com
furstgroup@furstgroup.com

Sherrie L. Barch, Principal
J. Robert Clarke, Principal

JAY GAINES & COMPANY, INC.†
(SPECIALIZE IN FINANCE & MIS)
450 Park Avenue
New York, NY 10022
(212) 308-9222
fax (212) 308-5146

Jay Gaines, President

GARDINER, TOWNSEND & ASSOCIATES†
101 East 52nd Street, 25th Floor
New York, NY 10022

(212) 838-0707
fax (212) 838-0424
www.gardinertownsend.com

E. Nicholas P. Gardiner, President
John Townsend, Partner

GILBERT & VAN CAMPEN INTERNATIONAL
420 Lexington Avenue
New York, NY 10170
(212) 661-2122
fax (212) 599-0839

Stephen B. Van Campen, President

GILBERT TWEED ASSOCIATES INC.
415 Madison Avenue, 20th Floor
New York, NY 10017
(212) 758-3000
www.gilberttweed.com
info@gilberttweed.com

Stephanie L. Pinson, President
Janet Tweed, Chief Executive Officer

GILREATH WEATHERBY INC.
Post Office Box 1483
50B Brook Street
Manchester-by-the-Sea, MA 01944
(978) 526-8771
www.GilreathWeatherby.com

James M. Gilreath, President

THE GLAZIN GROUP†
(SPECIALIZE IN REAL ESTATE & HOSPITALITY)
2300-1066 West Hasting Street
Vancouver, BC V6E 3X2
(604) 687-3875

Lynne Glazin, Partner

GOODRICH SHERWOOD ASSOCS., INC.
521 Fifth Avenue
New York, NY 10175
(212) 697-4131
fax (212) 983-7499

Andrew Sherwood, Chairman

Also:
Norwalk, CT (203) 847-2525
Richard E. Spann, Ex. Vice President
Charles Wright, Sr. Vice President
Parsippany, NJ (973) 455-7100
William Heald, Principal
Princeton, NJ (609) 452-0202
Donald C. Doele, Sr. VP & Manager
Rochester, NY (716) 262-4277
Cornelius J. Murphy, Sr. Vice President

GOODWIN & COMPANY
1150 Connecticut Ave., Suite 200
Washington, DC 20036
(202) 785-9292
fax (202) 785-9297

Tom L. Goodwin, President

GOULD, McCOY & CHADICK, INC.†
300 Park Avenue, 20th Floor
New York, NY 10022
(212) 688-8671
www.gmcsearch.com

gmc@gmcsearch.com
William E. Gould, Millington F.
McCoy & Susan Chadick, Mng. Partners

A. DAVIS GRANT & COMPANY
(SPECIALIZE IN MIS)
295 Pierson Avenue
Edison, NJ 08837
(732) 494-2266
fax (732) 494-3626
www.adg.net

Allan D. Grossman, Senior Partner

GRANT COOPER & ASSOCIATES
9900 Clayton Road
St. Louis, MO 63124-1102
(314) 567-4690
www.grantcooper.com
mail@grantcooper.com

Cynthia J. Kohlbry, Mng. Principal
Stephen H. Loeb, Principal
J. Dale Meier, Principal

GRANTHAM, GRIFFIN & BUCK, INC.
161Weaver Dairy Road
Chapel Hill, NC 27514
(919) 932-5650
fax (919) 942-1624
www.integritycareers.com

John D. Grantham, President
Charlie Griffin, Vice President
John Buck, Vice President

ANNIE GRAY ASSOCIATES, INC.
516 South Hanley
St. Louis, MO 63105
(314) 721-0205
www.anniegray.com
resume@anniegray.com

Annie Gray, President & CEO

GROSSBERG & ASSOCIATES
(SPECIALIZE IN MANUFACTURING & HEALTH CARE)
1100 Jorie Boulevard, Suite 301
Oak Brook, IL 60521
(630) 574-0066

Robert M. Grossberg, Mng. Partner

GUNDERSEN PARTNERS
230 West 17th Street, 6th floor
New York, NY 10011
(212) 675-2300
fax (212) 675-6965

Steven Gundersen, President & CEO

HALBRECHT LIEBERMAN ASSOCS., INC.†
(SPECIALIZE IN MIS & COMMUNICATIONS)
1200 Summer Street
Stamford, CT 06905-5573
(203) 327-5630
www.hlassoc.com
info@hlassoc.com

Beverly Lieberman, President

PLEASE NOTE: There's a trend toward accepting unsolicited resumes by e-mail. If e-mail and/or fax are shown, they were considered

W.L. HANDLER & ASSOCIATES
2255 Cumberland Pkwy. NW, Bldg. 1500
Atlanta, GA 30339
(770) 805-5000
www.wlhandler.com
resume@wlhandler.com

William Handler, President

HANDY PARTNERS
380 Lexington Avenue, Suite 2125
New York, NY 10168
(212) 697-5600
www.handypartners.com
info@handypartners.com

J. Gerald Simmons, President
Patrick Brennan, Managing Partner

HARVARD AIMES GROUP
(SPECIALIZE IN CORP. RISK MANAGEMENT &
SAFETY CLAIMS MANAGEMENT)
6 Holcomb Street
Post Office Box 16006
West Haven, CT 06516
(203) 933-1976
www.riskmanagementsearch.com
jlg@iskmanagementsearch.com

James J. Gunther, Principal

HASKELL & STERN ASSOCIATES INC.
380 Madison Avenue, 7th Floor
New York, NY 10017
(212) 856-4451

Allan D. R. Stern, Managing Director

HAYDEN GROUP, INC.
(SPECIALIZE IN FINANCIAL SERVICES)
One Post Office Square, Suite 3830
Boston, MA 02109
(617) 482-2445

Harry B. McCormick, Partner
Robert E. Hawley, Partner

HEATH/NORTON ASSOCIATES, INC.
545 Eighth Avenue, 7th Floor
New York, NY 10018
(212) 695-3600

Richard S. Stoller, President
Richard Rosenow, Senior Vice Pres.

HEIDRICK & STRUGGLES, INC.†
233 South Wacker Drive, Suite 7000
Chicago, IL 60606-6402
(312) 496-1000
fax (312) 496-1046
www.heidrick.com

Gerard R. Roche, Chairman (NY)
William J. Bowen, Chairman (Chicago)
Robert E. Hallagan, V.Chmn. (Boston)
John T. Thompson, V. Chmn. (Menlo Pk.)
Patrick S. Pittard, President & CEO
(Atlanta)

Also:
Atlanta, GA (404) 577-2410
A. Wayne Luke, Area Mng. Partner
Dale Jones, Office Managing Partner
Boston, MA (617) 423-1140

Carl Schaad, Office Managing Partner
Charlotte, NC (704) 335-1953
Eugene M. Rackley, Off. Mng. Partner
Chicago, IL (312) 496-1000
Linda Heagy, Office Mng. Partner
Caroline B. Ballantine, Partner
Michael D. Caver, Partner
Robert L. Heidrick, Partner
P. Frederick Kahn, Partner
Cleveland, OH (216) 241-7410
Charles E. Wallace, Off. Mng. Partner
Dallas, TX (214) 706-7700
David Pasahow, Off. Mng. Partner
Greenwich, CT (203) 629-3705
John DeRegt, Office Managing Partner
Houston, TX (713) 237-9000
David A. Morris, Off. Mng. Partner
Irvine, CA (949) 475-6500
Judy Klein, Off. Mng. Partner
Jacksonville, FL (904) 355-6674
Charles R. Hoskins, Off. Mng. Partner
Lexington, MA (781) 862-3370
Charles Polachi, Jr. , Off. Mng. Partner
Los Angeles, CA (213) 625-8811
Thomas M. Mitchell, Off. Mng. Partner
Menlo Park, CA (650) 234-1500
Wesley Richards, Office Mng. Partner
Miami, FL (305) 262-2606
Jean-Dominique Virchaux, Mng. Partner
New York, NY, *Park Ave* (212) 867-9876
Marvin Berenblum, North America Area
Mng. Partner
New York, NY, *Wall St.* (212) 699-3000
Barry Bregman. Off. Mng. Partner
Philadelphia, PA (215) 988-1000
Kenneth L. Kring, Off. Mng. Partner
San Francisco, CA (415) 981-2854
Jeffrey W. Hodge, Off. Mng. Partner
Toronto, ON (416) 361-4700
Jack Nederpelt, Office Mng. Partner
Washington, DC (202) 289-4450
Kevin McNerney, Managing Partner

G. W. HENN & COMPANY
42 East Gay Street, Suite 1312
Columbus, OH 43215
(614) 469-9666

George W. Henn Jr., President

THE HETZEL GROUP
1601 Colonial Parkway
Williamsburg Village
Inverness, IL 60067
(874) 776-7000

William G. Hetzel, President

HEYMAN ASSOCIATES, INC.†
(SPECIALIZE IN COMMUNICATIONS & PR)
11 Penn Plaza, Suite 1105
New York, NY 10001
(212) 784-2717
www.heymanassociates.com
hai@heymanassociates.com

William C. Heyman, President & CEO

HIGDON PRINCE INC.†
(SPECIALIZE IN FINANCIAL SERVICES)
230 Park Avenue, Suite 1455

New York, NY 10169
(212) 986-4662
www.higdonprince.com
contact@higdonprince.com

Henry G. Higdon, Marylin L. Prince &
Maryann C. Bovich, Managing Directors

HODGE-CRONIN & ASSOCIATES, INC.
(MEMBER, INDEPENDENT INTERNATIONAL
CONSULTANTS)
Post Office Box 309-0309
Des Plaines, IL 60016
(847) 803-9000

Richard J. Cronin, President
Kathleen A. Cronin, Vice President

HARVEY HOHAUSER & ASSOCIATES, LLC
5600 New King Street, Suite 355
Troy MI, 48098
(248) 641-1400
fax (248) 641 1929

Harvey Hohauser, President

Also
Okemos, MI (517) 349-7007
Kenneth F. Glickman, Senior VP

THE HOLMAN GROUP, INC.†
(SPECIALIZE IN CEO'S & VENTURE CAPITAL
PARTNERS)
1592 Union Street, Suite 239
San Francisco, CA 94123
(415) 751-2700
fax (415) 751-4897
www.holmangroup.net

Jonathan S. Holman, President

J.B. HOMER ASSOCIATES INC.†
(SPECIALIZE IN INFORMATION TECHNOLOGY)
420 Lexington Avenue, Suite 2328
New York, NY 10170-0002
(212) 697-3300
www.JBHomer.com
resumes@JBHomer.com

Judy B. Homer, President & Principal

HORTON INTERNATIONAL, INC.†
10 Tower Lane
Avon, CT 06001
(860) 674-8701
fax (860) 676-9753
Larry C. Brown, Managing Director
Robert H. Horton, Chairman (NY)
Michael Boxberger, CEO

Also:
Atlanta, GA (404) 459-5950
Sally Baker, Managing Director
Baltimore, MD (410) 625-3800
Timothy C. McNamara, Mng. Director
Chicago, IL (312) 332-3830
Dirk A. Himes, Managing Director
Los Angeles, CA (310) 454-4933
Susan Reynolds, Managing Director
New York, NY (212) 973-3780
Carolyn Dursi-Porteous, Mng. Director
Santa Clarita, CA (661) 222-2272
William H. Perry, Vice President

acceptable when this list was compiled. Regardless of what is shown, preference and/or other information may since have changed.

HOWE-LEWIS INTERNATIONAL
(SPECIALIZE IN HEALTH CARE)
521 Fifth Avenue, 36th Floor
New York, NY 10175
(212) 697-5000
fax (212) 697-6600

Anita Howe-Waxman, Chairman
Patricia Greco & Esther Rosenberg,
  Co-Managing Directors

HRD CONSULTANTS, INC.†
(SPECIALIZE IN HUMAN RESOURCES)
60 Walnut Avenue, Suite 100
Clark, NJ 07066
(908) 815-7825
www.hrdconsultants.com

Marcia Glatman, President

E.A. HUGHES & COMPANY†
(SPECIALIZE IN APPAREL & HOME FASHION)
146 East 37th Street
New York, NY 10016
(212) 689-4600
fax (212) 689-4975
www.eahughes.com
(online form to submit resumes)

Elaine A. Hughes, President

HUNT & HOWE INC.†
1 Dag Hammarskjold Plaza, 34th floor
New York, NY 10017
(212) 758-2800

James E. Hunt, Partner
William S. Howe, Partner

HUTCHINSON GROUP, INC.
235 Yorkland Boulevard, Suite 300
Toronto, ON M2J 4Y8
(416) 499-6621

Hamilton Hutchinson, President
David Hutchinson, Vice President

HVS EXECUTIVE SEARCH†
(SPECIALIZE IN THE HOSPITALITY INDUSTRY)
372 Willis Avenue
Mineola, NY 11501
(516) 248-8828
www.hvsinternational.com

Keith Kefgen, President

HYDE DANFORTH & COMPANY
5950 Berkshire Lane, Suite 1040
Dallas, TX 75225
(214) 691-5966
www.hdco.net
resume@hdco.net

W. Jerry Hyde, President
W. Michael Danforth, Executive VP

INGRAM & AYDELOTTE, INC.
430 Park Avenue , Suite 700
New York, NY 10022
(212) 319-7777

D. John Ingram, Partner
G. Thomas Aydelotte, Partner

INTERNATIONAL MGMT. ADVISORS, INC.
(MEMBER, INTERNATIONAL SEARCH ASSOCIATES, INC.)
P.O. Box 174, FDR Station
New York, NY 10150
(212) 758-7770

Constance W. Klages, President

ISAACSON, MILLER
334 Boylston Street, Suite 500
Boston, MA 02116
(617) 262-6500
www.imsearch.com

John Isaacson, Partner & Mng. Director
Arnie Miller, Partner

PENDLETON JAMES & ASSOCIATES, INC.†
200 Park Avenue, Suite 1600
New York, NY 10166
(212) 557-1599
www.penjames.com
pja@penjames.com

E. Pendleton James, Chairman
Also:
Boston, MA (617) 261-9696
Durant A. Hunter, President

JANUARY MANAGEMENT GROUP
432 East Rich Street, Suite 2F
Columbus, OH 43215
(614) 463-1820

Bruce M. Bastoky, President

JONAS, WALTERS & ASSOCIATES, INC.
1110 N. Old World Third St., Suite 510
Milwaukee, WI 53203-1102
(414) 291-2828

William F. Walters, President
Peter Flannery, Executive VP
Robert Denniston, Vice President

JONES-PARKER/STARR
(SPECIALIZE IN THE CONSULTING INDUSTRY)
207 South Elliott Road, Suite 155
Chapel Hill, NC 27514
(919) 542-5977

Janet Jones-Parker, Managing Director

KALUDIS CONSULTING GROUP, INC.
(SPECIALIZE IN HIGHER EDUCATION)
1055 Thomas Jefferson Street, N.W.
Washington, DC 20007
(202) 298-2800
www.kcg.com

George Kaludis, President

GARY KAPLAN & ASSOCIATES
201 South Lake Avenue, Suite 600
Pasadena, CA 91101
(626) 796-8100
www.gkasearch.com

Gary Kaplan, President

HOWARD KARR & ASSOCIATES INC.†
(SPECIALIZE IN FINANCE)
1777 Borel Place, Suite 408

San Mateo, CA 94402-3513
(650) 574-5277
www.karr.com
search@karr.com

Howard L. Karr, President
Cynthia L. Karr, Vice President

A. T. KEARNEY EXECUTIVE SEARCH†
222 West Adams Street
Chicago, IL 60606
(312) 648-0111
(312) 223-6369
www.atkearney.com

Charles W. Sweet, President

Also:
Alexandria, VA (703) 836-6210
Roger I. Sekera, VP & Mng. Director
Atlanta, GA (404) 760-6600
Richard Citarella, VP & Mng. Director
Cleveland, OH (216) 241-6880
David Lauderback, VP & Mng. Dir.
Dallas, TX (214) 969-0010
Rocky Johnson, VP & Mng. Director
Houston, TX (713) 222-1276
Les Csorba, VP & Mng. Director
Los Angeles, CA (213) 689-6800
Otis Booth III, VP & Mng. Director
Jill Faber, VP & Mng. Director
Miami, FL (305) 577-0046
John T. Mestepey, VP & Mng. Director
Minneapolis, MN (612) 921-8436
Don A. Hykes, VP & Mng. Director
New York, NY (212) 751-7040
James Abruzzo, VP & Mng. Director
Redwood City, CA (650) 637-6600
Carl Olsen, VP & Mng. Director
San Diego, CA (858) 646-3066
Susan Major, VP & Mng. Director
Stamford, CT (203) 969-2222
Mark J. McMahon, VP & Mng. Dir.

KENZER CORPORATION
777 Third Avenue
New York, NY 10017
(212) 308-4300
www.kenzer.com
ny@kenzer.com
(online form to submit resumes)
Robert D. Kenzer, Chairman & CEO
Eric B. Segal, President

Also:
Atlanta, GA (770) 955-7210
Marie Powell, Vice President
Chicago, IL (312) 266-0976
Barbara Kaufmann, Vice President
Dallas, TX (972) 620-7776
Don Jones, Vice President
Los Angeles, CA (310) 417-8577
Robert Armstrong, Vice President
Minneapolis, MN (612) 332-7700
Mary Jeanne Scott, Vice President

KETCHUM, INC.
(SPECIALIZE IN NONPROFIT & FUND-RAISING)
12770 Merit Drive, Suite 900
Dallas, TX 75251
(412) 281-1481

PLEASE NOTE: There's a trend toward accepting unsolicited resumes by e-mail. If e-mail and/or fax are shown, they were considered

Robert E. Carter, President

KINCANNON & REED†
(SPECIALIZE IN FOOD & AGRIBUSINESS)
2106-C Gallows Road
Vienna, VA 22182
(703) 761-4046
fax (703) 790-1533
www.krsearch.com
Mr. Kelly Kincannon, President & CEO

RICHARD KINSER & ASSOCIATES†
515 Madison Avenue, 36th Floor
New York, NY 10022
(212) 588-8801
Richard E. Kinser, President

KNAPP CONSULTANTS
(SPECIALIZE IN HIGH TECH & MANUFACTURING)
184 Old Ridgefield Road
Wilton, CT 06897
(203) 762-0790
fax (203) 762-0747
Ronald A. Knapp, President

KORN/FERRY INTERNATIONAL†
1800 Century Park East, Suite 900
Los Angeles, CA 90067-1593
(310) 552-1834
Richard M. Ferry, Chairman
Windle B. Priem, President & C.E.O.
(N.Y. Office)
Peter L. Dunn, Vice Chrmn. & C.O.O.
(L.A. Office)
Dr. John Moxley, Managing.Director
(L.A. Office)
Also:
Atlanta, GA (404) 577-7542
James E. Boone, Managing Director
Austin, TX (512) 236-1834
Robert Golding, Managing Director
Boston, MA (617) 345-0200
Dr. Mark L. Smith, VP & Office Mgr.
Chicago, IL (312) 466-1834
Scott Kingdom, VP & Office Manager
Dallas, TX (214) 954-1834
Robert William Funk, Mng. Director
Houston, TX (713) 651-1834
John R. Brock, Managing Director
Menlo Park, CA (415) 529-1834
Geoff Champion, Managing V.P.
Miami, FL (305) 377-4121
Bonnie Crabtree, Managing Director
Minneapolis, MN (612) 333-1834
Allan H. Raymond, Managing VP
New York, NY (212) 687-1834
Windle B. Priem, President & CEO -
Korn/Ferry International
Greg Coleman, V.P. - Fin'l. Svcs.
Michael A. Wellman, Managing Dir. -
New York Office
Newport Beach, CA (949) 851-1834
Elliot Gordon, Mng. Vice President
Philadelphia, PA (215) 496-6666
David Shabot, Managing Director
Princeton, NJ (609) 921-8811

Richard Arons, Managing Director
Redwood City, CA (650) 632-1835
Geoffrey Champion, Mng. Director
San Francisco, CA (415) 956-1834
James N. Heuerman, Mng. Director
David Nosal, Managing Director
Seattle, WA (206) 447-1834
Hershel V. Jones, VP & Office Mgr.
Stamford, CT (203) 359-3350
Terence P. McGovern, Mng. Director
Toronto, ON (416) 593-5776
P. J. Fennell, President - Canada
Vienna, VA (703) 761-7020
James M. Searing, Managing Director
Washington, DC (202) 822-9444
Mike Kirknan, Managing Director

KORS MONTGOMERY INTERNATIONAL
(SPECIALIZE IN CHEMICAL ENGINEERING, ENERGY & HIGH TECH)
1980 Post Oak Boulevard, Suite 2280
Houston, TX 77056-3810
(713) 840-7101
fax (713) 840-7280
www.korsmontgomery.com
research@korsmontgomery.com
R. Paul Kors, President

KPMG EXECUTIVE SEARCH
Commerce Court West
199 Bay Street
Toronto, ON M5L 1B2
(416) 777-8500
fax (416) 777-8070
James A. Parr, Vice President,
Executive Search
Also:
Calgary, AB (403) 691-8300
Brian Corbishley, Partner
Edmonton, AB (403) 429-7300
Allan Jacobson, Partner
Halifax, NS (902) 492-6062
Ken Hubbard, Principal
Montreal, PQ (514) 840-2500
Robert Nadeau, Partner
Ottawa, ON (613) 598-3700
Gary Reid, Partner
Saskatoon, SK (306) 934-6283
Roy Lloyd, Partner
Vancouver, BC (604) 669-4600
Anne Moore, Principal
Waterloo, ON (519) 747-8800
John Reid, Managing Partner

KRECKLO & ASSOCIATES INC.†
(SPECIALIZE IN MIS & TECHNOLOGY)
2 Bloor Street West, Suite 700
Toronto, ON M4W 3R1
(512) 573-2556
www.krecklo.com
Brian D. Krecklo, President

KREMPLE & MEADE INC.
Post Office Box 426
Pacific Palisades, CA 90272
(310) 459-4221
tomnet@gte.net

Thomas M. Meade, President & CEO

KREUTZ CONSULTING GROUP, INC.†
(SPECIALIZE IN HIGH TECH)
585 North Bank Lane, Suite 2000
Lake Forest, IL 60045
(847) 234-9115
Gary L. Kreutz, President

KRISTOPHERS CONSULTANTS
(SPECIALIZE IN HEALTH CARE, CONSUMER PRODUCTS & AUTOMOTIVE)
5551 North Osceola
Chicago, IL 60656
(773) 594-1301
Kevin Cabai, President

KUNZER ASSOCIATES, LTD.
1415 West 22nd Street, Suite 1180
Oak Brook, IL 60521
(630) 574-0010
William J. Kunzer, President

THE LAPHAM GROUP, INC.
80 Park Avenue, Suite 3-K
New York, NY 10016-2533
(212) 599-0644
www.thelaphamgroup.com
Lawrence L. Lapham, President

LARSEN, WHITNEY, BLECKSMITH, & ZILLIACUS
888 West Sixth Street, Suite 500
Los Angeles, CA 90017
(213) 243-0033
Richard F. Larsen, William A. Whitney
Edward L. Blecksmith & Patrick W.
Zilliacus, Principals

LAUER, SBARBARO ASSOCIATES
(EMA PARTNERS INTERNATIONAL)
30 North LaSalle, Suite 4030
Chicago, IL 60602-2588
(312) 372-7050
fax (312) 704-4393
www.emapartners.com
Richard D. Sbarbaro, President
William Yacullo, Exec. Vice President

LAWRENCE-LEITER & COMPANY
4400 Shawnee Mission Pkwy., Suite 204
Shawnee Mission, KS 66205
(913) 677-5500
David Bywaters, President
William B. Beeson, Vice President

LEVY / KERSON, INC.
(SPECIALIZE IN RETAIL)
200 Park Avenue, 37th Floor
New York, NY 10166
(212) 421-1133
Robert E. Kerson, Chairman

LOCKE & ASSOCIATES†
2410 Nations Bank Plaza
Charlotte, NC 28280

(704) 372-6600
M. Fred Locke Jr., President
Also:
Montgomery, AL (334) 272-7400
Glen Pruitt, Vice President

ROBERT LOWELL INTERNATIONAL
12200 Park Central Drive, Suite 120
Dallas, TX 75251
(972) 233-2270

Robert M. Bryza, Chairman

THE JOHN LUCHT CONSULTANCY INC.†
The Olympic Tower
641 Fifth Avenue
New York, NY 10022
(212) 935-4660

John Lucht, President

LYNCH MILLER MOORE PARTNERS INC.
10 South Wacker Drive, Suite 2935
Chicago, IL 60606
(312) 876-1505
www.lmminc.com

Michael C. Lynch, Michael Miller &
David Moore, Founding Partners

THE MACDONALD GROUP, INC.
301 Route 17, Suite 800
Rutherford, NJ 07070
(201) 939-2312
fax (201) 939-2312
macdgrp@aol.com

G. William Macdonald, President

THE MADISON GROUP
342 Madison Avenue, Suite 1060
New York, NY 10173
(212) 599-0032

David Soloway, Managing Director

MARK ADAM ASSOCIATES
*(SPECIALIZE IN INFORMATION SYSTEMS,
FINANCE & GENERAL MANAGEMENT)*
256 Canterbury Road
Westfield, NJ 07090-1905
(908) 654-8999
fax (908) 654-1136
www.markadamassoc.com

Donald A. Pizzi, Principal

J. L. MARK ASSOCIATES, INC.
2000 Arapahoe Street, Suite 505
Denver, CO 80205
(303) 292-0360
www.jlmark.com

John L. Mark, President
Ms. Lynne Mark, Senior Recruiter

MARK STANLEY
(EMA PARTNERS INTERNATIONAL)
1629 K Street N.W., Suite 1100
Washington, DC 20006
(202) 785-6711
fax (202) 331-4212

John H. Ramsey, President

MARRA PETERS & PARTNERS
Millburn Esplanade
Millburn, NJ 07041
(973) 376-8999
www.marrapeters.com
mpp@marrapeters.com

John V. Marra Jr., President

MARSHALL CONSULTANTS, INC.
(SPECIALIZE IN CORP. COMMUNICATIONS)
360 East 65th Street, Penthouse B
New York, NY 10021
(212) 628-8400
fax (212) 628-8449
www.marshallconsultants.com

Larry Marshall, President & C.E.O.

MARTIN PARTNERS†
224 South Michigan Avenue, Suite 620
Chicago, IL 60604
(312) 922-1800
www.martinptrs.com
webmaster@martinptrs.com

Theodore B. Martin, Founder & Partner
Sally Frantz, Partner
Thomas Jagielo, Partner

MASCHAL / CONNORS, INC.
(SPECIALIZE IN INDUSTRIAL PRODUCTS)
306 South Bay Avenue
Beach Haven, NJ 08008
(609) 492-3400

Charles E. Maschal Jr., President

MASON & ASSOCIATES
3000 Sand Hill Road
Building 1, Suite 155
Menlo Park, CA 94025
(650) 322-5288
fax (650) 347-3478

Robert G. Mason, President

THE MCAULAY FIRM†
Bank of America Corporate Center
100 North Tryon Street, Suite 5220
Charlotte, NC 28202
(704) 342-1880

Albert L. McAulay Jr., President

McBRIDE ASSOCIATES, INC.†
1511 K Street, N.W., Suite 819
Washington, DC 20005-1497
(202) 638-1150

Jonathan E. McBride, President

McCORMACK & ASSOCIATES†
*(SPECIALIZE IN NONPROFIT & DIVERSITY
EXECUTIVE SEARCH*
5042 Wilshire Boulevard, Suite 505
Los Angeles, CA 90036
(323) 549-9200
www.mccormackassociates.com

Joseph A. McCormack, Mng. Partner

McCORMACK & FARROW
695 Town Center Drive, Suite 660

Costa Mesa, CA 92626-1981
(714) 549-7222

Helen Friedman, Gene L. Phelps,
Kenneth Thompson, Jim Wade, Jeff
McDermott & Steve Treibel, Partners

G.E. McFARLAND & COMPANY
535 Colonial Park Drive
Roswell, GA 30075
(770) 992-0900
fax (770) 640-0067

Charles P. Beall, Managing Partner

CLARENCE E. McFEELY, INC.†
39 Brinker Road
Barrington, IL 60010
(847) 381-0475

Clarence E. McFeely, President

ROBERT McGRATH ASSOCIATES
*(SPECIALIZE IN CHEMICAL S & PAPER
INDUSTRIES)*
P.O. Box 2179
Westport, CT 06880
(203) 221-8335
fax (203) 221-8378

McNICHOL ASSOCIATES
*(SPECIALIZE IN ARCHITECTURE &
ENGINEERING)*
8419 Germantown Avenue
Philadelphia, PA 19118
(215) 922-4142
fax (215) 922-0178

John McNichol, President

JON McRAE & ASSOCIATES, INC.
*(SPECIALIZE IN PRESIDENTIAL & CABINET
SEARCHES FOR UNIVERSITIES)*
1930 N. Druid Hills Rd. N.E.,
Suite 200
Atlanta, GA 30319
(404) 325-3252
www.jonmcrae.com
jma@jonmcrae.com

Mr. O. Jon McRae, President

MDR ASSOCIATES
(SPECIALIZE IN HEALTH CARE)
9485 S.W. 72nd Street, Suite A270
Miami, FL 33173
(305) 271-9213
fax (305) 594-1053
www.mdrsearch.com

Judith Berger, President
Stephen Schoen, Executive Director

JAMES MEAD & COMPANY
(SPECIALIZE IN CONSUMER PCKGD GOODS)
15 Old Danbury Rd.,Suite 202
Wilton, CT 06897-2524
(203) 834-6300
mailbox@jmeadco.com

James D. Mead, President
Arthur S. Brown, Exec. VP & Partner

PLEASE NOTE: There's a trend toward accepting unsolicited resumes by e-mail. If e-mail and/or fax are shown, they were considered

MENG, FINSETH & ASSOCIATES, INC.
Del Amo Executive Plaza, Suite 202
3858 Carson Street
Torrance, CA 90503
(310) 316-0706
Charles M. Meng, President
Carl L. Finseth, Exec VP &Partner

MESSETT ASSOCIATES, INC.
*(PARTNER IN INTERNATIONAL EXECUTIVE
SEARCH, INC.)*
7700 North Kendall Drive, Suite 304
Miami, FL 33156
(305) 275-1000
www.messett.com
William J. Messett III, President

HERBERT MINES ASSOCIATES, INC.†
375 Park Avenue, Suite 301
New York, NY 10152
(212) 355-0909
www.herbertmines.com
Herbert Mines, Chairman
Harold D. Reiter, President & CEO
Jane Vergari, Senior Vice President

MIRTZ MORICE, INC.
One Dock Street, 3rd Floor
Stamford, CT 06902-5836
(203) 964-9266
P. John Mirtz, Partner
James L. Morice, Partner

M/J/A PARTNERS, INC.
(SPECIALIZE IN EXEC. MANAGEMENT)
1100 Jorie Boulevard, Suite 301
Oak Brook, IL 60521
(630) 990-0033
Manuel J. Alves, President
Victor R. Lindquist, Vice President

MONTGOMERY WEST
99 Almaden Boulevard, Suite 600
San Jose, CA 95113
(408) 292-9876
montgomerywest.com
resumes@montgomerywest.com
Greg Goodere, VP & Mng. Director

MORRIS & BERGER, INC.
(SPECIALIZE IN NONPROFIT)
201 South Lake Avenue, Suite 700
Pasadena, CA 91101
(626) 795-0522
fax (626) 795-6330
www.morrisberger.com
mb@morrisberger.com
Kristine A. Morris, Partner
Jay V. Berger, Partner

MOYER, SHERWOOD ASSOCIATES†
*(SPECIALIZE IN COMMUNICATIONS, PUBLIC
RELATIONS & INVESTMENT RELATIONS)*
1285 Ave. of the Americas, 35th floor
New York, NY 10019
(212) 554-4008
www.moyersherwood.com

research@moyersherwood.com
David S. Moyer, President

MRUK & PARTNERS
(EMA PARTNERS INTERNATIONAL)
230 Park Avenue, Suite 1000
New York, NY 10169
(212) 808-3076
Edwin S. Mruk, Senior Partner

MTA PARTNERS
(SPECIALIZE IN HEALTH CARE)
2828 West Parker Road, Suite 207
Plano, TX 75075
(972) 758-8646
Michael Tucker, Mng. Partner
Brian Ehringer, Partner

P. J. MURPHY & ASSOCIATES, INC.
735 North Water Street, Suite 915
Milwaukee, WI 53202
(414) 277-9777
www.pjmurphy.com
cszaff@pjmurphy.com
Dr. Patrick J. Murphy, Chairman

NADZAM, HORGAN & ASSOCIATES, INC.†
(SPECIALIZE IN HIGH TECH)
3211 Scott Boulevard, Suite 205
Santa Clara, CA 95054
(408) 727-6601
www.nhexecutivesearch.com
nh@nhexecutivesearch.com
Richard J. Nadzam, Partner
Thomas F. Horgan, Partner

NAGLER, ROBINS & POE, OMC
(SPECIALIZE IN HIGH TECH)
65 William Street
Wellesley Hills, MA 02181-3802
(781) 431-1330
fax (781) 431-7861
www.nrpinc.com
Leon G. Nagler, Ms. Jeri N. Robins, &
James B. Poe, Managing Directors

NORDEMAN GRIMM, INC.†
717 Fifth Avenue, 26th Floor
New York, NY 10022
(212) 935-1000
www.nordemangrimm.com
resume@nordemangrimm.com
Jacques C. Nordeman, Chairman
Peter G. Grimm, Vice Chairman

NORMAN BROADBENT INTERNAT'L. INC.†
*(SPECIALIZE IN NEW MEDIA, TECHNOLOGY,
COMMUNICATIONS & FINANCIAL SERVICES)*
200 Park Avenue, 20th Floor
New York, NY 10166-0011
(212) 953-6990
www.nbisearch.com
(online form to submit resumes)
Mr. Graham Durgan, CEO
Ms. Leah Peskin, Managing Director
Also:

Atlanta, GA (770) 955-9550
Charles J. Chalk, Managing Director
Chicago, IL (312) 876-3300
Thomas Higgins, COO
Reston, VA (703) 758 3528
Nicola Hasling, Managing Director
San Francisco,CA (415) 274-8333
Mark Brooke, Managing Director

OBER & COMPANY
11777 San Vicente Blvd., Suite 860
Los Angeles, CA 90049
(310) 207-1127
Ms. Lynn W. Ober, President

O'BRIEN & BELL
812 Huron Road, Suite 535
Cleveland, OH 44115
(216) 575-1212
fax (216) 575-7502
www.obrienbell.com
Timothy O'Brien, President

OLIVER & ROZNER ASSOCIATES, INC.†
823 Walton Avenue
Mamaroneck, NY 10543-4535
(914) 381-6242
Burton L. Rozner, President

THE ONSTOTT GROUP†
60 William Street
Wellesley, MA 02181-3803
(781) 235-3050
www.onstott.com
Joseph E. Onstott & Ben Beaver,
Managing Directors

OPALKA DIXON CONSULTANTS
(SPECIALIZE IN DIRECT MARKETING)
72 Cummings Point Road
Stamford, CT 06902
(623) 977-1135
Violet Dixon, President
Also:
Richmond, VA (804) 358-0119

OPPEDISANO & COMPANY, INC.
(SPECIALIZE IN INVESTMENT MANAGEMENT)
370 Lexington Avenue, Suite 1200
New York, NY 10017
(212) 696-0144
fax (212) 686-3006
opsearch@aol.com
Edward A. Oppedisano, Chrmn. & CEO

OPPORTUNITY RESOURCES INC.†
*(SPECIALIZE IN NONPROFIT & CULTURAL
ORGANIZATIONS)*
25 West 43rd Street, Suite 1017
New York, NY 10036
(212) 575-1688
Freda Mindlin, President

O'SHEA, DIVINE & CORPORATION
4 Civic Plaza, Suite 350
Newport Beach, CA 92660

(949) 720-9070
fax (949) 720-9628

Robert S. Divine, Principal

DENNIS P. O'TOOLE & ASSOCIATES, INC.†
(SPECIALIZE IN HOSPITALITY & LEISURE)
1865 Palmer Avenue, Suite 210
Larchmont, NY 10538
(914) 833-3712

Dennis P. O'Toole, President

OTT & HANSEN, INC.
136 South Oak Knoll, Suite 300
Pasadena, CA 91101
(626) 578-0551
fax (626) 578-0570

George W. Ott, President &CEO.
David G. Hansen, Executive Vice Pres.

D. P. PARKER & ASSOCIATES INC.†
(SPECIALIZE IN HIGH TECH)
372 Washington Street
Wellesley, MA 02481
(781) 237-1220
www.dpparker.com
information@dpparker.com

Dr. David P. Parker, President

PARKER, SHOLL AND GORDON, INC.
9 LaChance Drive, P.O. Box 10
Rindge, NH 03461
(603) 899-3267

Calvin K. Sholl, Chrmn. & CEO

THE PARTNERSHIP GROUP
(SPECIALIZE IN MGMT. CONSULTING)
7 Becker Farm Road
Roseland, NJ 07068
(973) 535-8566
www.partnershipgroup.com

Peter T. Maher, President.
Raymond Schwartz, Partner

PEOPLE MANAGEMENT INTERNAT'L LTD.
One Darling Drive, Avon Park South
Avon, CT 06001
(860) 678-8900

Steven M. Darter, President & CEO-
People Management Northeast
Also:
Nashville, TN (615) 463-2800
Tommy Thomas, President & CEO -
People Management Midsouth
Stillwater, MN (651) 351-7214
Robert Stevenson, President & CEO -
People Management Minnesota

PICARD INTERNATIONAL, LTD.
(SPECIALIZE IN FINANCE, TECHNOLOGY & HEALTH CARE)
125 East 38th Street
New York, NY 10016
(212) 252-1620
fax (212) 252-0973
www.piccardintl.com

Daniel A. Picard, President
William Kingore, Sr. VP & Director

RENÉ PLESSNER ASSOCIATES
(SPECIALIZE IN COSMETICS & FRAGRANCES)
375 Park Avenue
New York, NY 10152
(212) 421-3490
fax (212) 421-3999

René Plessner, President

PLUMMER & ASSOCIATES, INC.
(SPECIALIZE IN RETAIL, DIRECT MARKETING, FOOD SERVICE & E-COMMERCE)
65 Rowayton Avenue
Norwalk, CT 06853
(203) 899-1233
fax (203) 838-0887
www.plummersearch.com
resume@plummersearch.com

John Plummer, President
Also:
Marietta, GA (770) 429-9007
Susan Gill, Managing Director

POIRIER, HOEVEL & COMPANY
12400 Wilshire Boulevard, Suite 915
Los Angeles, CA 90025
(310) 207-3427
www.phandco.com
submissions@phandco.com

Roland Poirier, Partner
Michael J. Hoevel, Partner
Kristina Hoevel, Managing Director

DAVID POWELL, INC.
(SPECIALIZE IN HIGH TECH & BIOTECHNOLOGY)
2995 Woodside Road
Post Office Box 620109
Woodside, CA 94062
(650) 851-6000
fax (650) 851-5514
www.davidpowell.com

David L. Powell Sr., President

THE PRAIRIE GROUP
(SPECIALIZE IN FINANCE, MARKETING & HUMAN RESOURCES)
One Westbrook Corp Center, Suite 300
Westchester, IL 60154
(708) 449-7710
fax (708) 449-7708

James W. Kick, Principal
Mark Scott, Principal

PRATZER & PARTNERS INC.†
40 King Street West, Suite 4714
Toronto, ON M5H 3Y2
(416) 365-1841
fax (416) 365-0851
www.pratzer.com

Elan Pratzer, Partner

PRENG & ASSOCIATES, INC.†
(SPECIALIZE IN ENERGY)
2925 Briar Park, Suite 1111

Houston, TX 77042-3734
(713) 266-2600
fax (713) 266-3070
www.preng.com

David E. Preng, President

PRICEWATERHOUSECOOPERS, LLP†
Royal Trust Tower, Suite 3000
Toronto Dominion Centre
Toronto, ON M5K 1G8
(416) 863-1133
fax (416) 365-8215
www.pwcglobal.com

B. Keith McLean, Paul F. Crath & Bill
McFarland, Senior Vice Presidents

Also:
Calgary, AB (403) 267-1200
Irene Pfeiffer, Director - Exec. Search
Montreal, PQ (514) 938-5000
Joseph Beaupre, Principal
St. John, NB (506) 632-1810
Donald Moors, Partner
Toronto, ON (416) 869-1130
W. Tom Sinclair, Principal - Exec.
Search
Vancouver, BC (604) 806-7000
Robert McMillin, VP - Exec. Search

RAINES INTERNATIONAL INC.†
250 Park Avenue, 17th Floor
New York, NY 10177
(212) 997-1100
www.rainesinternational.com

Bruce R. Raines, President

RAY & BERNDTSON†
301 Commerce St., Suite 2300
Fort Worth, TX 76102
(817) 334-0500
fax (817) 334-0779
www.rayberndtson.com

Paul R. Ray Sr., Chairman
Paul R. Ray Jr., President & CEO
Breck Ray, Managing Partner

Also:
Atlanta, GA (404) 215-4600
Andrew E. Weidener, SVP & Manager
Chicago, IL (312) 876-0730
John Doyle, Managing Partner
Dallas, TX (214) 969-7620
Paul R. Ray Jr., Pres./CEO (Ft. Worth)
Los Angeles, CA (310) 557-2828
David B. Radden, Partner
Montreal, QB (514) 937-1000
B. F. Labrecque, Managing Partner
New York, NY (212) 370-1316
Kenneth M. Rich, Managing Partner
Ottawa, ON (613) 786-3191
Richard Morgan, Managing Partner
Palo Alto, CA (650) 494-2500
James A. McFadzean, Mng. Partner
Toronto, ON (416) 366-1990
W. Carl Lovas, Managing, Partner
Vancouver, BC (604) 685-0261
John Tanton & Kyle Mitchell, Partners,
Ray & Berndtson/Tanton Mitchell

PLEASE NOTE: There's a trend toward accepting unsolicited resumes by e-mail. If e-mail and/or fax are shown, they were considered

REDDEN & McGRATH ASSOCIATES, INC.
427 Bedford Road
Pleasantville, NY 10570
(914) 725-5566

Mary Redden, Partner
Laura McGrath Faller, Partner

REECE & MRUK PARTNERS
(EMA PARTNERS INTERNATIONAL)
75 Second Avenue
Needham, MA 02494
(781) 449-3603

Christopher S. Reece, Mng. Partner

REEDER & ASSOCIATES LTD.†
(SPECIALIZE IN HEALTH CARE)
1095 Old Roswell Road, Suite F
Roswell, GA 30076
(770) 649-7523
www.reederassoc.com
research@reederassoc.com
(online form to submit resumes)
Michael S. Reeder, President

REYNOLDS & PARTNERS
380 Madison Avenue, 7th Floor
New York, NY 10017
(212) 856-4466

Sydney Ann Reynolds, President

RUSSELL REYNOLDS ASSOCIATES, INC.†
200 Park Avenue, 23rd Floor
New York, NY 10166-0002
(212) 351-2000
fax (212) 370-0896
www.russellreynolds.com

Hobson Brown Jr., President & CEO
Gordon Grand lll, Mng Dir. / Area Mngr.
James M. Bagley & P. Clarke Murphy,
  Managing Directors
Also:
Atlanta, GA (404) 577-3000
Joseph T. Spence, Mng. Dir. / Area
Mngr.
Boston, MA (617) 523-1111
J. Nicholas Hurd, Mng. Dir. / Area Mgr.
Chicago, IL (312) 993-9696
Charles Tribbett III & Andrea
Redmond, Area Co-Managers
Dallas, TX (214) 220-2033
Joseph A. Baily III, Mng. Dir. / Area
Mngr.
Houston, TX (713) 658-1776
Stephen D. Newton, Mng. Director
Los Angeles, CA (213) 253-4400
Richard B. Krell, Mng. Dir / Area Mngr.
Menlo Park, CA (650) 233-2400
Barry S. Obrand, Mng. Dir./ Area Mngr.
Minneapolis, MN (612) 332-6966
Robert W. Macdonald, Jr., Mng. Dir. /
Area Mngr.
San Francisco, CA (415) 352-3300
P. Anthony Price, Mng. Dir. / Area
Mngr.
Toronto, ON (416) 364-3355
Richard C. E. Moore, Mng. Director /
Country Manager

Washington, DC (202) 628-2150
Eric L. Vautour, Mng. Dir. / Area Mngr.

ROBERTS RYAN AND BENTLEY, INC.
1107 Kenilworth Drive, Suite 208
Baltimore, MD 21204
(410) 321-6600
Richard Cappe, President
Richard Dannenberg, Sr. VP & Partner
Also:
Bethesda, MD (301) 469-3108
Gregory Reynolds, Vice President

BRUCE ROBINSON ASSOCIATES†
Harmon Cove Towers
Suite 8, A/L, Tower 1
Secaucus, NJ 07094
(201) 617-9595
Bruce Robinson, President
Eric B. Robinson, V.P. & Partner

ROBINSON, FRASER GROUP LTD.
10 Bay Street, Suite 700
Toronto, ON M5J 2R8
(416) 864-9174
Stephen A. Robinson, President

ROBISON & ASSOCIATES
128 South Tryon Street, Suite 1350
Charlotte, NC 28202
(704) 376-0059
John H. Robison Jr., Chairman & Pres.

R. ROLLO ASSOCIATES†
725 South Figueroa Street, Suite 440
Los Angeles, CA 90017
(213) 688-8358
fax (213) 688-8358
www.rolloassoc.com
Robert S. Rollo, Peter W. Kelly &
Jane Hurd, Managing Partners

ROPES ASSOCIATES, INC.†
(SPECIALIZE IN REAL ESTATE)
333 North New River Drive
East 3rd floor
Fort Lauderdale, FL 33301
(954) 525-6600
fax (954) 779-7279
www.ropesassociates.com
John Ropes, President

ROURKE LIZOTTE & ASSOCIATES
1130 Sherbrooke St. West, PH 1B
Montreal, PQ H3A 2M8
(514) 982-9000
Patrick Rourke, Senior Partner
André Lizotte, Senior Partner

RURAK & ASSOCIATES, INC.†
1350 Connecticut Ave. NW, Suite 801
Washington, DC 20036
(202) 293-7603
Zbigniew T. Rurak, President

RUSHER, LOSCAVIO & LOPRESTO†

142 Sansone Street, 5th Floor
San Francisco, CA 94104-4235
(415) 765-6600
fax (415) 397-2842
www.rll.com
resumes@rll.com
William H. Rusher Jr., Chrmn & CEO
J. Michael Loscavio, President & CFO
Also:
Palo Alto, CA (650) 494-0883
Robert L. LoPresto, President - High
  Technology Division

SALEY PARTNERS INTERNATIONAL
WaterPark Place
10 Bay Street, 14th Floor
Toronto, ON M5J 2R8
(416) 364-2020
Albert Saley, Chief Executive Officer

NORM SANDERS ASSOCIATES
(SPECIALIZE IN INFORMATION TECHNOLOGY)
2 Village Court
Hazlet, NJ 07730
(732) 264-3700
www.normsanders.com
ada@normsanders.com
Norman D. Sanders, Managing Director

ALLAN SARN ASSOCIATES, INC.
(SPECIALIZE IN HUMAN RESOURCES)
230 Park Avenue, Suite 1522
New York, NY 10169
(212) 687-0600
Allan G. Sarn, President

SATHE & ASSOCIATES, INC.
5821 Cedarlake Road
Minneapolis, MN 55416
(612) 546-2100
fax (612) 546-6930
www.sathe.com
Mark Sathe, President

SAVOY PARTNERS LTD.
1620 L Street, N. W., Suite 801
Washington, DC 20036
(202) 887-0666
Robert J. Brudno, Managing Director

SCHUYLER ASSOCIATES, LTD.
400 Perimeter Center Terrace, Suite 900
Atlanta, GA 30346
(770) 352-9414
www.Schuyler-Associates.com
Lambert Schuyler, President

SCHWEICHLER ASSOCIATES, INC.
(SPECIALIZE IN HIGH TECH)
200 Tamal Vista Boulevard, Suite 100
Corte Madera, CA 94925
(415) 924-7200
www.schweichler.com
search@schweichler.com
Lee J. Schweichler, President
Ann Peckenpaugh, Vice President

acceptable when this list was compiled. Regardless of what is shown, preference and/or other information may since have changed.

SCOTT EXECUTIVE SEARCH
(SPECIALIZE IN CONSUMER PRODUCTS & HIGH TECH)
61 Woodbury Place, Suite 200
Rochester, NY 14618
(716) 264-0330
Ms. E. Ann Scott, President

J. ROBERT SCOTT
27 State Street
Boston, MA 02109
(617) 563-2770
fax (617) 723-1282
www.jrobertscott.com
William A. Holodnak, President

THE SEARCH ALLIANCE
(SPECIALIZE IN HEALTH CARE, BANKING, MANUFACTURING & TECHNOLOGY)
311 1/2 Centre Street, Suite 206
Amelia Island, FL 32034
(904) 277-2535
fax (904) 277-7924
www.tsainc.net
Tom Byrnes, Managing Partner
Also:
Durham, NC (919) 806-2426
Tim Knechtel, Managing Partner
Greenwich, CT (203) 622-6903
Catherine deTuede, Managing Partner
West Hartford, CT (860) 232-2300
Bill Thomas, Managing Partner

SEARCH AMERICA
(SPECIALIZE IN PRIVATE CLUB MNGMT & HOSPITALITY)
5908 Meadowcreek Drive
Dallas, TX 75248-5451
(972) 233-3302
fax (972) 233-1518
Harvey M. Weiner, President

SECURA BURNETT COMPANY
(SPECIALIZE IN FINANCIAL SERVICES)
555 California Street, Suite 3950
San Francisco, CA 94104
(415) 398-0700
fax (415) 398-2274
www.securagroup.com
Mr. Louis C. Burnett, Managing Partner

SEIDEN KRIEGER ASSOCIATES
375 Park Avenue, Suite 1601
New York, NY 10152-3201
(212) 688-8383
Steven A. Seiden, President
Dennis F. Krieger, Managing Director

SEITCHIK CORWIN AND SEITCHIK
(SPECIALIZE IN TEXTILES, APPAREL, FOOTWEAR & RELATED INDUSTRIES)
3443 Clay Street
San Francisco, CA 94118-2008
(415) 928-5717
fax (415) 928-4424
Jack Seitchik, President
J. Blade Corwin, Vice President

Also:
330 East 38th Street, Suite 5-P
New York, NY 10016
(212) 370-3592
William Seitchik, Vice President

SENSIBLE SOLUTIONS, INC.
239 West Coolidge Avenue
Barrington, Il 60010-4211
(847) 382-0070
www.sensibleinc.com
(online form to submit resumes)
Patrick J. Delaney, Principal

M. B. SHATTUCK & ASSOCIATES, INC.†
(SPECIALIZE IN HIGH TECH & GEN'L. MFG.)
1904 Franklin Street, Suite 818
Oakland, CA 94612
(510) 663-8922
fax (510) 663-8924
www.mbshattuck.com
Mr. Merrill B. Shattuck, President

SHEPHERD BUESCHEL & PROVUS, INC.†
401 North Michigan Ave., Suite 3020
Chicago, IL 60611
(312) 832-3020
fax (312) 832-0001
Daniel M. Shepherd, David A Bueschel
& Barbara L. Provus, Principals

DAVID SHIPLACOFF & ASSOCIATES
2030 Fairburn Avenue, Suite 200-L
Los Angeles, CA 90025-5914
(310) 474-3600
www.dsasearch.com
David Shiplacoff, President

MICHAEL SHIRLEY ASSOCIATES, INC.
10709 Barkley, Suite B
Overland Park, KS 66211
(913) 341-7655
fax (913) 341-7657
Michael Shirley, President

SHOEMAKER & ASSOCIATES
1862 Independence Square, Suite A
Atlanta, GA 30338
(770) 395-7225
www.shoemakersearch.com
lcs@shoemakersearch.com
Larry C. Shoemaker, President

M. SHULMAN, INC.
44 Montgomery Street, Suite 3085
San Francisco, CA 94104
(415) 398-3488
fax (415) 398-2208
Melvin Shulman, President

JOHN SIBBALD & ASSOCIATES, INC.
7733 Forsyth Boulevard, Suite 2010
St. Louis, MO 63105
(314) 727-0227
fax (314) 727-2008
John R. Sibbald, President

Kathryn J. Costick, Vice President

SIGNIUM INTERNATIONAL GROUP, INC.†
44 North Virginia Street, Suite 3-B
Crystal Lake, IL 60014-4106
(815) 479-9415
www.signium.com
Sue Spate, Principal
Dorothy Marquelles, Principal

SILER & ASSOCIATES, LLC
11512 North Port Washington Road
Mequon, WI 53092
(262) 241-5041
fax (262) 241-9285
David J. Siler, President

DANIEL A. SILVERSTEIN ASSOCIATES INC.
(SPECIALIZE IN HEALTH CARE, PHARMACEUTICALS, BIOTECH & MEDICAL DEVICES)
5355 Town Center Road, Suite 1001
Boca Raton, FL 33486
(561) 391-0600
fax (561) 391-0180
Daniel A. Silverstein, President

SKOTT/EDWARDS CONSULTANTS
1776 On the Green
Morristown, NJ 07960
(973) 644-0900
fax (973) 644-0991
www.skottedwards.com
search@skottedwards.com
Skott B. Burkland, President
Charles R. Grebenstein, Senior VP

SLAYTON INTERNATIONAL, INC. / IIC PARTNERS
181 West Madison Street, Suite 4510
Chicago, IL 60602
(312) 456-0080
www.slaytonintl.com
Richard C. Slayton, President
Terence N. Burns, Vice President

SMITH & SAWYER INC.
230 Park Avenue, 33rd Floor
New York, NY 10169
(877) 490-4390
Robert L. Smith, Partner
Patricia L. Sawyer, Partner

SMITH & SYBERG INC.†
825 Washington Street, Suite 2A
Columbus, IN 47201
(812) 372-7254
www.smithandsyberg.com
mail@smithandsyberg.com
Joseph E. Smith, Partner
Keith A. Syberg, Partner

HERMAN SMITH EXECUTIVE INITIATIVES INC.
161 Bay Street, Suite 3600
Post Office Box 629
Toronto, ON M5J 2S1

PLEASE NOTE: There's a trend toward accepting unsolicited resumes by e-mail. If e-mail and/or fax are shown, they were considered

(416) 862-8830

Herman Smith, President

SOCKWELL & ASSOCIATES†
(SPECIALIZE IN FINANCE & BANKING)
227 West Trade Street, Suite 1930
Charlotte, NC 28202
(704) 372-1865
www.sockwell.com
email@sockwell.com
(online form to submit resumes)
J. Edgar Sockwell, Susan Jernigan,
Lyttleton Rich, Partners

SOLUTIONS GROUP
1512 Valley Place
Birmingham, AL 35209
(205) 663-1301
www.solutiongroupsearch.com
mike@solutiongroupsearch.com
Hinky Verchot, Principal
Michael E. Wheless, Principal

SPENCERSTUART†
277 Park Avenue, 29th Floor
New York, NY 10172-2998
(212) 336-0200
www.spencerstuart.com
resumes@spencerstuart.com
Robert A. Damon, Co-Managing
Director-U. S.
Dayton Ogden, Chairman & President
(Stamford)
Joseph E. Griesedieck Jr., CEO (San
Francisco)
Thomas J. Neff, Chairman - U.S. (NY)
Dennis C. Carey, U.S. Vice Chairman
(Philadelphia)
Also:
Atlanta, GA (404) 504-4400
William B. Reeves, Managing Director
Chicago, IL (312) 822-0080
Gail Vergara, Managing Director
Dallas, TX (214) 672-5200
O. Dan Cruse, Managing Director
Houston, TX (713) 225-1621
Tom Simmons , Managing Director
Los Angeles, CA (310) 209-0610
Michael Bruce, Managing Director
Menlo Park, CA (650) 234-4900
John Ware, Managing Director
Miami, FL (305) 443-9911
Ken Eckhart, Managing Director
Minneapolis, MN (612) 313-2000
Susan Boren, Principal
Matthew Christoff, Principal
Montreal, PQ (514) 288-3377
Ms. Manon Vennat, Chairman-Canada
Denis B. K. Lyons, Senior Director
E. Peter McLean, Senior Director
Philadelphia, PA (215) 814-1600
Connie McCann, Managing Director
San Francisco, CA (415) 495-4141
Jonathan O. White, Managing Director
Stamford, CT (203) 324-6333
Claudia Lacy Kelly, Managing Director
Toronto, ON (416) 361-0311

Andrew McDougall, Managing Director

SPLAINE & ASSOCIATES
(SPECIALIZE IN HIGH TECH)
15951 Los Gatos Boulevard, Suite 13
Los Gatos, CA 95032
(408) 354-366
fax (408) 356-6329
www.exec-search.com
Charles E. Splaine, President

SPRIGGS & COMPANY, INC.
1701 E. Lake Avenue, Suite 265
Glenview, IL 60025
(847) 657-7181
fax (847) 657-7186
Robert D. Spriggs, Chairman
John Goldrick, Partner
William Billington, Partner

STANTON CHASE INTERNATIONAL
100 East Pratt Street, Suite 2530
Baltimore, MD 21202
(410) 528-8400
www.stantonchase.com
(resumes to Web site only)
H. Edward Muendel, Managing Dir.
Also:
Chicago, IL (312) 422-8162
James R. Piper Jr., Managing Director
Dallas, TX (972) 404-8411
Ed Moerbe, Managing Director
Los Angeles, CA (310) 474-1029
Edward J. Savage, Managing Director

STAUB WARMBOLD ASSOCIATES, INC.
575 Madison Avenue, 10th Floor
New York, NY 10022
(212) 605-0554
fax (212) 759-7304
Robert A. Staub, President

STEPHENS ASSOCIATES, LTD., INC.
(SPECIALIZE IN HIGH TECH)
One German Village
480 South Third Street, 2nd Floor
Columbus, OH 43215
(614) 469-9990
fax (614) 469-0177
Stephen A. Martinez, President &
Managing Partner

MICHAEL STERN ASSOCIATES, INC.
70 University Avenue, Suite 370
Toronto, ON M5J 2M4
(416) 593-0100
www.michaelstern.com
search@michaelstern.com
Michael Stern, President

STEWART, STEIN & SCOTT, LTD.
1000 Shelard Parkway, Suite 606
Minneapolis, MN 55426
(952) 545-8151
fax (952) 545-8464
Jeffrey O. Stewart, President

LINFORD E. STILES ASSOCIATES
*(SPECIALIZE IN MANUFACTURING
COMPANIES, ALL FUNCTIONS)*
46 Newport Road, Suite 210
New London, NH 03257-4240
(603) 526-6566
fax (603) 526-6185
Linford E. Stiles, President

STONE MURPHY
5500 Wayzata Boulevard, Suite 1020
Minneapolis, MN 55416
(612) 591-2300
fax (612) 591-2301
Toni M. Barnum, Partner
Gary J. Murphy, Partner

STRATEGIC EXECUTIVES
980 Michigan Avenue, Suite 1400
Chicago, IL 60611-4501
(312) 988-4821
www.strategicexecutives.com
info@strategicexecutives.com
Randolph S. Gulian, Managing Dir.
Laurie R. Goldman, Director
James A Perry, Director

STRATFORDGROUP
6120 Parkland Boulevard
Cleveland, OH 44124
(440) 869-4600
Larry S. Imley, President
Eric Peterson, Managing Director

W. R. STRATHMANN ASSOCIATES†
(SPECIALIZE IN FINANCIAL SERVICES)
150 Fifth Avenue, Suite 626
New York, NY 10011
(212) 353-2034
Winfried R. Strathmann, Senior Partner

STRAUBE ASSOCIATES, INC.
855 Turnpike Street
North Andover, MA 01845
(978) 687-1993
fax (978) 687-1886
www.straubeassociates.com
sstraube@straubeassociates.com
Stanley H. Straube, President

**STRAWN, ARNOLD, LEECH &
ASHPITZ INC.**
(SPECIALIZE IN HEALTH CARE)
11402 Bee Caves Road West
Austin, TX 78733
(512) 263-1131
fax (512) 263-4149
www.salainc.com
genmail@salainc.com
William M. Strawn, Jerry M. Arnold,
David M. Leech, & Jeff Ashpitz,
Partners

SULLIVAN & ASSOCIATES†
344 N. Old Woodward Ave., Suite 304
Birmingham, MI 48009
(248) 258-0616

acceptable when this list was compiled. Regardless of what is shown, preference and/or other information may since have changed.

fax (248) 258-2823
www.sullivanassociates.com

Dennis B. Sullivan, Founder, Jeffrey A. Evans, Kevin E. Mahoney, Dodie C. David & Douglas R. Allen, Partners

SWEENEY, HARBERT, MUMMERT, & GALLAGHER

777 S. Harbour Island Blvd., Suite 130
Tampa, FL 33602
(813) 229-5360
fax (813) 223-1969

James W. Sweeney, David O. Harbert, Dennis D. Mummert & David A. Gallagher, Partners

SYNERGISTICS ASSOCIATES LTD.†

(SPECIALIZE IN INFORMATION TECHNOLOGY)
400 North State Street, Suite 400
Chicago, IL 60610
(312) 467-5450
fax (312) 822-0246
ajbsynerg@aol.com

Alvin J. Borenstine, President/Founder

TARNOW ASSOCIATES

150 Morris Avenue
Springfield, NJ 07081-1306
(973) 376-3900
fax (973) 376-0340
www.tarnow.com
evogel@tarnow.com

Emil Vogel, President

THORNE, BRIEGER ASSOCIATES INC.

11 East 44th Street, Suite 1502
New York, NY 10017
(212) 682-5424
fax (212) 557-4926
tba@thornebrieger.com

Steven Brieger, Mike Jacobs, & Jeffrey M. Stark, Principals

TMP WORLDWIDE†

565 Fifth Avenue, 18th Floor
New York, NY 10022
(212) 328-1100
www.tmpsearch.com

John F. Johnson, Senior Chairman (Cleveland)
Robert L. Pearson, Chief Executive Officer & Chairman (Dallas)
Steven Potter, President (NY)
Also:
Atlanta, GA (404) 688-0800
Joe D. Goodwin, Mng. Partner & EVP
William R. Robertson, Partner
Austin, TX (512) 425-3900
Tara Pettersson, Managing Partner
Barrington, IL (847) 382-2206
Michael J. Corey, Senior Partner
Douglas M. Smith, Senior Partner
Boston, MA (617) 292-6242
Walter E. Williams, Senior Partner
Kevin E. Conley , Partner
Chicago, IL (312) 782-3113

John S. Rothschild, Mng. Partner & EVP
Cleveland, OH (216) 694-3000
Mark P. Elliott, Regional Mng. Partner
Dallas, TX (214) 754-0019
Judy Stubbs, Managing Partner
Frederick A. Halstead, Partner
Encino, CA (818) 905-6010
Neal L. Maslan, Senior Partner
Houston, TX (713) 843-8600
Thomas H. Wilson, Managing Partner
Los Angeles, CA (310) 277-0550
Dr. Dana Beth Ardi, Senior Partner
Monterey, CA (831) 375-2676
Ronald W. Sills, Partner
New York, NY Fifth Ave.(212) 953-7900
Roderick C. Gow, EVP & Mng. Partner
New York, NY Park Ave.(212) 953-7900
Harold E. Johnson , Senior Partner
Stephen M. McPherson, Senior Partner
Phoenix, AZ (602) 955-3800
Vance A.Howe, Partner
Richard E. Nosky, Partner
Pittsburgh, PA (412) 255-3730
John E. Hughes, Jr., Partner
San Francisco, CA (415) 296-0600
David M. deWilde, Managing Partner
Stamford, CT (203) 324-4445
Lauren Gerken, Partner
Robert Simon, Partner
Tampa, FL (813) 221-7727
Walter U. Baker, Partner
Jack B. Henard, Partner
West Hartford, CT (860) 523-7100
David J. Beed, Partner

TNS PARTNERS, INC.

8140 Walnut Hill Lane, Suite. 301
Dallas, TX 75231
(214) 369-3565
fax (214) 369-3265

Craig C. Neidhart & John K. Semyan, Partners

SKIP TOLETTE EXECUTIVE SEARCH

(SPECIALIZE IN FINANCIAL SERVICES & INFORMATION TECHNOLOGY)
577 West Saddle River Road
Upper Saddle River, NJ 07458
(201) 327-8214
fax (201) 818-0970
www.tolettesearch.com
info@tolettesearch.com

Skip Tolette, President

TRAVIS & COMPANY

(SPECIALIZE IN MEDICAL, BIOTECHNOLOGY, COMPUTER HARDWARE & SOFTWARE)
325 Boston Post Road
Sudbury, MA 01776
(978) 443-4000
fax (978) 443-3251
www.travisandco.com

John A. Travis, President
Mary K. Morse & Michael J. Travis, Vice Presidents

TYLER & COMPANY

(SPECIALIZE IN HEALTH CARE)

1000 Abernathy Road, N.E.,
Suite 1400
Atlanta, GA 30328-5655
(770) 396-3939
fax (770) 396-6693
www.tylerandco.com

J. Larry Tyler, President

VANMALDEGIAM ASSOCIATES, INC.

500 Park Boulevard, Suite 800
Itasca, IL 60143
(630) 250-8338

Norman E. VanMaldegiam, President

VERKAMP-JOYCE ASSOCIATES, INC.

2443 Warrenville Road, Suite 600
Lisle, IL 60532
(630) 955-3750

Frank VerKamp & Sheila M. Joyce, Partners

VLCEK & COMPANY, INC.

(GENERALISTS WITH EMPHASIS IN CONSUMER GDS. & FOOD INDUSTRY)
620 Newport Center Drive, Suite 1100
Newport Beach, CA 92660
(714) 752-0661

Thomas J. Vlcek, President

WAKEFIELD TALABISCO INTERNATIONAL

342 Madison Avenue, Suite 1702
New York, NY 10173
(212) 661-8600
www.wtali.com

Barbara Talabisco, Managing Partner
Also:
Mendon Meadows, Suite 8
13 U.S. Route 4
Mendon, VT 05701-9706
(802) 747-5901
www.wakefieldtalabisco.com

J. Alvin Wakefield, Managing Partner

WALLING, JUNE & ASSOCIATES

(SPECIALIZE IN HIGH TECH, HEALTH CARE & FINANCIAL SERVICES)
716 Church Street
Alexandria, VA 22314
(703) 548-9660
fax (703) 836-1558
w716@erols.com

Gregory J. Walling, Senior Partner

WARD LIEBELT ASSOCIATES, INC.

(PREDOMINATELY SALES & MARKETING)
19 Ludlow Road, Suite 302
Westport, CT 06880-3040
(203) 454-0414
fax (203) 454-2310
wlacaruso@aol.com

Anthony C. Ward, President

R. J. WATKINS & COMPANY LTD.

3104 Fourth Avenue
San Diego, CA 92103
(619) 299-3094
www.rjwatkins.com

PLEASE NOTE: There's a trend toward accepting unsolicited resumes by e-mail. If e-mail and/or fax are shown, they were considered

info@rjwatkins.com
Robert J. Watkins, Chairman
Gary Saenger, President
Tom Murphy, Vice President

WATSON INTERNATIONAL, INC.
(SPECIALIZE IN ENERGY)
2124 Broadway, Suite 178
New York, NY 10023
(212) 362-2425
fax (212) 362-2460
www.watsoninternational.com
hwatson@watsoninternational.com
Ms. Hanan S. Watson, President

WEBB, JOHNSON ASSOCIATES, INC.
280 Park Avenue, 43rd Floor
New York, NY 10017
(212) 661-3700
fax (212) 986-4765

George H. Webb Jr., John W. Johnson Jr.,
& James K. Makrianes Jr., Mng. Directors

D. L. WEISS AND ASSOCIATES
18201 Von Karman Avenue, Suite 310
Irvine, CA 92612
(949) 833-5001
fax (949) 833-5073
www.dlweiss.com
(submit resumes through website)
David L. Weiss, President
Wendy A Worrell & Thomas D.
Mignanelli, Principal Consultants

WELLINGTON MANAGEMENT GROUP
*(GENERALISTS WITH EMPHASIS ON HIGH TECH,
TELECOMMUNICATIONS, HUMAN RESOURCES &
HEALTH CARE)*
1601 Market Street, Suite 2902
Philadelphia, PA 19103
(215) 569-8900
fax (215) 569-4902
www.wellingtonmg.com
wellington@wellingtonmg.com
Walter R. Romanchek,Robert S.
Campbell & Donald H Janssen,
Principals

THE WENTWORTH COMPANY, INC.
The Arcade Building
479 West Sixth Street
San Pedro, CA 90731-2656
(310) 519-0113
fax (310) 519-8402
www.wentco.com
info@wentco.com
John Wentworth, President

**WESTCOTT THOMAS & ASSOCIATES
LTD.**
*(SPECIALIZE IN GOVERNMENT, ASSOCIATIONS,
HUMAN RESOURCES, SALES & MARKETING)*
5650 Yonge Street, Suite 1500
Box 2412
Toronto, ON M2M 4G3
(416) 481-4471
Michael J. Thomas, President & C.E.O.

**WESTERN RESERVE SEARCH
ASSOCIATES, INC.**
*(EMPHASIS IN REORGANIZATIONS & START-UPS
IN EASTERN EUROPE)*
199 South Chillicothe Rd., Suite 200-6
Post Office Box 606
Aurora, OH 44202
(330) 562-4811
Darrell G. Robertson, President

WHEELER, MOORE & COMPANY
14800 Quorum Drive, Suite 200
Dallas, TX 75240
(972) 386-8806
Dr. Mark H. Moore, Managing Partner

THE WHITNEY GROUP
(SPECIALIZE IN FINANCIAL SERVICES)
850 Third Avenue (11th Floor)
New York, NY 10022
(212) 508-3500
fax (212) 508-3589
www.whitneygroup.com
recruiter@whitneygroup.com
Gary S. Goldstein, President & C.E.O.

KL WHITNEY COMPANY
(SPECIALIZE IN INVESTMENT MGMT.)
6 Aspen Drive
North Caldwell, NJ 07006
(973) 228-7124
Kenneth L. Whitney Jr., President

WHITTLESEY & ASSOCIATES, INC.
300 South High Street
West Chester, PA 19382
(610) 436-6500
James G. Hogg Jr., President

WILKINSON & IVES
(EMPHASIS ON HIGH TECHNOLOGY)
100 Shoreline Highway, Suite 275A
Mill Valley, CA 94941
(415) 289-7500
fax (415) 289-1506
www.w-ives.com
snyder@w-ives.com
Richard K. Ives, Partner
William R. Wilkinson, Partner

WILLIAMS EXECUTIVE SEARCH, INC.
4200 Norwest Center
90 South Seventh Street
Minneapolis, MN 55402-3903
(612) 339-2900
fax (612) 305-5040
www.williamsexec.com
resumes@williamsexec.com
William P. Dubbs, President
Christina Borchers, Principal

WILLIAMS, ROTH & KRUEGER, INC.
911 North Elm Street, Suite 328
Hinsdale, IL 60521
(630) 887-7771
fax (630) 323-4666
wrkinc@aol.com

Robert J. Roth, Partner
Alan Hanley, Partner

WILLIAM WILLIS WORLDWIDE, INC.†
P.O. Box 4444, 310 W. Lyon Farm Drive
Greenwich, CT 06831-4356
(203) 532-9292
fax (203) 532-1919
wwwinc@aol.com
William H. Willis, President & Mng. Dir.

WINGUTH, GRANT & DONAHUE
417 Montgomery Street, Suite 910
San Francisco, CA 94104
(415) 238-1970
fax (415) 986-1630
www.wgdsearch.com
cz@wgdsearch.com
Susan G. Grant, President,
Patrick D. Donahue, Vice President

**WITT/KIEFFER, FORD, HADELMAN &
LLOYD**
*(SPECIALIZE IN HEALTH CARE, HIGHER
EDUCATION & DEVELOPMENT)*
2015 Spring Road, Suite 510
Oak Brook, IL 60523
(630) 990-1370
fax (630) 990-1382
www.wittkieffer.com
(submit resumes through Web site)
Jordan M. Hadelman, Chairman & CEO
John S. Lloyd, Vice Chairman
Michael F. Doody, Senior Vice
President
J. Daniel Ford, Senior Vice President
Also:
Atlanta, GA (404) 233-1370
Martha Hauser, Managing Director
Bethesda, MD (301) 654-5070
Anna Phillips, Senior Vice President
Howard Jessamy, Vice President
Dallas, TX (972) 490-1370
Peter Doogsteed, Partner
Emeryville, CA (510) 420-1370
Elaina Genser, Senior Vice President
Houston, TX (713) 266-6779
Marvene M. Eastham, Senior VP
Irvine, CA (949) 851-5070
James W. Gauss, Senior Vice President
New York, NY (212) 686-2676
Alexander H. Williams, Sr. Vice President
Phoenix, AZ (602) 267-1370
Michael F. Meyer, Senior Vice President

WOJDULA & ASSOCIATES
700 Rayovac Drive, Suite 204
Madison, WI 53711
(608) 271-2000
fax (608) 271-7475
www.wojdula.com
wojdulaltd@wojdula.com
Andrew G. Wojdula, President

M. WOOD COMPANY
(SPECIALIZE IN INFORMATION TECHNOLOGY)
10 North Dearborn Street, Suite 700

Chicago, IL 60602
(312) 368-0633
fax (312) 368-5052
www.mwoodco.com
resume@mwoodco.com

Milton M. Wood, President

DICK WRAY & CONSULTANTS, INC.
(SPECIALIZE IN RESTAURANT CONSULTING)
3123 Hannan Lane
Soquel, CA 95073
(408) 436-9729
fax (800) 525-9697
www.dickwray.com
ray96@aol.com

Dick Wray, President

JANET WRIGHT & ASSOCIATES†
(SPECIALIZE IN PUBLIC & NONPROFIT)
21 Bedford Road. Suite 100
Toronto, ON M5R 2J9
(416) 923-3008

Janet Wright, President

WTW ASSOCIATES, INC.
*(CONCENTRATION IN MUSIC, BANKING, LEGAL
& TELECOMMUNICATIONS)*
675 Third Avenue, Suite 2808
New York, NY 10017
(212) 972-6990
fax (212) 297-0546
www.wtwassociates.com
wtwassoc@aol.com

Warren T. Wasp Jr., President

YELVERTON EXECUTIVE SEARCH
2465 E. Bayshore Rd.
Palo Alto, CA 94303
(415) 354-0231

Jack R. Yelverton, President

**ZAY & COMPANY INTERNATIONAL/
IIC PARTNERS**
Two Midtown Plaza, Suite 1740
1349 West Peachtree Street, NW
Atlanta, GA 30309
(404) 876-9986
fax (404) 872-5626
www.zaycointl.com
zaymail@zaycointl.com

Thomas C. Zay, Sr. President

EGON ZEHNDER INTERNATIONAL INC.
350 Park Avenue, 8th Floor
New York, NY 10022
(212) 519-6000
fax (212) 519-6060
www.zhender.com
EZI-NYC-Research@ezi.net
A. Daniel Meiland, CEO
Mark P. Schappell, Managing Partner
Also:
Atlanta, GA (404) 875-3000
Joel M. Koblentz, Managing Partner
Boston, MA (617) 535-3500
George L. Davis, Jr., Mng. Director

Chicago, IL (312) 782-4500
Louis Kacyn, Managing Partner
Los Angeles, CA (213) 621-8900
George Fifield, Managing Partner
Montreal, PQ (514) 876-4249
J. Robert Swidler, Managing Director
Palo Alto, CA (650) 847-3000
Jon Carter, Managing Partner
San Francisco, CA (415) 904-7800
Ross Brown, Managing Partner
Toronto, ON (416) 364-0222
Gregory T. Carrott, Managing Partner

ZINGARO & COMPANY
(SPECIALIZE IN HEALTH CARE)
21936 Briarcliff Drive
Briarcliff, TX 78669-2012
(512) 327-7277
fax (512) 327-1774
www.zingaro.com
search@zingaro.com

Ron Zingaro, President & CEO

MICHAEL D. ZINN & ASSOCIATES, INC.
601 Ewing Street, Suite C-8
Princeton, NJ 08540
(609) 921-8755
www.zinnassociates.com

Michael D. Zinn, President
Also:
New York, NY (212) 391-0070
Michael D. Zinn, President

This List Is Continually Updated and Available on *RITE*Site.com

Sadly, everything said on page 238 applies to this book too. The time-lag of publishing cannot be avoided by *any* information provider, no matter how well-intentioned.

Fortunately, these days the Internet can come to the rescue.

This list is continually updated on *RITE*Site.com, and is available to *RITE*Site's Custom Career Service participants in a *RITES*-Honored Download, which includes (1) e-mail addresses of all firms that accept resumes by e-mail, (2) fax numbers of all that accept by fax, (3) data for a personally addressed on-paper mailing to people at each office of every firm (works in any word-processing or database program on either PC or Mac), and (4) a *maximum efficiency combination*, which includes the e-mail addresses of all firms accepting by e-mail, plus fax numbers of firms accepting by fax but not e-mail, plus names and addresses for an on-paper mailing to firms accepting neither e-mail *nor* fax, plus Web site addresses of firms that require use of an intake mechanism on their sites.

There's much more to Custom Career Service on *RITE*Site.com, and the total cost is $94.

Please visit RITESite.com to view an array of searches being conducted by recruiters from the outstanding search firms honored both here and on RITESite.

600

Implementing RITES OF PASSAGE in a job search?

Save lots of time and and effort...and get a far better result. John Lucht removes most of the labor and all of the guess work from the executive-level job-changing process.

RITES OF PASSAGE deals with circumstances in the outside world.

This "twin" to RITES is focused in the opposite direction. Inwardly!

It deals with your own internal talents, motivations, goals, and achievements and helps you communicate them far more easily and effectively.

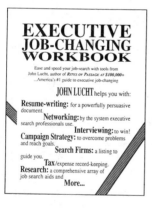

John is at your side as you map strategy, create a powerful resume and cover letter, and develop a convincing oral presentation. By means of pen-and-paper fill-ins, he helps you figure out how best to present yourself... what to emphasize and de-emphasize, and what to write, say, and do to surmount obstacles. You'll be far more persuasive on paper and in interviews if you take advantage of this "second half" of the RITES OF PASSAGE process.

Actually the "WORKBOOK" is two books in one. The first half you use at home to develop your strategy and paperwork. Although profound, the process becomes almost as easy as "paint by the numbers"!

The second half (which has a plain white cover after you sever it from the first half) you take to your interviews. Its handy "debriefer" questionnaires force you to remember absolutely everything you learn at each interview, so that—when you return as a second-round finalist—you will far outshine all of the other returnees who didn't have this secret weapon in their attaches initially.

The plain white cover prevents the possible embarrassment of accidentally showing you're carrying a commercial career aid, in case it slips out from under the WALL STREET JOURNAL in your attache as you reach for a pen or papers during an interview. (John doesn't think of everything, but he's on your side...and he DOES think of a lot.)

Why not take advantage?

PAPERBACK, 640 pages, 2 books in one, $29.95. THE VICEROY PRESS. *At local and online stores.* Tell them: ISBN No. 0-942785-22-3. Or phone: 1 800-JANUARY.

APPENDIX III

Sources of Information
for a Job Search

1. General Information on Companies and Their Executives; on Industries and Geographical Areas; and on Prominent People

National

America's Corporate Families (Vols. I & II) and **America's Corporate Families and International Affiliates** (Vol. III). Dun's Marketing Services (Three Sylvan Way; Parsippany, NJ 07054; 973-605-6174 in NJ, 800-526-0651 elsewhere) Annual. Two hardcover volumes. Vols. I &II, $560./year lease; Vol. III, $560./year lease; Vols. I, II, & III $1,020./year lease. Call for online and mailing list information.

> Vols. I & II: Information on more than 12,700 U.S. parent companies and with their subsidiaries and divisions. Address, phone, sales, no. of employees; primary bank, accounting, & law firm; net worth; fiscal year-end; subsidiary ownership percentage; founding date; change of ownership date; number of sites; major branch locations; stock exchange(s); lines of business; S.I.C. codes; and officers and directors. Vol. III: Information on over 12,000 U.S. subsidiaries and their ultimate parent companies outside the U.S., as well as 1,500 U.S. ultimate parent companies and their 15,000 foreign subsidiaries. 6,000 additional U.S. subsidiaries have been added to this volume. Other new information includes change of ownership date and global cross reference. Indexed geographically and by S.I.C. categories.

Business Rankings Annual. The Gale Group (P.O. Box 9187; Farmington Hills, MI 48333; 800-877-GALE; www.galegroup.com). Arranged by subject. Over 4,500 lists and rankings cover everything from sales, profit, market share, executive salaries, advertising budgets, and best-selling products. Annual. 2 Volume Set / $285.

The Career Guide; Dun's Employment Opportunities Directory. Dun's Marketing Services (Three Sylvan Way; Parsippany, NJ 07054; 973-605-6174 in NJ, 800-526-0651 elsewhere). Covers more than 5,000 major companies that plan to recruit during the publication year. Helpful in identifying companies opening new divisions or branches, or interested in hiring people with backgrounds of current interest to the company. Annual (October). One hardcover volume. $560.

Manufacturers Directories, such as *Ohio Register of Manufacturers*. Manufacturers News Inc. (1633 Central St.;Evanston, IL 60201; 800-752-5200). One book per state. Prices range from $40 to $179 depending on the number of manufacturers in that state. Regional and national lists, with over 500,000 manufacturers also available on CD-ROM.

> Information on manufacturers with more than 5 employees within the state/region. Organized by

city. Each company lists address, phone, products, incorporation date, employees, sales, plant size, officers and titles, primary bank, accounting, and law firm. Companies indexed (1) alphabetically and (2) by S.I.C. category.

Foreign Representatives Yellow Book. Leadership Directories (104 Fifth Avenue, 2nd Floor; New York, NY 10011; 212-627-4140). Lists the U.S. offices of Foreign Companies. $235 annual subscription for two softcover editions (Summer and Winter).

Directories in Print. The Gale Group (P.O. Box 9187; Farmington Hills, MI 48333; 800-877-GALE; www.galegroup.com). Two hardcover volumes. 2,187 pp. $499/set.

Organized by industry/discipline. Describes the contents of over 14,000 national and international publications, including directories, professional and scientific rosters, registers, and other lists and guides. Indexed by titles, key words, and "alternative format" availability, such as CD-ROM, diskette, and on-line database.

Directory of Corporate Affiliations. National Register Publishing Company / Reed Elsevier (122 Chanlon Road; New Providence, N.J. 07974; 800-521-8110). Annual. Volumes I & II, Master Index. Volume III, Public Companies, Volume IV, U.S. Private Companies, Volume V, International Public & Private Companies. Full set of 5 volumes, $1,159. Call for online and CD-ROM information.

Organized geographically by parent company, entries include "family trees" indicating subsidiaries. Also lists assets, liabilities, net worth, income/earnings, approximate sales, officers and board members of parent, plus chief officer of divisions/subsidiaries. Indexed by geography (state and city/country), S.I.C. codes, and people's names (linked with company), with a cross-reference index of divisions, subsidiaries, and affiliates. Also summarizes recent mergers, acquisitions, and name changes.

Select Guide to Human Resource Executives. Hunt-Scanlon Publishing (2 Pickwick Plaza; Greenwich, CT 06830; 203-352-2920). Covers over 15,000 human resource, personnel, compensation, benefits and training professionals at over 5,000 leading public and private companies. Cross-indexed alphabetically, geographically, and by industry specialization. One softcover volume. Annual (January). 1,250+ pp. $245 + $9.95 S & H.

Directory of Corporate Affiliations (U.S. Private). National Register Publishing Company / Reed Elsevier (122 Chanlon Road; New Providence, N.J. 07974; 800-521-8110). Profiles 22,000 companies with $10 million or more in annual sales. Includes information on department managers, pension fund managers, accounting, major professional service suppliers, and computer systems. Annual (March). One softcover volume. 1,353 pp. $1,159. Call for online and CD-ROM information.

Dun's Business Rankings. Dun's Marketing Services (3 Sylvan Way; Parsippany, NJ 07054; 201-605-6000 in NJ, 800-526-0651 elsewhere). Ranks over 25,000 companies in 67 industries. Each company is ranked nationwide, in its state, in its industry, and among other public or private companies. Annual. One hardcover vol. $545. Call for online information.

Dun's Regional Business Directories. Dun's Marketing Services (3 Sylvan Way; Parsippany, NJ 07054; 201-605-6758 in NJ, 800-526-0651 elsewhere). Covers the most prominent private and public businesses in one of 52 metro areas. Includes contact information for key executives. Each of the 52 editions is three softcover volumes. Vols. I and II profile the companies (size, sales rankings, etc.), and Vol. III is an alphabetical index and an industry index. Annual. $575 each regional edition. Call for online information.

Encyclopedia of Associations. The Gale Group (P.O. Box 9187; Farmington Hills, MI 48333; 800-877-GALE; www.galegroup.com) Annual (July). Provides detailed information on approx. 23,000 nonprofit U.S. membership organizations. Volume 1 - $505; Volume 2 - $390; Volume 3 - $415. Call for online information.

Volume 1: Encyclopedia of Associations ; National Organizations of the U.S. gives detailed entries on more than 23,000 U.S.-headquartered, nonprofit associations and organizations of all kinds (business and trade, political, social, fraternal, professional, ethnic, educational, etc.), arranged in 18 subject categories; includes address, phone, top officer, year founded, acronym, membership, subgroups, activities, committees, publications, meeting schedule, etc.

Volume 2: Geographic and Executive Index to Volume 1.

Volume 3: Supplement. A supplement, which updates information on more than 2,500 entries from the previous edition and provedes coverage on approximately 500 newly-formed or newly-found associations.

Encyclopedia of Associations: Regional, State, and Local Organizations. The Gale Group (P.O. Box 9187; Farmington Hills, MI 48333; 800-877-GALE; www.galegroup.com) Every other year (April). Hardcover. $600/set, $140/each individual volume.

Volume 1 - Great Lakes States (IL, IN, MI, MN, OH, WI). 713 pp.

Volume 2 - Northeastern States (CT, ME, MA, NH, NJ, NY, PA, RI, VT). 732 pp.

Volume 3 - Southern and Middle Atlantic States (AL, DE, DC, FL, GA, KY, MD, MS, NC, SC, TN, VA, WV, and U.S. territories of PR and VI). 699 pp.

Volume 4 - South Central and Great Plains States (AR, IA, KS, LA, MO, NE, ND, OK, SD, TX). 623 pp.

Volume 5 - Western States (AK, AZ, CA, CO, HI, ID, MT, NV, NM, OR, UT, WA, WY, and U.S. territories of GU). 658 pp.

Encyclopedia of Business Information Sources. The Gale Group (P.O. Box 9187; Farmington Hills, MI 48333; 800-877-GALE; www.galegroup.com) Every other year. About 1,200 pp / $330.

20,000 information sources on 1,280 highly specific subjects (from Abrasives Industry to Zinc Industry), including encyclopedias/dictionaries; handbooks/manuals; bibliographies; abstract services and indexes; trade associations and professional societies; periodicals; directories; biographical sources; price sources; almanacs/yearbooks; research centers/institutes; on-line data bases. Also lists sources of information on current trends in business policy and technology. Call for diskette information.

Fortune Magazine, "The Fortune Global 500" Issue. Time, Inc. (Fortune Single Copy Desk, P.O. Box 60001; Tampa, FL 33660; 800-621-8000). Ranks the top 500 businesses worldwide. August issue. Order by mail: $7.95, or view free online at www.fortune.com.

Hoover's Handbook of American Business. The Reference Press, Inc. (6448 Highway, 209 East, Suite E104; Austin, TX 78723; 512-374-4500). Profiles 500 companies. Includes contact information, brief history, current activity, products and brand names, key competitors, and ten-year financial history. Annual (November). $149.95/hardcover.

Hoover's Handbook of World Business. The Reference Press, Inc. (6448 Highway, 209 East, Suite E104; Austin, TX 78723; 512-454-7778). Profiles 200 companies. Includes contact info., brief history, current activity, products and brand names, key competitors, and ten-year financial history. Annual (February). $99.95/hardcover.

Industry Surveys. Standard & Poor's Corporation (25 Broadway; New York, NY 10004; 212-208-8786 in NY, 800-221-5277 elsewhere). Brief reviews of industries and the major companies in them. Issued two times a year. $500/year subscription. (Visit library).

Job Hunter's Sourcebook. The Gale Group (P.O. Box 9187; Farmington Hills, MI 48333; 800-877-GALE; www.galegroup.com). Lists reference materials and job-hunting services for 155 specific professions/occupations. Annual. One hardcover volume. 1,106 pp. $95.

Job Seeker's Guide to Private and Public Companies. The Gale Group (P.O. Box 9187; Farmington Hills, MI 48333; 800-877-GALE; www.galegroup.com). Annual (September).

Four hardcover volumes, about 2,000 pp. per volume. $105 per volume, $395/set. Call for diskette information.

> Gives detailed information on almost 15,000 companies, including company history, perspective, and goals, description of business operations, sales revenues, number of employees and employment practices. Also includes contact information for Human Resource and corporate officials. Five indexes in each volume. Volumes divided regionally: Vol. 1, Western United States; Vol. 2, Midwest; Vol. 3, Northeast; Vol. 4, South, Mid-Atlantic, and Great Plains.

Manufacturers' Directories. Manufacturers' News Inc. (1633 Central Street; Evanston, IL 60201; 888-752-5200).

> The leading specialist in state and regional directories of manufacturing companies. Manufacturers' News both publishes its own directories and distributes others, offering at least one—and often several—for each of the 48 contiguous states and various U.S. and foreign regions. Most directories organized alphabetically by line of business, by parent company with subsidiary listings, by product, by city, and by S.I.C. code. Call for information, including individual prices (ranging from $40 to $179). Call for CD-ROM information.

Million Dollar Directory Series. Dun's Marketing Services (3 Sylvan Way; Parsippany, NJ 07054; 201-605-6000 in NJ, 800-526-0651 elsewhere). A five-volume hardcover series. 9,200+ pp. $1,595 annual lease. Call for online and CD-ROM information.

> Lists over 160,000 public and private (over 90%) U.S. companies. Includes names and titles of principal officers, company size, lines of business, address, phone, parent company, divisions, incorporation, no. of employees, sales volume, types of business and applicable S.I.C. codes, primary bank, accounting & legal firm, import/export designation. Listed alphabetically, geographically, and by industry.

Million Dollar Directory Top 50,000 Companies. Dun's Marketing Services (3 Sylvan Way; Parsippany, NJ 07054; 201-605-6000 in NJ, 800-526-0651 elsewhere). Annual. One volume. 3,700 pp. $565 annual lease. Call for online and CD-ROM information.

> Covers the top 50,000 companies (net worth) from the Million Dollar Directory Series.

Moody's Industrial Manual and News Reports. Moody's Investors Service (99 Church Street; New York, NY 10007; 800-342-5647, ext. 0435). Annual. Two hardcover volumes. $1,895 (includes News Reports). Call for CD-ROM information.

> Full financial and operating data on every industrial corp. on the NYSE and ASE, plus over 500 on regional exchanges. Twice-weekly News Reports update developments on companies listed.

Moody's International Manual and News Reports. Moody's Investors Service (99 Church Street; New York, NY 10007; 800-342-5647, ext. 0435). Annual. Two hardcover volumes. $3,250 (includes News Reports). Call for CD-ROM information.

> Full financial and business data on over 5,000 international corporations. Twice-weekly News Reports update developments affecting companies covered.

Business Phone Book USA. Omnigraphics, Inc. (Penobscot Building; Detroit, MI 48226; 800-234-1340). Annual (October). Volume 1 - White pages, Alphabetical by organization name. And Volume 2 - Yellow pages, Alphabetical classified by subject. 2 Vol. Set / $165.

> Address and phone for major U.S. corporations. Also special sections listing address and phone for hotels, banks, agencies, county, state, and federal government entities in major U.S. cities.

Reference Book of Corporate Managements. Dun's Marketing Services (3 Sylvan Way; Parsippany, NJ 07054; 201-605-6000 in NJ, 800-526-0651 elsewhere). Annual. Four hardcover volumes. $910 annual lease. Call for online and CD-ROM information.

> Biographical profiles on 200,000 officers of more than 12,000 U.S. companies, arranged alphabetically by company name in three volumes. Fourth volume contains indexes by geography and

industry (S.I.C. codes), and by the names of officers and directors.

Standard & Poor's Register of Corporations, Directors and Executives. Standard & Poor's Corporation (25 Broadway; New York, NY 10004; 212-208-8786 in New York, 800-221-5277 elsewhere). Annual, with three cumulative supplements issued in April, July, and October. Three hardcover volumes. 5,000 pp. total. $895 annual lease.

> Volume 1 lists 55,000 public and private U.S. & Canadian (plus a few foreign) firms. Address, phone, sales, products/services, no. of employees, stock exchange, S.I.C. codes, officers and directors (including heads of personnel and industrial relations) principal bank, accounting, and law firm.

> Volume 2 sketches 70,000 key executives (year of birth, education, title/business affiliation, fraternal organizations, residence (if biographee permits), and directorships/trusteeships.

> Volume 3 contains S.I.C. (over 900 classifications) and geographical indexes of companies; index of subsidiaries/divisions cross-referenced to parent company; S&P 500 Composite Stock price index; obituary section; index of new individuals added since last publication; and index of companies added since last publication.

Standard Directory of Advertisers "The Red Books." National Register Publishing Company / Reed Elsevier (122 Chanlon Road; New Providence, N.J. 07974; 800-521-8110). Annual. Two editions ("Classified Edition," organized by product classification, and "Geographical Edition," organized by state and city), plus five cumulative Advertiser Supplements. One softcover volume, each book. Approximately 2,840 pp. per book. $659 each, plus pocket Index to the Geographical Edition included in the purchase of the Classified Edition (discount on either if purchased along with Standard Directory of Advertising Agencies). Call for CD-ROM information.

> Lists over 26,000 U.S. advertiser companies, with address, phone, sales, no. of employees, primary business(es), key managers, advertising agencies of record, account executives, time and amount of appropriations, and advertising media. Also lists subsidiaries/divisions.

Thomas' Register of American Manufacturers. Thomas Publishing Company (Five Penn Plaza, 9th Floor; New York, NY 10001; 212-695-0500). Annual (March). 27 hardcover volumes. 51,000+ pp. total. $149/set + $19.80 S & H. CD-ROM $149 + $9.80 S & H. Call for on-line information.

> Profiles 152,000 manufacturers, with their major products and services. Provides sourcing information on nearly 52,000 industrial products and services, along with comprehensive specifications and availability information from manufacturers. 1,400,000 individual product/service sources included in all. Contains a two-volume Company Profiles section and an eight-volume Catalog File section.

Top Executive Compensation. The Conference Board (845 Third Avenue; New York, NY 10022; 212-339-0345.) Annual (Dec.). One softcover volume. $195 for non-members.

Value Line Investment Survey. Value Line Publishing, Inc. (220 East 42nd Street; New York, NY 10017; 800-833-0046). Reports on and rates 1700 stocks in 96 industries, and gives analysis of industries. Weekly publication. $570./year subscription.

Wall Street Transcript. Wall Street Transcript Corporation (100 Wall Street, 9th Floor; New York, NY 10005; 212-952-7400). Reports industry and company financial news, and includes information on brokerage houses, analysts' discussions, and CEO interviews. Weekly publication. $1,890/year subscription.

Ward's Business Directory of U.S. Private and Public Companies. The Gale Group (P.O. Box 9187; Farmington Hills, MI 48333; 800-877-GALE; www.galegroup.com) Annual. Eight softcover volumes: $2,515/full set; Vols. 1-5 $2,125, Vols. 1-4 $2,162., Vol. 5 $950., Vols. 6-7 $950., Vol. 8 $463.68.

Demographic and financial business data on over 134,000 companies.

Volumes 1-3: Alphabetic listing of companies, including financial information, employee figures, and S.I.C. codes.

Volume 4: Companies listed in zip-code order within alphabetically arranged states, and include S.I.C. indexes, analysis of companies by state, sales rankings, and revenue rankings.

Volume 5: national rankings by sales volume within four digit S.I.C. codes.

Volumes 6-7: rank companies in each state by sales within 4-digit SIC codes and provide brief evaluations of the industry activity of leading companies for each state.

Vol. 8: Ranks companies within 6 digit NAICS codes. Sorts companies by cross-national agreements between the U.S., Canada, and Mexico.

Who's Who in America. Marquis, a division of Reed Elsevier Publishing (122 Chanlon Road; New Providence, N.J. 07974; 800-521-8110; www.marquiswhoswho.com). Three hardcover volumes (6,000 pp) $575. Call for online and CD-ROM information.

Profiles over 115,000 leaders, decision-makers, and innovators from a variety of fields (business, government, journalism, art, diplomacy, law, science, medicine, music, education, etc.), plus 30,000 emerging figures profiled for the first time. Biographies include education; career history; achievements, writings, and awards; civic and political activities; memberships; and address(es).

Who's Who in American Women. Marquis, a division of Reed Elsevier Publishing (122 Chanlon Road; New Providence, N.J. 07974; 800-521-8110; www.marquiswhoswho.com). Every two years. One hardcover volume. 1,172 pp. $269. Call for online and CD-ROM Information.

Profiles over 27,500 prominent women in the areas of business, government, law, and other professions.

Who's Who in Finance & Industry. Marquis, a division of Reed Elsevier Publishing (122 Chanlon Road; New Providence, N.J. 07974; 800-521-8110; www.marquiswhoswho.com). Every two years. One hardcover volume. 1,037 pp. $295. Call for online and CD-ROM information.

Profiles over 25,000 principal decision-makers from the fields of banking, insurance, transportation, government regulatory agencies, major corporations, etc. Biographies include education; career history; professional and social memberships; achievements, writings, and awards; and address(es).

Who's Who in Science and Engineering. Marquis, a division of Reed Elsevier Publishing (122 Chanlon Road; New Providence, N.J. 07974; 800-521-8110). Every two years. One hardcover volume. 1,500 pp. $269. Call for online and CD-ROM information.

Profiles over 22,000 leading international figures in aerospace, microcircuitry, lasers, genetics, biotechnology, etc. Includes published works, awards, notable findings, patents, and works in progress.

International

Dun's Europa. Dun's Marketing Services (3 Sylvan Way; Parsippany, NJ 07054; 201-605-6000 in NJ, 800-526-0651 elsewhere). Annual (October). Four hardcover volumes. 3,100 pp. $720/year lease. Call for on-line information.

Profiles top 50,000 European manufacturing, distribution, financial, and service companies. Listings in both English and indigenous language. Vols. I, II & III give information on companies; Vol. IV ranks the top 5,000 companies.

Dun's International Directories. Dun's Marketing Services (3 Sylvan Way; Parsippany, NJ 07054; 201-605-6758 in NJ, 800-526-0651 elsewhere). Individual country directories of the leading companies in Canada, Australia, Asia, Hong Kong, Singapore, Latin America, Austria, Denmark, Sweden, Norway, Belgium and Luxembourg, Europe, France, Italy, Spain, the United Kingdom, etc. Call for more information on individual prices.

Eastern Europe:A Directory and Sourcebook. The Gale Group (P.O. Box 9187; Farmington Hills, MI 48333; 800-877-GALE; www.galegroup.com). One hardcover volume. $590.

> Provides detailed information on top ranking companies in the region, as well as useful independent and government organizations.

International Directory of Company Histories. St. James/Available from The Gale Group (P.O. Box 9187; Farmington Hills, MI 48333; 800-877-GALE; www.galegroup.com) Five hardcover volumes: Vol. 1 published in 1988, Vol. 2 in 1990, Vol.3 in 1991, and Vol. 4, 5, and 6 in 1992. 800 pp. each. $180 each.

> Five volume set gives basic information and histories (1,500-3,000 words each) for about 1,250 companies in the U.S., Canada, U.K., Europe, and Japan. Volumes 1-5 are divided into groups alphabetically, so contain different industries (Vol. 1 begins with Advertising, and Vol. 5 ends with Utilities). Vol. 6 is Service Industries.

International Directory of Corporate Affiliations. National Register Publishing Company, a division of Reed Elsevier Publishing (122 Chanlon Road; New Providence, N.J. 07974; 800-521-8110). Volume V of Directory of Corporate Affiliations [see "National" section.]

> Two sections: (1) Non-U.S. holdings of U.S. parent companies; (2) U.S. and worldwide holdings of foreign enterprises. Includes address, telephone, types of business, S.I.C. codes, sales, number of employees, and key personnel. Indexes: (1) company names; (2) international trade names cross-referenced to product (S.I.C.) category and company name; (3) foreign companies by country; and (4) companies by S.I.C. categories.

Principal International Businesses. Dun's Marketing Services (3 Sylvan Way; Parsippany, NJ 07054; 201-605-6000 in NJ, 800-526-0651 elsewhere). Provides information on over 50,000 companies in 143 countries. Listings include contact information, parent company, lines of business, chief executives, number of employees, sales volume, S.I.C. code, and import/export indicator. Annual (September). One hardcover volume. $655.

Yearbook of International Organizations. Reed Elsevier Publishing (122 Chanlon Road; New Providence, N.J. 07974; 800-521-8110). Edited by the Union of International Associations, Brussels. Three hardcover volumes. Complete set, $1,280.

> Volume I: Organization Descriptions and Index. 1,700 pp. $440.
>
> Volume II: International Organization and Participation. 1,500 pp. $440.
>
> Volume III: Global Action Networks. 1,500 pp. $440.

2. Information on Particular Industries

Advertising/Market Research/Public Relations Industry

GREEN BOOK: International Directory of Marketing Research Houses and Services. American Marketing Association (60 East 42nd Street, Suite 1765; New York, NY 10165; 212-687-3280). Annual. $150 + $15 shipping and handling.

O'Dwyer's Directory of Public Relations Firms. J.R. O'Dwyer Company (271 Madison

Avenue; New York, NY 10016; 212-679-2471). Profiles 2,000 PR firms alphabetically, as well as specialists. Cross-indexed by client, ranked by fee income, and listed by area of specialty and by geographic region. Annual (May). One softcover volume. 288 pp. $175.

The Blue Book: Public Relations Journal Magazine . Public Relations Society of America (33 Irving Place, 3rd Floor; New York, NY 10003; 212-995-2230). Annual $100.

Standard Directory of Advertisers "The Red Books." [See listing in Section 1].

Standard Directory of Advertising Agencies "The Red Books." National Register Publishing, a division of Reed Reference Publishing (122 Chanlon Road; New Providence, N.J. 07974; 800-521-8110). Annual, plus at least one supplement. One softcover volume. 1,180 pp. $659 (discount if purchased with Standard Directory of Advertisers).

Aerospace/Defense Industry

World Aviation Directory & Buyer's Guide. McGraw-Hill, Inc. (P.O. Box 629; Hightstown, NJ 08520; 800-525-5003). Twice a year (Spring & Winter). Two volumes. $264.95/year.

Agribusiness/Foods Industry

Brewery Age Blue Book. Business Journals, Inc. (P.O. Box 5550; Norwalk, CT 06856; 203-853-6015). Annual (July). $275.

Directory of the Canning, Freezing and Preserving Industries. Edward E. Judge & Sons, Inc. (P.O. Box 866; Westminster, MD 21158; 410-876-2052). Even-numbered years. Standard Edition (720 pp.), $150; Deluxe Edition (1,360 pp.) $250.

Food Engineering's Directory of U.S. Food Plants. Chilton Company (Chilton Way; Radnor, PA 19089; 610-964-4447). Every other year. $295.

Fruit and Vegetable Blue Book Service. Produce Reporter Co. (845 E. Geneva Road; Carol Stream, IL 60188-3520; 630-668-3500). Twice a year (April & October). Also includes weekly updates by mail, on-line information access, and an individual 25-company updating service. One-year subscription $525. Also available on CD Rom

The National Frozen Food Association Directory. National Frozen Food Association (4755 Linglestown Road, Suite 300; Harrisburg, PA 17112; 717-657-8601). Annual. Member $25; non-member $195; previous year's edition $50.

Quick Frozen Foods Directory of Frozen Food Processors. Saul Beck Publications (271 Madison Avenue, Suite 1104; New York, NY 10016; 212-557-8600).Annual (August). $130.

Thomas Food Industry Register. Thomas Publishing Company (Five Penn Plaza, 14th Floor; New York, NY 10001; 212-290-7342). Annual. One hardcover volume $185. CD-ROM available and free online service to qualified subscribers. (Non-qualified $75.)

Apparel/Textiles Industry

Accessories Resources Directory. Business Journals, Inc. (P.O. Box 5550; Norwalk, CT 06856; 203-853-6015). Annual (December). One softcover volume. 200 pp. $25.

American Apparel Manufacturers Association Directory. American Apparel Manufacturers Association (2500 Wilson Boulevard, Suite 301; Arlington, VA 22201; 703-524-1864). Annual. One softcover volume. 284 pp. $100.

Davison's Textile Blue Book. Davison Publishing Company, Inc. (P.O. Box 1289; Concord, NC 28026; 704-785-8700). Annual (April), hardcover. 700 pp. $165.

Automotive Industry

Automotive News Magazine. Crain Communications (Attention:"Single Copies"; 965 East Jefferson Street; Detroit, MI 48207; 800-678-9595, ask for "single copy sales"). An annual (end of May), special issue of Automotive News magazine. 148 pp. $19.95 + $4. shipping & handling.

Ward's Automotive Yearbook. Ward's Communications, Inc. (28 West Adams; Detroit, MI 48226; 810-357-0800). Annual. One hardcover volume. 398 pp., including 100 page "Suppliers Directory" (a list of the automotive suppliers who advertised in the "yearbook" section). $205.

Banking/Finance/Venture Capital Industry

American Financial Directory. Thomson Financial Publishing (4709 West Golf; 6th Floor; Skokie, IL 60076; 800-321-3373; www.tfp.com). Twice a year (June and December). $455 per single copy (individual State reprints, $37 each, $12 for additional states); Call for online services.

America's Corporate Finance Directory. National Register Publishing, a division of Reed Reference Publishing (P.O. Box 31; New Providence, N.J. 07974; 800-521-8110). Annual (September). One softcover volume. 2,300 pp. $675.

America's Corporate Finance Sourcebook. National Register Publishing Company, a division of Reed Elsevier Publishing (122 Chanlon Road; New Providence, N.J. 07974; 800-521-8110). Lists over 20,000 financial experts in 3,645 organizations. "Mergers and acquisitions" section covers public offerings in the past three years, and M & A's over $100 million. Annual (September). One hardcover volume. 1,878 pp. $675.

Directory of Buyout Financing Sources. Venture Economics, Inc. (40 West 57th Street, 11th Floor; New York, NY 10019; 212-765-5311). Annual (November). One hardcover volume. 440+ pp. $395.

Directory of Institutional Investors. Vickers Associates, Inc. (226 New York Avenue; Huntington, NY 11743; 516-423-7710 in NY, 800-645-5043 elsewhere). Twice a year (April & October). One softcover vol. 100 pp. $195/year; $95 + S & H for one (April or October).

Directory of M and A Intermediaries. Venture Economics, Inc. (40 West 57th Street, 11th Floor; New York, NY 10019; 212-765-5311). Annual (November). One hardcover volume. 450 pp. $395.

Financial Yellow Book. Monitor Publishing Company (104 Fifth Avenue, 2nd Floor; New York, NY 10011; 212-627-4140). Semi-annual. One softcover volume. 600 pp. $235/year subscription.

Moody's Bank and Finance Manual. Mergent FTS (60 Madison Avenue; 6th Floor; New York, NY 10010; 212-553-0442). Annual (May), with weekly updates. Two hardcover volume set, plus updates, $1,175. Call for CD-ROM information.

Pratt's Guide to Venture Capital Sources. Venture Economics, Inc. (40 West 57th Street, 11th Floor; New York, NY 10019; 212-765-5311). Annual (February). One hardcover volume. 660+ pp. $575.

Securities Industry Yearbook. Securities Industry Association (120 Broadway; New York, NY 10271; 212-608-1500). Annual. One hardcover volume. 800+ pp. $102.84 for members, $146.14 for non-members.

Thomson/Polk Bank Directory. Thomson Financial Publishing (4709 West Golf; 6th

Floor; Skokie, IL 60076; 800-321-3373; www.tfp.com). Annual. One volume / $365. Call for online services.

Thomson Credit Union Directory. Thomson Financial Publishing (4709 West Golf; 6th Floor; Skokie, IL 60076; 800-321-3373; www.tfp.com). One hardcover volume. Semi-annual (June & December). $169. each edition. Call for online services.

Thomson Savings Directory. Thomson Financial Publishing (4709 West Golf; 6th Floor; Skokie, IL 60076; 800-321-3373; www.tfp.com). One hardcover volume. Semi-annual (June & December). $245. each edition. Call for online services.

Who's Who in International Banking. Marquis, a div. of Reed Elsevier Publishing (122 Chanlon Road; New Providence, N.J. 07974; 800-521-8110; www.marquiswhoswho.com). One hardcover volume. 652 pp. $249.

Biotechnology Industry

The Biotechnology Directory. Grove Dictionaries (49 West 24th Street; New York, NY 10010; 800-972-9892). Annual (December). One paperback volume. 710 pp. $295.

Biotechnology Guide U.S.A. Stockton Press (49 West 24th Street; New York, NY 10010; 800-972-9892). Gives financial, managerial, employee, affiliation, and product information on 742 biotechnology companies and 142 non-biotech corporations with biotechnology programs. Irregular. One paperback volume. 950 pp. $295

Chemicals/Plastics Industry

Directory of Chemical Producers - Canada. Stanford Research Institute (333 Ravenswood Avenue; Menlo Park, CA 94025; 650-859-3627). Annual, plus one supplement. $940 first annual subscription (includes inquiry privileges).

Directory of Chemical Producers - East Asia. Stanford Research Institute (333 Ravenswood Avenue; Menlo Park, CA 94025; 650-859-3627). Annual (October), plus one supplement. $2,440 first annual subscription (includes inquiry privileges).

Directory of Chemical Producers - Mexico. Stanford Research Institute (333 Ravenswood Avenue; Menlo Park, CA 94025; 650-859-3627). Annual (October), plus one supplement. $1,080 first annual subscription (includes inquiry privileges).

Directory of Chemical Producers - South America. Stanford Research Institute (333 Ravenswood Avenue; Menlo Park, CA 94025; 650-859-3627). Annual (October), plus one supplement. $1,520 first annual subscription (includes inquiry privileges).

Directory of Chemical Producers - U.S.A. Stanford Research Institute (333 Ravenswood Avenue; Menlo Park, CA 94025; 650-859-3627). Annual, plus one supplement. $2,030 first annual subscription (includes inquiry privileges).

Directory of Chemical Producers - Europe. Stanford Research Institute (333 Ravenswood Avenue; Menlo Park, CA 94025; 650-859-3627). Annual, plus one supplement. $2,660 first annual subscription (includes inquiry privileges).

Who's Who in World Petrochemicals & Plastics. Who's Who Information Services (17 S. Briar Hollow Lane, #401; Houston, TX 77027; 713-623-4627). 9,000 commercial people listed. Annual (October). One softcover volume. 250 pp. $165. + $30. shipping&handling.

[*See also*: Energy Industry.]

Communications Industry

Telecommunications Directory. The Gale Group (P.O. Box 9187; Farmington Hills, MI 48333; 800-877-GALE; www.galegroup.com). Annual. 1,033 pp. $415. Call for diskette information.

Telephone Industry Directory. Phillips Publishing (1201 Seven Locks Road, Suite 300; Potomac, MD 20854; 301-340-2100). Annual (December). 1,000 pp. $299.

[*See also*: Publishing/Information Industry, and Motion Picture/Broadcasting Industry.]

Computer/High-Tech Industry

The Corporate Technology Directory. CorpTech (12 Alfred Street, Suite 200; Woburn, MA 01801; 800-333-8036 elsewhere). Annual (March). Four-volume softcover set. $795. (Usually found in libraries.) Also, Regional Guide to High-Tech Companies, issued quarterly for thirteen regions.

[*See also specific high-tech categories*: Aerospace/Defense; Biotechnology; Communications; Electronics; Research & Development.]

Information Industry Directory. The Gale Group (P.O. Box 9187; Farmington Hills, MI 48333; 800-877-GALE; www.galegroup.com). Covers producers and vendors of electronic information (including CD-ROM databases and on-line services and networks). Every other year in December (even years). Two softcover volumes: Vol. 1, descriptive listings, 1,600 pp.; Vol. 2, Indexes, 750 pp. $620. Call for diskette information.

Telecommunications Directory. The Gale Group (P.O. Box 9187; Farmington Hills, MI 48333; 800-877-GALE; www.galegroup.com). Annual. 1,033 pp. $415. Call for diskette information.

Consulting Industry

Consultants and Consulting Organizations Directory. The Gale Group (P.O. Box 9187; Farmington Hills, MI 48333; 800-877-GALE; www.galegroup.com). Annual. Two hardcover volumes. 2,831 pp. $760. Call for on-line and diskette information.

The Directory of Management Consultants. Kennedy Publications (Templeton Road; Fitzwilliam, NH 03447; 603-585-6544). Profiles of 1,300 firms, with descriptions, billings, and staff. Four cross-indexes: 83 services offered, 107 industries served, geographic (including foreign), and key principals. Also information on consulting associations and advice on selecting consultants. Bi-annual. One hardcover volume. 840 pp. $295 + S & H.

Dun's Consultants Directory. Dun's Marketing Services (3 Sylvan Way; Parsippany, NJ 07054; 201-605-6000 in NJ, 800-526-0651 elsewhere). Annual (October). $480 lease.

Direct Mail Industry

Direct Marketing Market Place. National Register Publishing, a division of Reed Reference Publishing (P.O. Box 31; New Providence, N.J. 07974; 800-521-8110). Covers over 22,000 key executives in leading direct marketing companies, major firms, suppliers, and creative sources. Also lists advertising budgets, direct marketing expenditures, sales/billings, etc. Annual. 729 pp. $269 + 7.5% shipping, handling & tax..

Directory of Members. Direct Marketing Association, Inc. 11 West 42nd Street; New York, NY 10036; 212-768-7277, ext. 194). Annual. Not available to non-DMA members;

members receive one copy free and may purchase additional copies for $150 each.

Directory of Mail Order Catalogs. Grey House Publishing, Inc. (Pocket Knife Square; Lakeville, CT 06039; 203-435-0868). Annual (November). Three softcover volumes. $155.

Electronics Industry

Electronic Industry Telephone Directory. Harris Publishing Company (2057 Aurora Road; Twinsburg, OH 44087; 330-425-9000 in Ohio, 800-888-5900 elsewhere). Annual (September). Lists over 21,000 electronics firms worldwide. $55.

Electronics Manufacturers Directory. Harris Publishing Company (2057 Aurora Road; Twinsburg, OH 44087; 216-425-9000 in Ohio, 800-888-5900 elsewhere). Annual (June). $289. Also available on computer disc for $595.

Energy Industry

Brown's Directory of North American and International Gas Companies. Advanstar Data. (7500 Old Oak Boulevard; Cleveland, OH; 800-225-4569). Annual (November). One hardcover volume. $340 + $6 shipping and handling.

The Geophysical Directory. Geophysical Directory, Inc. (P.O. Box 130508; Houston, TX 77219; 713-529-8789). Annual (March). One softcover volume. 550 pp. $75.

Moody's Public Utility Manual. Moody's Investors Service, Inc. (99 Church Street; New York, NY 10007; 800-342-5647, ext. 0435). Annual (November), with weekly updates. Two hardcover volumes. 5500+ pp. $1,725. Call for CD-ROM information.

USA Oil and Gas Buyer. Geophysical Directory, Inc. (P.O. Box 130508; Houston, TX 77219; 713-529-8789). Annual (November). One softcover volume. 800 pp. $145.

U.S.A. Oilfield Service, Supply & Manufacturing Directory. PennWell Books (P.O. Box 21288; Tulsa, OK 74121; 800-752-9764). Annual. $165.

Worldwide Petrochemical Directory. PennWell Books (P.O. Box 21288; Tulsa, OK 74121; 800-752-9764). Annual. 300 pp. $155.

Worldwide Refining & Gas Processing Directory. PennWell Books (P.O. Box 21288; Tulsa, OK 74121; 800-752-9764). Annual. 475 pp. $155.

[*See also*: Chemicals/Plastics Industry.]

Executive Recruiting Industry

The Directory of Executive Recruiters Kennedy Information (One Kennedy Place, Fitzwilliam NH 03447; 800-531-0007 or 603-585-9555; www.kennedyinfo.com). In its 29th edition, this comprehensive listing of recruiting firms covers both retainer and contingency companies, has a 10-word self-description of each, and names one or more staff members at each...identifying a total of over 13,600 people working for executive recruiting organizations. It is extensively cross-indexed...alphabetically, by function and industry of activity, and geographically. 1,298 pp. paperback $47.95 plus $5.00 shipping.

Fine Arts & Performing Arts Industry

American Art Directory. R.R. Bowker, a division of Reed Elsevier (122 Chanlon Road; New Providence, N.J. 07974; 800-521-8110). A global directory of art institutions. Annual. One hardcover volume. 780 pp. $229.

International Directory of Arts. Reed Elsevier Publishing (122 Chanlon Road; New Providence, N.J. 07974; 800-521-8110). Contains over 150,000 names and addresses of art restorers, publishers, libraries, art dealers and galleries, museums, associations and more worldwide. Two hardcover volumes. 1,900 pp. $295.

Museums of the World. Reed Elsevier Publishing (122 Chanlon Road; New Providence, N.J. 07974; 800-521-8110). Includes museum name, person, and subject indexes. One hardcover volume. $450.

The Official Museum Directory. Reed Elsevier Publishing (122 Chanlon Road; New Providence, N.J. 07974; 800-521-8110). U.S. museums only. Annual (November). One softcover volume. 1,822 pp. $245.

Who's Who in American Art. Marquis, a division of Reed Elsevier Publishing (122 Chanlon Road; New Providence, N.J. 07974; 800-521-8110; www.marquiswhoswho.com). "Everyone who's anyone in the visual arts" in the U.S., Canada and Mexico. Every other year. 1,400 pp. $229. Call for online information.

Forest Products Industry

The Big Book. Random Lengths (P.O. Box 867; Eugene, OR 97440; 541-686-9925). Lists forest product producers, distributors, allied companies; company profiles, key personnel, products manufactured or distributed, special services, etc. Annual. One hardcover volume. $219.95.

Yearbook. Random Lengths (P.O. Box 867; Eugene, OR 97440; 503-686-9925). Lists market price information, including 11-year price histories, housing starts, production statistics, market activity timelines, and export information. Annual. $42.95.

Health Care Industry

American Hospital Association Guide to the Health Care Field. A.H.A. Services, Inc. (P.O. Box 92683; Chicago, IL 60675-2683; 800-242-2626). Annual (August). One softcover volume. $175 for members; $350 for non-members.

American Medical Directory of U.S. Physicians. American Medical Association (AMA Publications, P.O. Box 109050; Chicago, IL 60610; 312-464-5000). Annual. Four hardcover volumes. $695.

Directory of Medical Specialists. Marquis, a division of Reed Elsevier Publishing (122 Chanlon Road; New Providence, N.J. 07974; 800-521-8110; www.marquiswhoswho.com). Every other year. Three hardcover volumes. 6,300 pp. $525 + 7% S & H. Call for online and CD-ROM information.

Dun's Healthcare Reference Book. Dun's Marketing Services (3 Sylvan Way; Parsippany, NJ 07054; 201-605-6000 in NJ, 800-526-0651 elsewhere). Annual (July). One hardcover volume. 2,000+ pp. $480.

Medical and Health Information Directory. The Gale Group (P.O. Box 9187; Farmington Hills, MI 48333; 800-877-GALE; www.galegroup.com). Three hardcover volumes, published one per year in three-year cycles. Volume 1: Names of Medical & Health Organizations, Agencies, and Institutions; Volume 2: Publications and Other Information - AV Materials, Libraries, Databases; Volume 3: Health Services. 4,200 pages total. $225. per volume, $610/set.

Hotel/Motel/Resort Industry

Directory of Hotel and Motel Companies. American Hotel and Motel Association (1201 New York Avenue, N.W.; Washington, DC 20005; 202-289-3100). Annual (March). One softcover volume. 650 pp. $87 + $3.50 shipping & handling.

Official Cruise Guide. Reed Travel Group (P.O. Box 7653; Riverton, NJ 08077; 800-360-0015). Contains information on over 102 cruise lines and 308 ships. Annual. One softcover volume. $105 + tax.

Official Hotel and Resort Guide. Reed Travel Group (P.O. Box 7656; Riverton, NJ 08077; 800-360-0015). Annual (March). Three softcover volumes. $199 + tax.

[*See also*: Travel.]

Insurance Industry

Best's Insurance Reports: Life-Health. A.M. Best Company (A.M. Best Road; Oldwick, NJ 08858; 908-439-2200). Annual hardcover book plus monthly magazine, $600; plus weekly insurance management reports, $745 + $15.95 shipping & handling.

Best's Insurance Reports: Property-Casualty. A.M. Best Company (A.M. Best Road; Oldwick, NJ 08858; 908-439-2200). Annual hardcover book plus monthly magazine, $600; plus weekly insurance management reports, $745 + $15.95 shipping & handling.

Insurance Almanac. Underwriter Printing and Publishing Co. (50 East Palisades Avenue; Englewood, NJ 07631; 201-569-8808 in NJ, 800-526-4700 elsewhere). Annual (July). One hardcover volume. $150.

Who's Who in Insurance. Underwriter Printing and Publishing Co. (50 East Palisades Avenue; Englewood, NJ 07631; 201-569-8808 in NJ, 800-526-4700 elsewhere). Annual (Feb.). One hardcover volume. $130.

Who's Who in Risk Management. Underwriter Printing and Publishing Co. (50 East Palisades Avenue; Englewood, NJ 07631; 201-569-8808 in NJ, 800-526-4700 elsewhere). Annual (August). One hardcover volume. 200 pp. $80.

Legal Industry

Law and Legal Information Directory. The Gale Group (P.O. Box 9187; Farmington Hills, MI 48333; 800-877-GALE; www.galegroup.com). Every other year in September (even years). Two hardcover volumes. 2,252 pp. $385. Call for CD-ROM and online information.

Law Firms Yellow Book. Monitor Publishing Co. (104 Fifth Avenue, 2nd Floor; New York, NY 10011; 212-627-4140). Subtitled "Who's Who in the Management of the Leading U.S. Law Firms." Profiles over 13,000 key individuals, covering over 650 law firms. Semi-annual. One softcover volume. 750 pp. With annual subscription $223. One time buy $235.

Martindale-Hubbell Bar Register of Preeminent Lawyers. Reed Elsevier Publishing (122 Chanlon Road; New Providence, N.J. 07974; 800-521-8110). Lists over 8,000 outstanding members of the bar as designated by their fellow lawyers. Includes partnership contact information, as well as major clients represented. Annual (March). One hardcover volume. 2,500 pp. $195 + 7% shipping & handling.

Martindale-Hubbell Law Directory. Reed Elsevier Publishing (122 Chanlon Road; New Providence, N.J. 07974; 800-521-8110). Annual (March). 27 hardcover volumes. $695/set or $55/volume. Call for online and CD-ROM information.

Who's Who in American Law. Marquis, a division of Reed Elsevier Publishing (122 Chanlon Road; New Providence, N.J. 07974; 800-521-8110; www.marquiswhoswho.com). Every other year. One hardcover volume. 1,104 pp. $295 + 7% shipping & handling + tax.

Mining Industry

Keystone Coal Industry Manual. MacLean Hunter Publishing Company, Mining Information Services (P.O. Box 6500; Chicago, IL 60680; 312-726-2802 in IL; 800-247-8080 elsewhere). Every other year in December (even years). One hardcover volume. 926 pp. $295.

Motion Picture/Broadcasting Industry

AV Market Place. Reed Elsevier Publishing (122 Chanlon Road; New Providence, N.J. 07974; 800-521-8110). Annual. One softcover volume. 1,400 pp. $175.

Broadcasting and Cable Yearbook. Reed Elsevier Publishing (122 Chanlon Road; New Providence, N.J. 07974; 800-521-8110). Annual (March). Two softcover volumes. 2,015 pp. $179.95.

The Hollywood Reporter Studio Blu-Book Directory. The Hollywood Reporter Inc. (5055 Wilshire Boulevard, 6th Floor; Los Angeles, CA 90036; 323-525-2000). Annual (January). One hardcover volume. 500 pp. $82.22.

Standard Rate & Data publications, including *Radio Advertising Source* (monthly subscription $396, single copy $173), and *Television & Cable Source* (quarterly subscription $369, single copy $164). Standard Rate & Data Service, Inc. (3004 Glenview Road; Wilmette, IL 60091; 708-441-2210 in IL, 800-323-4601 elsewhere). Monthly subscription publications. Visit your library.

Talk Show Selects. Broadcast Interview Source (2233 Wisconsin Avenue, N.W., #540; Washington, DC 20007; 202-333-4904). Profiles over 700 top-rated radio and television talk shows. Includes six bi-monthly newsletter updates. Annual. Bound printed report, $185. Call for information on diskette and mailing labels.

Teleconferencing Resources Directory. Knowledge Industry Publications, Inc. (701 Westchester Avenue; White Plains, NY 10604; 914-328-9157 in NY, 800-248-5474 elsewhere). One softcover volume. $19.95.

Working Press of the Nation, Volume Three: Radio and Television Directory. Reed Reference Publishing Company (P.O. Box 31; New Providence, NJ 07974; 800-521-8110). Annual. $249. [See Publishing/Information Industry for other volumes.]

Nonprofit / Government

Associations Yellow Book. Monitor Publishing Co. (104 Fifth Avenue, 2nd Floor; New York, NY 10011; 212-627-4140). Each subscription includes two editions published semi-annually. 800 pp. With annual subscription $223. One time buy $235.

> Subtitled "Who's Who At The Leading U.S. Trade And Professional Associations." Provides information on over 30,000 officers, directors, managers, and professional staff. Includes information on association activities and company affiliations, board of directors, annual budget data, Washington representatives and PAC, publications, etc. Indexed by Master Association, Individual Names, Industry, Budget, Acronym, and PAC.

Congressional Yellow Book. Monitor Publishing Co. (104 Fifth Avenue, 2nd Floor; New York, NY 10011; 212-627-4140). Subtitled "Who's Who in Congress, Including Committees and Key Staff." New editions published quarterly. Four editions per subscription. One softcover volume. 700 pp. With annual subscription $290. One time buy $305.

Corporate Foundation Profiles. The Foundation Center (79 Fifth Avenue; New York, NY 10003; 212-620-4230 in NY; 800-424-9836 elsewhere). Profiles the 247 largest corporate foundations in the U.S. Includes data on previous grants awarded. Every other year. One softcover volume. $155.

Federal Yellow Book. Monitor Publishing Co. (104 Fifth Avenue, 2nd Floor; New York, NY 10011; 212-627-4140). Subtitled "Who's Who in Federal Departments and Agencies." New editions published quarterly. Four editions per subscription. One softcover volume. 800 pp. With annual subscription $290. One time buy $305.

Federal Regional Yellow Book. Monitor Publishing Co. (104 Fifth Avenue, 2nd Floor; New York, NY 10011; 212-627-4140). Subtitled "Who's Who in the Federal Government's Departments, Agencies, Courts, Military Installations and Service Academies Outside of Washington, DC." New editions published semi-annually. Two editions per subscription. 1300 pp. With annual subscription $223. One time buy $235.

The Foundation Directory. The Foundation Center (79 Fifth Avenue; New York, NY 10003; 212-620-4230 in NY; 800-424-9836 elsewhere). Profiles foundations that hold at least $1 million in assets, or give at least $100,000 in grants every year. Covers 8,700 foundations. Annual (March). Single volume. $215 hardcover.

The Foundation 1000. The Foundation Center (79 Fifth Avenue; New York, NY 10003; 212-620-4230 in NY; 800-424-9836 elsewhere). Profiles the 1000 largest foundations in the U.S., including data on the non-profit organizations they have funded. Annual. One softcover volume. $295.

Grant Guides. The Foundation Center (79 Fifth Avenue; New York, NY 10003; 212-620-4230 in NY; 800-424-9836 elsewhere). Describes foundation grants awarded ($100,000 or more) in 35 different titles; for example, children and youth, education, the environment, minorities, etc. Annual. All softcover volumes. $75 each. Call for more information.

Municipal & Government Manual and News Reports. Financial Institute Service (60 Madison Avenue; New York, NY 10010; 800-342-5647 x 7601). Annual. Three volumes, plus weekly News Reports. $2,595.

Municipal Yellow Book. Monitor Publishing Co. (104 Fifth Avenue, 2nd Floor; New York, NY 10011; 212-627-4140). Subtitled "Who's Who in the Leading City and County Governments and Local Authorities." New editions published semiannually. Two editions per subscription. 700 pp. With annual subscription $290. One time buy $305.

National Directory of Nonprofit Organizations. The Taft Group (835 Penobscot Building, Detroit, MI 48226; 800-877-TAFT). Annual (March). Two softcover volumes. Lists national nonprofit organizations with annual revenues of $100,000 or more. $535.

The National Directory of Corporate Giving. The Foundation Center (79 Fifth Avenue; New York, NY 10003; 212-620-4230 in NY; 800-424-9836 elsewhere). Profiles over 2,000 corporate funders, including information on key personnel, types of support usually granted, giving limitations, financial data, purpose and activities statements, and current giving reviews. Every other year. One softcover volume. $195.

State Yellow Book. Monitor Publishing Co. (104 Fifth Avenue, 2nd Floor; New York, NY 10011; 212-627-4140). Subtitled "Who's Who in the Executive and Legislative Branches of the 50 State Governments." New editions published quarterly. Four editions per subscription. 1,000 pp. With annual subscription $290. One time buy $305.

[*See also*: Encyclopedia of Associations]

Outplacement Industry

The Directory of Outplacement Firms. Kennedy Information (One Kennedy Place, Fitzwilliam NH 03447; 800-531-0007 or 603-585-9555; www.kennedyinfo.com). Full-page profiles of over 200 firms: staff size, revenues, fees, 750 key principals and where they work. Also feature articles, data, and statistics. Every other year. One hardcover volume. $129.95 + shipping & handling.

Packaging Industry

Official Container Directory. Advanstar Communications (7500 Old Oak Boulevard; Cleveland, OH 44130; 598-6008). Semi-annual (spring & fall). $60/issue.

Pharmaceutical Industry

Drug and Cosmetic Catalog. Advanstar Communications (131 West First Street; Duluth, MN 55802; 218-723-9558 in MN; 800-346-0085 elsewhere). Annual subscription (12 issues including "catalog issue"). $25.

Pharmaceutical Marketers Directory. CPS Communications (7200 West Camino Real; Boca Raton, FL 33433; 561-368-9301). Annual (May). One softcover volume. 1,500 pp. $162.50.

Publishing/Information Industry

American Book Trade Directory. Reed Elsevier Publishing (122 Chanlon Road; New Providence, N.J. 07974; 800-521-8110). Annual (July). One hardcover volume. 1,800 pp. $255 + 7% shipping & handling.

American Library Directory.. Reed Elsevier Publishing (122 Chanlon Road; New Providence, N.J. 07974; 800-521-8110). Annual (June). Two hardcover volumes. 2,200 pp. $269. Call for online and CD-ROM information.

American Wholesalers and Distributors Directory. Reed Elsevier Publishing (122 Chanlon Road; New Providence, N.J. 07974; 800-521-8110). Lists 63,000 publishers, distributors, wholesalers, software firms, museum and association imprints, and other trade organizations. Annual (October). Two hardcover volumes. 2,700 pp. $215. Call for online and CD-ROM information.

Gale Directory of Publications & Broadcast Media. The Gale Group (P.O. Box 9187; Farmington Hills, MI 48333; 800-877-GALE; www.galegroup.com). Annual (March). Three softcover volumes. 3,379 pp. $615. Call for online and diskette information.

Gebbie Press: All-in-One-Directory. Gebbie Press (P.O. Box 1000; New York, NY 12561; 914-255-7560). Gives complete address, circulation figures, editors, publishers, etc. in eight separate categories: daily and weekly newspapers, radio and TV stations, consumer magazines, business and financial papers, trade journals and magazines, farm publications, and news syndicates. Annual. One softcover volume, comb-bound. $90.

International Literary Market Place: The Directory of the International Book Publishing Industry. Reed Elsevier Publishing (122 Chanlon Road; New Providence, N.J. 07974; 800-521-8110). Annual (September). One softcover volume. 1,071 pp. $199.95. Call for CD-ROM information.

Literary Market Place: The Directory of the American Book Publishing Industry. Reed Elsevier Publishing (122 Chanlon Road; New Providence, N.J. 07974; 800-521-8110).

Annual (September). One softcover volume. 1,876 pp. $199.95. Call for CD-ROM information.

National Directory of Magazines. Oxbridge Communications, Inc. (150 Fifth Avenue; New York, NY 10011; 800-955-0231). Covers over 24,000 U.S. and Canadian magazines, including staff, advertising rates, circulation size, mailing list information, and production details. Annual. One softcover volume. $695.

News Media Yellow Book National. Monitor Publishing Company (104 Fifth Avenue, 2nd Floor; New York, NY 10011; 212-627-4140). Quarterly. One softcover volume. 800 pp. $305.

Power Media Selects. Broadcast Interview Source (2233 Wisconsin Avenue, N.W., #540; Washington, DC 20007; 202-333-4904). Provides contact information for over 3,000 leaders in the U.S. print and broadcasting industries. Annual. Bound printed report, $166.50. Floppy disk and book, $240. Mailing labels, $156.50.

Publishers Directory. The Gale Group (P.O. Box 9187; Farmington Hills, MI 48333; 800-877-GALE; www.galegroup.com). Covers 18,000 U.S. and Canadian publishers, including major publishing firms as well as small, independent presses. Annual. One softcover volume. 1,914 pp. $370. Call for online information.

The Standard Periodical Directory. Oxbridge Communications, Inc. (150 Fifth Avenue; New York, NY 10011; 800-955-0231). Annual (January). One hardcover volume. $495; CD-ROM Window or Dos, $995.

Ulrich's International Periodicals Directory. Reed Elsevier Publishing (122 Chanlon Road; New Providence, N.J. 07974; 800-521-8110). Information on 120,000 regularly and irregularly issued serials. Includes three supplements per year. Bi-annual (August). Three hardcover volumes. 7,200 pp. $525. Call for on-line, microfiche, and CD-ROM information.

Working Press of the Nation: Volume 1: Newspaper Directory; Volume 2: Magazine & Internal Publications Directory; Volume 3: Radio & TV Directory; Volume 4: Feature Writer & Photographer Directory. Reed Reference Publishing Company (P.O. Box 31; New Providence, NJ 07974; 800-521-8110). Annual (September). Softcover volumes. 2,880 pp. $439.95 / Full set.

World Guide to Libraries. Reed Elsevier Publishing (122 Chanlon Road; New Providence, N.J. 07974; 800-521-8110). One hardcover volume. 1,100 pp. $425.

The World News Media: A Comprehensive Reference Guide. Longman Group, available from The Gale Group (P.O. Box 9187; Farmington Hills, MI 48333; 800-877-GALE; www.galegroup.com). Gives a country-by-country overview of press and broadcast media and media organizations. Entries include contact information, circulation data, political orientation, editorial policies, historical background, and the restrictions and regulations under which they operate. Annual. One softcover volume. 480 pp. $198.

Yearbook of Experts, Authorities & Spokespersons. Broadcast Interview Source (2233 Wisconsin Avenue, N.W., #540; Washington, DC 20007; 202-333-4904). One softcover volume. 780 pp. $39.95 (free to all journalists; call for information).

Real Estate/Construction Industry

Constructor Magazine, "Directory Issue." Associated General Contractors of America (1957 E Street N.W.; Washington, D.C. 20006; 202-393-2040, ext. 204). Lists general contracting firms by state. Includes information on key officers and type of construction performed. July issue. $250.

The Executive Guide to Specialists in Industrial and Office Real Estate. Society of Industrial and Office Realtors (777 14th Street, N.W., #400; Washington, DC 20005; 202-737-1150). Annual (May). One softcover volume. 200 pp. No charge for members, $70 for non-members.

National Association of Real Estate Investment Trusts Directory of Members. National Association of Real Estate Trusts, Inc. (1129 20th Street N.W.; Washington, DC 20036; 202-785-8717). Annual (January). One softcover volume. 300 pp. Members, 1st copy free, additional copies $200. Non-members, $900/copy.

National Referral Roster. Stamats Communications, Inc. (427 Sixth Avenue, S.E.; P.O. Box 1888; Cedar Rapids, IA 52406; 319-364-6032). Annual (May). One softcover volume. 1,600 pp. $50.

Top Contacts. National Research Bureau, Inc. (3975 Fair Ridge Drive; Fairfax, VA 22033; 800-456-4555). One volume. $325. Discount if purchased along with 4-volume Shopping Center Directory in the United States (see "Retailing Industry").

U.S. Real Estate Register. Barry Inc. (P.O. Box 551; Wilmington, MA 01887; 978-658-0440). Annual (June). One softcover volume. 570 pp. $87.50, including shipping.

Research & Development Industry

American Men & Women of Science. Reed Reference Publishing (P.O. Box 31; New Providence, N.J. 07974; 800-521-8110). Biographical directory of U.S. & Canadian leaders in physical, biological, and related sciences. Annual. 8-volume hardcover set. 8,000 pp. total. $975. Call for on-line and CD-ROM information.

Research Centers Directory. The Gale Group (P.O. Box 9187; Farmington Hills, MI 48333; 800-877-GALE; www.galegroup.com). Annual (July). Two softcover volumes. 2,171 pp. $575. Call for diskette information.

Retailing Industry

The Chain Store Guides. The Chain Store Guides, Inc. CSG Information Services (3922 Coconut Palm Drive; Tampa, FL 33619-8321; 800-927-9292). Annual (month indicated in parentheses). Call for diskette, magnetic tape, and mailing label format information. Guides include:

Directory of Apparel Specialty Stores. (August) $260.
Directory of Automotive Aftermarket Suppliers. (September) $270.
Directory of Chain Restaurant Operators. (April) $290.
Directory of Consumer Electronics, Computer & Software Retailers. (December) $290.
Directory of Department Stores (November) $290.
Directory of Drug Store & HBC Chains (December) $300.
Directory of Foodservice Distributors. (May) $290.
Directory of General Merchandise/Variety, Specialty Stores & Discount Department Stores. (May) $300.
Directory of Hardlines Distributors. (July) $270.
Directory of High-Volume Independent Restaurants. (July) $300.
Directory of Home Center Operators & Hardware Chains. (June) $300.
Directory of Home Furnishings Retailers. (March) $290.
Directory of Single Unit Supermarket Operators. (August) $290.
Directory of Supermarket, Grocery & Convenience Store Chains. (September) $300.

Directory of Value Added Resellers. (August) $290.
Directory of Wholesale Grocers. (November) $300.

Franchise Annual. Info Press (728 Center Street, P.O. Box 550; Lewiston, NY 14092; 716-754-4669). Annual (January). One softcover volume. 352 pp. $39.95.

Shopping Center Directory. National Research Bureau, Inc. (3975 Fair Ridge Drive; Fairfax, VA 22033; 800-456-4555). Annual (October). Four regional volumes (East, South Midwest, West). Annual lease. Each volume/$335 each volume + top contact/$555; set/$655, set + top contact/$855.

Major Mass Market Merchandisers. Salesman's Guide, Inc. (P.O. Box 1009; Summit, NJ 07902; 908-464-6800 in NJ; 800-223-1797 elsewhere). Annual (June). One softcover volume. 600 pp. $189.

Travelware Suppliers Directory. Business Journals, Inc. (P.O. Box 5550; Norwalk, CT 06856; 203-853-6015). Annual (September). Two small softcover volumes. $25.

Service Industry

Dun's Directory of Service Companies. Dun's Marketing Services (3 Sylvan Way; Parsippany, NJ 07054; 201-605-6000 in NJ, 800-526-0651 elsewhere). One hardcover volume. 3,600+ pp. $565/year lease.

Training & Development Industry

Training and Development Organizations Directory. The Gale Group (P.O. Box 9187; Farmington Hills, MI 48333; 800-877-GALE; www.galegroup.com). Irregular. One softcover volume. 677 pp. $395. Call for on-line and diskette information.

Travel / Transportaion Industry

Air Freight Directory. Air Cargo, Inc. (1819 Bay Ridge Avenue; Annapolis, MD 21403; 410-280-5578, but no phone orders). Bi-monthly. $84/year subscription, or $34.50 per single issue.

Moody's Transportation Manual and News Reports. Moody's Investors Service (99 Church Street; New York, NY 10007; 212-553-0442 in NY; 800-342-5647, ext. 0442 elsewhere). Annual. One hardcover volume, plus weekly News Reports. $1,595

Logistics Management: The Directory. Cahners Publishing Company (275 Washington Street; Newton, MA 02158; 617-964-3030). An annual (July) special issue of Traffic Management Magazine. $10.

[*See also*: Hotel/Motel/Resort Industry.]

Wholesaling Industry

American Wholesalers and Distributors Directory. The Gale Group (P.O. Box 9187; Farmington Hills, MI 48333; 800-877-GALE; www.galegroup.com). Annual. One softcover volume. 1,678 pp. $215. Call for diskette information.

Provides descriptive listings of over 20,000 companies and their products. Lists top 50 companies, ranked by sales, for each four-digit SIC. Includes principal officers, address, and phone number for each company.

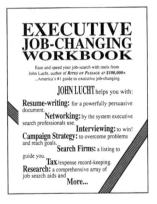
Implementing RITES OF PASSAGE in a job search?

Don't overlook the "second half" of the RITES program.

See page 600 for details.

624

INDEX

About the Author
and
Rites of Passage at $100,000 to $1 Million+

John Lucht is one of America's foremost executive recruiters. Since 1971 he has been bringing senior executives into major corporations in the U.S. and over-seas...as head of The John Lucht Consultancy Inc. in New York City since 1977, and for six prior years at Heidrick and Struggles, New York, where he was an officer. Earlier he was in general management or marketing with Bristol-Myers, J. Walter Thompson Co. and Tetley Tea. His B.S. and Law degrees are from the University of Wisconsin.

Rites of Passage was critically acclaimed and immediately achieved its continuing status as the #1 bestselling book of job-changing and lifetime career advice for executives when it first appeared in 1988. This current edition has been massively expanded, revised and rewritten by the author, who took a hiatus from all other activity for nearly a year to bring his classic up-to-the-minute in the 21st century technology and techniques of executive recruiting and job-changing.

Revised, expanded and updated with each new printing, *"Rites"* becomes more widely read and influential year after year.* With 300,000 copies in print, it has already helped hundreds of thousands of executives find new and better jobs and/or move up in their current company. Recently, *Rites* has become widely used among **non**-executives. It's the text for career courses in many business and professional schools and undergraduate colleges, and has become a favorite handbook to help people retiring from the armed forces find civilian jobs.

John Lucht has also written the EXECUTIVE JOB-CHANGING WORKBOOK, which further helps users implement his *Rites of Passage* principles. The WORKBOOK combined with *Rites* constitutes what John Drake, founder of Drake Beam Morin Inc., has called "the strongest, most comprehensive total program available in print."

With *Rites* "torn apart and totally renewed," John Lucht now returns to his active practice in senior executive recruiting and executive coaching. He also does a limited amount of high-level outplacement, and is a leading expert legal witness on matters involving executive careers and compensation.

---

*Rites has been in scores of publications (several times in many), including: Business Week, Wall Street Journal, Forbes, USA Today, New York Times, Working Woman, Self, Boston Globe, Denver Post, Chicago Tribune, The Philadelphia Inquirer, Los Angeles Times, Chief Executive, Seattle Times, American Way, Financial World, Portland Telegram, Dallas Morning News, Omaha World-Herald, New York Daily News, Savvy, Salt Lake City Tribune, American Banker, Women's Wear Daily, Psychology Today, Minneapolis Star & Tribune, Industry Week, Newsday, Success, Investor's Business Daily, St. Louis Post-Dispatch, Training, Publishers Weekly, San Antonio Express News, National Business Employment Weekly, Harper's Bazaar, Chicago Sun-Times, Board Room Reports, Newark Star-Ledger, Cleveland Plain Dealer, Baltimore Sun, El Paso Times, Wichita Eagle, Across the Board (The Conference Board), Men's Health, Personnel Executive, Training & Development Journal, Atlanta Journal/Constitution, Indianapolis Star & News, Executive Female, Manchester Union Leader, Personnel Administrator, Worcester Telegram, Akron Beacon Journal, Brandweek, Human Resource Executive, Madison State Journal & Capitol Times, Albany Times Union, Career News (Harvard Business School Alumni Career Services), Corpus Christi Caller-Times, The Bricker Bulletin, Canadian Industrial Relations & Personnel Development, World Executive's Digest (serving Asia from Singapore), China Technology Market News (mainland China), and many more.

RITES OF PASSAGE AT $100,000 TO $1 MILLION+ **and its companion** *EXECUTIVE JOB-CHANGING WORKBOOK* **are both available at better bookstores everywhere.**

Please visit and support your local booksellers, who save you both time and money in serving your reading needs. Phoning a few stores will surely locate both books, and any store that's out of stock can quickly get them for you.

But if that's inconvenient, you may order by mail. Just send $29.95* (plus $5.50 shipping / total $35.45*) for each RITES and $29.95* (plus $6.50 shipping / total $36.45*) for each WORKBOOK by check or money order to:

The Viceroy Press Inc.
P.O. Box 5356
New York, NY 10185
Phone: 1 (800) VICEROY

RITES OF PASSAGE, the WORKBOOK, and related career aids by author John Lucht may be ordered by phone. Merely dial:

1 800 JANUARY

*New York residents please add sales tax (NYC $2.47, outside NYC as applicable). All mail orders must be prepaid.